IMPACT
SOCIAL STUDIES

Our Communities

Teacher's Edition

Mc
Graw
Hill

IMPACT™
SOCIAL STUDIES

IMPACTO™
ESTUDIOS SOCIALES

mheducation.com/prek-12

Copyright © 2020 McGraw-Hill Education

Send all inquiries to:
McGraw-Hill Education
120 S. Riverside Plaza, Suite 1200
Chicago, IL 60606

ISBN: 978-0-07-691381-7
MHID: 0-07-691381-3

Printed in the United States of America.

4 5 6 7 8 9 LMN 23 22 21 20   E

Welcome to
IMPACT™
SOCIAL STUDIES

"We teach students to read the words and the world. To read the word, students need basic knowledge and skills. Reading the world requires students to question assumptions and paradigms and to use knowledge to make the world more just and humane. This is a critical goal of social studies education."

— James Banks, Ph.D., IMPACT Program Author

Reflect on the PAST, IMPACT™ the future.

Meet the Expert Team

IMPACT SOCIAL STUDIES ™

Program Authors

James Banks, Ph.D.
University of Washington
Seattle, Washington

Kevin P. Colleary, Ed.D.
Fordham University
New York, New York

William Deverell, Ph.D.
University of Southern California
Los Angeles, California

Daniel Lewis, Ph.D.
The Huntington Library
Los Angeles, California

Elizabeth Logan, Ph.D., J.D.
USC Institute on California and the West
Los Angeles, California

Walter C. Parker, Ph.D.
University of Washington
Seattle, Washington

Emily M. Schell, Ed.D.
San Diego State University
San Diego, California

Program Consultants

Tahira Dupree Chase, Ed.D.
Greenburgh Central School District
Hartsdale, New York

Jana Echevarria, Ph.D.
California State University
Long Beach, California

Douglas Fisher, Ph.D.
San Diego State University
San Diego, California

Nafees Khan, Ph.D.
Clemson University
Clemson, South Carolina

Jay McTighe
McTighe & Associates Consulting
Columbia, Maryland

Carlos Ulloa, Ed.D.
Escondido Union School District
Escondido, California

Rebecca Valbuena, M.Ed.
Glendora Unified School District
Glendora, California

Dinah Zike, M.Ed.
Dinah.com/Dinah Zike Academy
San Antonio, Texas

Program Reviewers

Gary Clayton, Ph.D.
Northern Kentucky University
Highland Heights, Kentucky

Lorri Glover, Ph.D.
Saint Louis University
St. Louis, Missouri

Thomas Herman, Ph.D.
San Diego State University
San Diego, California

Clifford Trafzer, Ph.D.
University of California
Riverside, California

Contents

Be a Social Studies Detective

Chapter Content

Reference Sources

Nerthuz/Shutterstock

Chapter Content

Chapter 1 Communities in Our Country and World

 Why Does It Matter Where We Live?

Dave Allen Photography/Shutterstock

Chapter 2 The Community and Its Environment

What Is Our Relationship With Our Environment?

sOUlsurfing - Jason Swain/Getty Images

Chapter 3 People and Communities

 What Makes a Community Unique?

Hisham Ibrahim/Photographer's Choice RF/Getty Images

Chapter 4 Communities Change Over Time

ESSENTIAL EQ QUESTION How Does the Past Impact the Present?

Michael Shake/Shutterstock

Chapter 5 American Citizens, Symbols, and Government

ESSENTIAL EQ QUESTION
Why Do Governments and Citizens Need Each Other?

Chapter 6 Economics of Communities

 How Do People in a Community Meet Their Wants and Needs?

gopixa/iStock/Getty Images

Skills and Features

xv

xvi

WHAT IS IMPACT™?

Reflect on the PAST, IMPACT the future.

McGraw-Hill Education's K–5 **IMPACT Social Studies** is a **coherent, knowledge-building program that promotes students' understanding of** the world and their individual place in it.

Research-based and student-centered, *IMPACT Social Studies* provides an engaging, **inquiry-based learning experience** that is grounded in significant social studies content.

IMPACT Social Studies provides a flexible, accessible, blended learning experience.

Student resources launch collaborative discovery.

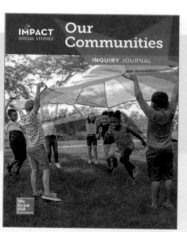

Inquiry Journal
Make meaning through engaging activities.

Research Companion
Explore primary and secondary sources.

Explorer Magazine
Enjoy captivating literature, real-world stories, and informational texts.

Use **IMPACT Social Studies** to **integrate rich social studies content, powerful analysis skills, and essential ELA skills and strategies** into lessons you are teaching.

- Students learn to think **historically, civically, spatially, and economically.**

- Students **analyze relevant information, critique arguments, develop opinions** and **make connections** through reading, writing, speaking, and listening in response to Essential Questions.

- Using **dynamic digital content,** students explore **activities with real-world applications**, both immediate and long-term.

IMPACTO provides equitable support for Spanish-speaking students.

Teacher support when—and how— you need it.

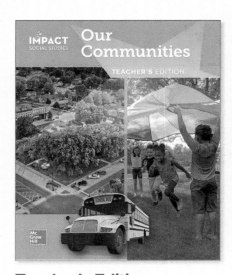

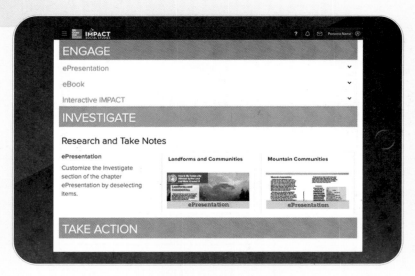

Teacher's Edition

Use this road map to plan how and when to teach social studies.

Explorer Magazine Teaching Guide

Follow a three-step instructional model to guide students through engaging texts.

WHY IMPACT?

Learning begins with curiosity.

IMPACT Social Studies is designed to spark students' interest, empower them to ask questions and think critically, and inspire them to make a difference. By taking an active role in their learning, students will enrich and deepen their content-specific knowledge and social studies skills.

IMPACT Social Studies blends **content, inquiry,** and **multiple perspectives** to help develop **citizenship in action**.

Using rich, **curated content resources** and **inquiry-based** instruction, *IMPACT Social Studies* helps students understand the **forces that shape the world** in which they live.

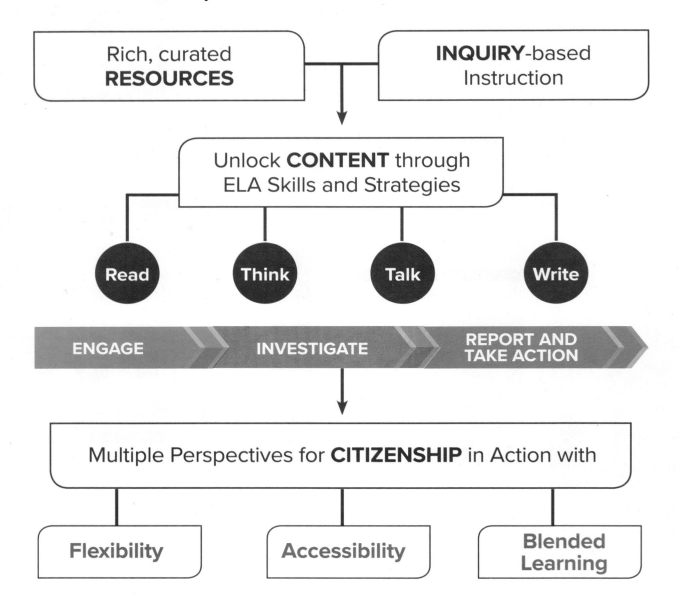

Students build a coherent base of knowledge about the world and how it works through rich, relevant, and rigorous social studies content that matters and makes an IMPACT.

Student-centered, inquiry-based learning expands thinking by considering multiple perspectives and understanding of core content.

CONTENT

INQUIRY

LITERACY

CITIZENSHIP

Using literacy skills, students read, think, talk, and write to unlock and demonstrate understanding of rich social studies content.

Students deepen their understanding of key issues about the world, share their ideas, reflect, and demonstrate democratic ideals by taking action in the classroom—and beyond.

IMPACT is CONTENT.

Explore social studies domains.

IMPACT Social Studies builds a solid grounding in the essential domains of social studies—**history, geography, economics,** and **civics**—with conceptually-coherent units of study that provide active engagement with a rich variety of informational texts, **primary sources,** media, and activities. In a spiraled, developmental approach across all grade levels, students learn and practice disciplinary tools and strategies to **think like a historian, a geographer, an economist—and as an informed and engaged citizen.**

Multiple perspectives are woven throughout the program—through the core text, primary sources, biographies, images, and literature connections. Articles and features in the Inquiry Journal and Research Companion showcase diverse perspectives and encourage students to engage with ideas and issues that have been debated throughout history. **As students form their own opinions** about these ideas and issues, they are reminded to **cite reliable sources to support their claims.**

History

Students learn to ask questions about the past using a variety of primary and secondary sources. When engaging with sources, students interact with an instructional strategy that requires them to **Inspect** the materials, **Find Evidence** to support claims, and **Make Connections** to other ideas and perspectives.

Geography

Exploring geography helps students understand how people have shaped our planet over the centuries and develops an appreciation for those things that connect us in spite of our geographic differences. Throughout the program, students use **Map Skills** as they explore the impact of geography on historical events.

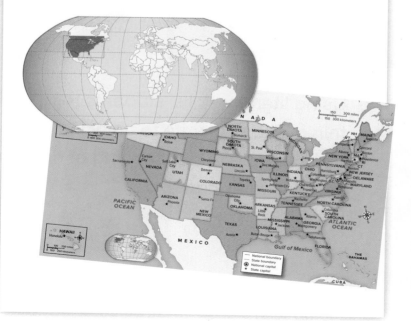

> "Social studies teaches us about ourselves: where we came from, who we are, where we are going. Primary sources allow us to peer into the past, and thinking and talking about them energizes our present and helps us all make decisions about a collective, shared future. Children of any and all ages can wrestle with the problems and mysteries we all wrestle with, and inviting them to do so in appropriate grade-level fashion is what great curriculum and great teaching is all about."

—William Deverell, Ph.D., IMPACT Program Author

Economics

Economics concepts are introduced across all grade levels to help students develop the fundamentals of economic thinking. **Graphs, Charts,** and **InfoGraphics** support key concepts and provide students with opportunities to build analysis and visual literacy skills. Teacher notes support interdisciplinary connections of key concepts to **Math** and **Science.**

Civics

The **IMPACT** instructional model encourages students to connect their learning to real world issues and apply problem-solving and communication skills. **Citizenship** features explore key concepts in civics and government and connect them to students' lives. **Biographies** tell the stories of people from the past and present who have made a difference in our communities, our country, and our world.

IMPACT is INQUIRY.

Curiosity is at the center of Inquiry.

Inquiry-based learning is **active** and **student-centered**. Teachers facilitate learning in the inquiry process with their students. The goal of inquiry is to **build knowledge** by **integrating content and skills** to **build deep knowledge grounded with evidence**.

Inquiry-based learning starts by **engaging learners and creating relevance** with a strong **Essential Question**. The essential questions help learners to **gather, organize, analyze,** and **synthesize** their ideas as they seek answers.

Inquiry blends **content, skills,** and **thinking** to help students **construct knowledge** as they put ideas together to **make meaning** and **ask more questions.**

Inquiry provides students and teachers **the opportunity to share the wonder of learning** on their knowledge-building journey. Inquiry is **deep and generative!**

> " When we teach with inquiry, we engage students in a way of thinking so that they will learn important content. "
>
> —Walter Parker, Ph.D.
> IMPACT Program Author

 ## Aligns to the C3 Framework's Inquiry Arc

IMPACT's instructional model scaffolds the inquiry process to make it easy to implement in your classroom!

1 ENGAGE	2 INVESTIGATE	3 REPORT AND TAKE ACTION
Learning begins with curiosity, and great questions are at the center of learning.	Sparking investigation of content, encouraging critical thinking, and inspiring more questions to research.	Building problem solvers, critical thinkers, and inspired innovators!
C3 **DIMENSION 1**	C3 **DIMENSION 2**	C3 **DIMENSION 4**
Framing Questions and Planning Inquiries	**Gathering Content Knowledge** Civics, Economics, Geography, History	**Applying and Expressing**
	C3 **DIMENSION 3** **Evaluating Sources and Using Evidence** Gathering and Evaluating Sources Making Claims Supported with Evidence	

Questions are the foundation of learning.

At all grade levels of *IMPACT Social Studies*, content is organized around inquiry-based chapters of study that are focused on engaging essential questions such as *"Why Does It Matter Where We Live?"* Questions spark curiosity and encourage students to find their voice and develop opinions.

Essential Questions are the starting point that shape the knowledge-building journey! The relevance and depth of these questions guide students toward unpacking core concepts of each chapter.

Lesson Questions continue the inquiry model and guide students toward unpacking historical concepts and discovering unique perspectives as they analyze high-quality primary and secondary sources. The Lesson Questions build the knowledge students need to address the chapter Essential Question.

Did You Know?

Students who collaborate in inquiry-based learning experiences become deeper thinkers and stronger communicators. These students develop principled, balanced, and more open views of the world which can lead to greater involvement in and active civic contributions to our global communities.

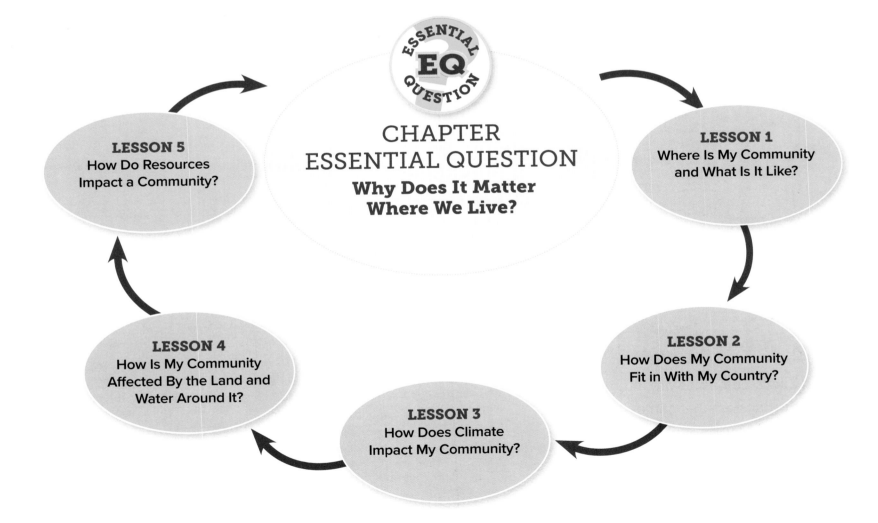

ESSENTIAL EQ QUESTION

CHAPTER ESSENTIAL QUESTION
Why Does It Matter Where We Live?

LESSON 1
Where Is My Community and What Is It Like?

LESSON 2
How Does My Community Fit in With My Country?

LESSON 3
How Does Climate Impact My Community?

LESSON 4
How Is My Community Affected By the Land and Water Around It?

LESSON 5
How Do Resources Impact a Community?

IMPACT is LITERACY.

Reading about the people and events that have shaped our world is relevant.

Literacy skills provide the foundation for inquiry. Students apply literacy tools—strategies for close reading, writing, and speaking and listening—to comprehend, critique, and synthesize social studies content.

Students **read, write,** and **investigate** for a purpose as they **analyze** primary and secondary sources; **explore** facts and figures; **form connections** to art and literary texts; and work with an array of texts written from **different perspectives** around an issue, problem, or question. Additionally, daily instruction is enhanced through text-based discussions, collaborative presentations, debates, games, and questioning.

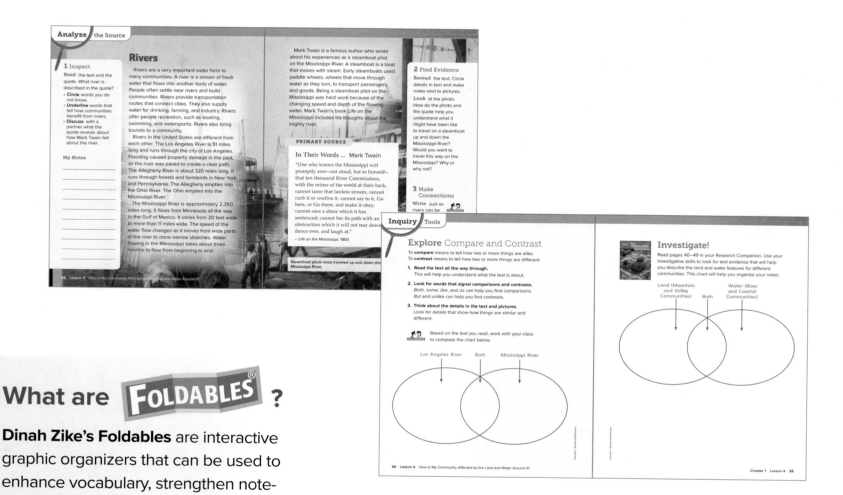

What are FOLDABLES®?

Dinah Zike's Foldables are interactive graphic organizers that can be used to enhance vocabulary, strengthen note-taking skills, and unlock content.

IMPACT is CITIZENSHIP.

Today's students are tomorrow's leaders.

A primary goal of *IMPACT Social Studies* is to prepare students to become **active citizens locally and globally** in an ever-changing world. Through **reading, writing,** and **conversation,** students are provided myriad opportunities to explore the **meaning of citizenship** and the qualities of good citizens, such as good sportsmanship, fair play, sharing, respect, integrity, and taking turns.

The texts and activities in *IMPACT Social Studies* focus on developing **civic values and democratic principles** as students build an understanding of their role in the **community,** the **nation,** and the **world.**

IMPACT Social Studies teaches students to **synthesize history** and use that knowledge to become **informed and engaged citizens.** At all grade levels, students learn about the **key factors of a democratic society.** They use **critical-thinking skills** to explore **multiple perspectives** on a variety of current and historical issues, and they learn to accept the ambiguity inherent in these issues.

IMPACT News is a current-events blogsite. Through rich, curated assets, the information provided on this site will enable students to develop new or different understandings of the world around them as they keep abreast of current events.

STUDENT EXPERIENCE
with **IMPACT**

Resources work together.

IMPACT's print and digital resources invite students to explore new people, places, and ideas and to engage with content; enhance students' critical-thinking skills; and inspire students to learn more.

The Inquiry Journal launches the inquiry by framing the chapter EQ and Inquiry Project.

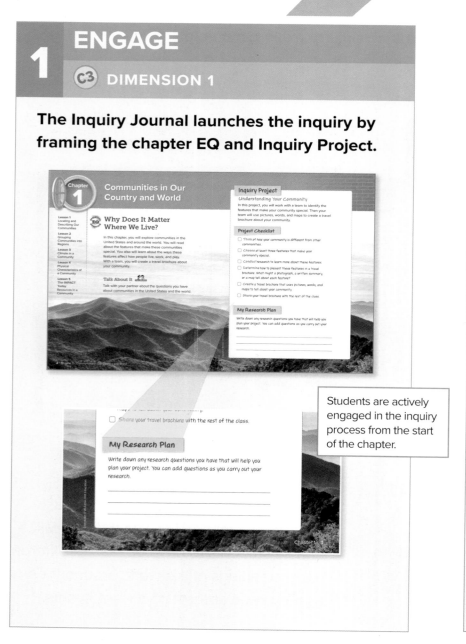

Students are actively engaged in the inquiry process from the start of the chapter.

The Research Companion is the primary collection of informational texts that deepens students' understanding of History, Geography, Civics, Economics, and Citizenship.

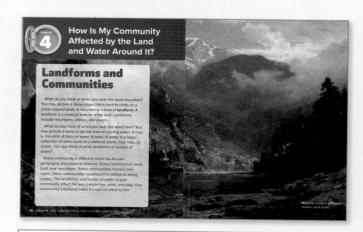

Texts of grade-appropriate complexity provide core social studies information and concepts for standards and framework expectations.

EXPLORER MAGAZINE

IMPACT's Explorer Magazine provides another route for all students to explore each chapter's key ideas through content written at a variety of grade-appropriate reading levels.

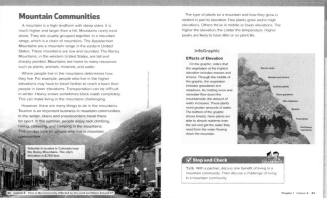

A variety of perspectives provide historical context for facts.

Students analyze a variety of sources, explore facts and figures, and examine issues and questions.

Foster critical thinking and deepen understanding through:

Anywhere.
Anytime.

- informational articles
- literary texts and graphic texts
- photographs, maps, and other visual resources
- additional questions and activities

3 REPORT AND TAKE ACTION

C3 DIMENSION 4

Students report their findings and then take action in the Inquiry Journal.

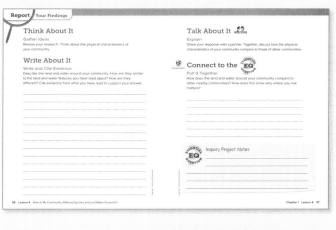

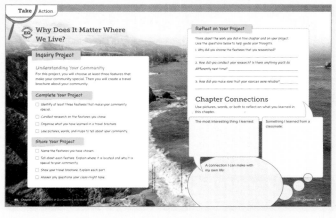

TEACHER EXPERIENCE
with **IMPACT**

Teach Social Studies with confidence.

| PLAN | 1 ENGAGE | 2 INVESTIGATE |

PLAN

The **IMPACT Social Studies** teacher materials offer you the flexibility to organize and expand the chapter content based around student inquiry. You can also easily integrate social studies into the literacy block.

IMPACT's scaffolded curriculum, instructional support, and assessment techniques make planning your **IMPACT** easy.

Start with an Essential Question.

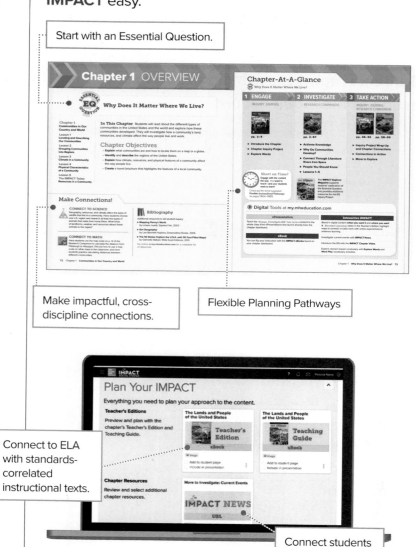

Make impactful, cross-discipline connections.

Flexible Planning Pathways

Connect to ELA with standards-correlated instructional texts.

Connect students to the community.

1 ENGAGE

IMPACT Social Studies provides daily opportunities for students to gain new knowledge, produce questions and ideas, and receive feedback to keep them immersed in a productive cycle of learning.

1 ENGAGE
C3 DIMENSION 1

The Inquiry Journal launches the inquiry by framing the chapter EQ and Inquiry Project.

Students are actively engaged in the inquiry process from the start of the chapter.

2 INVESTIGATE

Students read, write, investigate, and analyze primary and secondary sources; explore facts and figures; form connections to art and literary texts;

2 INVESTIGATE
C3 DIMENSIONS 2 AND 3

The Research Companion is the primary collection of informational texts that deepens students' understanding of History, Geography, Civics, Economics, and Citizenship.

Texts of grade-appropriate complexity provide core social studies information and concepts for standards and framework expectations.

EXPLORER MAGAZINE

IMPACT's Explorer Magazine provides another route for all students to explore each chapter's key ideas through content written at a variety of grade-appropriate reading levels.

3 REPORT AND TAKE ACTION

ASSESSMENT

and work with an array of texts written from different perspectives as they seek understanding and answers to the Essential and Lesson Questions.

Connecting what students are learning to why they are learning it and to how they will know they are successful creates meaning. As students report their findings by thinking, writing, and talking, they demonstrate citizenship in the classroom.

IMPACT's frequent and measurable assessment is the cornerstone of effective teaching as it shines a light on areas of mastery and helps to drive instruction.

Assessment of student learning is informed by formative discussion, writing prompts, and lesson-specific rubrics to measure student comprehension of the core content, engagement, and students' application of Inquiry Tools!

A variety of perspectives provide historical context for facts.

Students analyze a variety of sources, explore facts and figures, and examine issues and questions.

Foster critical thinking and deepen understanding through:

Anywhere. Anytime.

- informational articles
- literary texts and graphic texts
- photographs, maps, and other visual resources
- additional questions and activities

3 REPORT AND TAKE ACTION
C3 DIMENSION 4

Students report their findings and then take action in the Inquiry Journal.

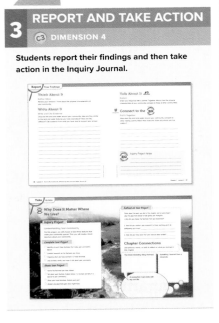

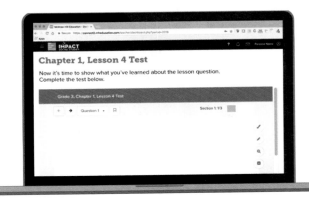

> **Effective social studies programs provide daily opportunities for students to gain new knowledge, produce questions and ideas, and receive feedback to keep them immersed in a productive cycle of learning.**
>
> —Emily Schell, Ph.D., IMPACT Program Author

BLENDED-LEARNING
with **IMPACT**

Enhance instruction with the right mix of print and digital resources.

IMPACT's digital and print resources can be used to personalize student learning according to their individual needs.

Through the use of the program components, you can assess and identify student strengths and areas of growth. Meet each student where they are by providing their perfect place, path, and pace!

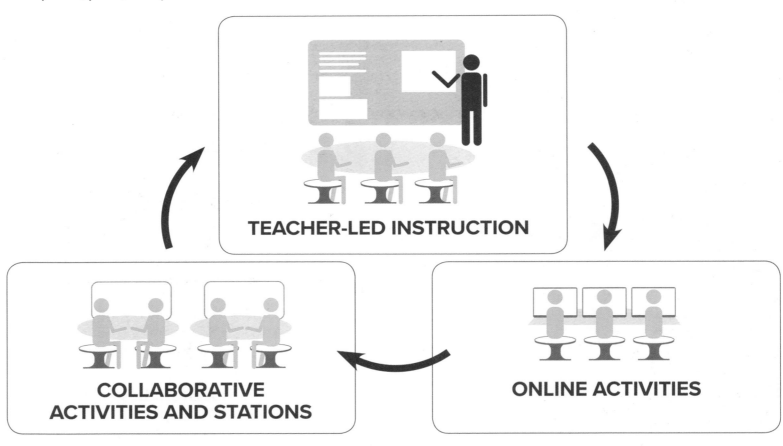

TEACHER-LED INSTRUCTION

COLLABORATIVE ACTIVITIES AND STATIONS

ONLINE ACTIVITIES

" Today's students are both witnesses to and participants in an ever-changing world. Access to modern technologies provides a constant flow of information from near and far. Our challenge is to help students understand themselves better by investigating the world, recognizing perspectives, communicating ideas, and taking action. "

—Emily Schell, Ph.D., IMPACT Program Author

Digital Tools at my.mheducation.com

1 ENGAGE

Resources in **Engage** will help you launch students on their investigative journeys.

ePresentation

Share a **Chapter** or **Lesson Video** to spark student interest.

Introduce content vocabulary with **Explore Words** and **Song Connections**.

Launch the **Inquiry Project** to promote collaboration.

eBook

Click on the icon to access the **Inquiry Journal** to start students on their journey.

Interactive IMPACT

Assign student content, including digital-only content.

Resources include:

- Engage with the EQ
- Chapter Video
- Inquiry Project
- Lesson Question
- Talk About It
- Analyze the Source
- Inquiry Tools Graphic Organizer (Printable and Online)

2 INVESTIGATE

The **Investigate** section includes chapter, lesson, and additional resources related to the topic.

ePresentation

Display chapter-level content for whole class instruction.

Model how to edit **Inquiry Tools Graphic Organizers**.

Display **Research It** tiles.

Share **Lesson Videos** for further enrichment on lesson topics.

Project and read **IMPACT Explorer Magazine** articles to deepen student understanding.

eBook

Access the **Research Companion** and **IMPACT Explorer Magazine** online.

Interactive IMPACT

Explore interactive **Time Lines, iMaps**, and **InfoGraphics**.

Stay up-to-date on current events with **IMPACT News**.

Access the **More to Investigate** section to extend student learning.

3 REPORT AND TAKE ACTION

In the **Report Your Findings** section, students demonstrate their understanding of the chapter content and vocabulary.

ePresentation

Provide a checklist to make sure students have covered all areas of the **Inquiry Project** with **EQ Take Action**.

Encourage students to find ways to make an **IMPACT** in their own communities with **Connections in Action**.

eBook

Click the icon to access the **Inquiry Journal** to **Take Action**.

Click the icon to access the **Research Companion** for **Connections in Action**.

Interactive IMPACT

Assign **Word Play** activities to give students the opportunity to demonstrate their understanding of chapter vocabulary.

Wrap up students' investigations with **Report Your Findings**.

IMPACT
BUILDS LANGUAGE.
IMPACT supports all Language Learners.

IMPACT Social Studies ensures that the language learning that occurs in social studies is especially valuable for ELs because it expands their language development in new directions as they engage with the content.

Students deepen their understanding of how language can be used for different purposes and in varied ways. By focusing on language development, all students can participate and engage in meaningful discussions. **IMPACT** supports teachers as they adapt the instruction to meet the language needs in their students.

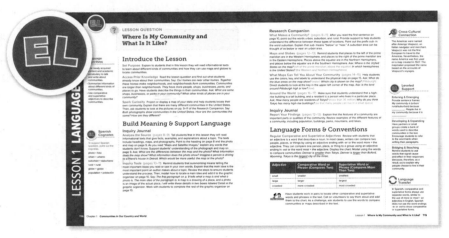

> " Providing access to social studies content for English learners requires attention to their language needs. Lessons should include a number of features to enhance their comprehension including clear, student-friendly definitions of terms, use of visuals, questions that are differentiated by proficiency level, and opportunities to discuss ideas with peers. Remember that these students are learning new content in a language they are still in the process of acquiring. "

—Jana Echevarria, Ph.D., IMPACT Program Author

McGraw-Hill Education is committed to providing English Learners appropriate support as they simultaneously learn content and language. As an organization, we recognize that the United States is culturally and linguistically diverse, and we value the backgrounds and experiences of all language learners.

Built upon McGraw-Hill's Guiding Principles for English Learners

- Provide Specialized Instruction
- Cultivate Meaning
- Teach Structure and Form
- Develop Language in Context
- Scaffold to Support Access
- Foster Interaction
- Create Affirming Cultural Spaces
- Engage Home to Enrich Instruction
- Promote Multilingualism

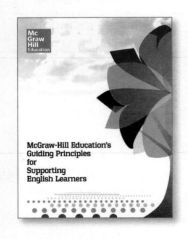

McGraw-Hill Education's Guiding Principles for Supporting English Learners

IMPACT TEACHES THE WHOLE CHILD.

Social Emotional Learning is one of the most important factors in predicting school success. **IMPACT Social Studies** supports students in mastering themselves and how they interact with the world. Social and emotional learning brings together affective and cognitive learning and social behavior.

IMPACT Social Studies provides children with the tools they need to complete daily tasks, meet challenges, and interact with others in positive, effective, and ethical ways. And to become globally competent citizens, our students need to know that they have a voice and when to use it.

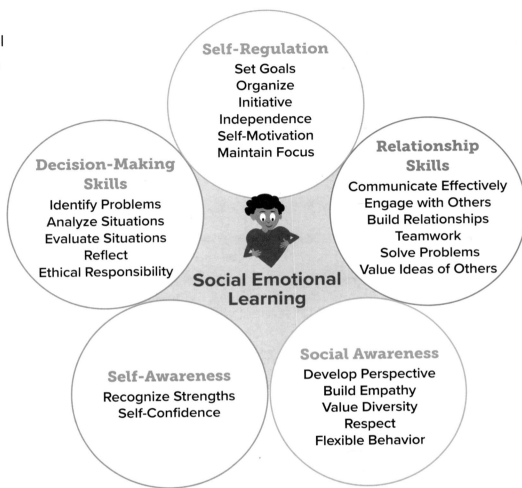

Self-Regulation
Set Goals
Organize
Initiative
Independence
Self-Motivation
Maintain Focus

Decision-Making Skills
Identify Problems
Analyze Situations
Evaluate Situations
Reflect
Ethical Responsibility

Relationship Skills
Communicate Effectively
Engage with Others
Build Relationships
Teamwork
Solve Problems
Value Ideas of Others

Social Emotional Learning

Self-Awareness
Recognize Strengths
Self-Confidence

Social Awareness
Develop Perspective
Build Empathy
Value Diversity
Respect
Flexible Behavior

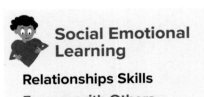

Social Emotional Learning

Relationships Skills

Engage with Others
Working closely with peers will help students develop their relationship skills. As students participate in the Talk About It activity, encourage them to listen carefully to their peers and respond respectfully.

Did You Know?

"**Social and emotional learning (SEL)** is the process through which children and adults acquire and effectively apply the knowledge, attitudes, and skills necessary to understand and manage emotions, set and achieve positive goals, feel and show empathy for others, establish and maintain positive relationships, and make responsible decisions."

—Collaborative for Academic, Social, and Emotional Learning

Chapter-level School-to-Home letters deepen the connection between community and classroom, supporting social and emotional development.

FLEXIBLE PACING
OPTIONS

Engage with content the way you want to teach—and your students want to learn!

Flexible options let you teach how you want, when you want.

You can mix and match to meet your needs and priorities!

1 The **FULL INQUIRY PATH** is ideal when you want to teach content with inquiry! Teaching with inquiry fosters curiosity and a love of learning. Inquiry teaches perseverance, growth mindset, and self-regulation.

2 The **READING PATH** is ideal for when you want to highlight the relationship between Social Studies, English Language Arts, and English Language Development.

3 The **SHORT-ON-TIME PATH** connects to the Chapter Inquiry Projects so students can have rich Social Studies investigations even when time is short!

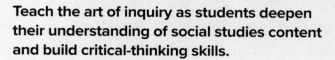

1 FOCUS ON FULL INQUIRY

Teach the art of inquiry as students deepen their understanding of social studies content and build critical-thinking skills.

ENGAGE

- Engagement begins with Essential Questions and images to spark curiosity.
- Read and write with specific purposes in mind.

INVESTIGATE

- Explore a rich range of informational texts including primary and secondary sources.

REPORT

- Cite evidence via text-based discussions, collaborative presentations, debates and questioning.

Inquiry Journal

Research Companion

Inquiry Journal

2 FOCUS ON READING SOURCES

While reading doesn't teach students social studies, teaching social studies during reading blocks teaches BOTH social studies AND reading.

IMPACT provides two options for teaching social studies content during reading. Use the **Explorer Magazine** for independent reading or small group time.

Explorer Magazine

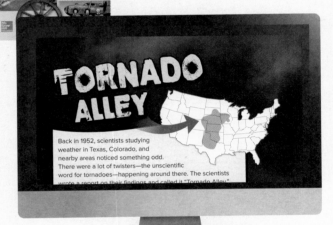

Use the **Research Companion** to explore important, carefully curated social studies content.

Research Companion

3 FOCUS ON TIME MANAGEMENT

IMPACT provides Short-on-Time Options to ensure you maximize the teaching time you have.

Chapter-Level Inquiry Projects

Chapter-level inquiry projects allow for whole-class time or small-group work.

Explorer Magazine

Explorer Magazine articles are brimming with a diverse range of literary selections about the topic of the chapter. Assign specific articles to students based on Lexile and reading levels.

Explorer Magazine

ASSESSMENT
with **IMPACT**

Know what your students know.

Frequent and measurable assessment is the cornerstone of effective teaching because it **informs instruction** and shines a light on **areas of mastery.** The flexible formal and informal paths included in the *IMPACT Social Studies* program are built on the understanding that **students thrive on feedback** from their teachers and peers.

IMPACT provides **daily opportunities** for students to **gain new knowledge, produce questions and ideas, and receive feedback** to keep them immersed in a productive **cycle of learning.**

IMPACT's data-driven, real-time information helps teachers make sound teaching decisions on the spot and across the school year. When decisions are informed by the right data at the right time, the needs of your students reside at the center.

The assessment of student learning is informed by state standards and national frameworks to help **all students** prepare now for **college, career, and civic life.**

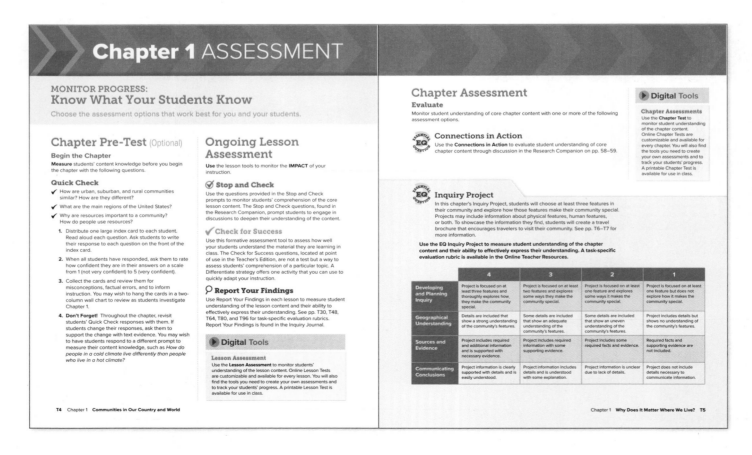

PROFESSIONAL
LEARNING with **IMPACT**

Teach with confidence.

At McGraw-Hill Education, we are your partner in professional learning. From point-of-use expert videos to point-of-use teacher support notes to Professional Development white papers, you will be well supported throughout the instructional journey.

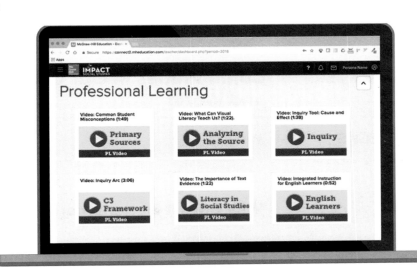

Getting Started

To get started with **IMPACT Social Studies**, you will find the Quick Start Guide, a brief, to-the-point description of how to use the program's components and how to customize content for individual, small-group, and whole-class needs.

Point-of-Use Teaching Support

Point-of-use quick tips and features designed to give you the confidence to be the expert in the subject area are found in both the print and digital Teacher's Editions. They are designed to provide support at the teaching moment.

Digital Tool notes help you determine how and why to blend your students' learning experience.

Ongoing Professional Learning

IMPACT Social Studies brings the experts to you by providing learning modules that focus on a set of best practices in social studies pedagogy, such as:

- How to teach with Primary and Secondary Sources
- How to support Language Learners in the content areas
- How to teach with and for inquiry in social studies
- How to address sensitive topics in your classroom

Professional Development White Papers are also available for review within the digital program and the print Teacher's Edition. These research-based white papers provide expert insight into how instruction can be optimized across a variety of topics.

CONTENT MAP

1
2

	1 Communities in Our Country and World	**2** The Community and Its Environment
CHAPTER TITLE	**Communities in Our Country and World**	**The Community and Its Environment**
WEEKS	**Weeks 1–6**	**Weeks 7–12**
ESSENTIAL QUESTION	**Why Does It Matter Where We Live?**	**What Is Our Relationship with Our Environment?**
LESSON QUESTIONS	**1.** Where Is My Community and What Is it Like? **2.** How Does My Community Fit in With My Country? **3.** How Does Climate Impact My Community? **4.** How Is My Community Affected By the Land and Water Around It? **5.** The IMPACT Today: How Do Resources Impact a Community?	**1.** How Does the Environment Change the Way People Live? **2.** How Do People Change Their Environment? **3.** The IMPACT Today: How Do We Meet Environmental Challenges?
CHAPTER INQUIRY PROJECT	Understanding Geography **Understanding Your Community** Students will work with a team to identify the features that make their community special. Then the team will use pictures, words, and maps to create a travel brochure about their community.	Understanding Geography **Improving the Environment** Students will think of a way to improve their community's environment. Their team will create a plan for an improvement and present it to the class.

3

4

	People and Communities	**Communities Change Over Time**
CHAPTER TITLE		
WEEKS	Weeks 13–18	Weeks 19–24
ESSENTIAL QUESTION 	**What Makes a Community Unique?**	**How Does the Past Impact the Present?**
LESSON QUESTIONS	**1.** What is Culture? **2.** How Do People Express Their Culture? **3.** What Do Immigrants Add to a Community? **4.** What Can Comparing Different Communities Tell Us About Global Cultures? **5.** The IMPACT Today: What Connects Communities Throughout the World?	**1.** How Did Conflict and Cooperation Shape Early Communities? **2.** What Makes a Community Grow? **3.** How Do Communities of the Past Compare to Today? **4.** How Can People and Events Change Communities? **5.** What Can Comparing Different Communities Tell Us About How Communities Change Over Time? **6.** The IMPACT Today: What Makes My Community Special?
CHAPTER INQUIRY PROJECT 	**Understanding Geography** **Planning a Cultural Event** Students will work with a team to create a plan for a holiday or festival for their school to celebrate the different cultures of their classmates.	**Understanding History** **Community Time Line** Students will work with a small group to create a time line showing the sequence of key events that played a role in the development of their community.

	5	6
CHAPTER TITLE	**American Citizens, Symbols, and Government**	**Economics of Communities**
WEEKS	**Weeks 25–30**	**Weeks 31–36**
 **ESSENTIAL QUESTION**	**Why Do Governments and Citizens Need Each Other?**	**How Do People in a Community Meet Their Wants and Needs?**
LESSON QUESTIONS	**1.** What Makes Democracy Work? **2.** What Are the Different Parts of Government? **3.** Why Do Communities Need Local Government? **4.** Why Do We Follow Rules? **5.** How Have Heroes Helped Communities? **6.** The IMPACT Today: How Can You Help Build Strong Communities?	**1.** How Can Communities Use Their Resources? **2.** How Do Businesses and Communities Provide Goods and Services? **3.** How Do People Get What They Want and Need? **4.** What Makes a Community's Economy Change? **5.** The IMPACT Today: How Can You Use Money Wisely?
 **CHAPTER INQUIRY PROJECT**	**Understanding Civics** **Creating a Classroom Constitution** Students will work with the class to create a classroom constitution that sets the rules everyone must follow to make their classroom a fair and safe community.	**Understanding Economics** **Blogging About a Local Business** Students will work with a small group to create a blog about a local business and describe how it helps their community.

Teacher Notes

BE A SOCIAL STUDIES DETECTIVE

Explore and Investigate

Activate Knowledge

Collaborate Launch a discussion about primary and secondary sources by presenting the following scenario.

You have walked into a classroom from 100 years ago. The room looks as if the teacher and students just left. There is writing on the blackboard and books are open on the teacher's and students' desks.

- Encourage partners to discuss what they would do to investigate this classroom and what they would hope to learn. Share responses with the class. (Possible responses: Read what's written on the blackboard. Look at the books to see what the students are studying. Look to see what other kinds of supplies are included in the room. Find out how school was the same and different 100 years ago.)

- Explain to students that learning about people, places, and events in the past and present is what social studies is all about. In this section, students will learn to read, think, talk, and write like Social Studies Detectives.

Investigate Primary Sources

Explain Primary Sources Have students read "What are Primary Sources?" on page 8a.

Ask partners to describe what a primary source is. Guide students to define a primary source as a piece of evidence from someone who saw something happen or official documents about people or things. Explain that a primary source is information that was recorded at the time it happened.

- Have students think about other things that can be considered primary sources. If necessary, mention items such as scrapbooks, photo albums, letters, emails, and audio and video recordings. Ask: *Why do you think these can be primary sources?* (These are things that can be from a different time period and can tell us more about that time.)

Explain Secondary Sources Have students read the information in the Did You Know? box on page 8a. Ask: *Who provides a secondary source?* (Someone who was not at the event.) Explain to students that textbooks, encyclopedias, and biographies are examples of secondary sources. Discuss with students how secondary sources differ from primary sources. Make sure they understand that secondary sources were written or told after the event by someone who didn't witness it as it was happening.

Be a Social Studies Detective

How do you learn about people, places, and events? Become a Social Studies Detective!

Explore! Investigate! Report!

Investigate Primary Sources

Detectives solve mysteries by asking questions and searching for clues to help them answer their questions. Where can you get clues that will help you learn about the past? By analyzing primary and secondary sources!

What are Primary Sources?

A **primary source** is a record of an event by someone who was present at whatever he or she is describing. **What are some primary sources?** Clothing, photographs, toys, tools, letters, diaries, and bank records are all examples of primary sources.

Did You Know?

A **secondary source** is information from someone who was not present at the event he or she is describing. Secondary sources are based on primary sources, such as a newspaper article.

8a

A classroom long ago

Social Studies Detective Strategies

Inspect
- Look closely at the source.
- Who or what is it?
- How would you describe it?

Find Evidence
- Where did the event take place?
- When did it happen?
- What are the most important details?

Make Connections
- Is this source like others you found?
- Are there other perspectives that you need to consider?
- What information supports your idea?

9a

RESEARCH COMPANION, pp. 8a–9a

Social Studies Detective Strategies

- Explain to students that they will use the Social Studies Detective Strategies throughout the year as they investigate social studies content in sources that include texts, maps, charts, art, photographs, audio, and video.
- Discuss each step with students and explain how these strategies can help us investigate both primary and secondary sources to develop a deeper understanding of content.

Inspect

Explain to students that in this step, they should look at the source to find out the topic that is being covered. Ask students what they think they can learn from the photograph on p. 9a. (Possible response: how people dressed at the time, or what a classroom in the past looked like)

Find Evidence

This step involves looking closely at a source to find details that help build the topic. Explain that details are smaller pieces of information in a source that help us understand and make sense of the topic.

Make Connections

Point out that this final step gives students the opportunity to ask themselves how this information builds on what they already know, helps them make a connection to their own lives, or gives them a new perspective. Discuss connections students can make between the photograph on p. 9a and their own classroom.

> " The task of using —and understanding —primary sources lies at the center of the social studies endeavor. To see and apply the undistilled stuff of history is to gain direct insight into social, cultural, economic, and political life as it played out in the past. Engagement with primary sources leads to understanding, which leads to direct action in our democratic processes. "
>
> —Daniel Lewis, Ph.D.
> IMPACT Program Author

Explore Primary Sources

Activate Knowledge

Review Ask students to discuss the difference between primary and secondary sources. Ask them to provide examples of both types of sources.

Engage Have partners discuss different ways we can learn about people who lived long ago. Then have them think about how people in the future will learn about us. What do they think our society will leave behind that will help people learn about us?

Explore Display the word *artifact*. Ask students if they know what an artifact is and where they might find one. Explain that artifacts are objects, such as cooking utensils, clothing, and tools, left behind by people in the past. Historians study artifacts to learn how people lived in the past.

- Why would a historian want to know where an artifact was found? (Possible answer: to identify which group of people used the artifact; to learn something about the lives of people who lived in an area.)

Investigate Have students investigate the tools on page 10a. If necessary, explain that the photo shows a collection of old tools. Have students identify the tools with which they are familiar. Explain that some of these tools are used for shoeing horses.

- What can you learn by knowing what these tools were used for? (You can learn how the person who owned the tools used them. You can learn something about the lives of the people in the past and the work they did.)

- What must a person infer when studying an artifact? (A person must infer how it could have been used.)

Talk About It Have partners discuss the supporting evidence they found in the photo. Remind them that they can also use their own knowledge about any of the tools to support their ideas.

Explore Explain to students that the Primary Source on p. 11a are letters from President Theodore Roosevelt to his children. Tell students that Sagamore Hill was the name of the Roosevelt home and the White House is the president's home in Washington, D.C. Explain that letters are important primary sources because they give historians a glimpse into the daily lives of people in the past. They can help us understand how people lived and what was important to them.

Investigate Have students investigate the letters on page 11a. Have them start by looking at the date, the location, and the greeting in each letter.

- When were the letters written? Who wrote the letters? (June 11, 1906, and November 22, 1908, by Theodore Roosevelt)

- What do you learn about Theodore Roosevelt and his family from these letters? (Possible responses: He looks forward to being with his family at Sagamore Hill, and he is concerned about his son Quentin who has a broken leg. They show that even though he is president of the United States, he's very much involved with his family.)

Report Have groups report their findings to the class. Discuss the steps students used to analyze the primary sources. After all groups present, discuss similarities and differences in the information from each group.

Social Studies Detectives make connections to learn about the past. Look closely at the image below. Use the Social Studies Detective Strategy to analyze the image.

PRIMARY SOURCE

Social Studies Detective Strategies

1. Inspect
2. Find Evidence
3. Make Connections

Talk About It   COLLABORATE

After you look closely and ask questions about the image, find evidence to support your ideas. Share your evidence and make connections to what you know.

10a

Here is another source. Inspect the source, and look for clues to answer your questions and make connections.

NO PLACE LIKE SAGAMORE HILL

(To Ethel, at Sagamore Hill)
White House, June 11, 1906.

BLESSED ETHEL:

I am very glad that what changes have been made in the house are good, and I look forward so eagerly to seeing them. After all, fond as I am of the White House and much though I have appreciated these years in it, there isn't any place in the world like home—like Sagamore Hill, where things are our own, with our own associations, and where it is real country.

MORE ABOUT QUENTIN

White House, Nov. 22, 1908.

DEAREST ARCHIE:

I handed your note and the two dollar bill to Quentin, and he was perfectly delighted. It came in very handy, because poor Quentin has been in bed with his leg in a plaster cast, and the two dollars I think went to make up a fund with which he purchased a fascinating little steam-engine, which has been a great source of amusement to him. He is out to-day visiting some friends, although his leg is still in a cast. He has a great turn for mechanics.

from Theodore Roosevelt's Letters to His Children

11a

RESEARCH COMPANION, pp. 10a–11a

TYPES OF PRIMARY SOURCES

Artifacts are objects that people make and use in their daily lives.

Official Documents are papers from a government or a government agency, such as a birth certificate, a population census, or a written law.

Letters are primary sources when they describe an event the writer saw or experienced.

Journal Entries and Diaries are primary sources when they describe events the writer saw or experienced.

Political Cartoons express the ideas or feelings of people at the time an event takes place. Political cartoons show opinions, not facts.

Photographs that show events as they happened are primary sources.

> " Primary sources are history. They reflect the thinking of the time and provide students an opportunity to gain a deeper understanding of the social, political, and economic environment in which our fore-parents lived. Studying primary sources ensures that students gain an appreciation for the actual historical context while also learning how to engage in research and investigation. "
>
> —Doug Fisher, Ph.D.
> IMPACT Program Author

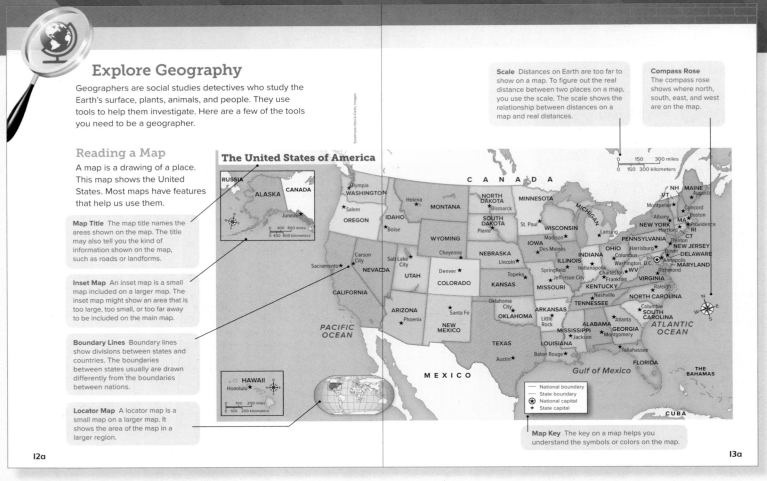

Explore Geography

Geographers are social studies detectives who study the Earth's surface, plants, animals, and people. They use tools to help them investigate. Here are a few of the tools you need to be a geographer.

Reading a Map

A map is a drawing of a place. This map shows the United States. Most maps have features that help us use them.

Map Title The map title names the areas shown on the map. The title may also tell you the kind of information shown on the map, such as roads or landforms.

Inset Map An inset map is a small map included on a larger map. The inset map might show an area that is too large, too small, or too far away to be included on the main map.

Boundary Lines Boundary lines show divisions between states and countries. The boundaries between states usually are drawn differently from the boundaries between nations.

Locator Map A locator map is a small map on a larger map. It shows the area of the map in a larger region.

Scale Distances on Earth are too far to show on a map. To figure out the real distance between two places on a map, you use the scale. The scale shows the relationship between distances on a map and real distances.

Compass Rose The compass rose shows where north, south, east, and west are on the map.

Map Key The key on a map helps you understand the symbols or colors on the map.

12a

13a

RESEARCH COMPANION, pp. 12a–13a

Explore Geography

Activate Knowledge

Engage Have students read pages 12a–13a. Ask students what they know about geography and what geographers do. Explain that geographers study how humans impact the earth and its atmosphere. Ask: *Why are maps important when we study geography?* (Answers will vary, but students should point out that maps show landforms, bodies of water, and physical features of the land.)

Investigate Maps

Reading a Map Explain that the map on pp. 12a–13a is called a *political map*. Political maps show features such as the names of states and countries, state and national borders, and capital cities. Review the map key with students and have them locate their state capital.

- Why are Alaska and Hawaii shown in inset maps? (They are separated from the main part of the United States.)

- What does the locator map tell us? (It shows where the United States is located in relation to the rest of the world.)

- Point to the compass rose on the right side of the map. Ask students why they think it's called a "compass rose"? (The points look like the petals on a rose.)

- Challenge students to use the map scale to estimate the distance across the United States from the Pacific Ocean to the Atlantic Ocean in both miles and kilometers. (Distances will vary, but the result should be 2800–3000 miles or 4400–4800 kilometers.)

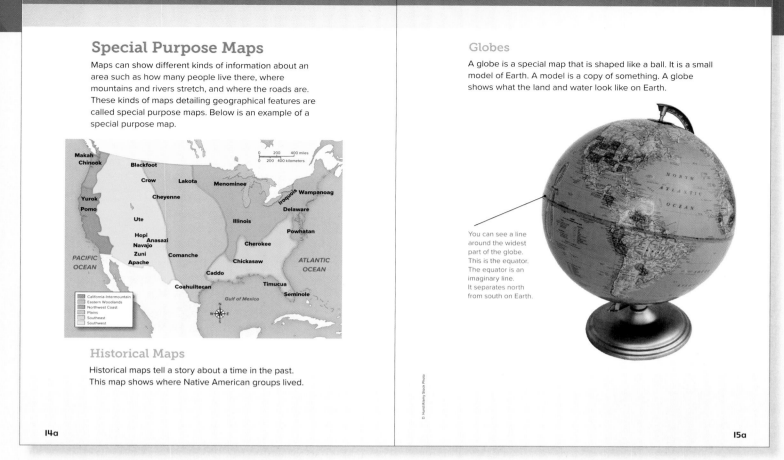

Special Purpose Maps

Maps can show different kinds of information about an area such as how many people live there, where mountains and rivers stretch, and where the roads are. These kinds of maps detailing geographical features are called special purpose maps. Below is an example of a special purpose map.

Historical Maps

Historical maps tell a story about a time in the past. This map shows where Native American groups lived.

Globes

A globe is a special map that is shaped like a ball. It is a small model of Earth. A model is a copy of something. A globe shows what the land and water look like on Earth.

You can see a line around the widest part of the globe. This is the equator. The equator is an imaginary line. It separates north from south on Earth.

14a

15a

RESEARCH COMPANION, pp. 14a–15a

Special Purpose Maps

Activate Knowledge

Engage Have students read pages 14a–15a. Explain that special purpose maps show specific kinds of information. Other kinds of special purpose maps provide information about climate and elevations of land.

Investigate the Historical Maps

Historical Maps Tell students that historical maps help us understand the past. The map on p. 14a shows where Native Americans lived throughout what is now the United States.

Investigate Have students study the map key and the colors on the map. Have partners discuss how these colors help someone who is using the map. (The colors help us understand which Native American people lived in each region.)

• Why are historical maps important for researchers today? (They can show where people lived in the past and help us understand how a place has changed over time.)

Globes Using a classroom globe, point out various features such as the equator, lines of latitude and longitude, and the north and south poles.

Investigate Have students discuss why they think a globe is tilted. If necessary explain that the tilt reflects the actual angle at which the earth is tilted on its axis.

• Which do you think provides a more accurate representation of the earth, a map or a globe? (Students should respond that a globe is more accurate because it is round like the earth.)

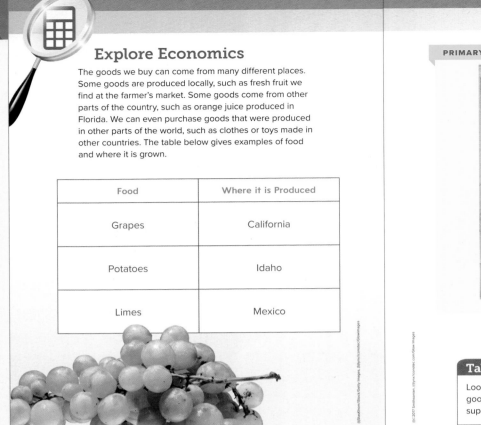

Explore Economics

The goods we buy can come from many different places. Some goods are produced locally, such as fresh fruit we find at the farmer's market. Some goods come from other parts of the country, such as orange juice produced in Florida. We can even purchase goods that were produced in other parts of the world, such as clothes or toys made in other countries. The table below gives examples of food and where it is grown.

Food	Where it is Produced
Grapes	California
Potatoes	Idaho
Limes	Mexico

PRIMARY SOURCE

136   B   1929   Advt No. 9771

COFFEE
..is..
America's Favorite Drink

and practically three-fourths
of all coffee consumed in the
United States comes from

B R A Z I L

COFFEE
AMERICA'S
favorite
DRINK

THE BRAZILIAN-AMERICAN COFFEE PROMOTION COMMITTEE
NEW YORK CITY

Talk About It

Look closely at the picture. Where do you think these goods were produced? What details in the picture support your ideas?

RESEARCH COMPANION, pp. 16a–17a

Explore Economics

Activate Knowledge

Engage Have students read page 16a. Explain that economics has to do with how goods and services are produced, distributed, and consumed. Tell students that goods may include things such as clothing, food, household items, and electronics. Services are things provided by other people, such as doctors, mechanics, and store owners.

Investigate Have partners work together to discuss goods that they use that are imported from other countries and goods that are exported to other countries. Ask students if they know of any goods that are produced in your area.

Investigate the Primary Source

Build Meaning Point to the Primary Source on p. 17a. Explain that this is an advertisement for coffee that was imported to the United States from Brazil. Call students' attention to the top of the image and ask what year the ad was printed. (1929)

- What is the purpose of the ad? (to promote coffee from Brazil)
- What does the ad tell people about coffee? (It is America's favorite drink and much of it comes from Brazil.)

Talk About It Have students note details in the advertisement that tell them where the coffee was produced and which group was responsible for the ad.

Explore Citizenship

You can make an impact by being a good citizen. The words below describe good citizens. They help us understand how to be good citizens in our home, neighborhood, school, community, country, and world.

Take Action!

You have learned to be a Social Studies Detective by investigating, finding evidence, and making connections. Then you practiced investigating geography, economics, and civics. Now it's time to explore and make an impact!

The Statue of Freedom sits atop the dome of the United States Capitol.

18a

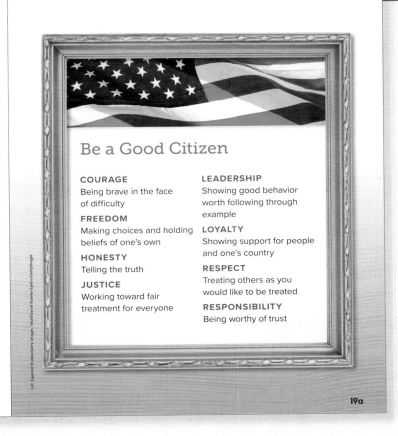

Be a Good Citizen

COURAGE
Being brave in the face of difficulty

FREEDOM
Making choices and holding beliefs of one's own

HONESTY
Telling the truth

JUSTICE
Working toward fair treatment for everyone

LEADERSHIP
Showing good behavior worth following through example

LOYALTY
Showing support for people and one's country

RESPECT
Treating others as you would like to be treated

RESPONSIBILITY
Being worthy of trust

19a

RESEARCH COMPANION, pp. 18a–19a

Explore Citizenship

Activate Knowledge

Engage Have students read pages 18a–19a. Explain that citizenship means belonging to a community. Point out that communities that we belong to can be as large as a country or as small as a neighborhood or school. Have students name different communities to which they belong. (Students may say the United States, their state or town, or their school.)

Discuss Tell students to choose the two or three qualities on page 19a that are most important to them. Have them talk with a partner about how they can embody those qualities at home, at school, or in the community.

Investigate the Primary Source

Build Meaning Explain to students that the photograph on p. 18a shows the Statue of Freedom that sits atop the dome of the U.S. capitol. The statue is 19 feet 6 inches tall and weighs about 15,000 pounds. It was designed by Thomas Crawford and was placed on the dome in 1863.

- Have students look closely at the photo and talk about what they see. (Students may say the statue, other pieces of sculpture in the room, and details of the room the statue is in.)

- Provide students with the option of finding out more about the Statue of Freedom by doing independent research.

Explain to students that they will learn more about citizenship and what it means to be a good citizen as they investigate social studies topics throughout the year.

Be a Social Studies Detective **FM49**

Why Does It Matter Where We Live?

In This Chapter Students will read about the different types of communities in the United States and the world and explore how these communities developed. They will investigate how a community's land, resources, and climate affect the way people live and work.

Chapter Objectives

- **Explain** what communities are and how to locate them on a map or a globe.
- **Identify** and **describe** the regions of the United States.
- **Explain** how climate, resources, and physical features of a community affect the way people live.
- **Create** a travel brochure that highlights the features of a local community.

Make Connections!

CONNECT TO SCIENCE

Geography, resources, and climate affect the types of wildlife that live in a community. Have students choose one U.S. region and research at least two types of animals that make their home there. What kinds of landforms, weather, and resources attract these animals to the region?

CONNECT TO MATH

Have students use the map scale on p. 14 of the Research Companion to calculate the distance from Pittsburgh to Aliquippa. Discuss how to use a map scale on other maps in the classroom, and have students practice calculating distances between different communities.

Bibliography

Additional resources to aid student inquiry:

▶ **Mapping Penny's World**
  by Loreen Leedy; Square Fish, 2003

▶ **Got Geography!**
  by Lee Bennett Hopkins; Greenwillow Books, 2006

▶ **The 50 States: Explore the U.S.A. with 50 Fact-Filled Maps!**
  by Gabrielle Balkan; Wide Eyed Editions, 2015

Go online at **my.mheducation.com** for a complete list of resources.

Chapter-At-A-Glance

 EQ Why Does It Matter Where We Live?

1 ENGAGE	**2 INVESTIGATE**	**3 TAKE ACTION**
INQUIRY JOURNAL	RESEARCH COMPANION	INQUIRY JOURNAL RESEARCH COMPANION

pp. 2–5

- ▶ **Introduce the Chapter**
- ▶ **Chapter Inquiry Project**
- ▶ **Explore Words**

pp. 2–57

- ▶ **Activate Knowledge**
- ▶ **Why Do Communities Develop?**
- ▶ **Connect Through Literature** Rivers from Space
- ▶ **People You Should Know**
- ▶ **Lessons 1–5**

pp. 46–53   pp. 58–59

- ▶ **Inquiry Project Wrap-Up and Chapter Connections**
- ▶ **Connections in Action**
- ▶ **More to Explore**

Short on Time?
Engage with the content the way YOU want to teach—and *your* students want to learn!

Check out the three suggested **Flexible Instructional Pathways** on pages FM34–FM35.

The **IMPACT Explorer Magazine** supports students' exploration of the Essential Question and provides additional resources for the EQ Inquiry Project.

Digital Tools at my.mheducation.com

ePresentation

Teach the Engage, Investigate, and Take Action content to the whole class from ePresentations that launch directly from the chapter dashboard.

eBook

You can flip your instruction with the **IMPACT eBooks** found on your chapter dashboard.

Interactive IMPACT

Blend in digital content **when you want it** and **where you want it**. Blended Learning notes in the Teacher's Edition highlight ways to connect in-class work with online experiences to enhance learning.

Investigate current events with **IMPACT News**.

Introduce the EQ with the **IMPACT Chapter Video**.

Explore domain-based vocabulary with **Explore Words** and **Word Play** vocabulary activities.

MONITOR PROGRESS:
Know What Your Students Know

Choose the assessment options that work best for you and your students.

Chapter Pre-Test (Optional)

Begin the Chapter

Measure students' content knowledge before you begin the chapter with the following questions.

Quick Check

✔ How are urban, suburban, and rural communities similar? How are they different?

✔ What are the main regions of the United States?

✔ Why are resources important to a community? How do people use resources?

1. Distribute one large index card to each student. Read aloud each question. Ask students to write their response to each question on the front of the index card.

2. When all students have responded, ask them to rate how confident they are in their answers on a scale from 1 (not very confident) to 5 (very confident).

3. Collect the cards and review them for misconceptions, factual errors, and to inform instruction. You may wish to hang the cards in a two-column wall chart to review as students investigate Chapter 1.

4. **Don't Forget!** Throughout the chapter, revisit students' Quick Check responses with them. If students change their responses, ask them to support the change with text evidence. You may wish to have students respond to a different prompt to measure their content knowledge, such as *How do people in a cold climate live differently than people who live in a hot climate?*

Ongoing Lesson Assessment

Use the lesson tools to monitor the **IMPACT** of your instruction.

✓ Stop and Check

Use the questions provided in the Stop and Check prompts to monitor students' comprehension of the core lesson content. The Stop and Check questions, found in the Research Companion, prompt students to engage in discussions to deepen their understanding of the content.

✔ Check for Success

Use this formative assessment tool to assess how well your students understand the material they are learning in class. The Check for Success questions, located at point of use in the Teacher's Edition, are not a test but a way to assess students' comprehension of a particular topic. A Differentiate strategy offers one activity that you can use to quickly adapt your instruction.

◯ Report Your Findings

Use Report Your Findings in each lesson to measure student understanding of the lesson content and their ability to effectively express their understanding. See pp. T30, T48, T64, T80, and T96 for task-specific evaluation rubrics. Report Your Findings is found in the Inquiry Journal.

▶ Digital Tools

Lesson Assessment

Use the **Lesson Assessment** to monitor students' understanding of the lesson content. Online Lesson Tests are customizable and available for every lesson. You will also find the tools you need to create your own assessments and to track your students' progress. A printable Lesson Test is available for use in class.

Chapter Assessment

Evaluate

Monitor student understanding of core chapter content with one or more of the following assessment options.

Connections in Action

Use the **Connections in Action** to evaluate student understanding of core chapter content through discussion in the Research Companion on pp. 58–59.

 Digital Tools

Chapter Assessments
Use the **Chapter Test** to monitor student understanding of the chapter content. Online Chapter Tests are customizable and available for every chapter. You will also find the tools you need to create your own assessments and to track your students' progress. A printable Chapter Test is available for use in class.

Inquiry Project

In this chapter's Inquiry Project, students will choose at least three features in their community and explore how those features make their community special. Projects may include information about physical features, human features, or both. To showcase the information they find, students will create a travel brochure that encourages travelers to visit their community. See pp. T6–T7 for more information.

Use the EQ Inquiry Project to measure student understanding of the chapter content and their ability to effectively express their understanding. A task-specific evaluation rubric is available in the Online Teacher Resources.

	4	3	2	1
Developing and Planning Inquiry	Project is focused on at least three features and thoroughly explores how they make the community special.	Project is focused on at least two features and explores some ways they make the community special.	Project is focused on at least one feature and explores some ways it makes the community special.	Project is focused on at least one feature but does not explore how it makes the community special.
Geographical Understanding	Details are included that show a strong understanding of the community's features.	Some details are included that show an adequate understanding of the community's features.	Some details are included that show an uneven understanding of the community's features.	Project includes details but shows no understanding of the community's features.
Sources and Evidence	Project includes required and additional information and is supported with necessary evidence.	Project includes required information with some supporting evidence.	Project includes some required facts and evidence.	Required facts and supporting evidence are not included.
Communicating Conclusions	Project information is clearly supported with details and is easily understood.	Project information includes details and is understood with some explanation.	Project information is unclear due to lack of details.	Project does not include details necessary to communicate information.

Why Does It Matter Where We Live?

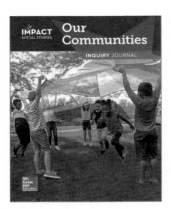

**INQUIRY JOURNAL,
pp. 2–3**

Background Information

Students will explore the different types of communities that are found in the United States and the world. As they investigate, students will discuss where their community is located and compare their community's features with the features in other communities.

Talk About It

Read Have students read the page together. Prompt students to list three questions they would like to know the answers to after reading about communities. Have students discuss their questions with partners. You may wish to list the questions and revisit the list throughout the chapter.

Inquiry Project

Understanding Your Community

Discuss the Inquiry Project with students. Review each step of the project and the **Project Checklist**. Tell students that they will use information from the chapter and from independent research to complete the project.

My Research Plan

Discuss the Essential Question with students and what life might be like in different communities in the United States and around the world. Have students work in pairs to read the Inquiry Project and think about research questions that focus on the geography, resources, and other important features in their community.

▶ Digital Tools

Blended Learning

Students engage with the chapter's Essential Question and launch their investigations.

Interactive IMPACT

Spark student interest with the **EQ Chapter Video**.

Design Your Own Inquiry Path (Optional)

You may wish to work with students to choose their own Essential Question, Inquiry Project, and related research questions. Have students preview chapter materials and discuss ideas with classmates to help develop possible questions, such as *How does the environment affect the way a community develops?*, *How is my community alike and different from other communities?*, or their own questions.

Have students explain why their Essential Question is important to them and to others. Have students record their question, project idea, and initial supporting research questions using the **Student EQ Inquiry Project** pages found at **my.mheducation.com**.

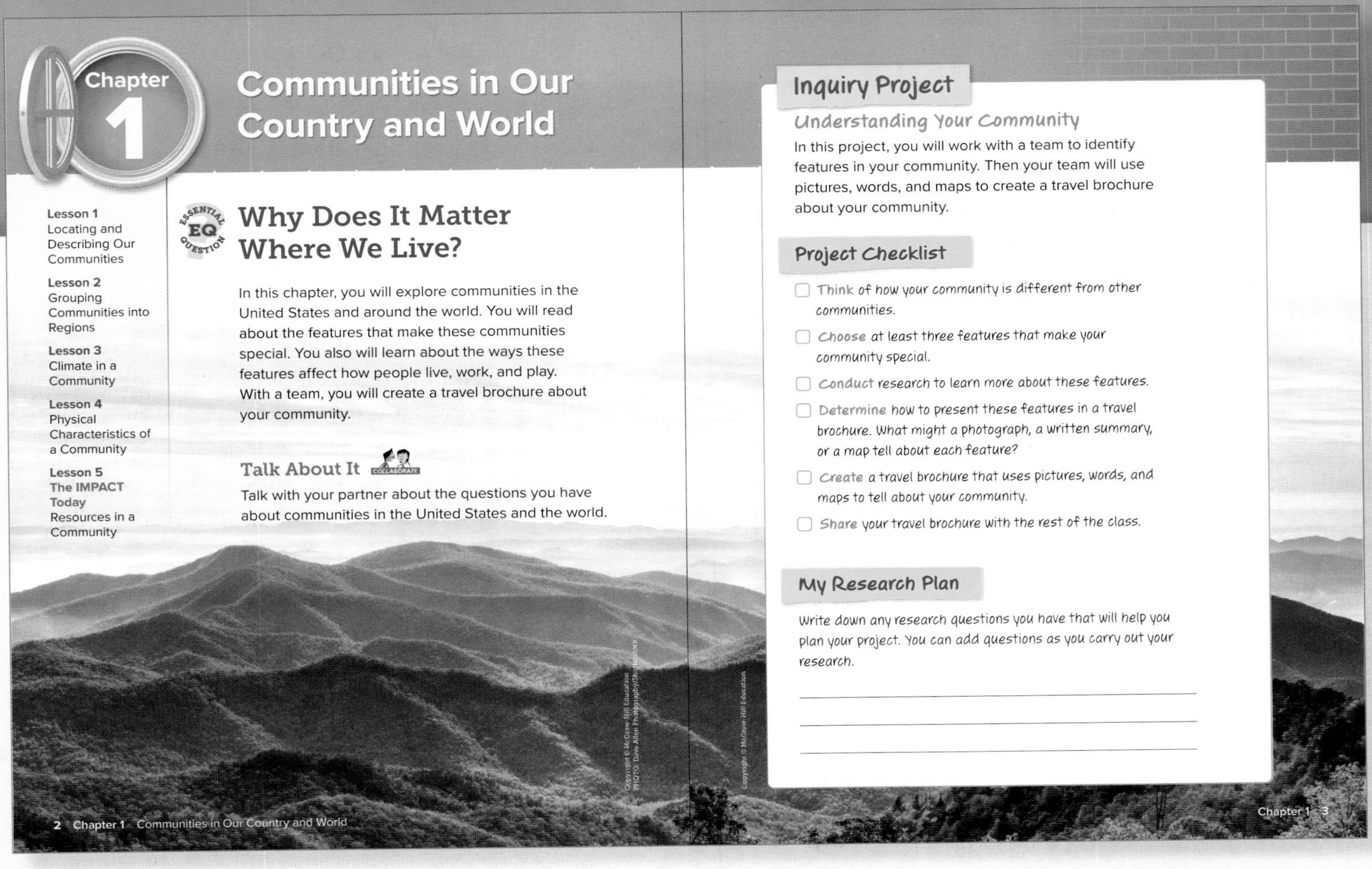

Chapter 1

Communities in Our Country and World

Lesson 1 Locating and Describing Our Communities

Lesson 2 Grouping Communities into Regions

Lesson 3 Climate in a Community

Lesson 4 Physical Characteristics of a Community

Lesson 5 The IMPACT Today Resources in a Community

ESSENTIAL QUESTION EQ

Why Does It Matter Where We Live?

In this chapter, you will explore communities in the United States and around the world. You will read about the features that make these communities special. You also will learn about the ways these features affect how people live, work, and play. With a team, you will create a travel brochure about your community.

Talk About It

COLLABORATE

Talk with your partner about the questions you have about communities in the United States and the world.

Inquiry Project

Understanding Your Community

In this project, you will work with a team to identify features in your community. Then your team will use pictures, words, and maps to create a travel brochure about your community.

Project Checklist

- ☐ **Think** of how your community is different from other communities.
- ☐ **Choose** at least three features that make your community special.
- ☐ **Conduct** research to learn more about these features.
- ☐ **Determine** how to present these features in a travel brochure. What might a photograph, a written summary, or a map tell about each feature?
- ☐ **Create** a travel brochure that uses pictures, words, and maps to tell about your community.
- ☐ **Share** your travel brochure with the rest of the class.

My Research Plan

Write down any research questions you have that will help you plan your project. You can add questions as you carry out your research.

____

____

____

INQUIRY JOURNAL, pp. 2–3

English Learners SCAFFOLD

Use the following scaffolds to support student understanding of the Inquiry Project.

Entering and Emerging

Show students examples of travel brochures. Point to different sections of the brochure and relate them to tasks that students will perform during the project. For example: *This brochure tells about places in Chicago, Illinois. The brochure shows a picture of a place and tells about it. You will choose three places in your community to tell about in your travel brochure.*

Developing and Expanding

Ask questions to check understanding of the Inquiry Project instructions. For example: *What is important in a travel brochure? What are some examples of features in your community that you could research?*

Bridging and Reaching

Have students read through the Inquiry Project instructions and talk about the types of information they will need to look for or the type of task they will need to complete each item in the Project Checklist. Write examples of the information on the board for each item in the Project Checklist.

Social Emotional Learning

Self-Awareness

Demonstrate Curiosity

Students need to express their curiosity and creativity. As students plan their Inquiry Project, encourage students to consider innovative ways to complete their project. Ask: *What are some interesting ways you could present information about the features in your community?*

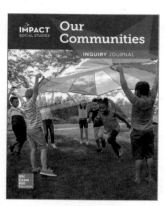

**INQUIRY JOURNAL,
pp. 4–5**

Explore Words

Academic/Domain-Specific Vocabulary Read the words aloud to students. Explain to students that these are words they will learn more about in the chapter.

Word Rater Have students place a checkmark in one of the three boxes below each word, indicating that they "Know It," "Heard It," or "Don't Know It." Explain to students that they will come back to this chart to add additional information about each word as they work through the chapter.

☐ **Know It!** Tell students that if they know the word, they should write its meaning on the lines provided.

☐ **Heard It!** Tell students that if they have heard, or are familiar with the word, they should write what they know about it on the lines provided. Remind them to take notes about the word as they encounter it.

☐ **Don't Know It!** If students do not know the word's meaning, tell them to write down its meaning when they encounter the word in the chapter.

Support Vocabulary

Return to the Word Rater as you come across vocabulary words in each lesson. Encourage students to use the "My Notes" section to include any of the following:

- definitions from the text
- deeper understandings
- synonyms
- other associations

Spanish Cognates

For Spanish speakers, point out the cognates.

community = comunidad

humidity = humedad

natural resources = recursos naturales

precipitation = precipitación

region = región

Content Words	
climate	the weather a place has over a long period of time
community	place where people live, work, and play
elevation	how high an area of land is above sea level
erosion	the gradual wearing away of something by forces such as water, wind, or ice
humidity	moisture in the air
landform	a natural feature on Earth's surface
natural resource	something found in nature that people use
population	the number of people who live in one place
precipitation	water that falls to the ground as rain, snow, sleet, or hail
region	an area of land with certain features that make it different from other areas

Complete this chapter's Word Rater. Write notes as you learn more about each word.

climate   My Notes
☐ Know It!
☐ Heard It!
☐ Don't Know It!

community   My Notes
☐ Know It!
☐ Heard It!
☐ Don't Know It!

elevation   My Notes
☐ Know It!
☐ Heard It!
☐ Don't Know It!

erosion   My Notes
☐ Know It!
☐ Heard It!
☐ Don't Know It!

humidity   My Notes
☐ Know It!
☐ Heard It!
☐ Don't Know It!

landform   My Notes
☐ Know It!
☐ Heard It!
☐ Don't Know It!

natural resource   My Notes
☐ Know It!
☐ Heard It!
☐ Don't Know It!

population   My Notes
☐ Know It!
☐ Heard It!
☐ Don't Know It!

precipitation   My Notes
☐ Know It!
☐ Heard It!
☐ Don't Know It!

region   My Notes
☐ Know It!
☐ Heard It!
☐ Don't Know It!

INQUIRY JOURNAL, pp. 4–5

EL English Learners SCAFFOLD

Use the following scaffolds to support student understanding of chapter vocabulary.

Entering and Emerging

Show a picture or object that depicts each vocabulary word. Help students identify each image or object using a term from the list. Use simple sentences to describe the terms in context. For example: *Look out the window. Do you see the hill? A hill is a landform.*

Developing and Expanding

Read aloud sentences that describe each term without saying the term itself. Have students work individually or in pairs to identify the terms. For example: *Water is found in nature. People use it for drinking, watering crops, and washing. Water is an example of this.* (natural resource)

Bridging and Reaching

Provide students with paper to create vocabulary flashcards. On one side, students can write the term. On the other side, students can write their own definition or draw a picture. Have them work in pairs and use the flashcards to quiz each other on the terms.

▶ Digital Tools

Blended Learning

Students investigate academic and domain specific words they encounter in each lesson.

Interactive IMPACT

Throughout the chapter, encourage students to interact with the **Explore Words** cards and games.

ESSENTIAL EQ QUESTION

Why Does It Matter Where We Live?

RESEARCH COMPANION, pp. 2–3

Activate Knowledge

Read and Discuss COLLABORATE Have students read the opening on page 2 together. Ask: *How do land, resources, and weather affect life in our community?* As students share their responses, you may wish to redirect misconceptions and inaccurate information.

Why Do Communities Develop?

- Have students read the text, focusing on both the photographs and the captions.
- How would you describe farming communities in the United States? (Answers will vary, but students might note that farming communities form around places that have fertile soil and get plenty of sunshine and rain. Students might also mention that people come to these communities to work on the farms.)
- How does the availability of jobs affect the growth of a town? Give an example. (Answers will vary, but students should understand that many towns develop around a specific industry. People will come to this town to find jobs. However, when businesses close, the town may shrink as people move away to find new jobs. An example is Braddock, Pennsylvania, which grew as people came to work in the steel mill. The town shrank when the steel mill closed.)

Make Connections

- Why do you think the shipbuilding industry came to Portland, Oregon? (Answers will vary, but students should use ideas from the text, such as Oregon's location along the Willamette River and the town becoming a trade center.)
- How was the growth of farming communities; Braddock, Pennsylvania; and Portland, Oregon, alike? How was it different? (Answers will vary but should include that all three grew because of their features: weather, land, available jobs, etc. However, when an important feature is taken away, like steel jobs in Braddock, the town shrank.)

Perspectives Would you rather live in an urban area or a rural area? Explain your answer. (Answers will vary, but students should give reasons to support their opinions.)

Chapter 1

Communities in Our Country and World

Lesson 1
Locating and Describing Our Communities

Lesson 2
Grouping Communities into Regions

Lesson 3
Climate in a Community

Lesson 4
Physical Characteristics of a Community

Lesson 5
The IMPACT Today Resources in a Community

Why Does It Matter Where We Live?

A community's land, resources, and weather affect how people live and work. In this chapter, you will read about the different types of communities in the United States. You will explore where communities developed in our country. You will also learn how people use the country's land and resources. As you read, think about your own community. How do land, resources, and weather affect life in your community?

The climate brings people to some cities and towns around the world.

2 Chapter 1 Communities in Our Country and World

Why Do Communities Develop?

Communities come in many different shapes and sizes. Some are small and rural. Others are huge cities with millions of people. Many things can affect how communities develop.

Some places in the United States are perfect for farming. These places have soil that is good for growing crops. They also get plenty of sunshine and rain. Small rural communities often developed around these farms. People came to these communities to work on the farms.

Some communities in the United States grew because of the steel industry. Many people settled in Braddock, Pennsylvania, when its steel mill opened in 1873. Workers came to the town to find jobs. Some of these communities shrunk once the steel mills closed. However, some continued to grow as new industries developed.

In 1846, Portland, Oregon, was a small town with only about a few dozen people. The town's location along the Willamette River helped Portland become a trading center. As trade grew, more rail lines were built in the area. Businesses including lumber mills, shipyards, and flour mills employed many people. Portland continued to grow in the 1940s as people came to build ships. Today, more than 600,000 people live in Portland.

Chapter 1 3

RESEARCH COMPANION, pp. 2–3

English Learners SCAFFOLD

Use these scaffolds to support students in activating their background knowledge.

Entering and Emerging

Help students understand any unfamiliar vocabulary words in the text. For example, explain that the word *rural* means "the countryside." A rural area is usually devoted to agriculture, or farming. Have each student draw a picture to help them understand the meaning of the word *rural*. Continue this activity with other words such *community* and *industry*.

Developing and Expanding

Ask partners to identify any unfamiliar vocabulary words in the text. Explain the meanings of these words or help students find the definitions of the words in a dictionary. Then have partners take turns using each word in a sentence.

Bridging and Reaching

Point out content-specific vocabulary words in the text, such as *rural, community*, and *industry*. Ask open-ended questions using these words to check students' understanding, such as: *What might you see in a rural community? What industries are important to our community?*

Connect Through Literature

Rivers from SPACE!

Usually we only see a little bit of a river—the bit flowing past where we are. But from space we can see all their amazing twists and turns. These photos of rivers were taken by satellites orbiting high above the Earth.

Mackenzie River, Canada, is the longest river in Canada. This picture shows the river near where it empties into the Arctic Ocean.

Think About It

1. What can you see in pictures of rivers taken from satellites that you cannot see normally?
2. What do the colors of the Lena River show?
3. How do these pictures change the way you think about rivers?

Betsiboka River estuary, Madagascar. The river dumps sediment as it reaches the sea, making little islands.

Green River, Utah. This river has carved deep canyons into the rock.

Mississippi River, Missouri, where it is joined by the Missouri and Illinois rivers (left and top right).

Lena River, Russia

The Lena is one of the longest rivers on Earth. This is the delta where it spreads out to meet the sea. This is an infrared picture, so the colors show different temperatures. Blue is colder—this water is pretty cold!

Ganges River delta, India. The dark green is the Sundarbands mangrove forest, home to many tigers.

Niger River, Mali. This river runs along the edge of the Sahara Desert.

4 Chapter 1 Communities in Our Country and World

Chapter 1 5

RESEARCH COMPANION, pp. 4–5

Connect Through Literature

| **GENRE** | Informational Article "Rivers from Space" is an informational article, or a short piece of nonfiction written for a newspaper, magazine, or website.

Have students read the selection on pp. 4–5. Then discuss the following question.

1. What can you see in pictures of rivers taken from satellites that you cannot see normally? (all of the ways that a river twists and turns)

Have students reread the selection; then ask:

2. What do the colors of the Lena River show? (different temperatures)

3. How do these pictures of rivers change what you think about rivers? (Answers will vary.)

Perspectives How can the use of satellite images help us better understand rivers? (Answers will vary but may suggest that satellite images can help show how diverse rivers are and how they can affect the landscape.)

▶ Digital Tools

Blended Learning
Students engage with the chapter's content by making connections to literature.

Have students use the **eBook** to interact with engaging literary selections.

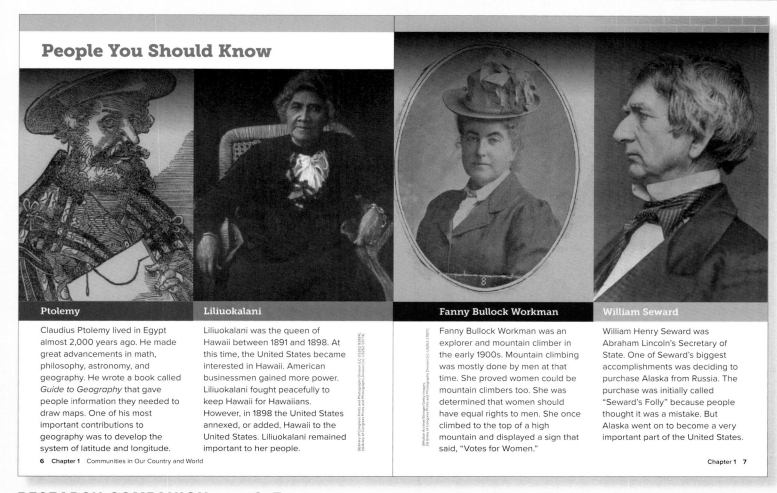

People You Should Know

Ptolemy

Claudius Ptolemy lived in Egypt almost 2,000 years ago. He made great advancements in math, philosophy, astronomy, and geography. He wrote a book called *Guide to Geography* that gave people information they needed to draw maps. One of his most important contributions to geography was to develop the system of latitude and longitude.

6   Chapter 1   Communities in Our Country and World

Liliuokalani

Liliuokalani was the queen of Hawaii between 1891 and 1898. At this time, the United States became interested in Hawaii. American businessmen gained more power. Liliuokalani fought peacefully to keep Hawaii for Hawaiians. However, in 1898 the United States annexed, or added, Hawaii to the United States. Liliuokalani remained important to her people.

Fanny Bullock Workman

Fanny Bullock Workman was an explorer and mountain climber in the early 1900s. Mountain climbing was mostly done by men at that time. She proved women could be mountain climbers too. She was determined that women should have equal rights to men. She once climbed to the top of a high mountain and displayed a sign that said, "Votes for Women."

William Seward

William Henry Seward was Abraham Lincoln's Secretary of State. One of Seward's biggest accomplishments was deciding to purchase Alaska from Russia. The purchase was initially called "Seward's Folly" because people thought it was a mistake. But Alaska went on to become a very important part of the United States.

Chapter 1   7

RESEARCH COMPANION, pp. 6–7

People You Should Know

How do personal stories IMPACT our understanding of communities in our country and the world?

Read Explain to students that they will learn about these people and others throughout the chapter. Then have students read through all the biographies and select one individual that interests them.

Research Instruct students to research that person's life, achievements, and opinions. Have students pick a particular incident from that person's life to examine in depth.

Respond Using the details from their research, students will write a newspaper article that tells about the event students selected. The article should give details that answer *who, what, where, when, why,* and *how.* Students may also wish to incorporate quotations and photographs into their newspaper articles.

Blended Learning

Students investigate and discuss curated news articles that extend the chapter content.

Interactive IMPACT

Connect to current events and people with **IMPACT News** and **More to Investigate.**

IMPACT EXPLORER MAGAZINE, pp. 2–15

WordBlast

Remind students to look for the Word Blasts as they read the *IMPACT Explorer Magazine.*

Extend Knowledge Building

The **IMPACT Explorer Magazine** provides students another route to explore each chapter's Essential Question from a variety of perspectives as they dig deeper into the subject of communities in the United States and the world. Additional questions and activities help students develop and deepen their understanding of the chapter's content.

Engage

Build background for students and share any information needed to provide a context for the chapter topic. Have students read the Essential Question and the Table of Contents.

Analyze the Visual Discuss the opening visual (photograph, photo essay, artwork) on the second page of the **IMPACT Explorer Magazine** chapter. Help students connect the visual to the chapter topic and the Essential Question.

Analyze the Sources

Students will read and analyze the leveled informational articles and literary texts, graphic texts, primary and secondary sources, photographs, maps, and other visual resources.

Read and Analyze Before reading, provide any additional information you think students will need about the topics. Then guide students through the three-step process to read and analyze the content.

1 Inspect

Have students skim the content on a page or multiple pages. Ask questions to help students recall and retell key ideas.

- What is this article mostly about?
- Who is _____?

2 Find Evidence

Have students reread the content and look for details they might have missed. Ask additional questions to help them read more closely.

- What details do you notice in the photographs?
- Why was _____ important?

3 Make Connections

Have students work in pairs or small groups to discuss prompts that help them connect the articles to other texts, their own lives, current ideas and issues, and other topics.

- How is _____ similar to what we do?
- How do you think _____ felt about what happened?
- What do you think about _____?

Chapter 1

Communities in Our Country and World

EQ Why does it matter where we live?

Table of Contents

2 Chapter 1 Communities in Our Country and World

Where Do Americans Live?

The United States is a big country with many different geographic features. Our communities are as varied as the land.

Van Horn, Texas, is in the Chihuahuan Desert.

This Oregon cabin is in the Cascade Mountains of the Pacific Northwest.

The vast Great Plains surround the town of Willow Lake, South Dakota.

Rockport, Massachusetts, overlooks the Atlantic Ocean.

- What details do you see in the photos?
- What details are similar to the place where you live?

Chapter 1 3

IMPACT EXPLORER MAGAZINE, pp. 2–15

How to Use the IMPACT Explorer Magazine

Use the following scaffolds to support students' understanding and your classroom needs.

Whole Class

Use the **IMPACT Explorer Magazine** Teaching Guide to read and discuss one or more articles with the whole class.

Small Group

Have partners or small groups read articles connected to the day's core lesson and report back to the whole class about what they read.

Independent Work

Assign articles for students to extend and enrich their understanding of a topic, including during center time and independent reading time.

The online **IMPACT Explorer Magazine** Teaching Guide provides support for various implementation models as well as a three-step lesson plan for each article. The lesson plan includes background information, meaningful questions, vocabulary activities, scaffolded support for English learners, and collaborative conversation prompts.

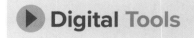

Blended Learning

Students extend the investigation of the Chapter Essential Question with highly-visual, leveled articles and video.

eBook

Use the **IMPACT Explorer Magazine eBook** to extend knowledge building.

LESSON QUESTION

Where Is My Community and What Is It Like?

Connect to the Essential Question

Tell students that this lesson provides key research into the Chapter Essential Question: **Why Does It Matter Where We Live?** Explain that they will learn how to read maps and globes and use them to locate their own community and communities around the world. They will become familiar with the different types of communities—urban, suburban, and rural—and understand why people choose to live in their community.

Lesson Objectives

- **Identify** the similarities and differences between urban, suburban, and rural communities.

- **Describe** the information that maps can tell about a community.

- **Locate** different places on a map or a globe using latitude and longitude.

- **Compare** a student's own community to communities in other parts of the world.

- **Write** a paragraph about what a student's own community is like and why people choose to live there.

Make Connections!

CONNECT TO ELA

Reading **Ask and answer** questions to demonstrate understanding of a text and refer explicitly to the text as the basis for the answers.

Research **Recall** information from experiences or gather information from print and digital sources; take brief notes on sources and sort evidence into provided categories.

Writing **Craft** informative/explanatory texts to examine a topic and convey ideas and information clearly.

Speaking and Listening **Follow** agreed-upon rules for discussions (e.g., gaining the floor in respectful ways, listening to others with care, speaking one at a time about the topics and texts under discussion).

Language **Acquire** and use accurately grade-appropriate conversational, general academic, and domain-specific words and phrases, including those that signal spatial and temporal relationships (e.g., *After dinner that night we went looking for them*).

COMMUNITY CONNECTIONS

To enrich what students have learned about urban, suburban, and rural communities, plan a field trip to a location in a community different from your own. For example, if your community is urban, plan a field trip to a farm in a rural area or a botanical garden in the suburbs. If your community is suburban or rural, consider planning a trip to a cultural center in the city.

Lesson-At-A-Glance

1 ENGAGE — INQUIRY JOURNAL

pp. 6–7

- ▶ **Talk About It:** Photographs of urban and rural communities
- ▶ **Analyze the Source:** Maps and Satellite Images
- ▶ **Inquiry Tools:** Explore Summarizing

2 INVESTIGATE — RESEARCH COMPANION

pp. 8–17

- ▶ **What Makes a Community?**
- ▶ **Urban, Suburban, and Rural Communities**
- ▶ **Maps and Globes**
- ▶ **What Maps Can Tell You About Your Community**
- ▶ **Around the World**

3 REPORT — INQUIRY JOURNAL

pp. 12–13

- ▶ **Think About It**
- ▶ **Write About It:** Write an Informational Text; Cite Evidence from Text
- ▶ **Talk About It**
- ▶ **Connect to the Essential Question**

ASSESSMENT

- ▶ **Online Lesson Test**
- ▶ **Printable Lesson Test**

For more details, see pages T4–T5.

Digital Tools

at **my.mheducation.com**

ePresentation

Teach the **Engage**, **Investigate**, and **Report** content to the whole class from **ePresentations** that launch directly from the lesson dashboard.

eBook

You can flip your instruction with the **IMPACT eBooks** found on your lesson dashboard.

Interactive IMPACT

Blend in digital content **when you want it** and **where you want it**.

Blended Learning features in the Teacher's Edition highlight ways to connect in-class work with online experiences to enhance learning.

Investigate current events with **IMPACT News**.

Explore domain-based vocabulary with **Explore Words** and **Word Play** vocabulary activities.

Go Further with IMPACT Explorer Magazine!

pp. 2–15

The **IMPACT Explorer Magazine** supports students' exploration of the Essential Question and provides additional resources for the EQ Inquiry Project.

LESSON 1 LANGUAGE LEARNERS

 LESSON QUESTION

Where Is My Community and What Is It Like?

Language Objectives

- Use newly acquired content and academic vocabulary to talk and write about communities.
- Summarize information about different kinds of communities.
- Use comparative and superlative adjectives to describe communities.

 Spanish Cognates

To support Spanish speakers, point out the cognates.

photo = foto

urban = urbano

suburban = suburbano

rural = rural

globe = globo

population = población

Introduce the Lesson

Set Purpose Explain to students that in this lesson they will read informational texts to learn about different kinds of communities and how they can use maps and globes to locate communities.

Access Prior Knowledge Read the lesson question and find out what students already know about their communities. Say: *Our homes are near other homes. Together these homes make neighborhoods, and neighborhoods form communities. Communities are larger than neighborhoods. They have more people, shops, businesses, parks, and places to go.* Have students describe the things in their communities. Ask: *What are some shops, businesses, or parks in your community? What other kinds of places are in your community?*

Spark Curiosity Project or display a map of your state and help students locate their own community. Explain that there are many different communities in the United States. Then, ask students to look at the pictures on pp. 9–11 of the Research Companion. Say: *Both photographs show communities in the United States. How are the communities the same? How are they different?*

Build Meaning & Support Language

Inquiry Journal

Analyze the Source (pages 8–9) Tell students that in this lesson they will read informational texts that give facts, examples, and explanations about a topic. The texts include headings, maps, and photographs. Point to the heading on page 8 and the photo and map on page 9. As you read "Maps and Satellite Images," explain any words that students don't know. Support students' understanding of the photograph and map on page 9. Ask: *What are the differences between the map and the photo? What information does the map show? What information does the photo show? Imagine a person is driving to a friend's house in Detroit. Which would be more useful: the map or the photo?*

Inquiry Tools (pages 10–11) Remind students that *summarizing* means telling the most important ideas you read or see in your own words. Explain that the main idea is the most important point an author makes about a topic. Review the steps to ensure students understand the process. Then, model how to locate a main idea and add it to the graphic organizer on page 10. Say: *The first paragraph on p. 9 tells what a map is and what a photo is. The main idea of the paragraph is:* A map is a drawing of a place, and a photo is an image of the actual place. *I will write these details in two boxes labeled* Detail *in the graphic organizer.* Work with students to complete the rest of the graphic organizer on page 10.

Research Companion

What Makes a Community? (pages 8–11) After you read the first sentence on page 10, point out the words *urban, suburban,* and *rural.* Provide support to help students understand the difference between these types of locations. Point out the prefix *sub-* in the word *suburban.* Explain that *sub-* means "below" or "near." A *suburban* area can be thought of as below or near an *urban* area.

Maps and Globes (pages 12–13) Remind students that places to the left of the prime meridian are in the Western Hemisphere, and places to the right of the prime meridian are in the Eastern Hemisphere. Places above the equator are in the Northern Hemisphere, and places below the equator are in the Southern Hemisphere. Ask: *Where is the United States on the map?* (left of the prime meridian; above the equator) *In which hemispheres is the United States?* (the Western and Northern Hemispheres)

What Maps Can Tell You About Your Community (pages 14–15) Help students use the colors, key, and labels to understand the physical map on page 15. Ask: *What do the blue areas on the map show?* (water) *Which city is shown on the map?* (Pittsburgh) Direct students to look at the key in the upper left corner of the map. Ask: *Is the land around Pittsburgh high or low?* (low)

Around the World (pages 16–17) Make sure that students understand that a *high-rise* building is a tall building, and a *resident* is a person who lives in a particular place. Ask: *How many people are residents of Tokyo?* (more than 36 million) *Why do you think Tokyo has many high-rise buildings?* (so that many people can live in a small space)

Inquiry Journal

Report Your Findings (pages 12–13) Explain that the *features* of a community are important parts or qualities of the community. Review examples of the different features of a community, including population, buildings, parks, mountains, and lakes.

Language Forms & Conventions

Regular Comparative and Superlative Adjectives Review with students that an adjective is a word that describes a noun. In most cases, writers can compare two people, places, or things by using an adjective ending with *-er* or the word *more* + the adjective. They can compare one person, place, or thing to a group using an adjective ending in *-est* or the word *most* + the adjective. Display the chart. Model using the words to compare communities: *Denver is smaller than Tokyo. Denver is larger than Buford, Wyoming. Tokyo is the largest city of the three.*

Adjective	Comparative Word or Phrase (Compares Two)	Superlative Word or Phrase (Compares More Than Two)
small	smaller	smallest
large	larger	largest
crowded	more crowded	most crowded

Have students work in pairs to locate other comparative and superlative words and phrases in the text. Call on volunteers to say them aloud and add them to the chart. As a challenge, ask students to use the words to compare communities or maps described in the text.

Cross-Cultural Connection

The Americas were named after Amerigo Vespucci, an Italian navigator and merchant. Vespucci was not the first European to travel to the Americas. Nevertheless, the name America was first used on a map created in 1507. The mapmaker proposed the name based on the accounts of Vespucci's voyages.

Leveled Support

Entering & Emerging
Provide sentence frames:
My community is (urban/ rural/suburban) because _____. People live in my community because it is _____.

Developing & Expanding
Have partners or small groups create a bank of words used to describe communities in the text. Encourage students to refer to the word bank when writing their paragraphs.

Bridging & Reaching
Remind students to use words that signal cause-and-effect in their responses (*because, therefore, as a result, so*) to explain why people choose to live in their community.

Language Transfer

In Spanish, comparative and superlative forms always use separate words, similar to the use of *more* or *most* + an adjective in English. Spanish does not use the word endings *-er* or *-est* to show comparative or superlative forms.

LESSON 1 ENGAGE

LESSON QUESTION

Where Is My Community and What Is It Like?

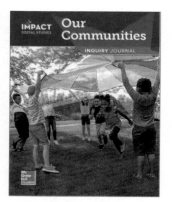

INQUIRY JOURNAL, pp. 6–7

Bellringer

Prompt students to begin a discussion about the topic. Say: *If someone asked you to describe where you live, what words would you use to describe it?* Be prepared to provide some examples of ways to describe a community. (Possible answers: crowded, busy, small, big, a city, a farm, in the mountains, near the ocean) *A community is a place where people live, work, and play. It can be a rural town or an urban city. A community can even be a neighborhood in the countryside.*

Lesson Outcomes

Discuss the lesson question and lesson outcomes with students.

- Confirm that students understand the word *community* as a place where people live, work, and play.

- To help students better understand the term, have them explain why the place where they live can be described as a community.

Talk About It

Explain that when we talk about photographs, we describe, analyze, and interpret them and present our ideas in our own words. Provide sentence frames to help students form sentences as they talk about the similarities and differences between the photographs and their own community.

- The photographs show _____ and _____.
- The photograph of _____ is like my community because _____.
- The photograph of _____ is different than my community because _____.

Collaborative Conversations

Take Turns Talking As students engage in partner, small group, and whole-class discussions, encourage them to

- wait for a person to finish before they speak.
- quietly raise their hand to let others know they would like a turn to speak.
- ask others to share their opinions so that all students have a chance to share.

Lesson 1

Where Is My Community and What Is It Like?

Lesson Outcomes

What Am I Learning?
In this lesson, you will use your investigative skills to explore different kinds of **communities** and where they are found.

Why Am I Learning It?
Reading and talking about different kinds of communities will help you understand more about your own community.

How Will I Know That I Learned It?
You will be able to write a paragraph about your community and why people choose to live there.

Talk About It COLLABORATE

Look closely at the pictures. Which place is more like your community? Explain your answer.

A rural community

An urban community

6 Lesson 1 Where Is My Community and What Is It Like?

Chapter 1 Lesson 1 7

INQUIRY JOURNAL, pp. 6–7

 English Learners SCAFFOLD

Use the following scaffolds to support student understanding of lesson outcomes.

Entering and Emerging

Explain that the word *urban* is used to describe a city and the word *rural* is used to describe the countryside. Then, provide students with a list of simple adjectives and nouns to use when identifying details: for example, *tall, building, tree, road, mountain.* Help students pronounce each word, as needed. Then, work with students to pair each word with the picture that word describes.

Developing and Expanding

Read aloud the captions for each picture. Ask partners to use a dictionary to find the meanings of *urban* and *rural.* Provide assistance, as needed. Then, guide partners to work together to describe details in each picture. Provide them with the following sentence frames to identify details:

- I see _____.
- There is/are _____ in the picture.

Bridging and Reaching

Ask students to read aloud the captions for each picture. Have them write definitions for *urban* and *rural* in their own words. Then, ask students to list adjectives that describe urban areas and rural areas. Have students write sentences that use those words to tell about these areas.

 Social Emotional Learning

Social Awareness

Respect In the classroom setting, students will be learning together as a community. As a result, respect will be a key aspect of facilitating a positive learning environment. Remind students that listening actively and politely whenever others speak is a sign of respect.

 Digital Tools

Blended Learning
Students engage with lesson question and discussion prompts.

Interactive IMPACT

Discuss the **Lesson Question** and **Talk About It.**

1 Inspect

Read the text and look at the map and the photos. What do maps and photos show?

Circle words you do not know.

Underline clues to help you answer these questions:
• What is a map?
• What is a satellite image?
• What community is shown in the satellite image and the map?

My Notes

_____
_____
_____
_____
_____
_____
_____

Maps and Satellite Images

A map is a helpful tool. It is a drawing that can show where streets, parks, and other landmarks are located in a community. A map is different from a photo. A photo shows an image of the actual community.

A satellite image is a photo of a place taken from high above it. In a satellite image, you can see the roofs of buildings, treetops, cars, and sometimes even people. If there are a lot of trees, some streets might be hard to see.

A map does not include every detail. A map shows only the things that make it a useful tool. For example, a street map shows clearly where streets are located. People use street maps to see how they can get from one place to another in their community.

A satellite image can also be a helpful tool. It shows what a place actually looks like from above. You can see where buildings are located and the type of land a place has.

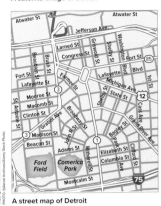

A satellite image of Detroit

A street map of Detroit

2 Find Evidence

Look Again How can you tell that the same community is shown both in the satellite image and on the map?

Circle a location in the photo. Then circle the same location on the map.

3 Make Connections

Talk Think about the communities shown in the photos on page 7. What might you use a street map of those communities for? What might you use satellite images for?

Analyze the Source

1 Inspect

Read Have students read the text and study the map and satellite images.

• **How are the map and satellite photos similar?** (They both show what places look like from above and can be used to locate things.) **How are they different?** (Maps are drawings that show details such as street names and landmark locations. Satellite images are actual photos and show the type of land a place has.)

2 Find Evidence

Look Again Have students look closely at the map and the satellite image to locate and circle a landmark that appears in both.

3 Make Connections

Talk Encourage partners to discuss how street maps and satellite images of these communities might be used. (Answers will vary, but students may suggest that street maps can help them get to particular places in their communities, and satellite images can help them see what the landscape or certain buildings really look like.)

EL Spotlight on Language

Understanding Language

The word *tool* may be familiar to students as a word describing an implement used for physical work, such as a hammer, shovel, or screwdriver. Point out that *tool* can be used more generally to describe any object that is useful for completing a task. Pencils, computers, and rulers are examples of familiar classroom tools.

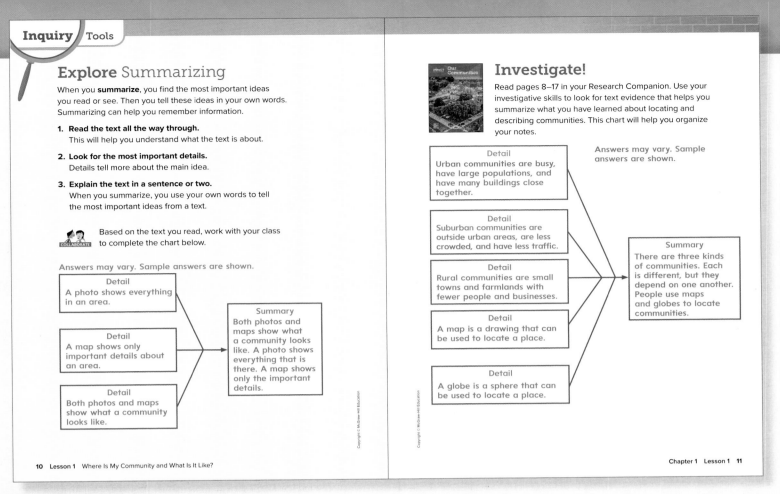

Inquiry Tools

Explore Summarizing

When you **summarize**, you find the most important ideas you read or see. Then you tell these ideas in your own words. Summarizing can help you remember information.

1. **Read the text all the way through.**
   This will help you understand what the text is about.

2. **Look for the most important details.**
   Details tell more about the main idea.

3. **Explain the text in a sentence or two.**
   When you summarize, you use your own words to tell the most important ideas from a text.

Based on the text you read, work with your class to complete the chart below.

Answers may vary. Sample answers are shown.

Detail
A photo shows everything in an area.

Detail
A map shows only important details about an area.

Detail
Both photos and maps show what a community looks like.

Summary
Both photos and maps show what a community looks like. A photo shows everything that is there. A map shows only the important details.

Investigate!

Read pages 8–17 in your Research Companion. Use your investigative skills to look for text evidence that helps you summarize what you have learned about locating and describing communities. This chart will help you organize your notes.

Answers may vary. Sample answers are shown.

Detail
Urban communities are busy, have large populations, and have many buildings close together.

Detail
Suburban communities are outside urban areas, are less crowded, and have less traffic.

Detail
Rural communities are small towns and farmlands with fewer people and businesses.

Detail
A map is a drawing that can be used to locate a place.

Detail
A globe is a sphere that can be used to locate a place.

Summary
There are three kinds of communities. Each is different, but they depend on one another. People use maps and globes to locate communities.

INQUIRY JOURNAL, pp. 10–11

Inquiry Tools

Explore Summarizing

Read Have students read the step-by-step instructions for how to summarize. Explain that the main idea is the most important point the author makes about a topic. Have them look for key words, such as *map* and *satellite image*, as they reread the text.

Guide Practice Have students review the text on pp. 8–9. Then work with them to complete the graphic organizer. Explain that they will use a similar graphic organizer to organize their independent research.

Check Understanding Confirm student understanding of the inquiry skill, Explore Summarizing. If students cannot summarize the most important ideas from the text, review the steps on p. 10.

Investigate!

Have students read pp. 8–17 in the Research Companion. Tell them the information will help them answer the lesson question *Where Is My Community and What Is It Like?*

Take Notes Tell students that they will take notes in the graphic organizer on p. 11 of the Inquiry Journal. Remind them that taking notes will help them understand and remember the information they learn. Explain to students the importance of paraphrasing, or using their own words, when they take notes. When students find the main idea in each paragraph, they will put the main idea into their own words to write the summary.

 Spotlight on Content

Scanning for Information

Have students work in pairs or small groups. Direct them to look in the text for the key words *shows* and *see* to help them locate information about what maps and satellite images show.

 **Digital Tools**

Blended Learning

Students prepare for the lesson investigation with step-by-step instruction about how to summarize.

ePresentation

Use the **Inquiry Tools** to model the lesson graphic organizer.

LESSON 1 INVESTIGATE

LESSON QUESTION

Where Is My Community and What Is It Like?

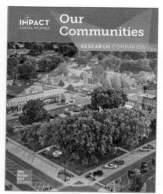

RESEARCH COMPANION, pp. 8–9

Background Information

Mapping the World Claudius Ptolemy is considered the founder of geography. During the second century A.D., his realistic maps of the Roman Empire were the first of their kind. He knew Earth was round, so he had to find ways to flatten the land he was mapping into a two-dimensional depiction. However, it was not until the 1500s that a successful solution to this problem was developed by Gerardus Mercator. The Mercator Projection is still used today for many world maps.

What Makes a Community?

1 Inspect Have students read pp. 8–9 and explain how some communities are alike and different.

2 Find Evidence Use the questions below to check comprehension. Remind students to support their answers with text evidence.

Classify Where are some places people work in your community? Where are some places people play? (Answers will vary, but may include that people work in a variety of local businesses and factories and that people play in parks, soccer fields, and school grounds.) **DOK 2**

3 Make Connections

Apply Concepts Who are some leaders in your community? What do they do in the community? (Answers will vary, but may include that city council members make laws or business people provide jobs.) **DOK 3**

Explain What are some ways your community is different from other communities in the United States and the world? (Answers will vary.) **DOK 3**

Lesson 1 · Where Is My Community and What Is It Like?

What Makes a Community?

You live in a **community**. A community is a place where people live, work, and play. The United States is a large country with many different communities. What is your community like?

All communities are alike in some ways. Every community has homes where people live. Communities also have places where people work. Most communities have schools, libraries, and places of worship. Many communities have fire and police departments to help keep people safe. All communities have leaders who help decide what the laws should be and what kinds of services the community needs.

Communities can also be different from each other. Some communities have larger **populations** than others. Population is the number of people who live in one place. Some communities are crowded with many homes, businesses, and buildings. Other communities have fewer people and more open space. These kinds of differences make each community in our country and the world special.

A community in Brooklyn, New York City

RESEARCH COMPANION, pp. 8–9

English Learners SCAFFOLD

Use the following scaffolds to support student understanding.

Entering and Emerging

Explain to students that this text tells how communities are alike and different. Help students understand the meanings and pronunciations of domain-specific vocabulary such as *community* and *population*. Then, guide students in using the following sentence frames to tell about their community:

- My community is like other communities because it has _____, _____, and _____.
- My community is different from other communities because it has _____, _____, and _____.

Developing and Expanding

Help individual students tell how their community is similar to and different from other communities. Ask questions such as: *What types of places does our community have that are in other communities?* Guide students to use domain-specific vocabulary, such as *community, population, services,* and *laws*.

Bridging and Reaching

Have small groups of students use information from the text to tell how their community is similar to and different from other communities. Encourage students to use domain-specific vocabulary, such as *community, population, services,* and *laws*, as they discuss.

 Digital Tools

Blended Learning

Guide students as they investigate the lesson content.

ePresentation

Investigate with the whole class or small groups.

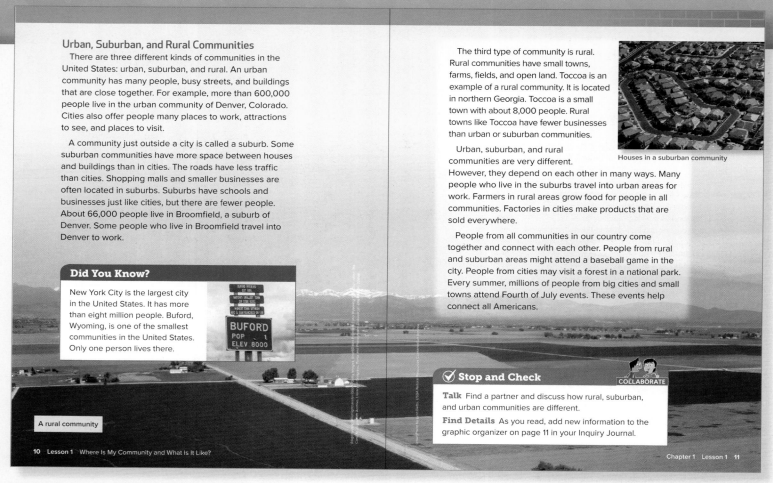

Urban, Suburban, and Rural Communities

There are three different kinds of communities in the United States: urban, suburban, and rural. An urban community has many people, busy streets, and buildings that are close together. For example, more than 600,000 people live in the urban community of Denver, Colorado. Cities also offer people many places to work, attractions to see, and places to visit.

A community just outside a city is called a suburb. Some suburban communities have more space between houses and buildings than in cities. The roads have less traffic than cities. Shopping malls and smaller businesses are often located in suburbs. Suburbs have schools and businesses just like cities, but there are fewer people. About 66,000 people live in Broomfield, a suburb of Denver. Some people who live in Broomfield travel into Denver to work.

Did You Know?

New York City is the largest city in the United States. It has more than eight million people. Buford, Wyoming, is one of the smallest communities in the United States. Only one person lives there.

A rural community

The third type of community is rural. Rural communities have small towns, farms, fields, and open land. Toccoa is an example of a rural community. It is located in northern Georgia. Toccoa is a small town with about 8,000 people. Rural towns like Toccoa have fewer businesses than urban or suburban communities.

Houses in a suburban community

Urban, suburban, and rural communities are very different. However, they depend on each other in many ways. Many people who live in the suburbs travel into urban areas for work. Farmers in rural areas grow food for people in all communities. Factories in cities make products that are sold everywhere.

People from all communities in our country come together and connect with each other. People from rural and suburban areas might attend a baseball game in the city. People from cities may visit a forest in a national park. Every summer, millions of people from big cities and small towns attend Fourth of July events. These events help connect all Americans.

✓ Stop and Check

Talk Find a partner and discuss how rural, suburban, and urban communities are different.

Find Details As you read, add new information to the graphic organizer on page 11 in your Inquiry Journal.

10   Lesson 1   Where Is My Community and What Is It Like?   Chapter 1   Lesson 1   11

RESEARCH COMPANION, pp. 10–11

Urban, Suburban, and Rural Communities

1 Inspect Have students read pp. 10–11 and identify the three different kinds of communities in the United States.

2 Find Evidence Use the questions below to check comprehension.

Compare and Contrast In what way are rural communities different from urban communities? (fewer people, more space, not as many sources of entertainment) **DOK 3**

Relate How do different communities depend on each other? (Possible answers: urban communities depend on suburban communities for workers; suburban and urban communities depend on rural communities for food.) **DOK 2**

3 Make Connections

Apply Concepts Based on what you have read, what type of community do you live in? Ask students to cite evidence from the text in their answers. (Students should correctly identify the type of community they live in, citing textual evidence.) **DOK 3**

✓ Stop and Check

Talk Encourage students to share their own knowledge of different communities as they discuss their answers. (Answers will vary, but students should discuss features from the text such as location, population, etc.)

Find Details Explain to students that after they read and take notes, they should review and think about how the facts and details will help them answer the Essential Question.

 Spotlight on Content

Using Maps

Display a map of the United States. Mark the locations of Denver, Colorado; Toccoa, Georgia; New York City, New York; and Buford, Wyoming. Then mark the location of the local community.

▶ Digital Tools

Blended Learning

Students investigate curated resources and find evidence to answer the Lesson Question.

Interactive IMPACT

Students **Research** and find evidence using digital format texts.

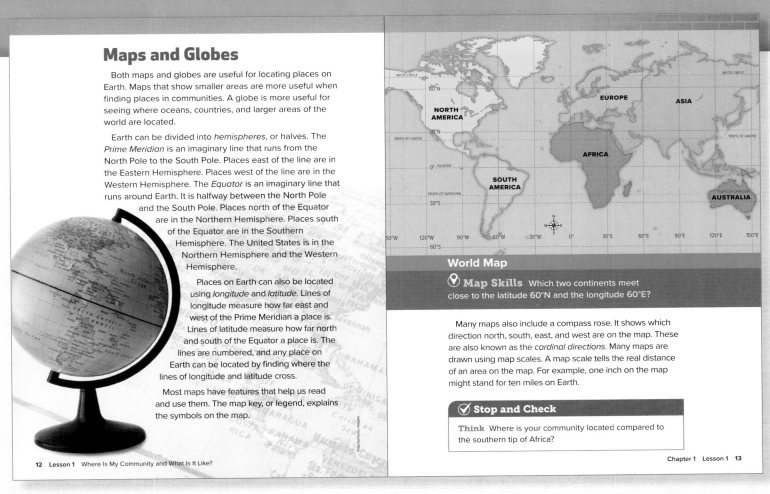

Maps and Globes

Both maps and globes are useful for locating places on Earth. Maps that show smaller areas are more useful when finding places in communities. A globe is more useful for seeing where oceans, countries, and larger areas of the world are located.

Earth can be divided into *hemispheres,* or halves. The *Prime Meridian* is an imaginary line that runs from the North Pole to the South Pole. Places east of the line are in the Eastern Hemisphere. Places west of the line are in the Western Hemisphere. The *Equator* is an imaginary line that runs around Earth. It is halfway between the North Pole and the South Pole. Places north of the Equator are in the Northern Hemisphere. Places south of the Equator are in the Southern Hemisphere. The United States is in the Northern Hemisphere and the Western Hemisphere.

Places on Earth can also be located using *longitude* and *latitude.* Lines of longitude measure how far east and west of the Prime Meridian a place is. Lines of latitude measure how far north and south of the Equator a place is. The lines are numbered, and any place on Earth can be located by finding where the lines of longitude and latitude cross.

Most maps have features that help us read and use them. The map key, or legend, explains the symbols on the map.

World Map

◉ Map Skills Which two continents meet close to the latitude 60°N and the longitude 60°E?

Many maps also include a compass rose. It shows which direction north, south, east, and west are on the map. These are also known as the *cardinal directions.* Many maps are drawn using map scales. A map scale tells the real distance of an area on the map. For example, one inch on the map might stand for ten miles on Earth.

> **✓ Stop and Check**
>
> **Think** Where is your community located compared to the southern tip of Africa?

RESEARCH COMPANION, pp. 12–13

Maps and Globes

1 Inspect Have partners read pp. 12–13, define *Prime Meridian* and *Equator,* and discuss how we divide Earth into hemispheres.

2 Find Evidence Use the questions below to check comprehension.

Contrast How do lines of longitude and latitude differ? (Lines of longitude run north and south and measure east and west. Lines of latitude run east to west and measure north and south.) **DOK 2**

Make Inferences Why does a map need a compass rose? (Without a compass rose, the map would be difficult to use because it would be unclear which parts of the map are north, south, east, or west.) **DOK 3**

3 Make Connections

Explain If you drew a map of your community, would it be better for one inch to stand for 5 miles or for 100 miles? Why? (5 miles; A map with one inch standing for 100 miles would not give enough detail for a community.) **DOK 3**

◉ Map Skills Project the map on p. 13. Guide students to identify the two continents that meet close to the latitude of 60°N and the longitude 60°E. (Europe and Asia)

 ✓ Stop and Check

Think Help students locate their community and the compass rose on the map. (Students should use cardinal directions—north, south, east, and west. United States communities are north and west of the southern tip of Africa.)

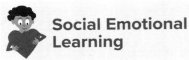

Social Emotional Learning

Relationship Skills

Engage with Others Students need to engage in positive interactions with other students and adults. Before students begin partner-reading the text, ask: *How can you show your partner that you are listening and interested in what they are saying?*

 **Digital Tools**

Blended Learning Students explore lesson content through interactive activities.

Interactive IMPACT

Use the **Lesson Video—** Google Maps.

What Maps Can Tell You About Your Community

Different kinds of maps give different kinds of information. For example, one map might show the streets in a place. Another map of the same place might show where resources are found.

A *political map* shows where cities, states, and countries are located. Each place is labeled with its name. The boundaries are marked with thin lines. Large bodies of water, such as rivers and oceans, are usually shown too.

A *physical map* may be similar to a political map, but it gives more details about what an area is like. Physical maps use different colors to show where things are located. Blue could show water, such as lakes, ponds, rivers, and creeks. A physical map of a large area will show mountain ranges, deserts, and forests. Physical maps also show **elevation**, or how high an area is.

A *vegetation map* is used to study how and where plants grow. Different colors on the map show forests, grasslands, swamps, and so on. A *resource map* shows where resources can be found. Different colors show areas with coal, water, trees, metals, and other things humans use from nature.

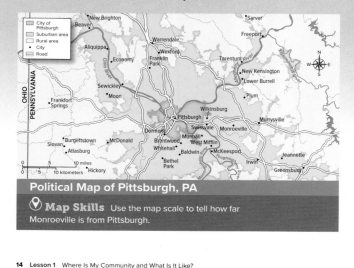

Political Map of Pittsburgh, PA

Map Skills Use the map scale to tell how far Monroeville is from Pittsburgh.

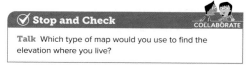

A physical map of Pittsburgh, Pennsylvania

Stop and Check

Talk Which type of map would you use to find the elevation where you live?

RESEARCH COMPANION, pp. 14–15

What Maps Can Tell You About Your Community

1 Inspect Have students read pp. 14–15 and describe political, physical, and vegetation maps.

2 Find Evidence Use the questions below to check comprehension.

Interpret Which type of map would be most useful to a scientist trying to locate desert scrub plants in a region? (a vegetation map) **DOK 2**

Draw Conclusions Why might it be necessary to have different kinds of maps for the same area? (A single map cannot show every detail. Different maps may be needed depending on the information someone wants to know about the area.) **DOK 3**

3 Make Connections

Assess If you were to make a map of your community, which type of map would you use? (Answers may vary, but students should support their responses with details from the text.) **DOK 3**

Map Skills Project a larger version of the map on p. 14. Guide students to determine how far Monroeville is from downtown Pittsburgh. (about 10 miles)

Stop and Check

Talk If possible, share different types of maps that show your community. (a physical map)

EL Spotlight on Vocabulary

Content Vocabulary

resources: things from nature that humans or animals use

boundaries: borders or edges where two places meet

forest rangers: people who protect and take care of forests

Around the World

Tokyo, Japan

Tokyo is the most populated city on Earth. More than 36 million people live in this urban area. In the main part of the city, about 16,000 people are packed into each square mile. What is life like in such a crowded urban community?

Many people in Tokyo live in apartments inside high-rise buildings. The tall buildings allow more people to have homes on a small amount of land. Many of the buildings also have grocery stores, shopping centers, and restaurants in them. Residents can walk to where they need to go. Very few people in Tokyo own cars. Instead, they take trains whenever they need to travel farther than they can walk.

The urban community of Tokyo, Japan

English Suburbs

In the 1800s, urban areas in England grew more crowded. People lived in the city where they worked. Some people wished they could live somewhere else. Eventually railroads were built, and later, cars were invented. By the early 1900s, people could travel quickly to and from cities like London. This allowed them to buy houses outside the city and still work inside it. As a result, suburban communities developed.

A commuter train connects Nottingham to the suburbs.

In cities like London, families often lived in apartments. Most of the time, they could also walk to nearby markets for shopping. In suburban communities, most families lived in a house, usually with a yard, too. All the houses took up a lot of space. The markets were farther away. Owning a car became important. People needed one to reach the markets and to travel to work.

Rural Ecuador

Rural areas have open land and fields. People in rural communities often work with the natural resources in the area. Coffee beans grow on plants in tropical areas. People in some rural communities in Ecuador grow coffee beans. People in the community grow coffee beans in their fields to sell to coffee companies. The community works together to make sure the crop is a success.

Rural communities in other parts of Ecuador have different natural resources. If the community is near open land, people in those communities might grow different crops or raise animals. If their community is near water, the people might use the water to catch fish or to create electricity.

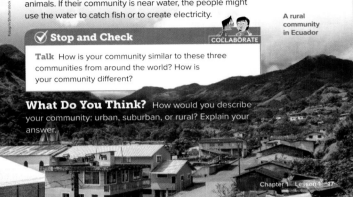
A rural community in Ecuador

✓ Stop and Check

Talk How is your community similar to these three communities from around the world? How is your community different?

What Do You Think? How would you describe your community: urban, suburban, or rural? Explain your answer.

RESEARCH COMPANION, pp. 16–17

Around the World: Communities Around the World

1 Inspect Have students read pp. 16–17 and explain how natural resources are important to rural Ecuador.

2 Find Evidence Use the questions below to check comprehension.

Analyze What is similar about the three communities? (Answers may vary, but will most likely focus on the way people work, play, and live together as a community.) **DOK 2**

Cause and Effect How does Tokyo's population affect the way the people live in that community? (Tokyo's large population causes many people to live in tall buildings or on land with a small amount of space.) **DOK 3**

3 Make Connections

Assess What are the advantages and disadvantages of living in each community? (Answers will vary, but students may consider criteria such as closeness to necessities, size of the population, sense of camaraderie among residents, and so on.) **DOK 3**

✓ Stop and Check

Talk Encourage students to use text evidence in their responses. (Answers will vary, but students should accurately describe the similarities and differences.)

What Do You Think? Have students compare where they live to the descriptions of communities they have read about in the lesson. (Answers will vary, but students should give reasons for their responses.)

✓ Check for Success

Categorize Can students identify their own community as urban, suburban, or rural and support their answer with details from the lesson?

Differentiate

If Not, Have students review the summaries and details about rural, urban, and suburban communities in their Inquiry Journal graphic organizers.

LESSON 1 REPORT

 LESSON QUESTION

Where Is My Community and What Is It Like?

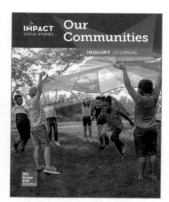

INQUIRY JOURNAL, pp. 12–13

Think About It

Students will review their research and determine the type of community they live in, and provide reasonable explanations as to why people may choose to live in their community. Encourage students to review the information about communities that they have included in their graphic organizers. Direct students back to pp. 8–17 of their Research Companion if they need more information.

Write About It

Write and Cite Evidence Remind students to include the following elements in their responses.

- Identify the type of community they live in, and include specific evidence and details.
- Provide ideas about why people settled in their community.
- Use chapter vocabulary as appropriate.

Discipline(s)	4	3	2	1
Geography	Student provides evidence and details showing the type of community (urban, suburban, or rural) they live in and why people chose to live there.	Student includes details for some evidence showing the type of community (urban, suburban, or rural) they live in and why people chose to live there.	Student includes evidence but few supporting details showing the type of community (urban, suburban, or rural) they live in and why people chose to live there.	Student does not support evidence with details showing the type of community (urban, suburban, or rural) they live in and why people chose to live there.

Talk About It

Share Your Ideas Remind students to take turns giving their opinions and to support their opinions with facts.

Assessment Students can check their understanding with feedback from the **Lesson Test** available online.

Connect to the Essential Question

Put It Together Before students respond, remind them that a community's location and landscape will have an impact on what people can and cannot do there.

Inquiry Project Update Remind students to turn to Inquiry Journal pp. 2–3 for project information. If necessary, review the Project Checklist with students. At this point in the chapter, students should focus on the first two items on the checklist.

Think About It

Give an Opinion
Based on your research, what kind of community do you live in: urban, suburban, or rural? Why do you think people choose to live in your community?

Write About It

Write and Cite Evidence
Based on your research, write a paragraph that identifies the type of community where you live. Why do you think people choose to live there? Use facts from your research to explain your answer.

Answers will vary, but students should
accurately identify the types of
communities they live in and provide
reasonable responses as to why people
want to live there.

Talk About It

Share Your Ideas
Share your paragraph with a partner. Discuss features of your type of community.

Geography **Connect to the**

Pull It Together
How do the features of where you live affect life in your community?

Answers will vary, but students should
accurately describe how the location and
features of the local community affect
people's lives.

 Inquiry Project Notes

INQUIRY JOURNAL, pp. 12–13

 # English Learners SCAFFOLD

Use the following scaffolds to support student writing.

Entering and Emerging

Guide students as they use the following sentence frames to help them write their paragraphs:

- My community is in a _____ area.
- People in my community live _____. (close together/far apart)
- Homes in my community are _____.

Developing and Expanding

Ask students to complete the sentence frames. Encourage students to provide details and use vocabulary from the text.

- My community is in a _____ area because it has _____ and _____.
- People choose to live in my community because _____.

Bridging and Reaching

Check for understanding. Ask: *What type of community do you live in? What information from the text did you use to determine this?*

✓ Check for Success

Summarize Are students able to write a paragraph about what their community is like and why people choose to live there?

Differentiate

If Not, Have students create a drawing to show what their community is like. Ask them to include captions to give reasons why people choose to live there.

How Does My Community Fit in With My Country?

Connect to the Essential Question

Tell students that this lesson asks them to think about the area where they live and helps them answer the Chapter Essential Question: **Why Does It Matter Where We Live?** Explain that they will explore the natural features, climate, and communities of the different regions of the United States and learn how people live in those regions.

Lesson Objectives

- **Describe** the five regions of the United States.
- **Explain** the similarities and differences among regions.
- **Identify** what makes each region unique.
- **Write** an opinion paragraph explaining what makes a student's region an interesting place to live.

Make Connections!

CONNECT TO ELA

Reading **Determine** the main idea of a text; recount the key details and explain how they support the main idea.

Ask and answer questions to demonstrate understanding of a text and refer explicitly to the text as the basis for the answers.

Research **Recall** information from experiences or gather information from provided sources to answer a question.

Writing **Craft** opinion pieces on familiar topics or texts, supporting a point of view with reasons.

Provide reasons that support the opinion.

Speaking and Listening **Engage** effectively in a range of collaborative discussions with diverse partners on grade level topics and texts, building on others' ideas and expressing students' own clearly.

COMMUNITY CONNECTIONS

To enrich what students have learned about regions, plan a virtual trip to a museum in their community or region that houses information about unique details of their community or region. Alternatively, plan a virtual trip to a museum in a different region to help students compare their region to one that is similar or different.

Lesson-At-A-Glance

1 ENGAGE
INQUIRY JOURNAL

pp. 14–19

- ▶ **Talk About It:** Photographs of the Southeast, Northeast, Midwest, Southwest, and West regions
- ▶ **Analyze the Source:** Going West! and Photographs of the Gateway Arch
- ▶ **Inquiry Tools:** Explore Main Ideas and Details

2 INVESTIGATE
RESEARCH COMPANION

pp. 18–29

- ▶ **What Is a Region?**
- ▶ **Northeast**
- ▶ **Southeast**
- ▶ **Midwest**
- ▶ **Southwest**
- ▶ **West**

3 REPORT
INQUIRY JOURNAL

pp. 20–21

- ▶ **Think About It**
- ▶ **Write About It:** Define a Region; Write an Opinion Paragraph
- ▶ **Talk About It**
- ▶ **Connect to the Essential Question**

ASSESSMENT

- ▶ **Online Lesson Test**
- ▶ **Printable Lesson Test**

For more details, see pages T4–T5.

▶ Digital Tools

at **my.mheducation.com**

ePresentation

Teach the Engage, Investigate, and Report content to the whole class from **ePresentations** that launch directly from the lesson dashboard.

eBook

You can flip your instruction with the **IMPACT eBooks** found on your lesson dashboard.

Interactive IMPACT

Blend in digital content **when you want it** and **where you want it**.

Blended Learning features in the Teacher's Edition highlight ways to connect in-class work with online experiences to enhance learning.

Investigate current events with **IMPACT News**.

Explore domain-based vocabulary with **Explore Words** and **Word Play** vocabulary activities.

Go Further with IMPACT Explorer Magazine!

pp. 2–15

The **IMPACT Explorer Magazine** supports students' exploration of the Essential Question and provides additional resources for the EQ Inquiry Project.

How Does My Community Fit in With My Country?

Language Objectives

- Use newly acquired content and academic vocabulary to talk and write about regions of the United States.
- Write a paragraph that supports an opinion with reasons or facts.
- Identify prepositions and prepositional phrases.

Spanish Cognates

To support Spanish speakers, point out the cognates.

arch = arco

expansion = expansión

monument = monumento

region = región

Introduce the Lesson

Set Purpose Explain to students that in this lesson they will read informational texts to learn about the regions of the United States, including the region where their community is located.

Access Prior Knowledge Read the Lesson Question and find out what students already know about their community and region. Remind students that they have already learned some things about their community, such as whether it is urban, suburban, or rural. Tell students that a state is larger than a community, and a region is larger than a state. Say: *The regions in the United States are the Northeast, Southeast, Midwest, West, and Southwest. All of these regions are made of states that share some things in common.* Show a compass rose. Ask students if they can identify the cardinal directions.

Spark Curiosity Have students study the map of the regions on page 19 of the Research Companion. Explain the color-coded map key and guide students to identify the region where their state is located. Explain that usually the states in a region share common land features and weather patterns. Ask: *What region is the farthest away from our region? What regions are next to our region?* Discuss features of your region with students. Then ask if students know about features of any other regions on the map.

Build Meaning & Support Language

Inquiry Journal

Analyze the Source (pages 16–17) Tell students that in this lesson they will read informational texts that give facts and explanations about regions of the United States. The texts include headings, maps, and photographs with captions. As you read "Going West!" explain any words students might not know, such as *gateway* and *arch*. Explain that a gateway is an entrance or way of getting to a new place. St. Louis was known as the "Gateway to the West" because it is where many people started their journey west. After discussing *gateway,* ask: *What does the photo show on page 16?* (the Gateway Arch) *What do you think an* arch *is?* (An arch is a curved structure.)

Inquiry Tools (pages 18–19) Tell students they will **Explore Main Idea and Details** as they read sections in the Research Companion. Explain that the graphic organizer will help them organize the information they read. Check to see that they understand the meaning of the column heads: *Region, Main Idea, Details.* Tell them that *Region* refers to the five main geographical areas in the United States. When filling in the *Main Idea* column, they should tell the main idea about each region. Ask: *What is the important idea about each region?* In the *Detail* column, students should add supporting facts about each region. Prompt them with questions: *What are common jobs people have in this region? Do a lot of people live in the region? When did people settle in the region?*

Research Companion

What Is a Region? (pages 18–19) As you read, explain any words that students don't know. To help students understand the difference between weather and climate, have students describe today's weather. Then ask: *What was the weather like yesterday?* Explain that weather is what we experience from day to day, such as temperature, rain, and wind. Climate is what the weather is like over a long period and changes depending on the season.

Northeast (pages 20–21) Unpack this sentence from page 20: *In fact, Native American peoples were the first to settle in all of the U.S. regions.* Ask: *Who were the Native Americans?* (the first people who lived in what is now the United States) Explain that the word *settle* means "to create a community in a particular place." The word *peoples* refers to people living in different communities or tribes. Help students restate the sentence in their own words.

Midwest (pages 24–25) Point out the words *nation's bread basket* on page 25. Ask students what they think a bread basket is. Then explain that in this sentence the term *bread basket* is used to mean a region that produces a large amount of food. Ask: *Why is the Midwest called the nation's bread basket?* (The land and climate are good for farming, or growing food.)

West (pages 28–29) Read aloud the second sentence on page 28. Explain that the Pacific Coast states are states that border, or are next to, the Pacific Ocean. Point out the phrase *inland states* later in the paragraph, and have students find the listed states on the map. Say: *The inland states include Idaho, Montana, Wyoming, Colorado, Utah, and Nevada. What do you notice about these states?* (They don't border the ocean.)

Inquiry Journal

Report Your Findings (pages 20–21) Review with students the difference between a fact, which can be proven to be true, and an opinion, which expresses a person's feelings about a topic. Provide examples, such as *The Southwest region has the fewest states* (fact) and *The Southwest is the best place to live* (opinion). Explain that students' paragraphs should express an opinion but also provide facts to support the opinion.

Language Forms & Conventions

Prepositions and Prepositional Phrases Remind students that prepositions are often short words that show the relationship between words in a sentence. A prepositional phrase starts with a preposition and includes a noun or a pronoun. A prepositional phrase can locate something in time or space, tell when something happened, or modify a noun. Write some common prepositions on the board, along with example sentences from the Research Companion that include prepositional phrases. Guide students to identify the prepositional phrase(s) in each sentence.

Prepositions	Sentence
to	People from states to the east came to the region...
along	People who live along the coast might enjoy the beach.
from, in	People from around the world visit communities in the Northeast.
for	Today the squares provide green space for the people.

 Have students work in pairs and find other prepositional phrases in the text. Ask them to list the prepositional phrases and circle the prepositions.

 Cross-Cultural Connection

Like the United States, many other countries have different geographical regions. For example, Mexico's regions include the Baja California peninsula in northwest Mexico, which has a dry climate and very dry land, and the southern Yucatán Peninsula, which has a wet climate and many caverns and sinkholes. The Mesa Central region, where most people live, has a mild climate and rich soil for farming.

 Leveled Support

Entering & Emerging
Provide sentence frames: *My region is an interesting place to live because _____.*

Developing & Expanding
Have small groups make a list of reasons why their region is an interesting place to live.

Bridging & Reaching
Have partners tell each other one opinion they have about their region and two facts to support their opinion.

 **Language Transfer**

Tell students that in both Spanish and English, prepositions are used to link nouns to other words in a sentence. Usually, prepositions function the same way in both English and Spanish.

LESSON 2 ENGAGE

 LESSON QUESTION

How Does My Community Fit in With My Country?

**INQUIRY JOURNAL,
pp. 14–15**

Bellringer

Prompt students to retrieve information from the previous lesson. Say: *You have learned about your community and different kinds of communities around the world. What type of community do you live in? What are some things that make your community special?* (Students should identify their community as urban, suburban, or rural and then name things that make their community special.)

Lesson Outcomes

Discuss the lesson question and lesson outcomes with students.

- Confirm that students understand the word *region* as an area of land with certain features that make it different from other areas.
- Tell students that their community is in a state (name state) in a specific region with unique features.

Talk About It

Explain that when we talk about photographs, we describe and interpret them and present our ideas in our own words. Provide sentence frames to help students form sentences as they talk about the photographs.

- The photographs show _____ of the United States.
- Some things in the photos that are the same are _____. Some things that are different are _____.

 Collaborative Conversations

Listen Carefully As students engage in partner, small-group, and whole-class discussions, encourage them to follow discussion rules by listening carefully to speakers. Remind students to

- look at the person who is speaking.
- respect others by not interrupting them.
- respect peers' ideas to promote understanding.

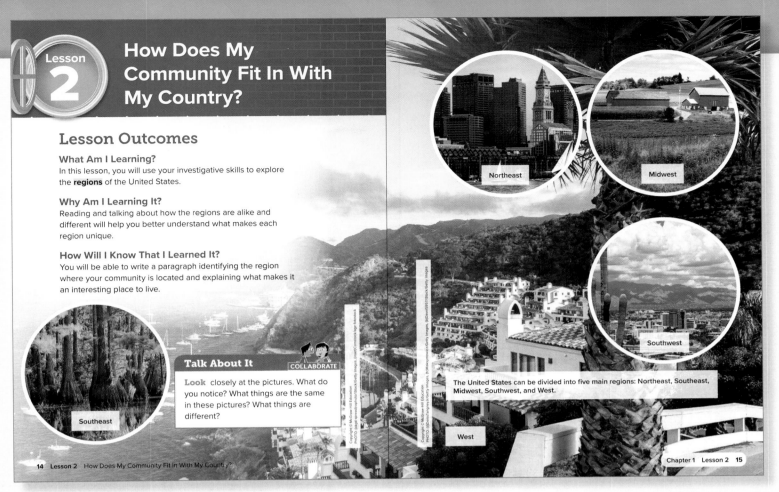

English Learners SCAFFOLD

Use the following scaffolds to support student understanding of the lesson outcomes.

Entering and Emerging

Have students study the photographs of the five regions. Provide sentence frames to help students describe each region:

- In the _____ region, there is/are _____.

Provide words such as *mountains, desert, fields,* and *buildings* as needed.

Developing and Expanding

Have small groups study the photograph of each region. Have groups write a list of words that describe details they see in each picture, such as *farm, cactus, mountains, ocean,* and *cities.*

Bridging and Reaching

Have partners compare and contrast what they see in the photos. Then have students write a sentence explaining which region they think they'd like to live in based on what they see in the photo. Provide the following sentence frame as needed:

- I would like to live in the _____ because_____. Encourage students to include details from the photos.

Social Emotional Learning

Relationship Skills

Value Ideas of Others
To develop their relationship skills, students need to engage in positive interactions with others. Before students engage in collaborative conversations, ask: *How can you show others that you value their ideas?*

 Digital Tools

Blended Learning
Students engage with the lesson question and discussion prompts.

ePresentation

Discuss the **Lesson Question** and **Talk About It** with the whole class.

Going West!

1 Inspect

Read the title. What do you think this text will be about?

- **Circle** words you do not know.
- **Underline** clues that help you answer the following questions:
  - Why do many people go to visit the Gateway Arch?
  - Why was the arch built?
  - What does the arch look like?

My Notes

_____

_____

_____

_____

_____

_____

_____

The Gateway Arch is located in St. Louis, Missouri. The arch is named for the role St. Louis played as the Gateway to the West in the 1800s. Many people who traveled to the West started their journey in this midwestern city.

The arch reaches 630 feet across and stands 630 feet tall. That is twice the height of the Statue of Liberty. It is made of 5,199 tons of steel. That is over one million pounds. The arch can sway up to eighteen inches in high winds.

The Gateway Arch is part of the Jefferson National Expansion Memorial. This place honors President Thomas Jefferson's plan to make the country larger. He wanted Americans to settle the land to the west. The arch also honors the people who set out from St. Louis to reach the West. Underneath the arch, a museum tells visitors the story of Westward Expansion. Six areas feature interactive exhibits that celebrate the spirit of those who made the journey west.

The Gateway Arch was completed in 1965.

The Museum of Westward Expansion is underneath the Gateway Arch.

Visitors can ride in a special train through a tube to the top of the arch. The arch has sixteen windows that face east and sixteen windows that face west. People can look out on the city and the surrounding land.

Monuments help us to understand the role history plays in everyday life. An arch is a type of doorway. Think about the choice to make a monument to the journey westward by building such a structure. Why do you think this is important?

2 Find Evidence

Look at the pictures. **Reread** the text. What do you learn about the Gateway Arch that you do not learn from the pictures?

Underline the details that describe the way the arch is built.

3 Make Connections

Talk Turn back to page 15. Find the pictures that show the Midwest and the West. What does the Gateway Arch help you understand about how these regions are connected?

INQUIRY JOURNAL, pp. 16–17

Analyze the Source

Background Information

The Gateway Arch stands on the west bank of the Mississippi River. Eero Saarinen, a Finnish-born American architect, designed the arch in 1948. It was built from 1963 to 1965. In addition to the arch and the Museum of Westward Expansion, the Jefferson National Expansion Memorial includes the Old Courthouse, where trials were held that led to the Dred Scott decision.

1 Inspect

Read Have students read the text and look at the photographs on pp. 16–17 to get a general idea of the topic. Remind them to circle words they are unfamiliar with.

- Underline clues about why the arch was built (to honor President Jefferson's plan to expand the country and to honor people who went west to live) and what the arch looks like (steel monument, 630 feet tall).

2 Find Evidence

Look and Reread Have students look at the photographs, captions, and reread the text. Students should underline the details about how the arch was built.

3 Make Connections

Talk Ask students what *mid* in *Midwest* means. Then ask students what that tells them about where St. Louis is located in the United States. (the middle part of the United States)

▶ Digital Tools

Blended Learning

Students read informational texts and analyze primary sources.

Interactive IMPACT

Have students practice and apply the strategy of close reading as they analyze text.

Explore Main Idea and Details

The topic is what a piece of writing is about. The **main idea** is the most important point the author makes about a topic. **Details** tell about the main idea.

1. **Read the text once all the way through.**
   This will help you understand what the text is about.

2. **See if there is a sentence that states the main idea.**
   This is often the first sentence of a paragraph. Sometimes other sentences in a paragraph can state the main idea.

3. **Now look for details.**
   Sentences with details give more information about the main idea.

Based on the text you read, work with your class to complete the chart below.

Topic	Main Idea	Details
Gateway Arch	The Gateway Arch is a monument in St. Louis, Missouri.	630 feet across and 630 feet tall 5,199 tons of steel Honors Jefferson's plan to make the country bigger In the city where settlers left from on their trips to the west

Investigate!

Read pages 18–29 in your Research Companion. Use your investigative skills to look for text evidence that tells you the main idea and details about each of the five main regions in the United States. This chart will help you organize your notes.

Region	Main Idea	Details
Northeast	The Northeast is made up of eleven states that offer many types of jobs and things to do.	Many people live in cities. People work in business, manufacturing, fishing, farming, mining, and other jobs. The Northeast contains many monuments, museums, parks, and beaches.
Southeast	The Southeast is made up of twelve states where farming is important and where there are many activities.	Farmers grow cotton, peanuts, and tobacco. Jobs include farming, fishing, tourism, business, and manufacturing. Entertainment includes water sports, museums, monuments, parks, and amusement parks.
Midwest	The Midwest is made up of twelve states that play important roles in farming and manufacturing.	The region is known as the nation's "Bread Basket" and "Corn Belt" because of its contribution to the nation's food supply. The region is also known as the "Rust Belt" because of manufacturing.
Southwest	The Southwest is made up of four states that have important land resources.	Oil, cattle, and cotton are the main products. National parks and monuments support tourism jobs in New Mexico. Farming, manufacturing, and tourism are jobs in Arizona. Copper mining is also important.
West	The West is made up of eleven states that Americans settled slowly, but the region has grown because of resources and jobs.	Many states have much land but few people. Settlement was slow but was helped by the Oregon and California Trails, the growth in railroads, and people searching for gold. Jobs include tourism, fishing, farming, ranching, and technology.

INQUIRY JOURNAL, pp. 18–19

Inquiry Tools

Explore Main Idea and Details

Read Have students read the step-by-step instructions about how to find the main idea of a passage. Tell students that the topic of a piece of writing answers the question *What is the passage about?* The main idea answers the question *What is the author's most important point about the topic?* Details are not the main idea, but they tell more about the main idea. Point out that one way to figure out the main idea is to ask *What do the details tell me?*

Guide Practice Have students review the text on pp. 16–17. Then work with them to complete the graphic organizer. Explain that they will use a similar graphic organizer to organize their independent research.

Check Understanding Confirm understanding of the inquiry skill, Explore Main Idea and Details. If students cannot identify the main idea and related details, review the steps on p. 18.

Investigate!

Have students read pp. 18–29 in the Research Companion. Tell them the information will help them answer the lesson question **How Does My Community Fit in With My Country?**

Take Notes Tell students they will use the graphic organizer on p. 19 of the Inquiry Journal to take notes on main ideas and supporting details for the main U.S. regions.

Remind students that good note taking will help them understand and remember the information they learn.

Spotlight on Content

Scanning for Information

Have students work in pairs to find and list the number of states in each region and one important activity or resource before entering the main ideas into the chart. Then have them continue with supporting details.

LESSON 2 INVESTIGATE

How Does My Community Fit in With My Country?

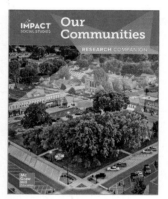

RESEARCH COMPANION, pp. 18–19

What Is a Region?

1 Inspect Have students read pp. 18–19 and explain what a region is.

2 Find Evidence Use the questions below to check comprehension. Remind students to support their answers with text evidence.

Explain How do the features of an area affect people? (The features of each area or region affect how people live, what they wear, and what they do.) **DOK 2**

Apply Concepts How might some features of an area affect the population? Could features bring more people to the area? Are there any features that make life more difficult? (Answers will vary, but students should identify landforms, bodies of water, or climate that might encourage people to move to a region or might make daily life in a region more challenging.) **DOK 3**

3 Make Connections

Point of View Think about how the features of your region affect your life. What features in your region play an important part in your life? (Answers will vary but should include how features impact how they live.) **DOK 3**

Infer Using the map and what you already know about the regions in our country, is there another region in which you think you'd like to live? (Answers will vary but should include specific details about the region students choose.) **DOK 3**

⊙ Map Skills Guide students to locate the five regions on the map. Then have students identify the region with the largest land area (West) and the two regions with the most states (Southeast and Midwest).

• Look at the shapes and the borders of the different regions. What can you say about the borders of the regions in the United States? (Answers will vary, but students should give some detail about locations of regions, such as which regions have an ocean as one of their borders.)

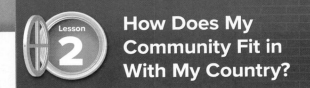

Lesson 2
How Does My Community Fit in With My Country?

What Is a Region?

Think about where you live. Is it hilly or flat? Do you live near an ocean or a river? Is it cloudy, foggy, or sunny most of the time? Your answers will depend on the **region** where you live. A region is an area of land with certain features that make it different from other areas. Each region has its own unique land and water features, as well as its own unique **climate**. Climate is the weather a place has over a long period of time.

The United States has five main regions. These five regions are the Northeast, Southeast, Midwest, West, and Southwest. The features of each region affect how people live. People who live in a place with a cold climate need different kinds of clothes and houses than people who live where it is warm.

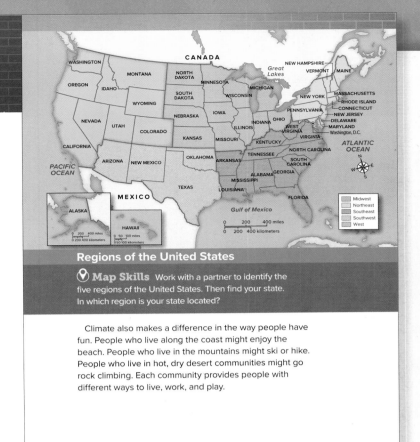

Regions of the United States

📍 **Map Skills** Work with a partner to identify the five regions of the United States. Then find your state. In which region is your state located?

Climate also makes a difference in the way people have fun. People who live along the coast might enjoy the beach. People who live in the mountains might ski or hike. People who live in hot, dry desert communities might go rock climbing. Each community provides people with different ways to live, work, and play.

RESEARCH COMPANION, pp. 18–19

 English Learners SCAFFOLD

Use the following scaffolds to support student understanding of lesson content.

Entering and Emerging

Discuss with students the features of their region, including such things as bodies of waters, land features, and climate. List the features on the board and say each word as you write it. Provide the following sentence frames as needed:

- Bodies of water in our region include _____.
- The land in our region is _____.
- The climate where we live is _____.

Developing and Expanding

Have small groups work together to identify and describe features in their region. Ask: *What lakes or rivers are in your region? What land features are in your region? What activities do people like to do in your region because of the features?*

Bridging and Reaching

Have partners identify activities that people like to do in their region and write each activity on a strip of paper. Put the strips in a container. Have partners take turns choosing one and identifying whether the activity relates to a landform, body of water, or climate.

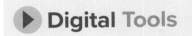 **Digital Tools**

Blended Learning
Students explore lesson content through interactive activities.

Interactive IMPACT

Use the **Explore a Map**— Regions of the United States.

Northeast

Eleven states make up the Northeast. They are Maine, Vermont, New Hampshire, Massachusetts, New York, Connecticut, Rhode Island, Delaware, New Jersey, Maryland, and Pennsylvania. Canada borders the region to the north. The Atlantic Ocean borders the region to the east. Two U.S. regions also border the Northeast—the Midwest to the west and the Southeast to the south.

Thousands of years ago, Native Americans began to settle in what is now the Northeast. In fact, Native American peoples were the first to settle in all of the U.S. regions. Europeans began to settle in the Northeast in the early 1600s. All of the states in this region were among the original thirteen colonies of the United States. However, Maine was part of Massachusetts at that time. Vermont was part of New York. Today, people have come from all over the world to live, work, and play in the Northeast. Many people in the region live in large urban areas, such as Boston, Philadelphia, and Pittsburgh. Many also live in New York City, which is the biggest city in the United States.

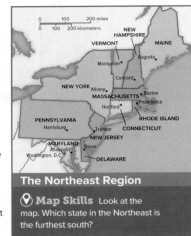

The Northeast Region

Map Skills Look at the map. Which state in the Northeast is the furthest south?

InfoGraphic

Look at the infographic. It shows the population density of Connecticut in the Northeast and Oklahoma in the Southwest. *Population density* means the number of people living per square mile of land. The Northeast is the most densely populated region in the country.

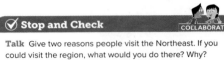

People in the Northeast have many kinds of jobs. Some people work in business, manufacturing, or technology. Others work in fishing, farming, mining, or forestry. Still others work in the arts or education. The Northeast is home to many of the nation's oldest universities, such as Harvard University and Yale University.

People from around the world visit communities in the Northeast. They come to see monuments, such as the Statue of Liberty and the Liberty Bell. They enjoy the museums, parks, and beaches. These visitors make more jobs for the people who live in the Northeast. Some of those jobs are in food service, hotels, and transportation.

✓ Stop and Check

Talk Give two reasons people visit the Northeast. If you could visit the region, what would you do there? Why?

Find Details As you read, add new information to the graphic organizer on page 19 in your Inquiry Journal.

RESEARCH COMPANION, pp. 20–21

Northeast

1 Inspect Have students read pp. 20–21 and identify a unique feature or characteristic of the Northeast region.

2 Find Evidence Use the question below to check comprehension.

Interpret Why do you think the Northeast is the most densely populated region in the United States? (Answers will vary, but students might suggest the variety of jobs that are available and that it includes major cities, such as Boston, New York, Philadelphia, and Washington, D.C.) **DOK 3**

3 Make Connections

Interpret What does the sentence "All the states in this region were among the original thirteen colonies of the United States" mean? (The states in the Northeast region were some of the first colonies of Europeans that eventually became the United States.) **DOK 2**

Map Skills Guide students to identify Maryland as the southernmost state.

✓ Stop and Check

Talk Have students discuss the questions with a partner. Remind them to use the text and map when discussing their answers. (People visit the Northeast to see monuments and visit museums, parks, and beaches. Students' answers to the second part of the question will vary, but they should provide reasons to support their answers.)

EL Spotlight on Language

Understanding Language

forestry: the practice of caring for forests or woods

original: happening first or at the beginning

Southeast

There are twelve states in the Southeast. They are Virginia, West Virginia, North Carolina, South Carolina, Georgia, Florida, Kentucky, Tennessee, Alabama, Mississippi, Arkansas, and Louisiana. The Atlantic Ocean sits to the east of the region. The Gulf of Mexico lies to the south. Two other US regions, the Southwest to the west and the Midwest to the north, also border the Southeast.

The oldest European settlement in the United States is in the Southeast. Explorers from Spain founded St. Augustine, Florida, in 1565. Later, in 1607, Jamestown, Virginia, became the first permanent English settlement in North America. Virginia was one of the original thirteen colonies of the United States. North Carolina, South Carolina, and Georgia also were among the original thirteen colonies.

The Southeast Region

📍 **Map Skills** Look at the map. Which state in the Southeast is farthest north?

The Southeast's hot summers and warm-to-cool winters make the region ideal for farming. Cotton, peanuts, and tobacco grow in the Southeast. Soybeans, wheat, oats, and hay grow there, too. Many fruits and vegetables also grow on farms there, including apples, oranges, watermelon, peaches, potatoes, tomatoes, and pumpkins.

People in the Southeast also work in fishing, tourism, business, and manufacturing. Many people have jobs making cars, trucks, buses, trains, and airplanes.

Many people visit the Southeast. They come to enjoy water sports, hike, and visit museums and monuments. They also enjoy the state and national parks and the many amusement parks in this region.

Did You Know?

Savannah, Georgia, was originally laid out in a square and grid pattern. In the center of each section is a square. The roads that border the square to the north and south were divided into ten large lots. Homes were built on these lots. Public buildings, such as churches or courthouses, were built on the roads on the east and west sides of the square. Today the squares provide green space for the people. The squares have gardens and parks.

✓ **Stop and Check** COLLABORATE

Think What is the climate like in the Southeast? How does the climate affect the way people live and work there?

RESEARCH COMPANION, pp. 22–23

Southeast

1 Inspect Have students read pp. 22–23 and identify something people enjoy about living in the Southeast.

2 Find Evidence Use the questions below to check comprehension.

Explain How does the climate of the Southeast impact farming? (The Southeast has warm-to-cool winters and hot summers, so it is good for farming.) **DOK 2**

3 Make Connections

Compare and Contrast In what ways are the Northeast and Southeast regions similar and different? (Similar: settled by Europeans, some states in each region were among the original thirteen colonies, both regions border the Atlantic Ocean; Different: milder climate in the Southeast, more farming in the Southeast, population density less in the Southeast.) **DOK 3**

📍 **Map Skills** Guide students to locate which state in the Southeast is farthest north (West Virginia) and what the states of West Virginia, Kentucky, Tennessee, and Arkansas have in common. (They do not border the Atlantic Ocean or the Gulf of Mexico.)

✓ **Stop and Check** COLLABORATE

Think Have students discuss the question with a partner. Remind them to use the text when discussing their answers. (The summers are hot and the winters are warm to cool, although the northernmost states and the mountains do get colder. The climate makes it possible to grow many different crops. It also likely brings more visitors to the area.)

▶ **Digital Tools**

Blended Learning
Students explore lesson content through interactive activities.

Interactive IMPACT

Use the **Explore a Map**—The Northeast Region and The Southeast Region.

Midwest

The Midwest is the center of the continental United States. There are twelve states in the region. They are Ohio, Indiana, Michigan, Illinois, Missouri, Wisconsin, Minnesota, Iowa, Kansas, Nebraska, South Dakota, and North Dakota.

Immigrants and people from the Northeast settled in the Midwest. An immigrant is a person who moves from one country to live in another country. At first the people settled along canals and waterways in what would become Ohio, Indiana, Michigan, Illinois, and Wisconsin. By the mid-1800s, people began to settle in states that are part of the Great Plains. By 1890, Chicago, Illinois, was the second biggest city in the country.

The Midwest Region

◉ Map Skills Look at the map. Which state in the Midwest lies farthest east?

The Midwest is known as the "nation's bread basket" and the Corn Belt. This is because the region has good soil and weather for farming. The growing season is long. Farmers grow corn, wheat, soybeans, and vegetables. Their crops are sold around the country and around the world.

Many people also work in manufacturing. About thirty percent of the manufacturing done in the United States is done in the Midwest. The region is well-known for making cars.

Citizenship

A good citizen takes action to make his or her community strong. The Midwest has very snowy winters. Look at the people in the picture helping each other shovel the snow from sidewalks and driveways. Are they being good citizens? Think about your community. What action can you take to help make your community stronger?

✓ Stop and Check

Talk In what ways does the Midwest help the country? Cite information in the text to support your answers.

RESEARCH COMPANION, pp. 24–25

Midwest

1 Inspect Have students read pp. 24–25 and list crops grown in the Midwest.

2 Find Evidence Use the questions below to check comprehension.

Hypothesize Why do you think people first settled along waterways in the Midwest? (Answers will vary, but students might say waterways provided transportation, fishing, or water for farming.) **DOK 3**

Explain Why is the Midwest called the "nation's bread basket"? (Much of our food is grown in this region.) **DOK 2**

3 Make Connections

Differentiate Why might it be more difficult to ship crops around the world from the Midwest, compared with the other regions in the United States? (It is in the center of the United States, and it has no ocean borders.) **DOK 3**

◉ Map Skills Guide students to identify which state in the Midwest lies farthest east (Ohio) and to explain why some borders are straight lines and some are not straight lines. (Possible response: Rivers and lakes make up many natural borders in the Midwest.)

✓ Stop and Check

Talk Have students discuss the question with a partner. Remind them to use the text to cite information when discussing their answers. (The Midwest helps provide the country with food. It has a long growing season that helps farmers produce crops. There is also manufacturing throughout the region.)

 Spotlight on Language

Understanding Language

growing season: the period of time for growing crops

soybeans: a plant that has a large amount of protein and is used for food

 Social Emotional Learning

Relationship Skills

Teamwork In order to work together in a team, students need to understand team goals and what each team member needs to contribute. Teamwork requires communication and cooperation. Ask: *How are the people in the photograph working as a team? What do you think their goal is?*

Southwest

The Southwest is the U.S. region with the fewest states. Only four states belong to the region. They are Texas, Oklahoma, New Mexico, and Arizona. The Southwest is bordered by the Southeast to the east. The Gulf of Mexico and Mexico border the region to the south. The West runs along the western and northern borders. The Midwest lies to the north.

Many groups have settled in the Southwest. Native American peoples have lived in this region for thousands of years. Europeans began to explore and settle in the Southwest in the late 1500s. In the 1800s, immigrants and people from states to the east came to the region.

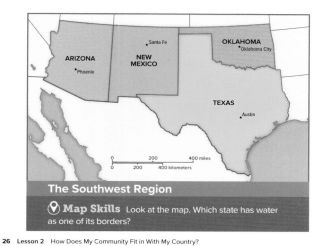

The Southwest Region

📍 **Map Skills** Look at the map. Which state has water as one of its borders?

26 Lesson 2 How Does My Community Fit in With My Country?

Today, though there are large open spaces in the region, most of the people in the Southwest live in urban areas, such as Houston, Oklahoma City, Albuquerque, and Phoenix.

Many people in the Southwest work in jobs based on the land resources in each state. In Texas and Oklahoma, many people grow cotton, raise cattle, and remove oil from underground. Many people in New Mexico work in tourism. Many people in Arizona have jobs in farming, manufacturing, and tourism. Copper mining is especially important in Arizona. Visitors come to the Southwest to enjoy the region's environment. People can hike in the mountains and see rock formations in the deserts. They can also come to fish, camp, and attend local festivals and rodeos. Many people visit Carlsbad Caverns in New Mexico and the Grand Canyon in Arizona. People can also learn about the history of the region at places such as the Alamo in San Antonio, Texas.

Did You Know?

The Grand Canyon is located in northwestern Arizona. A canyon is a deep valley with steep sides. Often, a river or stream flows through a canyon. The Colorado River runs through the Grand Canyon. The Grand Canyon stretches a distance of about 270 miles. Its width ranges from about 175 yards to 18 miles. In some places the canyon is more than a mile deep. Each year, millions of people visit the Grand Canyon. They come to hike on trails, ride mules into the canyon, and ride rafts on the Colorado River.

✓ **Stop and Check**

Talk With a partner, discuss what makes the Southwest different from the other regions you've read about so far.

Chapter 1 Lesson 2 27

Southwest

1 Inspect Have students read pp. 26–27 and identify a special landform located in the Southwest.

2 Find Evidence Use the question below to check comprehension.

Explain Why do some people in New Mexico and Arizona work in tourism? (New Mexico is the home of Carlsbad Caverns, and Arizona is the home of the Grand Canyon. People come to visit these places. There are also mountains to hike and rock formations to see in the desert areas.) **DOK 3**

3 Make Connections

Draw Conclusions What conclusions can you make about what life is like for people who live in the Southwest? (Answers will vary, but students should mention the types of jobs people have, the major population centers, and the opportunities for outdoor activities.) **DOK 3**

📍 **Map Skills** Guide students to locate the state that borders both the Midwest and the West (Oklahoma), the state that extends farthest south in the region (Texas), and the state that shares borders with all of the other states in the Southwest region (New Mexico).

✓ **Stop and Check**

Talk (Answers will vary, but students might suggest the Southwest has the fewest states of any region, there is a lot of open space, raising cattle and drilling for oil is important to the Southwest, and the unique environment attracts many visitors.)

EL Spotlight on Language

Understanding Language

raise cattle: to look after cows until they can be sold

rodeos: events in which people compete by riding horses and bulls, and catching animals with ropes

▶ **Digital Tools**

Blended Learning

Guide students as they investigate the lesson content.

Interactive IMPACT

Use the **Explore a Map**—The Midwest Region and The Southwest Region.

West

1 Inspect Have students read pp. 28–29 and explain how the West was settled.

2 Find Evidence Use the questions below to check students' comprehension.

Infer Why were railroads and gold important to the West region? (New railroads made it possible for people to come to the region easily, and gold in California brought many people into the region.) **DOK 2**

Differentiate How are the states of Hawaii and Alaska different from the other states in the West region? (They both are separated from the connected states in the West region. Hawaii is a group of islands in the Pacific Ocean, and Canada separates Alaska from the connected states in the region.) **DOK 3**

3 Make Connections

Infer What impact did the discovery of gold have on the city of San Francisco? (As more people came to settle in California, San Francisco grew rapidly. Businesses in the city grew quickly, especially those that supported the gold industry and the new settlers.) **DOK 3**

Map Skills Guide students to locate the states in the West that do not border any other states (Alaska, Hawaii), the state that extends the farthest east (Colorado), and the states that border the Pacific Ocean (California, Oregon, Washington, Alaska, Hawaii).

Stop and Check

Talk Remind students to review the text and map when discussing their answers. (People could not reach Hawaii by wagon or train, so it was isolated from the rest of the country. However, because Hawaii was located on early shipping routes, the news of its warm climate and rich soil spread and attracted people from all over the world.)

What Do You Think? Discuss the features that make up your region. (Answers will vary but should reflect what students know about their region and other regions.)

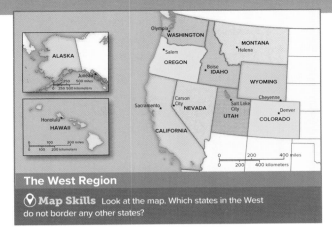

The West Region

 Map Skills Look at the map. Which states in the West do not border any other states?

West

Eleven states belong to the region known as the West. The Pacific Coast states include Washington, Oregon, and California. Hawaii is a group of islands surrounded by the Pacific Ocean. Canada separates Alaska from the connected states. Idaho, Montana, Wyoming, Colorado, Utah, and Nevada are inland states.

In the early 1800s, settlers from the East traveled the Oregon and California Trails. By the mid-1800s, the railroads reached the West. This brought more people. The discovery of gold in California caused the largest movement of people in U.S. history.

Hawaii is located on shipping routes. Sailors stayed on the islands for the winter. News of the islands spread. People from all over the world moved there.

Most people in the West live in urban areas. However, in some states people live far apart from each other. Many people work in tourism, fishing, farming, and ranching. Jobs in technology bring people to the West Coast.

Then and Now

The Settlement of the West

Communities along the West Coast changed as more people settled in them. San Francisco is one community that has changed. It started as a tiny settlement near the coast. But San Francisco grew quickly during the mid-1800s. Gold seekers from all over the world came to try to strike it rich. Other people came to San Francisco to start businesses that sold tools and other things to the miners. San Francisco is now one of California's largest cities.

Stop and Check

Think How was the settlement of Hawaii different from the rest of the West?

What Do You Think? How is your region similar to other regions in the United States? How is it different?

RESEARCH COMPANION, pp. 28–29

EL English Learners SCAFFOLD

Use the following scaffolds to support student understanding of lesson content.

Entering and Emerging

Have students describe features of their region that are in or near their community. Provide sentence frames: *In our region, there are _____ and _____. In my community, there are _____ and _____.* Encourage students to say word phrases or sentences to describe where they have seen one of the landforms or bodies of water.

Developing and Expanding

Have small groups each choose one of the five regions. Ask: *What activities do people enjoy in the region you chose?* Have each group make a list of phrases describing the activities. Then have a student from each group read each item from their list, and have the class guess which region it is before the student finishes reading the list.

Bridging and Reaching

Have partners take turns describing a region with one example and one non-example. "My region has _____ but does not have _____." The other partner should guess the region.

✓ Check for Success

Connect Can students identify locations and features of the different regions of the United States and explain how their community fits geographically with the rest of the country?

Differentiate

If Not, Guide students to review the features of each region (the main idea) and the supporting details identified in the graphic organizer on p. 19 of their Inquiry Journals.

LESSON 2 REPORT

 LESSON QUESTION

How Does My Community Fit in With My Country?

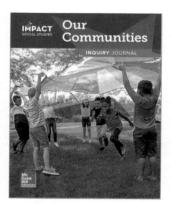

INQUIRY JOURNAL, pp. 20–21

Think About It

Remind students to review their research and think about what they learned about each of the five regions. Encourage students to review the main ideas and details they have included in their graphic organizer. Direct students back to pages 18–29 of their Research Companion if they need more information.

Write About It

Write and Cite Evidence Have students include the following elements in their opinion paragraphs.

- Identify why they think their region is an interesting place to live.
- Describe their region using information from the text and maps and their own knowledge about the region.
- Include facts based on their research.
- Use chapter vocabulary as appropriate.

Disciplines	4	3	2	1
Geography History	Student provides evidence and details as to why their region is an interesting place to live.	Student includes details to provide some evidence as to why their region is an interesting place to live.	Student includes evidence but few supporting details as to why their region is an interesting place to live.	Student does not support evidence with details as to why their region is an interesting place to live.

Talk About It

Consider Opinions Encourage students to connect their personal experiences or prior knowledge to the conversation.

Assessment Students can check their understanding with feedback from the **Lesson Test** available online.

Connect to the Essential Question

Take Action Encourage students to think about the features of their region, how their community is affected by the region, and how their community is similar to or different from other communities around them.

Inquiry Project Update Remind students to turn to Inquiry Journal pp. 2–3 for project information. If necessary, review the Project Checklist with students. At this point in the chapter, students should focus on the second two items on the Checklist.

Think About It

Review your research. Based on the information you have gathered, in what region do you live? What features describe your region?

Write About It

Define
What is a region?

A region is an area of land with certain features that make it different from other areas.

Write and Cite Evidence
Write an opinion paragraph explaining what makes your region an interesting place to live. Support your opinion with reasons.

Answers will vary but should be supported with facts from the text.

Talk About It

Consider Opinions
Find a partner who chose a different reason than you did for why your region is a good place to live. Take turns discussing your opinions and the evidence used to support them. Do you agree or disagree with your partner's opinion? Why?

Geography Connect to the EQ

Take Action
What are some characteristics of your region? Why do these characteristics matter to your community? List ideas to share with others.

Answers will vary, but students should list characteristics of their region and how they affect their community.

EQ Inquiry Project Notes

20 Lesson 2 How Does My Community Fit in With My Country?

Chapter 1 Lesson 2 21

INQUIRY JOURNAL, pp. 20–21

English Learners SCAFFOLD

Use the following scaffolds to support student writing.

Entering and Emerging

Help students think about why their region is an interesting place to live. Provide sentence frames to help students describe their regions:

- The _____ region is a good place to live because the climate is _____.
- Fun places to visit include _____ and _____.
- In this region, people like to _____ and _____.

Developing and Expanding

Remind students that opinions should be supported with reasons. Ask questions to help students describe what is interesting about their region and why. For example: *What is the climate in your region? Why do you like it? What are some activities to do in your region? Where do people like to go in your region? Why? What do you like most about where you live?*

Bridging and Reaching

Have partners discuss what is most interesting about their region and why. Have them create a T-chart with opinions in one column and reasons for their opinions in the other column. Guide students to write a paragraph that includes details about climate, landforms, bodies of water, activities, or special features of their region.

✔ Check for Success

Explain Can students write an opinion paragraph in which they explain why they think their region is an interesting place to live in, with reasons and evidence for those reasons?

Differentiate

If Not, Have students make a chart with three columns. Have them list items they like about their region in the first column, phrases explaining their reasons in the second column, and examples of those items in a third column.

LESSON QUESTION

How Does Climate Impact My Community?

Connect to the Essential Question

Tell students that this lesson will help them answer the Chapter Essential Question: **Why Does It Matter Where We Live?** Explain that they will learn about climates in different parts of the United States and how climate affects the people, plants, and animals that live there.

Lesson Objectives

- **Describe** different climates found in the United States.

- **Explain** how the climates in other regions compare to that of the student's own region.

- **Identify** ways climate affects people, plants, and animals in a student's life.

- **Write** a diary entry that explains how climate affected a student's activity in the community.

Make Connections!

CONNECT TO ELA

Reading **Determine** the main idea of a text; recount the key details and explain how they support the main idea.

Research **Recall** information from experiences or gather information from print and digital sources; take brief notes on sources and sort evidence into provided categories.

Writing **Develop** the topic with facts, definitions, and details.

Speaking and Listening **Engage** effectively in a range of collaborative discussions with diverse partners on grade 3 topics and texts, building on others' ideas and expressing students' own clearly.

Language **Determine** or clarify the meaning of unknown and multiple-meaning words and phrases based on grade-level reading and content, choosing flexibly from a range of strategies.

COMMUNITY CONNECTIONS

To enrich what students have learned about climate in different parts of the United States, have them talk to friends or relatives who have visited or lived in different communities. Have students ask what the climate is like there and how it affects the way people live.

Lesson-At-A-Glance

1 ENGAGE — INQUIRY JOURNAL

pp. 22–27

- ▶ **Talk About It:** Photograph of a Snowy Climate
- ▶ **Analyze the Source:** Climate Helps Describe a Region
- ▶ **Inquiry Tools:** Explore Main Idea and Details

2 INVESTIGATE — RESEARCH COMPANION

pp. 30–39

- ▶ **Climates of the United States**
- ▶ **Life in Dry and Desert Climates**
- ▶ **Life With Cold Winters**
- ▶ **Life With Humid Summers**
- ▶ **Perspective: Gladesmen**
- ▶ **Life With Mild Seasons**

3 REPORT — INQUIRY JOURNAL

pp. 28–29

- ▶ **Think About It**
- ▶ **Write About It:** Write and Cite Evidence; Write a Diary Entry
- ▶ **Talk About It**
- ▶ **Connect to the Essential Question**

ASSESSMENT

- ▶ **Online Lesson Test**
- ▶ **Printable Lesson Test**

For more details, see pages T4–T5.

Digital Tools

at **my.mheducation.com**

ePresentation

Teach the Engage, Investigate, and Report content to the whole class from ePresentations that launch directly from the lesson dashboard.

eBook

You can flip your instruction with the **IMPACT eBooks** found on your lesson dashboard.

Interactive IMPACT

Blend in digital content **when you want it** and **where you want it.**

Blended Learning features in the Teacher's Edition highlight ways to connect in-class work with online experiences to enhance learning.

Investigate current events with **IMPACT News.**

Explore domain-based vocabulary with **Explore Words** and **Word Play** vocabulary activities.

Go Further with IMPACT Explorer Magazine!

pp. 2–15

The **IMPACT Explorer Magazine** supports students' exploration of the Essential Question and provides additional resources for the EQ Inquiry Project.

LESSON 3 LANGUAGE LEARNERS

How Does Climate Impact My Community?

Introduce the Lesson

Set Purpose Explain to students that in this lesson they will read informational texts to learn about how climates affect life in different regions of the United States.

Access Prior Knowledge Before presenting the lesson outcomes, read the lesson question and remind students that climate is the usual weather in a place. Ask students to look at the map on page 31 of the Research Companion, and list words in the map key that describe different climates. Say: *Different parts of the United States have different climates.* Ask: *What pairs of opposites can you find in this map key?* (tropical/desert; long/short; humid/dry) *What word means that it is neither very hot nor very cold?* (mild)

Spark Curiosity Have students study the Climate Map of the United States on page 31 of the Research Companion. Encourage them to describe the patterns of different climates. Ask: *Do you see any patterns on the map? What do you notice about the West region compared to the Northeast and Southeast regions? Do people live differently because of their region's climate?*

Build Meaning & Support Language

Inquiry Journal

Analyze the Source (pages 24–25) Discuss the heading "Climate Helps Describe a Region." Say: *The word* describe *means "tell about" or "help people understand." What does climate help you understand about a region?* (what the weather is usually like in the region) Read aloud the first sentence of the section. Explain that when something "makes a big difference," it is very important. Ask: *Why is climate very important?* (It affects how people live, including what kinds of buildings there are, what jobs people have, and how much time people can spend outside.)

Inquiry Tools (pages 26–27) Tell students they will **Explore Main Idea and Details** as they read sections in the Research Companion. Explain that the graphic organizer will help them organize the information they read. Check to see that they understand the meaning of the column heads: *Climate, Main Idea, Details*. Then have students scan the photos and section headings in the Research Companion. For each section, ask what regions of the country might have that type of climate.

Language Objectives

- Use newly acquired content and academic vocabulary to talk and write about the effect of climate on people's lives.
- Write a diary entry about the effects of climate on a community.
- Identify pronouns and antecedents.

Spanish Cognates

To support Spanish speakers, point out the cognates.

arctic = ártico

desert = desierto

precipitation = precipitación

temperature = temperature

volcano = volcán

Research Companion

Climates of the United States (pages 30–31) As you read, explain any words that students don't know. In the first paragraph, explain that the phrase *make a living* means "to earn enough money to support oneself or one's family." Ask: *What does it mean to "tell about the ways people in your community make a living"?* (It means to tell what jobs people in your community have.)

Life in Dry and Desert Climates (pages 32–33) After you read page 33, discuss this sentence in detail: *Natural resources also draw people.* Explain that *draw people* means "convince people to live in the area." Say: *Natural resources are materials such as gold and oil. They can be sold or used to make products. Why do natural resources draw people to an area?* (The resources can help them make products and earn money.)

Life With Cold Winters (pages 34–35) Remind students that a main idea is what a text or part of a text is mostly about, and that details in the text support the main idea. Have students identify the main idea and details of this section by completing these sentence frames: *The climate in the Northeast and Midwest is _____.* (cold in the winter) *One detail about the climate is that _____.* (Blizzards bring cold wind and snow.) *Another detail is that _____.* (Nor'easter storms can bring heavy rain and snow.)

Life With Humid Summers/Life With Mild Seasons (pages 36–39) Read the first paragraph on page 38 and point out the final sentence: *This can lead to dangerous wildfires.* Explain that *lead to* is another way of saying "cause." Ask: *What leads to the dangerous wildfires?* Guide students to identify the causes in the previous sentence. (When plants and grasses dry up, they burn more easily.)

Inquiry Journal

Report Your Findings (pages 28–29) Explain that the word *impact* means "to affect or change." Review with students the elements of a diary entry, including the use of the first-person pronoun *I* to express personal feelings and thoughts. Explain that often diary entries include the date and a greeting such as "Dear Diary" or "Dear Journal."

Language Forms & Conventions

Pronouns and Antecedents Remind students that a *pronoun* is a word that replaces a noun in a sentence. Explain that an *antecedent* is the word that the pronoun replaces. Tell students that to figure out what a pronoun means, they should look for a noun that is most likely to match the pronoun that appears later in the sentence or in the next sentence. If there is more than one, they can use clues to identify the noun that best fits. Display the chart. Help students identify the antecedent for each pronoun. (it: state or community; They: Deserts; these: pineapples and sugarcane)

Pronoun	Sentences
it	Locate your state or community on the map. What color is <u>it</u>?
They	Deserts in the region are even drier. <u>They</u> can be hot or cold.
these	Early settlers brought pineapples and sugarcane to Hawaii. The tropical climate was ideal for growing <u>these</u>.

 COLLABORATE Have pairs of students find other pronouns and antecedents in the text.

 Cross-Cultural Connection

Some communities live in areas with extremely cold climates. The Inuit people of the Canadian Arctic have traditionally lived in areas where winters are long and the ground remains frozen year-round. In Inuit communities, people live in houses designed to withstand very cold weather and wear thick, warm clothes to hunt and fish. Ask: *What would you need to change to live in a place with a very cold climate?*

 EL Leveled Support

Entering & Emerging
Help students complete the sentence frames: *The summers in my community are _____. The winters in my community are _____. I like to _____ in the summer and _____ in the winter.*

Developing & Expanding
Have small groups create a list of words used to describe the climate in their community.

Bridging & Reaching
Encourage students to work with partners to describe the climate in their community and list three ways climate affects how people live there.

 **Language Transfer**

In several languages, including Spanish and Korean, subject pronouns like *I, they,* or *we* can be omitted since the ending of a verb gives information about the subject's number or gender.

LESSON 3 ENGAGE

LESSON QUESTION

How Does Climate Impact My Community?

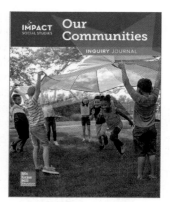

INQUIRY JOURNAL, pp. 22–23

Bellringer

Prompt students to retrieve information from the previous lesson. Ask: *In which region of the United States is your community? What are the other four regions?* (The five regions are Northeast, Southeast, Midwest, Southwest, and West.)

Lesson Outcomes

Discuss the lesson question and lesson outcomes with students.

- Make sure students understand that the term *climate* refers to the weather a region usually has over many years.

- To help students make connections between climate and their community, have them describe some plants or animals they see in their community. Remind students that each region of the United States has specific features that make it different from other regions of the country. Explain that learning about different climates will help them understand how climate affects the people, plants, and animals in a region.

Talk About It

Guide students to look at the photograph, read the caption, and answer the following questions about the weather that is shown:

- What is happening in this picture? (A snowstorm is occurring.)

- What can you tell about the climate in this region of the United States? (It has snowy, cold winters.)

- What are some ways the climate affects this community? (Answers will vary, but students should understand that people might play in the snow, cities might need to clear ice and snow, and people need to dress warmly in the winter.)

 Collaborative Conversations

Take Turns Talking As students engage in partner, small-group, and whole-class discussions, encourage them to

- wait for a person to finish before they speak. They should not speak over others.
- quietly raise their hand to let others know they would like a turn to speak.
- ask others in the group to share their opinions so that all students have a chance to share.

Lesson 3

How Does Climate Impact My Community?

Lesson Outcomes

What Am I Learning?
In this lesson, you will use your investigative skills to learn about climates in the United States.

Why Am I Learning It?
Reading and talking about different climates will help you understand how climate affects the people, plants, and animals around you.

How Will I Know That I Learned It?
You will be able to write a diary entry that explains how climate affects your community.

Talk About It COLLABORATE

Look closely at the picture. What do you think is happening? How could this impact the community in the picture?

In some climate regions of the United States, snowstorms like this are common.

INQUIRY JOURNAL, pp. 22–23

English Learners SCAFFOLD

Use the following scaffolds to support student understanding of the lesson outcomes.

Entering and Emerging

Read the photo caption and then provide a sentence frame to help students describe the photograph:

- There is/are _____ in the photograph.

Ask: *What will happen later? What do you think happened earlier? Where are other people now?*

Developing and Expanding

Have small groups work together to read the caption and consider the word *common*. Encourage students to look for clues in the photograph that show that the community is familiar with snowstorms. Ask: *What clues in the photograph tell you that snowstorms are common in this climate region?*

Bridging and Reaching

Have student pairs write a three-sentence story about the person pictured in the photo. Encourage them to think about the climate, where the person might be going, and what the person might be thinking.

Social Emotional Learning

Social Awareness

Build Empathy To empathize with others and understand their feelings, students need to learn how to put themselves in someone's shoes. Ask students to briefly role-play the thoughts of the person pictured in the photograph.

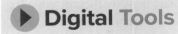 **Digital** Tools

Blended Learning

Students engage with the lesson question and discussion prompts.

ePresentation

Discuss the **Lesson Question** and **Talk About It** with the whole class.

1 Inspect

Read Look at the titles of the two graphs. Based on the titles, what do you expect to see in the graphs?

Circle the month with the highest average low temperature in International Falls, Minnesota.

Discuss with a partner how the weather described in the graphs compares to the weather in your region.

My Notes

_____

_____

_____

_____

_____

_____

_____

_____

Climate Helps Describe a Region

The climate of a region makes a big difference! Climate is the weather a region has over a long period of time. California's Death Valley is the hottest and driest place in the United States. There is very little **precipitation**. In an average year, there may be less than two inches of rain. This can be very challenging.

Living in a cold climate can also be challenging. Keeping homes, offices, and schools warm in a cold climate can be expensive. Blizzards can cause power outages.

Average Monthly Low Temperature in International Falls, MN

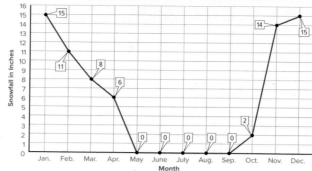

Average Monthly Snowfall in International Falls, MN

One of the coldest communities in the continental United States is International Falls, Minnesota. In an average year, International Falls gets almost six feet of snow and over two feet of rain. This amount of precipitation is challenging, too. Snow can make it difficult to get to school and to stores. Rain can cause flooding.

2 Find Evidence

Look How does the information in the graphs help you understand the climate of International Falls?

Reread According to the text, how are Death Valley and International Falls similar?

3 Make Connections

Talk Look at the photo on page 23. With a partner, discuss the climate shown in the photo. How is it similar to the climate of International Falls, Minnesota?

24 Lesson 3 How Does Climate Impact My Community?

Chapter 1 Lesson 3 25

INQUIRY JOURNAL, pp. 24–25

Analyze the Source

1 Inspect

Read Have students read the text and study the graphs on pp. 24–25.

- Underline words and phrases in the text that tell about the climate in International Falls, Minnesota. (one of the coldest communities, six feet of snow, two feet of rain)
- What month has the highest average low temperature in International Falls, Minnesota? (July, 53 degrees)
- What two months have the greatest amount of snowfall? (December and January, 15 inches)

2 Find Evidence

Look Have students discuss with a partner how the graphs help them understand about the environment of International Falls.

Reread Students should understand that precipitation levels make both Death Valley and International Falls challenging places to live.

3 Make Connections

Talk Encourage partners to discuss if the photo on page 23 could be a photo from International Falls. Make sure they use evidence from the photo, the chart, and the text to make their argument.

EL Spotlight on Language

Superlative Adjectives

Explain that a superlative adjective compares three or more nouns. It shows the highest degree of something. To make a superlative, add the ending -est to an adjective with one syllable to show comparison of three or more things. For example, if you say "Jenna is the fastest runner I know," you are comparing Jenna to all the people you've ever met. Have students locate words in the text that use the suffix -est.

Explore Main Idea and Details

The **main idea** is the most important point the author makes about a topic. **Details** tell more about the main idea.

1. **Read the text all the way through.**
   This will help you understand what the text is about.

2. **Look carefully at the pictures and charts.**

3. **See if there is a sentence that states the main idea.**
   This is often the first sentence of a paragraph. Sometimes other sentences in a paragraph can state the main idea.

4. **Now look for details.**
   Sentences with details give more information about the main idea.

Based on the text you read, work with your class to complete the chart below.

Topic	Main Idea	Details
climate	Climate creates challenges.	Death Valley is challenging because it is hot and dry. International Falls is challenging because it is cold and gets lots of precipitation.

Investigate!

Read pages 30–39 in your Research Companion. Use your investigative skills to look for text evidence that tells you the main idea and supporting details. This chart will help you organize your notes.

Climate	Main Idea	Details
Dry and desert	Little precipitation makes life difficult.	Not many people live in this climate. People need to find or bring in water.
Warm summers and cold winters	Cold winters affect people, plants, and animals.	People wear warm clothing and make their houses warm for winter. Some animals hibernate or migrate. Trees drop their leaves before winter arrives.
Humid summers and mild winters	The heat and humidity can create dangerous weather.	Tornadoes and hurricanes can cause damage and injuries.
Mild seasons	Mild weather is good for tourism and farming.	Tourists visit these areas to enjoy the mild weather and the sights. Farmers grow crops all year round.

INQUIRY JOURNAL, pp. 26–27

Inquiry Tools

Explore Main Idea and Details

Read Have students read the step-by-step instructions for finding the main idea and details of a text. Explain that they can find details by asking *wh-* questions about the text.

Guide Practice Have students review the text on pp. 24–25. Then work with students to complete the graphic organizer. Explain that they will use a similar graphic organizer to organize their independent research.

Check Understanding Confirm understanding of the inquiry skill, Explore Main Idea and Details. If students cannot identify a main idea and its related details, review the steps on p. 26.

Investigate!

Have students read pp. 30–39 in the Research Companion. Tell them the information will help them answer the lesson question *How Does Climate Impact My Community?*

Take Notes Tell students that they will take notes in the graphic organizer on p. 27 of the Inquiry Journal. Remind them that taking notes will help them understand and remember the information they learn. Remind students that they should use their own words when taking notes.

 Digital Tools

Blended Learning

Students prepare for the lesson investigation with step-by-step instructions about how to determine the main idea and details.

ePresentation

Use the **Inquiry Tools** to model the lesson graphic organizer.

LESSON 3 INVESTIGATE

How Does Climate Impact My Community?

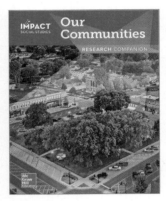

RESEARCH COMPANION, pp. 30–31

Climates of the United States

1 Inspect Have students read pp. 30–31 and explain what humidity is.

2 Find Evidence Use the questions below to check comprehension. Remind students to support their answers with text evidence.

Summarize How does humidity influence the climate of a region? (Humidity makes the air feel warmer; humid regions are also more likely to have rain.) **DOK 2**

Infer Do you think Hawaii has a humid climate? Why or why not? (Hawaii is warm with lots of precipitation; humid climates are also warm and rainy, so Hawaii probably has a fairly humid climate.) **DOK 3**

3 Make Connections

Hypothesize How do you think houses in the Midwest or Northeast regions are different than houses in the Southwest region? (Answers will vary, but students should understand that houses in the Midwest or Northeast need to be made with features that keep them warm because the climates there have cold winters; the climate in Arizona is dry and hot, so houses there don't need as many features to keep them warm.) **DOK 3**

Map Skills Guide students to locate their states or communities and to use the map key to find the climate where they live. Have students compare their experience with the typical weather where they live with the climate from the map. (Answers will vary.)

Lesson 3

How Does Climate Impact My Community?

Climates of the United States

How would you describe your community to someone from another state? You might tell about the weather, or you might describe your summer and winter activities. You could tell about the ways people in your community make a living. You might describe the plants and animals around you. All of these things are related to the climate where you live.

The climate map shows the different climates in the United States. In some parts of the United States, the summers are hot and humid and the winters are mild. In other parts of the country, the summers are warm and humid, but the winters are very cold. **Humidity** is a measure of how much moisture is in the air. Humidity makes the air feel warmer. A humid climate is also more likely to have rain. Some areas of the United States are dry and some are desert. In regions with very mild seasons, summer and winter weather are very similar. Most of Alaska has cold, arctic temperatures. Hawaii is tropical, with warm weather and lots of **precipitation**, which falls as rain.

The climate of a community affects how people live and how many people live there. It also affects the kinds of homes people build and the type of work they do.

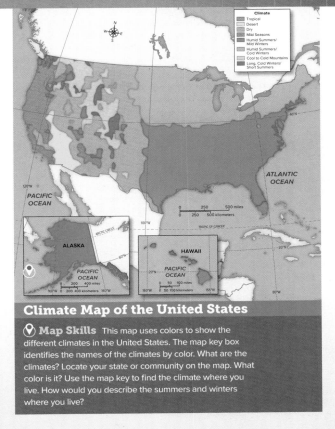

Climate Map of the United States

Map Skills This map uses colors to show the different climates in the United States. The map key box identifies the names of the climates by color. What are the climates? Locate your state or community on the map. What color is it? Use the map key to find the climate where you live. How would you describe the summers and winters where you live?

RESEARCH COMPANION, pp. 30–31

English Learners SCAFFOLD

Use the following scaffolds to support student understanding of lesson content.

Entering and Emerging

Work with students to understand *humidity* and *precipitation*. Say: Humidity *and* precipitation *are both words that talk about water*.

- Humidity/Precipitation is water that stays in the air.
- Humidity/Precipitation is water that falls out of the air, like rain or snow.

Developing and Expanding

Help students describe *humidity* and *precipitation*. Ask: *What does it feel like when it is humid outside? Does humidity make it warmer or colder? What is the weather like when there is precipitation? What kind of precipitation falls in warm climates?*

Bridging and Reaching

Have partners discuss and define *humidity* and *precipitation* in their own words. Ask: *How are humidity and precipitation alike? How are they different?*

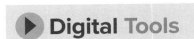

Digital Tools

Blended Learning
Students explore lesson content through interactive activities.

Interactive IMPACT

Use the **Lesson Video** Severe Weather.

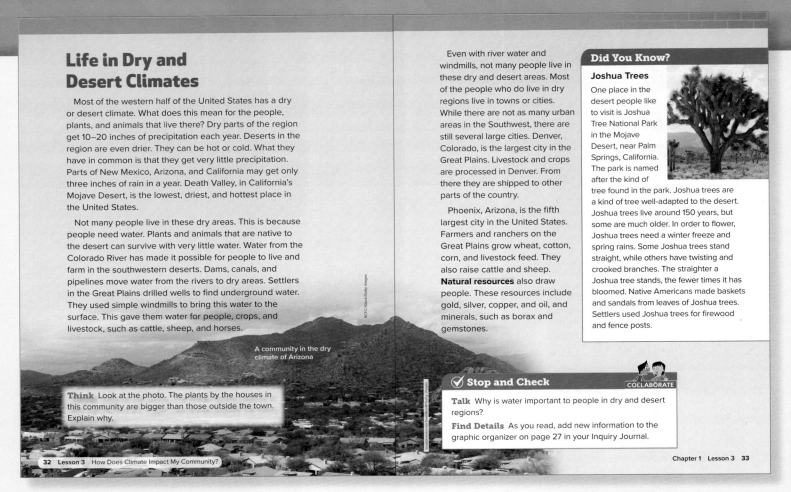

Life in Dry and Desert Climates

Most of the western half of the United States has a dry or desert climate. What does this mean for the people, plants, and animals that live there? Dry parts of the region get 10–20 inches of precipitation each year. Deserts in the region are even drier. They can be hot or cold. What they have in common is that they get very little precipitation. Parts of New Mexico, Arizona, and California may get only three inches of rain in a year. Death Valley, in California's Mojave Desert, is the lowest, driest, and hottest place in the United States.

Not many people live in these dry areas. This is because people need water. Plants and animals that are native to the desert can survive with very little water. Water from the Colorado River has made it possible for people to live and farm in the southwestern deserts. Dams, canals, and pipelines move water from the rivers to dry areas. Settlers in the Great Plains drilled wells to find underground water. They used simple windmills to bring this water to the surface. This gave them water for people, crops, and livestock, such as cattle, sheep, and horses.

A community in the dry climate of Arizona

Think Look at the photo. The plants by the houses in this community are bigger than those outside the town. Explain why.

Even with river water and windmills, not many people live in these dry and desert areas. Most of the people who do live in dry regions live in towns or cities. While there are not as many urban areas in the Southwest, there are still several large cities. Denver, Colorado, is the largest city in the Great Plains. Livestock and crops are processed in Denver. From there they are shipped to other parts of the country.

Phoenix, Arizona, is the fifth largest city in the United States. Farmers and ranchers on the Great Plains grow wheat, cotton, corn, and livestock feed. They also raise cattle and sheep. **Natural resources** also draw people. These resources include gold, silver, copper, and oil, and minerals, such as borax and gemstones.

Did You Know?

Joshua Trees

One place in the desert people like to visit is Joshua Tree National Park in the Mojave Desert, near Palm Springs, California. The park is named after the kind of tree found in the park. Joshua trees are a kind of tree well-adapted to the desert. Joshua trees live around 150 years, but some are much older. In order to flower, Joshua trees need a winter freeze and spring rains. Some Joshua trees stand straight, while others have twisting and crooked branches. The straighter a Joshua tree stands, the fewer times it has bloomed. Native Americans made baskets and sandals from leaves of Joshua trees. Settlers used Joshua trees for firewood and fence posts.

✓ Stop and Check

Talk Why is water important to people in dry and desert regions?

Find Details As you read, add new information to the graphic organizer on page 27 in your Inquiry Journal.

RESEARCH COMPANION, pp. 32–33

Life in Dry and Desert Climates

1 Inspect Have students read pp. 32–33 and identify characteristics of a desert climate.

2 Find Evidence Use the questions below to check comprehension.

Explain Why are there fewer large urban areas in the Southwest United States? (The climate is hot and dry and there is not much water, making it somewhat challenging to live there.) **DOK 2**

Infer If the climate is so hot and dry, why might people still move to places like a desert? (Answers will vary but could include that other natural resources may draw people or that some people might like warmer and less crowded locations.) **DOK 3**

3 Make Connections

Apply Concepts Suppose you visited the Mojave Desert. What kind of clothes would you wear? What would you take with you? (Answers will vary but should show that the Mojave Desert is hot and dry.) **DOK 3**

✓ Stop and Check

Talk Students should support their answers using details from the photo and the text. (There is not much water and people need water to live.)

Find Details As students discuss details, have them note how Native Americans, settlers from the past, and people today all adapted to this climate. (Answers should include bringing water from rivers and digging wells to bring groundwater to the surface.)

Spotlight on Vocabulary

Content Vocabulary

crops: plants such as grains, fruits, or vegetables that farmers grow in large amounts

livestock: animals that are kept on a farm

urban: relating to a town or city

▶ Digital Tools

Blended Learning

Students investigate curated resources and find evidence to answer the lesson question.

Students choose from print or digital **Inquiry Tools** to take notes.

Life With Cold Winters

Winters in the Northeast and Midwest states are much colder than the rest of the country. These two regions have four seasons. Winters are cold, with fewer daylight hours. In spring and summer, with more hours of daylight, plants grow and flower. Spring and summer are busy times for farmers in the Midwest. Corn and soybeans are important crops in Indiana, Michigan, and Illinois. Wheat and hay are also grown in this region. Wisconsin is known for its dairy products.

In fall, the air cools, and the days become shorter. The leaves change color and drop from the trees. People, plants, and animals prepare for another cold winter.

In the winter, blizzards bring cold wind and heavy snow. Cities around the Great Lakes have especially heavy snowfalls. In Indiana, for instance, areas near Lake Michigan average five feet more snow in a year than areas in southern Indiana. Chicago, Illinois, gets about three feet of snow each winter. The Atlantic Ocean also affects climate. A storm called a nor'easter brings heavy rain, snow, and strong winds to the Northeast. Nor'easters can cause major damage to property and businesses.

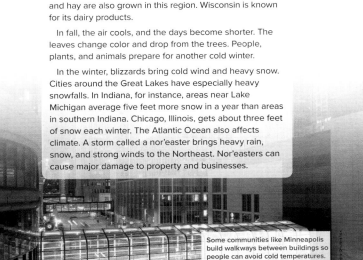

Some communities like Minneapolis build walkways between buildings so people can avoid cold temperatures.

Pine and hardwood trees cover northern regions of the Northeast and Midwest. Deer, elk, caribou, gray wolves, and black bears make their homes there. Bears, raccoons, squirrels, and other animals hibernate, or sleep, through the cold months. Birds, such as ducks and geese, fly to warmer areas before winter. They return in the spring to build nests and raise their young.

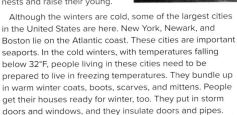

During cold winters in Indiana and other midwestern and eastern states, people need warm outdoor clothing.

Although the winters are cold, some of the largest cities in the United States are here. New York, Newark, and Boston lie on the Atlantic coast. These cities are important seaports. In the cold winters, with temperatures falling below 32°F, people living in these cities need to be prepared to live in freezing temperatures. They bundle up in warm winter coats, boots, scarves, and mittens. People get their houses ready for winter, too. They put in storm doors and windows, and they insulate doors and pipes.

Lots of snow brings winter activities. These winter sports include ice skating, sledding, and cross-country skiing. People build snowmen, throw snowballs, and fish through holes cut in the ice. Sometimes they sit outside in the cold beside the holes. Other times, fishermen stay warm by sitting in shacks built over the ice holes.

✓ Stop and Check

Think How do people and animals in cold regions get ready for winter?

RESEARCH COMPANION, pp. 34–35

Life With Cold Winters

1 Inspect Have students read pp. 34–35 and describe winter in the Northeast and Midwest.

2 Find Evidence Use the questions below to check comprehension.

Explain How does geography affect the climate in the Midwest and Northeast? (Northern states get less sunlight in the winter, so they have a colder climate with four seasons. Also, the bodies of water around these states can mean heavy snow or rain.) **DOK 2**

Cause and Effect Why are farmers in the Midwest busy in the spring and summer? (The days are shorter and colder in the fall and winter. Farmers take care of their crops during the spring and summer when crops are planted and grow.) **DOK 2**

3 Make Connections

Cite Evidence Why are some of the largest cities in the United States located along the cold Atlantic coast of the Northeast? (Answers will vary, but students might state that these cities are important seaports. Some might mention that this part of the country was one of the first areas settled by people sailing across the Atlantic from Europe.) **DOK 3**

✓ Stop and Check COLLABORATE

Think Have students discuss the question with a partner. (Possible answers: People put on their winter clothes and make their homes warmer. Some animals hibernate, and some birds fly to warmer areas.)

Social Emotional Learning

Decision-Making Skills

Evaluate Situations Students can strengthen their decision-making skills by thinking about activities that need to be carried out in specific situations. After students read pp. 34–35, prompt them to think more deeply about life in cold, snowy climates. Ask: *What do you think cities do during major snowfalls?*

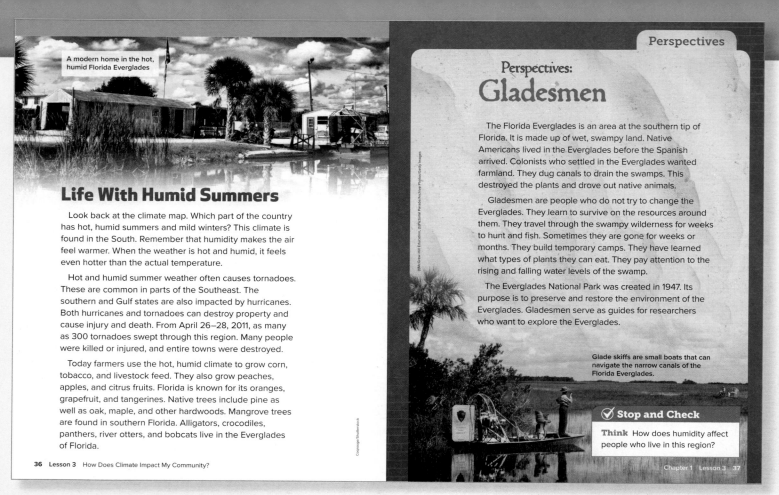

A modern home in the hot, humid Florida Everglades

Life With Humid Summers

Look back at the climate map. Which part of the country has hot, humid summers and mild winters? This climate is found in the South. Remember that humidity makes the air feel warmer. When the weather is hot and humid, it feels even hotter than the actual temperature.

Hot and humid summer weather often causes tornadoes. These are common in parts of the Southeast. The southern and Gulf states are also impacted by hurricanes. Both hurricanes and tornadoes can destroy property and cause injury and death. From April 26–28, 2011, as many as 300 tornadoes swept through this region. Many people were killed or injured, and entire towns were destroyed.

Today farmers use the hot, humid climate to grow corn, tobacco, and livestock feed. They also grow peaches, apples, and citrus fruits. Florida is known for its oranges, grapefruit, and tangerines. Native trees include pine as well as oak, maple, and other hardwoods. Mangrove trees are found in southern Florida. Alligators, crocodiles, panthers, river otters, and bobcats live in the Everglades of Florida.

36 Lesson 3 How Does Climate Impact My Community?

Perspectives:
Gladesmen

The Florida Everglades is an area at the southern tip of Florida. It is made up of wet, swampy land. Native Americans lived in the Everglades before the Spanish arrived. Colonists who settled in the Everglades wanted farmland. They dug canals to drain the swamps. This destroyed the plants and drove out native animals.

Gladesmen are people who do not try to change the Everglades. They learn to survive on the resources around them. They travel through the swampy wilderness for weeks to hunt and fish. Sometimes they are gone for weeks or months. They build temporary camps. They have learned what types of plants they can eat. They pay attention to the rising and falling water levels of the swamp.

The Everglades National Park was created in 1947. Its purpose is to preserve and restore the environment of the Everglades. Gladesmen serve as guides for researchers who want to explore the Everglades.

Glade skiffs are small boats that can navigate the narrow canals of the Florida Everglades.

✓ Stop and Check

Think How does humidity affect people who live in this region?

Chapter 1 Lesson 3 37

RESEARCH COMPANION, pp. 36–37

Life With Humid Summers/
Perspective: Gladesmen

1 Inspect Have students read pp. 36–37 and describe how humidity affects weather.

2 Find Evidence Use the questions below to check comprehension.

Explain How do the heat and humidity in the South cause problems? How are they helpful? (Hot, humid weather can cause tornadoes that destroy property and cause injury. But hot, humid weather also helps farmers grow citrus fruit.) **DOK 2**

Draw Conclusions Why are the warm winters of the South good for tourism? From what parts of the United States do you think many of the tourists come? (In the winter, people who live in cold places like the Midwest and Northeast like to visit places with a warmer climate.) **DOK 3**

3 Make Connections

Compare How do people have outdoor fun in the South? How are these activities different from those in the communities of the Midwest and Northeast? (The beaches of the South are warm, and people can play in the water and on the sand during most months of the year. In the Midwest and Northeast, people might play in the water during warm months, but in winter they can ice skate, sled, ski, and build snowmen.) **DOK 3**

✓ Stop and Check

Think (People must prepare more often for warmer and dangerous weather.)

 Spotlight on Language

Tornadoes and Hurricanes
Some students may not understand the difference between tornadoes and hurricanes. Explain that both are destructive storms involving high winds. They differ mainly in size and location.

▶ **Digital Tools**

Blended Learning
Students investigate curated resources and find evidence to answer the lesson question.

Interactive IMPACT
Students **Research** and find evidence using digital format texts.

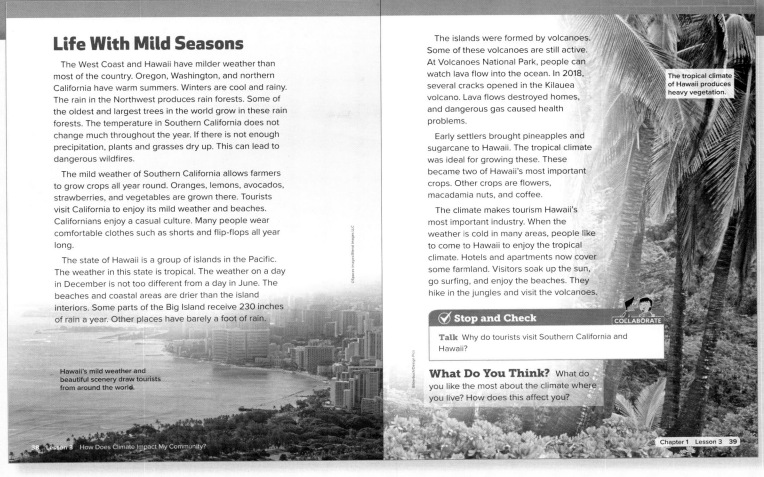

Life With Mild Seasons

The West Coast and Hawaii have milder weather than most of the country. Oregon, Washington, and northern California have warm summers. Winters are cool and rainy. The rain in the Northwest produces rain forests. Some of the oldest and largest trees in the world grow in these rain forests. The temperature in Southern California does not change much throughout the year. If there is not enough precipitation, plants and grasses dry up. This can lead to dangerous wildfires.

The mild weather of Southern California allows farmers to grow crops all year round. Oranges, lemons, avocados, strawberries, and vegetables are grown there. Tourists visit California to enjoy its mild weather and beaches. Californians enjoy a casual culture. Many people wear comfortable clothes such as shorts and flip-flops all year long.

The state of Hawaii is a group of islands in the Pacific. The weather in this state is tropical. The weather on a day in December is not too different from a day in June. The beaches and coastal areas are drier than the island interiors. Some parts of the Big Island receive 230 inches of rain a year. Other places have barely a foot of rain.

Hawaii's mild weather and beautiful scenery draw tourists from around the world.

The islands were formed by volcanoes. Some of these volcanoes are still active. At Volcanoes National Park, people can watch lava flow into the ocean. In 2018, several cracks opened in the Kilauea volcano. Lava flows destroyed homes, and dangerous gas caused health problems.

Early settlers brought pineapples and sugarcane to Hawaii. The tropical climate was ideal for growing these. These became two of Hawaii's most important crops. Other crops are flowers, macadamia nuts, and coffee.

The climate makes tourism Hawaii's most important industry. When the weather is cold in many areas, people like to come to Hawaii to enjoy the tropical climate. Hotels and apartments now cover some farmland. Visitors soak up the sun, go surfing, and enjoy the beaches. They hike in the jungles and visit the volcanoes.

The tropical climate of Hawaii produces heavy vegetation.

✓ Stop and Check

Talk Why do tourists visit Southern California and Hawaii?

What Do You Think? What do you like the most about the climate where you live? How does this affect you?

RESEARCH COMPANION, pp. 38–39

Life With Mild Seasons

1 Inspect Have students read pp. 38–39 and identify how the climate along the West Coast differs from the rest of the country.

2 Find Evidence Use the questions below to check comprehension.

Compare How does the climate along the West Coast change from south to north? (The temperature in Southern California does not change much and there is little rain. The Northwest winters are cooler and rainy.) **DOK 2**

Explain How does the tropical climate affect life in Hawaii? (The tropical climate is good for growing crops like pineapples, sugarcane, flowers, nuts, and coffee. It makes Hawaii a popular tourist destination.) **DOK 2**

3 Make Connections

Connect What region or area besides Hawaii is the most similar to the West Coast in terms of climate? Explain. (Answers may vary, but students may say the Southeast with its hot, humid summers and mild winters is closest to the West Coast.) **DOK 3**

✓ Stop and Check

Talk Have students discuss reasons tourists visit California and Hawaii. (People visit these areas because of the mild climate, beautiful scenery, and tourist activities.)

What Do You Think? Have students discuss the climate in their area and how it affects daily life. (Answers will vary.)

✓ Check for Success

Explain Can students cite details from the text to explain how climate impacts their communities?

Differentiate

If Not, Work with students to use details from their Inquiry Journals to make a list of activities or experiences they have had that were impacted by climate.

LESSON 3 REPORT

How Does Climate Impact My Community?

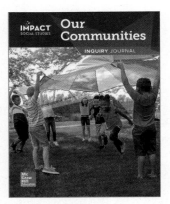

INQUIRY JOURNAL, pp. 28–29

Think About It

Remind students to review their research and think about what they learned about the climate in different parts of the United States. Encourage students to review the information they have included in their graphic organizer. Direct students back to pages 30–39 of their Research Companion if they need more information.

Write About It

Write and Cite Evidence Remind students to include the following elements in their responses.

- Introduce their experience in the form of a diary entry.
- Explain how an activity they participated in was affected by the local climate.
- Use descriptive words and details from the text.

Discipline(s)	4	3	2	1
Geography	Student provides evidence and details showing a strong understanding of local climate and climate in different regions of the U.S.	Student includes details for some evidence showing an adequate understanding of local climate and climate in different regions of the U.S.	Student includes evidence but few supporting details showing an uneven understanding of local climate and climate in different regions of the U.S.	Student does not support evidence with details showing little or no understanding of local climate and climate in different regions of the U.S.

Talk About It

Explain Remind students to use evidence as they tell how the local climate has had an impact on something they have done in the past.

Assessment Students can check their understanding with feedback from the **Lesson Test** available online.

Connect to the Essential Question

Pull It Together Before they respond, remind students to think about the different climates in the United States and how they impact the people who live there.

Inquiry Project Update Remind students to turn to Inquiry Journal pp. 2–3 for project information. If necessary, review the Project Checklist with students. At this point in the chapter, students should focus on the second and third items on the Checklist.

Think About It

Describe
Review your research. Based on the information you have gathered, what are the different climates found in the United States? How would you describe the climate of your community?

Write About It

Write and Cite Evidence
Write a diary entry describing how the climate in your community impacted something you have done in the past.

Students should accurately describe the climate where they live. Answers should be in the form of a diary entry and should describe the impact of climate on a community and local activities.

Talk About It

Explain
Share your diary entry with a partner. Then ask and answer questions about how climate where you live affects each of you.

Geography

Connect to the EQ

Pull It Together
Think about how climate affects your community. How does this help you understand why it matters where you live?

Answers should reflect the local climate.

EQ Inquiry Project Notes

INQUIRY JOURNAL, pp. 28–29

English Learners SCAFFOLD

Use the following scaffolds to support student writing.

Entering and Emerging

Help students think of a past experience to write about for their diary entries. Help them create complete sentences, providing sentence frames as needed:

- The climate here is _____. I (like/do not like) the climate.

- When it is _____, I _____. Other people _____.

- Climate in my region is _____, people in my community like to _____.

Developing and Expanding

Explain that a diary entry usually retells a recent personal experience. Ask questions to help students connect climate to a past experience. For example: _How does the climate affect what people in your community do in the summer? In the winter? What is something you did in the past that was because of climate?_

Bridging and Reaching

Have partners discuss how climate impacts what people do in their communities. Then ask for volunteers to share how climate affected a past activity or experience. Guide students to write a diary entry, including details about how climate impacted what they did and how they felt about it.

✓ Check for Success

Describe Can students create a diary entry about an experience that shows how climate impacts life in their community?

Differentiate

If Not, Have students present their experiences with climate in their communities in a different way, such as in a drawing or comic strip, or as an oral presentation.

LESSON QUESTION

How Is My Community Affected by the Land and Water Around It?

Connect to the Essential Question

Tell students that this lesson will help them answer the Chapter Essential Question: **Why Does It Matter Where We Live?** Explain that they will examine how the geography surrounding a community affects the people who live there. Tell them that they will compare and contrast the ways people work and play in mountain, river, valley, and coastal communities across the United States.

Lesson Objectives

- **Describe** how the land and water around a community affect the people who live there.

- **Compare** physical characteristics of different communities.

- **Write** a paragraph that describes similarities and differences between the land and water around different communities.

Make Connections!

CONNECT TO ELA

Reading **Determine** the main idea of a text; recount the key details and explain how they support the main idea.

Compare and contrast the most important points and key details presented in two texts on the same topic.

Describe the logical connection between particular sentences and paragraphs in a text.

Research **Conduct** short research projects that build knowledge about a topic.

Writing **Craft** informative/explanatory texts to examine a topic and convey ideas and information clearly.

Speaking and Listening **Engage** effectively in a range of collaborative discussions (one-on-one, in groups, and teacher-led) with diverse partners on grade 3 topics and texts, building on others' ideas and expressing their own clearly.

Language **Determine or clarify** the meaning of unknown and multiple-meaning words and phrases based on grade-level reading and content, choosing flexibly from a range of strategies.

COMMUNITY CONNECTIONS

To enrich student learning about the geography of their community, invite a scientist from a local college or a park ranger to talk to your students about the region's landforms and water forms.

Lesson-At-A-Glance

1 ENGAGE — INQUIRY JOURNAL

▶ **Talk About It:** Photograph of a River Community

▶ **Analyze the Source:** Rivers

▶ **Inquiry Tools:** Compare and Contrast

pp. 30–35

2 INVESTIGATE — RESEARCH COMPANION

▶ **Landforms and Communities**

▶ **Mountain Communities**

▶ **River Communities**

▶ **Valley Communities**

▶ **Coastal Communities**

pp. 40–49

3 REPORT — INQUIRY JOURNAL

▶ **Think About It**

▶ **Write About It:** Write and Cite Evidence; Compare and Contrast Communities

▶ **Talk About It**

 ▶ **Connect to the Essential Question**

pp. 36–37

ASSESSMENT

▶ **Online Lesson Test**

▶ **Printable Lesson Test**

For more details, see pages T4–T5.

▶ Digital Tools

at **my.mheducation.com**

ePresentation

Teach the Engage, Investigate, and Report content to the whole class from **ePresentations** that launch directly from the lesson dashboard.

eBook

You can flip your instruction with the **IMPACT eBooks** found on your lesson dashboard.

Interactive IMPACT

Blend in digital content **when you want it** and **where you want it**.

Blended Learning features in the Teacher's Edition highlight ways to connect in-class work with online experiences to enhance learning.

Investigate current events with **IMPACT News**.

Explore domain-based vocabulary with **Explore Words** and **Word Play** vocabulary activities.

Go Further with IMPACT Explorer Magazine!

pp. 2–15

The **IMPACT Explorer Magazine** supports students' exploration of the Essential Question and provides additional resources for the EQ Inquiry Project.

How Is My Community Affected by the Land and Water Around It?

Language Objectives

- Use newly acquired content and academic vocabulary to talk and write about how communities are affected by land and water.
- Describe similarities and differences among communities' land and water.
- Write a paragraph about a familiar physical landscape, using common and proper nouns.

Spanish Cognates

To support Spanish speakers, point out the cognates.

community = comunidad

affect = afectar

elevation = elevación

transport = transporte

coast = costa

industry = industria

Introduce the Lesson

Set Purpose Explain to students that in this lesson they will read informational texts to learn how the land and water around a community affect the people who live in the community.

Access Prior Knowledge Remind students that a community is a place where people live and work. Point out that every community has different physical features. Ask: *What is the land or water like? What sorts of activities have you done on the land or water?*

Spark Curiosity Project or display the photo on pages 40–41 of the Research Companion. Explain that this photo shows mountains, a river, and land. These are all part of what is called the "physical landscape." Tell students that the physical landscapes of communities do not all look the same. Ask: *What does the physical landscape of your community look like?* Discuss with students how the physical landscape of your area is similar to or different from what they see in the image on pages 40–41.

 Have pairs of students with different language proficiency levels discuss similarities and differences between the physical landscape in the photo and their own community.

Build Meaning & Support Language

Inquiry Journal

Analyze the Source (pages 32–33) To help students unlock the Primary Source on page 33, first explain that River Commissions were people who made sure the river could be used safely. Then, use the chart below to help students understand Mark Twain's words. Reread the passage using the translations. Then discuss with students what Mark Twain is saying about the Mississippi River.

Primary Source Text	Everyday English
aver	say it is true
the mines of the world at their back	a lot of information available to them
tame	make less wild
lawless	violent or unruly
save a shore which it has sentenced	keep safe a coastal area that is flooded
bar its path	put something in its way

Inquiry Tools (pages 34–35) Tell students they will **Compare and Contrast** as they read the selections in the Research Companion. Tell them that the graphic organizer will help them organize the information as they read. Review some words used to compare and contrast such as *both*, *some*, and *like* for comparing and *but*, *however*, and *unlike* for contrasting. Then provide support as students fill in the graphic organizer.

Research Companion

Mountain Communities (pages 42–43) As you read page 43, help students understand the graphic. Explain that *elevation* means how high something is. Say: *Look at the chart on page 43. What is found at the highest elevations?* (barren rocks, mosses and lichens) Guide students down the graphic to the middle and lower elevations. Ask: *What grows best at the lowest elevation? What grows in the middle?*

River Communities (pages 44–45) Read the first sentence on page 45. Explain that it asks a question, and the rest of the paragraph answers the question. Ask: *What is one reason people like living in river communities?* (fertile land, fresh water, fish, reliable way to transport goods) Read aloud the first sentence of paragraph 2 on page 45. Point out that the word *similar* shows how river and mountain communities are alike. Ask: *How are mountain and river communities alike?* (They are great places for recreation.)

Valley Communities (pages 46–47) Read aloud the last sentence of the first paragraph on page 46. Explain that this sentence shows a cause-and-effect relationship. Point to the second part of the sentence, *because the soil has many minerals that help plants to grow.* Explain that this part tells the cause: the soil has helpful minerals. Ask: *What is the effect the minerals have?* (The valley is good for farming.)

Coastal Communities (pages 48–49) Discuss the terms *coast, coastal,* and *coastline* with students. Explain that *coast* is a noun, and it refers to the land along or near the ocean. *Coast* is also used when talking about land near large lakes, such as the Great Lakes. *Coastline* refers to the outline of the coast. It is also used as a synonym for *coast. Coastal* is an adjective that is used to describe things that are near a coast, such as a coastal highway. Work with students to use each word in a sentence.

Inquiry Journal

Report Your Findings (pages 36–37) Explain to students that when they compare and contrast, they provide information that describes how two or more things are alike or different. Remind them to include facts and examples about their own communities. They should also include evidence from the text to support the similarities and differences they describe. Encourage them to use the new vocabulary words they have learned. Check their work for spelling and punctuation errors.

Language Forms & Conventions

Common and Proper Nouns Remind students that nouns name people, places, and things. Proper nouns name a specific person, place, or thing. Common nouns are not specific. Remind students that proper nouns are capitalized, but common nouns are not. Display a version of the chart for students.

Common Nouns	Proper Nouns
river	Mississippi River
ocean	Atlantic Ocean
city	Pittsburgh
state	Ohio

 Have students work in pairs to locate some proper nouns in the texts. Call on volunteers to say them aloud and add them to the chart. As a challenge, ask them to name the common noun for each proper noun.

 Cross-Cultural Connection

St. Louis, Missouri, was settled by French explorer Pierre Laclede in 1764. Its location on the Mississippi River proved to be important to traders and travelers alike. According to legend, on a single day in 1803, St. Louis flew under three flags: Spanish, French, and American. This is because the Spanish transferred the city to the French, who sold it to the United States in the Louisiana Purchase.

 Leveled Support

Entering & Emerging
Help students form complete sentences from their notes.

Developing & Expanding
Encourage students to use words such as *both, like,* and *some* to compare and *however, unlike,* and *but* to contrast.

Bridging & Reaching
Encourage students to include an introduction, key details comparing and contrasting physical characteristics, and a concluding sentence.

 **Language Transfer**

Point out that names of cities, states, and named landforms and bodies of water are capitalized in English.

LESSON 4 ENGAGE

How Is My Community Affected by the Land and Water Around It?

INQUIRY JOURNAL, pp. 30–31

Bellringer

Prompt students to retrieve information from the previous lesson. Say: *You have learned about different climates in the United States. How does climate affect farming? How does climate affect recreation or tourism?* (Different climates determine where farming is possible, the length of the growing season, and the types of crops planted; people engage in swimming and boating in warm climates, and people may travel to snowy climates to ski or snowboard.) Say: *Climate affects the way people live, work, and play. The land and water features of a region also affect how people live.*

Lesson Outcomes

Discuss the lesson question and lesson outcomes with students.

- Make sure students understand that the term *landform* refers to the physical features of the land.

- Tell students that each region of the United States has specific landforms and bodies of water that make it different from other regions of the country. Learning about different landforms and bodies of water will help them understand how geography affects the people, plants, and animals in a region.

Talk About It

Discuss with students that a photograph can provide a great deal of information. Have students look at the photograph, read the caption, and answer the questions to better understand what the image shows. Provide sentence frames as needed as students complete the activity.

- The image shows _____.
- I see a _____ over the water.
- This is a _____ community because _____.

 Collaborative Conversations

Add New Ideas As students engage in partner, small-group, and whole-class discussions, encourage them to

- stay on topic.
- connect their ideas to points their classmates have made.
- look for ways to connect relevant personal experiences or prior knowledge to the conversation.
- build on what they have already learned when presenting new ideas.

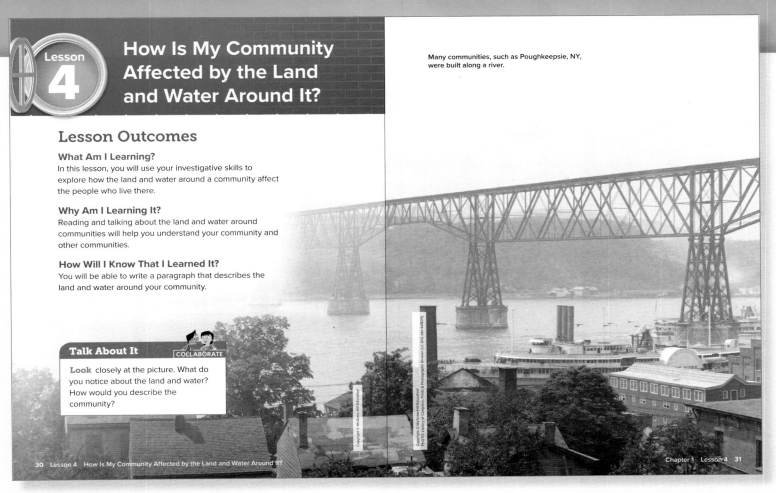

Lesson 4

How Is My Community Affected by the Land and Water Around It?

Many communities, such as Poughkeepsie, NY, were built along a river.

Lesson Outcomes

What Am I Learning?
In this lesson, you will use your investigative skills to explore how the land and water around a community affect the people who live there.

Why Am I Learning It?
Reading and talking about the land and water around communities will help you understand your community and other communities.

How Will I Know That I Learned It?
You will be able to write a paragraph that describes the land and water around your community.

Talk About It COLLABORATE

Look closely at the picture. What do you notice about the land and water? How would you describe the community?

30   Lesson 4   How Is My Community Affected by the Land and Water Around It?

Chapter 1   Lesson 4   31

INQUIRY JOURNAL, pp. 30–31

(EL) English Learners SCAFFOLD

Use the following scaffolds to support student understanding of lesson outcomes.

Entering and Emerging

Encourage students to study the photograph. Then point to different details in the photograph and say: *This is a* _____. Have students repeat the sentences or say their own sentences using the same word. Provide vocabulary support as needed for words used to describe details in the photo.

Developing and Expanding

Have partners brainstorm and write a list of words about the community in the photograph. Encourage partners to take turns using those words in sentences that describe river communities.

Bridging and Reaching

Have partners study the photograph and discuss the details they see. Then have them work together to write three sentences that describe details in the photo. Have partners share their sentences. Encourage students to build on each other's sentences.

Social Emotional Learning

Relationship Skills

Value Ideas of Others Explain to students that it is important to value diversity and to consider multiple perspectives and opinions. As students discuss their views about life in river communities, urge them to listen respectfully to their partner's reasons.

 Digital Tools

Blended Learning

Students engage with the lesson question and discussion prompts.

Interactive IMPACT

Discuss the **Lesson Question** and **Talk About It** with the whole class.

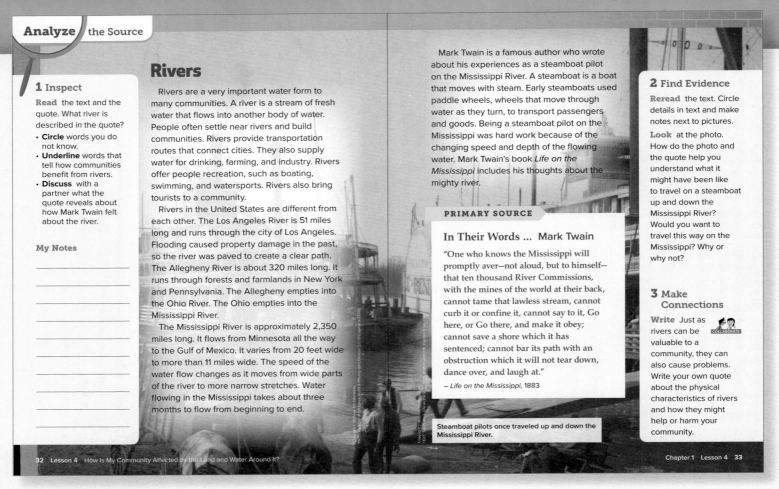

Analyze the Source

1 Inspect

Read the text and the quote. What river is described in the quote?

- **Circle** words you do not know.
- **Underline** words that tell how communities benefit from rivers.
- **Discuss** with a partner what the quote reveals about how Mark Twain felt about the river.

My Notes

_____
_____
_____
_____
_____
_____
_____
_____
_____

Rivers

Rivers are a very important water form to many communities. A river is a stream of fresh water that flows into another body of water. People often settle near rivers and build communities. Rivers provide transportation routes that connect cities. They also supply water for drinking, farming, and industry. Rivers offer people recreation, such as boating, swimming, and watersports. Rivers also bring tourists to a community.

Rivers in the United States are different from each other. The Los Angeles River is 51 miles long and runs through the city of Los Angeles. Flooding caused property damage in the past, so the river was paved to create a clear path. The Allegheny River is about 320 miles long. It runs through forests and farmlands in New York and Pennsylvania. The Allegheny empties into the Ohio River. The Ohio empties into the Mississippi River.

The Mississippi River is approximately 2,350 miles long. It flows from Minnesota all the way to the Gulf of Mexico. It varies from 20 feet wide to more than 11 miles wide. The speed of the water flow changes as it moves from wide parts of the river to more narrow stretches. Water flowing in the Mississippi takes about three months to flow from beginning to end.

Mark Twain is a famous author who wrote about his experiences as a steamboat pilot on the Mississippi River. A steamboat is a boat that moves with steam. Early steamboats used paddle wheels, wheels that move through water as they turn, to transport passengers and goods. Being a steamboat pilot on the Mississippi was hard work because of the changing speed and depth of the flowing water. Mark Twain's book *Life on the Mississippi* includes his thoughts about the mighty river.

PRIMARY SOURCE

In Their Words ... Mark Twain

"One who knows the Mississippi will promptly aver—not aloud, but to himself—that ten thousand River Commissions, with the mines of the world at their back, cannot tame that lawless stream, cannot curb it or confine it, cannot say to it, Go here, or Go there, and make it obey; cannot save a shore which it has sentenced; cannot bar its path with an obstruction which it will not tear down, dance over, and laugh at."

– *Life on the Mississippi*, 1883

Steamboat pilots once traveled up and down the Mississippi River.

2 Find Evidence

Reread the text. Circle details in text and make notes next to pictures.

Look at the photo. How do the photo and the quote help you understand what it might have been like to travel on a steamboat up and down the Mississippi River? Would you want to travel this way on the Mississippi? Why or why not?

3 Make Connections

Write Just as rivers can be valuable to a community, they can also cause problems. Write your own quote about the physical characteristics of rivers and how they might help or harm your community.

32 Lesson 4 How Is My Community Affected by the Land and Water Around It?

Chapter 1 Lesson 4 33

INQUIRY JOURNAL, pp. 32–33

Analyze the Source

1 Inspect

Read Have students read the text and photo caption and read the excerpt from Mark Twain. Remind them to circle words in the text with which they are unfamiliar.

- Underline words and phrases in the text that tell about how communities benefit from rivers. (Answers should include: provide transportation routes; supply water for drinking, farming, and industry; offer people recreation; bring tourists)

2 Find Evidence

Reread Students should recognize that Twain calls the Mississippi a "lawless stream" that cannot be curbed or confined; that no one can "make it obey." Twain suggests that the river "laughs at" any attempts to control it. Ask students what they think Twain is saying about the Mississippi. (It's a powerful river that will do what it wants.)

Look Have students reread the text and complete the Look activity. Make sure students cite evidence from the text to support their opinions. Ask: *How do Twain's words make you feel about the river?*

3 Make Connections

Write Before they write their quotes, encourage students to work with a partner to discuss the physical characteristics of rivers. Have students talk about any personal experiences they have had with rivers (e.g., boating, fishing) and what they have heard about problems rivers have caused (e.g., flooding).

EL Spotlight on Content

Using Maps Use a map or an atlas to identify the rivers mentioned in the text. Show students the paths of the different rivers and the spots where the Allegheny empties into the Ohio River and where the Ohio empties into the Mississippi. Help students locate and identify rivers in their state.

▶ Digital Tools

Blended Learning

Students read informational texts and analyze primary sources.

Interactive IMPACT

Have students practice and apply the strategy of close reading as they analyze text.

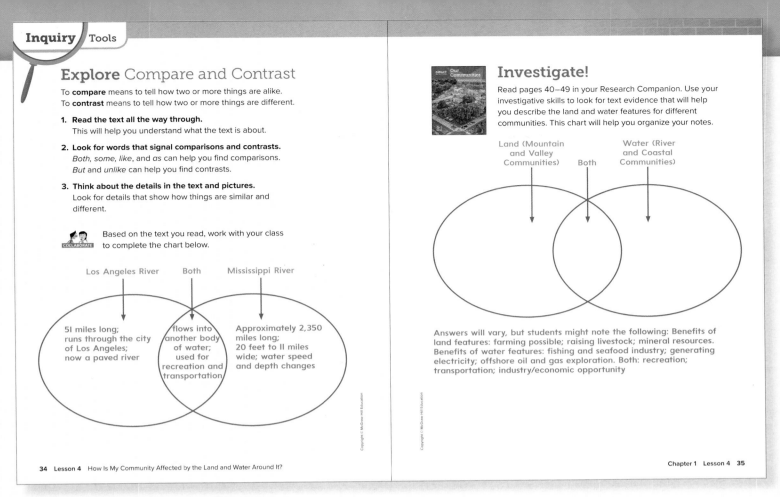

Inquiry Tools

Explore Compare and Contrast

Read Review with students the meanings of the words *compare* and *contrast*. Discuss the step-by-step instructions found on p. 34 of the Inquiry Journal for comparing and contrasting details in a text. Review signal words such as *both*, *same*, *like*, and *as* along with *but* and *unlike*.

Guide Practice Have students review the text on pp. 32–33. Then work with them to complete the graphic organizer on p. 34. Explain that they will use the graphic organizer on p. 35 to organize their independent research.

Check Understanding Confirm understanding of the inquiry skill, Explore Compare and Contrast. If students cannot effectively compare and contrast details from the text, review the steps on Inquiry Journal p. 34.

Investigate!

Have students read pp. 40–49 in the Research Companion. Tell them the information will help them answer the lesson question *How Is My Community Affected by the Land and Water Around It?*

Take Notes Tell students that they will use the graphic organizer on p. 35 of the Inquiry Journal to take notes as they read. Guide students to watch for compare and contrast words as they read the text in each section. Remind them that taking notes will help them understand and remember the information they learn. Remind students that they should use their own words when taking notes.

 Spotlight on Content

Comparing and Contrasting Explain how a Venn diagram is used. Then have students work in pairs or small groups to find and list facts about the Mississippi, Allegheny, and Los Angeles rivers on pp. 32–33 of the Inquiry Journal before entering them into the graphic organizer. Guide students in determining which facts about the Mississippi are the same as the other two rivers and which are different.

LESSON 4 INVESTIGATE

How Is My Community Affected by the Land and Water Around It?

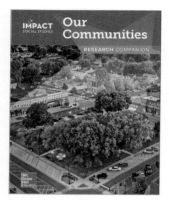

RESEARCH COMPANION, pp. 40–41

Landforms and Communities

1 Inspect Have students read pp. 40–41 and define *landform*. Discuss local landforms with students.

2 Find Evidence Use the questions below to check comprehension. Remind students to support their answers with text evidence.

Cause and Effect Why do athletes get tired more quickly when they compete in the mountains rather than on flat ground? (Mountains are steeper than flat ground.) **DOK 2**

Hypothesize Why do you think people form communities near different landforms and bodies of water? (Possible answer: People like to work and play at different activities. Some activities can only be carried out near certain types of landforms and bodies of water.) **DOK 3**

3 Make Connections

Interpret Look at a physical map of your state. Find a landform or a body of water near your community. Tell one way that this geographic feature affects your community. (Answers will vary; students should correctly identify a nearby geographic feature.) **DOK 3**

How Is My Community Affected by the Land and Water Around It?

Landforms and Communities

What do you think of when you hear the word *mountain*? You may picture a steep slope that is hard to climb, or a snow-capped peak. A mountain is a kind of **landform**. A landform is a physical feature of the land. Landforms include mountains, valleys, and coasts.

What do you think of when you hear the word *river*? You may picture a wide or narrow area of running water. A river is one kind of body of water. A body of water is a large collection of water such as a wetland, pond, river, lake, or ocean. Can you think of other landforms or bodies of water?

Every community is different. Each has its own geography and physical features. Some communities were built near mountains. Some communities formed near rivers. Other communities developed in valleys or along coasts. The landforms and bodies of water in your community affect the way people live, work, and play. Your community's features make it a special place to live.

Mountains have different shapes and sizes.

40 Lesson 4   How Is My Community Affected by the Land and Water Around It?

Chapter 1   Lesson 4   41

RESEARCH COMPANION, pp. 40–41

English Learners SCAFFOLD

Use the following scaffolds to support student understanding of lesson content.

Entering and Emerging

Explain to students that a *physical feature* is a natural part of the earth's surface. Physical features include things such as mountains, hills, rivers, and lakes. Then have students locate the definition of *landform* on p. 40 of the Research Companion and complete this sentence starter: *A landform is _____.*

Developing and Expanding

Have students identify the landforms specified in the text. (mountains, valleys, coasts) Encourage them to think of different types of bodies of water by using sentence starters such as: *A river is a body of water. Another body of water is _____.*

Bridging and Reaching

Have students work with partners to list the landforms and bodies of water mentioned in the text and then add others with which they are familiar. Challenge students to list specific landforms or bodies of water, such as the Rocky Mountains, Mississippi River, or Ohio Valley.

Digital Tools

Blended Learning

Guide students as they investigate the lesson content.

ePresentation

Students choose from print or digital **Inquiry Tools** to take notes.

Mountain Communities

A mountain is a high landform with steep sides. It is much higher and larger than a hill. Mountains rarely exist alone. They are usually grouped together in a mountain range, which is a chain of mountains. The Appalachian Mountains are a mountain range in the eastern United States. These mountains are low and rounded. The Rocky Mountains, in the western United States, are tall and sharply pointed. Mountains are home to many resources such as plants, animals, minerals, and water.

Where people live in the mountains determines how they live. For example, people who live in the higher elevations may have to travel farther to reach a town than people in lower elevations. Transportation can be difficult in winter. Heavy snows sometimes block roads completely. This can make living in the mountains challenging.

However, there are many things to do in the mountains. Tourism is an important business in mountain communities. In the winter, skiers and snowboarders travel there for sport. In the summer, people enjoy rock climbing, hiking, canoeing, and camping in the mountains. This creates jobs for people who live in mountain communities.

Telluride is located in Colorado near the Rocky Mountains. The city's elevation is 8,750 feet.

The type of plants on a mountain and how they grow is related in part to elevation. Few plants grow well in high elevations. Others thrive in middle or lower elevations. The higher the elevation, the colder the temperature. Higher peaks are likely to have little or no plant life.

InfoGraphic

Effects of Elevation

On the graphic, notice that the vegetation at the highest elevation includes mosses and lichens. Through the middle of the graphic, the vegetation includes grasslands and meadows. As melting snow and rainwater flow down the mountainside, the amount of water increases. These plants need greater amounts of water. The bottom of the graphic shows forests. Here plants are able to absorb nutrients from the soil and get the water they need from the water flowing down the mountain.

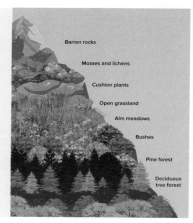

- Barren rocks
- Mosses and lichens
- Cushion plants
- Open grassland
- Alm meadows
- Bushes
- Pine forest
- Deciduous tree forest

✓ Stop and Check

Talk With a partner, discuss one benefit of living in a mountain community. Then discuss a challenge of living in a mountain community.

RESEARCH COMPANION, pp. 42–43

Mountain Communities

1 Inspect Have students read pp. 42–43 and tell what a chain of mountains is called.

2 Find Evidence Use the questions below to check comprehension.

Infer Have students use the diagram on p. 43 and the text to make an inference about mosses, lichens and cushion plants. Ask: *Why do you think these plants grow at the highest elevations?* (These plants thrive in colder temperatures.) **DOK 3**

Compare and Contrast How are the Appalachian Mountains different from the Rocky Mountains? Use details from the text to support your answer. (The Appalachians are in the eastern United States and are low and rounded, while the Rockies are tall and sharply pointed and located in the western United States.) **DOK 2**

3 Make Connections

Analyze Study the image on p. 42. What could you imagine would draw people to that community? What types of recreational activities might they participate in? Use text evidence to support your answer. (Answers will vary, but students should respond with reasons and descriptions related to a mountain community.) **DOK 3**

✓ Stop and Check

Talk Share and have students share any experirce they have had visiting mountain communities. (Answers may vary, but students could say that one benefit is a variety of recreational activities, such as skiing, snowboarding, and rock climbing. A disadvantage could be difficult transportation in the winter.)

 Spotlight on Language

Academic Language
Have students use context and the image to explain the meaning of *vegetation, grasslands,* and *meadows.*

 Digital Tools

Blended Learning
Flip the research approach and find evidence in a digital format.

eBook

Students investigate using their **Research Companion** and **IMPACT Explorer Magazine eBooks** to find evidence.

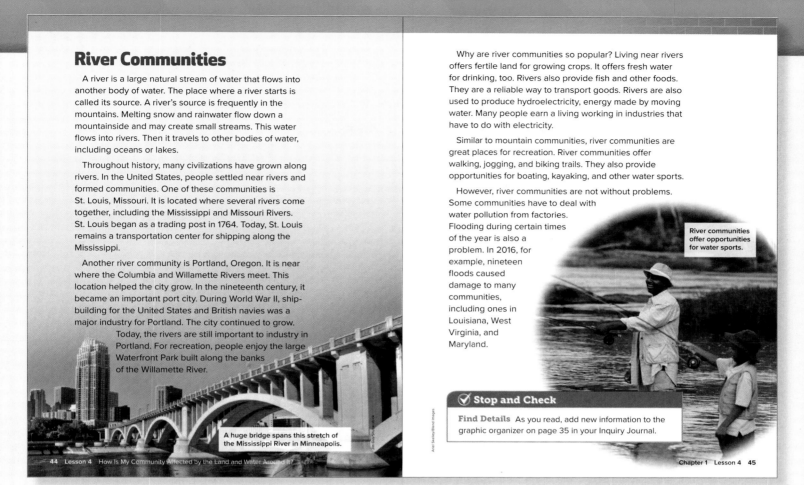

River Communities

A river is a large natural stream of water that flows into another body of water. The place where a river starts is called its source. A river's source is frequently in the mountains. Melting snow and rainwater flow down a mountainside and may create small streams. This water flows into rivers. Then it travels to other bodies of water, including oceans or lakes.

Throughout history, many civilizations have grown along rivers. In the United States, people settled near rivers and formed communities. One of these communities is St. Louis, Missouri. It is located where several rivers come together, including the Mississippi and Missouri Rivers. St. Louis began as a trading post in 1764. Today, St. Louis remains a transportation center for shipping along the Mississippi.

Another river community is Portland, Oregon. It is near where the Columbia and Willamette Rivers meet. This location helped the city grow. In the nineteenth century, it became an important port city. During World War II, ship-building for the United States and British navies was a major industry for Portland. The city continued to grow. Today, the rivers are still important to industry in Portland. For recreation, people enjoy the large Waterfront Park built along the banks of the Willamette River.

A huge bridge spans this stretch of the Mississippi River in Minneapolis.

44 Lesson 4 How Is My Community Affected by the Land and Water Around It?

Why are river communities so popular? Living near rivers offers fertile land for growing crops. It offers fresh water for drinking, too. Rivers also provide fish and other foods. They are a reliable way to transport goods. Rivers are also used to produce hydroelectricity, energy made by moving water. Many people earn a living working in industries that have to do with electricity.

Similar to mountain communities, river communities are great places for recreation. River communities offer walking, jogging, and biking trails. They also provide opportunities for boating, kayaking, and other water sports.

However, river communities are not without problems. Some communities have to deal with water pollution from factories. Flooding during certain times of the year is also a problem. In 2016, for example, nineteen floods caused damage to many communities, including ones in Louisiana, West Virginia, and Maryland.

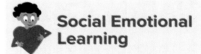
River communities offer opportunities for water sports.

✓ Stop and Check

Find Details As you read, add new information to the graphic organizer on page 35 in your Inquiry Journal.

Chapter 1 Lesson 4 45

River Communities

1 Inspect Have students read pp. 44–45 and describe pros and cons of living along a river.

2 Find Evidence Use the questions below to check comprehension.

Explain Why have so many communities throughout history originated along rivers? (Rivers offer fertile land for growing crops and fresh water for drinking, provide fish and other foods, and are a reliable way to transport goods.) **DOK 2**

Cite Evidence Use evidence from the text to explain the relationship between mountains and rivers. (Rivers usually begin in the mountains; melting snow and rainwater flow down mountainsides and create streams, which in turn flow into rivers.) **DOK 3**

3 Make Connections

Infer In which industries are residents of river communities likely to find jobs? (Answers will vary, but students should mention transportation, shipbuilding, energy, and tourism/recreation.) **DOK 3**

✓ Stop and Check COLLABORATE

Find Details Guide students to add information to the graphic organizer on p. 35 of the Inquiry Journal. Students should have information about mountain communities. Encourage them to think about the differences and the similarities between these types of communities as they complete the Venn diagram.

Social Emotional Learning

Relationship Skills

Build Relationships Direct students' attention to the photo of the people fishing. Call on students to tell about special things they do with the adults in their lives. Ask what those experiences have taught them about building positive relationships with others.

Valley Communities

A valley is low land between hills or mountains. Most valleys are long but not very wide. Many valleys have rivers flowing through them. A valley forms when water from glaciers or rivers flows through an area of land and wears it down. It takes thousands of years for valleys to form. The land in a valley is usually good for farming because the soil has many minerals that help plants grow.

There are many valleys in the United States. The Shenandoah Valley is in Virginia and West Virginia. It is about 150 miles long and 25 miles wide. It is located between the Blue Ridge and Allegheny Mountains. The Shenandoah Valley has many resources, including fertile soil and water. Many of its farms produce livestock, apples, and dairy products. The area is known for its limestone caverns, too. The Shenandoah Valley and Shenandoah National Park are busy tourist destinations. The Ohio Valley is the area that surrounds the Ohio River. Farms across the Ohio Valley produce soybeans, corn, dairy products, and livestock.

Fertile soil and an abundance of water have contributed to the success of farming in valley communities.

Then and Now

Farming

New inventions have changed the way people farm. At first, farmers relied on oxen and horses to pull plows. Eli Whitney invented the cotton gin in 1793. It created a simple way to remove seeds from cotton. Cyrus McCormick introduced the reaper in London in 1851. Workers no longer had to harvest crops by hand. In 1892, the first motorized tractor made plowing even easier. Today, some farms have machines similar to tractors that steer themselves.

It is clear to see why people settled in valley communities. Valleys had flat, fertile land and were close to water. This made it possible for people to farm the land. Over time, people took advantage of the area's resources. They built towns that grew into cities.

Valley communities today offer people many different opportunities. They provide existing homes and good places to build new homes. There are usually jobs in service and high-tech industries. In addition, national and state parks are nearby. These include Cuyahoga Valley National Park in Ohio and Iao Valley State Park in Hawaii. These parks offer everyone living or visiting these areas a look at each valley area's natural beauty.

✓ Stop and Check

Talk What are the most important reasons people live in valley communities?

RESEARCH COMPANION, pp. 46–47

Valley Communities

1 Inspect Have students read pp. 46–47 and describe the Shenandoah Valley.

2 Find Evidence Use the questions below to check comprehension.

Cause and Effect What causes a valley to form? (Over time, water from glaciers or rivers flows through an area of land and wears it down.) **DOK 2**

Infer Why are valleys important for farming? (Valleys provide flat, fertile soil and access to an abundance of water, which support growing crops and raising livestock.) **DOK 2**

3 Make Connections

Compare How are valley communities related to mountain and river communities? (Possible answers could include that valleys have nearby mountains and often contain rivers.) **DOK 3**

✓ Stop and Check

Talk Have students share any experiences they have had in visiting or living in valley communities. (Answers will vary. People live in valley communities for soil and water access, which makes them suitable for farming. They also live in valley communities because they offer many recreation and work opportunities.)

 Spotlight on Text

Content Vocabulary

service industry: jobs that involve doing work for customers but not making products

high-tech industry: jobs that involve the most modern equipment, often involving electronics or computers

 Digital Tools

Blended Learning
Students investigate curated resources and find evidence to answer the lesson question.

Interactive IMPACT

Students **Research** and find evidence using digital format texts.

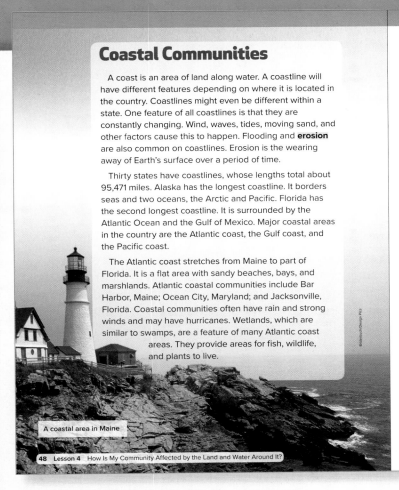

Coastal Communities

A coast is an area of land along water. A coastline will have different features depending on where it is located in the country. Coastlines might even be different within a state. One feature of all coastlines is that they are constantly changing. Wind, waves, tides, moving sand, and other factors cause this to happen. Flooding and **erosion** are also common on coastlines. Erosion is the wearing away of Earth's surface over a period of time.

Thirty states have coastlines, whose lengths total about 95,471 miles. Alaska has the longest coastline. It borders seas and two oceans, the Arctic and Pacific. Florida has the second longest coastline. It is surrounded by the Atlantic Ocean and the Gulf of Mexico. Major coastal areas in the country are the Atlantic coast, the Gulf coast, and the Pacific coast.

The Atlantic coast stretches from Maine to part of Florida. It is a flat area with sandy beaches, bays, and marshlands. Atlantic coastal communities include Bar Harbor, Maine; Ocean City, Maryland; and Jacksonville, Florida. Coastal communities often have rain and strong winds and may have hurricanes. Wetlands, which are similar to swamps, are a feature of many Atlantic coast areas. They provide areas for fish, wildlife, and plants to live.

A coastal area in Maine

48 Lesson 4 How Is My Community Affected by the Land and Water Around It?

The Gulf Coast is located in the southern part of the United States along the Gulf of Mexico. It is a large, flat area. In certain seasons tropical storms and hurricanes batter the Gulf Coast. Much of the land along the Gulf coast is low and marshy. Gulf coastal communities include New Orleans, Louisiana; Biloxi, Mississippi; and Mobile, Alabama.

The Pacific coast is made up of California, Washington, and Oregon. Much of the land is mountainous. This is because the coastal region is part of the Coast Ranges. These mountains start in Washington. They extend south through Oregon and into California. The land is rocky and the seawater is cold along the northern coast. The southern coast has sandy beaches and warm water. Pacific coastal communities include Seattle, Washington, and San Diego, California.

Many people who live along coasts work in the fishing and shipping industries. Cities such as Houston, Texas and Tacoma, Washington have major ports. Ports are places where ships load and unload people and goods. For fun, people go to the many beaches to swim and surf. Others enjoy water sports and boating.

Fishermen on the Sausalito waterfront in California

✓ Stop and Check

Talk How do people have fun in coastal communities? Discuss with a partner something you think would be most enjoyable to do.

Find Details As you read, add new information to the graphic organizer on page 35 in your Inquiry Journal.

What Do You Think? What is the land and water around your community like? Explain your answer.

Chapter 1 Lesson 4 49

RESEARCH COMPANION, pp. 48–49

Coastal Communities

1 Inspect Have students read pp. 48–49 and identify some features of coastal communities.

2 Find Evidence Use the question below to check comprehension.

Infer How does the temperature of ocean water affect the climate along the Pacific Coast? (Ocean water along the northern part of the Pacific Coast is cold, so the climate is colder in Washington, Oregon, and in parts of northern California; ocean water along the southern coast is warm, so the climate in southern California is warmer.) **DOK 3**

3 Make Connections

Hypothesize Look at the photograph of the coast of Maine. How might the land and buildings along the coast of southern California look different? (Possible answer: Buildings along the coast of southern California might have lots of windows so people can enjoy the warm weather. The land would look sandier and less rocky.) **DOK 3**

✓ Stop and Check

Talk (Answers will vary, but students should note that, for fun, people go to the beaches to swim, surf, enjoy water sports and boating.)

Find Details Guide students to add information to the graphic organizer on p. 35 of the Inquiry Journal.

What Do You Think? Have students discuss your local community. (Answers will vary, but students should provide support for their choices.)

✔ Check for Success

Describe Can students describe how land and water affect their communities?

Differentiate

If Not, Review with students the benefits of the land and water features of the communities that they compared and contrasted in the graphic organizers of their Inquiry Journals.

LESSON 4 REPORT

How Is My Community Affected by the Land and Water Around It?

INQUIRY JOURNAL, pp. 36–37

Think About It

Remind students to review their research and think about what they learned about landforms and bodies of water in their community compared to those in different parts of the United States. Encourage them to review the information they have included in their graphic organizers. Direct students back to pp. 40–49 of their Research Companion if they need more information.

Write About It

Write and Cite Evidence Remind students to include the following elements as they craft their description from their notes:

- Describe the physical characteristics of their community.
- Compare and contrast those characteristics with landforms and bodies of water they have read about.
- Use descriptive words and details from the text.

Discipline(s)	4	3	2	1
Geography Understanding	Shows strong understanding of local geographic features and how they compare to geographic features in different parts of the United States.	Shows adequate understanding of local geographic features and how they compare to geographic features in different parts of the United States.	Shows uneven understanding of local geographic features and how they compare to geographic features in different parts of the United States.	Shows no understanding of local geographic features and how they compare to geographic features in different parts of the United States.

Talk About It

Explain Remind students to compare their communities to other communities they have learned about in this lesson.

Assessment Students can check their understanding with feedback from the **Lesson Test** available online.

Connect to the Essential Question

Pull It Together Before they respond, remind students to think about the different landforms and bodies of water in their communities and how those features impact the way people live, work, and play there.

Inquiry Project Update Remind students to turn to Inquiry Journal pp. 2–3 for project information. If necessary, review the Project Checklist with students. At this point in the chapter, students should focus on the second, third, and fourth items on the Checklist.

Report Your Findings

Think About It

Gather Ideas

Review your research. Think about the physical characteristics of your community.

Write About It

Write and Cite Evidence

Describe the land and water around your community. How are they similar to the land and water features you have read about? How are they different? Cite evidence from what you have read to support your answer.

Answers will vary, but students should describe how the physical characteristics found in their community are similar to and different from those they have read about.

Talk About It

Explain

Share your response with a partner. Together, discuss how the physical characteristics of your community compare to those of other communities.

Connect to the EQ

Geography

Pull It Together

How does the land and water around your community compare to other nearby communities? How does this show why where you live matters?

Answers will vary, but students should demonstrate an understanding of how the land and water in their community compares to other communities.

EQ Inquiry Project Notes

INQUIRY JOURNAL, pp. 36–37

EL English Learners SCAFFOLD

Use the following scaffolds to support student writing.

Entering and Emerging

Help students review their notes about the physical characteristics of their community. Have them talk with partners about the characteristics in their community and how these compare to those they've read about. To help students write, provide sentence frames such as these: *My community is like the _____ community. Some physical characteristics of my community include _____.*

Developing and Expanding

Have partners review the notes in their graphic organizers. Then have them list some physical characteristics of their community. Pose the following questions: *What are some of the physical characteristics of our community? What kind of community do these characteristics remind you of?*

Bridging and Reaching

Before they begin writing, have students work with partners to brainstorm a list of words that describe the physical characteristics of their community. They can discuss which community they read about most closely resembles theirs. Have students use words from their list in their writing.

✔ Check for Success

Compare and Contrast

Can students compare the geography of their community with that of one of the communities they read about?

Differentiate

If Not, Have students use drawings and captions to compare and contrast their community with communities around them.

LESSON 5 OVERVIEW

LESSON QUESTION

How Do Resources Impact a Community?

Connect to the Essential Question

Tell students that this lesson provides key research into the Chapter Essential Question: **Why Does It Matter Where We Live?** Explain that they will learn how the land, water, and other natural resources in an area shape the communities that develop there. Tell them that they will discover how people use natural resources and how natural resources help populations grow.

Discuss The IMPACT Today

Tell students that a key goal of this lesson is to investigate the impact of natural resources on their community today. Identify and discuss key resources in your area as you investigate the lesson question.

Lesson Objectives

- **Describe** uses for various natural resources, including land, water, minerals, and fossil fuels.
- **Explain** the difference between renewable and nonrenewable resources.
- **Describe** how location affects the availability of natural resources.
- **Identify** benefits of, and drawbacks to, the use of specific natural resources.
- **Describe and provide** evidence on the most important resource to a community.

Make Connections!

CONNECT TO ELA

Reading **Ask and answer** questions to demonstrate understanding of a text, referring explicitly to the text as the basis for the answers.

Research **Recall** information from experiences or gather information from print and digital sources; take brief notes on sources and sort evidence into provided categories.

Writing **Craft** informative/explanatory texts to examine a topic and convey ideas and information clearly.

Speaking and Listening **Engage** effectively in a range of collaborative discussions (one-on-one, in groups, and teacher-led) with diverse partners on grade 3 topics and texts, building on others' ideas and expressing their own clearly.

COMMUNITY CONNECTIONS

To build on what students have learned about natural resources, plan an investigation of state and local print and online materials, including newspapers, the state department of natural resources, and maps of the community or region. Guide students to use these materials to identify natural resources in the community, their uses, and jobs associated with those resources.

Lesson-At-A-Glance

1 ENGAGE — INQUIRY JOURNAL

pp. 38–43

- ▶ **Talk About It:** Photograph of a waterwheel
- ▶ **Analyze the Source:** Photograph of coal mining and infographic of a coal mine
- ▶ **Inquiry Tools:** Explore Drawing Conclusions

2 INVESTIGATE — RESEARCH COMPANION

pp. 50–57

- ▶ **The Land as a Resource**
- ▶ **Beneath the Surface**
- ▶ **Water as a Resource**
- ▶ **Resources and Tourism**

3 REPORT — INQUIRY JOURNAL

pp. 44–45

- ▶ **Think About It**
- ▶ **Write About It:** Write an Informational Paragraph; Cite Evidence from Text; Define
- ▶ **Talk About It**
- ▶ **Connect to the Essential Question**

ASSESSMENT

- ▶ **Online Lesson Test**
- ▶ **Printable Lesson Test**

For more details, see pages T4–T5.

▶ Digital Tools

at **my.mheducation.com**

ePresentation

Teach the **Engage**, **Investigate**, and **Report** content to the whole class from **ePresentations** that launch directly from the lesson dashboard.

eBook

You can flip your instruction with the **IMPACT eBooks** found on your lesson dashboard.

Interactive IMPACT

Blend in digital content **when you want it** and **where you want it**.

Blended Learning features in the Teacher's Edition highlight ways to connect in-class work with online experiences to enhance learning.

Investigate current events with **IMPACT News**.

Explore domain-based vocabulary with **Explore Words** and **Word Play** vocabulary activities.

pp. 2–15

Go Further with IMPACT Explorer Magazine!

The **IMPACT Explorer Magazine** supports students' exploration of the Essential Question and provides additional resources for the EQ Inquiry Project.

How Do Resources Impact a Community?

Language Objectives

- Use newly acquired content and academic vocabulary to talk and write about natural resources.
- Draw conclusions and cite the supporting evidence, using a graphic organizer for support.
- In a group setting, discuss how jobs shape life in a community, using *-ing* words and their roots.

 Spanish Cognates

To support Spanish speakers, point out the cognates.

community = comunidad

climate = clima

agriculture = agricultura

mineral = mineral

mine = mina

metal = metal

Introduce the Lesson

Set Purpose Explain to students that in this lesson they will read informational texts to learn why natural resources are important and how they influence a community.

Access Prior Knowledge Remind students of the different types of communities they learned about in Lesson 4: *mountain, river, valley,* and *coastal.* Ask which type of community they live in. Then explain to students that in this lesson they will learn about how people in communities use the *natural resources* around them. Tell students that *natural* means things that occur in nature. *Natural resources* are things that we find in nature and are useful to people, such as water, forests, minerals, and animals. Ask: *What natural resources are found in our community?* Guide students to name local resources such as farmland, forests, or bodies of water.

Spark Curiosity Have students examine the photograph on page 51 of the Research Companion. Discuss the natural resources they see in the photograph, including land, water, and plants. Ask: *Why is water being used in the picture?* (to help the crops grow)

Have pairs of students with different language proficiency levels discuss ways they use water in their lives. Have them discuss other ways that water is important in our lives.

Build Meaning & Support Language

Inquiry Journal

Analyze the Source (pages 40–41) Point out that a *mine* is a tunnel or pit where workers dig out coal or other materials, and a *deposit* is a place where coal or another substance is found. Discuss the sentence *Coal mining is hard and dangerous work, but it shapes life in many communities.* Point out the photograph of a coal miner. Explain that the miner's helmet and safety gear show the need for protection from falling objects or breathing in coal dust. Ask: *Why is coal mining important?* (People use energy from coal.) Explain that when a job or activity *shapes life* in a community, it affects the way people live. Ask: *How might coal mining shape life in a community?* (Many people in the community might work in the mine.) Ask students to name jobs or activities that shape life in their community.

Inquiry Tools (pages 42–43) Tell students they will **Draw Conclusions** as they read the selections in the Research Companion to find out how resources impact a community. Explain that the graphic organizer on page 43 will help them organize information to draw conclusions as they read. Review the four steps on page 42, and clarify any words or phrases as needed. Remind students that when we draw a conclusion, we use information from the text and what we already know to make a judgment about something. We can also use information from sources such as photos, charts, graphs, and maps. Use the graphic organizer on page 42 to model for students how to draw conclusions.

Research Companion

The Land as a Resource (pages 50–51) Read aloud the first paragraph on page 50. Explain that *for their own gain* means "to help themselves." Read the last sentence of the second paragraph. Ask: *What is agriculture?* (using plants and animals for food) Read aloud the third paragraph, and explain that *to settle* means "to stay in one place." Ask: *How did agriculture change the way people lived?* (It helped them settle and create communities.) After you finish reading the page, review how communities trade with each other to get things they need.

Beneath the Surface (pages 52–53) After reading the first paragraph on page 52, explain that dirt, rock, clay, and sand are all types of earth and that copper, gold, and silver are types of metals. Ask: *How have people used types of earth?* (in tools, bricks, and pottery) Have students focus on the different ways to use resources as they read pages 52–53. Create a T-chart listing resources in one column and how they are used in the other column. Encourage students to add to the list with details from the text.

Water as a Resource (pages 54–55) Ask students to focus on the ways water is used as they read the second paragraph. Ask: *What are examples of water resources?* (rivers, lakes, oceans) *How did the water resources help villages grow?* (People moved near the water resources so they could trade.) Then discuss the word *waterway* with students. Explain that *waterway* is a compound word, and point out the two words in the compound. Help students determine the meaning of *waterway* from the words *water* and *way*. Then discuss various kinds of waterways with students.

Resources and Tourism (pages 56–57) Read aloud the third sentence of the first paragraph on page 56. Ask students what types of places they think would be fun to visit. Then read the second paragraph. Remind students that different regions have different climates, or common weather patterns. Ask: *Why might people go to a place with a warm climate?* (to swim or walk outside) *Why might people go to a place with a cold climate?* (for skiing, snowboarding, or ice-skating) Then read the final two paragraphs. Ask: *What types of jobs does tourism provide?* (selling food, souvenirs, and supplies, working at hotels or campgrounds)

Inquiry Journal

Report Your Findings (pages 44–45) Have students review their entries in the chart on page 43 and circle a resource they can find in their community. Then have them brainstorm ideas about how it affects their lives. Explain that a resource is *present* in a community when it can be found in that community. A resource is *absent* when it is not found in a community.

Language Forms & Conventions

-ing Words and Their Roots Explain to students that words with *-ing* endings usually tell about an action. Sometimes these words name things. In this lesson, many *-ing* words name specific industries. For example, *farming* names the industry created by people who farm. The following sentences give examples of how the forms are related.

Verb: *The man is <u>farming</u> his field.*   Noun: *<u>Farming</u> is an important industry.*

Have pairs scan the text for examples of *-ing* words. Then have them identify the *-ing* words that name industries or types of work. Call on volunteers to share their examples. Challenge students to use their words in sentences.

Cross-Cultural Connection

A historical example of a trade route is The Camino Real (Royal Road) located in Mexico and New Mexico. It was established by the Spanish to transport crops and livestock 1,600 miles to and from Mexico City and Santa Fe from 1598 to 1882. Although this route was a difficult trail in the desert, communities benefitted from the exchange of goods that the route enabled. Today Spanish, Mexican, and Native American influences can be seen in many aspects of life in the area. The National Park Service maintains information online and in Santa Fe where people can learn about the history of the route.

Leveled Support

Entering & Emerging
Guide students in understanding and responding to the questions posed in the writing prompt.

Developing & Expanding
Have students work in a group to choose a resource that affects life in their community and list its effects.

Bridging & Reaching
Encourage students to support their ideas about the effects of a resource on a community by using detailed examples.

Language Transfer

The word *resource* conveys key concepts in the lesson. Students from some Asian languages may confuse the sounds of *r* and *l*. You may want to model the pronunciation of *resource*. Have students repeat as needed.

LESSON 5 ENGAGE

LESSON QUESTION

How Do Resources Impact a Community?

INQUIRY JOURNAL, pp. 38–39

Bellringer

Prompt students to access information from the previous lesson. Ask: *What are some reasons that people live in mountain communities? Why do people live in river communities?* (Answers will vary, but students should understand that mountains have many natural resources and support tourism and recreation, while rivers move people and goods, provide fresh water, supply fish and other foods, produce fertile land for growing crops, and can be used to generate hydroelectricity.)

Lesson Outcomes

Discuss the lesson question and lesson outcomes with students.

- Make sure that students understand that *natural resources* are things found in nature that people can use.
- Guide students to identify examples of natural resources, such as land and water.
- To help students understand the term *natural resources*, ask them to think of something they find in nature and to describe one way they might use that resource. If they need more support, invite them to describe one or more ways they use water.

Talk About It

Guide students to study the image and read the caption. Have partners or groups take turns identifying something shown in the picture. Ask guiding questions as needed as students complete the activity.

- What is the water doing?
- Does the wheel move the water or does the water move the wheel?
- According to the caption, what does moving water do?

Challenge each student pair or group to discuss the image and write one sentence explaining what they think the wheel does.

 Collaborative Conversations

Activate Prior Knowledge Have students work with one or two partners to identify the following:

- how our daily activities are affected by natural resources
- one landform and one waterway in or near their community

Then challenge groups to discuss how they have seen people use the waterways and landforms identified. If time permits, ask them to draw one or more pictures showing these natural resources in use and to write an appropriate caption for each picture.

THE IMPACT TODAY

Lesson 5 — How Do Resources Impact a Community?

Lesson Outcomes

What Am I Learning?
In this lesson, you will use your investigative skills to explore different types of natural resources and how people use those resources.

Why Am I Learning It?
Reading and talking about how communities use land, water, and other resources will help you understand how location affects how people live in different communities.

How Will I Know That I Learned It?
You will be able to give an opinion with reasons about the most important resource for communities.

Talk About It COLLABORATE

Look closely at the picture. Describe what you see. How do you think the wheel generates energy?

Waterwheels turn energy from moving water into power that people can use for other things.

INQUIRY JOURNAL, pp. 38–39

EL English Learners SCAFFOLD

Use the following scaffolds to support student understanding of lesson outcomes.

Entering and Emerging

Remind students that natural resources are things we find in nature that we can use in our lives. List some natural resources on the board, such as water, fertile land, and forests. Then discuss with students how we can use each resource and why it is valuable to people. To promote discussion, provide sentence frames such as *Water is important because we use it to _____. We use land to _____. Forests provide _____.*

Developing and Expanding

Discuss the term *natural resources* with students, and work with them to write a definition. Then brainstorm with students a list of natural resources. Have students work with partners to write a sentence that explains why each natural resource is important to people. Provide the following sentence frame if needed: *_____ is an important natural resource because _____.*

Bridging and Reaching

Have students work with partners to make a two-column chart listing natural resources in one column and a brief explanation of what each resource can provide to people in the other. If necessary, provide students with general categories, such as water, minerals, and land, to use as headings for their lists. Have partners share their lists and explain how each resource is useful to people.

Social Emotional Learning

Relationship Skills

Communicate Effectively
Before students discuss the image, help them plan for their collaborative conversation. Ask: *How can you show other students that you are listening to their ideas? How can you ask for clarification or help in understanding their ideas?*

 Digital Tools

Blended Learning
Students engage with the lesson question and discussion prompts.

Interactive IMPACT

Discuss the **Lesson Question** and **Talk About It** with the whole class.

1 Inspect

Look at the images carefully. What do you expect to read about?

- **List** three adjectives that describe what you see in the first image.
- **Identify** the three types of mines shown in the second image.
- **Circle** examples of shaft mining.
- **Underline** examples of slope mining.

My Notes

_____

_____

_____

_____

_____

_____

_____

_____

Where Does Our Energy Come From?

When you turn on a light or use a computer, you are using energy. Most energy used by machines comes from natural resources called fossil fuels. In 2017, the top three fossil fuels used in the United States were oil, natural gas, and coal. People dig wells to pump oil and natural gas up to the surface of the ground. People also dig mines to reach coal deposits. Coal is found on every continent and in many countries, but not in every community. Coal is often found in mountainous regions.

The United States has some of the largest coal deposits in the world. They are found in the Appalachian Mountains, the Rocky Mountains, and in other areas. Many communities in the United States depend on coal. They use coal to power their homes and businesses. They also sell and trade coal to other places. Coal mining is hard and dangerous work, but it shapes life in many communities.

To reach coal, miners dig hundreds, even thousands, of feet underground. They use special equipment to travel in and out of the mines.

Copyright © McGraw-Hill Education
PHOTO: Monty Rakusen/Getty Images

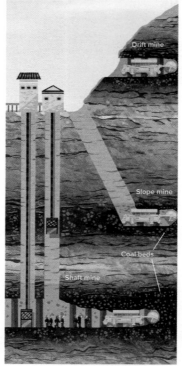

Drift mine

Slope mine

Coal beds

Shaft mine

Copyright © McGraw-Hill Education

Coal deposits can be far underground and deep within mountains. Shaft mines go straight down a long way beneath the surface. Slope and drift mines tunnel into mountainsides. Surface mining for coal, not shown here, involves removing large areas of earth.

2 Find Evidence

Underline the sentence that describes what work in a coal mine is like.

Reread How do the images support this description?

Read the captions and study the images again. How else might you describe the work done by coal miners?

3 Make Connections

Talk As you know, landforms and water impact nearby communities. How might having a mountain with coal deposits impact nearby communities?

COLLABORATE

INQUIRY JOURNAL, pp. 40–41

Analyze the Source

Background Information

The United States has about a quarter of the world's known supply of coal. Most of this coal formed more than 300 million years ago. Then much of what is now the United States was covered in lush vegetation, wetlands, and inland seas. The vegetation decayed to form peat. Over long periods of time, this peat became covered by sediment at the bottom of sea basins. Plate tectonics lifted some of these deposits closer to the surface and pushed others farther underground. As they did, the pressure squeezed water from the peat while heat from the planet's core baked the material—producing coal.

1 Inspect

Look Have students read the text, study the images, and read the image captions. Remind them to list and circle three adjectives that describe what they see in the first image. Help them as needed to identify the different types of mining.

2 Find Evidence

Reread Have students reread the text and complete the activity.

3 Make Connections

Talk Have students work with partners to make inferences about the possible different impacts of coal mines on communities. Guide them to think about impacts on jobs and the environment.

EL Spotlight on Language

Understanding Language

Have students locate the words *deposit* and *power*. Both can be verbs or nouns. Here, *deposit* is a noun meaning a supply of something that piled up over time, while *power* is a verb meaning to give something energy to enable it to move or do work.

Explore Drawing Conclusions

A **conclusion** is a judgment about events or conditions. To **draw a conclusion**, you use text clues and your own knowledge to make a judgment. This judgment might be about why something happens, how something works, or what something is like. You can also use visual clues in images, charts, graphs, and maps.

1. **Read the text and study the images.**
   This will help you understand what the text and images are about. You will draw your conclusion about the overall subject.

2. **Highlight or underline important details in the text and images.**
   Think about how these details relate to one another and to the subject.

3. **Recall what you already know about the subject.**
   Connect your knowledge to the ideas in the text and images.

4. **Ask yourself,** *What do the details and my own knowledge make me think about this subject?* Use what you have learned and what you know to draw a conclusion.

Based on the text you read, work with your class to complete the chart below.

Text Clues	Conclusion
People dig different types of mines to reach coal in different places.	Shaft mining looks more difficult than drift mining.
Coal mines look dark, dirty, deep, and tight.	Coal mines are difficult places to work. They can be dangerous.

Investigate!

Read pages 50–57 in your Research Companion. Use your investigative skills to look for text evidence that helps you draw conclusions about how communities use natural resources. This chart will help you organize your notes.

Text Clues	Conclusion
People stopped moving around when they started growing their own food.	People need a food source to live in towns and cities.
Communities trade to get things they need and want.	Many places don't have all the resources needed to support all the people who live there.
Workers separate metal from ore through smelting, which uses heat.	Smelting is hard work and can be uncomfortable and dangerous.
Steel makes it possible to build skyscrapers.	Iron was too heavy to make buildings that high.
Communities need water.	Communities that don't have a ready supply of water must find a way to get this vital resource.
People tend to settle near harbors.	Ports are less likely to be located on rocky coastlines that don't have sheltered harbors.
High elevations tend to be colder.	Most ski resorts are probably in the mountains.
Tourism is a business.	If a place loses tourism, businesses might shut down and people might lose their jobs.

INQUIRY JOURNAL, pp. 42–43

Inquiry Tools

Explore Drawing Conclusions

Read Discuss with students the steps for drawing conclusions from information provided in a text. Guide students to understand that a conclusion relies on existing information from the text to form a judgment, or opinion, about the topic of that information. If students already know something about the topic, they can also use that information as they draw conclusions.

Guide Practice Have students review the text on pp. 40–41. Then work with them to complete the graphic organizer on p. 42. Explain that they will use a similar graphic organizer to organize their independent research.

Check Understanding Confirm understanding of the inquiry skill, Drawing Conclusions. If students cannot draw an appropriate conclusion, review the steps on p. 42.

Investigate!

Have students read pp. 50–57 in the Research Companion. Tell them the information will help them answer the lesson question ***How Do Resources Impact a Community?***

Take Notes Tell students they should use the graphic organizer on p. 43 of the Inquiry Journal to record key details in the text and to draw conclusions from those details. Remind students that good note-taking is about finding the most important information and writing key words or phrases about it.

Spotlight on Content

Understanding Language

The verb *conclude* is related to the noun *conclusion*. *To conclude* means to use reason to reach a judgment or to form an opinion.

 **Digital Tools**

Blended Learning

Students prepare for the lesson investigation with step-by-step instructions about how to draw conclusions.

ePresentation

Use the **Inquiry Tools** to model how to complete the lesson graphic organizer.

How Do Resources Impact a Community?

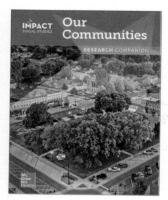

RESEARCH COMPANION, pp. 50–51

Background Information

In early North America, Native Americans often lived near lakes and rivers on which they relied for drinking, farming, fishing, and trade. In the Northeast, Great Lakes, and Southeast regions, fresh waterways, abundant rainfall, and seasonally warm temperatures supported agriculture. In the hot, dry conditions of the Southwest, Native Americans used irrigation to bring water from rivers to crops. Corn, beans, and squash grew well together and became the main crops. The ocean and forests along the Pacific Coast provided food for Native Americans who fished, hunted, and gathered. On the Great Plains, Native Americans followed herds of bison and gathered wild plants.

Today, farming thrives in most parts of the United States. European and then American settlers used steel plows to turn the hard soil of the Great Plains. There, farmers grew much of the nation's grains like wheat. Today, corn and soybeans are the main crops in other parts of the Midwest, while much of the nation's fruits and vegetables come from states like California and Florida that have fertile soil and warm temperatures year-round. Water scarcity is a growing concern in Southern California and in the Southwest where growing populations use more than the rain and snow can replenish.

The Land as a Resource

1 Inspect Have students read pp. 50–51 and explain what a natural resource is.

2 Find Evidence Use the questions below to check comprehension. Remind students to support their answers with text evidence.

Cause and Effect How did agriculture affect early people? (Answers should include that agriculture enabled people to settle in one place and build communities.) **DOK 2**

Cite Evidence Why do you think it was important for people to establish communities where there was fresh water and fertile soil? (Answers should include that communities needed fresh water to survive and fertile soil for farming.) **DOK 3**

3 Make Connections

Analyze Why would people want to grow their own food? (Answers should include the idea that people might want to control their food supply and not travel around in search of food.) **DOK 3**

Connect Do you live in a community and surrounding area known for growing food? Or do you live in a community where most food has to be brought in from other places? Explain possible reasons for your answer. (Answers will vary but may reflect whether the community is an urban, rural, or suburban community, as well as landforms and climate of the community.) **DOK 3**

Lesson 5

How Do Resources Impact a Community?

The Land as a Resource

Natural resources are things people can use for their own gain. The land, water, and climate of a place give a community its natural resources.

Farming as we know it started 10,000 years ago. People learned how to keep seeds from plants to grow their own crops. Raising plants and animals for food and other uses is known as agriculture.

Agriculture changed how people lived. Instead of moving around, they began to settle. They built communities in areas that had fresh water, fertile soil, and a climate that was suited to growing crops. As people grew more of their own food, populations grew. More people meant bigger communities. Eventually, the first cities developed.

Much of the world as we know it today would not have developed without agriculture. Today, humans still depend on growing crops and raising animals. Some communities are still centered on farming and ranching.

Other communities focus on other kinds of activities. These communities must trade to get the food they need. Trade means exchanging, or buying and selling, goods.

Like the first farmers, farmers today rely on soil, water, and sunlight. Communities that lack easy access to fresh water might use irrigation methods. Irrigation brings water to fields for farming.

50 Lesson 5 How Do Resources Impact a Community?

Chapter 1 Lesson 5 51

RESEARCH COMPANION, pp. 50–51

 English Learners SCAFFOLD

Use the following scaffolds to support student understanding of lesson content.

Entering and Emerging

Read aloud the text about agriculture. Ask: *Why did people move from place to place?* (to get food and other things they needed to survive) *What happened when they started growing crops?* (They settled in one place.) Have students draw a picture showing people who are farming.

Developing and Expanding

Have partners take turns reading aloud the text on pp. 50–51. Ask: *How did agriculture change life?* (People grew their own crops for food and other things so they settled in one place. Communities developed.)

Bridging and Reaching

Tell students to read the text on pp. 50–51. After reading, have students work with partners to chart the events that led to the formation of communities and cities. Encourage them to use words such as *first, next,* and *then* in their charts.

 **Digital Tools**

Blended Learning

Students investigate curated resources and find evidence to answer the lesson question.

Interactive IMPACT

Students **Research** and find evidence using digital format texts.

Beneath the Surface

Minerals are important resources found in dirt, rock, clay, and sand. Some minerals come from deep underground, and others are found on the Earth's surface. Examples of minerals include salt, copper, gold, and even the graphite in your pencil. Early people made tools and weapons from different minerals. They made bowls and jars from clay. They also made bricks from mud or clay to build their homes. Today, people still use clay to make pottery. Many dishes and glasses are made with minerals. The red brick found in some homes is made from clay and rock ground together.

Over time, people found metal in mineral ores. Ore is a mineral with something inside it that people want, such as copper or iron. First, miners dig up the ore. Next, workers heat the ore. Then they separate the metal from the ore. This process is called smelting. Finally, the melted metal can be shaped and cooled. Once cooled, it gets very hard. Metal goods are harder and stronger than things made from dirt, clay, or wood.

Most iron ore comes from mines close to Earth's surface.

One of most common metals on Earth is iron. For thousands of years, people made weapons, tools, and other things from iron. Then people learned to make steel from iron. Steel is stronger and lighter than iron. Steel makes it possible to build skyscrapers. Steel is also used in bridges, trains and train tracks, cars, ships, and airplanes.

Mills are industrial plants. Steel mills turn iron from iron ore and carbon from coal into steel.

Many communities in the United States started in areas where minerals could be mined and milled. Today, people across the country rely on mining and milling for goods, jobs, and trade. Minerals are found in goods we use every day from jewelry to mirrors and computers to toilets!

Some underground resources called fossil fuels, form over long periods of time from dead plants and animals. Fossil fuels include oil, natural gas, and coal. Fossil fuels are the largest source of energy in the United States. However, they are nonrenewable resources. They take a long time to replace. Many people worry about running out of these resources. Some people and communities have begun using more renewable resources for power. These include water, wind, and solar energy from the sun.

✓ Stop and Check

Talk Where might you look in your home to find things made from minerals?

Find Details As you read, add new information to the graphic organizer on page 43 in your Inquiry Journal.

RESEARCH COMPANION, pp. 52–53

Beneath the Surface

1 Inspect Have students read pp. 52–53 and identify renewable energy resources.

2 Find Evidence Use the question below to check comprehension.

Infer Why might many communities in the United States have started in areas where minerals could be mined and milled? (The minerals could be used to create goods and for trade, and the mining and milling of minerals could provide jobs.) **DOK 3**

3 Make Connections

Draw Conclusions Why might some communities want to reduce fossil fuel use? Cite evidence from the text in your response. (Answers should include that fossil fuels are nonrenewable resources that can't be replenished easily and that using them causes pollution.) **DOK 3**

Apply Using what you know about coal mining from Inquiry Journal pp. 40–41, what do you think work in other types of mines is like? (Answers should include that mining jobs probably involve hard, dangerous work with machinery.) **DOK 3**

✓ Stop and Check

Talk Bring in and share items made from minerals. Then have students discuss items from their homes. (Answers will vary but students may look at the walls, floors, and ceilings for building materials made of metals or in the kitchen for utensils, dishware, glassware, and metal pots and pans.)

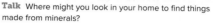

Spotlight on Content

Scanning for Information

Have student pairs scan the text to find examples of fossil fuels and examples of other types of minerals.

Spotlight on Language

Content Vocabulary

Explain that *fossils* are remains of plants and animals that lived long ago and *fuel* is a substance that produces heat or power when it burns. Ask students to use these meanings to write a sentence explaining what *fossil fuels* are.

Water as a Resource

Communities need water as a resource for drinking, washing, fishing, and raising crops. Waterways also serve as roads. Before trains, cars, trucks, and airplanes, people traveled more quickly by water than over land. People settled where they found good water resources. Over time, villages grew into towns and cities.

Communities use their rivers, lakes, and oceans to help them trade and grow further. Often, communities trade resources that they have for those that they do not. They trade goods that they make to get things that they do not make. Jobs in trade help towns and cities grow even more. People are also attracted by the easy availability of different goods.

Because water is such an important resource, people tend to settle near harbors. A harbor is part of an ocean or lake. Harbors are next to land and are protected from rough waters. Because the water in harbors is deep enough for ships, they are good places for ports where ships load and unload people and goods.

Large boats such as this barge use rivers to transport goods to communities around the country.

People also settle and build communities near the mouths of rivers. This is where rivers empty into a larger body of water. That way, people can be connected by both the river and the larger bodies of water.

Many of the largest cities in the United States were built on waterways. Boston, New York City, and Miami are on the Atlantic Ocean. Los Angeles, San Francisco, and Seattle are on the Pacific Ocean. New Orleans is at the mouth of the Mississippi River where it empties into the Gulf of Mexico. The Mississippi River also flows through the northern city of Minneapolis. Chicago and Milwaukee each border Lake Michigan.

The busiest ports in the United States are found at Los Angeles and Long Beach in California, New York City in New York, and Newark, New Jersey. The Port of Los Angeles alone employs half a million people.

Port cities are busy. Some people have jobs loading and unloading goods on the ships as they come and go. Other people own shops and businesses that support shipping. Today, the large ships that travel in and out of our ports can carry as many as 18,000 containers! Each container might be the size of a classroom.

Waterways have been important resources for people for thousands of years. They provide food, water, and an important source for transporting goods around the world.

✓ Stop and Check

Talk How does the availability of water resources impact a community?

54 Lesson 5 How Do Resources Impact a Community?

Chapter 1 Lesson 5 55

RESEARCH COMPANION, pp. 54–55

Water as a Resource

1 Inspect Have students read pp. 54–55 and explain what a waterway is. Have them give examples of waterways mentioned in the text. (rivers, lakes, oceans, harbors)

2 Find Evidence Use the questions below to check comprehension.

Make Inferences Why might communities trade to get things they need or want? (Answers should reflect that communities trade because they cannot make everything they need or want themselves.) **DOK 2**

Interpret Why are waterways such an important resource? (Communities need water for drinking, washing, fishing, raising crops, and so on. Waterways also serve as roads and allow for boats to transport people and goods.) **DOK 2**

3 Make Connections

Apply Reread the second paragraph. Think about a time that you traded something with a friend. Why did you both decide to make the trade? (Answers will vary but students might suggest that each person had something the other wanted, such as a baseball card, toy, or article of clothing.) **DOK 3**

✓ Stop and Check

Talk Discuss whether your community has nearby water and how the availability or lack of water affects the community. (Answers will vary but could include that the availability of water is useful for drinking water, fishing, farming, trade, and transport.)

Social Emotional Learning

Decision-Making Skills

Identify Problems When people trade goods and services, they do so to solve a problem. Ask students to explain a problem that can be solved by conducting trade.

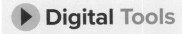 **Digital Tools**

Blended Learning

Students explore lesson content through interactive activities.

Interactive IMPACT

Use the **More to Explore**.

Academic Vocabulary Make sure students understand the meanings of the terms *tour, tourist,* and *tourism.*

tour = a journey for pleasure

tourist = a person traveling for pleasure

tourism = the business of providing services for travelers

Resources and Tourism

1 Inspect Have students read pp. 56–57 and identify two things they learned about tourism.

2 Find Evidence Use the questions below to check comprehension.

Explain How do community businesses support tourism? (They provide goods and services, such as food and lodging, to tourists.) **DOK 2**

Apply What tourist activities might you expect to find in a region with forests? Why? (Answers may vary, but should include activities such as hiking and camping because people would go there to enjoy nature and explore the woods.) **DOK 3**

3 Make Connections

Analyze What does tourism in national parks suggest about the importance of natural resources? (Answers should include that people not only want to use natural resources to make things, but also enjoy the beauty and experience of exploring natural areas.) **DOK 3**

 Stop and Check

Talk Have students discuss resources, climate, and tourism in their community. (Answers should reflect the opportunities available in the local community. Area parks may be important sources of tourism. The landscape might attract tourists, and tourism might be highest during certain seasons.)

What Is the IMPACT Today?

Revisit the different resources—land, water, minerals, climate, and other natural resources—discussed in the lesson. Have students discuss which are most important for survival. (Answers should reflect that a community needs water and other resources to survive. Students may note that some missing resources could be brought in through trade.)

 Digital Tools

Blended Learning
Students investigate curated resources and find evidence to answer the lesson question.

Interactive IMPACT

Students choose from print or digital **Inquiry Tools** to take notes.

Resources and Tourism

You know that people use natural resources to make food, tools, and other things. People can also enjoy natural resources in other ways. Tourism means visiting places for fun. Think about the places you might like to visit. Maybe you want to make sandcastles at a beach or hike in a forest of tall trees. You might want to ski down a mountain. These are examples of tourism. Landforms are important natural resources for tourism.

Tourism is also affected by climate, or the usual weather that a place has. Some climates are warm and wet. Some are cold and dry. Others change with the seasons. The climate of a place depends on many factors. These include its latitude, its nearness to large bodies of water, and its elevation, or height above sea level. Higher elevations, such as mountains, tend to be colder. Low elevations near the equator tend to be hot.

Beaches provide another important resource to communities. They attract tourism.

Many tourists like to visit places with warm climates, especially if they live in places with cold winters. Communities in warm states, such as Florida and California, benefit from year-round tourism where people come to enjoy the beaches. Other tourists flock to snow-covered mountains where they can enjoy cold-weather sports, such as skiing, snowboarding, and ice skating.

Tourism is not just an activity. It is also a business. Many people work in jobs that support tourists. They sell food, souvenirs, and supplies. Others find jobs at businesses that provide places to stay, such as campgrounds or hotels.

Some communities rely almost entirely on tourism. In the Rocky Mountains, the town of Aspen, Colorado, got its start in silver mining. Later, ski resorts made tourism the town's main business. Across the country, millions of people visit national and state parks each year. Among these are Yellowstone National Park in Wyoming, Yosemite National Park in California, and the Everglades National Park in Florida. Communities nearby benefit from the jobs and money that tourists bring.

In 2016–2017, more than 20 million people participated in ski activities in the Rocky Mountains. Millions more visited other ski spots across the nation during that time.

✓ Stop and Check

COLLABORATE

Talk How does climate and natural resources affect tourism in a community?

What Is the IMPACT Today? What resources do communities need to survive and grow?

RESEARCH COMPANION, pp. 56–57

 # English Learners SCAFFOLD

Use the following scaffolds to support student understanding of the content.

Entering and Emerging

Make a word web on the board with *tourism* in the center. Ask students to give examples of tourist activities, such as hiking, skiing, camping, and boating, and add them to the web. Encourage students to name activities they have done or would like to do. Then help students describe the climate and landscape needed for each activity, and add those terms to the web.

Developing and Expanding

Ask the following guiding questions: *What tourist activities could you do in hot and warm climates? What tourist activities might you find in the mountains? What tourist activities could you do on the coastline of an ocean or sea?* Tell partners to write and take turns saying their responses.

Bridging and Reaching

Divide students into groups. Have each student select a geographic region on the map of the United States to visit. Challenge students to draw a picture and write a caption that shows what type of tourism they would find if they visited that region. Ask students to take turns sharing their paragraphs and pictures in their groups.

✓ Check for Success

Explain Can students describe how different resources impact communities?

Differentiate

If Not, Have students review the text clues and related conclusions they noted about resources and communities in their Inquiry Journals.

LESSON 5 REPORT

LESSON QUESTION

How Do Resources Impact a Community?

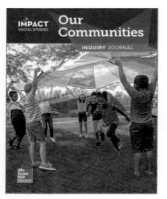

INQUIRY JOURNAL, pp. 44–45

Think About It

Remind students to review their research and consider how different natural resources have affected communities in the past and present. Encourage students to review the conclusions drawn in their graphic organizers about the natural resources they have chosen. Direct students back to pp. 50–59 of their Research Companion if they need more information.

Write About It

Write and Cite Evidence Read aloud the prompt to students. Remind students to include the following as they craft their responses.

- Introduce the resource that was chosen.
- Organize key details about the resource's location in or absence from the community.
- Identify how that resource has impacted life in the community.
- Use chapter vocabulary as appropriate.

Discipline(s)	4	3	2	1
Geography Economics	Student includes evidence and details to show the importance of a resource to a community.	Student includes some evidence to show the importance of a resource to a community.	Student includes the importance of a resource to the community with little evidence to support thinking.	Student provides no evidence to support his or her discussion of a resource in the community.

Talk About It

Explain Students may find it challenging to support their own conclusions if there are different opinions regarding the importance of different resources. Encourage students to back up their opinions with text evidence or with knowledge about their own community.

Assessment Students can check their understanding with feedback from the **Lesson Test** available online.

Connect to the Essential Question

Pull It Together Help students connect the availability of resources with why it matters where people live. Discuss how the availability of some resources may make a location more attractive to settlers in the past and people today.

Inquiry Project Update Remind students to turn to Inquiry Journal pp. 2–3 for project information. If necessary, review the Project Checklist with students. At this point in the chapter, students should focus on the last two items on the checklist.

Think About It

Recall Details

Think about these five different resources that impact communities—land, minerals, fossil fuels, water, and climate. What makes each resource important for a community?

Write About It

Write and Cite Evidence

Of the five resources you have considered, what do you think is the most important resource for a community? Provide evidence to support your opinion. You can use the importance of the resources to your own community to help support your argument.

Answers will vary but students should give their opinion on the most imporant resource for a community with reasons to support their thinking.

Talk About It

Explain

Share your response with a partner. Compare and contrast your opinions of the most important resources for a community. Do you agree or disagree with your partner's opinion? Why?

Economics

Connect to the EQ

Pull It Together

How does the availability of resources make an impact on how people live or where people choose to live? Describe why the availability of resources matters to where we live.

Answers may vary but should reflect how the availability of resources affects people's daily lives or choices on where to live.

Inquiry Project Notes

INQUIRY JOURNAL, pp. 44–45

English Learners SCAFFOLD

Use the following scaffolds to support students as they write their paragraphs.

Entering and Emerging

On the board, list words and phrases to describe amounts, such as *few, a lot, a little, some,* and *no.* Give students sentence frames such as the following, and have them choose from words on the board to complete the sentences: *My community has _____ fresh water resources. My community has _____ fossil fuel resources. My community has _____ mineral resources.*

Developing and Expanding

Ask students to brainstorm a list of natural resources discussed in the lesson. Have them categorize the resources by their presence in the community. For example, you might provide the categories *many, some,* and *few* or *none.* Tell partners to choose a resource and to take turns describing its presence or absence in the community.

Bridging and Reaching

Have students make a T-chart listing resources that the community has and resources that the community lacks. Ask these questions to help them prepare to write their paragraphs: *What does the community do with the resources it has? What does the community do about the resources it does not have?*

✔ Check for Success

Analyze Can students provide evidence to support their discussion of the importance of different resources to the community?

Differentiate

If Not, Have students list the resources in the community and possible benefits of those resources to help them cite specific evidence.

EQ ESSENTIAL QUESTION

Why Does It Matter Where We Live?

**INQUIRY JOURNAL,
pp. 46–47**

Inquiry Project Wrap Up

Remind students that they created a travel brochure to showcase three features that make their community special.

Assessment Use the rubric on p. T5 to assess students' Inquiry Projects.

Complete Your Project

Have students work individually to review the Complete Your Project checklist. Remind them that if they have missed any of the criteria, now is their opportunity to make corrections or additions.

Share Your Project

If time allows, you may want to have students present their projects to the class. Provide the following presentation tips for students.

- Prepare and rehearse.
- Use notes to help you stay on topic.
- Speak slowly and clearly. Make sure everyone can hear you.
- Make eye contact and speak directly to the audience.

Reflect on Your Project

Student reflections begin with thinking about the process for how they chose the features in their community that they wanted to research. Students should focus on the results of the inquiry as well as the challenges and successes of the inquiry process. Discuss examples of reliable or trustworthy sources such as official government sites, education sites, and sites with primary source materials. Discuss less reliable sources such as advertisements or opinion pieces not backed by facts. Ask students to tell whether their sources include facts, opinions, or both as you work with them to find reliable sources. Students can apply these ideas on research to future projects.

Chapter Connections can focus on anything that resonated with students about their study of the features in their community. These connections may spark students to do further research on their own.

▶ **Digital Tools**

Blended Learning
Students use online checklists to prepare, complete, and reflect on their Inquiry Projects.

Chapter Assessments
Students can demonstrate chapter content mastery with the feedback from the online **Chapter Test**.

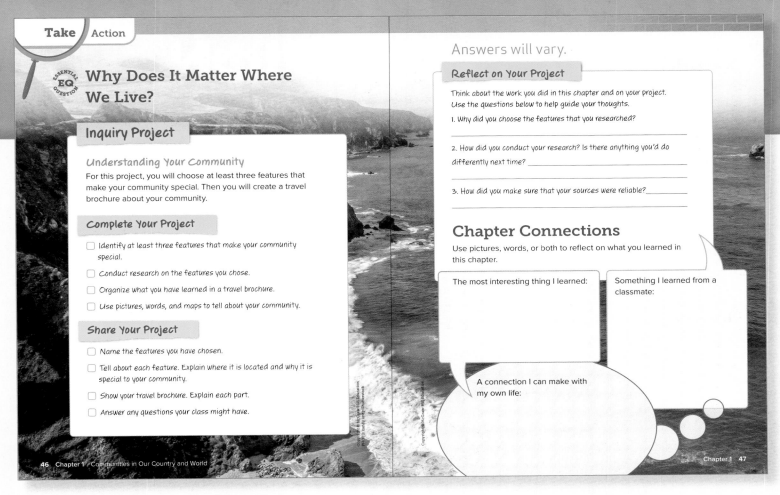

INQUIRY JOURNAL, pp. 46–47

 # English Learners SCAFFOLD

Use the following scaffolds to support student presentation of their projects.

Entering and Emerging
Review the project checklist with students, and check for understanding. Discuss any unfamiliar language. Help students practice reading their travel brochures. Focus on fluency: pronunciation and reading at an appropriate pace. Have students work with partners. Each partner can take turns reading his or her brochure.

Developing and Expanding
Have students work in pairs to read the project checklist. As a class, make a list of question words or stems that could be used for discussing important features of their community. Have partners take turns reading their travel brochures to each other. Tell each partner to ask one question about the brochure.

Bridging and Reaching
Have partners read the project checklist and brainstorm ways to make a interesting presentation. Give students time to practice presenting their travel brochures with their partners.

✓ Check for Success

Describe Use your online rubric or the rubric found on p. T5 to record student progress. Can students create a travel brochure describing special features about their community?

Differentiate

If Not, Have students create an oral presentation or write an essay describing what makes their community special.

TAKE ACTION
with RESEARCH COMPANION

**RESEARCH COMPANION,
pp. 58–59**

Connections in Action

Analyze Lead a discussion about the geography in your community and the surrounding area. Have students identify features of the land and climate and available natural resources, and list these on the board. Then have students work with partners to discuss the impact of these features on the community.

Talk To help focus students' conversations, you may want to discuss the EQ with the entire class before students discuss their ideas with a partner. Remind students to think about evidence they can provide that will support their ideas.

Share Invite students to share their small-group discussions with the class.

More to Explore

How Can You Make an IMPACT?

Mix and match the More to Explore activities to meet the needs of your classroom. Stretch students' thinking by offering alternative ways to demonstrate what they learned during the chapter.

These activities are flexible enough that you can assign one, two, or three activities to specific students or have students work in small groups. Remind students to use proper collaborative procedures when they work with partners.

Brainstorm Synonyms

Before students begin, choose one vocabulary word and ask volunteers to come up with examples of synonyms. As an extra challenge, have partners come up with synonyms for words that are not in the vocabulary list.

Teacher Tip! **Use this activity to monitor students' understanding of chapter vocabulary.**

Create a Television Ad

Organize students into groups, and have them brainstorm ideas before they begin their ads. Ask them to think about why people would want to visit their community. Discuss both physical and human features. Invite each group to perform its ad for the class.

Teacher Tip! **This activity can be used to monitor students' relationship skills.**

Compose a Song

Review the vocabulary words and the ideas and examples presented in the chapter. Write one or two of the words on the board, and ask students for words that rhyme with them. Then as a class, create the first two lines of a song, using those words.

Teacher Tip! **This activity can be used to help students practice speaking and listening skills.**

▶ Digital Tools

Blended Learning

Students apply chapter concepts to extension activities and connect them to the Essential Question.

Interactive IMPACT

Review chapter vocabulary with **Word Play.**

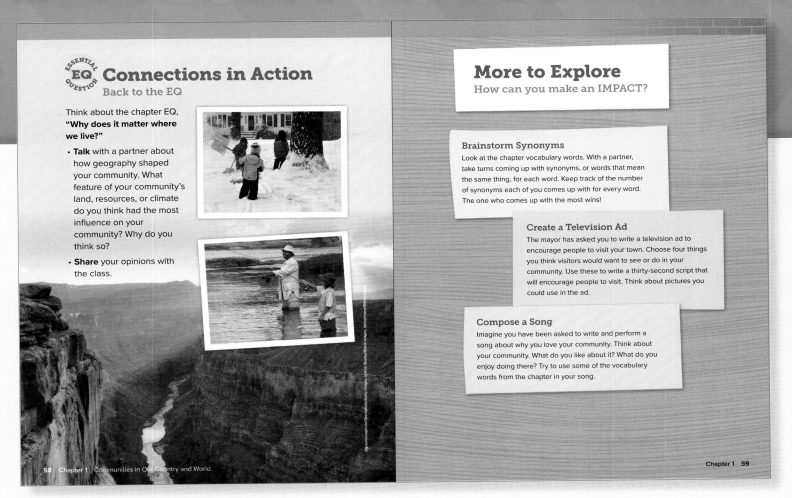

RESEARCH COMPANION, pp. 58–59

 # English Learners SCAFFOLD

Use the following scaffolds to support student understanding of chapter content.

Entering and Emerging

Provide visual support for identifying features that influence the local community. Draw a graphic organizer with the heads *Land, Climate,* and *Resources.* Use images from the book or elsewhere to elicit language that helps students identify the various features of their community. Have students list the words in the correct column on the graphic organizer.

Developing and Expanding

Have students work in pairs or small groups to create a graphic organizer to identify the land, climate, and resources of their community. Then have volunteers explain some of the information in the graphic organizer, speaking in complete sentences.

Bridging and Reaching

Have students work in pairs or small groups to list information they found interesting about the land, climate, and resources in their community. Have groups report back to the class and write information about their community on the board to discuss.

 ## Social Emotional Learning

Relationship Skills

Communicate Effectively
Remind students that it is important to communicate their ideas clearly and to listen carefully to the ideas of others. Discuss ways that students can build their communication skills to make their group work more productive, such as clarifying their own ideas and asking questions to clarify the ideas of others.

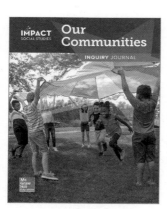

**INQUIRY JOURNAL,
pp. 48–53**

Extend Learning

Deepen students' understanding of how the land, climate, and resources can affect a community with the Reader's Theater selection "Exploring Planet Ava."

> | **GENRE** | Reader's Theater Reader's Theater is a form of drama in which actors do not memorize their lines. They use their voices rather than sets or costumes to help listeners understand the text.

Perform the Reader's Theater

Model the reading. Project the play with an interactive whiteboard or projector, and read aloud as students follow along. As you read, use your voice to show how expression and rate can communicate meaning. Explain how exclamation points should affect expression.

Choose a few lines to examine. Discuss how a reader should read the lines:

- **Robb:** Look at the three moons!
  How should the character read this line? Why do you think so? (The exclamation point means that the line should be read loudly, in an excited voice.)

- **Robb:** (*disappointed*) We saw lots of trees but not many were Kottowool. We didn't find too much cordromite, either.
  What does the word in parentheses tell you to do? How would you read these lines? (The word in parentheses is a stage direction that tells how the character feels. I would read the words as if I were feeling let down.)

Practice the reading. Before students read aloud on their own, give them time to practice reading. Use techniques such as the following:

- Echo Read—Read a line and then have students repeat it.
- Partner Read—Have pairs of students take turns reading aloud the lines of the play.

Assign roles. Consider these strategies:

- Pair up students to take turns reading a role if some of your students are reluctant to participate.
- Put students into performance groups, and let students try out different roles when rehearsing.
- Have students mark up their scripts. They can highlight their dialogue, underline stage directions, and circle words they should emphasize when they speak.

Talk About It

Have students think about the reasons people might have settled in their community. As they discuss their ideas with partners, have them think about the features that make their community a good place to live.

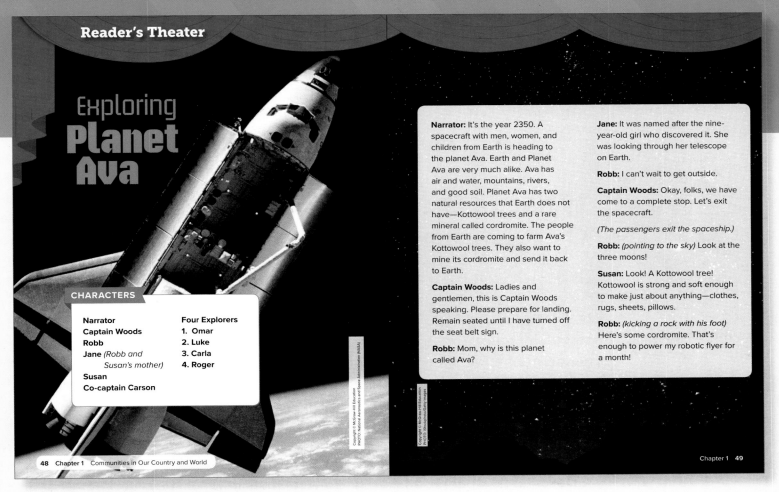

INQUIRY JOURNAL, pp. 48–53

Reader's Theater

Exploring Planet Ava

CHARACTERS

Narrator
Captain Woods
Robb
Jane *(Robb and Susan's mother)*
Susan
Co-captain Carson

Four Explorers
1. Omar
2. Luke
3. Carla
4. Roger

48 Chapter 1 Communities in Our Country and World

Narrator: It's the year 2350. A spacecraft with men, women, and children from Earth is heading to the planet Ava. Earth and Planet Ava are very much alike. Ava has air and water, mountains, rivers, and good soil. Planet Ava has two natural resources that Earth does not have—Kottowool trees and a rare mineral called cordromite. The people from Earth are coming to farm Ava's Kottowool trees. They also want to mine its cordromite and send it back to Earth.

Captain Woods: Ladies and gentlemen, this is Captain Woods speaking. Please prepare for landing. Remain seated until I have turned off the seat belt sign.

Robb: Mom, why is this planet called Ava?

Jane: It was named after the nine-year-old girl who discovered it. She was looking through her telescope on Earth.

Robb: I can't wait to get outside.

Captain Woods: Okay, folks, we have come to a complete stop. Let's exit the spacecraft.

(The passengers exit the spaceship.)

Robb: *(pointing to the sky)* Look at the three moons!

Susan: Look! A Kottowool tree! Kottowool is strong and soft enough to make just about anything—clothes, rugs, sheets, pillows.

Robb: *(kicking a rock with his foot)* Here's some cordromite. That's enough to power my robotic flyer for a month!

Chapter 1 49

Reader's Theater Tips

- Students should have time to practice their lines before performing.
- Have students sit in a circle so they can hear each other.

Remind students of these strategies for reading aloud:

- Speak loudly so everyone can hear your voice.
- Speak at an appropriate pace.
- Use expression. Pay attention to punctuation.

Connect to the Essential Question

Have students connect the Reader's Theater to the Essential Question. Ask: *How did the land, climate, and resources of Planet Ava affect where the explorers chose to settle?* (Answers will vary, but students should understand that the explorers chose to settle in the area that had the best land, climate, and resources for their needs.)

 Digital Tools

Blended Learning

Students investigate why people settle a community with the online Reader's Theater.

Interactive IMPACT

Use the printable script for whole-class or small-group presentations.

Chapter 2 OVERVIEW

What Is Our Relationship With Our Environment?

In This Chapter Students will investigate how people in a community relate to their environment. They will explore both how the environment affects the community and how the community affects the environment. Students also will propose ways to improve their community's environment.

Chapter Objectives

- **Describe** how people adapt to the environment in which they live.
- **Tell** how people change their environment to meet their needs.
- **Describe** environmental challenges that people face.
- **Explain** how communities respond to environmental challenges.
- **Use information** from a variety of sources to develop a plan for improving the community's environment.

Make Connections!

CONNECT TO SCIENCE

Some of the ways that people interact with the environment can harm plants and animals. Have students research an endangered animal or plant to find out why that organism is endangered and how people are working to protect it.

CONNECT TO MATH

Recycling is one way to help the environment and to make money. Recyclers often pay between 30 and 40 cents per pound for aluminum cans. Have students calculate how much they can make for different weights of aluminum cans. Extend the activity by connecting with a recycling center to buy cans students collect in the class.

Bibliography

Additional resources to aid student inquiry:

▶ **Finder, A Coal Mine Dog**
by Alison Hart; Peachtree Publishers, 2015

▶ **One Plastic Bag: Isatou Ceesay and the Recycling Women of the Gambia**
by Miranda Paul; Millbrook Press, 2015

▶ **Ada's Violin: The Story of the Recycled Orchestra of Paraguay**
by Susan Hood; Simon & Schuster Books for Young Readers, 2016

Go online at **my.mheducation.com** for a complete list of resources.

Chapter-At-A-Glance

 EQ ESSENTIAL QUESTION What Is Our Relationship With Our Environment?

1 ENGAGE

INQUIRY JOURNAL

pp. 54–57

▶ **Introduce the Chapter**

▶ **Chapter Inquiry Project**

▶ **Explore Words**

Short on Time?
Engage with the content the way YOU want to teach—and *your* students want to learn!

Check out the three suggested **Flexible Instructional Pathways** on pages FM34–FM35.

2 INVESTIGATE

RESEARCH COMPANION

pp. 60–87

▶ **Activate Knowledge**

▶ **How Do Communities and the Environment Depend on Each Other?**

▶ **Connect Through Literature**
   Earth Day Birthday

▶ **People You Should Know**

▶ **Lessons 1–3**

The **IMPACT Explorer Magazine** supports students' exploration of the Essential Question and provides additional resources for the EQ Inquiry Project.

3 TAKE ACTION

INQUIRY JOURNAL
RESEARCH COMPANION

pp. 82–83   **pp. 88–89**

▶ **Inquiry Project Wrap-Up and Chapter Connections**

▶ **Connections in Action!**

▶ **More to Explore**

▶ Digital Tools at my.mheducation.com

ePresentation

Teach the Engage, Investigate, and Take Action content to the whole class from ePresentations that launch directly from the chapter dashboard.

eBook

You can flip your instruction with the **IMPACT eBooks** found on your chapter dashboard.

Interactive IMPACT

Blend in digital content **when you want it** and **where you want it**. Blended Learning notes in the Teacher's Edition highlight ways to connect in-class work with online experiences to enhance learning.

Investigate current events with **IMPACT News**.

Introduce the EQ with the **IMPACT Chapter Video**.

Explore domain-based vocabulary with **Explore Words** and **Word Play** vocabulary activities.

Chapter 2 ASSESSMENT

MONITOR PROGRESS:
Know What Your Students Know
Choose the assessment options that work best for you and your students.

Chapter Pre-Test (Optional)

Begin the Chapter

Measure students' content knowledge before you begin the chapter with the following questions.

Quick Check

✔ How does weather affect the clothes people wear and the houses they build?

✔ What are some examples of ways that people change the environment?

✔ What is a natural disaster? Give some examples.

✔ How have people responded to pollution?

1. Write each question on a piece of poster paper. Ask students to write their answers on the poster paper below the question.

2. When all students have responded, ask them to rate the answers on a scale from 1 (not very confident) to 5 (very confident).

3. Review students' responses for misconceptions, factual errors, and to inform instruction. You may wish to display the posters to review responses later as students investigate Chapter 2.

4. **Don't Forget!** Revisit students' Quick Check responses with them. If students change their response, ask them to support the change with text evidence. You may wish to have students respond to a different prompt to measure students' content knowledge, such as *What are some ways that people have adapted to environments in which they live?*

Ongoing Lesson Assessment

Use the following lesson tools to monitor the **IMPACT** of your instruction.

☑ Stop and Check

Use the questions provided in the Stop and Check prompts to monitor student comprehension of the lesson content.

✔ Check for Success

Use this formative assessment tool to assess how well your students understand the material they are learning in class. The Check for Success questions, located at point of use in the Teacher's Edition, are not a test but a way to assess students' comprehension of a particular topic. A Differentiate strategy offers one activity that you can use to quickly adapt your instruction.

○ Report Your Findings

Use each lesson task to measure students' understanding of the lesson content and their ability to effectively express their understanding. See the Lesson Assessment pp. T130, T144, and T160 for task-specific evaluation rubrics.

▶ Digital Tools

Lesson Assessments
Use the **Lesson Test** to monitor students' understanding of the lesson content. Online Lesson Tests are available for every lesson. You will also find the tools you need to create your own assessments and to track your students' progress. A printable Lesson Test is available for use in class.

Chapter Assessment

Evaluate

Monitor student understanding of core chapter content with one or more of the following assessment options.

Connections in Action

Use the **Connections in Action** to evaluate student understanding of core chapter content through discussion in the Research Companion, pp. 88–89.

Inquiry Project

In this chapter's Inquiry Project, students will explore an issue that affects their community's environment and create a plan for an improvement. Projects will include a description of the issue, a plan for improvement, and an explanation of why this plan will improve the community. To showcase the information they researched, students will give a presentation to the class. See pp. T108–T109 for more information.

Use the EQ Inquiry Project to measure students' understanding of the chapter content and their ability to effectively express their understanding. A task-specific evaluation rubric is available in the Online Teacher Resources.

	4	3	2	1
Developing and Planning Inquiry	Presentation is focused on an issue in the community and gives a specific plan to improve the issue.	Presentation is focused on an issue in the community and gives a general plan to improve the issue.	Presentation is focused on an issue in the community but gives only a basic idea to improve the issue.	Presentation is focused on an issue in the community but gives no plan to improve the issue.
Geographic Understanding	Details are included that show a deep understanding of the environmental issue and a possible solution.	Some details are included that show a deep understanding of the issue and a possible solution.	Includes the issue and a possible solution but few supporting details show understanding.	Includes the issue and a possible solution but no supporting details.
Sources and Evidence	Presentation includes required and additional information and is supported with necessary evidence.	Presentation includes required information with some supporting evidence.	Presentation includes some required facts and evidence.	Required facts and supporting evidence are not included.
Communicating Conclusions	Information is clearly supported with details and easily understood.	Information includes details and is understood with some explanation.	Information is unclear due to lack of details.	Presentation does not include details necessary to communicate information.

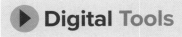

▶ Digital Tools

Chapter Assessments

Use the **Chapter Test** to monitor student understanding of the chapter content. Online Chapter Tests are customizable and available for every chapter. You will also find the tools you need to create your own assessments and to track your students' progress. A printable Chapter Test is available for use in class.

What Is Our Relationship With Our Environment?

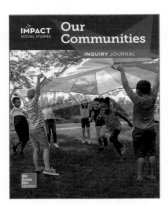

INQUIRY JOURNAL, pp. 54–55

Talk About It

Read Have students read the page together. Ask students: *How does the environment affect the way people live? How do people change the environment to meet their needs?* Encourage students to share their responses with the class. You may wish to list students' responses and revisit the list throughout the chapter.

Inquiry Project

Improving the Environment

Discuss the Inquiry Project with students. Review each step of the project and the **Project Checklist** evaluation rubric. Tell students that they will use information from the chapter and from independent research to complete the project.

My Research Plan

Discuss the Essential Question with students, and discuss ways that the environment affects people and people affect the environment. Have students work in pairs to read the Inquiry Project and think about research questions that could connect the environment with people's actions.

Design Your Own Inquiry Path (Optional)

You may wish to work with students to choose their own Essential Question, Inquiry Project, and related research questions. In addition to your feedback, have students preview chapter materials and discuss ideas with classmates to help develop possible questions, such as *How does your community interact with the environment?, What problems with your community's environment need to be solved?,* or their own questions.

Once chosen, have students explain why their Essential Question is important to them and to others. Have students record their question, project idea, and initial supporting research questions using the **Student EQ Inquiry Project** pages found at **my.mheducation.com**.

▶ Digital Tools

Blended Learning
Students engage with the chapter's Essential Question and launch their investigations.

Interactive IMPACT
Spark student interest with the **EQ Chapter Video**.

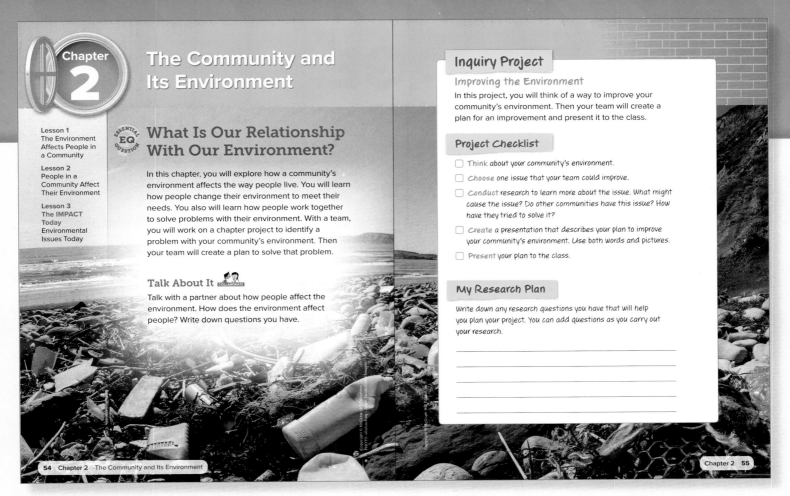

INQUIRY JOURNAL, pp. 54–55

 English Learners SCAFFOLD

Use the following scaffolds to support student understanding of the Inquiry Project.

Entering and Emerging

To help students understand what they'll need to do in the Inquiry Project, discuss the term *environment*. Say: *The word* environment *refers to the natural world, including the land, water, and resources that are in a community. Talk with a partner about what features make up your community's environment.* Guide students in thinking about the land, water, and resources in their community.

Developing and Expanding

Ask questions to check understanding of the Inquiry Project instructions, and elicit answers. For example, *How do you define the word* environment? *Can you name some land features, water features, and resources in your community? How have people affected these features? Is there a problem in your community's environment that you think needs to be addressed?*

Bridging and Reaching

Read through the Inquiry Project instructions with students. Have partners work together to define the word *environment*. Then have them list features of their community's environment and discuss an environmental issue in the community that they think needs to be addressed.

 Social Emotional Learning

Social Awareness

Develop Perspective
Students need to develop perspective in order to analyze the world around them. As students plan their Inquiry Project, encourage them to ask and consider the perspective of others. Ask: *Why might people consider this to be a problem with our community's environment? Why might some people think this is not a problem?*

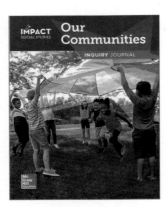

**INQUIRY JOURNAL,
pp. 56–57**

Explore Words

Academic/Domain-Specific Vocabulary Read the words aloud to students. Explain to students that these are words they will learn more about in the chapter.

Word Rater Have students place a checkmark in one of the three boxes below each word, indicating that they "Know It," "Heard It," or "Don't Know It." Explain to students that they will come back to this chart to add additional information about each word as they work through the chapter.

☐ **Know It!** Tell students that if they know the word, they should write its meaning on the lines provided.

☐ **Heard It!** Tell students that if they have heard, or are familiar with the word, they should write what they know about it on the lines provided. Remind them to take notes about the word as they encounter it.

☐ **Don't Know It!** If they do not know the word's meaning, tell them to write down its meaning when they encounter the word in the chapter.

Support Vocabulary

Return to the Word Rater as you come across vocabulary words in each lesson. Encourage students to use the "My Notes" section to include any of the following:

- definitions from the text
- deeper understandings
- synonyms
- other associations

EL Spanish Cognates

For Spanish speakers, point out the cognates.

atmosphere = atmósfera

habitat = habitat

natural disaster = desastre natural

technology = tecnología

Content Words	
atmosphere	the whole mass of air that surrounds Earth
deforestation	the loss of forests
ecosystem	all of the living things in an environment
endangered	describes a plant or animal that is rare and could die out
extinct	describes a plant or animal that has died out
habitat	the home of an animal or plant
hydroelectric dams	dams that are built to produce electricity using machines that are powered by moving water
natural disaster	an event in nature that damages the environment and may hurt living things
ozone layer	the part of the atmosphere that protects Earth from ultraviolet rays
technology	the use of science to create something useful or to solve problems

Explore Words

Complete this chapter's Word Rater. Write notes as you learn more about each word.

atmosphere — My Notes
- ☐ Know It!
- ☐ Heard It!
- ☐ Don't Know It!

deforestation — My Notes
- ☐ Know It!
- ☐ Heard It!
- ☐ Don't Know It!

ecosystem — My Notes
- ☐ Know It!
- ☐ Heard It!
- ☐ Don't Know It!

endangered — My Notes
- ☐ Know It!
- ☐ Heard It!
- ☐ Don't Know It!

extinct — My Notes
- ☐ Know It!
- ☐ Heard It!
- ☐ Don't Know It!

habitat — My Notes
- ☐ Know It!
- ☐ Heard It!
- ☐ Don't Know It!

hydroelectric dam — My Notes
- ☐ Know It!
- ☐ Heard It!
- ☐ Don't Know It!

natural disaster — My Notes
- ☐ Know It!
- ☐ Heard It!
- ☐ Don't Know It!

ozone layer — My Notes
- ☐ Know It!
- ☐ Heard It!
- ☐ Don't Know It!

technology — My Notes
- ☐ Know It!
- ☐ Heard It!
- ☐ Don't Know It!

INQUIRY JOURNAL, pp. 56–57

EL English Learners SCAFFOLD

Use the following scaffolds to support student understanding of chapter vocabulary.

Entering and Emerging

Work with students to use a dictionary to find definitions for each word. Display each definition and read each one aloud as students follow along. Then guide students to provide a definition for each word in their own words. Help students find examples or synonyms for each word, such *tornado* for *natural disaster*.

Developing and Expanding

Have students work with partners to look up each word in a dictionary and write the definition. Then have partners work together to write definitions in their own words, write context sentences, or draw an image to represent the word.

Bridging and Reaching

Have students create vocabulary flashcards for each word. On the front, have them write the word. On the back, have them write a definition in their own words, a context sentence using the word, or draw an image to represent the word. Have them quiz partners using their flashcards.

▶ Digital Tools

Blended Learning

Explore Words engages students in the investigation of academic and domain-specific words they encounter in each lesson.

Interactive IMPACT

Throughout the chapter, encourage students to interact with the **Explore Words** cards and games.

What Is Our Relationship With Our Environment?

ESSENTIAL **EQ** QUESTION

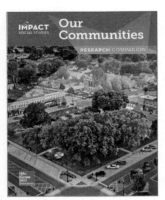

RESEARCH COMPANION, pp. 60-61

Activate Knowledge

Read and Discuss COLLABORATE Have students read the opening on p. 60 together. Ask: *How might building a road change the environment?* As students share their responses, you may wish to redirect misconceptions and inaccurate information.

How Do Communities and the Environment Depend on Each Other?

Have students read the text, focusing on both the photographs and the captions.

- How does the environment affect the way people live? (Answers will vary, but students may point out that the work people do, the clothes they wear, and the things they do for fun depend on where they live.)

- Why do people change their environment? (Answers will vary, but students may point out that people change their environment to make space to live and work and to use available resources.)

- What is the difference between regular weather and extreme weather? (Answers will vary, but students should note that extreme weather is weather that can cause damage to the environment and harm people. Regular weather does not harm people.)

Make Connections

- In what kind of environment do you think the people in the first photograph live? (Answers will vary, but students may point out that since the people in the first image are working on a farm, they probably live in an environment that has warm weather, good soil, and rain.)

- Look at the photographs and text again. What do they tell you about how people and the environment are connected? (Answers will vary, but students should point out that people depend on the environment to meet their needs and that the changes people make can have an important impact on the environment.)

- Is it important that people work to protect the environment? (Answers will vary but should include reasons to support students' opinions about the importance of protecting the environment.)

Chapter 2
The Community and Its Environment

Lesson 1
The Environment Affects People in a Community

Lesson 2
People in a Community Affect Their Environment

Lesson 3
The IMPACT Today
Environmental Issues Today

ESSENTIAL EQ QUESTION
What Is Our Relationship With Our Environment?

A community's environment can affect the way people live. People who live in a coastal town may fish to earn a living. People can also affect the environment by changing it to meet their needs. They may clear land to build roads that make it easier to travel from one place to another. In this chapter, you will explore ways that people and the environment can impact each other.

People use solar panels to collect energy from the sun.

60   Chapter 2   The Community and Its Environment

How Do Communities and the Environment Depend on Each Other?

There are many ways that people and the environment affect each other.

The way people work, live, and play depends on where they live. People must adapt to their environment. People who live in areas with good soil and lots of rain may farm for a living. People who live in areas with hot weather likely wear light clothing to stay cool. People who live in areas with lots of snow may sled or ski for fun.

People change the environment to meet their needs. They may clear land to build places for people to live or work. They may cut down trees and dig canals to grow crops. They may build dams to create electricity. These changes can have a big effect on the environment.

Sometimes the environment can cause harm to a community. Extreme weather such as hurricanes can damage buildings with heavy rain and high winds. When this happens, communities may come together to solve problems with their environment.

Chapter 2   61

RESEARCH COMPANION, pp. 60–61

 English Learners **SCAFFOLD**

Use these scaffolds to support students in activating their background knowledge.

Entering and Emerging

Ask partners to identify any unfamiliar vocabulary words in the text. Explain the meanings of these words or help students find the definitions of the words in a dictionary. Then have partners take turns using each word in a sentence. Provide the following sentence frames as needed: *The word _____ means _____. An example of _____ is _____.*

Developing and Expanding

Ask partners to identify any unfamiliar vocabulary words in the text. Have students discuss the meanings of these words or help students find the definitions of the words in a dictionary. Then have partners take turns creating context sentences for each word.

Bridging and Reaching

Point out content-specific vocabulary words in the text, such as *adapt, environment,* and *hurricane*. Ask open-ended questions using these words to check students' understanding, such as: *How do people adapt to cold weather? What land and water features are part of our community's environment? How can a hurricane harm a community?*

Connect Through Literature

EARTH DAY BIRTHDAY

by Jody Jensen Shaffer
Art by Roger Simo

"I just want a normal birthday party," April told Bailey as they walked home from school. Bailey knew what April meant. April's parents loved the environment. And because April happened to be born on Earth Day, all her parties had an Earth Day theme.

"Remember when you turned seven?" Bailey said.

"How could I forget the Throw-Out Blowout?" said April.

"We helped out at your garage sale and donated the money to charity. And when you turned eight—"

"It was a Tree Spree," finished April. "We planted maples."

Later that night, as April loaded the dishwasher, she said, "I'd like to plan my own party this year."

"Sure," said Mom. "We could have a Compost Carnival."

"Great idea!" said Dad.

April cleared her throat. "I'd like to go to Maze Craze instead."

"Really?" said Dad, surprised.

"I guess we could do that," said Mom.

The following weekend, everyone gathered in the parking lot outside of Maze Craze.

62 Chapter 2 The Community and Its Environment

"Thanks for coming," said April. "I've been so excited about my party. No shovels. No collecting recyclables. Nothing earthy about it." She shifted her feet. "Then I got here this morning and saw this parking lot."

April's friends glanced around. Plastic bottles bounced across the cement. Newspapers and fast-food sacks clogged the storm drain. Shopping bags rustled in the trees.

"Even though I wanted a non-Earth Day birthday, I couldn't have fun knowing this mess was out here. Can we pick up the garbage in the parking lot first, then go through the maze?"

"Of course!" said her friends. April's parents grabbed some gloves and trash bags from the trunk of their car.

The kids fanned out across the parking lot while their parents watched for traffic. Before long, they had filled three bags with bottles, cans, and paper to recycle.

April looked at the bags and smiled. It felt good to do something for the earth. And with everyone pitching in, it didn't take long.

"Happy Earth Day, everyone," said April. "Now I'm ready for Maze Craze."

"Happy birthday, April!" shouted her friends.

Think About It

1. How did April help the environment on past birthdays?

2. Why did April and her friends decide to clean up when they arrived at the maze?

3. Would you spend your birthday helping the environment? What are some other ways you could pitch in?

Chapter 2 63

RESEARCH COMPANION, pp. 62–63

Connect Through Literature

| **GENRE** | Short Story "Earth Day Birthday" is a short story. A short story is a work of fiction where the characters and the plot are made up.

Have students read the selection on pp. 62–63. Then discuss the following questions.

1. How did April help the environment on past birthdays? (held a garage sale and donated money to charity, planted maple trees, collected newspapers to recycle)

Have students reread the selection and ask:

2. Why did April and her friends decide to clean up when they arrived at the maze? (The parking lot was littered with trash, and April couldn't have fun knowing that she didn't try to clean it up.)

Perspectives What are some ways that you can celebrate Earth Day? (Answers will vary, but students could mention activities such as gathering items to recycle, organizing a cleanup of a local park, and so on.)

Background Information

In the United States, Earth Day is observed on April 22 each year. On this day, millions of people celebrate the accomplishments of the environmental movement and work to raise awareness of the importance of protecting Earth and its resources.

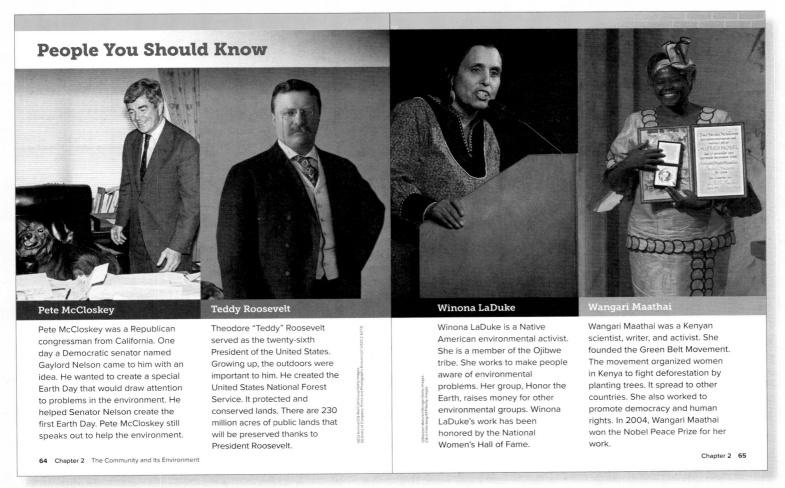

People You Should Know

Pete McCloskey

Pete McCloskey was a Republican congressman from California. One day a Democratic senator named Gaylord Nelson came to him with an idea. He wanted to create a special Earth Day that would draw attention to problems in the environment. He helped Senator Nelson create the first Earth Day. Pete McCloskey still speaks out to help the environment.

Teddy Roosevelt

Theodore "Teddy" Roosevelt served as the twenty-sixth President of the United States. Growing up, the outdoors were important to him. He created the United States National Forest Service. It protected and conserved lands. There are 230 million acres of public lands that will be preserved thanks to President Roosevelt.

Winona LaDuke

Winona LaDuke is a Native American environmental activist. She is a member of the Ojibwe tribe. She works to make people aware of environmental problems. Her group, Honor the Earth, raises money for other environmental groups. Winona LaDuke's work has been honored by the National Women's Hall of Fame.

Wangari Maathai

Wangari Maathai was a Kenyan scientist, writer, and activist. She founded the Green Belt Movement. The movement organized women in Kenya to fight deforestation by planting trees. It spread to other countries. She also worked to promote democracy and human rights. In 2004, Wangari Maathai won the Nobel Peace Prize for her work.

64 Chapter 2 The Community and Its Environment

Chapter 2 65

RESEARCH COMPANION, pp. 64–65

People You Should Know

How do personal stories IMPACT our understanding of the relationship between people and the environment?

Read Explain to students that they will learn about the relationship between people and the environment. Have students read the four biographies and think about how these people worked to help others better understand their relationship with the environment.

Research Ask students to research people who have worked to improve the environment. Tell students to gather facts about each person as well as a memorable story that helps reveal what each person was like.

Respond Have students create a class infographic display board to showcase the people they researched. Students can draw, download, or photocopy portraits for the display. Have students assemble the infographic display board and refer to it throughout the chapter.

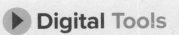

Digital Tools

Blended Learning

Students investigate and discuss curated news articles that extend the chapter content.

Interactive IMPACT

Connect to current events and people with **IMPACT News** and **More to Investigate**.

IMPACT EXPLORER MAGAZINE, pp. 16–29

WordBlast

Remind students to look for the Word Blasts as they read the *IMPACT Explorer Magazine.*

▶ Digital Tools

Blended Learning
Students investigate Magazine content in video format.

ePresentation

Use the **IMPACT Explorations Video**.

Extend Knowledge Building

The **IMPACT Explorer Magazine** provides students another route to explore each chapter's Essential Question from a variety of perspectives as they dig deeper into the subject of the relationship between people and the environment. Additional questions and activities help students develop and deepen their understanding of the chapter's content.

Engage

Build background for students and share any information needed to provide a context for the chapter topic. Read aloud the Essential Question and the Table of Contents.

Analyze the Visual Discuss the opening visual (photograph, photo essay, artwork) on the second page of the **IMPACT Explorer Magazine** chapter. Help students connect the visual to the chapter topic and the Essential Question.

Analyze the Sources

Students will read and analyze the leveled informational articles and literary texts, graphic texts, primary and secondary sources, photographs, maps, and other visual resources.

Read and Analyze Before reading, provide any additional information about the topics you think students will need. Then guide students through the three-step process to read and analyze the content.

1 Inspect

Have students skim the content on a page or multiple pages. Ask questions to help students recall and retell key ideas.

- What is this article mostly about?
- Who is _____?

2 Find Evidence

Have students reread the content and look for details they might have missed. Ask additional questions to help them read more closely.

- What details do you notice in the photographs?
- Why was _____ important?

3 Make Connections

Have students work in pairs or small groups to discuss prompts that help them connect the articles to other texts, their own lives, current ideas and issues, and other topics.

- How is _____ similar to what we do?
- How do you think _____ felt about what happened?
- What do you think about _____?

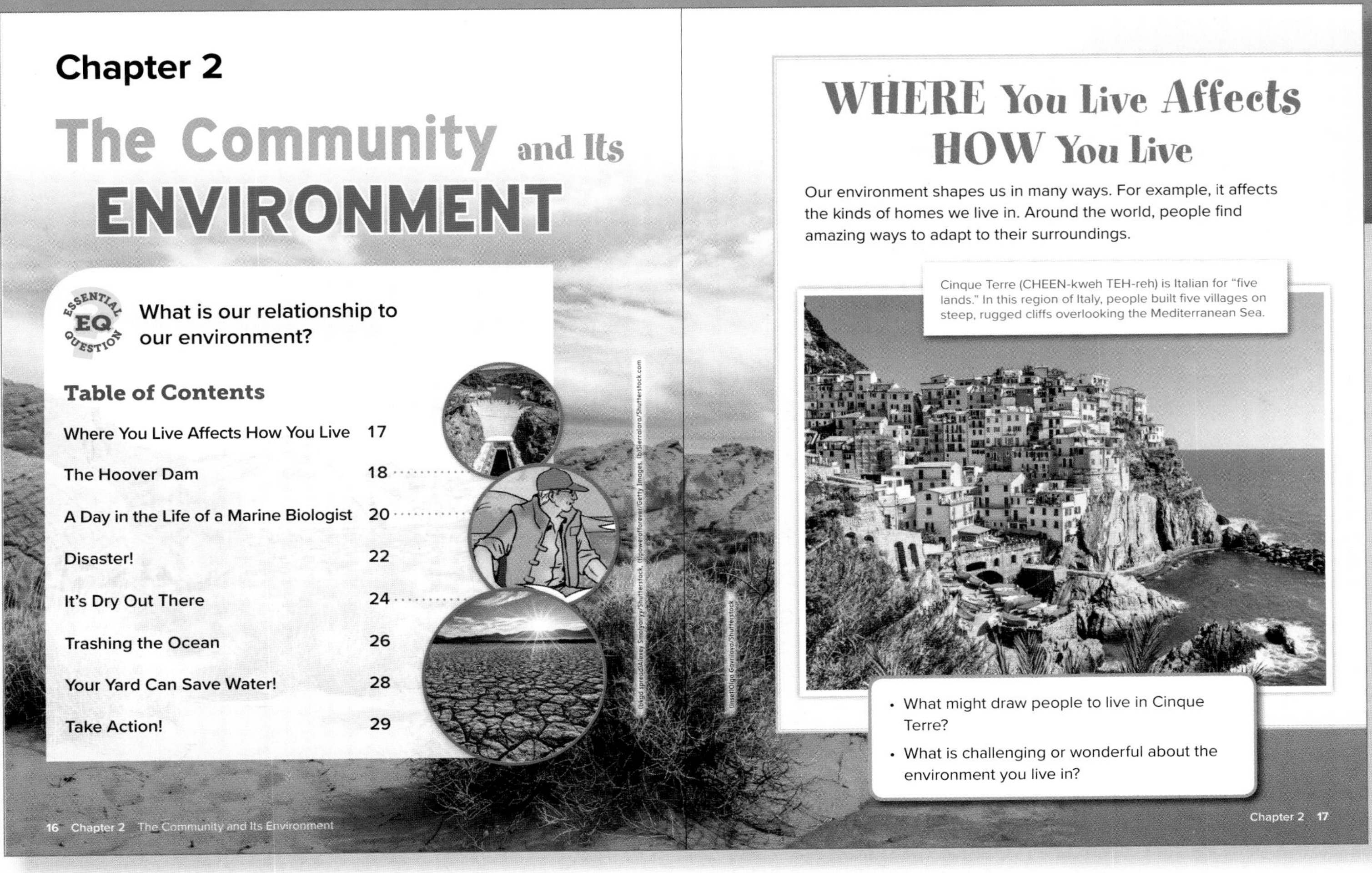

Chapter 2

The Community and Its ENVIRONMENT

ESSENTIAL QUESTION EQ What is our relationship to our environment?

Table of Contents

WHERE You Live Affects HOW You Live

Our environment shapes us in many ways. For example, it affects the kinds of homes we live in. Around the world, people find amazing ways to adapt to their surroundings.

Cinque Terre (CHEEN-kweh TEH-reh) is Italian for "five lands." In this region of Italy, people built five villages on steep, rugged cliffs overlooking the Mediterranean Sea.

- What might draw people to live in Cinque Terre?
- What is challenging or wonderful about the environment you live in?

IMPACT EXPLORER MAGAZINE, pp. 16–29

How to Use IMPACT Explorer Magazine

Use the following scaffolds to support students' understanding and your classroom needs.

Whole Class

Use the **IMPACT Explorer Magazine** Teaching Guide to read and discuss one or more articles with the whole class.

Small Group

Have partners or small groups read articles connected to the day's core lesson and report back to the whole class about what they read.

Independent Work

Assign articles for students to extend and enrich their understanding of a topic, including during Center Time and Independent Reading time.

The online **IMPACT Explorer Magazine** Teaching Guide provides support for various implementation models as well as a three-step lesson plan for each article. The lesson plan includes background information, meaningful questions, vocabulary activities, scaffolded support for English learners, and collaborative conversation prompts.

Digital Tools

Blended Learning

Students extend the investigation of the Chapter Essential Question with highly-visual, leveled articles and video.

eBook

Use the **IMPACT Explorer Magazine eBook** to extend knowledge building.

LESSON QUESTION

How Does the Environment Change the Way People Live?

 EQ ESSENTIAL QUESTION

Connect to the Essential Question

Tell students that this lesson provides key research into the Chapter Essential Question: **What Is Our Relationship to Our Environment?** Explain that they will learn how people adapt to their environment. Tell them they will explore how people's homes and daily activities are shaped by the climates and landscapes around them.

Lesson Objectives

- **Compare** how people adapted to their environments with and without modern technology.
- **Explain** how cultures are shaped by the land and climate around them.
- **Identify** how technology helps people today adapt to their surroundings.
- **Write** a list of natural resources from the student's own region and how they can be used.

Make Connections!

CONNECT TO ELA

Reading **Determine** the meaning of words and phrases as they are used in a text, distinguishing literal from nonliteral language.

Research **Recall** information from experiences or gather information from print and digital resources; take brief notes on sources and sort evidence into provided categories.

Writing **Craft** informative/explanatory texts to examine a topic and convey ideas and information clearly.

Speaking and Listening **Engage** effectively in a range of collaborative discussions with diverse partners on grade 3 topics and texts, building on others' ideas and expressing students' own ideas clearly.

COMMUNITY CONNECTIONS

To further students' understanding of how communities are affected by their environments, have them research what their local government does to adapt to the environment in their community. Have students research the websites of local agencies, or invite a local official to talk about public resources such as snowplows, tree trimmers, lawnmowers, and fire trucks and how they are used to aid the public.

Lesson-At-A-Glance

1 ENGAGE — INQUIRY JOURNAL

pp. 58–63

▶ **Talk About It:** Primary Source by **Jane Dumas**

▶ **Analyze the Source:** Using Natural Resources: Then and Now

▶ **Inquiry Tools:** Explore Making Inferences

2 INVESTIGATE — RESEARCH COMPANION

pp. 66–71

▶ **How Native Americans Adapted to Their Environment**

▶ **How People Today Adapt to Their Environment**

▶ **How Cambodian Rice Farmers Adapt to Their Environment**

3 REPORT — INQUIRY JOURNAL

pp. 64–65

▶ **Think About It**

▶ **Write About It:** Write a List; Identify Natural Resources

▶ **Talk About It**

 ▶ **Connect to the Essential Question**

ASSESSMENT

▶ **Online Lesson Test**

▶ **Printable Lesson Test**

For more details, see pages T106–T107.

▶ Digital Tools

at **my.mheducation.com**

ePresentation

Teach the Engage, Investigate, and Report content to the whole class from **ePresentations** that launch directly from the lesson dashboard.

eBook

You can flip your instruction with the **IMPACT eBooks** found on your lesson dashboard.

Interactive IMPACT

Blend in digital content **when you want it** and **where you want it.**

Blended Learning features in the Teacher's Edition highlight ways to connect in-class work with online experiences to enhance learning.

Investigate current events with **IMPACT News.**

Explore domain-based vocabulary with **Explore Words** and **Word Play** vocabulary activities.

pp. 16–29

Go Further with IMPACT Explorer Magazine!

The **IMPACT Explorer Magazine** supports students' exploration of the Essential Question and provides additional resources for the EQ Inquiry Project.

How Does the Environment Change the Way People Live?

Language Objectives

- Use newly acquired content and academic vocabulary to talk and write about how people adapt to their environment.
- Write a list of natural resources that can be used for daily life.
- Recognize and use the irregular past tense verb forms *made* and *was*.

Spanish Cognates

To support Spanish speakers, point out the cognates.

adapt = adaptar

native = nativo

group = grupo

animal = animal

region = región

police = policía

Introduce the Lesson

Set Purpose Explain to students that in this lesson, they will read informational texts to find out how people adapt to their environment.

Access Prior Knowledge Have students think about the communities and regions they studied in Chapter 1. Have them work with a partner to list characteristics of a community. Then have two pairs share their ideas with each other. Review ideas as a class. Be sure to discuss climate, land formations, water, and natural resources. Then ask students to describe important characteristics of their own community.

Spark Curiosity Have students study the photograph on p. 67 of the Research Companion. Explain that the word *cattails* refers to a plant that looks like a cat's tail. Encourage students to describe the environment they see in the photo. Ask: *What do you think is happening here? How are the people in the photo using or adapting to their environment?* (Native Americans are traveling on water in a boat made of cattails, using poles maybe made of wood. They might be going to fish.)

  Have groups of four students with different language proficiency levels brainstorm ways they travel in their own lives. Have them compare what they know about boats to the type of boat shown (type of construction, how the boat is moved, and so on).

Build Meaning & Support Language

Inquiry Journal

Analyze the Source (pages 60–61) Unpack the sentence: *Even though today's tools are different from long ago, people still adapt to their environment by using the land around them.* Tell students that the phrase *even though* means the same as *though* or *although* and is used to introduce the clause *today's tools are different.* Explain that *even though* is used to point out that while some things might be different, there are still similarities. Ask: *What does this sentence tell us is different and what does it tell us is the same?* (The tools are different, but people still adapt to their environment.) Ask students how the photos on page 61 support the information in the sentence.

Inquiry Tools (pages 62–63) Tell students they will use what they know about **Making Inferences** as they read about how the environment changes the way people live. Review the four steps with students and clarify any words or phrases as needed. Remind students that in order to make an inference, we use information from the text and what we already know about something. Explain that the chart on p. 63 will help them organize information to make inferences as they read. If necessary, show students how to enter text in the left column that supports their inference in the right column.

Research Companion

How Native Americans Adapted to Their Environment (pages 66–67) As you read, explain any words that students don't know. In the first paragraph on page 66, explain that *adapted* means "changed your ways." Ask: *From what environments did Native Americans get their food?* (rivers, forests, fields, deserts) In the second paragraph, explain that *bodies of water* can be used to refer to such things as rivers, ponds, lakes, or oceans. Ask: *How did Native Americans use water?* (travel, trade, food source) *How did they use forests?* (materials for homes, baskets, wood for fires, food source) Discuss the different ways they could use the animals they hunted. (food, clothes, tools) Then help students summarize the different ways that Native Americans adapted to their environment.

How People Today Adapt to Their Environment (pages 68–69) As you read page 68, explain that *suit* means "to be a good match for." Ask students how the homes in the Northeast "suit" the climate there. Compare the types of homes described, and clarify words such as *steep roofs, snow, stormy, stilts*, and *flood* as needed. Ask: *How does technology change the way people eat?* (variety of food, food from other regions) Discuss examples. Read p. 69 and discuss how climate affects the clothing people wear. Ask students how the climate where they live determines the type of clothing they wear and how the clothing they wear changes with the climate.

How Cambodian Rice Farmers Adapt to Their Environment (pages 70–71) Read the first paragraph on p. 70. Help students identify the things needed to grow rice. (warm weather, sunlight, soil, water) Clarify key words such as *challenges, water buffalo, harvest, grain*, and *stalks* as needed. Read the second paragraph aloud and say: *Describe the work of rice farmers.* (They use water buffalo, work by hand, separate grain from stalk, and work hard.) Read the last paragraph on p. 71. Ask students to tell what happens if there is not enough rain.

Inquiry Journal

Report Your Findings (pages 64–65) Have students work in pairs to brainstorm resources from their environment they could use for food, shelter, tools, and transportation. Then have students write a list of natural resources with details about how they would use them. Invite partners to discuss their lists. Have them discuss how people may have used these resources in the past and how people have adapted their food, shelter, tools, and transportation because of new technology.

Language Forms & Conventions

Irregular Past-Tense Forms Explain that many verbs that we use to talk about things that happened in the past end in *-ed*. Use examples from the first paragraph on p. 66: *lived, adapted, used*, and *provided*. Help students understand and use verbs that have irregular past-tense forms. Use the chart below to teach some irregular past-tense verbs.

Present	Past
make	made
build	built
go	went
hear	heard
make	made
see	saw
think	thought

Cross-Cultural Connection

The native people of Mexico domesticated corn about ten thousand years ago, and Native Americans introduced it to European colonists. Today, Latin Americans use it to make masa, a kind of dough used in tortillas and tamales. In the United States, corn is also boiled, roasted on the cob, creamed, or made into hominy, puddings, polenta, cornbread, or scrapple—depending on where you live. Ask: *Do you eat corn? How does your family use/cook corn?*

Leveled Support

Entering & Emerging
Provide sentence frames to help students describe resources: _____ *is a resource we use today for _____. In the past, people used _____.*

Developing & Expanding
Ask: *What resources do people use today to build homes? What resources did people use in the past?*

Bridging & Reaching
Have partners write a paragraph describing the reason a resource is used differently today than it was in the past.

Language Transfer

It is common for students to use incorrect past-tense verb forms by overgeneralizing the use of the *-ed* ending. Introduce appropriate forms when hearing words such as *heared* (heard), *goed* (went), or *maked* (made) by restating the student's idea using the correct verb form.

LESSON 1 ENGAGE

How Does the Environment Change the Way People Live?

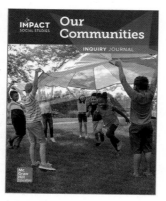

**INQUIRY JOURNAL,
pp. 58–59**

Bellringer

Prompt students to think about tools they need in the classroom to do their work. Ask: *What kinds of resources do you need to help you learn in school?* (pencils, paper, computers, and books; resources to help read, write, do activities) Say: *Communities need resources to live. What are some resources they need?* (Answers will vary but should include food, water, and materials to build homes.)

Lesson Outcomes

Discuss the lesson question and lesson outcomes with students.

- Make sure that students understand the word *environment*. This word includes both the physical landscape in which people live as well as the climate.

- Have students list a few features of their environment that impact them. These might include temperature, amount of rainfall, and whether the landscape is flat or mountainous.

Talk About It

Guide students to look at the photograph and read the selection by Jane Dumas. Discuss the questions in the Talk About It box:

- What does Dumas say the willow tree provides for people? (clothes, wood for homes, aspirin) Explain that aspirin, a pain medication, contains an ingredient that comes from willow bark.

- What are some other things we get from plants? (fruit, vegetables, other medicines, cotton, linen, oils)

Point out to students that they encounter things made from plants every day. These include more than food. They include desks made of wood, clothes made of cotton, paper made of wood pulp, and so on.

 ## Collaborative Conversations

Activate Prior Knowledge Have students discuss the following questions as a group. Remind them to engage with each other in a respectful way. This includes letting others finish their statements before they begin theirs.

- What are some things in our environment, such as climate, land, and water, that determine the way we live?

- How might those things have been more difficult to deal with one hundred years ago than they are today?

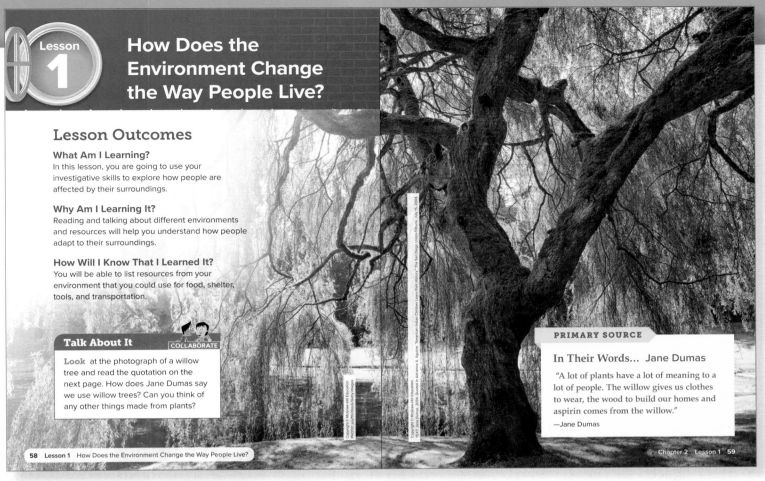

Lesson 1

How Does the Environment Change the Way People Live?

Lesson Outcomes

What Am I Learning?
In this lesson, you are going to use your investigative skills to explore how people are affected by their surroundings.

Why Am I Learning It?
Reading and talking about different environments and resources will help you understand how people adapt to their surroundings.

How Will I Know That I Learned It?
You will be able to list resources from your environment that you could use for food, shelter, tools, and transportation.

Talk About It COLLABORATE

Look at the photograph of a willow tree and read the quotation on the next page. How does Jane Dumas say we use willow trees? Can you think of any other things made from plants?

PRIMARY SOURCE

In Their Words... Jane Dumas

"A lot of plants have a lot of meaning to a lot of people. The willow gives us clothes to wear, the wood to build our homes and aspirin comes from the willow."
—Jane Dumas

58 Lesson 1 How Does the Environment Change the Way People Live?

Chapter 2 Lesson 1 59

INQUIRY JOURNAL, pp. 58–59

English Learners SCAFFOLD

Use the following scaffolds to support student understanding of lesson outcomes.

Entering and Emerging

Read the quotation from Jane Dumas. Provide sentence frames to help students talk about how plants are used in everyday life:

- Plants give us _____ and _____.
- We use plants for _____.
- We eat _____ from plants/trees.

Developing and Expanding

Have small groups read the quote and identify other ways we depend on plants in our lives. Ask: *What are some plants that you depend on every day? How would your life be different if you could not use these plants?* Have groups write their responses and share with another group.

Bridging and Reaching

Have partners think about different plants that they depend on in their daily lives and the kinds of resources they get from those plants. Then have them use a two-column chart to make a list of three to five of these plants and the resources each plant provides.

Social Emotional Learning

Social Awareness

Build Empathy To develop empathy, students should be encouraged to think about how others have lived in environments other than their own. Ask: *What do you think it would be like to live in a desert? How would that life be challenging?*

 Digital Tools

Blended Learning

Students engage with the lesson question and discussion prompts.

ePresentation

Discuss the **Lesson Question** and **Talk About It** with the whole class.

1 Inspect

Look Compare the two images. What do you think this text will be about?

Circle words that tell when something happened or is happening.

Underline clues that tell you:

- for what purposes people use natural resources
- how people gathered seeds long ago
- how people can harvest seeds now

My Notes

_____

_____

_____

_____

_____

_____

_____

Using Natural Resources: Then and Now

Long ago, Native Americans adapted to their environment. Their food, shelter, transportation, and tools were shaped by the natural resources around them. They learned which plants were safe to eat and how to gather them. They knew how to fish and hunt.

Today, people still adapt to their environment. We also use natural resources for food, shelter, transportation, and tools. Modern **technology** has changed the way we use our resources, though. Farmers use modern tools to plant, irrigate, and harvest crops.

Before modern machines, people gathered seeds by hand. They had to separate the seeds from the rest of the plant. Then they had to remove the hard shells from the seeds. It took a long time and a lot of work to produce a small amount of edible seeds.

Instead of harvesting seeds by hand, farmers now use powerful machines. This seed harvester automatically picks, separates, and cleans the seeds. It can harvest more than three bushels of seeds per second!

Even though today's tools are different from long ago, people still adapt to their environment by using the land around them.

A Native American woman gathering seeds

A modern seed harvesting machine

2 Find Evidence

Look The photo shows a woman gathering seeds. How is she using the resources around her? What can you tell about the tools she is using?

3 Make Connections

Talk What are the differences between using machinery to harvest seeds and harvesting seeds by hand? Why do you think using machines is more important today than it was 150 years ago?

INQUIRY JOURNAL, pp. 60–61

Analyze the Source

1 Inspect

Look Have students read the text and study the photographs on pp. 60–61. Remind them to circle words that tell when something has happened or is happening.

- Underline clues about natural resources. (Natural resources are used for food, shelter, transportation, and tools. People used to gather seeds by hand; now they use machines.)

- Have students look closely at the two photographs and identify what they have in common. (Both show a method of harvesting.)

2 Find Evidence

Look Tell students that the photograph of the woman is a historical artifact. When analyzing an artifact, they should look very closely at the details. Have students describe the tools the woman is using and how they think these helped her in gathering seeds.

3 Make Connections

Collaborate Have students work in pairs to discuss other examples of how technology lets us access natural resources today more easily than people could in the past. Have them consider such things as bringing water, heat, and light to our homes. (Examples will vary but may include such things as running water provided by a municipality, central heat, and electricity.)

Spotlight on Language

Academic Language

Have students use context to find synonyms for *technology* as used in the text. "Modern *technology* has changed the way we . . . "

Explore Making Inferences

When you read, you often **make inferences** about the text. An **inference** is a decision you make about the meaning of the text. To make an inference:

1. **Read the text once all the way through.**
   This will help you understand what the text is about.

2. **Think about what you read.**
   An author may not always tell you everything. What questions do you have?

3. **Think about what you already know about this topic.**

4. **Make a decision about the text.**
   Base your decision on what you know and what you read.

Based on the text you read, work with your class to complete the chart below.

Text Clues and What I Already Know	Inferences
It took a long time and a lot of work to produce a small amount of edible seeds. I know: Answers will vary, but students may know that many people have a limited amount of time to do a lot of work.	This text means: Answers will vary, but students should understand that using machines to gather seeds might allow people to do other activities that take time and work.

 Investigate!

Read pages 66–71 in your Research Companion. Use your investigative skills to look for text evidence that tells you how people adapt to their environment. This chart will help you organize your notes.

Text Clues and What I Already Know	Inferences
In different regions, Native Americans made boats out of tall grasses, hollowed-out tree trunks, or animal skins. I know: Answers will vary, but students should understand that objects can be made out of natural resources found in the environment.	This text means: Answers will vary, but students should infer that Native Americans used natural resources found in their environment to build their boats.
People in New York can buy potatoes from Idaho and oranges from Florida. I know: Answers will vary, but students may know that the food they eat comes from many different places.	This text means: Answers will vary, but students should infer that because of transportation and technology, people have food from different places more available to them.
The photograph shows a house on stilts and the tells about houses with steep roofs. I know. Answers will vary, but students may know that houses are built in different ways.	The photo and text mean: Answers will vary, but students should infer that building houses in a way that meets a challenge in the environment is one example of how people adapt to their environment.

INQUIRY JOURNAL, pp. 62–63

Inquiry Tools

Explore Making Inferences

Read Discuss with students the steps involved in making an inference. Point out that making an inference requires them to think closely about what they have read. In other words, they will not be able to *find* an inference while reading a text—they have to look at the information in the text and draw a conclusion using that information. If they already know something about the topic, they can use that information, too.

Guide Practice Have students review the text and captions on pp. 60–61. Then work with students to complete the graphic organizer on p. 62. Explain that they will use a similar organizer to organize their independent research.

Check Understanding Confirm understanding of the inquiry skill, Making Inferences. If students cannot generate inferences from the text, review the steps on p. 62.

Investigate!

Have students read pp. 66–71 in the Research Companion. Tell them the information will help them answer the lesson question *How Does the Environment Change the Way People Live?*

Take Notes Tell students they should use the graphic organizer on p. 63 of the Inquiry Journal to take notes on how different people have adapted to their environments throughout history. Explain that they should gather relevant information that will help them make inferences about how people adapt to their environments.

 Spotlight on Content

Scanning for Information
Point out language that introduces a fact an an inference. As an example, compare a fact about Venice to an inference about living there. Then have students scan the text in the Research Companion for language that indicates a fact or inference.

 Digital Tools

Blended Learning
Students prepare for the lesson investigation with step-by-step instruction about how to make inferences.

ePresentation
Use the **Inquiry Tools** to model and complete the lesson graphic organizer.

LESSON 1 INVESTIGATE

How Does the Environment Change the Way People Live?

RESEARCH COMPANION, pp. 66–67

How Native Americans Adapted to Their Environment

1 Inspect Have students read p. 66 and provide examples of how Native Americans used the environment around them.

2 Find Evidence Use the questions below to check comprehension. Remind students to support their answers with text evidence.

Infer Why did Native American groups throughout the United States wear different kinds of clothes and eat different foods? (Each region had its own environment and resources. People used the resources that were available to them.) **DOK 3**

Infer Why were water resources important for Native American groups? (Life was dependent on water. Without water, there were fewer resources for food. Travel and trade might have been easier and quicker for groups who lived near a body of water.) **DOK 3**

3 Make Connections

Analyze Visuals Look carefully at the size and depth of the boat in the picture on p. 67. Where and how do you think this boat was used? (Answers will vary, but students should point out that it was probably used for hunting or fishing on calm bodies of water.) **DOK 3**

Infer What else can you infer about these Native Americans from the image? (They used the water to travel and maybe for fishing. It looks like their clothes were made from animal skins.) **DOK 3**

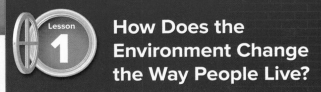

Lesson 1

How Does the Environment Change the Way People Live?

How Native Americans Adapted to Their Environment

For thousands of years, Native Americans lived in different regions of the United States. Each group adapted to its environment and used the resources around it. Groups made clothes to suit the climates where they lived. They used nearby resources to build homes and make tools. The rivers, forests, fields, and deserts provided food.

Groups that lived near bodies of water used that water in many ways. It allowed for travel and trade between villages. Native Americans made boats out of tall grasses, hollowed-out tree trunks, or animal skins. The water was also a source of food. It provided fish, clams, oysters, ducks, and geese. Some Native American groups learned how to preserve fish so they would have food to eat in the winter.

Forests provided Native Americans with vegetation, such as trees, plants, and grasses. These could be used to build homes and weave baskets. People burned wood to cook and to keep warm. Women gathered nuts, berries, and roots in the forest. Men hunted animals for food, clothes, and tools.

A Native American boat made of cattails

66 Lesson 1 How Does the Environment Change the Way People Live?

Chapter 2 Lesson 1 67

RESEARCH COMPANION, pp. 66–67

English Learners SCAFFOLD

Use the following scaffolds to support student understanding of the lesson content.

Entering and Emerging

Help students talk about how Native Americans adapted to their environment. Provide sentence frames:

- Native Americans who lived near water used the water for _____.
- Native Americans who lived near forests used _____ for _____.

Developing and Expanding

Have students describe how Native Americans adapted to their environment. Ask: *How did Native Americans who lived near bodies of water use that water to live? What resources did Native Americans who lived near forests use for everyday life?*

Bridging and Reaching

Have partners make a list of environmental factors that affected Native Americans' lives. (Lists will vary but might include factors such as temperature, rainfall, amount of sunshine, severe weather, landscape, soil quality, and so on.) Ask: *How did the location of different Native American groups affect what they ate and what they did?*

 Digital Tools

Blended Learning
Flip the research approach and find evidence in a digital format.

eBook

Students investigate using their **Research Companion** and **IMPACT Explorer Magazine eBooks** to find evidence.

How People Today Adapt to Their Environment

People today still adapt to their environment. They build homes to suit the climates in their regions. In the Northeast, houses have steep roofs that let snow slip off. The Southeast can be stormy. Some homes there are built on stilts to keep them dry during floods. Modern **technology** lets us heat and cool our homes.

Technology also lets us enjoy foods from outside our region. People in New York can buy potatoes from Idaho or oranges from Florida. This kind of trade means we have more variety in our diets than people did long ago. People still celebrate food from their local region though.

Mississippi homes built on stilts to protect them from floodwaters

Did You Know?

Every summer, the city of Traverse City, Michigan, holds the National Cherry Festival. A parade, concerts, events, and awards all celebrate this local food favorite that is a major crop in Michigan. In fact, Michigan produces over 100,000 tons of cherries per year!

People also adapt their clothing to their climate. In hot, sunny regions, people wear shorts and short-sleeved shirts. They use light fabrics to make clothes. They also use sunglasses and sunscreen. In regions with colder climates, people bundle up in warm, heavy clothing. They wear jeans and sweaters. To go outside, they might add boots, hats, gloves, and even snow pants. People often wear one type of clothing in summer and another type in winter.

People in cold climates must adapt to their environment in the way they dress.

Around the World

Venice, Italy, is an island city built on a lagoon. Instead of cars and roads, people use boats to travel the many canals. Boats are even used as public buses and police vehicles. The lagoon brings tourists to Venice. It also supplies fish and salt to the city. However, people have to monitor the lagoon carefully and deal with flooding.

✓ Stop and Check

Talk What are some of the ways people adapt to bodies of water in their environment?

68   Lesson 1   How Does the Environment Change the Way People Live?

Chapter 2   Lesson 1   69

RESEARCH COMPANION, pp. 68–69

How People Today Adapt to Their Environment

1 Inspect Have students read pp. 68–69 and explain how technology has helped people adapt to their environment.

2 Find Evidence Use the questions below to check comprehension.

Summarize How have people adapted their homes to the environment in which they live? (People who live in cold climates build their homes so that snow can slide off the roofs. In areas that flood, they sometimes build their homes on stilts.) **DOK 2**

Explain Think about the environment where you live. How does the climate help you decide what clothes to wear? (Answers will vary, but students should explain that they dress for the weather.) **DOK 3**

3 Make Connections

Apply Concepts How has technology impacted what we wear in cold and hot climates? (Answers will vary, but students might suggest the development of fabric that is cooler and protects against UV rays, clothing that is warmer but not heavy, sunglasses that better protect our eyes, and waterproof clothing.) **DOK 3**

✓ Stop and Check

Talk Students should think about how people interact with water. (Answers will vary, but students may mention transportation, structures, industries, food, and recreation.)

Spotlight on Vocabulary

Content Vocabulary

technology: tools or devices that help us do things

▶ Digital Tools

Blended Learning

Students explore lesson content through interactive activities.

Interactive IMPACT

Use the **More to Explore.**

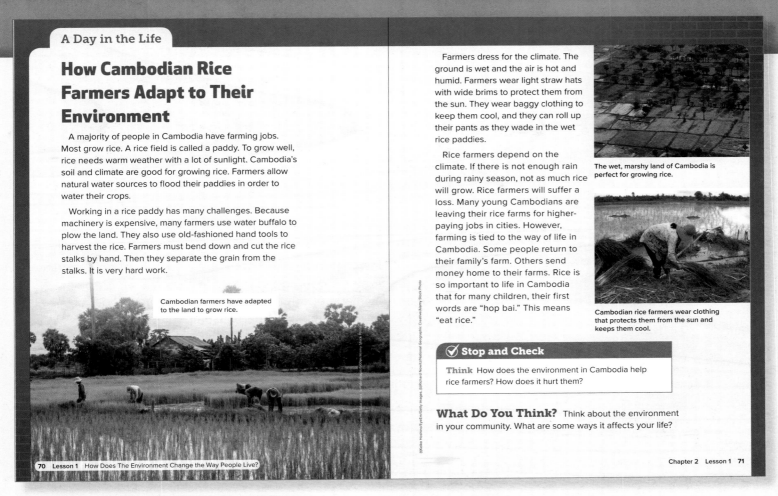

A Day in the Life

How Cambodian Rice Farmers Adapt to Their Environment

A majority of people in Cambodia have farming jobs. Most grow rice. A rice field is called a paddy. To grow well, rice needs warm weather with a lot of sunlight. Cambodia's soil and climate are good for growing rice. Farmers allow natural water sources to flood their paddies in order to water their crops.

Working in a rice paddy has many challenges. Because machinery is expensive, many farmers use water buffalo to plow the land. They also use old-fashioned hand tools to harvest the rice. Farmers must bend down and cut the rice stalks by hand. Then they separate the grain from the stalks. It is very hard work.

Cambodian farmers have adapted to the land to grow rice.

Farmers dress for the climate. The ground is wet and the air is hot and humid. Farmers wear light straw hats with wide brims to protect them from the sun. They wear baggy clothing to keep them cool, and they can roll up their pants as they wade in the wet rice paddies.

Rice farmers depend on the climate. If there is not enough rain during rainy season, not as much rice will grow. Rice farmers will suffer a loss. Many young Cambodians are leaving their rice farms for higher-paying jobs in cities. However, farming is tied to the way of life in Cambodia. Some people return to their family's farm. Others send money home to their farms. Rice is so important to life in Cambodia that for many children, their first words are "hop bai." This means "eat rice."

The wet, marshy land of Cambodia is perfect for growing rice.

Cambodian rice farmers wear clothing that protects them from the sun and keeps them cool.

✓ Stop and Check

Think How does the environment in Cambodia help rice farmers? How does it hurt them?

What Do You Think? Think about the environment in your community. What are some ways it affects your life?

RESEARCH COMPANION, pp. 70–71

How Cambodian Rice Farmers Adapt to Their Environment

1 Inspect Have students read pp. 70–71 and describe the climate in Cambodia.

2 Find Evidence Use the questions below to check comprehension.

Compare How would you compare your environment to the one in Cambodia? (Students should include a description of both environments.) **DOK 2**

Explain How do Cambodian farmers dress in order to adapt to their environment? (They wear light straw hats to protect them from the sun. Baggy clothes help them stay cool. They roll up their pants when the fields are wet.) **DOK 3**

3 Make Connections

Draw Conclusions What do you think would happen to farmers if the climate in Cambodia changed permanently and it was no longer rainy? (Farmers would no longer be able to grow rice the way they have been.) **DOK 3**

✓ Stop and Check

Think Students should find specific evidence to support their answers. (Answers will vary, but students might mention the climate and soil as being helpful, while a lack of rain could result in losses for the farmers.)

What Do You Think? Think about the environment in your community. What are some ways it affects your life? (Answers will vary but students should describe their environment and clearly connect how it affects them)

✔ Check for Success

Explain Can students explain how the environment shapes people's actions and behaviors?

Differentiate

If Not, Have students review the inferences they drew about the environment and people's behavior from their notes in their Inquiry Journals.

LESSON 1 REPORT

LESSON QUESTION

How Does the Environment Change the Way People Live?

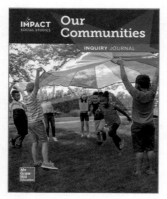

INQUIRY JOURNAL, pp. 64–65

Think About It

Reflect Remind students to review their notes and to think about how people around the world adapt to their environments. Encourage students to review their graphic organizers and the inferences they made about the subject. If students need more information, have them review pp. 66–71 of the Research Companion.

Write About It

Identify Remind students to include the following elements in their lists.

- Identify details about their region's land and climate and available natural resources.
- Decide which natural resources would be most useful for food, shelter, tools, and transportation.
- Use chapter vocabulary as appropriate.

Discipline(s)	4	3	2	1
Geography	Student provides a list of natural resources from the region that would be useful for food, shelter, tools, and transportation.	Student provides a list of natural resources from the region, some of which would be useful for the needs listed.	Student provides a list of natural resources, some of which are available and some of which would be useful.	Student does not provide a list of available and useful resources.

Talk About It COLLABORATE

Consider Different Ideas Suggest that students share their full lists with their partners before discussing them. This will show them the similarities and differences in their lists.

Assessment Students can check their understanding with feedback from the **Lesson Test** available online.

Connect to the Essential Question

Explain Before students respond, have them think about what it must have been like to live in their region two hundred years ago. How does it compare to today? Have them think about the forms of technology they have now that were not available then. If needed, have students return to p. 68 in the Research Companion to review the information about technology.

Inquiry Project Update Remind students to turn to Inquiry Journal pp. 54–55 for project information. If necessary, review the Project Checklist with students. At this point in the chapter, students should focus on the first two items on the checklist.

Think About It

Reflect

Imagine that there are no stores to buy things. What resources from your environment would you use for food, shelter, tools, and transportation in the region where you live?

Write About It

Identify

Write a list telling which natural resources from your region you would use for food, shelter, tools, and transportation.

Answers will vary but should include at least one example for each need: food, shelter, tools, and transportation.

Talk About It

Consider Different Ideas

Share your list with a partner. How do your ideas for using natural resources differ?

Economics **Connect to the EQ**

Explain

How has technology changed the way people adapt to the environment?

Answers will vary but should somehow mention the use of technology, whether it be machinery, such as farming equipment, or electronics, such as computers and the Internet.

EQ Inquiry Project Notes

64 **Lesson 1** How Does the Environment Change the Way People Live?

Chapter 2 **Lesson 1** 65

INQUIRY JOURNAL, pp. 64–65

English Learners SCAFFOLD

Use the following scaffolds to support student writing.

Entering and Emerging

Have students think about resources from their region that they use or need every day. Be prepared to give examples. Provide sentence frames as needed:

- My region has _____ that I can use for food.
- I can use _____ from my region to build a shelter.
- For transportation, I can use _____ found in my region.
- I can make tools from _____ resources in my region.

Developing and Expanding

Explain that natural resources are things that are found in nature that can be used to live. Ask: *What are some natural resources available in your community or region?* (Answers will vary but might include good soil, clean water, forests, and mountains.) *Which of these natural resources could you use for food? Which could you use for shelter? Which could you use to make tools? How would you use natural resources for transportation?*

Bridging and Reaching

Have partners discuss ways people used natural resources in the past. Guide them to create a list of the natural resources found in their community or region today. Then have them explain how they would use each resource for food, shelter, tools, or transportation.

✔ Check for Success

Identify Can students create a list of natural resources from their region? Can they think of resources that could be used as food, shelter, tools, and transportation?

Differentiate

If Not, Have students present their information in another way, such as in a collage, or with examples brought in as part of an oral presentation.

LESSON QUESTION

How Do People Change Their Environment?

Connect to the Essential Question

Tell students that this lesson provides key research into the Chapter Essential Question: **What Is Our Relationship With Our Environment?** Explain that they will learn why and how communities in the past and present have changed their environment. They will also examine and evaluate the consequences of some of those changes to better understand the relationship between people and the world around them.

Lesson Objectives

- **Explain** how and why people change the environment.
- **Identify** ways human activities impact the environment.
- **Describe** the consequences and benefits of environmental changes.
- **Write** an informational paragraph describing the relationship between environmental changes and people.

Make Connections!

CONNECT TO ELA

Reading **Ask and answer** questions to demonstrate understanding of a text and refer explicitly to the text as the basis for the answers.
Use language that pertains to time, sequence, and cause/effect to describe the relationship between a series of historical events, scientific ideas or concepts, or steps in technical procedures in a text.

Research **Recall** information from experiences or gather information from print and digital sources; take brief notes on sources and sort evidence into provided categories.

Writing **Craft** informative/explanatory texts to examine a topic and convey ideas and information clearly.

Speaking and Listening **Engage** effectively in a range of collaborative discussions with diverse partners on grade 3 topics and texts, building on others' ideas and expressing students' own ideas clearly.

COMMUNITY CONNECTIONS

To enrich what students have learned about the effects of human activities on the environment, explore past and present maps of the local community. Challenge students to identify changes in the community over time. Ask them to detail how human developments like roads, bridges, buildings, and even parks and playgrounds changed the natural landscape of the area. Discuss how changes may have affected plant, animal, and human life.

Lesson-At-A-Glance

1 ENGAGE   INQUIRY JOURNAL

pp. 66–71

- ▶ **Talk About It:** Photograph of Erie Canal construction
- ▶ **Analyze the Source:** Changing a Waterway
- ▶ **Inquiry Tools:** Explore Cause and Effect

2 INVESTIGATE   RESEARCH COMPANION

pp. 72–77

- ▶ **How Native Americans Changed Their Land**
- ▶ **How People Today Change the Land**
- ▶ **InfoGraphic: Bringing Water to the Desert**
- ▶ **Unintended Consequences**

3 REPORT   INQUIRY JOURNAL

pp. 72–73

- ▶ **Think About It**
- ▶ **Write About It:** Write an Informational Paragraph; Cite Evidence
- ▶ **Talk About It**
- ▶ **Connect to the Essential Question**

▶ Digital Tools

at **my.mheducation.com**

ePresentation

Teach the Engage, Investigate, and Report content to the whole class from ePresentations that launch directly from the lesson dashboard.

eBook

You can flip your instruction with the **IMPACT eBooks** found on your lesson dashboard.

Interactive IMPACT

Blend in digital content **when you want it** and **where you want it**.

Blended Learning features in the Teacher's Edition highlight ways to connect in-class work with online experiences to enhance learning.

Investigate current events with **IMPACT News**.

Explore domain-based vocabulary with **Explore Words** and **Word Play** vocabulary activities.

ASSESSMENT

- ▶ **Online Lesson Test**
- ▶ **Printable Lesson Test**

For more details, see pages T106–T107.

pp. 16–29

Go Further with IMPACT Explorer Magazine!

The **IMPACT Explorer Magazine** supports students' exploration of the Essential Question and provides additional resources for the EQ Inquiry Project.

How Do People Change Their Environment?

Language Objectives

- Use newly acquired content and academic vocabulary to talk and write about how people change the environment.
- Write a paragraph describing examples of causes of environmental changes and their effects.
- Distinguish the correct meaning of homophone.

Spanish Cognates

To support Spanish speakers, point out the cognates.

community = comunidad

construct = construír

energy = energía

human = humano

control = controlar

generate = generar

Introduce the Lesson

Set Purpose Explain to students that in this lesson, they will read informational texts to learn how people change their environment.

Access Prior Knowledge Have students brainstorm what they have learned about how people use resources from their environment. Have them work in small groups to list what natural resources people use and how they use them. Review ideas as a class. Discuss the use of minerals for tools, wood for fuel and building, bricks from clay for building, grasses to make boats, animals for food and clothes, and water to grow crops. Explain that in this lesson, they will learn how the use of resources changes the environment.

Spark Curiosity Have students study the illustration of the Native American community on page 73 of the Research Companion. Read the caption aloud. Encourage students to describe what they see in the image. Ask: *Where is the man standing?* (on a dam) *How does this help him fish?* (He's closer to the water and the fish.)

Have pairs of students discuss ways they use local resources. Have them think about ways people have adapted to help them access the resources more easily. Suggest that they think about different kinds of machines or technology that helps with this.

Build Meaning & Support Language

Inquiry Journal

Analyze the Source (pages 68–69) Unpack the sentences: *Many people and businesses produced a lot of waste. This waste polluted the Chicago River and flowed into Lake Michigan.* Explain that the waste created by people made the river and lake dirty. Explain that *produced* means "made." Examples of *waste* are trash and garbage. *Polluted* means "made dirty." *Flowed* means "went." Then discuss the cause and effect in the two sentences. If necessary, explain that the actions of people caused a problem of too much waste. The effect was a polluted river and lake. Then have students identify cause and effect in the last paragraph.

Inquiry Tools (pages 70–71) Tell students they will explore Cause and Effect as they read the selections in the Research Companion. Explain that the chart on page 71 will help them record causes and their effects as they read. Say: *On page 72 of the Research Companion, we will read that Native Americans used fire to clear land for farming. The action of setting a fire is the cause, and the effect is that the land is cleared.* Show students how to enter causes in the left column and effects in the right column.

Research Companion

How Native Americans Changed Their Land (pages 72–73) Explain that the word *survive* means "stay alive" and the word *settle* means "stay in one place." Read aloud the first two sentences on page 72. Explain that Native Americans changed their environment. The rest of the paragraph gives examples of change. Describe how fire was used to clear land. Explain that *dammed* means "blocked the water." Ask: *How did Native Americans change their environment?* (cleared land with fire, dammed rivers) *How did this help them obtain food?* (planted crops, fished easily) Clarify key vocabulary such as *canals*, *mud*, *clay*, and *bundles* as you complete the page.

How People Today Change the Land (pages 74–75) Explain that the first paragraph gives examples of how we change the environment today. Preview the words *blast*, *crops*, *raise*, *wind farms*, *power*, and *energy*. Read the paragraph. Ask students what they think "blast through mountains" means. (use explosives to create tunnels or openings in mountains) Read the second paragraph aloud, and explain the meaning of the phrase and words *control the flow*, *dependable*, and *generates*. Discuss with students how the Hoover Dam changed the land and the effects of building this dam. Then review the diagram on page 75 with students and discuss how water is brought to the desert.

Unintended Consequences (pages 76–77) Explain that *unintended consequences* means "unplanned effects." Read the first paragraph on page 76. Explain that in this context, *weigh* means "compare." Ask: *What is affected when people change an ecosystem?* (everything) Preview and clarify key words such as *rapid*, *provide*, *erosion*, and *grazing*. Read the rest of the page. Explain that the phrase *wearing away* means "disappearing." Say: *Describe some effects of changes in the environment.* (loss of habitat, deforestation, changes in the air, erosion) Read the first paragraph on page 77 and discuss how new species affect the environment. Clarify that *extinct* and *endangered* describe the situation for all individuals of a species, not just one animal.

Inquiry Journal

Report Your Findings (pages 72–73) Have students write sentences using the causes and effects they listed in their graphic organizers. Then have them read their sentences to a partner. If their meaning is unclear, have partners ask questions to help clarify the meaning.

Language Forms & Conventions

Homophones Explain that English has different ways to spell the same words. Words that sound the same may be written differently and will have different meanings. Monitor student responses for any misunderstandings that students might have.

Examples from the Reading	Homophones
to	two (2), too (also)
through	threw (tossed)
meet	meat (animal flesh you can eat)
some	sum (total of addition problem)
build	billed (charged)
new	knew (had knowledge of)

 Have pairs find examples of homophones in the text and explain their meaning. Then have them rewrite sentences using synonyms to demonstrate understanding.

Cross-Cultural Connection

Teotihuacán is an ancient city near modern-day Mexico City. It is unknown exactly who built the city, but its structures, which include platforms and pyramids, made a striking change to the existing landscape. Evidence of the use of natural resources includes obsidian tools, clay pottery, metal jewelry, seeds for crops, and the bones of animals used for food. Ask: *Have you ever visited a place and found evidence that it was once something else?*

Leveled Support

Entering & Emerging
Provide sentence frames: People changed _____ in my community. This change caused _____.

Developing & Expanding
Have small groups describe actions people took in their community and how those actions impacted the environment.

Bridging & Reaching
Have partners describe two ways people's actions have changed their community and what the effects of those actions were on their environment.

Language Transfer

It is common for homophones and multiple-meaning words to confuse students. For example, students may know the meaning of the word *foot*, then look for a picture of a foot when they hear the phrase "look at the foot of the page." Identify and clarify words that sound alike but have different meanings.

LESSON 2 ENGAGE

 LESSON QUESTION

How Do People Change Their Environment?

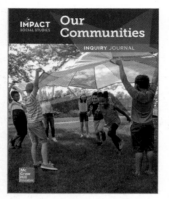

INQUIRY JOURNAL, pp. 66–67

Bellringer

Say: *In this lesson, you will learn how the adaptations that people make to the environment affect it. Think about your community. It did not always look this way. What are some ways people have changed the environment?* Have students discuss their ideas in small groups. (Answers will vary but should include ideas such as clearing land for farming and building, mining and drilling, building roads and bridges, and polluting land, air, and water resources.)

Lesson Outcomes

Discuss the lesson question and lesson outcomes with students.

- Invite volunteers to list things that make up the natural environment.
- Encourage students to think about environmental changes in their own region and community as they learn about ways people have changed the environment in other places.

Talk About It

Have students study the image of the construction of the Erie Canal and read the caption. Ask students to describe what is shown:

- What is happening in this image? (Many people are working on the construction of a canal.)
- How would you describe the people, equipment, and landscape? (many workers, massive equipment, the landscape is being dug up)
- How does this image help answer the lesson question? (It shows one way people change the environment—construction of something new to allow them to do something different or overcome an obstacle.)

 ## Collaborative Conversations

Text-Based Discussions Have students work in pairs to discuss the information conveyed by the image and caption. After they discuss the image, have students discuss events they might know about that changed the landscape in their own region or community. These could include building such things as parks, shopping centers, or housing subdivisions. Then combine pairs to share responses. Provide sentence frames such as the following to help students with their discussion:

- This photograph shows _____.
- The photograph and caption help me understand _____.
- In my community/region, one thing that changed the landscape is _____.

Lesson 2

How Do People Change Their Environment?

The Erie Canal is a human-made waterway in New York. It was completed in 1825. The canal was used for moving people and goods from the Great Lakes to the Atlantic Ocean.

Lesson Outcomes

What Am I Learning?
In this lesson, you are going to use your investigative skills to explore how people have changed the environment to survive and to support their communities.

Why Am I Learning It?
Reading and talking about how people affect the environment will help you understand the relationship between humans, human activity, and plant and animal life.

How Will I Know That I Learned It?
You will be able to write a paragraph describing how people have changed their environment.

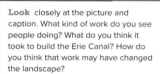

Talk About It   COLLABORATE

Look closely at the picture and caption. What kind of work do you see people doing? What do you think it took to build the Erie Canal? How do you think that work may have changed the landscape?

66   Lesson 2   How Do People Change Their Environment?

Chapter 2 · Lesson 2   67

INQUIRY JOURNAL, pp. 66–67

English Learners SCAFFOLD

Use the following scaffolds to support student understanding of the lesson outcomes.

Entering and Emerging

Explain that the environment includes landforms, waterways, weather conditions, plants, and animals. Read the photo caption and then provide sentence frames to help students describe what is happening in the photo:

- People in the photo are _____.
- They are changing the environment to _____.
- These changes to the environment will also change _____.

Developing and Expanding

Have small groups discuss what *environment* means. Then have them study the photograph and read the caption. Ask: *How are people changing the environment in this image? How do you think these changes will affect the plants and animals that live there? What else might be affected in the environment?*

Bridging and Reaching

Have partners define *environment* and list what makes up an environment. Say: *Natural forces like wind, water, and fire can change the environment. How do people change the environment?* Challenge partners to write a few sentences about what is happening in the photo and how they think people's actions will impact the environment.

Social Emotional Learning

Relationship Skills

Communicate Effectively
Effective discussions are most successful when students take turns speaking (to share their ideas) and listening (to learn others' ideas). Ask students: *How can you show that you are listening? What can you do if you don't understand or you disagree with something?*

Lesson 2   **How Do People Change Their Environment?**   T137

Changing a Waterway

In the 1800s, Chicago grew quickly. Many people and businesses produced a lot of waste. This waste polluted the Chicago River and flowed to Lake Michigan. The lake supplied the city's drinking water. It also supplied fish. Many people started to get sick from the lake water.

People in Chicago wanted to stop pollution from reaching the lake. They decided to reverse, or change the direction of, the Chicago River's flow. To do this, pumps pushed water from the river to a canal. The job was too big for those pumps, though. So workers built a new canal called the Chicago Sanitary and Ship Canal. The Chicago River flowed through this second canal to the Des Plaines River.

The Chicago Sanitary and Ship Canal helped solve one problem but caused others. Fewer people in Chicago got sick, but wastewater flowed to other communities. Reversing the river also meant that water flowed from the Lake Michigan to the Mississippi River. As a result the **habitat**, or home, of plants and animals changed. It also caused new sources of flooding.

The Chicago River was changed so it flows away from its mouth.

INQUIRY JOURNAL, pp. 68–69

Analyze the Source

Background Information

In 1885, a powerful storm raised water levels and flushed the polluted water of the Chicago River into Lake Michigan. To redirect the river, engineers built the Chicago Sanitary and Ship Canal, connecting the southern branch of the Chicago River to the Des Plaines River that feeds into the Illinois River that flows into the Mississippi River. The completed canal stretches nearly thirty miles and has a minimum depth of about nine feet.

1 Inspect

Read Have students read the text and study the image. Remind them to circle the names of natural waterways and to draw a box around the human-made waterway.

2 Find Evidence

Underline Have students skim the text and complete the activity.

Reread Ask student pairs to reread the text and discuss effects of changing waterways. Have students highlight words and phrases that describe the effects.

3 Make Connections

Talk Direct partners to discuss the potential benefits of canals. In their discussion, they should talk about what canals can be used for and how those uses can help people.

Draw Guide students to visualize a part of their community with which they are most familiar. Ask: *What are the human and natural elements of that place?* Have them draw a picture that reflects what they visualize and write a caption describing the human impact.

Spotlight on Language

Understanding Language

waste: In this context, *waste* is a noun meaning "material left over or thrown away, such as garbage or sewage."

reverse: to turn around or move in a different direction

wastewater: water carrying waste like sewage or garbage

▶ Digital Tools

Blended Learning

Students read informational texts and analyze primary sources.

Interactive IMPACT

Have students practice and apply the strategy of close reading as they analyze text.

Explore Cause and Effect

An **effect** is something that happens. A **cause** is why it happens. As you read, look out for something that causes another thing to happen.

1. **Read the text all the way through.**
   This will help you understand what the text is about.

2. **Understand how causes and effects are related.**
   A cause happens before an effect. As you read, look for clue words that tell the order in which the events happened. Sometimes a cause may have many effects.

3. **Watch for words that signal a cause or effect.**
   Words such as *so, since, because,* and *as a result* often indicate a cause-and-effect relationship.

4. **Ask yourself:** *What happened? Why did it happen?*
   The answer to *Why did it happen?* is a cause.

 Based on the text you read, work with your class to complete the chart below.

Cause	Effect
People want a waterway to travel across New York.	New York builds the Erie Canal.
Wastewater from the Chicago River pollutes Lake Michigan.	Chicago decides to reverse the flow of the Chicago River.
Chicago decides to reverse the flow of the Chicago River.	Chicago builds a canal from the Chicago River to the Des Plaines River.

 ## Investigate!

Read pages 72–77 in your Research Companion. Use your investigative skills to look for text evidence that tells you about things that happened (effects) and why they happened (causes). This chart will help you organize your notes.

Answers will vary. Possible answers are provided.

Cause	Effect
Native Americans dam rivers.	They catch more fish.
People clear land.	They change ecosystems and destroy habitats.
The Hoover Dam is built.	Lake Mead is created. Hydroelectric power is provided.
People clear forest lands.	Deforestation spreads.
People dig irrigation canals.	They can live and farm in desert regions.
Habitats are destroyed by development.	Some plants and animals become endangered or extinct.

INQUIRY JOURNAL, pp. 70–71

Inquiry Tools

Explore Cause and Effect

Read Review the definitions of *cause* and *effect*. Discuss with students the step-by-step instructions for finding causes and effects. Ask: *What words or phrases provide clues that you are reading about causes or effects?* (since, because, as a result)

Guide Practice Have students review the text on pp. 68–69. Then work with them to complete the graphic organizer on p. 70. Explain that they will use a similar graphic organizer to organize their independent research.

Check Understanding Confirm understanding of the inquiry skill, Explore Cause and Effect. If students cannot identify and differentiate between causes and effects, review the steps on p. 70.

Investigate!

Have students read pp. 72–77 in the Research Companion. Tell them the information will help them answer the lesson question *How Do People Change Their Environment?*

Take Notes Tell students they should use the graphic organizer on p. 71 of the Inquiry Journal to record causes and effects as they read each section in the Research Companion. Advise students that they will use these notes to write a paragraph explaining how human changes to the environment affect the people that live there.

 ## Spotlight on Content

Understanding Cause and Effect

Draw a cause-and-effect diagram on the board. Demonstrate that causes come *before* effects and effects come *after* causes. You may wish to extend the diagram into a chain to show that effects can also become causes that have new effects.

LESSON 2 INVESTIGATE

LESSON QUESTION

How Do People Change Their Environment?

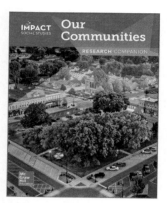

RESEARCH COMPANION, pp. 72–73

Background Information

Humans throughout history have modified the landscape to accommodate their needs.

Early Native American groups studied the natural world to learn ways of survival. They learned fire could be used to clear land; crops could be grown by gathering, planting, and tending seeds; and dams could be built to control the flow of rivers and streams. They learned to use materials from nature like wood, stone, grass, and mud to build shelters just as many animals did.

Over time, people experimented and developed more advanced technologies. The first waterwheels and mills were invented thousands of years ago. They harnessed the power of moving water to grind grains for food.

During the First Industrial Revolution in the 1700s, innovators learned to use massive waterwheels to turn machines in factories that wove textiles. By the end of the 1800s, British and American inventors had developed water turbines and built them into massive dams to turn a river's momentum into electric power.

How Native Americans Changed Their Land

1 Inspect Have students read the text and caption and study the image on pp. 72–73 and explain how Native Americans used their environment to survive.

2 Find Evidence Use the questions below to check comprehension. Remind students to support their answers with evidence from the text.

Explain According to the text, what are some ways that Native Americans changed the environment? (using fires to clear land, building dams, and digging canals) **DOK 2**

Compare and Contrast How are the canals dug by Native Americans similar to and different from the Chicago Sanitary and Ship Canal? (Both types of canals are human-made waterways dug to meet human needs. However, the Chicago Sanitary and Ship Canal was dug to help reverse the flow of a river and protect drinking water from pollution, while the canals dug by Native Americans were dug to carry fresh water to crops for farming.) **DOK 3**

3 Make Connections

Analyze How did the people in the image change their environment in order to build their shelters and the dam? (Answers should include cutting down trees for building materials, clearing land for shelters, and changing the river flow with the dam.) **DOK 3**

Predict What might you expect to happen if people hunted, fished, or gathered too much from one area? (Answers should include that they might run out of animals to hunt and plants to gather. This might force people to go elsewhere to look for food or to find other ways, such as farming, to obtain food.) **DOK 3**

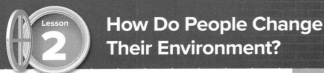

How Do People Change Their Environment?

How Native Americans Changed Their Land

People use the resources around them to survive. When they travel through a place or settle there, they change the environment. In the past, Native Americans changed their environments to meet their needs. They used fires to clear land for building and farming. They dammed rivers to make it easier to catch fish. Both changes provided people with food.

Native Americans in other parts of the country also learned to use resources from their environments. Some hunted animals and gathered wild plants, nuts, seeds, and berries. Others dug canals to bring water to their crops. Some used mud or clay bricks to build homes, while others used wood and bundles of grass.

Wherever Native Americans lived, the environment affected how they lived. They, in turn, affected the land, water, plants, and animals around them.

A Native American community sits beside a river. A man stands on a small dam. He uses a net to catch fish.

72   Lesson 2   How Do People Change Their Environment?

Chapter 2   Lesson 2   73

RESEARCH COMPANION, pp. 72–73

English Learners SCAFFOLD

Use the following scaffolds to support student understanding of the lesson content.

Entering and Emerging

Have students study the image and describe what they see. Guide students to complete the following sentence frames:

- These Native Americans lived near _____.
- They built homes made from _____.
- They dammed rivers to _____.

Developing and Expanding

Have small groups study the image and read the caption. Ask questions to help students describe how Native Americans used the environment to live. Ask: *Where do these Native Americans live? What resources did they use to build their homes? How did they change the environment to get food?*

Bridging and Reaching

Have partners study the image and then describe two causes and effects based on what is shown. If students need help, ask questions similar to these: *What did Native Americans need to survive? What did they do because they needed food/shelter/water? How did the changes to the environment help them survive?*

Digital Tools

Blended Learning
Students explore lesson content through interactive activities.

Interactive IMPACT

Use the **More to Explore**.

How People Today Change the Land

Just as Native Americans cleared lands, dammed rivers, and changed their environments, so do we. Technology has made those changes even bigger. People blast through mountains to build roads and railroads. We cut down forests to build houses and businesses. We plant crops and raise animals on farms. We construct bridges to cross waterways. We build wind farms, **hydroelectric dams,** and other power plants to provide energy. Hydroelectric dams turn the energy of moving water into electric power. Other kinds of dams are used to control flooding or to create human-made lakes. The new lakes provide water for people.

One of the most famous dams in the United States is the Hoover Dam. When it was completed in 1939 it was the world's tallest dam. If you took all the concrete used to build the Hoover Dam, you could pave a highway between New York City and San Francisco. The Hoover Dam controls the flow of the Colorado River. It helps provide a dependable water supply for southern California and Arizona. It also generates enough energy for 1.3 million people in Nevada, Arizona, and California to use.

The Hoover Dam was built on the Colorado River in the 1930s. It created Lake Mead. It also provides electricity.

Bridges make it easier for people to cross waterways.

74 Lesson 2 How Do People Change Their Environment?

InfoGraphic

Bringing Water to the Desert

Water is hard to find in desert regions. To live and work in a desert, people must have water brought to them. Many farms in the Southwest exist because technology brings them water. Canals, or human-made waterways, carry water to irrigate crops. They also provide water for farm animals. How do canals and other types of irrigation in desert areas work?

Water source
A major water source, such as the Colorado River, provides the water.

Canals
Hundreds of miles of canals transport the water to places in the desert.

Pipes
Pipes lead from the canals to the farmers' fields.

Irrigation
Drip and sprinkler irrigation systems water crops, such as vegetables, grains, and fruit trees.

✓ Stop and Check

Compare and Contrast Name one similarity between how early Native Americans affected their environment and how people do so today. Then name one difference.

Find Details As you read, add new information to the graphic organizer on page 71 in your Inquiry Journal.

Chapter 2 Lesson 2 75

RESEARCH COMPANION, pp. 74–75

How People Today Change the Land

1 Inspect Have students read pp. 74–75 and give two examples of how people have changed the land.

2 Find Evidence Use the questions below to check comprehension.

Summarize Why do people make changes to the land? (to enable transportation, to provide food and shelter, to produce electricity or power) **DOK 2**

Explain and Hypothesize What are some benefits of building dams? What are some drawbacks? (Benefits: They can provide electricity and water, control floods, and create lakes; Drawbacks: Students may say that dams can change the ecosystem of a river or that people have to relocate.) **DOK 3**

3 Make Connections

Hypothesize Study the image of the Hoover Dam. How would the land and water look without the dam? (Answers should reflect that the river would flow continually through the canyon, lowering the water level on one side of the dam and raising the water level on the other side.) **DOK 3**

✓ Stop and Check

Compare and Contrast Have students discuss the similarities and differences they identified with a partner. Remind them to use the text when discussing their answers. (Answers may vary, but students should support their answers with text evidence.)

 Spotlight on Vocabulary

Understanding Word Parts

Explain that the prefix *hydro-* means "water." The word *hydroelectric* describes things that generate electricity from moving water.

 Digital Tools

Blended Learning
Students investigate curated resources and find evidence to answer the lesson question.

Interactive IMPACT

Students choose from print or digital **Inquiry Tools** to take notes.

T142 Chapter 2 **The Community and Its Environment**

Unintended Consequences

Everything that lives in a place makes up an **ecosystem**. When people change one thing in an ecosystem, everything is affected. This means many human actions have unintended consequences. These are changes that people do not mean to make. As humans continue to change the world around them, they must weigh the benefits of what they build against their consequences.

Your home and other places in your community sit on land that had to be cleared. Clearing this land changes the **habitat** of plants and animals. A habitat is the home of an animal or plant. Over time, humans have cleared a lot of land across the world. However, this activity has led to rapid **deforestation**, or the loss of forests. Forests are important because they provide resources. They also help clean the air we need to breathe. Without forests and other plants, humans could not live on Earth.

Another effect of clearing land is soil erosion. Erosion is the wearing away of rock and soil by wind or flowing water. Much erosion is natural. However, people can cause too much erosion too quickly. This happens because of deforestation, too much farming, or grazing too many farm animals on the land.

To make way for development, people first clear the natural landscape of trees and other plant life.

Sometimes humans bring new plants and animals to a habitat. These can push out the original ones. For example, a beetle brought from East Asia called the emerald ash borer has destroyed large numbers of ash trees across the nation.

Many species of animals have become **endangered** or **extinct** because of human activity. *Extinct* means a type of animal has died out. *Endangered* means the animal is at risk of becoming extinct. The mammoth, an animal related to the elephant, is extinct. In the United States, the gray wolf and red wolf are endangered because of loss of habitat.

Soil erosion strips the land of nutrients needed for farming.

Did You Know?

The bald eagle is the national symbol of the United States. Not long ago, it had almost become extinct. This is because people had destroyed much of the eagles' habitats. Eagles could not hunt and nest as they needed to. Some were poisoned by pollution. Others were hunted. Laws to protect the eagles and their habitats have helped them recover.

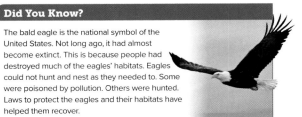

✓ Stop and Check   COLLABORATE

Think of a building in your community. Were there unintended consequences to building it? Did the benefits outweigh those consequences?

What Do You Think? What are advantages of changing the environment? What are disadvantages?

RESEARCH COMPANION, pp. 76–77

Unintended Consequences

1 Inspect Have students read pp. 76–77 and describe one consequence of changing the environment.

2 Find Evidence Use the questions below to check comprehension.

Explain Why is the heading for this spread appropriate to the content? (Answers should reflect that human changes to the environment have led to harmful effects, or consequences, that people did not necessarily mean, or intend, to cause.) **DOK 2**

Identify Cause and Effect What does the text say are unintended consequences of clearing land and deforestation? (loss of animal habitat and forests, soil erosion) **DOK 2**

3 Make Connections

Analyze What do you think is the purpose of this text? Cite evidence from the text to support your conclusions. (to inform readers of the potential harmful effects humans can have on the environment, including deforestation, soil erosion, and animal endangerment or extinction) **DOK 3**

✓ Stop and Check

Think Some students may need a specific example of a building project in their community. (Answers will vary, but students should consider appropriate examples from their community—new housing development, construction of a superstore, or the paving of a new road—and consider how each development has impacted the environment.)

✓ Check for Success

Cause and Effect Can students identify ways in which people change their environment?

Differentiate

If Not, Guide students in reviewing the graphic organizer on p. 71 of their Inquiry Journals, and discussing one cause-and-effect relationship identified from the reading.

LESSON 2 REPORT

LESSON QUESTION

How Do People Change Their Environment?

**INQUIRY JOURNAL,
pp. 72–73**

Think About It

Remind students to review their research and consider how people change their environments. Encourage students to review the information that they have included in their graphic organizers. Direct students back to pp. 72–77 of their Research Companion if they need more information.

Write About It

Write and Cite Evidence Remind students to include the following as they craft their responses.

- Cite a specific example from the text to explain one way that people change their environment.
- Explain any positive and negative effects of this change for the people who live there.
- Use chapter vocabulary as appropriate.

Disciplines	4	3	2	1
Geography **History** **Economics**	Student cites appropriate, specific examples from the text and the community and provides detailed descriptions of several potential effects for each example.	Student cites appropriate but general examples from the text and the community and provides adequate descriptions of at least two potential effects for each example.	Student cites somewhat appropriate examples from the text and the community and provides basic descriptions of at least one potential effect for each example.	Student cites inappropriate or vague examples from the text and the community and fails to provide appropriate descriptions of potential effects for each example.

Talk About It

Express Your Opinion Remind students to consider the causes and the effects of the changes in their communities.

Assessment Students can check their understanding with feedback from the **Lesson Test** available online.

Connect to the Essential Question

Describe and Predict Suggest students brainstorm ideas for their drawings before they begin. As an alternative, you may wish to challenge students to find visual examples of changes in the community through local news media and archival resources.

Inquiry Project Update Remind students to turn to Inquiry Journal pp. 54–55 for project information. If necessary, review the Project Checklist with students. At this point in the chapter, students should focus on the first three items on the checklist.

Think About It

Explain

Review your research. Based on the information you have gathered, why do you think people change things in their environment?

Write About It

Write and Cite Evidence

Use what you read to describe an example of how people affect the environment. Then describe an example of how changes to the environment affect people.

Answers will vary. Students might point out that people changed the landscape by clearing and digging up land for the Erie Canal. This change made it easier and faster for people to travel. They might also describe how people changed plants' and animals' habitats by reversing the flow of the Chicago River. This change reduced pollution in Lake Michigan but increased pollution for other communities.

Talk About It

Express Your Opinion

Talk to your partner about changes in your community that have affected the environment. Which do you think have been most helpful and why? Which do you think have caused new challenges and why?

 Connect to the

Geography

Describe and Predict

Think about how your community has changed over time and how it might change in the future. Draw and label three pictures that show physical and human-made features in your community.

1. What do you think your community looked like before people settled there?

2. What does your community look like today?

3. How might your community look in the future?

Pictures will vary but should show ways communities change.

Inquiry Project Notes

INQUIRY JOURNAL, pp. 72–73

EL English Learners SCAFFOLD

Use the following scaffolds to support student writing.

Entering and Emerging

Guide students to think about the relationship between people and the environment. Provide sentence frames such as the following:

- Native Americans cleared land to _____. They dammed rivers to _____.

- When people clear and build on land, they change _____. These changes can lead to _____.

Developing and Expanding

Help small groups identify how and why people changed the environment. Ask: *What are some ways that people in the past changed the environment? Why did they make those changes? What were some effects of those changes? How have people changed the environment in your community? Why did they change it? What is one effect of that change?*

Bridging and Reaching

Have partners take turns asking and answering these questions: *What changes did Native Americans make to their environments? What were the effects of these changes to the environment and to the people? What changes have people today made to their environments? What are the effects of these changes?* Guide students to list changes and their effects for their communities.

✔ Check for Success

Describe Can students write a paragraph explaining how people change the environment and how those changes, in turn, affect people's lives? Can they cite specific examples as evidence to support their explanation?

Differentiate

If Not, Have students present their ideas as a visual report or in a question-and-answer discussion.

LESSON 3 OVERVIEW

How Do We Meet Environmental Challenges?

Connect to the Essential Question

Tell students that this lesson provides key research into the Chapter Essential Question: **What Is Our Relationship to Our Environment?** Explain that they will learn how local and global communities respond to both natural and human-made environmental challenges.

Discuss The IMPACT Today

This lesson provides students with a way for them to learn about how to make an impact today in their communities. Tell them they will identify environmental challenges and suggest ways humans can solve the problems or reduce their impact.

Lesson Objectives

- **Identify** environmental issues and concerns.
- **Describe** specific examples of people meeting environmental challenges.
- **Identify** the steps taken to meet an environmental challenge.
- **Debate** the pros and cons of different energy sources.
- **Write** a paragraph about possible solutions to an environmental problem.

Make Connections!

CONNECT TO ELA

Reading **Ask and answer** questions to demonstrate understanding of a text and refer explicitly to the text as the basis for the answers.

Research **Conduct** short research projects that build knowledge about a topic.

Writing **Write** informative/explanatory texts to examine a topic and convey ideas and information clearly.

Speaking and Listening **Explain** students' own ideas and understanding in light of the discussion.

COMMUNITY CONNECTIONS

To enrich students' experience in learning about how people work together to address environmental problems, help them research a local environmental group and how it positively impacts the community. If possible, invite a member of the group to visit the classroom and share the group's successes and challenges.

Lesson-At-A-Glance

1 ENGAGE — INQUIRY JOURNAL

pp. 74–79

- ▶ **Talk About It:** Photograph of Ocean Pollution
- ▶ **Analyze the Source:** Rachel Carson and Primary Source
- ▶ **Inquiry Tools:** Explore Problem and Solution

2 INVESTIGATE — RESEARCH COMPANION

pp. 78–87

- ▶ **How Communities Respond to Natural Disasters**
- ▶ **How Communities Respond to Pollution**
- ▶ **The Impact of Energy**
- ▶ **The Ozone Layer and the International Community**

3 REPORT — INQUIRY JOURNAL

pp. 80–81

- ▶ **Think About It**
- ▶ **Write About It:** Write an Informational Text; Write and Cite Evidence
- ▶ **Talk About It**
- ▶ **Connect to the Essential Question**

ASSESSMENT

- ▶ **Online Lesson Test**
- ▶ **Printable Lesson Test**

For more details, see pages T106–T107.

▶ Digital Tools

at **my.mheducation.com**

ePresentation

Teach the Engage, Investigate, and Report content to the whole class from **ePresentations** that launch directly from the lesson dashboard.

eBook

You can flip your instruction with the **IMPACT eBooks** found on your lesson dashboard.

Interactive IMPACT

Blend in digital content **when you want it** and **where you want it**.

Blended Learning features in the Teacher's Edition highlight ways to connect in-class work with online experiences to enhance learning.

Investigate current events with **IMPACT News**.

Explore domain-based vocabulary with **Explore Words** and **Word Play** vocabulary activities.

pp. 16–29

Go Further with IMPACT Explorer Magazine!

The **IMPACT Explorer Magazine** supports students' exploration of the Essential Question and provides additional resources for the EQ Inquiry Project.

How Do We Meet Environmental Challenges?

Language Objectives

- Use newly acquired content and academic vocabulary to talk and write about how people solve problems related to the environment.
- Write about how to solve a problem in the environment.
- Identify adjectives and their function in a sentence.

Spanish Cognates

To support Spanish speakers, point out the cognates.

event = evento

natural = natural

protect = proteger

disaster = desastre

hurricane = huracán

recover = recobrar

impact = impacto

energy = energía

Introduce the Lesson

Set Purpose Explain to students that in this lesson, they will read informational texts to find out how people solve problems that are related to the environment.

Access Prior Knowledge Tell students that people and other living things have had to learn how to survive events that occur in nature that they cannot control. Ask: *Have you ever experienced a natural event, such as a flood, a blizzard, or an earthquake?* Have students discuss any natural events they have experienced, including what the experience was like and how they prepared for it.

Spark Curiosity Project or display the photo on page 79 of the Research Companion. Explain that this photo shows a flooded street. Tell students that there are several types of natural disasters that can affect a community, depending on its location. Each type may have different effects and require different solutions. Ask: *How are the people traveling?* (in a boat) *Why are they using a boat to travel along a street?* (There has been a flood.)

Have students work in pairs of different proficiency levels to discuss what they would do to stay safe if their community faced a situation like the one in the photo.

Build Meaning & Support Language

Inquiry Journal

Analyze the Source (pages 76–77) Point out that *overuse* means "to use something too much." Ask: *Why might overusing something be harmful to the environment?* (It could kill living things or lessen the supply of something.) Point out that *sparked* means "set in motion." Ask: *How could a book spark people's interest?* (It could make them aware of what has been happening so they know that something needs to be done.) Unpack the sentence: *One solution to the problem of pollution was that people started using "green," or sustainable, products.* Point out that *the problem of pollution* refers to an environmental problem. Explain that the word *green* is in quotes because it is an informal meaning for the words *sustainable products.* "Green" refers to products that do not cause harm to the environment. Break down the word *sustainable.* Point out that the root of the word is *sustain,* which means "to allow something to continue for a period of time." The suffix *-able* means "capable of." So *sustainable* means "able to continue for a long time." Ask: *What are some products you use that you think are "green" or sustainable?*

Inquiry Tools (pages 78–79) Tell students they will identify **Problems** and **Solutions** as they read the selections in the Research Companion. Tell them that the graphic organizer will help them organize the information as they read. Explain that there are steps to take when solving a problem. Say: *First, you identify the problem. Then, you identify details that tell what was done to solve the problem. Finally, you look for ways that the problem was solved.* Ask: *Why was the book* Silent Spring *one step toward solving the pesticide problem?* (It made people aware that there was a problem.) Provide support as students fill in the graphic organizer.

Have student pairs discuss a problem they faced and the steps they took to solve it. Was the problem solved?

Research Companion

How Communities Respond to Natural Disasters (pages 78–81) Discuss the first sentence in the second paragraph on page 80: *After natural disasters, local governments make sure that people have water, power, shelter, and medical care.* Explain that the words "make sure" mean to "ensure that something is done or happens." Say: *Local governments do what is necessary to help citizens after natural disasters.* Point out the prepositional phrase at the beginning of the sentence. In this case, *after* is a preposition indicating when something happens.

How Communities Respond to Pollution (pages 82–83) Explain to students that carbon dioxide is an odorless, colorless gas that occurs naturally in the atmosphere. It's what creates the fizz in carbonated beverages. However, too much carbon dioxide can cause warming of the earth's atmosphere and can lead to climate change. Point to the second sentence in the second paragraph: Ask: *What do the words* for example *indicate?* (an example that relates to the previous sentence)

Pros and Cons of Energy (pages 84–85) Work with students to develop a two-column chart that identifies the pros and cons of each type of energy discussed. Then have students discuss the type of energy they think is most useful.

The Ozone Layer and the International Community (pages 86–87) Point out that the words *International Community* refer to all countries in the world as a group. In this case, it refers to those countries who agreed to the Montreal Protocol and who work to protect the ozone layer from harmful chemicals. Read aloud the word *human-made* on page 86. Explain that it is a compound word, or a word that uses two or more words as one single word. Tell students that if they know the meaning of the individual words, they can sometimes figure out the meaning of the compound word. Ask: *What does* human-made *mean?* (things that are made by humans)

Inquiry Journal

Report Your Findings (pages 80–81) Explain to students that when they write about a problem and a solution, they should first state the problem and then provide steps and examples to show how they would solve that problem. Students should include evidence and details from the text in their writing. Encourage them to use the new vocabulary words they have learned. Check their writing for spelling and punctuation errors.

Language Forms & Conventions

Adjectives Remind students that an adjective is a word that describes, or tells more about, a noun. Most adjectives come before the nouns they describe. Adjectives can tell *what kind, which one,* or *how many.* Display the chart.

Adjective	Noun It Describes	Type
common	natural disaster	what kind
one	event	how many
heavy	rains	what kind
powerful	winds	what kind
this	event	which one

 Have students work in pairs to locate some adjectives in the text. Call on volunteers to say them aloud and add them to the chart.

LESSON 3 ENGAGE

 LESSON QUESTION

How Do We Meet Environmental Challenges?

INQUIRY JOURNAL, pp. 74–75

Bellringer

Prompt students to draw on information learned in the previous lesson. Ask: *What are some ways that people in a community affect their environment both positively and negatively?* Have students read the lesson question. Then ask: *What are some environmental challenges, or problems, that people in a community might need to deal with?* (Answers will vary but may include pollution, weather-related issues, or animals and insects.)

Lesson Outcomes

Discuss the lesson question and lesson outcomes with students.

- Make sure students understand that environmental challenges are problems in nature that affect humans or other organisms. Some environmental challenges, such as pollution, can be prevented by addressing the cause. Others, such as weather events, generally cannot be prevented. Instead, humans address the effects to solve the problem.

- Talk with students about natural disasters with which they are familiar, such as rainstorms or blizzards, and the problems that can result from those disasters. Then discuss possible solutions to those problems. Remind students that solutions can be actions we take before or after the event.

Talk About It

Guide students to look at the image. Explain to them that the connected plastic rings came from a six-pack of cans. Ask: *Is this something that is supposed to be part of the environment shown in the photo?* (no) Read the caption and the questions in the box. Then have partners or groups briefly discuss why they think the plastic is dangerous for the animals in the photograph. Come together again as a whole class, and have students report back with their ideas.

 ## Collaborative Conversations

Listen Carefully As students engage in partner, small-group, and whole-class discussions, encourage them to follow discussion rules by listening carefully to speakers. Remind students to

- always look at the person who is speaking.
- respect others by not interrupting them.
- repeat peers' ideas as necessary to check understanding.

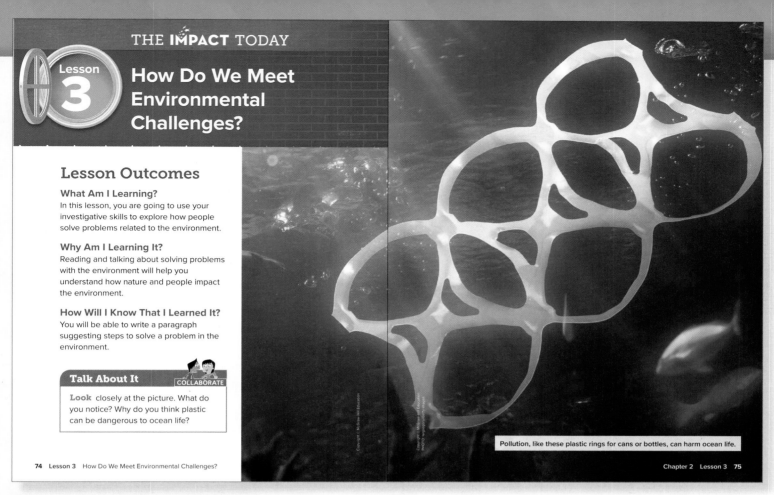

THE **IMPACT** TODAY

Lesson 3 How Do We Meet Environmental Challenges?

Lesson Outcomes

What Am I Learning?
In this lesson, you are going to use your investigative skills to explore how people solve problems related to the environment.

Why Am I Learning It?
Reading and talking about solving problems with the environment will help you understand how nature and people impact the environment.

How Will I Know That I Learned It?
You will be able to write a paragraph suggesting steps to solve a problem in the environment.

Talk About It COLLABORATE

Look closely at the picture. What do you notice? Why do you think plastic can be dangerous to ocean life?

74 Lesson 3 How Do We Meet Environmental Challenges?

Pollution, like these plastic rings for cans or bottles, can harm ocean life.

Chapter 2 Lesson 3 75

INQUIRY JOURNAL, pp. 74–75

English Learners SCAFFOLD

Use the following scaffolds to support student understanding of lesson outcomes.

Entering and Emerging

Display an idea web with *Pollution* written in the center. Discuss with students some causes of pollution that they know about. Then have them suggest words and phrases related to pollution to complete the web.

Developing and Expanding

Have small groups discuss how litter and other kinds of pollution affect the environment. Have groups choose one member to be the group's speaker. Have each speaker share the main ideas from the discussion. Provide a sentence frame to help students respond:

- Pollution causes problems such as _____, _____, and _____.

Bridging and Reaching

Have partners describe their personal experiences of seeing litter or other kinds of pollution. Ask them to think about how the pollution affected the specific environment where they saw it. Choose one student from each pair to share the main ideas of their discussion.

Social Emotional Learning

Self-Awareness

Self-Confidence In the classroom environment, students will have multiple opportunities for action and reflection, both as individuals and in teams. Self-confidence plays a key role in whether the student approaches these opportunities positively or negatively. As often as possible, praise students' efforts and provide positive feedback to reinforce their sense of accomplishment.

Analyze the Source — THE IMPACT TODAY

1 Inspect

Read the title. What do you think this text will be about?

Circle words you do not know.

Underline words that tell answers to these questions:

- Who was Rachel Carson?
- What problems did she describe?
- How did Rachel Carson help the environment?

My Notes

_____

_____

_____

_____

_____

_____

_____

Rachel Carson and the Environment

Rachel Carson was a biologist and nature writer. A biologist studies plant and animal life. Her mother loved nature. She inspired Rachel's interest in the environment. In the 1930s, Carson created radio programs about sea life for the United States Bureau of Fisheries. Later, she wrote pamphlets on protecting natural resources. Then she began to write books about the environment. In 1962, she wrote the book *Silent Spring*. The book told how the overuse of pesticides was harming the environment. A pesticide is a substance used to kill insects that harm plants and crops. Pesticides can also cause animals and people to become ill. In *Silent Spring*, Carson said that the government and scientists working in agriculture needed to take better care of the environment. To solve this, she wanted rules that would protect the environment and people from these dangerous chemicals. Many pesticides are no longer used today because of Rachel Carson.

PRIMARY SOURCE

In Their Words... Rachel Carson

"Only within the moment of time represented by the present century has one species—man—acquired significant power to alter the nature of his world."

—from *Silent Spring*

Rachel Carson's book sparked national interest in the environment. In 1970, the first Earth Day was held. It addresses some problems in the environment. It led people to clean up pollution, to recycle, and to conserve, or protect, the environment. The environmental movement had begun. One solution to the problem of pollution was that people started using "green," or sustainable, products. A sustainable product does not harm Earth or the environment. It helps conserve it for the future. Another solution was that the government passed laws such as the Clean Water Act, the Safe Drinking Water Act, and the Endangered Species Act. Carson is often referred to as the "Mother of the Environmental Movement."

Rachel Carson

2 Find Evidence

Reread the Primary Source quote. Who did Rachel Carson say is causing the problems with the environment? Why do you think she said this?

Think about the phrase "moment of time." What does the phrase mean? Is it still happening? Name a word that has a similar meaning.

3 Make Connections

Talk Think about the ocean shown in the photo on page 75. How could people solve the problem shown in the photo?

Rachel Carson wanted to preserve natural environments like this spring.

INQUIRY JOURNAL, pp. 76–77

Analyze the Source

Background Information

During the 1960s, Americans grew increasingly concerned about their impact on the environment. In response, Congress consolidated several federal regulatory groups handling environmental concerns into a single entity—the Environmental Protection Agency (EPA)—in 1970.

1 Inspect

Read Have students read the text, study the images, and read the image captions. Remind them to circle words in the text with which they are unfamiliar.

- Underline details that tell who Rachel Carson was (a biologist and nature writer) and why she is an important part of environmental history (Rachel Carson's book sparked national interest in the environment).

2 Find Evidence

Reread Have students reread the Primary Source quote.

Think Guide students to understand that "moment of time" refers to the time when Carson was writing. A similar word might be "now."

3 Make Connections

Talk Have partners discuss how people could solve the problem of pollution in the oceans. Remind them to consider Rachel Carson's actions and ideas in their discussion.

Spotlight on Language

Understanding Language

Movement may be more commonly understood as a noun describing a change in location. However, it is also used for a group of people working to effect change in society, politics, or the arts.

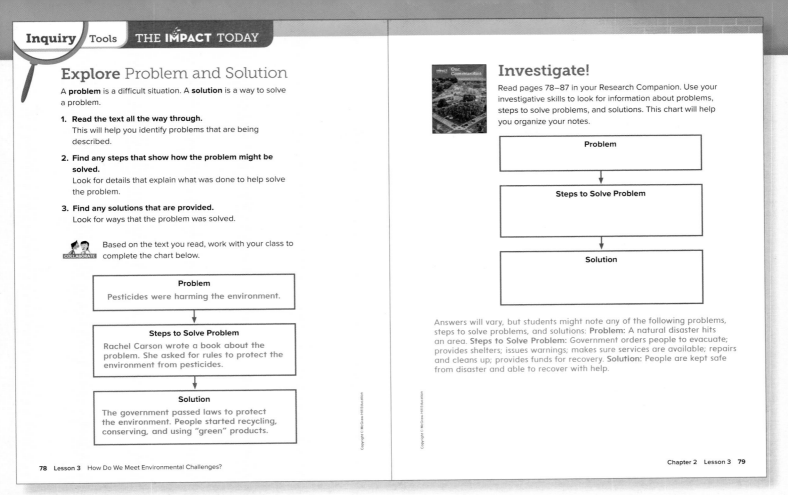

Explore Problem and Solution

A **problem** is a difficult situation. A **solution** is a way to solve a problem.

1. **Read the text all the way through.**
   This will help you identify problems that are being described.

2. **Find any steps that show how the problem might be solved.**
   Look for details that explain what was done to help solve the problem.

3. **Find any solutions that are provided.**
   Look for ways that the problem was solved.

Based on the text you read, work with your class to complete the chart below.

Problem
Pesticides were harming the environment.

↓

Steps to Solve Problem
Rachel Carson wrote a book about the problem. She asked for rules to protect the environment from pesticides.

↓

Solution
The government passed laws to protect the environment. People started recycling, conserving, and using "green" products.

Investigate!

Read pages 78–87 in your Research Companion. Use your investigative skills to look for information about problems, steps to solve problems, and solutions. This chart will help you organize your notes.

Problem

↓

Steps to Solve Problem

↓

Solution

Answers will vary, but students might note any of the following problems, steps to solve problems, and solutions: **Problem:** A natural disaster hits an area. **Steps to Solve Problem:** Government orders people to evacuate; provides shelters; issues warnings; makes sure services are available; repairs and cleans up; provides funds for recovery. **Solution:** People are kept safe from disaster and able to recover with help.

INQUIRY JOURNAL, pp. 78–79

Inquiry Tools

Explore Problem and Solution

Read Discuss with students the meaning of *problem* and *solution* and how they are related. Pose a real-life problem, such as oversleeping on a school day or missing the school bus, and discuss possible solutions with students.

Guide Practice Have students review the text on pp. 76–77. Then work with them to complete the graphic organizer. Explain that they will use a similar graphic organizer to organize their independent research.

Check Understanding Confirm students' understanding of the inquiry skill, Explore Problem and Solution. If students cannot recognize a problem and its related solution, review the steps on p. 78.

Investigate!

Have students read pages 78–87 in the Research Companion. Tell them the information will help them answer the lesson question *How Do We Meet Environmental Challenges?*

Take Notes Tell students that they should use the graphic organizer on p. 79 of the Inquiry Journal to take notes on the different environmental challenges or problems described in the Research Companion.

Remind students to look for the solutions people have developed to prevent or to address the effects of environmental challenges.

 Spotlight on Content

Content Vocabulary

Students may be more familiar with *steps* as a synonym for *stairs* or as part of walking. Help clarify the meaning here by drawing a comparison between steps on a staircase and the steps in a process.

 Digital Tools

Blended Learning

Students prepare for the lesson investigation with step-by-step instruction about how to recognize problems and solutions.

ePresentation

Use the **Inquiry Tools** to model and complete the lesson graphic organizer.

LESSON 3 INVESTIGATE

How Do We Meet Environmental Challenges?

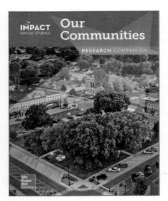

RESEARCH COMPANION, pp. 78–79

Background Information

- As Earth's average temperatures rise, the chance for severe storms—in particular, hurricanes—has risen as well. The majority of scientists agree that the devastating flooding that has accompanied some recent hurricanes, such as Katrina and Harvey, was intensified due to warmer ocean temperatures.

- Between 2008 and 2017, the percentage of electricity generated by renewable sources in the United States doubled. During that same period, the share of electricity produced by coal dropped from 48 percent to 30 percent.

How Communities Respond to Natural Disasters

1 Inspect Have students read pp. 78–79 and identify the types of natural disasters described in the text.

2 Find Evidence Use the questions below to check comprehension. Remind students to support their answers with text evidence.

Compare How are tornadoes and hurricanes similar? How are they different? (Both tornadoes and hurricanes have strong winds. Tornadoes mostly happen in the Midwest. Hurricanes happen along the coasts and in Hawaii.) **DOK 3**

Generate Based on the details you read, why are these events called *natural* disasters? (They are disasters caused by events that happen in nature.) **DOK 2**

3 Make Connections

Interpret Based on what you read, which natural disasters could most likely affect the area where you live? (Answers will vary.) **DOK 3**

THE IMPACT TODAY

Lesson 3
How Do We Meet Environmental Challenges?

How Communities Respond to Natural Disasters

Has your community ever experienced a **natural disaster**? A natural disaster is an event that occurs in nature. It damages the environment and may harm living things. Each natural disaster is different. How a community and the local, state, or federal government respond to each natural disaster is different as well.

Hurricanes, tornadoes, and earthquakes can cause natural disasters. People living along the Gulf Coast, the Atlantic Coast, and in Hawaii are at risk for hurricanes. These tropical storms have heavy rains and strong winds. Tornadoes are funnel-shaped windstorms. They are common in the Midwest but have occurred everywhere. Earthquakes are the sudden shaking of the ground. The Pacific Coast is at the highest risk for earthquakes.

Like other natural disasters, wildfires can occur in most states. However, they are most common in the West. High temperatures, drought, and thunderstorms can cause wildfires. Wildfires burn millions of acres of land every year. Floods can also happen in every state. Areas around the Mississippi and Missouri Rivers are most likely to have flooding. Coastal areas may also flood, especially during a hurricane.

78 Lesson 3   How Do We Meet Environmental Challenges?

Floods can occur throughout the United States, but areas near bodies of water are more likely to have them.

Chapter 2   Lesson 3   79

RESEARCH COMPANION, pp. 78–79

English Learners SCAFFOLD

Use the following scaffolds to support student understanding of lesson content.

Entering and Emerging
Clarify the meaning of *challenge* by providing synonyms, such as *problem* or *difficulty*. Then display several images of nature, including some that show pollution or damage to the environment. Have students use single words, short phrases, or gestures to identify which photos show environmental challenges.

Developing and Expanding
On the board, list words that describe environmental challenges, such as *flood, litter, tornado, pollution,* and so on. Ask: *Why are these considered environmental challenges?* Have students discuss their ideas with a partner before calling on individual volunteers. Provide students with the following sentence frame to help them respond:

- _____ is an environmental challenge because _____.

Bridging and Reaching
Have students write three ways they think people in a community might respond to a natural disaster. Tell students to write their ideas using complete sentences. Then have them exchange their writing with a partner. Ask partners to read the ideas aloud.

▶ Digital Tools

Blended Learning
Flip the research approach and find evidence in a digital format.

eBook

Students investigate using their **Research Companion** and **IMPACT Explorer eBooks** to find evidence.

THE IMPACT TODAY

Who helps a community when a natural disaster happens? Local and state governments help rescue people. The federal government may order people to leave the area before a natural disaster occurs. It may open shelters for these people. Federal and state governments may keep order and help protect people's property. They also provide money to communities to help recover from disasters and try to solve problems related to disasters.

After natural disasters, local governments make sure that people have water, power, shelter, and medical care. They remove tree branches and other materials from areas near fallen power lines. They repair roads and bridges.

Volunteer organizations are part of the solution to natural disasters, too. They help with shelter, food, and clothing. They provide household items, repairs, and help with clean-up efforts.

Workers and volunteers pass out supplies to people suffering from the effects of a natural disaster.

Citizenship

Cajun Navy Sets Out to Solve Disaster Problems

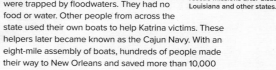

The Cajun Navy operates flood rescue missions after disasters in Louisiana and other states.

Hurricane Katrina hit New Orleans and the eastern Gulf coast in 2005. It was one of the worst disasters in the country's history. People were trapped by floodwaters. They had no food or water. Other people from across the state used their own boats to help Katrina victims. These helpers later became known as the Cajun Navy. With an eight-mile assembly of boats, hundreds of people made their way to New Orleans and saved more than 10,000 people.

The Cajun Navy didn't stop with Katrina. Members have continued to help others. They helped flooding victims in Baton Rouge, Louisiana, in 2016. The group traveled to Houston, Texas, during Hurricane Harvey in 2017. Their actions have saved hundreds of lives.

 Stop and Check

Talk With a partner, discuss one problem caused by a natural disaster. What can your community or government do to lessen its effect on people?

Find Details As you read, add new information to the graphic organizer on page 79 in your Inquiry Journal.

80 Lesson 3 How Do We Meet Environmental Challenges?

Chapter 2 Lesson 3 81

RESEARCH COMPANION, pp. 80–81

How Communities Respond to Natural Disasters/Cajun Navy Sets Out to Solve Disaster Problems

1 Inspect Have students read pp. 80–81 and identify some ways that governments respond to natural disasters.

2 Find Evidence Use the questions below to check comprehension.

Summarize Why is help from volunteers, such as the Cajun Navy, important during natural disasters? (Volunteers can help bring supplies, clean up damage, rescue people in danger, and support federal and state agencies with recovery efforts.) **DOK 3**

3 Make Connections

Cause/Effect What effect do you think a natural disaster has on the businesses and workers in a community? (Answers will vary but may include the disruption of business operations and the effect that it would have on people's ability to earn a living.) **DOK 3**

 Stop and Check

Talk Remind students to use the text when comparing their answers. (Temporary shelters and funds to rebuild would lessen the effect of home loss.)

 Spotlight on Content

American Communities

Students may be unfamiliar with the term *Cajun*. Explain that the Cajun community consists of people who descended from French Canadians who settled in the bayou region of Louisiana, near New Orleans.

▶ **Digital Tools**

Blended Learning
Students investigate curated resources and find evidence to answer the lesson question.

Interactive IMPACT
Students **Research** and find evidence using digital format texts.

How Communities Respond to Pollution

Pollution is the presence of something harmful in the environment. There are several types of pollution: air pollution, water pollution, and littering.

Anything that is put into the air that might harm the environment and living things is air pollution. For example, the carbon dioxide from cars and airplanes causes air pollution. The smoke and fumes from chemicals can cause a kind of air pollution called smog.

Water pollution occurs when harmful chemicals, gases, and waste are put into bodies of water. These materials cause harm to the water. Living things are unable to use it. Some substances cause diseases. In 2015, many people in Flint, Michigan, got sick from drinking water. It was from a water source with high amounts of lead pollution.

Littering is another form of pollution. A person litters when he or she does not properly get rid of trash or harmful substances. Animals can be harmed by litter.

These children are doing their part to help the environment.

Individuals, communities, businesses, and governments can take action to respond to these forms of pollution.

People can combat air pollution by reducing the amount of carbon dioxide and other gases they put in the air. They can ride bikes or take buses instead of driving. Governments have passed laws like the Pollution Prevention Act in 1990. Some presidents have issued orders about air pollution.

People can reduce water pollution by not throwing cleaning products or cooking oil down the sink. They can help clean up beaches and waterways. Businesses can follow the rules of the Clean Water Act and other laws.

Many communities have laws against littering. People and businesses that break these laws face consequences. They may be fined, put in jail, or have to do community service. Some communities put up signs reminding people not to litter. Other communities have added garbage and recycling bins in public places. This is meant to make it easier for people to stop littering.

Exhaust from cars leads to air pollution.

✓ Stop and Check

Talk If you were a government official, what form of pollution would you first work to reduce? What steps would you take to do this?

RESEARCH COMPANION, pp. 82–83

How Communities Respond to Pollution

1 Inspect Have students read pp. 82–83 and identify three types of pollution.

2 Find Evidence Use the questions below to check comprehension.

Compare How are the effects of water, air, and land pollution similar? (All three types of pollution can cause humans and animals to become sick.) **DOK 2**

Hypothesize How could more people riding bikes instead of driving cars help the environment? (Bikes do not produce carbon dioxide, so there would be less pollution, and less pollution helps the environment.) **DOK 3**

3 Make Connections

Construct If you saw another student littering, what could you say to convince them that they should not litter? (Answers will vary but should use text evidence to support the idea that littering is a form of pollution.) **DOK 3**

✓ Stop and Check

Talk Remind students to use the text when discussing their answers. (Answers will vary, but students should discuss the problems associated with the different forms of pollution and ways they might solve the issues.)

Social Emotional Learning

Decision-Making Skills

Identify Problems Every day, students are faced with problems that need to be solved. Having the skills to evaluate evidence in order to find solutions is key to creating positive outcomes. Ask: *What evidence is there that littering is a problem?*

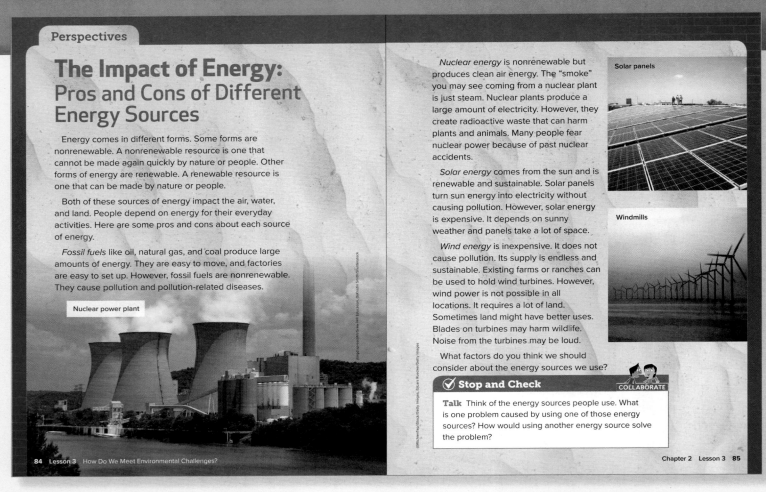

The Impact of Energy: Pros and Cons of Different Energy Sources

Energy comes in different forms. Some forms are nonrenewable. A nonrenewable resource is one that cannot be made again quickly by nature or people. Other forms of energy are renewable. A renewable resource is one that can be made by nature or people.

Both of these sources of energy impact the air, water, and land. People depend on energy for their everyday activities. Here are some pros and cons about each source of energy.

Fossil fuels like oil, natural gas, and coal produce large amounts of energy. They are easy to move, and factories are easy to set up. However, fossil fuels are nonrenewable. They cause pollution and pollution-related diseases.

Nuclear power plant

Nuclear energy is nonrenewable but produces clean air energy. The "smoke" you may see coming from a nuclear plant is just steam. Nuclear plants produce a large amount of electricity. However, they create radioactive waste that can harm plants and animals. Many people fear nuclear power because of past nuclear accidents.

Solar energy comes from the sun and is renewable and sustainable. Solar panels turn sun energy into electricity without causing pollution. However, solar energy is expensive. It depends on sunny weather and panels take a lot of space.

Wind energy is inexpensive. It does not cause pollution. Its supply is endless and sustainable. Existing farms or ranches can be used to hold wind turbines. However, wind power is not possible in all locations. It requires a lot of land. Sometimes land might have better uses. Blades on turbines may harm wildlife. Noise from the turbines may be loud.

What factors do you think we should consider about the energy sources we use?

Solar panels

Windmills

✓ Stop and Check COLLABORATE

Talk Think of the energy sources people use. What is one problem caused by using one of those energy sources? How would using another energy source solve the problem?

RESEARCH COMPANION, pp. 84–85

The Impact of Energy

1 Inspect Have students read pp. 84–85 and explain the difference between a renewable and a nonrenewable resource.

2 Find Evidence Use the questions below to check comprehension.

Compare and Contrast What are some similarities and differences between fossil fuels and nuclear energy? (Both produce large amounts of energy, are nonrenewable, and produce waste that is harmful to people and the environment; fossil fuels cause pollution, but nuclear energy produces clean air energy) **DOK 2**

Draw Conclusions Based on the information in the text, which energy source do you think is the least harmful to the environment? (Answers will vary but should be supported by evidence from the text.) **DOK 3**

3 Make Connections

Analyze If you were in charge of choosing an energy source for a community, what factors would you need to consider? (Possible answers: cost, space, where the energy source is located in relation to the community) **DOK 3**

Predict Which energy source do you think most people will use one hundred years from now? (Answers will vary.) **DOK 3**

✓ Stop and Check COLLABORATE

Talk What is one problem caused by using one of those energy sources? How would using another energy source solve the problem? (Answers will vary, but students might say that fossil fuels cause pollution. Using solar or wind power would solve that problem.)

EL Spotlight on Language

Understanding Language

space the area something occupies or takes up

pros positive aspects of something

cons negative aspects of something

▶ Digital Tools

Blended Learning
Students explore lesson content through interactive activities.

Interactive IMPACT

Use the **More to Explore**.

The Ozone Layer and the International Community

The layers of air and gases between Earth and space make up the **atmosphere**. The part of the atmosphere that protects Earth from dangerous sun rays called ultraviolet rays is called the **ozone layer**. It acts like Earth's sunscreen. The ozone layer is in a part of the atmosphere called the stratosphere. This is right above the troposphere, where most human activity takes place. In the 1970s, scientists realized the ozone layer was getting thinner over Antarctica. They referred to this thinning as the "ozone hole." Scientists realized that human-made chemicals were destroying ozone and causing this hole.

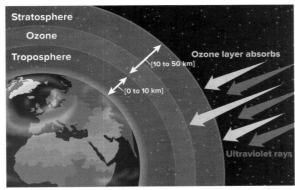

The ozone layer protects Earth from about 97 percent of the sun's harmful ultraviolet rays.

What action was needed to fix the problem of the ozone layer? No country could take on the job alone. It required cooperation. An agreement called the Montreal Protocol was created in 1987. Leaders of 46 countries agreed not to use chemicals that harmed the ozone layer. Today, about 200 countries have signed the agreement. In January of 2018, scientists were able to find that there was less ozone being destroyed than in 2005. Scientists think that the ozone layer might recover between 2060 and 2080.

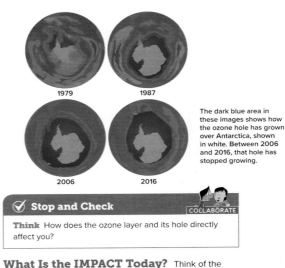

The dark blue area in these images shows how the ozone hole has grown over Antarctica, shown in white. Between 2006 and 2016, that hole has stopped growing.

✓ Stop and Check

Think How does the ozone layer and its hole directly affect you?

What Is the IMPACT Today? Think of the problems discussed in this lesson. Which problem affects your community the most? How could your community solve the problem?

RESEARCH COMPANION, pp. 86–87

The Ozone Layer and the International Community

1 Inspect Have students read pp. 86–87 and define *ozone layer*.

2 Find Evidence Use the questions below to check comprehension.

Draw Conclusions How was the Montreal Protocol a solution to the problem of the ozone hole? (Many countries agreed to stop using chemicals that harm the ozone layer, and now scientists think the ozone layer will recover in the future.) **DOK 3**

3 Make Connections

Assess Why did the author of the text include explanations about the different layers of the atmosphere? (Answers may vary but should make the point that this information helps the reader understand why the ozone layer is important.) **DOK 3**

✓ Stop and Check

Think Have students discuss the question with a partner. (Answers will vary, but students should include text evidence in their responses.)

What Is the IMPACT Today?

Discuss environmental problems or events in your community with students. (Answers will vary, but students should present a problem and workable solutions.)

✓ Check for Success

Summarize Can students identify environmental challenges covered in the text and describe at least one way communities respond to them?

Differentiate

If Not, Have students review one problem and a related solution noted in the graphic organizer on p. 79 of their Inquiry Journals.

LESSON 3 REPORT

LESSON QUESTION

How Do We Meet Environmental Challenges?

INQUIRY JOURNAL, pp. 80–81

Think About It

Have students review their research and think about the issues they explored about environmental challenges. Remind them to review the notes about problems and solutions they wrote in their graphic organizers. Direct students back to pp. 78–87 of their Research Companion if they need more information.

Write About It

Write and Cite Evidence Remind students to include the following elements in their responses:

- Identify an environmental problem featured in the text.
- Organize key evidence and facts from the text describing why it is a problem.
- Include possible solutions to the problem.
- Use chapter vocabulary as appropriate.

Discipline(s)	4	3	2	1
Geography	Student shows strong understanding of environmental challenges and how communities can respond to them.	Student shows adequate understanding of environmental challenges and how communities can respond to them.	Student shows vague understanding of environmental challenges and how communities can respond to them.	Student shows no understanding of environmental challenges and how communities can respond to them.

Talk About It

Explain Pair classmates who have chosen to write about different environmental challenges. After students have shared their ideas about the steps needed to solve the problem, have them discuss with their partners which steps are most important and why.

Assessment Students can check their understanding with feedback from the **Lesson Test** available online.

Connect to the Essential Question

Pull It Together Before students respond, remind them that people in communities can work together in different ways to address environmental challenges.

Inquiry Project Update Remind students to turn to Inquiry Journal pp. 54–55 for project information. If necessary, review the Project Checklist with students. At this point in the chapter, students should focus on the last items on the checklist.

Think About It

Examine
Review your research. What are some problems related to the environment? How have some of these problems been solved?

Write About It

Write and Cite Evidence
Think of a problem in the environment you have read about or heard about. Write some steps you would suggest to solve it.

Answers will vary, but students should identify a problem from the chapter or from their own environment and provide steps that show how they would go about solving the problem.

Talk About It

Explain
Share your response with a partner. Together, discuss the steps suggested to solve the problem. What step do you think is most important? Why?

Geography — Connect to the EQ

Pull It Together
Think about how and why people solve problems with the environment. How have these solutions affected the environment?

Answers will vary, but students should demonstrate an understanding of the importance of governments and people working together to solve problems, and of how the solutions have benefited the environment and the world in general.

Inquiry Project Notes
EQ

INQUIRY JOURNAL, pp. 80–81

English Learners SCAFFOLD

Use the following scaffolds to support students' understanding of writing about problems and solutions.

Entering and Emerging

Explain to students that when we describe the steps in doing something, we can use time-order words, such as _first, second, next, then,_ and _finally._ Model using time-order words to describe the steps of a simple process, such as brushing your teeth or making a sandwich. Then display the following sentence starters for students to use in their writing: First _____. Then _____. Next _____. Finally _____.

Developing and Expanding

List time-order words on the board: _first, second, third, then, next, last, finally._ Have volunteers use the words to describe the steps of a simple process, such as making a bed or doing the dishes. Remind students that they should be using time-order words to show the steps they would take to solve an environmental problem.

Bridging and Reaching

Work with students to generate a list of time-order words, as well as a list of words and phrases used to show cause-and-effect relationships, such as _because, as a result, therefore,_ and _then._ Remind students that they should be using these signal words to organize the ideas in their writing.

✓ Check for Success

Connect Are students able to identify a community's environmental challenge and write a possible solution for that challenge?

Differentiate

If Not, Have students present their solutions in a different format, such as in a public service announcement or commercial.

TAKE ACTION
with INQUIRY JOURNAL

What Is Our Relationship With Our Environment?

INQUIRY JOURNAL, pp. 82–83

Inquiry Project Wrap-Up

Remind students that they are to have created a plan to improve their community's environment.

Assessment Use the rubric on p. T107 to assess students' Inquiry Projects.

Complete Your Project

Have students work individually or with their groups to review the Complete Your Project checklist. Remind them that if they have missed any of the criteria, now is their opportunity to make corrections or additions.

Share Your Project

If time allows, you may want to have students present their projects to the class. Provide the following presentation tips for students.

- Prepare and rehearse.
- Use notes to help you stay on topic when you present.
- Speak slowly and clearly. Make sure everyone can hear you.
- Make eye contact and speak directly to the audience.

Reflect on Your Project

Student reflections begin with thinking about the process for how they decided which problem with their community's environment they wanted to solve and how they conducted their research. Students should focus not only on the results of the inquiry but also on the challenges and successes in the inquiry process. Students can apply those findings to future projects.

Chapter Connections can focus on anything that resonated with students about their study of their community's environment. These connections may spark students to do further research on their own.

Blended Learning
Students use online checklists to prepare, complete, and reflect on their Inquiry Projects.

Chapter Assessments
Students can demonstrate chapter content mastery with the feedback from the online **Chapter Test**.

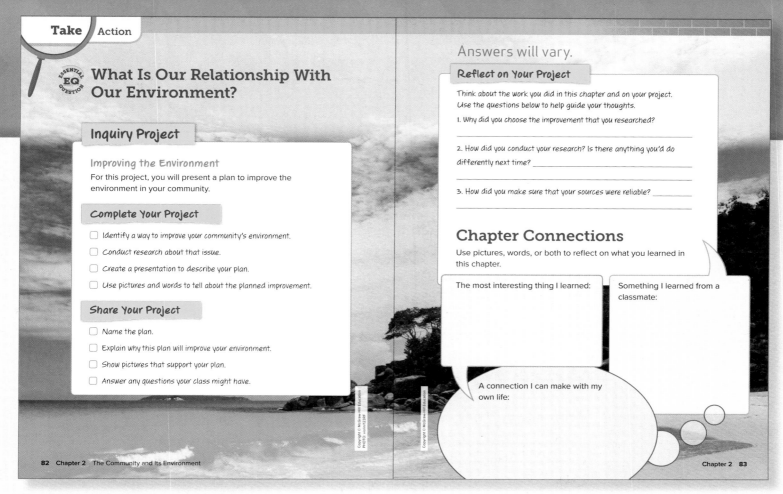

INQUIRY JOURNAL, pp. 82–83

 # English Learners SCAFFOLD

Use the following scaffolds to support student presentation of their projects.

Entering and Emerging

Review the project checklist with students. Make sure students understand key terms, including *conduct*, *research*, and *presentation*. Explain any other unfamiliar vocabulary.

Developing and Expanding

Have partners read the project checklist and circle any unfamiliar words. Have partners work together to define the unfamiliar words they circled.

Bridging and Reaching

Have partners read the project checklist. Ask them to brainstorm ways to make their presentations compelling and persuasive. Allow time for students to practice their presentations with their partners and discuss ways to improve them.

✓ Check for Success

Use Rubric Use your online rubric or the rubric found on p. T107 to check students' progress. Did students' presentations identify a problem with their community's environment and propose a solution to that problem?

Differentiate

If Not, Have students list and describe the evidence they used to identify the problem and solution to see how their presentation could be improved.

**RESEARCH COMPANION,
pp. 88–89**

Connections in Action!

Think Lead a discussion about how the environment can affect the way people live and how people can change the environment. Students should also consider the environmental challenges people face and how people respond to those challenges.

Talk To help focus students' conversations, you may want to discuss the EQ with the entire class before students discuss their ideas with a partner. Remind students to think about evidence they can provide that will support their ideas.

Share Invite students to share their small-group discussions with the class.

More to Explore

How Can You Make an IMPACT?

Mix and match the More to Explore activities to meet the needs of your classroom. Stretch students' thinking by offering alternative ways to demonstrate what they learned during the chapter.

These activities are flexible enough that you can assign one, two, or three activities to specific students or have students work in small groups. Remind students to use proper collaborative procedures when they work with partners.

Make a Crossword Puzzle
Have students create crossword puzzles using vocabulary from the chapter. Review the definitions with students or have them look up the words in the glossary.

Teacher Tip! **This activity can be used to monitor students' understanding of chapter vocabulary.**

Write a Letter to the Editor
Guide students to write letters to the editor of the local newspaper, expressing their opinions about how their community affects the environment. Invite volunteers to share their letters with the class.

Teacher Tip! **Use this activity to monitor students' ability to use evidence to support their opinions.**

Create a Poster
Have partners create posters using words and images that show ways people adapt to the environment. Display completed posters around the classroom.

Teacher Tip! **Use this activity as an independent assignment to monitor students' understanding of how people adapt to the environment.**

▶ Digital Tools

Blended Learning
Students apply chapter concepts to extension activities and connect them to the Essential Question.

Interactive IMPACT

Review chapter vocabulary with **Word Play**.

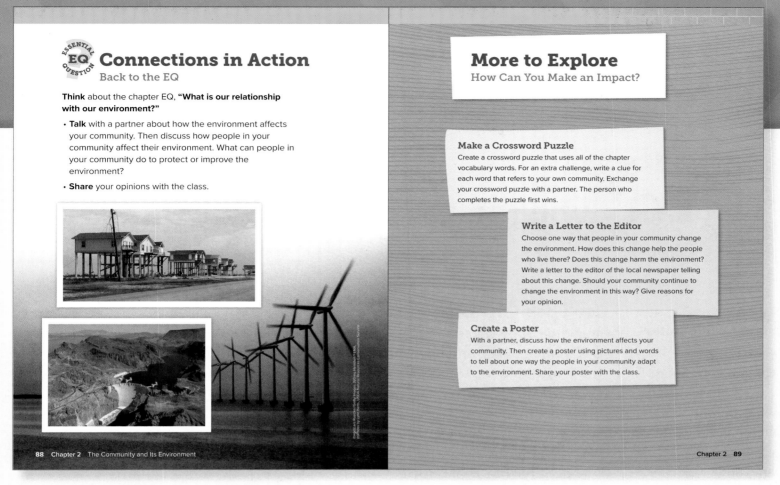

RESEARCH COMPANION, pp. 88–89

The page 88–89 content includes:

EQ Connections in Action
Back to the EQ

Think about the chapter EQ, **"What is our relationship with our environment?"**

- **Talk** with a partner about how the environment affects your community. Then discuss how people in your community affect their environment. What can people in your community do to protect or improve the environment?
- **Share** your opinions with the class.

88 Chapter 2 The Community and Its Environment

More to Explore
How Can You Make an Impact?

Make a Crossword Puzzle
Create a crossword puzzle that uses all of the chapter vocabulary words. For an extra challenge, write a clue for each word that refers to your own community. Exchange your crossword puzzle with a partner. The person who completes the puzzle first wins.

Write a Letter to the Editor
Choose one way that people in your community change the environment. How does this change help the people who live there? Does this change harm the environment? Write a letter to the editor of the local newspaper telling about this change. Should your community continue to change the environment in this way? Give reasons for your opinion.

Create a Poster
With a partner, discuss how the environment affects your community. Then create a poster using pictures and words to tell about one way the people in your community adapt to the environment. Share your poster with the class.

Chapter 2 89

 # English Learners SCAFFOLD

Use the following scaffolds to support student understanding of chapter content.

Entering and Emerging
Work with students to identify how the environment affects people and how people affect the environment. Write headings on the board, such as *Environmental Effects on Community* and *Community Effects on Environment*. Help students list ideas under each heading. Then have students discuss ideas with a partner.

Developing and Expanding
Write headings on the board, such as *Environmental Effects on Community* and *Community Effects on Environment*. Have partners discuss ideas they could list for each heading. Then have them present their ideas to the class.

Bridging and Reaching
Have partners choose one way the environment affects people or one way that people affect the environment. Have them discuss whether that relationship exists in their community, citing text evidence from the reading and examples as support. Have them share their ideas with the class.

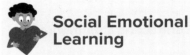 ## Social Emotional Learning

Social Awareness

Respect Remind students that as they discuss their community's environment with a partner, it is important to value each other's ideas. Showing respect for someone's opinion helps build good relationships with others. It also helps us build new understandings and perspectives.

What Makes a Community Unique?

In This Chapter Students will explore how a community's culture makes it unique. They will read about what culture is, what cultures are found in different U.S. communities, and how immigrants add to a community's culture. They also will investigate the similarities and differences between two communities and what connects communities throughout the world.

Chapter Objectives

- **Identify** ways that people around the world express their cultures.

- **Explain** how people in the United States express culture through art, stories, music, dance, and religion.

- **Describe** how immigrants contribute to a community's culture.

- **Compare** the cultures of Lima, Peru, and Johannesburg, South Africa.

- **Describe** how transportation, tourism, trade, and media connect communities around the world.

- **Create** a plan for a holiday or festival that celebrates the different cultures at school.

Make Connections!

CONNECT TO SCIENCE

Students will read about Johnny Appleseed on p. 98 of the Inquiry Journal. Show students an apple and discuss its parts, including the skin, stem, pulp, core, and seeds. On a separate sheet of paper, have each student draw an apple and label its parts.

CONNECT TO MATH

Tell students that about 40 million Americans were foreign born, and the U.S. population is about 328 million. Help students calculate the percentage of Americans born in another country. (40/328 = 12%)

Bibliography

Additional resources to aid student inquiry:

▶ **50 Cities of the U.S.A.**
by Gabrielle Balkan and Sol Linero; Wide Eyed Editions, 2017

▶ **The Map of Good Memories**
by Fran Nuño and Zuzanna Celej; Cuento de Luz, 2017

▶ **Mama Africa!**
by Kathryn Erskine; Farrar, Straus and Giroux Books for Young Readers, 2017

Chapter-At-A-Glance

 What Makes a Community Unique?

1 ENGAGE	2 INVESTIGATE	3 TAKE ACTION
INQUIRY JOURNAL	RESEARCH COMPANION	INQUIRY JOURNAL RESEARCH COMPANION

pp. 84–87

pp. 90–133

pp. 128–129   pp. 134–135

▶ **Introduce the Chapter**

▶ **Chapter Inquiry Project**

▶ **Explore Words**

▶ **Activate Knowledge**

▶ **How Do People Shape Their Communities?**

▶ **Connect Through Literature**
Fire to the People

▶ **People You Should Know**

▶ **Lessons 1–5**

▶ **Inquiry Project Wrap-Up and Chapter Connections**

▶ **Connections in Action!**

▶ **More to Explore**

Short on Time?
Engage with the content the way YOU want to teach—and *your* students want to learn!

Check out the three suggested **Flexible Instructional Pathways** on pages FM34–FM35.

The **IMPACT Explorer Magazine** supports students' exploration of the Essential Question and provides additional resources for the EQ Inquiry Project.

▶ Digital Tools at my.mheducation.com

ePresentation

Teach the Engage, Investigate, and Take Action content to the whole class from ePresentations that launch directly from the chapter dashboard.

eBook

You can flip your instruction with the **IMPACT eBooks** found on your chapter dashboard.

Interactive IMPACT

Blend in digital content **when you want it** and **where you want it**. Blended Learning notes in the Teacher's Edition highlight ways to connect in-class work with online experiences to enhance learning.

Investigate current events with **IMPACT News**.

Introduce the EQ with the **IMPACT Chapter Video**.

Explore domain-based vocabulary with **Explore Words** and **Word Play** vocabulary activities.

Chapter 3 ASSESSMENT

MONITOR PROGRESS:
Know What Your Students Know

Choose the assessment options that work best for you and your students.

Chapter Pre-Test (Optional)

Begin the Chapter

Measure students' content knowledge before you begin the chapter with the following questions.

Quick Check

✔ What are some ways that people express their culture?

✔ What are some cultural contributions in your own community?

✔ How can immigrants contribute to the culture of a community?

✔ How can communities share their cultures?

1. When all students have responded, ask them to rate how confident they are in their answers on a scale from 1 (not very confident) to 5 (very confident).

2. Ask students to compare their responses. Discuss with students some commonly held beliefs about culture. Ask students to keep these in mind as they progress through the chapter.

3. **Don't Forget!** Throughout the chapter, revisit students' quick-check responses with them. If students change their responses, ask them to support the change with text evidence. You may wish to have students respond to a different prompt to measure their content knowledge, such as *How do art, music, and stories help people express their culture?*

Ongoing Lesson Assessment

Use the lesson tools to monitor the **IMPACT** of your instruction.

☑ Stop and Check

Use the questions provided in the Stop and Check prompts to monitor students' comprehension of the lesson content. The Stop and Check questions, found in the Research Companion, prompt students to engage in discussions to deepen their understanding of the content.

✔ Check for Success

Use this formative assessment tool to assess how well your students understand the material they are learning in class. The Check for Success questions, located at point of use in the Teacher's Edition, are not a test but a way to assess students' comprehension of a particular topic. A Differentiate strategy offers one activity that you can use to quickly adapt your instruction.

◯ Report Your Findings

Use each lesson task to measure student understanding of the lesson content and their ability to effectively express their understanding. See pp. T192, T206, T222, T238, and T254 for task-specific evaluation rubrics. Report Your Findings is found in the Inquiry Journal.

▶ Digital Tools

Lesson Assessments

Use the **Lesson Test** to monitor students' understanding of the lesson content. Online Lesson Tests are customizable and available for every lesson. You will also find the tools you need to create your own assessments and to track your students' progress. A printable Lesson Test is available for use in class.

Chapter Assessment

Evaluate

Monitor student understanding of core chapter content with one or more of the following assessment options.

Connections in Action

Use the **Connections in Action** to evaluate student understanding of core chapter content through discussion in the Research Companion, pp. 134–135.

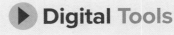 **Digital Tools**

Chapter Assessments
Use the **Chapter Test** to monitor student understanding of the chapter content. Online Chapter Tests are customizable and available for every chapter. You will also find the tools you need to create your own assessments and to track your students' progress. A printable Chapter Test is available for use in class.

Inquiry Project

In this chapter's Inquiry Project, students choose three cultures of their classmates and investigate how people express these cultures. Projects will include information about each of these cultures and explain how they help make the school unique. To showcase the information they find, students will present a plan for a holiday or festival that celebrates these cultures. See pp. T170–T171 for more information.

Use the EQ Inquiry Project to measure students' understanding of the chapter content and their ability to effectively express their understanding. A task-specific evaluation rubric is available in the Online Teacher Resources.

	4	3	2	1
Developing and Planning Inquiry	Project is focused on three different cultures and explores specific aspects of each.	Project is focused on three different cultures and explores some aspects of each.	Project is focused on three different cultures but explorations lack details.	Project is focused on three different cultures but does not explore aspects of them.
Cultural Understanding	Details are included that show a deep understanding of the cultures explored.	Some details are included that show a deep understanding of the cultures explored.	Includes information on cultures explored but few supporting details to show understanding.	Includes information on cultures explored but no supporting details.
Sources and Evidence	Project includes required and additional information and is supported with necessary evidence.	Project includes required information with some supporting evidence.	Project includes some required facts and evidence.	Required facts and supporting evidence are not included.
Communicating Conclusions	Project information is clearly supported with details and is easily understood.	Project information includes details and is understood with some explanation.	Project information is unclear due to lack of details.	Project does not include details necessary to communicate information.

EQ What Makes a Community Unique?

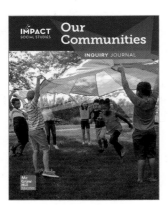

INQUIRY JOURNAL, pp. 84–85

Talk About It

Read Have students read the opening page together. Prompt students to write three questions they would like to be able to answer after reading about the features that make communities special. Give them a chance to share their questions with a partner. You may wish to record these questions and refer back to them throughout the chapter.

Inquiry Project
Planning a Cultural Event

Discuss the Inquiry Project with students. Review each step of the project from the **Project Checklist**. Tell students that they will use information from the chapter and from independent research to complete the project.

My Research Plan

Discuss the Essential Question with students. Have students think about how people and their cultures have made their community special. Then have students work in pairs to brainstorm research questions that are "just right," neither too general nor too specific.

Design Your Own Inquiry Path (Optional)

You may wish to work with students to choose their own Essential Question, Inquiry Project, and related research questions. Have students preview chapter materials and discuss ideas with classmates to help develop possible questions, such as *How do immigrants contribute to the culture of our community?, How is our community similar to and different from a community in another country?,* or their own questions.

Have students explain why their Essential Question is important to them and to others. Have students record their question, project idea, and initial supporting research questions using the **Student EQ Inquiry Project** pages found at **my.mheducation.com**.

▶ Digital Tools

Blended Learning
Students engage with the chapter's Essential Question and launch their investigations.

Interactive IMPACT
Spark student interest with the **EQ Chapter Video**.

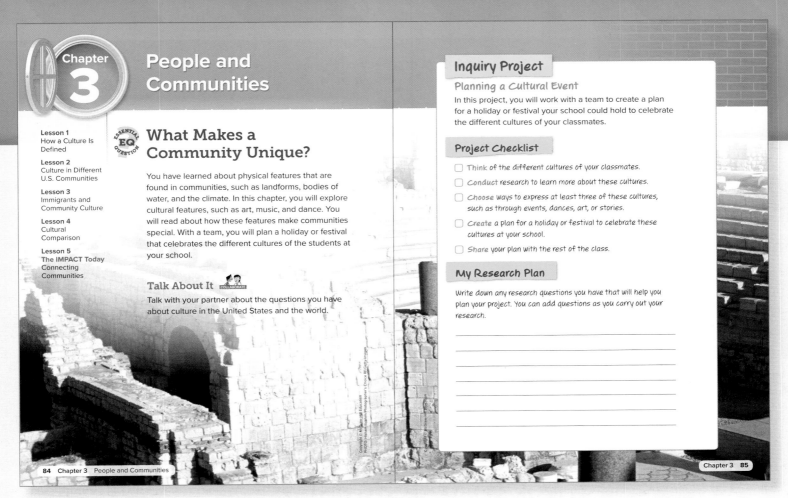

INQUIRY JOURNAL, pp. 84–85

English Learners SCAFFOLD

Use the following scaffolds to support student understanding of the Inquiry Project.

Entering and Emerging

Help students understand the Inquiry Project checklist. Explain the word *express*. Say: Express *can mean "to make known" or "to show." People can express, or make known, cultural ideas through their holidays, festivals, music, dances, art, and stories. With a partner, tell one way that your family expresses its culture.* Have students use the following sentence frame:

- My family expresses its culture through _____.

Developing and Expanding

Ask questions to check understanding of the Inquiry Project instructions and elicit answers. For example: *You're going to plan a holiday or festival that celebrates the cultures of your classmates. Can you identify some of the cultures of the students at our school? This festival will also feature ways that people express their cultures. Can you name some ways that people express their cultures?*

Bridging and Reaching

Have partners read through the Inquiry Project instructions and checklist. Have them talk about different cultures that are present in the classroom and discuss ways that they can research more about these cultures. Have them consider local resources that might be available and compile a list of potential Internet search terms they could use.

Social Emotional Learning

Self-Regulation

Organize As students plan their Inquiry Projects, stress the importance of being organized. Explain that organizing information will help them identify the most relevant information for their projects and determine additional information to find. Being organized will also ensure that students complete their work in a timely manner.

ENGAGE
with INQUIRY JOURNAL

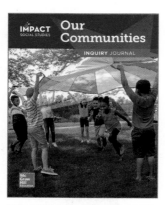

**INQUIRY JOURNAL,
pp. 86–87**

Explore Words

Academic/Domain-Specific Vocabulary Read the words aloud to students. Explain to students that these are words they will learn more about in the chapter.

Word Rater Have students place a checkmark in one of the three boxes below each word, indicating that they "Know It," "Heard It," or "Don't Know It." Explain to students that they will come back to this chart to add additional information about each word as they work through the chapter.

☐ **Know It!** Tell students that if they know the word, they should write its meaning on the lines provided.

☐ **Heard It!** Tell students that if they have heard or are familiar with the word, they should write what they know about it on the lines provided. Remind them to take notes about the word as they encounter it.

☐ **Don't Know It!** If students do not know the word's meaning, tell them to write down its meaning when they encounter the word in the chapter.

Support Vocabulary

Return to the Word Rater as you come across vocabulary words in each lesson. Encourage students to use the "My Notes" section to include any of the following:

- definitions from the text
- deeper understandings
- synonyms
- other associations

 Spanish Cognates

For Spanish speakers, point out the cognates.

culture = cultura

pioneer = pionero

tolerance = tolerancia

Content Words	
apartheid	a system of racial inequality and discrimination against black people
artifact	an object that was used by people in the past
citizen	a person who lives in a community or is a member of a country
culture	the way of life a group of people share
ethnic group	people who have come from the same place and often share the same language, history, and other aspects of culture
folktale	a story that is handed down over the years
heritage	tradition or background of a group of people
oral tradition	stories or poems that are spoken aloud rather than written
pioneer	people who settled in wilderness areas
tolerance	respecting something different from your own beliefs and customs

Complete this chapter's Word Rater. Write notes as you learn more about each word.

apartheid

☐ Know It!
☐ Heard It!
☐ Don't Know It!

My Notes
_____
_____
_____

artifact

☐ Know It!
☐ Heard It!
☐ Don't Know It!

My Notes
_____
_____
_____

citizen

☐ Know It!
☐ Heard It!
☐ Don't Know It!

My Notes
_____
_____
_____

culture

☐ Know It!
☐ Heard It!
☐ Don't Know It!

My Notes
_____
_____
_____

ethnic groups

☐ Know It!
☐ Heard It!
☐ Don't Know It!

My Notes
_____
_____
_____

folktale

☐ Know It!
☐ Heard It!
☐ Don't Know It!

My Notes
_____
_____
_____

heritage

☐ Know It!
☐ Heard It!
☐ Don't Know It!

My Notes
_____
_____
_____

oral tradition

☐ Know It!
☐ Heard It!
☐ Don't Know It!

My Notes
_____
_____
_____

pioneer

☐ Know It!
☐ Heard It!
☐ Don't Know It!

My Notes
_____
_____
_____

tolerance

☐ Know It!
☐ Heard It!
☐ Don't Know It!

My Notes
_____
_____
_____

INQUIRY JOURNAL, pp. 86–87

 # English Learners SCAFFOLD

Use the following scaffolds to support student understanding of chapter vocabulary.

Entering and Emerging

Display the word list and definitions for students. Pronounce each word and read the definitions. Then point to each word and definition and have students read along with you. Work with them to write context sentences for each word.

Developing and Expanding

Review vocabulary terms and definitions with students. Then provide sentence frames such as the following to help them understand the meaning of each word:

- The people who first settled in our town are called _____.
- Fireworks on the Fourth of July are an example of American _____.

Have students work with partners to write context sentences for each word.

Bridging and Reaching

Have students work in small groups to create vocabulary flashcards. On one side of the card, have students write the term. On the other side, have students write their own definition of the term or draw a picture. Then have groups quiz one another using their flashcards.

 **Digital** Tools

Blended Learning

Explore Words engages students in the investigation of academic and domain-specific words they encounter in each lesson.

Interactive IMPACT

Throughout the chapter, encourage students to interact with the **Explore Words** cards and games.

What Makes a Community Unique?

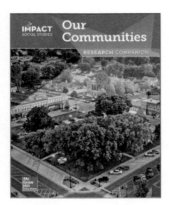

RESEARCH COMPANION, pp. 90–91

Activate Knowledge

Read and Discuss COLLABORATE Have students read the opening on p. 90 together. Ask: *How would our country be different if every community had the same culture?* As students share their responses, you may wish to redirect misconceptions and inaccurate information.

How Do People Shape Their Communities?

- Have students read the text, focusing on both the photographs and captions.
- What is the purpose of telling stories? (Answers should note that people tell stories to educate or entertain, to express hopes and fears, and to tell about people and events from the past.)
- What is the relationship between food and cultural holidays? (Students should point out that for some cultures, certain foods are eaten to celebrate holidays.)
- What types of art do people create? (Answers will vary but may include paintings, drawings, photographs, and sculptures.)

Make Connections

- What do a culture's stories have in common with its art, music, and dance? (Answers will vary, but students should understand that people communicate ideas and emotions that are important to their culture through stories, art, music, and dance.)
- How do people in your community express their different cultures? (Answers will vary, but students may describe how different cultures in their community are expressed through stories, food, art, music, and dance.)

Perspectives How does living and working with people from different cultures affect all the people in a community? (Students should include reasons that support their opinions.)

People and Communities

ESSENTIAL EQ QUESTION

What Makes a Community Unique?

You have read about how the location, climate, and environment make a community special. In this chapter, you will find out how people and their cultures, or ways of life, also make a community unique. You will explore how stories, art, music, food, dance, and other things help form a community's culture. As you read, think about the cultures in your community. How do these cultures make your community special?

Communities in the United States celebrate Independence Day on July 4.

90 Chapter 3 People and Communities

How Do People Shape Their Communities?

People shape their communities through the stories they tell, the food they share, and the art, music, and dance they create.

People from all over the world share stories. Stories can educate or entertain. People sometimes tell stories to express their hopes and fears. They also use stories to tell about important people and events from the past. Storytelling is one way that people keep their cultures alive.

Everyone needs food to survive. However, food also plays an important role in a community's culture. This includes the types of food people eat as well as the way the food is prepared and how it is eaten. People may eat certain foods to celebrate holidays or festivals. For example, many families in the United States eat turkey on Thanksgiving Day.

A community's culture can be expressed through the art, music, and dance people create. People can view art, such as paintings, drawings, photographs, or sculptures. They can listen and dance to many kinds of music, such as rock, pop, and hip-hop. Art, music, and dance allow people to communicate ideas and emotions that are important to their cultures.

Chapter 3 91

RESEARCH COMPANION, pp. 90–91

 English Learners SCAFFOLD

Use these scaffolds to support students in activating their background knowledge.

Entering and Emerging

Point to each picture on p. 91, and ask: *What are the people in this picture doing?* Provide students with the following sentence frame:

- In this picture, the people are _____.

Then point out that each picture shows people who are sharing their culture. Ask students to draw a picture to show how they share their cultures with others in their community. Have students share their pictures with a partner and tell what it shows using the sentence frame above.

Developing and Expanding

Have students tell a partner what the people in each picture on p. 91 are doing. Then explain that each picture shows people who are sharing their culture. Ask students to think of ways that people in their community share their cultures, and have them discuss their ideas with a partner.

Bridging and Reaching

Ask students to look at the pictures on p. 91 and read the captions. With a partner, have students discuss what the pictures have in common. Then ask partners to discuss how people in their community share their culture through stories, food, art, music, and dance.

Connect Through Literature

FIRE TO THE PEOPLE

Retold by Donna Henes

There are many myths around the world that describe the origin of fire. Though each is different, many share a common theme: a brave young person steals fire from the gods, gives it to the people, and is then punished for doing it. Here, you can read fire myths from two different cultures.

Greece

Zeus ordered that only the gods should have fire. So the world of people was sad and dark. There was no fire to light their lives. There was no fire for cooking, for warmth, or to make metal tools and weapons. The god Prometheus felt sorry for the people.

He decided he would steal fire for them. He did this in secret, because he knew that Zeus would be angry with him. Prometheus knew he would never be allowed to return to his home once Zeus discovered his plan. So he said goodbye to Mount Olympus.

Prometheus broke off a glowing coal from the Sun. Hiding it in the hollowed-out stalk of a fennel plant, Prometheus carried the coal down to Earth. He showed people how to use it. Zeus was furious. He ordered Prometheus to be captured and chained to the side of a cliff. There, a vulture was sent to peck at Prometheus's liver all day long. Each night, his liver grew back. There was no end to his suffering.

92 Chapter 3 People and Communities

Nigeria

Obassi Osaw, the creator god, provided humankind with everything but fire. The people complained that he was cruel for not giving them the means to keep warm. The chief of the village pleaded with the god for fire. But Obassi Osaw turned him down. So the chief sent his youngest son to beg for fire. He, too, was denied. Then the boy returned once again to the god. He was determined to get fire even if he had to steal it.

That night, Obassi Osaw asked his wife to bring him the lamp, but she was busy. She asked the chief's son to take the lantern to her husband, and she showed him how to light it with a long stick. The boy took the stick, wrapped it in leaves so it wouldn't burn out, and hid it in the forest.

Later, when all was quiet, the boy went back to get the burning stick. Then, he ran to Earth, where he showed the people how to use fire.

When Obassi Osaw awoke in the morning, he saw smoke and went to investigate. The chief's son confessed that he had stolen the fire. Obassi Osaw punished him, forcing him to walk forevermore as if he had been burnt.

Chapter 3 93

Think About It

1. What is similar about these two stories?

2. What is different about these two stories?

3. Which fire myth do you like better? Why?

RESEARCH COMPANION, pp. 92–93

Connect Through Literature

| **GENRE** | **Myth** "Fire to the People" tells two stories that explain the origin of fire. A myth is a story that is told to explain a practice, belief, or something in nature.

Have students read the text on pp. 92–93. Then discuss the following questions.

1. What is similar about these two stories? (Both stories tell how people got fire and that the character who stole fire was punished.)

Have students reread the selection and ask:

2. What is different about these two stories? (Answers will vary but may discuss the different ways that Prometheus and the chief's son obtained fire.)

3. Why do you think different cultures have different stories to explain the same things? (Answers will vary.)

Perspectives Why do you think myths were an important part of the culture of ancient people such as the Greeks and Nigerians? (Answers will vary.)

▶ Digital Tools

Blended Learning
Students explore the chapter content by making connections to literature.

eBook

Have students use the eBook to interact with engaging literary selections.

People You Should Know

Sandra Cisneros

Sandra Cisneros is an author from Chicago, Illinois, who writes books and poems, often shaped by her own cultural experiences. Her first book, *The House on Mango Street*, was written in 1984 and won an American Book Award. Her book *Hairs/Pelitos* is written with both English and Spanish words on the same page.

Keith Haring

Keith Haring was a graphic artist and designer. He made large outdoor murals, or paintings on a wall. Children often helped him complete the murals. In 1986, 900 children helped him create a mural for the 100th anniversary of the Statue of Liberty. Keith Haring's work can be seen today in many museums around the world.

Gloria Estefan

Gloria Estefan is a singer who moved from Cuba to the United States when she was very young. Her songs are known for mixing both Cuban and American styles. Gloria Estefan and her husband, Emilio, have been awarded the Presidential Medal of Freedom for their contribution to music and Latin American culture.

Harper Lee

Harper Lee was an author who wrote the book *To Kill a Mockingbird*. The story is known in many countries. It has also been made into a film. *To Kill a Mockingbird* has been praised for its message on tolerance.

94 Chapter 3 People and Communities

Chapter 3 95

RESEARCH COMPANION, pp. 94–95

People You Should Know

How do personal stories IMPACT our understanding of people and communities?

Read Explain to students that they will learn about how people and their cultures make communities unique. Have students read the four biographies and think about how each person contributed to the culture of his or her community.

Research Instruct students to select one of these individuals and do more research about his or her life and cultural contributions. Tell students to gather facts about a specific piece of writing, art, or music the person created, and examine how the work reflected his or her culture.

Respond Have each student write a series of three diary entries from the point of view of the person he or she researched. Each entry should detail the creation of the specific work the student researched. One entry could detail how the person came up with the idea, another could describe the process of creating the work, and the last could explain the effect of that work on the person's community.

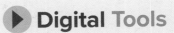 **Digital Tools**

Blended Learning

Students investigate and discuss curated news articles that extend the chapter content.

Interactive IMPACT

Connect to current events and people with **IMPACT News** and **More to Investigate**.

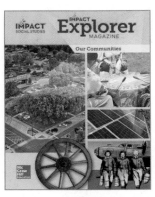

**IMPACT EXPLORER
MAGAZINE, pp. 30–41**

WordBlast

Remind students to look for the Word Blasts as they read the *IMPACT Explorer Magazine*.

Extend Knowledge Building

The **IMPACT Explorer Magazine** provides students another route to explore each chapter's Essential Question from a variety of perspectives as they dig deeper into the subject of people and communities. Additional questions and activities help students develop and deepen their understanding of the chapter's content.

Engage

Build background for students and share any information needed to provide a context for the chapter topic. Read aloud the Essential Question and the Table of Contents.

Analyze the Visual Discuss the opening visual (photograph, photo essay, artwork) on the second page of the **IMPACT Explorer Magazine** chapter. Help students connect the visual to the chapter topic and the Essential Question.

Analyze the Sources

Students will read and analyze the leveled informational articles and literary texts, graphic texts, primary and secondary sources, photographs, maps, and other visual resources.

Read and Analyze Before reading, provide any additional information you think students will need about the topics. Then guide students through the three-step process to read and analyze the content.

1 Inspect

Have students skim the content on a page or multiple pages. Ask questions to help students recall and retell key ideas.

- What is this article mostly about?
- Who is _____?

2 Find Evidence

Have students reread the content and look for details they might have missed. Ask additional questions to help them read more closely.

- What details do you notice in the photographs?
- Why was _____ important?

3 Make Connections

Have students work in pairs or small groups to discuss prompts that help them connect the articles to other texts, their own lives, current ideas and issues, and other topics.

- How is _____ similar to what we do?
- How do you think _____ felt about what happened?
- What do you think about _____?

IMPACT EXPLORER MAGAZINE, pp. 30–31

How to Use the IMPACT Explorer Magazine

Use the following scaffolds to support students' understanding and your classroom needs.

Whole Class
Use the **IMPACT Explorer Magazine** Teaching Guide to read and discuss one or more articles with the whole class.

Small Group
Have partners or small groups read articles connected to the day's core lesson and report back to the whole class about what they read.

Independent Work
Assign articles for students to extend and enrich their understanding of a topic, including during center time and independent reading time.

The online **IMPACT Explorer Magazine** Teaching Guide provides support for various implementation models as well as a three-step lesson plan for each article. The lesson plan includes background information, meaningful questions, vocabulary activities, scaffolded support for English learners, and collaborative conversation prompts.

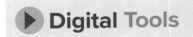

Digital Tools

Blended Learning
Students extend the investigation of the Chapter EQ with highly visual, leveled articles and video.

eBook

Use the **IMPACT Explorer Magazine eBook** to extend knowledge building.

LESSON QUESTION

What Is Culture?

Connect to the Essential Question

Tell students that this lesson provides key research into the Chapter Essential Question: **What Makes a Community Unique?** Explain that they will explore the meaning of *culture*, how cultures form, and why a community, state, and nation can comprise many cultures. They will also investigate how cultures from all over the world are different and alike, how culture groups overlap, and how culture relates to *ethnicity* and other aspects of society.

Lesson Objectives

- **Define** culture and explain the difference between culture and ethnicity.
- **Describe** how culture groups form and how they express and share their cultures.
- **Explain** how culture affects schools and families in a community.
- **Write** an informative paragraph to explain culture and why it is important to communities.

Make Connections!

CONNECT TO ELA

Reading **Ask and answer** questions to demonstrate understanding of a text and refer explicitly to the text as the basis for the answers.

Demonstrate understanding of the text (e.g., *where, when, why,* and *how* key events occur) by using information gained from illustrations and the words in a text.

Research **Recall** information from experiences or gather information from print and digital sources; take brief notes on sources and sort evidence into provided categories.

Writing **Craft** informative/explanatory texts to examine a topic and convey ideas and information clearly.

Speaking and Listening **Follow** agreed-upon rules for discussions (e.g., gaining the floor in respectful ways, listening to others with care, speaking one at a time about the topics and texts under discussion).

Language **Demonstrate** command of the conventions of standard English capitalization, punctuation, and spelling when writing.

COMMUNITY CONNECTIONS

To enrich students' learning about culture, have them conduct a guided online research project in which they investigate and learn about nearby cultural festivals and other cultural events. Challenge students to create a Culture Calendar to share with their community showing dates and summaries of cultural celebrations throughout the year. You may wish to extend the activity by having students identify holidays celebrated by different culture groups.

Lesson-At-A-Glance

1 ENGAGE
INQUIRY JOURNAL

pp. 88–93

- ▶ **Talk About It:** Photograph of sculpture "The Thinker"
- ▶ **Analyze the Source:** How Cultures Form
- ▶ **Inquiry Tools:** Explore Summarizing

2 INVESTIGATE
RESEARCH COMPANION

pp. 96–101

- ▶ **Culture and Ethnicity**
- ▶ **Cultures Across the Globe**
- ▶ **Around the World: Schools and Families**

3 REPORT
INQUIRY JOURNAL

pp. 94–95

- ▶ **Think About It**
- ▶ **Write About It:** Write an Informational Paragraph; Cite Evidence from Text
- ▶ **Talk About It**
- ▶ **Connect to the Essential Question**

ASSESSMENT

- ▶ **Online Lesson Test**
- ▶ **Printable Lesson Test**

For more details, see pp. T168–T169.

▶ Digital Tools
at **my.mheducation.com**

ePresentation

Teach the Engage, Investigate, and Report content to the whole class from **ePresentations** that launch directly from the lesson dashboard.

eBook

You can flip your instruction with the **IMPACT eBooks** found on your lesson dashboard.

Interactive IMPACT

Blend in digital content **when you want it** and **where you want it**.

Blended Learning features in the Teacher's Edition highlight ways to connect in-class work with online experiences to enhance learning.

Investigate current events with **IMPACT News**.

Explore domain-based vocabulary with **Explore Words** and **Word Play** vocabulary activities.

pp. 30–41

Go Further with IMPACT Explorer Magazine!

The **IMPACT Explorer Magazine** supports students' exploration of the Essential Question and provides additional resources for the EQ Inquiry Project.

LESSON 1 LANGUAGE LEARNERS

What Is Culture?

Language Objectives

- Use newly acquired content and academic vocabulary to talk and write about culture.
- Explain in writing the meaning and importance of culture, using examples from the text.
- Analyze a text to determine if two ideas are alike or different by identifying comparing and contrasting words.

 Spanish Cognates

To support Spanish speakers, point out the cognates.

custom = costumbre

important = importante

education = educación

Introduce the Lesson

Set Purpose Explain to students that in this lesson, they will read informational texts to learn about cultures and how they change and grow over time.

Access Prior Knowledge Read the Lesson Question. Remind students that a community is a place where people live, work, and play. Ask students what people in their community have in common with each other. Say: *What do people in your community do together? How are people in your community alike?*

Spark Curiosity Have students study the photograph of the Yee Peng Lantern Festival on p. 99 of the Research Companion. Ask students what they think the people in the photo are doing. Explain that holidays and festivals are an important part of many cultures, and that these celebrations help bring people together. Say: *This photo shows a festival in Thailand. During the festival, people release lanterns into the air and wish for good fortune in the new year.* Ask students to name other holidays and festivals they are familiar with. Ask who celebrates each holiday or festival and why.

Build Meaning & Support Language

Inquiry Journal

Analyze the Source (pp. 90–91) Tell students that in this lesson they will read informational texts that give facts, examples, and explanations about cultures around the world. As you read "How Cultures Form," explain any words that students don't know. Support students' understanding using the photographs on p. 91. Say: *Culture includes people's way of life, or how they live and what they do every day. Clothing is one part of culture. What do you notice about the clothing in each photograph? What does it tell you about the people's culture?*

Inquiry Tools (pp. 92–93) Remind students that when they **Summarize** information, they should focus on the main idea and important supporting details. Explain that the graphic organizer will help them organize the information they read. Have students preview the Research Companion text by reading the heading on p. 96 and scanning each paragraph. Ask what they think this part of the text will be about. Check that students understand how to find the main idea of a paragraph. You may wish to have students work with a partner to write down the main idea of each paragraph and compare their ideas in small groups.

Research Companion

Culture and Ethnicity (pp. 96–97) After you read the first paragraph on p. 96, draw students' attention to the words *customs* and *traditions*. Explain that customs and traditions are common beliefs and actions that members of a culture pass down over time. In paragraph 2, point out this sentence: "These help bind together the community." Say: *The words* bind together *mean "to join or unite people." Why do traditions join people together?* (because they are beliefs or activities that people share)

Cultures Across the Globe (pp. 98–99) Explain to students that this section provides examples of cultures and traditions. Draw a T-chart on the board. As you read, add to the left column names of cultures described in the text (such as Japanese, Eastern European, and West African cultures). Have students identify the traditions of each culture (such as haikus, polkas, and stories about Anansi). Add these to the right column. Model the pronunciation of the cultures and traditions, and have students repeat them after you.

Schools and Families (pp. 100–101) Point out the word *resources* on p. 100. Remind students that resources are things that benefit people, and explain that the resources in a school include anything that helps students learn. Ask: *What are some examples of resources you use in school?* Encourage students to mention examples such as books, paper, pencils, and computers. On p. 101, explain that a *family* is any group of people who live together as a family. Review the words for family members on this page and explain any terms that are unfamiliar (such as *caregiver* and *stepparent*).

Inquiry Journal

Report Your Findings (pp. 94–95) Remind students that *evidence* is facts or details that support an idea or opinion. Explain that students can use connecting words such as *because* and *since* to introduce reasons and evidence to support their opinions.

Language Forms & Conventions

Compare and Contrast Words Explain that there are some key words that give a clue that a sentence is showing two ideas that are alike or different. Throughout this lesson, there are comparisons of cultures. Point out this sentence in the "Did You Know?" box on p. 99: "Unlike some countries, the United States does not have an official language." Display the chart.

Comparison Words	Contrasting Words
like	unlike
both	none, neither
same	different
too	but, however

 Have students work in pairs to locate comparison words that appear in the lesson. Call on partners to say them aloud and add them to the chart. Ask volunteers to use the words in sentences.

 Cross-Cultural Connection

The Anansi stories play an important role in West African oral tradition. Often they are shared with children, and they teach a lesson or moral. Many of the stories began in what is now Ghana but spread to other places, including Jamaica, the United States, and the northern parts of South America. Ask: *What stories were you told as a child?*

 Leveled Support

Entering & Emerging
Provide sentence frames: *Culture is _____. Culture is important because it _____.*

Developing & Expanding
Have small groups make a list of reasons culture is important.

Bridging & Reaching
Have partners identify a culture in their community and give two reasons why it is important to the community.

 **Language Transfer**

Many languages, including Spanish, also use certain suffixes to indicate nationality. In Spanish, these suffixes include *-és, -o,* and *-ense*. Unlike English, Spanish nouns and adjectives often have different masculine and feminine forms. Therefore, words used to describe nationalities may change based on the gender of the person or the word being described.

LESSON QUESTION

What Is Culture?

INQUIRY JOURNAL, pp. 88–89

Bellringer

Say: *You have learned about the physical characteristics of communities, like land and water features and things that humans have made and built. Now, we are going to take a look at culture in our communities. What do people in your community have in common? What do people in your community do together?* Invite students to call out examples or other ideas. (Responses may include ways of life, customs, traditions, religion and other beliefs, language, stories, songs and music, art, architecture, dance, clothing, and food.)

Lesson Outcomes

Discuss the lesson question and lesson outcomes with students.

- Make sure that students notice that the term *culture* can be both a big idea and a smaller idea that is specific to a community. When we speak about specific communities, we can use a plural noun (*cultures*). When we speak about culture as a big idea, even though it is a universal idea, we use a singular noun (*culture*).

- Remind students that the United States has many diverse, or different, communities. The people in the communities may speak different languages and practice a variety of religions or no religion.

Talk About It

Have small groups list as many types of art as they can in one minute. Then call on each group to share one type of art. Keep going until all groups have shared. Ask students to study and describe the photograph of "The Thinker," read the caption, and discuss what the sculpture tells them about culture. Provide sentence frames as needed to help students complete the activity.

- The sculpture is a kind of _____. It shows _____.
- The sculpture tells me that culture means/includes _____.
- People express, or share, their culture by/through _____.

 Collaborative Conversations

Ask Questions to Deepen Understanding As students engage in small group and whole-class discussions, encourage them to

- ask questions about things they don't understand or to clarify what others are saying.
- form a clear answer to another student's question before giving it.
- show respect by allowing other students to ask questions.

What Is Culture?

Lesson Outcomes

What Am I Learning?
In this lesson, you will use your investigative skills to explore what *culture* means and how cultures around the world are different and similar.

Why Am I Learning It?
Reading and talking about cultures will help you make connections between people and places.

How Will I Know That I Learned It?
You will be able to write a paragraph that defines *culture* and explains why culture matters.

Talk About It

Look closely at the sculpture. What does the picture lead you to believe *culture* might mean?

88 Lesson 1 What Is Culture?

Art makes up just one part of culture.

Chapter 3 Lesson 1 89

INQUIRY JOURNAL, pp. 88–89

English Learners SCAFFOLD

Use the following scaffolds to support student understanding of lesson outcomes.

Entering and Emerging

Tell students that the photograph shows a type of art called a sculpture. It might also be called a statue. Read the caption aloud. Provide sentence frames to help students connect art to culture.

- Many people can make art. Some people I know who make art are _____.
- Art is one part of _____.
- Culture is important to our _____.

Developing and Expanding

Have small groups work together to make a list of different types of art (e.g., sculpture, painting, drawing, weaving, pottery, engraving, woodworking, carving). Ask: *Who makes art? How can art be an important part of a culture? What types of art are important to the culture in your community?*

Bridging and Reaching

Guide students to identify the picture as a sculpture. Explain that sculptures are one type of art. They can be made from stone, metal, clay, wood, or other materials. Ask: *What does this sculpture show? What else might be part of culture?* Have partners talk about the question and write their answers in complete sentences.

Social Emotional Learning

Self-Regulation

Set Goals and Maintain Focus
Students must learn to hold productive discussions with one another and with teachers. Part of having a productive discussion is staying on topic. Set goals for class discussions. As conversations proceed, remind students to maintain focus.

Analyze the Source

How Cultures Form

1 Inspect

Read the article and look at the images. How do the images help you understand the text?

Circle words you do not know.

Underline words you have already learned.

List parts of culture.

My Notes

_____
_____
_____
_____
_____
_____
_____
_____
_____
_____
_____
_____

When people began forming communities, they also developed **cultures**. _Culture_ means the values, beliefs, and other ways of life shared by a group of people.

Cultures can be as big as a world culture linked by trade and technology. Cultures can also be as small as a family group. Some communities and nations have one main culture. They might have a few smaller cultures. Others, like the United States, are home to many different cultures.

Many culture groups have come to the United States over time. Native Americans were the earliest people to live here. They formed unique, or special, cultures across the continent. Their environments shaped their cultures. People in the east, like the Cherokee, learned to make clothing from plants that grew around them. People further north learned to make clothes from the animals that lived there. Some cultures used plant dyes to decorate themselves and their goods. Others used stones, shells, or other resources found nearby.

Clothing, music, jewelry, tools, and food all express, or show, culture.

Later, people from Asia, Europe, and other parts of the world also came to the Americas. African people were brought as enslaved people. They, too, brought their cultures. Then and now, culture groups work to preserve, or keep, their cultures alive. They do so through shared activities. These include art, music, stories, games, celebrations, and religious gatherings.

2 Find Evidence

Reread Where are cultures found?

Highlight ways that environment affects culture.

Describe How do people preserve culture?

3 Make Connections

Talk Think about the cultural activities shown in the photographs on this page. Turn back to page 89. How do the photographs on both pages show what culture is?

Analyze the Source

Background Information
The word _culture_ is related to the word _cultivate_, which means "to raise, take care of, or grow crops or other things." Both come from a Latin word meaning "to guard, nurture, or tend." A culture is made up of all the ideas, beliefs, and ways of life that a group of people have tended, nurtured, or grown together over time.

1 Inspect

Read Have students read the text and study the images on pp. 90–91. Remind them to circle unfamiliar words and underline words they have already learned.

- Have students list parts of culture described in the text.

2 Find Evidence

Reread Have students reread the text and highlight ways that the environment affects culture.

Describe Tell partners to skim the text for the word _preserve_, and list ways that people preserve culture.

3 Make Connections

Talk Direct students to look at the pictures on pp. 89 and 91, and discuss the question. Ask: _What do these images have to do with how people preserve culture?_
(Answers will vary.)

Spotlight on Language

Comparing with Opposites

Have students skim the text to find words that describe size and quantity. Point out the words that have opposite meanings: _big/small_ and _few/many_. Say: _These words are antonyms. They show differences._ Ask partners to take turns using antonyms to compare culture groups.

Explore Summarizing

To **summarize** means to retell something in your own words. A **summary** tells the main idea and a few important details.

1. **Read the text and look at any pictures and maps.**
   Ask yourself: *What is this about?* This will help you understand the topic.

2. **Look for main ideas and details.**
   Titles, labels, images, and words on the page will help you understand what you are learning.

3. **Say in a few words what it is about.**
   Explain it in your own words. What does this section teach you?

 Based on the text you read, work with your class to complete the chart below. Then summarize the information in the text and the images.

Topic	Main Idea	Details
The topic is culture, what it is, and how it forms.	Different groups of people develop their own cultures.	Culture includes art, music, stories, language, beliefs, values, customs, tools, and clothing. Environment shapes cultures. Cultures can be big or small. A nation can have one main culture or many different cultures.

Summary: Answers will vary, but summaries should explain that cultures are the ways of life, including the beliefs and values, of different groups of people. The U.S. is home to many cultures.

 ## Investigate!

Read pages 96–101 in your Research Companion. Use your investigative skills to look for evidence that helps you understand what the topic of each section of text is. The evidence will include main ideas and details. This chart will help you organize your notes.

Answers will vary. Sample answers shown below.

Topic	Main Idea	Details
culture and ethnicity	Culture and ethnicity are closely related.	Elements of culture include language, religion, and customs. Ethnic groups have shared geographic origins and often share a culture. Cultures change over time as communities change.
cultures around the world	People around the world preserve and express culture in many ways.	Expressions of culture include art, music, stories, festivals and holidays, and religious and spiritual beliefs and gatherings. When people from different cultures interact, their cultures mix. Mass media connects people in a global culture.
education in different cultures	Culture shapes ideas about education.	Not all schools have the same resources. Dress codes, types of classes, and other things differ from culture to culture. Schools are one way that cultures pass on important ideas, values, and skills.
family in different cultures	Culture shapes ideas about family.	Family size and relationships differ across the United States and around the world.

Summary: Answers will vary but should include each of the main ideas recorded in the chart.

INQUIRY JOURNAL, pp. 92–93

Inquiry Tools

Explore Summarizing

Read Have students read the step-by-step instructions about how to summarize an informational text. Emphasize that students should read a text completely to get an overall idea of what the text is about. Then they can go back and identify the main idea. Point out the importance of retelling the information in their own words.

Guide Practice Have students review the text on pp. 90–91. Then work with students to complete the graphic organizer and write a summary. Explain that they will use a similar graphic organizer to organize their independent research.

Check Understanding Confirm student understanding of the inquiry skill, Explore Summarizing. If students cannot identify main ideas and important details and then write a summary in their own words, review the steps on p. 92.

Investigate!

Have students read pp. 96–101 in the Research Companion. Tell them the information will help them answer the lesson question **What Is Culture?**

Take Notes Tell students they should use the graphic organizer on p. 93 of the Inquiry Journal to take notes on the main ideas and important details about culture and ethnicity, cultures around the world, and family and education in different countries.

Remind students that the main idea of a text, or a section of text, is the most important idea on the topic covered. Important details are those that provide evidence or examples for the main idea.

 ### Spotlight on Content

Following Instructions

Remind students to read step-by-step instructions in the order in which they are listed. Start with the first step, then the next. Have students read the instructions. Ask: *What's the first thing you do when summarizing a text? Why do you reread?*

 ### Digital Tools

Blended Learning

Students prepare for the lesson investigation with step-by-step instructions about how to summarize information.

ePresentation

Use the **Inquiry Tools** to model the lesson graphic organizer.

LESSON 1 INVESTIGATE

LESSON QUESTION

What Is Culture?

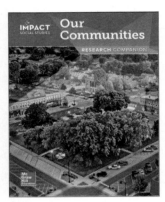

RESEARCH COMPANION, pp. 96–97

Background Information

Terms like *culture, ethnicity, nationality,* and *race* sometimes overlap, but they are distinct.

- People who share an ethnicity may have the same national origins or different nationalities. For example, ethnic Arabs and ethnic Jews live in many nations all over the world. Also, most nations comprise people from multiple ethnic groups. Most people in Russia are ethnic Russians, but the nation also includes several smaller ethnic groups, such as Chechens and Tatars. Many American citizens have more than one ethnic background.
- National and ethnic groups often share cultural characteristics, but many people belong to more than one culture group. A popular misconception is that all Muslims, or followers of Islam, are Arab or come from Southwest Asia. Yet the nation with the world's largest Muslim population is Indonesia, located in *Southeast* Asia. This nation has three major ethnic groups, none of them Arab, and many smaller ones. Even in Southeast Asia, Muslims might be Arab, Persian, Turkish, Kurdish, or another ethnicity.
- Race reflects shared physical characteristics but tends to be broader than ethnicity. For example, a person considered Caucasian might come from any number of ethnic groups originating in Europe, Asia, or North Africa.

Culture and Ethnicity

1 Inspect Have students read pp. 96–97 and explain how culture groups differ from ethnic groups. (Culture groups share customs and ways of life while ethnic groups come from the same place.)

2 Find Evidence Use the questions below to check comprehension. Remind students to support their answers with text evidence.

Explain How do communities develop their own cultures? (When people form communities they develop shared customs that bind them together. These customs become their culture.) **DOK 2**

Draw Conclusions Why do ethnic groups often share cultural characteristics? (Ethnic groups come from the same place so they likely share language, history, and other cultural characteristics.) **DOK 2**

3 Make Connections

Categorize To what culture groups do you belong? Identify at least two, and describe a custom or characteristic of each culture. (Answers should reflect students' individual cultural backgrounds.) **DOK 2**

Apply What can you assume about culture and ethnicity in the United States? (Answers may vary, but students should conclude that the United States has people from many cultures and many ethnic groups because people from many different places helped build the nation.) **DOK 3**

Lesson 1

What Is Culture?

Culture and Ethnicity

Did you know that **cultures** grow and change over time? A culture is the shared customs of a group of people. A custom is a way of life practiced over a long period of time. Customs can also be called traditions.

Cultures form when people come together to create communities. As well as shared customs and traditions, they adopt shared practices, like language, and beliefs, like religion. These help bind together the community.

When a community grows large, people might leave to start new communities. These different communities may now share a culture. This is one way that nations grow. It is why culture spreads from place to place with different **ethnic groups**.

Ethnic groups are made up of people who have come from the same place. For example, ethnic groups like the Irish, Germans, and Slavs came to North America from Europe. Ethnic groups often share a language, history, and other aspects of culture. People who belong to the same ethnic group have the same ethnicity. Some nations have one main ethnic group and culture. Others have many. People of the same ethnicity and culture can live in many countries.

Dancers celebrating their culture in traditional dress at a festival in Bolivia, a country in South America

RESEARCH COMPANION, pp. 96–97

English Learners SCAFFOLD

Use the following scaffolds to support student understanding of lesson content.

Entering and Emerging

Direct students' attention to the picture, and read aloud the caption. On the board, draw a concept web for *culture*. On the web, list words to describe the picture, such as *clothing, dress, hat, women, dancing, music,* and *celebration.* Act out a word, point to it, and say it aloud. Ask students to say it aloud in a sentence.

Developing and Expanding

Have small groups study the picture and read the caption. Remind students that the picture reflects a South American culture. Then ask questions to help students describe the clothing in the picture and how it fits in with the environment: *What do you notice about the dress? What do you notice about the hat? Do you think the climate in this area is always hot? How do you know?*

Bridging and Reaching

Guide partners to study and describe the people shown in the picture. Ask them to predict the type of climate in which this culture group lives. Have partners identify specific parts of the clothing that makes sense for the environment they have identified. Have them use the picture and the text to write one sentence in response to this question: *How does the environment help form culture?*

Social Emotional Learning

Social Awareness

Value Diversity To respect others in a global community and value differences, students need to learn about others' cultural expressions. Ask students about the photograph: *What could you do to understand why this cultural tradition is important to the people in the picture?*

 Digital Tools

Blended Learning

Students investigate curated resources and find evidence to answer the lesson question.

Interactive IMPACT

Students choose from print or digital **Inquiry Tools** to take notes.

Cultures Across the Globe

All cultures find ways to express, or show, their values and practices. Parts of Japanese culture include peaceful gardens to show a love of nature and three-line poems called haiku. These poems are meant to express big ideas with only a few words. Hindu temples and sculptures of gods and goddesses show part of Indian culture. Czechs, Poles, Slovaks, and other Eastern European cultures enjoy the polka. The polka is a kind of folk music and dance.

Some cultures share their ideas and customs through **oral tradition**. Oral tradition refers to stories and poems that are spoken rather than written. Stories of Anansi, a clever spider, are popular in West African cultures. Anansi tales are part of an oral tradition that enslaved African people brought to the Americas.

Cultures also share their values through art. Diego Rivera was a Mexican artist. He made large paintings called murals. These paintings cover walls, ceilings, and entire buildings. They show scenes from Mexican history and ways of life.

Ink drawings that show a love of nature are a part of Japanese culture.

98 Lesson 1 What Is Culture?

Another way people express their culture is through festivals and holidays. The people of Thailand celebrate the Yee Peng Lantern Festival. People send paper lanterns into the sky. When people from many different cultures live in one place, their cultures mix. People pick up ideas and customs from one another. Today, trade and mass media, like television and the Internet, connect many people globally.

Yee Peng Lantern Festival in Chiang Mai, Thailand

Did You Know?

More than 300 languages are spoken in the United States. Unlike some countries, the United States does not have an official language. English is the most widely spoken, followed by Spanish. Tagalog, the third most spoken language, is the language of the Philippines. Multiple Chinese languages are widely spoken in the United States as well, including Mandarin and Cantonese. Many people speak more than one language.

✓ Stop and Check

Talk If you were to paint a mural about your community's culture, what would you include?

Find Details As you read, add new information to the graphic organizer on page 93 in your Inquiry Journal.

Chapter 3 Lesson 1 99

Cultures Across the Globe

1 Inspect Have students read pp. 98–99 and list several ways that people around the world share their cultures. (People share cultures through art, music, dance, stories, festivals, holidays, language, and other customs.)

2 Find Evidence Use the questions below to check comprehension.

Draw Conclusions Where might you expect to hear Anansi stories? Why? (in West Africa and in the Americas; Anansi stories are part of the oral tradition of West African cultures, and Africans brought this tradition with them to the Americas.) **DOK 2**

Explain Why do people celebrate festivals such as the Yee Peng Lantern Festival? (People want to express their culture and share their customs with one another.) **DOK 2**

3 Make Connections

Synthesize The United States does not have an official language. How does this reflect the nation's history and culture? (People from many different countries helped build the United States. They brought different languages to the country. Today, people from different backgrounds with different languages still come to the nation. The United States does not have an official language because it has a diverse history and is home to many cultures.) **DOK 3**

✓ Stop and Check

Talk Have students discuss the question with a partner. (Answers should reflect the students' community and should show an understanding of the cultures there.)

 Spotlight on Vocabulary

Content Vocabulary

temple: a place of worship

custom: way of life, tradition

mural: a large painting

festival: event where many people celebrate something

holiday: a special day when people celebrate something

▶ **Digital Tools**

Blended Learning
Students explore lesson content through interactive activities.

Interactive IMPACT

Use the **More to Explore.**

Around the World

Schools and Families

Children all over the world attend school. Some walk long distances to reach schools. In Kenya, students might walk as far as ten miles to reach a school. Others ride to school on bicycles, buses, trains, or in cars with family members.

Different schools have different resources. In some places, students attend many classes in large buildings. Others go to school in small schoolhouses or even outside. Some schools require uniforms. In some places, boys and girls go to separate schools. Technology also varies. While one school uses modern computers, another will do more work with books and paper.

All schools work to pass on knowledge and values that are important to their culture.

Most schools in Japan require uniforms.

Some students in Bangladesh have classes on floating schools. There, seasonal flooding makes roads impassable, so students cannot reach regular schools.

Families come in all sizes, too. Families can include two parents, one parent, stepparents, and other adult caregivers. Some share one home, while others are split between homes. Some families include different races, ethnicities, or cultures. In some cultures, extended families, like grandparents, aunts, uncles, and cousins, are very important. How families live and work together is also shaped by culture.

✓ Stop and Check COLLABORATE

Talk With a partner, discuss how schools around the world are different and the same as yours.

What Do You Think? Explain to a partner in your own words what culture means. How are your explanations similar? How are they different?

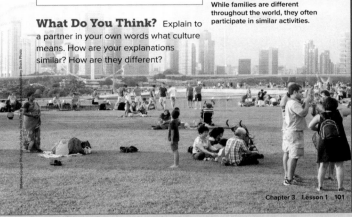

While families are different throughout the world, they often participate in similar activities.

RESEARCH COMPANION, pp. 100–101

Around the World: Schools and Families

1 Inspect Have students read pp. 100–101 and describe how families are different around the world. (Answers should include descriptions of family size, family homes, diversity, and extended families.)

2 Find Evidence Use the questions below to check comprehension.

Draw Conclusions What do the pictures tell you about schools around the world? (People in diverse places wear different clothing to school, go to school in many types of buildings, and have different resources.) **DOK 2**

Distinguish How does a nuclear family differ from an extended family? (A nuclear family refers to one or more parents and their children. An extended family also includes other relatives, such as grandparents, aunts and uncles, and cousins.) **DOK 2**

3 Make Connections

Analyze You have learned that culture shapes or impacts people. How do you think families and schools affect culture? (Families and schools shape culture by helping pass on cultural practices, values, and traditions. Culture is shown and taught in schools and families just as in other parts of the community.) **DOK 3**

 Stop and Check

Talk Have students discuss the question with a partner. (Similarities and differences may relate to dress, buildings, transportation to school, rules, resources, and technology.)

LESSON 1 REPORT

LESSON QUESTION

What Is Culture?

INQUIRY JOURNAL, pp. 94–95

Think About It

Remind students to review their research and consider how culture develops in communities, how communities preserve culture, and how cultures are different and similar in communities around the world. Encourage students to review the main ideas and details they have included in their graphic organizers. Direct students back to pp. 96–101 of their Research Companion if they need more information.

Write About It

Write and Cite Evidence Remind students to include the following elements in their responses.

- Provide a definition of culture.
- Cite examples or characteristics of culture.
- Explain why communities develop and benefit from culture.

Discipline(s)	4	3	2	1
Geography **History** **Civics**	Provides an appropriate and detailed definition of culture and cites many cultural characteristics; gives an insightful explanation of the role of culture in uniting communities	Provides an appropriate definition of culture and cites some cultural characteristics; gives an adequate explanation of the role of culture in uniting communities	Provides a basic definition of culture and cites one or two cultural characteristics; gives a general explanation of the role of culture in communities	Fails to provide a definition of culture or cite any cultural characteristics; explanation of role of culture is vague, confusing or incorrect

Talk About It

Explain Remind students to identify the culture groups in their community. Challenge them to think of how they know these different cultures exist in their communities. Remind them of examples from the lesson text as needed.

Assessment Students can check their understanding with feedback from the **Lesson Test** available online.

Connect to the Essential Question

Pull It Together Before they respond, remind students to think about the distinct culture groups they learned about, the places these culture groups lived, and the characteristics of their own cultures.

Inquiry Project Update Remind students to turn to Inquiry Journal pp. 84–85 for project information. If necessary, review the Project Checklist with students. At this point in the chapter, students should focus on the first item on the Checklist.

Think About It

Gather Evidence
Review your research. Based on the information you have gathered, how do you think culture affects communities?

Write About It

Write and Cite Evidence
What is culture? What do you think about when you describe the culture of a community? Use information from the texts to explain your response.

Answers will vary, but students should explain the idea that culture is the way of life and beliefs shared by groups of people. Culture includes values, art, music, language, stories, tools, clothing, food, games, celebrations, religious ideas, and other customs.

Talk About It

Explain
Share your response with a partner. Together, discuss different culture groups that exist in your community. Describe how those groups show and preserve their cultures.

Geography

Connect to the **EQ**

Pull It Together
Why is culture important to your community? List three ideas to share with others.

Answers will vary but might include the following:

1. *Culture reflects the effect of the environment on our community.*
2. *Culture shows how the people in our community relate to one another and what they have in common.*
3. *Culture gives our community a way to express its values and practices.*

Inquiry Project Notes
_____
_____
_____

Copyright © McGraw-Hill Education

INQUIRY JOURNAL, pp. 94–95

 English Learners **SCAFFOLD**

Use the following scaffolds to support student writing.

Entering and Emerging

Help students define culture and talk about why it is important. Provide the following sentence frames:

- _____ is how a group of _____ live and what they believe.
- We can see culture in art. We can hear culture in _____.
- Sharing a culture makes a community feel _____.

Developing and Expanding

Before students write their paragraph, ask: *What is culture? How do people express, or show, culture? How did cultures form? Why do communities have/ need culture? What purpose does culture serve?* Remind students to cite facts from the texts to explain what culture is and why it is important.

Bridging and Reaching

Before writing their paragraph, have partners discuss the meaning of culture, examples of culture, and its importance. Have partners share why culture matters to them and how they see culture benefiting their community. Guide students to write a paragraph about culture that includes a definition, expressions of culture, and its importance to the community.

✔ Check for Success

Summarize Can students write an informative paragraph summarizing the meaning and importance of culture to communities?

Differentiate

If Not, Have students present their ideas in another format, such as a collage that includes drawings/ photographs of cultural expressions with captions explaining the importance of those customs or traditions.

LESSON QUESTION

How Do People Express Their Culture?

Connect to the Essential Question

Tell students that this lesson provides key research into the Chapter Essential Question: **What Makes a Community Unique?** Explain that they will take a closer look at how people in communities express their culture and how those expressions shape their communities. Students will also compare and contrast different culture groups within and among global communities.

Lesson Objectives

- **Explain** how and why people express culture in different ways.
- **Describe** how art, stories, music, dance, and religion are expressions of cultures in the United States.
- **Compare and contrast** how cultures shape communities around the world.
- **Write** a news report to describe ways in which different groups express their cultures.

Make Connections!

CONNECT TO ELA

Reading **Ask and answer** questions to demonstrate understanding of a text and refer explicitly to the text as the basis for the answers.
Compare and contrast the most important points and key details presented in two texts on the same topic.

Research **Recall** information from experiences or gather information from print and digital sources; take brief notes on sources and sort evidence into provided categories.

Writing **Craft** informative/explanatory texts to examine a topic and convey ideas and information clearly.
Develop the topic with facts, definitions, and details.

Speaking and Listening **Follow** agreed-upon rules for discussions (e.g., gaining the floor in respectful ways, listening to others with care, speaking one at a time about the topics and texts under discussion).

COMMUNITY CONNECTIONS

To enhance students' understanding of diverse cultural groups and events in their community or region, guide them to search online community events calendars and websites. You may also wish to review with students the life and community sections in their local newspapers. These will give insight into cultural events as well as prepare students to write their own news reports at the end of the lesson.

Lesson-At-A-Glance

1 ENGAGE
INQUIRY JOURNAL

- ▶ **Talk About It:** Photograph of a theater
- ▶ **Analyze the Source:** The Story of Johnny Appleseed
- ▶ **Inquiry Tools:** Explore Compare and Contrast

pp. 96–101

2 INVESTIGATE
RESEARCH COMPANION

- ▶ **Many Cultures in One**
- ▶ **Art**
- ▶ **Music and Dance**
- ▶ **Citizenship: Religious Tolerance**

pp. 102–107

3 REPORT
INQUIRY JOURNAL

- ▶ **Think About It**
- ▶ **Write About It:** Local News Report
- ▶ **Talk About It**
- **EQ** ▶ **Connect to the Essential Question**

pp. 102–103

ASSESSMENT

- ▶ **Online Lesson Test**
- ▶ **Printable Lesson Test**

For more details, see pp. T168–T169.

▶ Digital Tools
at **my.mheducation.com**

ePresentation
Teach the Engage, Investigate, and Report content to the whole class from **ePresentations** that launch directly from the lesson dashboard.

eBook
You can flip your instruction with the **IMPACT eBooks** found on your lesson dashboard.

Interactive IMPACT
Blend in digital content **when you want it** and **where you want it**.

Blended Learning features in the Teacher's Edition highlight ways to connect in-class work with online experiences to enhance learning.

Investigate current events with **IMPACT News**.

Explore domain-based vocabulary with **Explore Words** and **Word Play** vocabulary activities.

Go Further with IMPACT Explorer Magazine!

The **IMPACT Explorer Magazine** supports students' exploration of the Essential Question and provides additional resources for the EQ Inquiry Project.

pp. 30–41

How Do People Express Their Culture?

Language Objectives

- Use newly acquired content and academic vocabulary to talk and write about cultural expressions.
- Write a news report describing how people express their culture, using details that answer *wh-* questions.
- Communicate about cultural expressions orally and in writing using active and passive voice.

Spanish Cognates

To support Spanish speakers, point out the cognates.

compare = comparar

contrast = contrastar

different = diferente

express = expresar

religion = religión

Introduce the Lesson

Set Purpose Explain to students that in this lesson they will read informational texts to learn how people and communities express or show their culture.

Access Prior Knowledge Read the Lesson Question, and remind students that culture includes the beliefs, traditions, and ways of life of a group of people. Explain that people express something by communicating it to another person, and that people express themselves through talking, writing, singing, dancing, or drawing. Say: *What are some ways that people express their culture?* (through art, music, dance, stories, games, clothing, and holidays) Point out that people can belong to more than one culture. Their cultures can be associated with their family's heritage, traditions, or with communities where they live. Ask volunteers to name a culture that they or their families share.

Spark Curiosity Have students study the photographs on p. 104 of the Research Companion. Point out the two photos of art and explain that both show people's ways of expressing their culture. Ask: *What do you see in each photo? How is the art similar? How is it different?* Tell students that the top illustration was likely painted in the past. Say: *Often, cultures preserve or keep important pieces of art in museums.*

Build Meaning & Support Language

Inquiry Journal

Analyze the Source (pp. 98–99) Take a closer look at this sentence from p. 98: "A folktale is a story handed down over the years." Explain the meaning of *handed down.* Say: *Families hand things down, from a parent to a child, or from an older sibling to a child. Things that are handed down are special, because they stay in that family.* Explain that when a story is handed down, it is told many times. Often, parents or older people in a community tell it to children, who later tell it to their children. Then point out that Johnny Appleseed valued living simply and sharing with others. Explain that values are ideas or beliefs that are important to a person or group of people. Ask: *How does a folktale show a community's values?* (It is about things that are important to them.) Provide examples of values that a folktale might express, such as the importance of family or education.

Inquiry Tools (pp. 100–101) Tell students they will **Compare and Contrast** cultures as they read the selections in the Research Companion. Point out the signal words listed on p. 100 (such as *like, alike, unlike,* and *different*) that students can use to identify comparisons and contrasts in the texts. Provide examples of these words in a comparison of Johnny Appleseed to John Chapman: <u>Both</u> *Johnny Appleseed and John Chapman traveled a long way.* <u>Unlike</u> *Johnny Appleseed, John Chapman owned land.* Ask volunteers to find other ways that Johnny Appleseed and John Chapman were alike and different. Guide them to use comparison and contrast words to describe the similarities and differences.

Research Companion

Many Cultures in One (pp. 102–103) After you read p. 102, explain any unfamiliar words. Tell students that a person's *background* is his or her family history or traditions. Point out that the words *descended from* in the second paragraph refer to people's ancestors, or relatives from the past. Use an example to check comprehension. Say: *Imagine you know a girl who has parents from Mexico. Who is the girl descended from?* (people from Mexico)

Art (pp. 104–105) Read the first paragraph on p. 104. Help students take a closer look at this sentence: *Some come from hundreds of years ago.* Explain that in this sentence, the word *some* is a pronoun that refers to a noun in a previous sentence. Help students identify the noun that is the antecedent. Ask: *What comes from hundreds of years ago?* (works by artists) Explain that the words *comes from hundreds of years ago* mean that the artworks were painted hundreds of years ago. Ask: *Why do cultures want to save or keep old art and stories?* (They think the art and stories are important.)

Music and Dance (p. 106) Remind students that earlier in the lesson, they learned that the United States is home to many cultures. Ask: *How does music show that the United States has many cultures?* (People in the United States play music from European, African, and Native American cultures.) Explain that when a type of music *blends* different cultures, it uses parts or qualities from each culture.

Religious Tolerance (p. 107) Read aloud the paragraph on p. 107 and make sure students understand what the word *religion* means. Then read aloud the third sentence. Ask: *What is religious freedom?* (people's right to practice their own beliefs) *Why is religious freedom important?* (It helps people respect others' beliefs.) Help students use details from the paragraph to answer the question.

Inquiry Journal

Report Your Findings (pp. 102–103) Review what a local news report includes. Tell students that often news reports answer the questions *who, what, when, where, why,* and *how.* Explain that their reports should answer several of these questions.

Language Forms & Conventions

Active and Passive Voice Remind students that a subject is the noun or pronoun that a sentence is mostly about, and the verb is the what the subject is or does. Explain that sometimes we say what the subject does: *Luis caught the baseball.* Sometimes, we say what someone or something did to the subject: *The baseball was caught by Luis.* Other times, we do not say who did something to the subject: *The baseball was caught.* Provide the following examples. Guide students to identify the subject of each sentence. Ask if the subject is doing the action being described.

Passive Sentence	Active Sentence
Songs are shared between families and friends.	Families and friends share songs.
Culture is expressed by people.	People express their culture.
Traditional patterns are seen in blankets.	Blankets have traditional patterns.

Show partners the photo captions on p. 106. Have partners change the active sentences to use the passive voice, and change the passive sentences to use the active voice.

LESSON 2 ENGAGE

How Do People Express Their Culture?

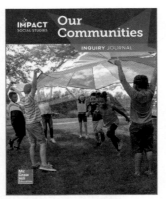

INQUIRY JOURNAL, pp. 96–97

Bellringer

Prompt students to retrieve information from the previous lessons. Ask: *What is culture? What are some characteristics of culture?* (Answers should include that culture is the shared customs, or ways of life, of a group of people. Cultural characteristics include art and architecture, music and dance, language and literature, customs, beliefs, food, and styles of dress). Challenge student groups to identify three things in the classroom or their school that show culture.

Lesson Outcomes

Have students read the lesson question and lesson outcomes in pairs.

- Make sure students understand that *express* means "to show" or "to communicate."
- Have partners brainstorm a list of ways that people express their culture.

Talk About It

Explain that buildings reflect the resources and interests of the cultures that created them. Have students identify types of buildings in their community and think about the purposes the different buildings serve. Ask: *What does a library tell you about the values of a community?* (Answers should include that the community thinks learning, literature, or access to books and resources is important.)

Have students study the image and discuss the questions in small groups. Provide sentence frames as needed.

- I see _____ in this picture.
- I think people go here to _____.
- The caption helps me answer the question by _____.

 Collaborative Conversations

Follow Rules for Discussion As students prepare to engage in partner and small-group discussions, remind them to
- calculate how long each student can speak based on the time allotted.
- decide who will speak first.
- take turns listening and speaking, and stay on topic.
- ask questions to clarify information.

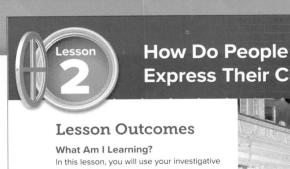

Lesson 2
How Do People Express Their Culture?

People show their cultures through dance, music, and plays.

Lesson Outcomes

What Am I Learning?
In this lesson, you will use your investigative skills to find out how people and groups in the community express their cultures.

Why Am I Learning It?
Reading and talking about how communities show their diverse cultures will help you understand how people shape communities over time.

How Will I Know That I Learned It?
You will be able to write a news report showing how two people or groups in your community express their cultures.

Talk About It   COLLABORATE

Look closely at the picture. Have you been in a building like this? What do you think this place is for?

INQUIRY JOURNAL, pp. 96–97

 English Learners SCAFFOLD

Use the following scaffolds to support student understanding of lesson outcomes.

Entering and Emerging
Read the photo caption and identify the building as a theater. Label parts of the theater for students: stage, curtains, seats. Name performers who might be on stage: dancer, musician, actor. Provide sentence frames to help students describe the photograph.

- Theaters have _____ and _____.
- People go to theaters to see _____.

Developing and Expanding
Have small groups study the photograph and label things that they see, such as the stage, seats, and curtains. Have them discuss what events take place at theaters. Ask: *What kinds of performances take place in a theater? Why do communities have theaters? What would you like to see at a theater?*

Bridging and Reaching
Have partners discuss the types of shows or performances that take place at theaters, such as movies, plays, dance recitals, and music or concerts. Then have them describe a performance or show that they would like to attend.

 Social Emotional Learning

Social Awareness

Respect Remind students that they will not always agree with one another. It is natural for people to have different ideas and opinions. Ask: *What are some ways you can show respect even when you disagree?*

 **Digital Tools**

Blended Learning
Students engage with the lesson question and discussion prompts.

Interactive IMPACT

Discuss the **Lesson Question** and **Talk About It.**

The Story of Johnny Appleseed

1 Inspect

Read Look at the title and the images. What do you think this text will be about?

Circle words you do not know.

Underline clues that tell you:
- what folktales and folksongs are
- why they matter

My Notes

_____
_____
_____
_____
_____
_____
_____
_____
_____
_____

Have you heard a song or a story about Johnny Appleseed? Appleseed is an American folk hero. His good deeds are the subject of folktales. A deed is something you do. A **folktale** is a story handed down over the years.

According to folktales, Appleseed was a friendly man who walked across parts of the United States planting apple trees. He had very few belongings and walked barefoot. He wore a pan for a hat, a coffee sack for a shirt, and ragged pants. As he traveled, he scattered apple seeds across the land.

The story of Johnny Appleseed is based on the life of John Chapman. Chapman lived in the United States more than one hundred years ago.

Born in Massachusetts, Chapman worked in an apple orchard at an early age. An orchard is a tree farm. As a teenager, Chapman traveled west. On the way, he bought land and planted apple trees. Like Appleseed, he gave away many seeds and young trees to **pioneers**. Pioneers were early Americans who settled in wilderness areas. Unlike Appleseed, Chapman owned land and sold his seeds and trees to make money. Chapman helped many farmers in Pennsylvania, Ohio, and Indiana get started. Both Chapman and Appleseed were known for their kindness to people and to animals.

Today, communities from Massachusetts to California hold festivals to celebrate Johnny Appleseed.

The real John Chapman sold many seeds and trees to pioneers.

2 Find Evidence

Reread the text and captions. What parts of the story of Johnny Appleseed are based on the life of Chapman? What are made up?

3 Make Connections

Talk Why do you think people make folktales out of true stories?

INQUIRY JOURNAL, pp. 98–99

Analyze the Source

 Spotlight on Language

Background Information

John Chapman was born in 1774 in Massachusetts and died around 1845 in Indiana. He was not only a gardener known for planting trees and sharing seeds, but he was also a missionary. Wherever he traveled, Chapman shared religious teachings while also encouraging early white settlers to live peacefully with Native Americans who lived on the land before them.

1 Inspect

Read Have students read the text and captions and study the images on pp. 98–99. Remind them to circle unfamiliar words.

- Underline words that tell the meaning of *folktales*. (stories handed down over the years)

2 Find Evidence

Reread Have students reread the text and captions.

- How do you know what information is fact and what information is made up? (The words "According to folktales" let the reader know that what follows is probably made up.)

3 Make Connections

Talk Draw students' attention to the information they underlined about the meaning of folktales. Ask student pairs to discuss and write a response to the question.

Introductory Phrases

A *phrase* is a group of two or more words that expresses an idea but does not form a complete sentence. Introductory phrases appear at the start of sentences and are set off by a comma. They modify the rest of the sentence after the comma.

▶ Digital Tools

Blended Learning

Students read informational texts and analyze primary sources.

Interactive IMPACT

Have students practice and apply the strategy of close reading as they analyze text.

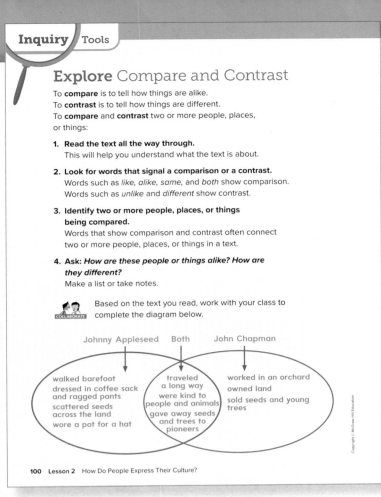

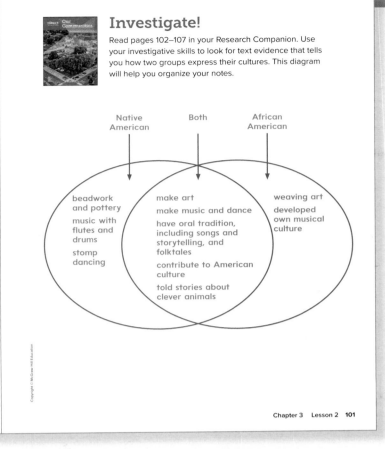

INQUIRY JOURNAL, pp. 100–101

Inquiry Tools

Explore Compare and Contrast

Read Have students work in small groups to read the step-by-step instructions. Explain that when you compare, you look for similarities, or things that are alike. When you contrast, you look for differences, or things that are not alike. Ask: *What are some words that signal comparisons?* (alike, like, similar, same, both) *What are some words that signal contrasts?* (unlike, different, not)

Guide Practice Have students review the text on pp. 98–99. Then work with students to complete the graphic organizer. Explain that they will use a similar graphic organizer to organize their independent research.

Check Understanding Confirm student understanding of the inquiry skill, Explore Compare and Contrast. If students cannot compare and contrast effectively, review the steps on p. 100.

Investigate!

Have students read pp. 102–107 in the Research Companion. Tell them the information will help them answer the lesson question *How Do People Express Their Culture?*

Take Notes Tell students they should use the graphic organizer on p. 101 of the Inquiry Journal to take notes about similarities and differences between two cultures.

Remind students that good note taking is about finding the most important information and writing key words or phrases about it.

Spotlight on Content

Using Prepositions and Conjunctions Model ways students can use prepositions and conjunctions to write sentences to compare and contrast.

_____ is similar to _____.

_____ is different from _____.

_____ is like _____ because _____.

_____ is unlike _____ because_____.

_____ is the same as _____.

LESSON 2 INVESTIGATE

How Do People Express Their Culture?

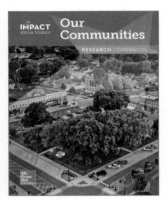

RESEARCH COMPANION, pp. 102–103

Background Information

Culture and heritage are related concepts, and often, the words are used interchangeably. Culture can refer to a group of people who share beliefs, values, and ways of life. It can also mean the body of beliefs, values, and ways of life shared by a group of people. Heritage refers to ideas and traditions handed down from one group of people to another. Heritage includes aspects of culture, but a people's culture comprises more than just its heritage. Think of heritage as coming from the past. In contrast, culture comprises not only ideas and customs inherited from those who came before us but also the ways of life that we actively create in the present. For this reason, American culture today reflects many distinct cultural heritages from the past.

Many Cultures in One

1 Inspect Have student partners read pp. 102–103 and summarize what they learn about culture in the United States.

2 Find Evidence Use the questions below to check comprehension. Remind students to support their answers with text evidence.

Explain How do stories, songs, and games become part of a culture? (They are handed down over time from one person to the next.) **DOK 2**

Analyze Images How does the image show the connection between culture and heritage? (Answers should explain that the image shows a storyteller; storytelling is one way that groups pass on their cultural heritage.) **DOK 2**

Draw Conclusions Why do people in the United States express culture in different ways? (The United States has many different culture groups with diverse heritages.) **DOK 2**

3 Make Connections

Make Inferences Why do many Americans today come from multiple cultures and ethnic groups? (Many different ethnic groups with different cultures came to the United States. People from different groups have married, combined families, and had children of their own.) **DOK 3**

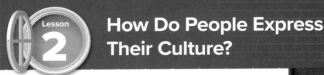

How Do People Express Their Culture?

Many Cultures in One

Do you sing songs, dance, make art, tell stories, or play games? These are ways of expressing your culture. Songs, dance, art, stories, and even games are shared among families and friends. They are passed down over time from one person to the next. Over time, they become part of a culture.

Today, the United States has the third largest population in the world. It is made up of many people with various **heritages**. Heritage means background or tradition. Some people in the United States are descended from people in Europe, Africa, Asia, and other parts of the Americas. Some have Native American heritage. Many are from more than one ethnic group. People brought many different religions, languages, stories, dances, songs, and customs to the nation. Because of this, people express their cultures in our communities in many ways.

Storytelling is an important part of many cultures.

RESEARCH COMPANION, pp. 102–103

 ## English Learners SCAFFOLD

Use the following scaffolds to support student understanding of lesson content.

Entering and Emerging

To help students understand the meaning of *heritage*, have them circle the names of continents in the text. Explain that most continents have many countries with many cultures. On the board, write the continent names as well as adjectives and nouns that describe people from those continents (e.g., *Europe, European, Europeans*).

Developing and Expanding

Have small groups list the continents. Explain that most continents have many countries with different cultures. Ask: *Which continents are discussed in the text?* (Africa, Asia, Europe, and the Americas, or North America and South America) *From which continent might people with African heritage come from? European heritage? Asian heritage? Where might people come from who have Native American heritage?*

Bridging and Reaching

Have partners identify the continents discussed in the text and review what the word *heritage* means. Then guide students to choose a continent (or a country in it). Encourage them to write three sentences about the culture or background a family from that continent/country might bring to the United States. Ask: *When Europeans came to the United States, what kinds of cultural things did they bring?* (traditions and customs from the European country they left)

 ## Spotlight on Language

Academic Language

Have students use context to explain the meaning of *descended from* in the sentence that begins "Some people in the United States." Guide them to understand that *descend* means to "come from." People descend from family who came before them.

 ## Digital Tools

Blended Learning

Students investigate curated resources and find evidence to answer the lesson question.

Interactive IMPACT

Students choose from print or digital **Inquiry Tools** to take notes.

Art

Art is one way people express culture. People create art to show their ideas, feelings, and values. Visual art includes paintings, drawings, and sculptures. In museums in the United States today, you can see different types of works by artists. Some come from hundreds of years ago. Some were made today. Museums show art from many different cultures. These include oil paintings that show the influence of European heritage. They include ink drawings that reflect East Asian cultures. Some art looks like things you would see in real life. Other art might not look like anything you would see in real life.

Sometimes artists do not mean for their work to be in museums. Norman Rockwell drew illustrations for newspapers and advertisements. Now his art is shown in museums all over the world. Andy Warhol made art for museums that sometimes looked like it was made for advertisements.

Some paintings in museums show how people lived long ago.

Art exists outside of museums as well. Today, Native American peoples still make beadwork and pottery as they have for hundreds of years. African Americans use traditional weaving patterns from Africa in blankets and in clothing. People paint murals in cities all over the country that show the influence of different cultures. Art is everywhere in our communities.

Murals show the importance of local cultures in communities.

Storytelling

Poems, songs, and stories are written art. Originally, people talked and sang to each other. Eventually, people began to write these stories and songs. **Folktales** have been handed down over time. Many began as tales of true events and real people. Over time, stories changed.

American **pioneers** told folktales that showed their adventurous spirit. Pioneers were people who settled in wilderness areas. They told folktales about the lumberjack Paul Bunyan and the railroad worker John Henry. Many believe these stories are exaggerations of real-life events.

Stories are often sacred to cultures. Native Americans tell stories about clever animals solving problems. So do African Americans. Enslaved people in America passed down stories that came from their African ancestors. Some of those stories are about a spider escaping danger. Stories are still very important to our culture today.

Folktales tell how the giant Paul Bunyan made the Grand Canyon, the Black Hills, and the Great Lakes.

Stop and Check

Talk Why do people tell stories and make art?

Find Details As you read, add new information to the graphic organizer on page 101 in your Inquiry Journal.

RESEARCH COMPANION, pp. 104–105

Art

1 Inspect Have students read pp. 104–105 and explain what a folktale is.

2 Find Evidence Use the questions below to check comprehension.

Cite Evidence What evidence in the text supports the conclusion that the different types of art in the United States are similar to the different cultures of people in the United States? (Since people in the United States make and study art, and there are many different types of art and stories that reflect diverse heritages, the art in the United States must come from diverse cultures.) **DOK 2**

3 Make Connections

Synthesize How can visual and written art work together to express culture? (Answers should indicate that visual art can show what written art tells about or describes, and that written art can give more information or tell the stories behind visual art.) **DOK 3**

Hypothesize How do you think oral, or spoken, stories differ from written stories? (Answers might note that oral stories probably change more with each telling.) **DOK 3**

Stop and Check

Talk Have students discuss the question with a partner. (People make art and tell stories to share ideas, pass on values and other cultural information, and record events in their lives.)

Draw Encourage students to add a caption to their drawings.

Social Emotional Learning

Relationship Skills

Value Ideas of Others Students learn to value the ideas of others by actively listening and sharing their own ideas appropriately. Ask: *How can you show that you value ideas or beliefs that are different from yours?*

▶ Digital Tools

Blended Learning Students investigate curated resources and find evidence to answer the lesson question.

Interactive IMPACT

Use the **Lesson Video**.

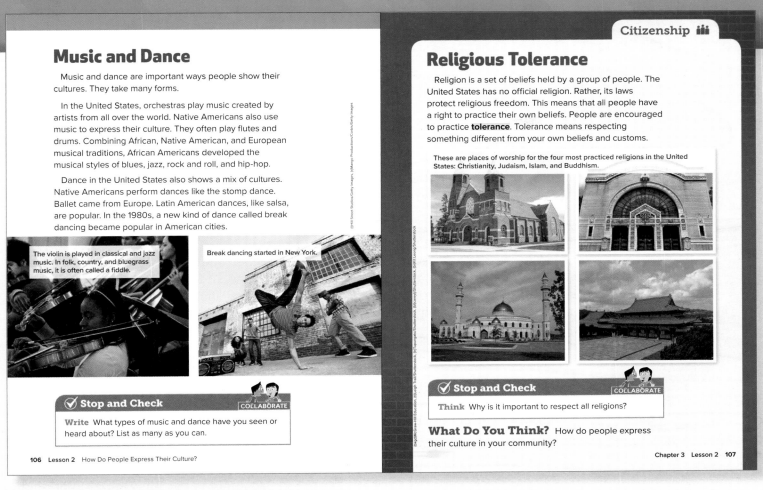

RESEARCH COMPANION, pp. 106–107

Music and Dance/ Religious Tolerance

1 Inspect Have students read pp. 106–107 and explain how music and dance reflect culture.

2 Find Evidence Use the questions below to check comprehension.

Analyze Images Study the images on p. 106. Which sentence in the text does the first image best support? Which sentence does the second image best support? (First: "In the United States, orchestras play music created by artists from all over the world." Second: "Break dancing started in American cities.") **DOK 2**

Compare and Contrast How are music and dance alike and different? (Both are ways people show their culture, and they take many forms. Music uses instruments and voices to make sounds, while dance uses body movements for expression.) **DOK 2**

3 Make Connections

Hypothesize How might a community without religious freedom look different from communities in the United States? (The community would probably have one type of religious building, and other traditions and laws might reflect that religion.) **DOK 3**

Stop and Check

Write Page 106 (Answers will vary but might include bluegrass, jazz, hip-hop, rock and roll, classical, folk; stomp, ballet, salsa, or break dancing.)

Think Page 107 (Answers should note that diversity and tolerance help communities.)

LESSON 2 REPORT

How Do People Express Their Culture?

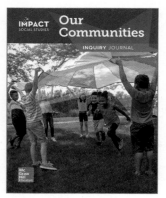

INQUIRY JOURNAL, pp. 102–103

Think About It

Remind students to review their research and consider what characteristics two different cultural groups have in common and what customs and art forms are unique to each. Encourage students to review the information they have included in their graphic organizers. Direct students back to pp. 102–107 of their Research Companion if they need more information.

Write About It

Local News Report Remind students to include the following in their responses.

- Introduce two culture groups in your community.
- Describe one way in which each group expresses their culture in your community.
- Provide details about the location and events for each culture group.
- Summarize what you might experience when encountering these cultural expressions.

Discipline(s)	4	3	2	1
Geography	Student provides thorough information and relevant details about two ways that local culture groups express themselves in the community.	Student provides accurate information and mostly relevant details about two ways that local culture groups express themselves in the community.	Student provides basic information and a few relevant details about one way that a local culture group expresses itself in the community.	Student fails to provide appropriate information or details about cultural expressions in the community.

Talk About It

Explain Remind students to point out similarities and differences between the two expressions of culture during their conversations.

Assessment Students can check their understanding with feedback from the **Lesson Test** available online.

Connect to the Essential Question

Pull it Together Before they respond, remind students to think about the groups they wrote about and how each group expressed its culture.

Inquiry Project Update Remind students to turn to Inquiry Journal pp. 84–85 for project information. If necessary, review the Project Checklist with students. At this point in the chapter, students should focus on the second and third items on the Checklist.

Think About It

Gather Evidence
How do different groups express their cultures?

Answers will vary but should reflect
the content in the lesson. For example,
students might point out art, music,
folktales and other oral tradition, as well
as religious gatherings and festivals as
ways to express culture.

Write About It

Local News Report
Imagine traveling through your community and observing two ways in which
different groups express their cultures. Write a short local news report in
which you describe what you see, hear, and experience. Be sure to describe
the location in your community, the culture group, and the events.

Answers will vary but should explain
specific examples of cultural expression in
the community in a creative way. Students
should identify and describe locations
and culture groups within the community.
Their reports should provide details
about the artwork, music, dance, theater,
architecture, or events observed.

Talk About It

Explain
Share your news story with a partner. Together, discuss how different groups
of people in your community express their cultures.

Geography **Connect to the EQ**

Pull It Together
How do the expressions of culture in your community make your
community unique?

Answers will vary but should include how
different communities express culture in
ways that are unique to both the community
and to the aspect of culture being
expressed.

Inquiry Project Notes
_____
_____
_____
_____
_____

INQUIRY JOURNAL, pp. 102–103

English Learners SCAFFOLD

Use the following scaffolds to support student writing.

Entering and Emerging

Encourage students to use descriptive words and phrases as they write their
reports. Provide the following sentence frames as needed:

- In this community, _____ express their culture by/through
  _____.

- People who visit _____ can see/hear _____.

- This _____ shows how _____ express culture.

Developing and Expanding

Explain that a news report usually answers *what? when? where? why?* and
how? Ask questions to help students think about the details their reports
should include. For example: *What cultural groups live in your community?
What do you see or hear about their culture? What events do they have to
express their culture? Where can you experience their culture?*

Bridging and Reaching

Have partners brainstorm what they might see, hear, feel, taste, or smell when
they experience different cultures in their community. Then ask volunteers
to describe a cultural event they experienced. Guide students to write their
reports using descriptive words and phrases to answer the *what? when?
where? why?* and *how?* questions.

✔ Check for Success

Synthesize Can students
write a news report in
which they provide detailed
information about two culture
groups in their community?

Differentiate

If Not, Have students
present their information in
an alternate format, such as
presenting and describing
visual resources and
community notices about the
ways these cultures express
themselves in the community.

LESSON QUESTION

What Do Immigrants Add to a Community?

Connect to the Essential Question

Tell students that this lesson provides key research into the Chapter Essential Question: **What Makes a Community Unique?** Explain that they will learn about how immigrants from the past and in the present enhance the communities in which they live. They will explore the ways immigrants have shaped American culture and recognize contributions made by immigrants to their own local communities.

Lesson Objectives

- **Explain** the meaning of the quote that appears on the Statue of Liberty.
- **Describe** the history of immigration to America.
- **Identify** the ways in which immigrants have contributed to American culture.
- **Write** a letter to the editor about how immigrants have enriched a community.

Make Connections!

CONNECT TO ELA

Reading **Distinguish** a student's own point of view from that of the author of a text.

Research **Recall** information from experiences or gather information from print and digital sources.

Writing **Craft** opinion pieces on familiar topics or texts, supporting a point of view with reasons.

Speaking and Listening **Explain** students' own ideas and understanding in light of the discussion.

Language **Form and use** regular and irregular verbs.

COMMUNITY CONNECTIONS

To enhance what students are learning about immigrant experiences, consider inviting someone who is new to America to address the class and explain how and why he or she immigrated to the United States.

Lesson-At-A-Glance

1 ENGAGE — INQUIRY JOURNAL

pp. 104–109

- ▶ **Talk About It:** A quote from Emma Lazarus's "The New Colossus"
- ▶ **Analyze the Source:** Ellis Island: Gateway to a New Life
- ▶ **Inquiry Tools:** Explore Point of View

2 INVESTIGATE — RESEARCH COMPANION

pp. 108–115

- ▶ **Melting Pot or Quilt?**
- ▶ **Immigration Throughout American History**
- ▶ **Contributions of Immigrants to American Culture**
- ▶ **Around the World in the USA**

3 REPORT — INQUIRY JOURNAL

pp. 110–111

- ▶ **Think About It**
- ▶ **Write About It:** Point of View
- ▶ **Talk About It**
- ▶ **Connect to the Essential Question**

ASSESSMENT

- ▶ **Online Lesson Test**
- ▶ **Printable Lesson Test**

For more details, see pp. T168–T169.

▶ Digital Tools

at **my.mheducation.com**

ePresentation

Teach the Engage, Investigate, and Report content to the whole class from **ePresentations** that launch directly from the lesson dashboard.

eBook

You can flip your instruction with the **IMPACT eBooks** found on your lesson dashboard.

Interactive IMPACT

Blend in digital content **when you want it** and **where you want it**.

Blended Learning features in the Teacher's Edition highlight ways to connect in-class work with online experiences to enhance learning.

Investigate current events with **IMPACT News**.

Explore domain-based vocabulary with **Explore Words** and **Word Play** vocabulary activities.

pp. 30–41

Go Further with IMPACT Explorer Magazine!

The **IMPACT Explorer Magazine** supports students' exploration of the Essential Question and provides additional resources for the EQ Inquiry Project.

What Do Immigrants Add to a Community?

Language Objectives

- Use newly acquired content and vocabulary to talk and write about what immigrants add to a community.
- Use nuances in words to identify and describe the point of view of an author.
- Chronicle an immigrant's background in America by writing using irregular past tense verbs like *came* and *became*.

Spanish Cognates

To support Spanish speakers, point out the cognates.

immigrant = immigrante

immigrate = immigrar

enter = entrar

symbol = símbolo

recipe = receta

ethnic = étnico

Introduce the Lesson

Set Purpose Explain to students that in this lesson, they will read informational texts to learn about immigrants and the contributions they have made and continue to make to American culture.

Access Prior Knowledge Read the Lesson Question and find out what students already know about immigrants in their communities. Ask: *Do you know any immigrants in your community? Where do they come from? How are their experiences the same as those of someone born in America? How are they different?*

Spark Curiosity Project or display a map of the world and help students locate where any immigrants in their community may come from. Then locate Turkey on the map and say: *Mr. Hamdi Ulukaya immigrated to New York from Turkey. He did not speak any English when he arrived. Later, he bought an old yogurt factory in New York and started making Greek-style yogurt there. He wanted Americans to taste yogurt as he had known it as a boy.*

Build Meaning & Support Language

Inquiry Journal

Analyze the Source (pp. 104–107) Tell students that in this lesson they will read informational texts that give facts, dates, and explanations about immigrants' first stop in the United States. To support understanding of the Primary Source poem on p. 105, read the excerpt and explain the following phrases. Say: Huddled masses *describes crowded groups of people, possibly on ships that brought immigrants to America.* Yearning *means having a strong want or desire.* Wretched refuse *refers to poor, unwanted people.* Teeming shore *reminds us that the area where ships let people off was crowded.* Tempest-tost *means thrown around, possibly by storms or other bad situations.* As you read "Ellis Island: Gateway to a New Life" on pp. 106–107, explain any words students don't know.

Inquiry Tools (pp. 108–109) Remind students that they will explore **Point of View** as they read the selections in the Research Companion. Tell them that often they have to look at the particular words the author uses in order to recognize his or her point of view. Review the process on p. 108 for determining point of view. Then work with students to complete the graphic organizer. Point out how "scary and uncomfortable" describes negative aspects of the process at Ellis Island, while "usually lasted only a few hours" is positive.

Research Companion

Melting Pot or Quilt? (pp. 108–109) After you read the first paragraph on 108, ask what might happen in a melting pot. (Everything blends together.) Show a photo of a quilt and describe what a quilt is. Explain that a quilt is made of many pieces of fabric to make a whole blanket. Each piece of a quilt could be one culture in America, while the whole quilt represents a mix of various cultures that live and work together side by side.

Immigration Throughout American History (pp. 110–111) Read the sentence "Immigrants continue to seek a new life in America" in the last paragraph on p. 111. Review with students what the phrase "new life" means. Ask: *What does a new life in America mean? What were immigrants' old lives if they were seeking a new life in America?*

Contributions of American Immigrants to American Culture (pp. 112–113) As you read, explain any words or expressions students may not know. Provide support to help them understand the meaning of *biography*. Explain that it is the story of someone's life. Ask: *Where did Madeleine Albright come from?* (Czechoslovakia) *Why did she make history?* (She was the first woman to be the United States Secretary of State.) Point out that she was an immigrant.

Around the World in the USA (pp. 114–115) Have students preview the headings and photos and predict which multicultural celebrations will be discussed in the text. Ask: *Which celebrations are shown in the photos on pages 114 and 115? Which cultures do they represent? How are the celebrations the same and different?*

Inquiry Journal

Report Your Findings (pp. 110–111) Explain that a newspaper article usually starts with the most important idea, and supporting details come next. Sentences in a newspaper article are often short. Students will write a newspaper article that explains something immigrants have added to American culture. Students should use examples from the texts to support their point of view. Encourage students to use the new vocabulary words they have learned.

Language Forms & Conventions

Past Tense of Irregular Verbs: *came, became, began* Remind students that the past tense is used to show that an action was completed in the past. Review with students that many verbs in English have irregular past tense forms and that these forms must be memorized. Display the chart. Model using the past tense form to talk about a past action. Say: *Nikola Tesla <u>came</u> from Croatia. Ellis Island <u>became</u> a symbol of the immigrant story. St. Patrick's Day <u>began</u> as a religious holiday.*

Irregular Verb	Past Tense
come	came
become	became
begin	began

Have students work in pairs to locate some examples of these verbs in the texts. Call on volunteers to say them aloud. As a challenge, ask pairs to find any other irregular verbs on 106 of the Inquiry Journal. (had, chose, knew)

LESSON 3 ENGAGE

What Do Immigrants Add to a Community?

INQUIRY JOURNAL, pp. 104–105

Bellringer

Prompt students to retrieve information from previous lessons. Ask: *What are some examples of people expressing their culture in our community?* (Answers will vary but should describe art, music, food, or other aspects of people's cultures.) Then explain that immigrants are people who come to live in a new country. Ask: *What do you think you will learn about what immigrants add to our community?* (Answers will vary, but students should connect what they know about culture and diversity to the idea that America is made up of immigrants as well as many people whose ancestors came from other places.)

Lesson Outcomes

Discuss the lesson question and lesson outcomes with students.

- Make sure students understand that *immigrants* describes people who were born in other countries and moved to the United States.

- Have students recall what they know about American history and the origins of the United States. Point out that, with the exception of Native Americans, all Americans are descendants of people who came to this country from another part of the world.

Talk About It

Point out to students that this quote appears on the Statue of Liberty. Explain that poems, particularly older ones, sometimes contain difficult or unusual language. As a result, it is important to read slowly and to carefully decode the poem's meaning. Provide sentence frames to help students form sentences as they discuss the quote.

- I think the huddled masses are _____.
- I think the golden door is _____.
- The poet is talking to _____.

 Collaborative Conversations

Analyze Details As students engage in partner, small group, and whole-class discussions, encourage them to
- think about who is speaking in the poem.
- use a dictionary as needed to find meanings of unfamiliar words.
- analyze the imagery in the poem and recognize it as symbolic rather than literal.

Lesson 3

What Do Immigrants Add to a Community?

. . . "Give me your tired, your poor,
Your huddled masses yearning to breathe free,
The wretched refuse of your teeming shore.
Send these, the homeless, tempest-tost to me,
I lift my lamp beside the golden door!"

—*from* "The New Colossus"
by Emma Lazarus

Lesson Outcomes

What Am I Learning?
In this lesson, you will use your investigative skills to look at the history of immigrants in the United States and what they have added to American life.

Why Am I Learning It?
Reading and talking about immigrants will help you understand how their contributions help make the United States a strong and diverse nation.

How Will I Know That I Learned It?
You will be able to write a newspaper article describing ways in which immigrants have enriched your community.

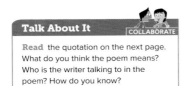

Talk About It

COLLABORATE

Read the quotation on the next page. What do you think the poem means? Who is the writer talking to in the poem? How do you know?

The Statue of Liberty on Liberty Island in New York Harbor

INQUIRY JOURNAL, pp. 104–105

 # English Learners SCAFFOLD

Use the following scaffolds to support student understanding of lesson outcomes.

Entering and Emerging
Paraphrase the poem quotation to help clarify its meaning. For example, say: *Give me your people who want to be free. Send them to me. I will shine a light that shows them where to find freedom.* Ask simple questions to guide their understanding: *Who is holding the light? What is the statue a symbol for?*

Developing and Expanding
Have students underline words or phrases in the quotation that are unfamiliar or difficult to understand. Provide more familiar synonyms or rewordings to help clarify meanings. Ask a volunteer to reread the poem using the synonyms.

Bridging and Reaching
Have students work together to act out the descriptions in the poem to show more clearly what is meant. One student can be the Statue of Liberty, and other students can play roles that demonstrate *tired, poor, huddled masses,* being *tempest-tost,* and so on.

 ### Social Emotional Learning

Social Awareness

Build Empathy As students read and discuss the poem, ask them to think about what it must have been like for people who had to flee a dangerous place to seek safety in America. Trying to understand how others feel and relating to what they have experienced can help students become more caring, empathetic individuals.

Ellis Island: Gateway to a New Life

1 Inspect

Read the title. What do you think this text will be about?

Circle words you do not know.

Underline words and phrases that the author uses to describe Ellis Island.

My Notes

_____

_____

_____

_____

_____

_____

_____

_____

_____

_____

During the 1800s, millions of immigrants arrived in the United States. They came to America seeking work, freedom, and a safe place to live. Toward the end of the 1800s, so many immigrants arrived here each year that some states had a hard time keeping track of the new arrivals. As a result, the US government made a change. In 1890, President Benjamin Harrison chose Ellis Island as the site of the first federal immigration station.

Ellis Island sits in New York Harbor. After a weeks-long journey by ship, new immigrants from Europe would spot the Statue of Liberty. They knew they had arrived in their new land. For most of them, the first stop would be Ellis Island.

Inside the Ellis Island station, immigrants waited in long lines to be inspected. These new arrivals had to present official papers showing who they were and where they came from. Immigrants were also examined for illnesses or diseases. For many, this process could be scary and uncomfortable. Then the immigrants were allowed to enter the country.

Ellis Island operated from 1892 to 1954. During that time, more than 12 million immigrants passed through its doors. At its busiest, more than 5,000 people entered the United States through Ellis Island each day.

The immigration station was crowded and was not always a pleasant place to be. But it was the gateway to a new and hopefully better life. Ellis Island became a powerful symbol of the immigrant experience.

2 Find Evidence

Reread How was Ellis Island both a positive and a negative experience for immigrants?

Underline one good thing and one bad thing about arriving as an immigrant at Ellis Island.

3 Make Connections

Talk about the reasons why an immigrant family might choose to come to the United States today. Does the poem on page 105 still describe those reasons? Why or why not? Explain your answer.

The Statue of Liberty on Liberty Island and the immigration center on Ellis Island in New York Harbor

INQUIRY JOURNAL, pp. 106–107

Analyze the Source

Background Information
Wealth played a major role in determining which immigrants had to pass through the screening process on Ellis Island. Passengers who traveled first or second class on the ships were usually inspected onboard. If they were deemed healthy and legal, they were allowed entry to the United States at once. In contrast, all third class, or "steerage" passengers had to be processed at the Ellis Island station.

Understanding Language

keeping track of: knowing where someone or something is

sits in: is located in

spot: see

1 Inspect

Read Have students read the title, text, and photo caption. Remind them to circle words in the text that they do not know.

- Underline words and phrases that the author uses to describe Ellis Island. (sits in New York Harbor; long lines; scary and uncomfortable; usually lasted only a few hours; crowded and not always a pleasant place; gateway to a new and hopefully better life; powerful symbol of the immigrant experience)

2 Find Evidence

Reread Have students reread the text.

Underline Students should underline one good and one bad thing about Ellis Island.

3 Make Connections

Talk Guide students in comparing the reasons an immigrant family might want to move to America today to those reasons described in the poem. (Students should recognize that many immigrants still come to America today to seek freedom and safety.)

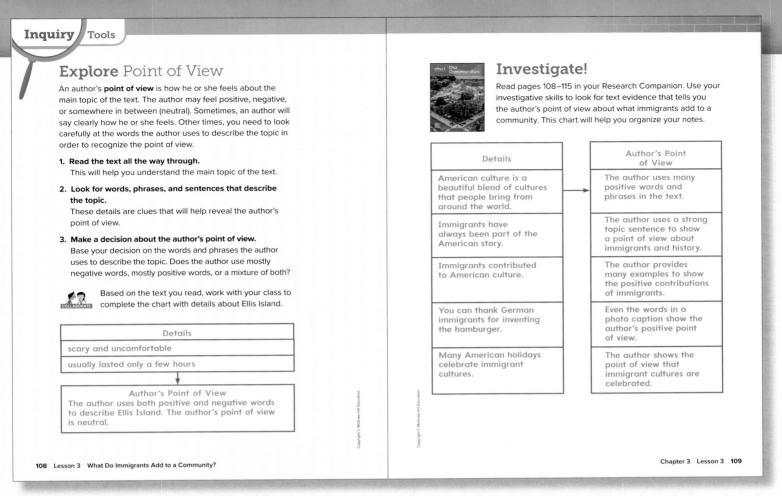

INQUIRY JOURNAL, pp. 108–109

Inquiry Tools

Explore Point of View

Read Discuss with students the steps for determining an author's point of view. Remind them that they should be looking closely at the kinds of words and phrases the author uses.

Guide Practice Have students review the text on pp. 106–107. Then work with them to complete the graphic organizer. Explain that they will use a similar graphic organizer to organize their independent research.

Check Understanding Confirm student understanding of the inquiry skill, Explore Point of View. If students cannot identify the author's point of view, review the steps on p. 108.

Investigate!

Have students read pages 108–115 in the Research Companion. Tell them the information will help them answer the lesson question ***What Do Immigrants Add to a Community?***

Take Notes Tell students they should use the graphic organizer on p. 109 of the Inquiry Journal to record words and phrases the author uses to describe what immigrants have added to America.

Remind students to pay particular attention to positive and/or negative words and phrases, because they will help students determine the author's point of view.

 Spotlight on Content

Details

Have students discuss with a partner how to differentiate between main ideas and details. Then have them work together to identify and take notes about the details in the Ellis Island text.

 **Digital Tools**

Blended Learning

Students prepare for the lesson investigation with step-by-step instruction about how to identify an author's point of view.

ePresentation

Use the **Inquiry Tools** to model the lesson graphic organizer.

LESSON 3 INVESTIGATE

LESSON QUESTION

What Do Immigrants Add to a Community?

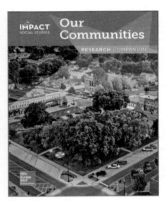

RESEARCH COMPANION, pp. 108–109

Melting Pot or Quilt?

1 Inspect Have students read pp. 108–109 and define *citizen*.

2 Find Evidence Use the questions below to check comprehension. Remind students to support their answers with text evidence.

Summarize How would you summarize the reason why American culture can be compared to a quilt? (American culture is made up of many contributions from other cultures in the same way a quilt is made up of many different kinds of fabric.) **DOK 2**

Draw Conclusions How can an immigrant be part of American culture, while at the same time still be part of his or her original culture? (An immigrant can take part in American cultural experiences, such as celebrating the Fourth of July, while also keeping some of their original culture, such as foods and music.) **DOK 3**

3 Make Connections

Identify Cause and Effect If a large number of immigrants from the same culture move into a community, how do you think the community might be affected? (Answers will vary but should touch on the idea that the community's existing culture may be, at least to some degree, influenced or altered by the new immigrants' culture.) **DOK 2**

Lesson 3

What Do Immigrants Add to a Community?

Melting Pot or Quilt?

Over one hundred years ago, a man named Israel Zangwill wrote a play called *The Melting Pot*. The play showed how people from many places came together in the United States. These people helped build a new American culture. Since that time, people have used the term *melting pot* to describe the mix of people and cultures in the United States.

Other people prefer to think of American culture as a quilt. Each piece of the quilt represents a unique culture. Although the pieces are all very different, each one is beautiful in its own way. When the pieces are stitched together, the result is a bright and colorful quilt unlike any other. In the same way, American culture is a beautiful blend of cultures that people bring from around the world.

About 40 million Americans were born in another country. Every year, about one million immigrants become American **citizens**. Some come by boat, some on foot, others on airplanes. They often face hardships when they arrive in the United States. Each person brings the food, clothing styles, music, holidays, and customs from his or her homeland. What they bring becomes part of the American quilt.

Chinatown in San Francisco, California

108   Lesson 3   What Do Immigrants Add to a Community?

Chapter 3   Lesson 3   109

RESEARCH COMPANION, pp. 108–109

English Learners   SCAFFOLD

Use the following scaffolds to support student understanding of lesson content.

Entering and Emerging

Ask students to name some of their favorite foods. Choose one of the foods that consists of different ingredients, mixed and then cooked together, like bread or a cake. Point out that that food is made up of different parts that are combined to make something new. Explain that this is similar to a melting pot. Show a picture of a quilt and point out the different fabrics that are still visible.

Developing and Expanding

Provide the following sentence frames to help students express how America is like a quilt: America is like a quilt because _____. Immigrants take part in American culture by _____. Immigrants take part in their own culture by _____.

Bridging and Reaching

Have students work with partners or in small groups to answer the Find Evidence questions. After you ask each question, have partners or groups discuss their ideas about the answer. Then call on one student from each pair or group to provide an answer.

 Digital Tools

Blended Learning

Flip the research approach and find evidence in a digital format.

eBook

Students investigate using their **Research Companion** and **IMPACT Explorer Magazine eBooks** to find evidence.

Immigration Throughout American History

Immigrants have always been a part of the American story. Even the founders of our country were descended from people from another country (Great Britain). During the early 1800s, millions of Irish immigrants came to America. The potato crops in Ireland had failed, and many people were starving. The Irish came here by boat to escape hunger and to look for work. They faced many challenges and unfair treatment when they arrived in the United States.

During the mid-1800s, news that there was gold in California traveled around the world. Thousands of Chinese crossed the Pacific Ocean, searching for economic opportunities. Many found work building railroads across the West, even though railroad companies did not treat Chinese workers equally.

Chinese immigrants worked building railroads.

Irish immigrants arriving in America

Did You Know?

The Cedar-Riverside neighborhood in Minneapolis, Minnesota, is nicknamed Little Mogadishu. Mogadishu is the capital of Somalia, a country in East Africa. This Minneapolis community has a large population of Somali immigrants.

Immigrants from Europe arrived in record numbers during the early 1900s. The total included more than four million Italians. About two million Jewish people also came in that time. They were fleeing hatred and violence.

Whenever immigrants arrive in America, they often look for communities that share their culture. Many cities have areas named after ethnic groups. Chinatown, Germantown, Little Italy, and Little India are just a few examples.

Immigrants continue seek a new life in America. Today, Mexico is where most immigrants were born. People from the Caribbean, China, and India also immigrate to the United States in large numbers. Though they may face many challenges, they are also part of the American story.

Ethnic neighborhoods are home to immigrants who share a culture.

✓ Stop and Check

Think Why did different groups of immigrants come to the United States?

Find Details As you read, add new information to the graphic organizer on page 109 in your Inquiry Journal.

RESEARCH COMPANION, pp. 110–111

Immigration Throughout American History

1 Inspect Have partners read pp. 110–111 and list some of the reasons immigrants have come to the United States.

2 Find Evidence Use the questions below to check comprehension.

Analyze What evidence does the author present to support the idea that immigrants have always been part of America's history? (The founders were descended from immigrants, and immigrants arrived during the 1800s, the 1900s, and still come today.) **DOK 2**

Formulate Why do you think the countries where the most immigrants come from have changed through time? (Answers will vary, but should note that places that were troubled or poor in the past may have improved, and that today different places in the world are having difficulties.) **DOK 3**

3 Make Connections

Draw Conclusions Recall what you read previously about American culture being like a quilt. How do ethnic neighborhoods support this idea? (Each ethnic neighborhood is culturally different, like the different fabrics used to make a quilt.) **DOK 3**

✓ Stop and Check COLLABORATE

Think Encourage students to review the text if they do not know the answer. (to escape starvation and find work)

 Spotlight on Content

American History

Locate and display a simple time line of American history with a few major events shown, such as the nation's founding, the Civil War, World War I, and World War II. Refer to the time line as you review the text and when the various large groups of immigrants arrived in America.

 Digital Tools

Blended Learning
Students explore lesson content through interactive activities.

Interactive IMPACT
Use the **More to Explore**.

Contributions of Immigrants to American Culture

Food is one way we experience other cultures. Immigrants from all over the world bring their favorite recipes with them when they come here. In most cities, people have a wide variety of ethnic food choices. Japanese sushi, Mexican tacos, Thai curries, and Italian pizzas are popular foods to eat. Even many foods that we think of as American today were originally introduced by immigrants. Hamburgers and hot dogs, for example, were both made popular by German Americans.

Immigrants have also influenced American music, dance, games, and art. K-pop music comes from South Korea. The game mancala comes from Africa. Anime is a type of animation that comes from Japan. Salsa dancing comes from the Caribbean.

You can thank German immigrants for giving us the hamburger.

This sushi burrito combines Japanese sushi with a Mexican burrito!

Many American inventors immigrated to the United States. For example, Nikola Tesla came from Croatia. He developed a better way to power motors and lighting systems. Recently, immigrants from Russia, Syria, Brazil, Taiwan, Cuba, and South Africa have had important roles in creating the largest American technology companies. Immigrants continue to help our nation succeed. They add their ideas, energy, and expertise to make America stronger.

Immigrants developed many computer technologies we use every day.

Biography

In 1997, **Madeleine Albright** made history when she became the first female secretary of state. Madeleine was born in 1937 in Czechoslovakia. In 1948, Madeleine and her family moved to America. She attended college in the United States, became a citizen, and began working for the government. Her specialty was foreign affairs, or working with other nations. In 1997, President Bill Clinton chose her as secretary of state. The secretary of state is in charge of the department that helps the president handle our relationships with other countries. She served until 2001.

✓ **Stop and Check**   COLLABORATE

Talk How have immigrants helped make America a great place to live?

Draw a picture of your favorite ethnic food.

RESEARCH COMPANION, pp. 112–113

Contributions of Immigrants to American Culture

1 Inspect Have students read pp. 112–113 and identify some popular American foods that were introduced by immigrants.

2 Find Evidence Use the questions below to check comprehension.

Make Observations How would America be different without immigrants and their contributions to American culture? (Answers will vary but may suggest that America would be less interesting or successful.) **DOK 2**

Summarize Why is Madeleine Albright an example of an immigrant helping to make America a better place to live? (She worked hard as part of the government to handle America's relationships with other countries.) **DOK 3**

3 Make Connections

Infer Why do you think the author chose to write first about foods brought to America by immigrants? (Most people are already familiar with these foods, so it is a good way to start discussing what immigrants add to American culture.) **DOK 3**

✓ **Stop and Check**   COLLABORATE

Talk Encourage students to summarize the main point of the text. (Answers will vary, but should include concrete examples of cultural contributions from different ethnic groups.)

Social Emotional Learning

Self-Regulation

Independence Learning to think and work independently builds character in students and prepares them for success when faced with challenging peer-pressure situations. As students draw their favorite ethnic foods, praise their individual choices of subject matter.

Around the World in the USA

1 **Inspect** Have partners read pp. 114–115 and describe the four holidays featured in the text.

2 **Find Evidence** Use the questions below to check comprehension.

Compare What are some things all of these celebrations have in common? (Answers may include being with family or with others who share a similar culture, parties, and costumes.) **DOK 2**

Explain Why are these holidays important to the people who take part in them? (They're fun; they bring people together; they allow people to celebrate their heritage while still being part of American culture.) **DOK 3**

3 **Make Connections**

Draw Conclusions How are these celebrations examples of immigrants adding to American culture? (Many Americans from different cultures take part in the celebrations, so they are not just celebrations of their original cultures. They are now part of American culture.) **DOK 3**

 Stop and Check

Talk Help students identify similarities and differences between Día de Los Muertos and Chinese New Year. (Both holidays bring families together. Parades are held on Chinese New Year; people go on picnics for Day of the Dead.)

What Do You Think? (Answers will vary but should include examples of cultural diversity in the community.)

 Digital Tools

Blended Learning

Students investigate curated resources and find evidence to answer the lesson question.

Interactive IMPACT

Students **Research** and find evidence using digital format texts.

Around the World in the USA

Many American holidays celebrate immigrant cultures. Today, Americans of many different backgrounds take part in the celebrations. These celebrations are a great way to recognize the diversity of American culture.

St. Patrick's Day

St. Patrick's Day began as a religious holiday in Ireland. In the United States, it has become a way to celebrate Irish culture. During the 1800s, many poor Irish immigrants came to America. They were often met with prejudice. St. Patrick's Day made them feel proud of their culture. Today, many cities have large parades. The city of Chicago even dyes the Chicago River green for a day!

Wearing green is a tradition on St. Patrick's Day.

Chinese New Year

The Chinese New Year begins between late January and late February each year. This Chinese holiday brings families together to feast and prepare for the new year. Everyone in the family works to clean the home. This task brings good luck for the coming year. America's biggest cities hold festive Chinese New Year parades. The parades feature dancing dragons, traditional clothing, and lots of fireworks.

A Chinese New Year celebration

Día de los Muertos

Día de los Muertos, or Day of the Dead, is a Mexican holiday. Families come together to remember their ancestors and relatives who have died. Families and friends light candles for those who have passed away. They also display the favorite foods and objects of their ancestors. Later in the day, families bring picnics to cemeteries so they can be close to their deceased loved ones.

People celebrating Día de los Muertos

Mardi Gras

Mardi Gras is a celebration in New Orleans. Mardi Gras means "Fat Tuesday" in French. It happens each year on the last day before the Christian season of Lent. People eat big meals. They parade through the streets in costumes and dance to loud marching jazz bands. The first Mardi Gras celebrations in the Americas were held in 1699.

Wild costumes are a common sight during Mardi Gras.

> ### ✓ Stop and Check COLLABORATE
>
> **Talk** How are Día de los Muertos and the Chinese New Year similar? How are they different?

What Do You Think? How have immigrants added to your community?

114 Lesson 3 What Do Immigrants Add to a Community?

Chapter 3 Lesson 3 115

RESEARCH COMPANION, pp. 114–115

 ## English Learners SCAFFOLD

Use the following scaffolds to support student understanding of lesson content.

Entering and Emerging

Gather photographs or illustrations for vocabulary related to the descriptions of the celebrations, such as *parade, candles, passed away, cemetery, skeleton*. Use the images to help clarify the meanings. Provide sentence frames to help students describe what is happening in the photographs in the text.

- I see _____.
- The people are _____.

Developing and Expanding

Assign holidays from the text to student pairs. Have them practice together reading aloud the text about their assigned holiday. One student will read the section aloud while the other student listens and provides polite, constructive feedback about pronunciation. Then have students switch roles. Afterward, call on individual students to read aloud parts of the text.

Bridging and Reaching

Provide a list of comparison and contrast signal words and phrases, such as *both, like, same, in common, similar, not alike, but, in contrast, different*. Display the list so students can refer to it. Have student pairs take turns to describe similarities and differences between the different holidays.

✔ Check for Success

Identify Can students list some ways that immigrants have added to American culture?

Differentiate

If Not, Refer students to the notes they have taken about immigrants in the graphic organizer on p. 109 of their Inquiry Journals. Remind them that these notes will either include descriptions of what immigrants have added or point them to places in the text where they can review specific contributions.

LESSON 3 REPORT

What Do Immigrants Add to a Community?

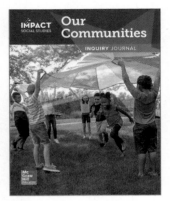

INQUIRY JOURNAL, pp. 110–111

Think About It

Remind students to review their research and consider how the words and phrases that appeared in the text are clues to the author's point of view. Encourage students to think about whether the author has shown immigrant contributions to American culture as being positive or negative. Direct students back to pp. 108–115 of their Research Companion if they need more information.

Write About It

Point of View Remind students to include the following elements in their responses:

- Cite evidence and examples from the text showing how immigrants have contributed to American culture.
- Introduce words and phrases that show your point of view.
- Use vocabulary from the lesson when appropriate.

Discipline(s)	4	3	2	1
Civics	Student provides evidence that shows a strong understanding of ways immigrants have contributed to American culture.	Student provides evidence that shows adequate understanding of ways immigrants have contributed to American culture.	Student provides evidence that shows a weak understanding of ways immigrants have contributed to American culture.	Student provides evidence that shows no understanding of ways immigrants have contributed to American culture.

Talk About It

Explain Have students identify specific examples of ways immigrants have contributed to American culture.

Assessment Students can check their understanding with feedback from the **Lesson Test** available online.

Connect to the Essential Question

Look at Our Community Before they respond, remind students to think about the examples of immigrant contributions that they read about in the text. Encourage them to identify similar examples they have seen or experienced in their own community.

Inquiry Project Update Remind students to turn to Inquiry Journal pp. 84–85 for project information. If necessary, review the Project Checklist with students. At this point in the chapter, students should focus on the third bullet point on the Checklist.

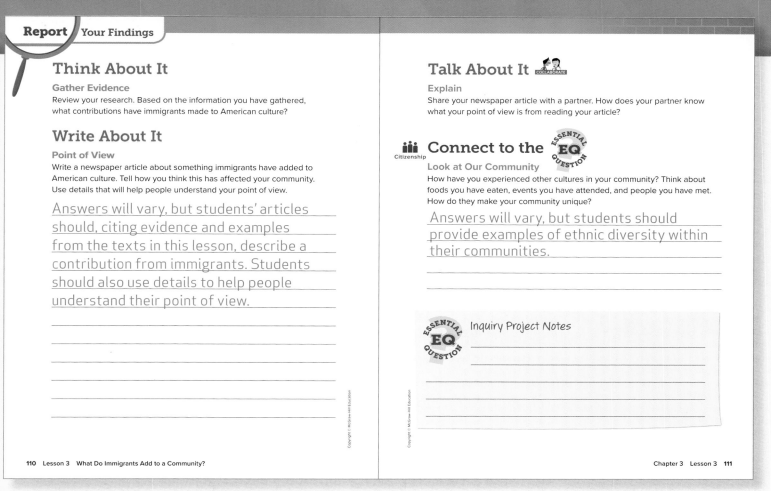

Report / Your Findings

Think About It

Gather Evidence

Review your research. Based on the information you have gathered, what contributions have immigrants made to American culture?

Write About It

Point of View

Write a newspaper article about something immigrants have added to American culture. Tell how you think this has affected your community. Use details that will help people understand your point of view.

Answers will vary, but students' articles should, citing evidence and examples from the texts in this lesson, describe a contribution from immigrants. Students should also use details to help people understand their point of view.

Talk About It

Explain

Share your newspaper article with a partner. How does your partner know what your point of view is from reading your article?

Connect to the EQ
Citizenship

Look at Our Community

How have you experienced other cultures in your community? Think about foods you have eaten, events you have attended, and people you have met. How do they make your community unique?

Answers will vary, but students should provide examples of ethnic diversity within their communities.

Inquiry Project Notes

INQUIRY JOURNAL, pp. 110–111

 # English Learners SCAFFOLD

Use the following scaffolds to support student writing.

Entering and Emerging

Before students begin the *Look at Our Community* activity, write the following sentence frames on the board:

- I ate _____. I saw _____. I met _____.

Model using the sentence frames to describe examples of other cultures in your community. Ask volunteers to use them to share their own examples. Write the sentences on the board and allow students to use them in their writing.

Developing and Expanding

Before students begin the *Look at Our Community* activity, organize them into three small groups assigned as *food, events,* and *people*. Have each group discuss examples from other cultures related to their topic. Allow students to use their original languages as needed during the discussions. Ask volunteers to share some of the examples they identified. List the examples on the board, and have students refer to these examples as they write.

Bridging and Reaching

Before students begin the *Write About It* activity, review the format for a newspaper article. Remind students to avoid using first person pronouns like *I* and *we*. Display a graphic organizer that shows the format with the following sections labeled: main idea, support 1, support 2. Have students follow this format when writing their newspaper article.

✔ Check for Success

Describe Can students write a newspaper article describing how immigrants have added to their community's culture?

Differentiate

If Not, Have students present the information in another way, such as in a mock news segment.

LESSON QUESTION

What Can Comparing Different Communities Tell Us About Global Cultures?

Connect to the Essential Question

Tell students that this lesson provides key research into the Chapter Essential Question: **What Makes a Community Unique?** Explain that they will compare and contrast communities in Peru and South Africa to learn about the culture that makes each place unique. Tell them they will explore different aspects of culture and express an opinion about what people can learn from other cultures.

Lesson Objectives

- **Explain** what artifacts can reveal about cultures of the past.
- **Compare and contrast** cultures from different parts of the world.
- **Identify** lifestyles, traditions, holidays, and additional aspects of other cultures.
- **Write** an opinion paragraph stating the most important aspects of culture.

Make Connections!

CONNECT TO ELA

Reading **Compare and contrast** the most important points and key details presented in two texts on the same topic.

Determine the main idea of a text; recount the key details and explain how they support the main idea.

Research **Recall** information from experiences or gather information from print and digital sources; take brief notes on sources and sort evidence into provided categories.

Writing **Craft** opinion pieces on familiar topics or texts, supporting a point of view with reasons.

Speaking and Listening **Follow** agreed-upon rules for discussions (e.g., gaining the floor in respectful ways, listening to others with care, speaking one at a time about the topics and texts under discussion).

Language **Determine or clarify** the meaning of unknown and multiple-meaning words and phrases based on grade 3 reading and content, choosing flexibly from a range of strategies.

COMMUNITY CONNECTIONS

To enrich what students have learned about different cultures, invite a local dance or music group to do a traditional performance in class, such as folk dancing or African drumming. You can also locate online cultural performances for students to view.

Lesson-At-A-Glance

1 ENGAGE — INQUIRY JOURNAL

pp. 112–117

- **Talk About It:** Photographs of Landscapes in Peru and South Africa
- **Analyze the Source:** Cultural Artifacts
- **Inquiry Tools:** Explore Compare and Contrast

2 INVESTIGATE — RESEARCH COMPANION

pp. 116–125

- **Two Vibrant Cultures**
- **The Stories Cultures Tell About Themselves**
- **Arts, Music, Dance, Food**
- **Traditional Holidays and Festivals**

3 REPORT — INQUIRY JOURNAL

pp. 118–119

- **Think About It**
- **Write About It:** Write and Cite Evidence; Write an Opinion
- **Talk About It**
- **Connect to the Essential Question**

ASSESSMENT

- **Online Lesson Test**
- **Printable Lesson Test**

For more details, see pp. T168–T169.

▶ Digital Tools

at **my.mheducation.com**

ePresentation

Teach the **Engage**, **Investigate**, and **Report** content to the whole class from **ePresentations** that launch directly from the lesson dashboard.

eBook

You can flip your instruction with the **IMPACT eBooks** found on your lesson dashboard.

Interactive IMPACT

Blend in digital content **when you want it** and **where you want it**.

Blended Learning features in the Teacher's Edition highlight ways to connect in-class work with online experiences to enhance learning.

Investigate current events with **IMPACT News**.

Explore domain-based vocabulary with **Explore Words** and **Word Play** vocabulary activities.

pp. 30–41

Go Further with IMPACT Explorer Magazine!

The **IMPACT Explorer Magazine** supports students' exploration of the Essential Question and provides additional resources for the EQ Inquiry Project.

LESSON 4 LANGUAGE LEARNERS

LESSON QUESTION

What Can Comparing Different Communities Tell Us About Global Cultures?

Introduce the Lesson

Set Purpose Explain to students that in this lesson they will read informational texts about two different cultures to learn about various aspects of people's lives, including art, music, dance, food, and holidays.

Access Prior Knowledge Read the lesson question and ask students what they know about culture. Remind them that culture relates to the beliefs, customs, and way of life of a group. Ask: *Have you ever been to a festival that celebrates another culture? Did you see special clothing or dances? Have you heard examples of traditional music from different places?* Ask students if they can name foods that came from different cultures.

Spark Curiosity Have students look at the photographs on p. 117 of the Research Companion. Read the caption for students and help students identify the different items they see that are for sale in the markets in Peru and South Africa. Provide a list of words to describe aspects of culture (such as *traditional, ethnic group,* and *crafts*). Use the words to ask questions about the photographs: *What types of items are for sale?* (clothing, blankets, tote bags) *Are these items you would purchase at a market?* (Answers will vary.)

Build Meaning & Support Language

Inquiry Journal

Analyze the Source (pp. 114–115) Explain to students that an *artifact* is a simple object, such as a tool or an ornament from the past. Artifacts are made by people and can help us understand how people lived in the past. Work with students to list examples of artifacts, such as arrowheads, old schoolbooks or toys, or cooking utensils. Explain that the photos on pp. 114 and 115 show artifacts. Each provides a look at the way life was lived centuries ago. Ask: *What benefits do you think people today get from an artifact?* (They can learn how people lived.)

Inquiry Tools (pp. 116–117) Tell students they will **Compare and Contrast** as they read sections in the Research Companion. Review words used to compare, such as *both, same,* and *like,* and contrast, such as *but, however,* and *unlike.* Then discuss similarities (size, how the culture ended) and differences (location, artifacts) between the Inca and Mapungubwe cultures and guide students to fill in the graphic organizer on p. 116. Explain that the graphic organizer will help them organize the information as they read. Explain to students how to use the Venn diagram, pointing to each circle, the intersection, and the caption below each circle. Say: *We will look at the Inca and Mapungubwe cultures to learn how they are alike and how they are different.*

Language Objectives

- Use newly acquired content and academic vocabulary to talk and write about different cultures and what people can learn from other cultures.
- Write an opinion about what culture means to a community.
- Participate in group discussions, using abstract nouns.

Spanish Cognates

To support Spanish speakers, point out the cognates.

tradition = tradición

art = arte

music = música

dance = danza

Research Companion

Two Vibrant Cultures (pp. 116–117) In the first paragraph on p. 116, read aloud sentences three and four, beginning with "Many Peruvians." Point out that sentence three describes how the Inca influenced the culture. Then in the next sentence, the word *also* signals a similarity. That sentence tells about Spanish influence. Ask: *How can you describe Peru's culture?* (It is a mix of Inca and Spanish influences.)

The Stories Cultures Tell About Themselves (pp. 118–121) Read aloud the first sentence on p. 120 and write it on the board. Point out that the word *while* indicates a contrast between Lima and Johannesburg. On the board, cross out the word *while* and insert *but* after the first comma. Explain that these are two ways to express a contrast. Ask: *Which city is influenced more by recent history?* (Johannesburg)

Arts, Music, Dance, Food (pp. 122–123) Read aloud the first sentence on p. 122. Explain that this sentence compares the two cultures by stating how they are alike. Guide students to understand that the word *both* signals that the two cultures share something—a blend of ancient traditions with those of settlers. Show that the text describes how Peru and South Africa are alike because they each have art, music, dance, and food traditions.

Traditional Holidays and Festivals (pp. 124–125) Provide students the following definitions before reading the text: patron (a special protector or supporter), flag-raising ceremony (a ceremony in which a nation's or organization's flag is officially raised and honored), twenty-one gun salute (a military honor in which cannon or other artillery are fired), reconciliation (two people or groups becoming friendly again). Then have students look at each photo as you read the captions. Discuss similarities and differences in the photos.

Inquiry Journal

Report Your Findings (pp. 118–119) Review with students the difference between a fact, which can be proven to be true, and an opinion, which expresses a person's feelings about a topic. Provide examples, such as *Johannesburg is the largest city in South Africa* (fact) and *Johannesburg is the best place to live* (opinion). Remind students that their paragraphs should express an opinion and also include evidence from the text to support the opinion. Encourage students to use the new vocabulary words they have learned.

Language Forms & Conventions

Abstract and Concrete Nouns Remind students that nouns name a person, a place, or a thing. Say: *We can talk about some nouns that people can touch or see. People can only think about other nouns. Nouns people cannot touch or see are abstract nouns. Concrete nouns can be experienced through one's senses. Feelings, ideas, and concepts are abstract nouns.* Write the chart on the board.

Abstract Nouns	Concrete Nouns
pride	award
holiday	parade
tradition	dress
happiness	friend

 Have students work in pairs to locate some abstract nouns in the lesson. Call on volunteers to say them aloud and add them to the chart. Have students name a concrete noun that is related to the abstract noun.

 Cross-Cultural Connection

Political activist Albertina Sisulu worked against apartheid policies in South Africa beginning in the 1960s. She was jailed frequently and held in solitary confinement a few times because of her activities. After apartheid ended, Albertina was a member of the first democratically elected parliament. She and her husband were honored with several humanitarian awards.

 Leveled Support

Entering & Emerging
Provide sentence frames:
I think _____ is the most important part of culture because it shows a community's _____.

Developing & Expanding
Have students work in small groups to state their opinions and to list their supporting evidence for their opinions.

Bridging & Reaching
Have partners tell each other their opinion and the key details that support their opinion. Then work together on conclusions that restate their opinion in different words.

 Language Transfer

Point out that sometimes abstract nouns have both a singular and a plural form. The singular form has a more general meaning, like *culture*. The plural form is more specific, like *cultures*.

LESSON 4 ENGAGE

What Can Comparing Different Communities Tell Us About Global Cultures?

INQUIRY JOURNAL, pp. 112–113

Bellringer

Prompt students to recall that millions of people came to the United States in the 1800s seeking work and freedom. Ask: *What is an immigrant? How do immigrants contribute to the culture of a community?* (An immigrant is someone who leaves their original country to live permanently in a different country. Students should recognize that immigrants share their traditions, food, music, and other aspects of culture with their new community.)

Lesson Outcomes

Discuss the lesson question and lesson outcomes with students.

- Make sure that students understand the term *culture* as the way of life a group of people share.
- Help students understand what they will be comparing by having them identify various aspects of culture and give specific examples. Students may mention traditional foods, holidays, or music and give examples such as Peruvian panpipe music.

Talk About It

Explain that when we talk about photographs, we describe, analyze, and interpret them and present our ideas in our own words. Provide sentence frames to help students talk about the similarities and differences between the photographs.

- The photographs show _____ and _____.
- The photograph from Peru is like the one from South Africa because it shows _____.
- The photograph from Peru is not like the one from South Africa because _____.

 Collaborative Conversations

Rules for Discussion Remind students of your class expectations for partner, small-group, and whole-class discussions. Give suggestions such as these:

- Express your ideas clearly.
- Listen carefully to what others say.
- Build on the ideas shared by others.

Lesson 4 — What Can Comparing Different Communities Tell Us About Global Cultures?

Lesson Outcomes

What Am I Learning?
In this lesson, you will use your investigative skills to compare and contrast cultures in two different countries.

Why Am I Learning It?
Reading and talking about different cultures help you understand people's lifestyles, traditions, holidays, and other aspects of culture.

How Will I Know That I Learned It?
You will be able to write a paragraph that compares and contrasts cultures and offer an opinion about what people can learn from other cultures.

Mapungubwe Cultural Landscape in South Africa

Talk About It COLLABORATE

Look closely at the photos. What do you notice about each of these images? How are they similar? How are they different?

Machu Picchu in Peru

112 Lesson 4 What Can Comparing Different Communities Tell Us About Global Cultures?

Chapter 3 Lesson 4 113

INQUIRY JOURNAL, pp. 112–113

English Learners SCAFFOLD

Use the following scaffolds to support student understanding of lesson outcomes.

Entering and Emerging

Read the photo captions aloud to students. Make sure they understand that Peru and South Africa are different places. Show a world map and point to Peru and South Africa. Teach vocabulary for the features seen in the photographs, if necessary. Point to different features in the photograph. Ask students to describe what they see, using sentence frames as needed:

- I see a _____.

- This is a _____.

Developing and Expanding

Ask students to share their observations about the photographs, using compare/contrast words such as *same*, *like*, *also*, *different*, *but*, and *however*. Provide sentence starters such as: *The picture of Peru is like the picture of South Africa because . . .* and *The two pictures are different because . . . .*

Bridging and Reaching

Have partners work together to answer the questions about the photographs. Then have student pairs write two sentences that describe how the pictures are different and two sentences that tell how they are similar. Ask volunteers to read their sentences aloud.

Social Emotional Learning

Social Awareness

Respect Remind students that we live in an increasingly multicultural nation that can be greatly enriching if we learn to understand and respect one another's differences. Ask: *What are some ways you can show respect to people whose cultures differ from your own?*

▶ Digital Tools

Blended Learning
Students engage with the lesson question and discussion prompts.

Interactive IMPACT

Discuss the **Lesson Question** and **Talk About It**.

Cultural Artifacts

1 Inspect

Read the title. What do you think this text will be about?

Underline words or phrases that tell about the Inca civilization.

Circle words or phrases that tell about the Mapungubwe Cultural Landscape.

Discuss with a partner what you notice about the different artifacts.

My Notes

_____

_____

_____

_____

_____

_____

_____

An **artifact** is an object that was used by people in the past. The artifacts pictured below are from the Inca civilization of ancient Peru. This civilization was the largest empire in the Americas at the time. The Inca were known for creating new farming and building methods. They built the city of Machu Picchu without using sand or cement, and without the help of the wheel. Long ago, Machu Picchu was abandoned. No one knows why this happened, but it might have been the result of disease.

These tools and pottery are artifacts found in the ancient Inca city of Machu Picchu. They were rediscovered in 1911.

The artifact below is from the Mapungubwe Cultural Landscape. Mapungubwe was a large kingdom in southern Africa. Some of the people who lived there were gold and ivory traders. Others were successful farmers. However, the kingdom was abandoned in the fourteenth century. It is believed that climate change caused the people to leave the kingdom. The Mapungubwe Cultural Landscape is preserved so people can see the remains of this civilization.

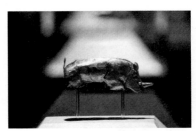

This rhinoceros artifact from the Mapungubwe Cultural Landscape is made of gold foil. It was found buried with a king.

2 Find Evidence

Reread What was unique about the Inca and the Mapungubwe Cultural Landscape? What was the same about their cultures? Look for details that show these differences and similarities.

Look at the captions. What conclusions can you draw about each artifact? How was each artifact used? Was the purpose similar or different? Why?

3 Make Connections

Talk What comparisons can you make between these cultures based on their artifacts?

Connect to Now How do these artifacts compare to objects that are important to you?

INQUIRY JOURNAL, pp. 114–115

Analyze the Source

1 Inspect

Read Have students read the text, study the photos, and read the photo captions. Remind them to underline words that tell about the Inca civilization. (ancient Peru, largest empire, new farming and building methods, Machu Picchu) Circle words that tell about the Mapungubwe Cultural Landscape. (large, southern African kingdom; abandoned in fourteenth century due to climate change)

2 Find Evidence

Reread Have students reread the text and photo captions.

Look Students should understand that the Inca artifacts were made of common materials and were likely used by ordinary people in their daily lives. The artifact from the Mapungubwe Cultural Landscape was made of gold, a valuable metal, and used in a king's burial as a decorative or symbolic object.

3 Make Connections

Talk Encourage students to work with a partner to make comparisons between the two cultures. (Answers will vary, but students' observations should be based on evidence from the text and photos.)

Connect to Now Encourage students to think of both common and special objects that are important to them and to compare them with the artifacts. (Answers will vary, but students should name contemporary objects and compare them to the artifacts.)

Spotlight on Content

Using Maps

Use an atlas or map of South America and Africa to show students where the Inca and Mapungubwe civilizations were located. Help students name the present-day countries where these civilizations existed.

▶ Digital Tools

Blended Learning

Students read informational texts and analyze primary sources.

Interactive IMPACT

Have students practice and apply the strategy of close reading as they analyze text.

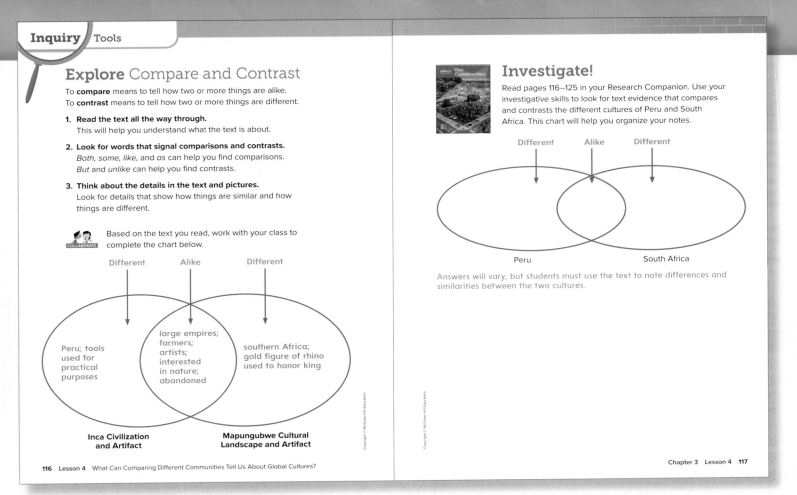

Explore Compare and Contrast

To **compare** means to tell how two or more things are alike.
To **contrast** means to tell how two or more things are different.

1. **Read the text all the way through.**
   This will help you understand what the text is about.

2. **Look for words that signal comparisons and contrasts.**
   Both, some, like, and *as* can help you find comparisons.
   But and *unlike* can help you find contrasts.

3. **Think about the details in the text and pictures.**
   Look for details that show how things are similar and how things are different.

Based on the text you read, work with your class to complete the chart below.

Different → Alike → Different

- Peru; tools used for practical purposes
- large empires; farmers; artists; interested in nature; abandoned
- southern Africa; gold figure of rhino used to honor king

Inca Civilization and Artifact   **Mapungubwe Cultural Landscape and Artifact**

Investigate!

Read pages 116–125 in your Research Companion. Use your investigative skills to look for text evidence that compares and contrasts the different cultures of Peru and South Africa. This chart will help you organize your notes.

Different → Alike → Different

Peru   South Africa

Answers will vary, but students must use the text to note differences and similarities between the two cultures.

INQUIRY JOURNAL, pp. 116–117

Inquiry Tools

Explore Compare and Contrast

Read Review with students the meanings of *compare* and *contrast*. Have students read the step-by-step instructions for how to compare and contrast. Have them look for key words, such as *both, same, like,* and *as* along with *but* and *unlike* as they reread the text.

Guide Practice Have students review the text on pp. 114-115. Then work with them to complete the graphic organizer on p. 116. Explain that they will use a similar graphic organizer to organize their independent research.

Check Understanding Confirm student understanding of the inquiry skill, Explore Compare and Contrast. If students cannot compare and contrast the most important details from the text, review the steps on p. 116.

Investigate!

Have students read pp. 116–125 in the Research Companion. Tell them the information will help them answer the lesson question **What Can Comparing Different Communities Tell Us About Global Cultures?**

Take Notes Tell students they should use the graphic organizer on p. 117 of the Inquiry Journal to take notes on the key similarities and differences between the cultures of Peru and South Africa. Remind students that they should use their own words when taking notes.

EL Spotlight on Language

Comparing and Contrasting

Use sentence frames to help students compare and contrast details. To compare, suggest frames such as:

_____ and _____ both have _____.

_____ and _____ are the same because _____.

_____ is like _____ because _____.

To contrast, use frames such as:

_____ has _____ but _____ doesn't.

_____ and _____ are different because _____.

LESSON 4 INVESTIGATE

LESSON QUESTION

What Can Comparing Different Communities Tell Us About Global Cultures?

RESEARCH COMPANION, pp. 116–117

Background Information

Peru sits on the west coast of South America, bordered on the north by Ecuador and Colombia, on the east by Brazil, and on the south by Bolivia and Chile.

- The Inca Empire was the most sophisticated in pre-Columbian America, but Peru was also home to the Norte Chico, the oldest civilization in the Americas, in 3200 BC.
- The Spanish conquered the Inca in the 16th century, and Lima became the capital of Spain's South American colonies.
- Peru proclaimed independence from Spain in 1821.

South Africa is the southernmost country in Africa. Its southern coastline is 1700 miles long, stretching from the Atlantic Ocean to the Indian Ocean. Its northern neighbors are Namibia, Botswana, and Zimbabwe. Mozambique and Swaziland border the east and northeast.

- Two of South Africa's 11 official languages are of European origin. Afrikaans developed from Dutch and is the first language of most South Africans. English reflects the era of British colonialism and is the fourth most common language.
- Apartheid, which was imposed in 1948 by the ruling white minority, legalized racial segregation and institutionalized racism in the country.
- South Africa has some of the oldest archaeological sites in the world.
- An area of caves in Guateng Province is a UNESCO World Heritage site and is called the "Cradle of Humankind."
- South Africa was colonized by the Portuguese in the 15th century, the Dutch in the 17th century, and the British in the 18th and 19th century. It became a fully independent nation in 1931.

Two Vibrant Cultures

1 Inspect Have students read pp. 116-117. Ask: *What parts of culture in Peru and South Africa does the text describe?* (ethnic groups, language, religion)

2 Find Evidence Use the questions below to check comprehension. Remind students to support their answers with text evidence.

Assess Which two cultural groups have had the greatest impact on life in Peru? (Inca and Spanish) **Give an example of each.** (Inca—Quechua is one of the official languages, and traditional religious beliefs are common. Spanish—The Spanish language is one of the official languages, and Catholicism is the main religion.) **DOK 3**

Compare and Contrast How is the ethnic diversity similar in Peru and South Africa? How is it different? (Both cultures are ethnically diverse. Peru's main ethnic groups are Amerindians and mestizos. South Africa's main ethnic groups are black, white, multiethnic, and Asian.) **DOK 3**

3 Make Connections

Explain Think about your own community. What groups have influenced the culture there? How would you describe your community's culture to someone who has never been there? (Answers will vary, but should show that students understand that culture involves such things as art, music, food, and holiday traditions.) **DOK 3**

Lesson 4
What Can Comparing Different Communities Tell Us About Global Cultures?

Two Vibrant Cultures

Comparing cultures in different communities can help us learn more about culture. The third largest country in South America is Peru. Many Peruvians are descended from the Inca. The Spanish have also influenced the country. Peru's main ethnic groups are Amerindians, the name for Native Americans on the continent of South America, and Mestizos descendant of Amerindians and Europeans. Asians, Peruvians descended from Africans, and many other ethnic groups live in Peru. The country's main religion is Catholicism. Many Amerindians combine traditional religious beliefs with Catholic ideas. Peru's official languages are Spanish and Quechua. Quechua is spoken by Amerindians in Peru and other South American countries. Most Peruvians live near the capital, Lima.

South Africa is Africa's ninth largest country. It is on Africa's southern tip. South Africa's main ethnic groups are black South Africans, multiethnic South Africans, white South Africans, and Asian South Africans. The country has eleven official languages because of its ethnic diversity. The majority are Christians. Others are Hindus, Muslims, Jews, and Buddhists. Most of the people live in cities, such as Johannesburg and Pretoria.

People from South Africa and Peru (smaller photo) make purchases at markets.

RESEARCH COMPANION, pp. 116–117

 # English Learners SCAFFOLD

Use the following scaffolds to support student understanding of lesson content.

Entering and Emerging
Read the title of the selection aloud to students. Explain that *vibrant* means "lively" or "exciting." Ask students to name things they see in the photographs, and list the items on the board. Then guide students in discussing how the photographs reflect the ways in which the cultures of Peru and South Africa are vibrant. Guide students to complete this sentence frame:

- _____ and _____ have vibrant cultures.
- *The photographs show _____.*

Developing and Expanding
Have students work in groups to list what they see in the photographs. Then ask groups to discuss how the photographs reflect the ways in which Peru and South Africa have vibrant cultures. Ask two groups to come together to compare their ideas.

Bridging and Reaching
Ask students to discuss with a partner how the photographs support the idea that Peru and South Africa are countries with a great deal of cultural and ethnic diversity. Remind them to cite evidence from the photographs to support their opinion.

 **Digital** Tools

Blended Learning
Guide students as they investigate the lesson content.

Interactive IMPACT

Use the **More to Explore**.

The Stories Cultures Tell About Themselves

Lima

Myths, legends, and stories from the past tell much about a culture. In Peru's capital, Lima, and throughout Peru, people share stories about their history. The stories connect people to their Peruvian heritage and culture. Many of these stories tell about the origin of the world. Other stories tell about when the Inca ruled, or about life after the Spanish came to Peru. People tell stories to explain events that occurred in the past and to relate those events to modern life.

Lima and its surrounding areas have been important to Peru's culture for thousands of years. For example, Pachacamac was an important religious site near Lima long ago. Many pilgrims visited the site. It was named after the god Pachacamac. His name means "Maker of the Earth." According to legend, the god Pachacamac represented all living things. One story about him describes how he created the first man and woman. Today, much of the ancient religious site of Pachacamac has been restored so visitors can learn about Inca culture.

In Lima Centro, people share an identity and heritage that goes back thousands of years.

Did You Know?

Many **artifacts** have been found in Peru. The Museo Larco has many ancient objects including tools, highly detailed figures, and jewelry. Museo de la Nación is also in Peru and contains similar artifacts from ancient civilizations. Museums help people in Peru learn about their history.

Museo Larco in Lima

The most important of the Inca creator gods was Viracocha. According to legend, he created the sun, the moon, and the stars from Lake Titicaca. His first attempt at human life produced stone giants. They could not be controlled. So Viracocha got rid of them. Then he made people who were smaller and more manageable. This group turned out to be too proud and greedy. So Viracocha sent a great flood to destroy everything. However, he let three humans live. These humans brought about the human race. Many Amerindians continue to tell this story as part of their cultural heritage.

Inca god Viracocha

✓ Stop and Check

COLLABORATE

Talk Why is history so important to today's Peruvians? What evidence in the lesson supports this?

RESEARCH COMPANION, pp. 118–119

The Stories Cultures Tell About Themselves

1 Inspect Have students read pp. 118–119 and name two important Inca gods.

2 Find Evidence Use the questions below to check comprehension.

Summarize How would you summarize the story of Viracocha? (Possible response: Legend says that Viracocha created the sun, moon, stars, and humans. He destroyed the first people because they could not be controlled. He created smaller people, but they were proud and greedy. Viracocha sent a flood to destroy all but three people, who are the ancestors of the human race.) **DOK 2**

Draw Conclusions Name two reasons why people share myths and legends. (Answers may include: to explain how things came to be, to teach lessons, to unify a group or define a group's identity, to connect people to their heritage and culture.) **DOK 3**

3 Make Connections

Compare Are the stories of Pachacamac and Viracocha similar to other stories you have heard? In what way? (Answers will vary.) **DOK 3**

✓ Stop and Check

COLLABORATE

Talk Remind students to cite evidence in the text when discussing their answers. (Answers will vary, but students should recognize that history gives people a sense of their past and relates past events to their beliefs and way of life.)

Spotlight on Vocabulary

Content Vocabulary

heritage: traditions and achievements that are part of a group's history

origin: the source or beginning of something

pilgrims: people who travel to a religious place

attempt: the effort of trying to do something

▶ Digital Tools

Blended Learning

Students investigate curated resources and find evidence to answer the lesson question.

Interactive IMPACT

Students choose from print or digital **Inquiry Tools** to take notes.

Johannesburg

While citizens of Lima identify with heritage that goes back thousands of years, more recent history influences the identity of the citizens of Johannesburg, South Africa. Johannesburg is the largest city in South Africa. Different groups of people live freely there. But at one time the black population in South Africa was denied rights and freedom. White leaders ruled the country even though most South Africans were black. The country followed a system of racial inequality and segregation called **apartheid**.

Protests against apartheid lasted for many years. Police and government officials arrested protest leaders. One leader was Nelson Mandela. His arrest caused the rest of the world to notice what was happening in South Africa. In 1989, South Africa's government made a change. Leaders wrote a new constitution. Blacks won their freedom and rights back. Then in 1990, Mandela was released from prison. He continued to fight for reforms. South Africa's first democratic election took place in 1994. Nelson Mandela was elected president.

People with the flag of the Rainbow Nation

With the end of apartheid, Archbishop Desmond Tutu of Cape Town, South Africa, began using the phrase *Rainbow Nation* to describe his country. Once a country that separated whites and blacks, it now united many cultures. Groups from different backgrounds had joined together to begin better lives in South Africa.

Nelson Mandela talked about Tutu's *Rainbow Nation* idea early in his presidency. With his words, South Africa's nickname, *Rainbow Nation*, was set.

South Africa's stories have been told for generations. South Africa's writers have also recorded apartheid events. These writings mean people will always remember what life was like in South Africa.

> **PRIMARY SOURCE**
>
> ### In Their Words... Nelson Mandela
>
> "Each one of us is as intimately attached to the soil of this beautiful country as are the famous jacaranda trees of Pretoria . . . a rainbow nation at peace with itself and the world."
>
> —Nelson Mandela, 1994

Biography

Nelson Mandela

Nelson Mandela

Nelson Mandela organized nonviolent protests against South Africa's apartheid government. The government sentenced him to life in prison for treason. In prison, Mandela became a symbol of apartheid's injustice. He was thought of as a hero. After 27 years, Mandela was released from prison as apartheid ended. Nelson Mandela became South Africa's first black president. During his presidency, he worked for unity and peace.

> ☑ **Stop and Check**
>
> **Talk** How did Nelson Mandela influence the country?

120 Lesson 4 What Can Comparing Different Communities Tell Us About Global Cultures?

Chapter 3 Lesson 4 **121**

RESEARCH COMPANION, pp. 120–121

The Stories Cultures Tell About Themselves

1 Inspect Have students read pp. 120–121 and define the term *apartheid*.

2 Find Evidence Use the questions below to check comprehension.

Explain What were black South Africans protesting under the system of apartheid? (lack of rights and freedom, racial inequality, segregation) **DOK 2**

Cause and Effect Why was Nelson Mandela arrested? (He protested apartheid) What effect did his arrest have on South Africa? (The world began to speak out against apartheid, and South Africa's government was forced to abolish it.) **DOK 2**

Interpret Why is "Rainbow Nation" a good description of South Africa? (because South Africa is made of many different cultures, just as a rainbow is made of many different colors) **DOK 3**

3 Make Connections

Assess Why do you think it is important to read about people like Nelson Mandela and Desmond Tutu? (Answers will vary, but students should understand that reading about such people can inspire others to behave ethically and heroically.) **DOK 3**

☑ Stop and Check
COLLABORATE

Talk Have students discuss the question with a partner. (Answers will vary, but students should include his nonviolent methods and the end of apartheid.)

Social Emotional Learning

Social Awareness

Build Empathy Students who can imagine how others feel in different situations can begin to develop empathy. Ask students to think of questions they would ask black South Africans who lived through apartheid.

Arts, Music, Dance, Food

Cultural Arts and Food in Lima and Throughout Peru

The cultures of both Peru and South Africa blend ancient traditions with newer ones. Many Peruvians still make traditional arts and crafts. For example, some Amerindians make clothing from llama hair or sheep's wool.

The Ayacucho made *retablos*, wooden altars, for religious ceremonies in their homes. Today, craftspeople continue carving religious scenes for these altars. Spanish and Italian artists in Peru created paintings and sculptures for churches.

Peru's music and dance also blend its history. Music from Peru's mountains, or Andean music, uses flutes and panpipes. Andean dances include the *huayno*, a fast dance with colorful costumes. Criollo music from Peru's coast includes the *marinera*, a slow and romantic dance accompanied by guitar.

People living on the coast enjoy seafood. In the Amazon Jungle, people eat tropical fruits and fish. Traditional Andean dishes include potatoes and meat. Potatoes originally came from Peru.

This Peruvian plays the panpipes.

Potatoes came from Peru and are still very important to Peruvian food.

Cultural Arts and Food in Johannesburg and Throughout South Africa

A person traveling to South Africa might stumble across rock art. These prehistoric works show animals, tools, and activities of ancient times. Black folk art, such as beadwork, is tied to South African customs. Today, it is used in clothing and may be part of ceremonies.

Popular South African music often combines traditional music, jazz, religious music, and other forms. Miriam Makeba was a black South African singer who introduced Xhosa and Zulu songs to Western audiences.

Gumboot dancing began with gold miners who worked and lived under terrible conditions. They began beating out rhythms with their boots in order to communicate with each other. Gumboot dancing spread outside the mines and is still performed today.

People in South Africa enjoy traditional and modern foods. *Bobotie*, a meat pie with apricots, raisins, and curry flavoring, comes from the Dutch and English. *Braii* is barbeque with beef, chicken, ostrich, or other game.

Zulu bead art

> **✓ Stop and Check** COLLABORATE
>
> **Talk** What are two ways both Peruvians and South Africans show their traditions through art, music, dance, or food?
>
> **Find Details** As you read, add new information to the graphic organizer on page 117 in your Inquiry Journal.

RESEARCH COMPANION, pp. 122–123

Arts, Music, Dance, Food

1 Inspect Have students read pp. 122–123 and describe Gumboot dancing.

2 Find Evidence Use the questions below to check comprehension.

Compare and Contrast How is Peruvian music similar to South African music? How is it different? (Both use elements of traditional ethnic music; Peruvian music varies by region and uses flutes, panpipes, and guitars; popular South African music incorporates traditional, jazz, and religious music.) **DOK 3**

Cite Evidence What do the cultural arts and food in South Africa communicate about the country's history? (Modern clothing has beadwork that shows that black folk art is part of the culture and history of South Africa; South African music is a combination of many forms of music; gumboot dancing began because of difficult conditions; food in South Africa has Dutch, English, and local influences.) **DOK 3**

3 Make Connections

Differentiate How does reading about the art, music, dance, and food of Peru and South Africa help you understand the cultures of each country? (Answers will vary, but students should point out that they learn how the culture of each country is a blend of different influences over the centuries.) **DOK 3**

 Stop and Check

Talk Remind students to use the text when discussing their answers. (Answers should provide two specific examples of ways Peruvians and South Africans use arts, music, dance, or food to express their traditions.)

 Spotlight on Language

Understanding Language

The word *stumble* may be familiar to students as a word that means "to miss a step while walking and almost fall down." Point out that in this text, *stumble across* means "to find something by accident."

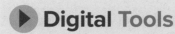 **Digital Tools**

Blended Learning

Students investigate curated resources and find evidence to answer the lesson question.

Interactive IMPACT

Students **Research** and find evidence using digital format texts.

Traditional Holidays and Festivals

Holidays Throughout Peru

Many people in Peru celebrate Catholic religious holidays. Día de Santa Rosa de Lima honors Saint Rose of Lima, the first person born in the Americas to be made a saint. She is also the patron saint of South America. Another holiday is Día de San Pedro y San Pablo (Feast of Saint Peter and Saint Paul). People attend special masses on this day. Saint Peter is the patron saint of fishermen. Many decorate their boats in his honor.

People in Lima celebrating

Peruvians celebrate their independence from Spain every year in a two-day celebration on July 28 and July 29. Independence was not complete until 1824. However, July 28, 1821, was the day it was first declared. The celebration is known as Fiestas Patrias. In Lima, there is a flag-raising ceremony and a twenty-one-gun salute. People watch large military parades.

An important festival during September in Lima is Mistura. It is South America's largest food festival. Chefs and restaurants from around the world serve some of Peru's best foods. Quinoa, a grain grown in the Andes Mountains, is served in stew. People eat fish from the Amazon River and ceviche, a fish dish, from the coast. About five hundred thousand people attend this event.

Parade to honor the heroism of the Peruvian navy

South Africa

The Makhanda National Arts Festival is Africa's largest cultural event. It includes arts, crafts, and entertainment. It lasts for eleven days. More than two hundred thousand attend.

National Arts Festival in South Africa

People in South Africa also celebrate seven new national holidays. These began in 1994 when apartheid ended. They are Human Rights Day, Freedom Day, Worker's Day, Youth Day, National Women's Day, Heritage Day, and Day of Reconciliation. These days celebrate important values in South Africa. Some are updates of older apartheid holidays. For example, December 16 used to be a holiday called the Day of the Vow. In 1995, it became the Day of Reconciliation. Two important events happened on this day. In 1839, the Zulu army was defeated by the Voortrekkers in the Battle of Blood River. In 1961, the military branch of the African National Congress was created. The new name for the day was meant to build national unity.

A group of women celebrating Zulu culture during a Freedom Day Parade.

> ### ✓ Stop and Check
> COLLABORATE
>
> **Talk** How are holidays in Peru and South Africa similar? How are they different?

What Do You Think? What do you learn about culture by comparing these cultures?

124 Lesson 4 What Can Comparing Different Communities Tell Us About Global Cultures?

Chapter 3 Lesson 4 125

RESEARCH COMPANION, pp. 124–125

Traditional Holidays and Festivals

1 Inspect Have students read pp. 124–125 and name an important festival in both Peru and South Africa.

2 Find Evidence Use the questions below to check comprehension.

Relate The Peruvian holiday of Fiestas Patrias is similar to which American holiday? (Independence Day or the Fourth of July) **DOK 2**

Draw Conclusions Why do you think South Africans changed the Day of the Vow holiday's name to the Day of Reconciliation? (The new name came into effect after the end of apartheid to help build national unity.) **DOK 3**

3 Make Connections

Assess How can you use the photographs and the text to understand holidays and festivals in Peru and South Africa? (Students should point out that the text explains holidays in each country and the photos show how people celebrate on various holidays.) **DOK 3**

✓ Stop and Check

Talk Have students discuss the question with a partner. (Students should recognize that holidays in both countries reflect the culture of each. However, many of Peru's holidays have a religious basis, while many of South Africa's are related to apartheid struggles.)

✓ Check for Success

Compare Can students cite details from the text to compare and contrast the cultures of Peru and South Africa?

Differentiate

If Not, Have students review their completed Venn diagrams on p. 117 of the Inquiry Journal and discuss the similarities and differences between the cultures of Peru and South Africa.

LESSON 4 REPORT

What Can Comparing Different Communities Tell Us About Global Cultures?

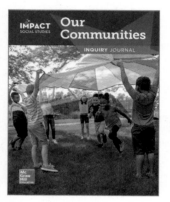

INQUIRY JOURNAL, pp. 118–119

Think About It

Have students review their research and consider the various expressions of culture in Peru and South Africa. Encourage students to review the data they have included in their graphic organizers. Direct students back to pp. 116–125 of their Research Companion if they need more information.

Write About It

Write and Cite Evidence Remind students to include the following in their responses:

- Identify the most important aspects of a culture in the form of an opinion.
- Include evidence from the lesson to support their opinion.
- Use chapter vocabulary as appropriate.

Discipline(s)	4	3	2	1
Historical Understanding	Student provides evidence and details to show an understanding of what culture means to a community.	Student includes details for some evidence to show an understanding of what culture means to a community.	Student includes evidence but few supporting details to show an understanding of what culture means to a community.	Student does not support evidence with details showing an understanding of what culture means to a community.

Talk About It

Explain Pair classmates who have different opinions about the most important aspects of a culture.

Assessment Students can check their understanding with feedback from the **Lesson Test** available online.

Connect to the Essential Question

Pull It Together Before students respond, ask them to think about the cultures of Peru and South Africa, the different ways the cultures are expressed, and what we can learn from them.

Inquiry Project Update Remind students to turn to Inquiry Journal pp. 84–85 for project information. If necessary, review the Project Checklist with students. At this point in the chapter, students should focus on the second, third, and fourth items on the checklist.

Think About It

Gather Evidence

Review your research. Compare and contrast the cultures you learned about. What do you think are the most important things people can learn from a culture?

Write About It

Write and Cite Evidence

Based on the two cultures you learned about, write an opinion about how comparing two cultures helps you understand what culture means to a community. Cite evidence from what you have read to support your answer.

Answers will vary, but students should state their opinions about how comparing cultures helps them understand more about each community. They should use evidence from the lesson to support their reasons.

Talk About It

Explain

Share your opinion with a partner. Together, discuss some important things people can learn from a culture and why they are important.

Connect to the EQ
Geography

Pull It Together

Think about what the cultures of Peru and South Africa tell about culture. In what ways do their cultures show how cultures make a community unique?

Answers will vary, but students should demonstrate an understanding that cultures have similar qualities but each group has unique customs, holidays, language, religions, and other aspects of culture.

Inquiry Project Notes

INQUIRY JOURNAL, pp. 118–119

EL English Learners SCAFFOLD

Use the following scaffolds to support student writing.

Entering and Emerging

Make sure students understand the difference between fact and opinion. Say: *A fact is something that can be proven. An opinion is your belief.* Provide some examples for students. Say: *People in South Africa celebrate seven new national holidays. Is this a fact or an opinion?* (fact) Then say: *Freedom Day is the most enjoyable holiday in South Africa. Is this a fact or an opinion?* (opinion) Provide additional examples for students to sort, using a T-chart.

Developing and Expanding

Draw a two-column table on the board. Label one column *Facts* and the other *Opinions*. Invite students to make a statement about something they have learned or something they think about the information they have read in this lesson. Then have students decide if the statement should be written in the *Facts* column or the *Opinions* column. Students should give evidence to support their answer.

Bridging and Reaching

Teach students about opinion "signal words" such as *believe*, *think*, *feel*, *might*, *should*, and *good/bad*. Encourage students to use such words as they write their paragraphs about aspects of culture, and as they discuss the question with classmates.

✓ Check for Success

Explain Can students express an opinion about which aspects of culture are most important and cite evidence in support of their views?

Differentiate

If Not, Have students present their information in a different way, such as in an oral presentation.

LESSON 5 OVERVIEW

LESSON QUESTION

What Connects Communities Throughout the World?

Connect to the Essential Question

Tell students that this lesson provides key research into the Chapter Essential Question: **What Makes a Community Unique?** Explain that they will learn how changes in transportation and media have changed the way people within a community relate to one another and to communities around the world.

Discuss The IMPACT Today

Today's world is connected in more ways than ever before. Students will look at how the forces that shape culture in a community are changing rapidly because of these connections. They will also examine the ways in which culture still makes different communities unique.

Lesson Objectives

- **Identify** ways in which revolutions in transportation and media have changed communities.
- **Explain** how improved communication methods have brought together communities around the world.
- **Describe** ways that technology has changed how people spend their free time.
- **Write** a scene or dialogue about cultures connecting through technology.

Make Connections!

CONNECT TO ELA

Reading **Use** language that pertains to time, sequence, and cause/effect to describe the relationship between a series of historical events, scientific ideas or concepts, or steps in technical procedures in a text.

Research **Conduct** short research projects that build knowledge about a topic.

Writing **Craft** narratives to develop real or imagined experiences or events using effective technique, descriptive details, and clear event sequences.

Speaking and Listening **Engage** effectively in a range of collaborative discussions with diverse partners on grade 3 topics and texts, building on others' ideas and expressing students' own ideas clearly.

COMMUNITY CONNECTIONS

Help students research online or with local historical societies to identify ways in which revolutions in transportation and media have impacted the community. For instance, did railroads or highways change the community? What local attractions draw visitors from other communities?

Lesson-At-A-Glance

1 ENGAGE — INQUIRY JOURNAL

- ▶ **Talk About It:** Photograph of railroad
- ▶ **Analyze the Source:** A Railroad from Sea to Shining Sea
- ▶ **Inquiry Tools:** Making Inferences

pp. 120–125

2 INVESTIGATE — RESEARCH COMPANION

- ▶ **Revolutions in Transportation:** Tourism; Trade
- ▶ **Revolutions in Media:** Communication; International Events; Entertainment

pp. 126–133

3 REPORT — INQUIRY JOURNAL

- ▶ **Think About It**
- ▶ **Write About It:** Write a scene or dialogue
- ▶ **Talk About It**
- ▶ **Connect to the Essential Question**

pp. 126–127

ASSESSMENT

- ▶ **Online Lesson Test**
- ▶ **Printable Lesson Test**

For more details, see pp. T168–T169.

▶ Digital Tools

at **my.mheducation.com**

ePresentation

Teach the Engage, Investigate, and Report content to the whole class from **ePresentations** that launch directly from the lesson dashboard.

eBook

You can flip your instruction with the **IMPACT eBooks** found on your lesson dashboard.

Interactive IMPACT

Blend in digital content **when you want it** and **where you want it**.

Blended Learning features in the Teacher's Edition highlight ways to connect in-class work with online experiences to enhance learning.

Investigate current events with **IMPACT News**.

Explore domain-based vocabulary with **Explore Words** and **Word Play** vocabulary activities.

Go Further with IMPACT Explorer Magazine!

The **IMPACT Explorer Magazine** supports students' exploration of the Essential Question and provides additional resources for the EQ Inquiry Project.

pp. 30–41

 LESSON QUESTION

What Connects Communities Throughout the World?

Language Objectives

- Use newly acquired content and academic vocabulary to talk and write about how communities are connected.
- Make inferences about the meanings of images and texts.
- Use regular and irregular verbs to talk about how communities are connected.

Spanish Cognates

To support Spanish speakers, point out the cognates.

connect = conectar

revolution = revolución

automobile = automóvil

vacation = vacación

communication = comunicación

international = internacional

Introduce the Lesson

Set Purpose Explain to students that in this lesson they will read informational texts to explore different ways that communities throughout the world are connected.

Access Prior Knowledge Read the Lesson Question and find out what students already know about ways that communities around the world are connected. Ask: *Do you ever travel to places far away? How do you get there? Do you communicate with people from other places? How do you communicate with them? Do you watch international sporting events or concerts? How can watching those help you communicate with others around the world?*

Spark Curiosity Display or project the photograph of Machu Picchu on p. 128 of the Research Companion. Explain that the famous Inca city of Machu Picchu is very high in the Andes Mountains at 7,972 feet above sea level. The city was built in the fifteenth century and later abandoned. Then it was rediscovered in 1911. It includes more than 150 buildings ranging from houses to temples, or holy places. Today, it is a UNESCO World Heritage Site and many tourists from all over the world visit it each year.

 Have students work in pairs to discuss the picture. Ask: *How would people be able to travel to this site today?* (Answers will vary, but students should talk about transportation technologies such as flying to Peru and different ways people could go up the mountain to the site.) *What do you think you could learn by going to this site?* (Answers will vary, but students should mention the history of a different culture and how people lived 500 years ago.)

Build Meaning & Support Language

Inquiry Journal

Analyze the Source (pp. 122–123) Tell students that in this lesson they will read informational texts that give facts, examples, and explanations about a topic. Point out the photo on p. 123 as you read "A Railroad from Sea to Shining Sea" on p. 122. Explain any words that students don't know. Support students' understanding of the passive sentences, "Rock had to be blasted away to make the road" and "Fifteen tunnels were built through rock." Rephrase them as: "Workers had to blast the rock away to make the road" and "Workers built fifteen tunnels through rock." Explain that workers had to blast, or make a hole, in the mountains with explosions to make a place for tunnels to go through the mountains.

Inquiry Tools (pp. 124–125) Tell students that they will **Make Inferences** as they read the selections in the Research Companion. Remind them that an inference is a kind of guess, but it is based on information that they have, such as a text, a picture, or a caption. Model how to make an inference based on the photo and caption on p. 123. Ask: *What are the people doing? Do they look happy? How do you know?* (I think they are celebrating because they are shaking hands.) Then work with students to complete the chart on p. 124. Say: *I know that spikes are large nails that join things together.* Infer: *Gold is valuable, so a gold spike must join together very important things.*

Research Companion

Revolutions in Transportation (pp. 126–129) Have students follow along as you read the headings and photo captions on pp. 126–129. Then have them predict the topics that will be discussed. (transportation, tourism, and trade) Tell students that *revolution* is a word that has several different meanings. Explain that in this context *revolution* means a complete change in how something is done, usually because of improvements. Tell students that the transcontinental railroad is an example of a revolution in transportation. Point out the prefix *trans-* in the words *transcontinental* and *transportation*. Explain that *trans-* means "across" and that *transcontinental* means "across the continent" or from the East Coast to the West Coast. Explain that *transportation* means "moving something from one place to another." Ask: *How was the transcontinental railroad a revolution in transportation?*

Revolutions in Media (pp. 130–133) Explain to students that *media* is any means that people use for mass communication, such as television and radio. Work with students to name other kinds of media. Then preview the headings and photos on pp. 130–133 with students and have them predict the topics that will be discussed. (media, communication, international events, entertainment) As you read, explain any words that students don't know. Be sure that students understand that the word *instantly* means "immediately" or "at that same moment." Ask: *What was the first kind of instant communication?* (the telegraph) Explain that the prefix *tele-* means "far" and the suffix *-graph* means "written." Ask: *What other word uses the prefix tele-?* (telephone) Explain that *phone* comes from a Greek word that means voice. Have them write definitions for *telegraph* and *telephone* using those language clues.

Inquiry Journal

Report Your Findings (pp. 126–127) Explain to students that a scene is one part of a play or movie where the events happen in one place, and a dialogue is a conversation between people in a play, movie, or book. Share examples of scenes from a play with students and explain how these are structured. Encourage students to use the new vocabulary words they have learned. Check their work for spelling and punctuation errors.

Language Forms & Conventions

Regular and Irregular Verbs Remind students that regular verbs end in *-ed* in the past tense but irregular verbs have their own special forms that must be memorized. Display the chart. Model using the verbs to talk about how communities are connected: *When communities connected, cultures began to mix.*

Regular Verbs	Irregular verbs
face - faced	bring - brought
belong - belonged	buy - bought
cross - crossed	drive - drove
connect - connected	have - had

Have students work in pairs to find other regular and irregular verbs in the text. Call on volunteers to say them aloud and add them to the chart. As a challenge, ask students to use the verbs in a sentence to describe how communities are connected.

Cross-Cultural Connection

Have students discuss whether they think there can be too much connection between cultures to a point where the cultures become too much alike. Would the world be as interesting?

Leveled Support

Entering & Emerging
Provide sentence frames such as: *Our communities are connected by* _____.

Developing & Expanding
Have small groups create a bank of words used to show how communities are connected. Encourage students to refer to the word bank when writing their responses.

Bridging & Reaching
Remind students to use words that signal cause and effect in their responses (*because, therefore, so*) to explain how communities are connected.

Language Transfer

Point out that while English uses a different form of the verb to show past time, in some languages, such as Chinese, Hmong, and Vietnamese, verbs do not change form to show past tense. Past time can be indicated by context or by adding an adverb of time, such as *yesterday*.

LESSON QUESTION

What Connects Communities Throughout the World?

INQUIRY JOURNAL, pp. 120–121

Bellringer

Prompt students to retrieve information from the previous lessons. Say: *What are some aspects of culture? What makes cultures different? How do cultures become like one another?* (Answers may include art, stories, food, music, dance, family structure, celebrations, and literature. All cultures share these basic traits, but they express them differently. For instance, all cultures have food, but each culture has unique ingredients and recipes. As cultures come into contact with each other, they blend together.)

Lesson Outcomes

Discuss the lesson question and lesson outcomes with students.

- Make sure that students understand the term *revolution* as describing a sudden, fundamental change to something.

- To help students understand how the word is used in this lesson, have them identify ways they remember in which some form of technology, such as cars or electronic devices, has changed.

Talk About It

Explain that a photograph can present both a scene and an idea. Have students work with a partner or in a small group to discuss the following questions. Then invite them to share their ideas with the whole class. Remind them to be respectful of the opinions of others.

- Describe the physical scene in the picture. (railroad tracks in a straight line through open country)

- What is the purpose of the tracks? Where are they going? (The tracks connect with a nearby city, and their purpose is transporting people and goods.)

 Collaborative Conversations

Add New Ideas As students engage in partner, small-group, and whole-class discussions, encourage them to add new ideas to their conversations. Remind students to

- stay on topic.
- connect their own ideas to things their peers have said.
- look for ways to connect relevant personal experiences or prior knowledge to the conversation.

THE IMPACT TODAY

Lesson 5
What Connects Communities Throughout the World?

Lesson Outcomes

What Am I Learning?
In this lesson, you will use your investigative skills to explore how communities around the world are connected to one another.

Why Am I Learning It?
Reading and talking about ways that communities are connected will help you understand ways that your own community is connected to the world.

How Will I Know That I Learned It?
You will be able to describe how these connections change cultures.

Talk About It   COLLABORATE

Look closely at the picture. What do you see? How can this connect communities?

Railroad tracks connect communities that are distant from one another.

Copyright © McGraw-Hill Education

120   Lesson 5   What Connects Communities Throughout the World?

Chapter 3   Lesson 5   121

INQUIRY JOURNAL, pp. 120–121

English Learners SCAFFOLD

Use the following scaffolds to support student understanding of the lesson outcomes.

Entering and Emerging

Draw four dots on the board and connect them with lines to form a square. Say: *I connected the dots with lines. To connect is to join things together. Railroads made it possible to move people and goods among communities easily. In that way, the railroads connected communities.*

Developing and Expanding

Read aloud the photo caption and ask students to circle the word *connect*. Explain that the word has many meanings. Write on the board: *Students connect with each other when they work in small groups. The Internet connects our classroom to the rest of the world. The hallway connects the classroom and the office.* Have students tell what the word *connect* means in each sentence. Encourage them to use a dictionary for synonyms.

Bridging and Reaching

Have students read the lesson question and the photo caption and circle the word *connect* in each. Have them work with a partner to list different ways that they connect with people at home, in school, in the community, or in other parts of the world. Have partners share their lists with the larger group.

Social Emotional Learning

Social Awareness

Build Empathy
Understanding how others feel in different situations helps students build empathy. As they read about the railroad workers, ask students to think about the challenges and dangers of the work.

Digital Tools

Blended Learning

Students engage with the lesson question and discussion prompts.

Interactive IMPACT

Discuss the **Lesson Question** and **Talk About It** with the whole class.

Lesson 5   **What Connects Communities Throughout the World?**   T245

1 Inspect

Read the title. What do you think this text will be about?

Circle the names of the railroad companies.

Underline clues that will help you answer these questions:

- What happened on May 10, 1869?
- Why was this event important?
- How did it change the United States?

My Notes

_____

_____

_____

_____

_____

_____

_____

_____

_____

_____

A Railroad from Sea to Shining Sea

On May 10, 1869, two railroad engines faced one another in Utah. The transcontinental railroad was one link away from joining the Atlantic and Pacific coasts. When it was finished, people would be able to ride a train from Washington, D.C. to San Francisco, a 2,800-mile journey.

The train engine from the west belonged to the Central Pacific Railroad. This company's line began in Sacramento, California, and crossed the Sierra Nevada. Building a railroad through the mountains was difficult and dangerous. Rock had to be blasted away to make the road. Fifteen tunnels were built through rock. Most of this hard work was done by men who came from China.

The train engine from the east belonged to the Union Pacific Railroad. This company's line began near Omaha, Nebraska. The tracks crossed the Great Plains. The ties, steel rails, spikes, food, and other supplies were brought in by train. Most of the

Railroad officials pounded this spike into the ground to show that a transportation line joined the East and West Coasts of the United States and all the communities between. How did this change life for people in the United States?

Locomotives and crews from the two railroad companies face each other at Promontory Point, Utah.

Union Pacific Railroad workers were Civil War veterans, Chinese immigrants, or Irish immigrants. Native Americans did not want a train going through their lands. Because the railroad companies claimed the land where the track was laid, native peoples defended the right to their land.

At the ceremony, a special wooden tie joined the two sections of railway. Two gold spikes, a silver spike, and a gold-and-silver-plated spike were driven into this special tie. This was only for show. The special tie and the spikes were quickly replaced with a regular wooden tie and iron spikes. The final iron spike was driven in by an ordinary worker who had helped build the railroad. The United States was now connected by a railroad.

2 Find Evidence

Look How do the pictures help explain the text?

Reread What was done at a special ceremony to join the section of railway?

3 Make Connections

Talk Look at the people celebrating. Why do you think the railroad officials are celebrating? Why do you think the workers are celebrating? Why would the country be celebrating?

INQUIRY JOURNAL, pp. 122–123

Analyze the Source

Background Information

- The Golden Spike National Historic Site in Utah commemorates the joining of the Union Pacific and Central Pacific Railroads.
- The location of the joining of the two railroads was actually Promontory Summit, about 35 miles from Promontory Point.

1 Inspect

Read Have students read the lesson title and the photo captions. Remind students to circle the names of the railroad companies.

2 Find Evidence

Look Have students reread the text and study the pictures.

Reread Have students circle details that show what was done at the ceremony at Promontory Point, Utah. (special wooden tie joined two sections, two gold spikes, a silver spike, a gold-and-silver-plated spike, final iron spike driven in by an ordinary worker)

3 Make Connections

Talk Encourage students to think about what the completion of the transcontinental railroad meant to the people who had been working on it. Ask them to think about how people across the country might have felt about this new means of cross-country transportation.

 Spotlight on Content

Using Maps

Use a physical map of the United States to show students where each railroad line began and the geography each covered. Trace the line with your finger and have students identify possible difficulties of the terrain.

Making Inferences

When you read or look at a picture, you often make inferences about the text you read or the picture you see. An **inference** is a decision you make about the meaning of a text or a picture. How do you make an inference?

1. **Read the text carefully all the way through. Look closely at any pictures. Read the captions as you study the pictures.**
   This will help you understand what the text and pictures are about.

2. **Think about what you read and the pictures you studied.**
   An author may not always tell you everything. What questions do you have?

3. **Think about what you already know about this topic.**

4. **Make a decision about the text and pictures.**
   Base your decision on what you know and what you read or see.

Based on the text you read and the pictures you studied, work with your class to complete the chart below.

Text and Picture Clues and What I Already Know	Inferences
The tie was made of beautiful wood. Two gold spikes, a silver spike, and a gold and silver plated spike were driven into this special tie. I know: gold is rare	This text means: Answers will vary, but students may infer that connecting the railroad was a special event and an important achievement.

Investigate!

Read pages 126–133 in your Research Companion. Use your investigative skills to make inferences about how communities throughout the world are connected to one another. This chart will help you organize your notes.

Text and Picture Clues and What I Already Know	Inferences
There have been huge changes to transportation in the past two hundred years. These changes make it possible for people and goods to travel farther and faster. I know: Cars and airplanes help people around the world connect.	This text means: Answers will vary, but students should observe that transportation connects their community to a bigger world.
The photographs that show a telegraph operator and students using a computer. I know: Telegraphs are no longer used and computers are smaller now.	These photographs mean: Answers will vary, but students should observe that technology has advanced and instant communication has become more accessible.
Americans watch foreign movies, too, and they affect how we view other cultures. Many people think of anime or Godzilla movies when they think of Japanese culture. I know: American movies are not always accurate.	This text means: Answers will vary, but students should observe that what they learn about other cultures from movies and television might not be accurate.

INQUIRY JOURNAL, pp. 124–125

Inquiry Tools

Making Inferences

Read Review with the students the meaning of the word *inference*. Remind them that when they make inferences they use information provided in the text and what they might already know. Have students read the step-by-step instructions for how to make inferences.

Guided Practice Have students review the text on pp. 122–123. Then work with them to complete the graphic organizer. Explain that they will use a similar graphic organizer to organize their independent research.

Check Understanding Confirm student understanding of the inquiry skill, Making Inferences. If students do not understand how to make inferences, review the steps on p. 124.

Investigate!

Have students read pp. 126–133 in the Research Companion. Tell them the information will help them answer the lesson question *What Connects Communities Throughout the World?*

Take Notes Tell students that they will use the graphic organizer on p. 125 of the Inquiry Journal to take notes about how communities throughout the world are connected to one another. Explain to students that making inferences is a way of reading actively. It helps them apply their knowledge of the topic and think about what they are learning.

Remind students that taking notes will help them understand and remember the information they learn.

Spotlight on Language

Understanding Language

To help students understand the words *infer* and *inference*, explain that *infer* is a verb meaning to form an opinion, something they actively do. *Inference* is a noun, a thing. It is a conclusion they make from what they read.

Digital Tools

Blended Learning

Students prepare for the lesson investigation with step-by-step instruction about how to make inferences.

ePresentation

Use the **Inquiry Tools** to model the lesson graphic organizer.

LESSON 5 INVESTIGATE

LESSON QUESTION

What Connects Communities Throughout the World?

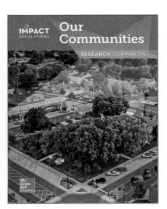

RESEARCH COMPANION, pp. 126–127

Background Information

Advances in technology and transportation connected communities throughout the United States and the world.

- Several possible routes for a transcontinental railroad were originally surveyed. The Northern Pacific Railroad, completed in 1883, ran between St. Paul, MN and Seattle, WA. In the same year, the Southern Pacific Railroad completed its route connecting New Orleans to California.

- Founded in 1872 as a mail order catalog, Montgomery Ward flourished for over a century. Later, the company expanded to retail stores. The last Montgomery Ward retail stores closed in 2001. The company was bought by a mail order business and is once again selling merchandise and delivering it by mail. This time, it is an Internet-based company.

Revolutions in Transportation

1 Inspect Have students read pp. 126–127 and describe what the word *revolution* means in this context.

2 Find Evidence Use the questions below to check comprehension. Remind students to support their answers with text evidence.

Infer Study the picture. How would you describe these roads? Why do you think they might be like this? (Answers will vary, but students may point out how complicated these highway interchanges are and may infer that they need to connect many drivers to many different places.) **DOK 3**

Differentiate What are some ways in which travel by horse and wagon was different from travel by train? (Travel by horse and wagon was much slower than by train. Train travelers could go to new communities on the plains and bring along more supplies.) **DOK 2**

3 Make Connections

Compare How would building a highway be similar to building a railroad line? (Both require moving people and supplies to the construction area; both can be difficult and dangerous; both require many workers.) **DOK 3**

THE IMPACT TODAY

Lesson 5
What Connects Communities Throughout the World?

Revolutions in Transportation

There have been huge changes to transportation in the past two hundred years. These changes make it possible for people and goods to travel farther and faster. Cultures are more connected today than ever before.

The first European colonists arrived in America on sailing ships. This trip took about two months. When settlers moved inland, they traveled by horse, on boats, or in covered wagons. People could take only what they could carry with them. The transcontinental railroad changed this. Railroads carried immigrants and settlers to new homes on the plains and beyond. The trains also carried supplies to communities along the way.

At first, immigrant groups stayed close together. This way, they could keep the language and culture of their home country. As communities connected, cultures mixed and blended together.

This maze of roads connects several different highways, each leading to other communities across the country. The automobile led to major changes in the ways people lived.

RESEARCH COMPANION, pp. 126–127

EL English Learners SCAFFOLD

Use the following scaffolds to support student understanding of lesson content.

Entering and Emerging

Read aloud the first sentences on pp. 126 and 130. Write the words *transportation* and *communication* on the board. Underline the root words. Tell students that *transport* means to take something from one place to another, and that *communicate* means to exchange information or ideas. Have students work in pairs to act out these two actions.

Developing and Expanding

Have students read the first sentences on p. 126 and 130. Write the words *transportation* and *communication* on the board and underline the root words in each. Discuss the meanings of each root word with students. Then have them look up the words *transportation* and *communication* in the dictionary and write a simple definition for each in their own words.

Bridging and Reaching

Have students read the first sentence on pp. 126 and 130. Help them determine the root words in each word. Have them work with partners to discuss the meanings of each root. Then have them write definitions for *transportation* and *communication* using their own words. Challenge students to provide a context sentence for each word.

 Digital Tools

Blended Learning
Flip the research approach and find evidence in a digital format.

eBook

Students investigate using their **Research Companion** and **IMPACT Explorer Magazine eBooks** to find evidence.

Tourism

Cars transformed the way people lived, worked, and played. With a car, people did not need to live close to their workplaces. Families bought houses in suburbs. People drove to work in their cars. People drove to shopping centers. For vacations, Americans visited national parks, such as the Great Smoky Mountains, the Indiana Dunes, and the Grand Canyon. Tourism became an important source of income in many communities.

This passenger airplane is taking off. How do airplanes make it easy to travel long distances?

Today, it is faster and easier than ever to travel long distances. American families may vacation in another state or in another country. Americans visit Machu Picchu in Peru and Mount Fuji in Japan. At tourist sites around the world, Americans can learn about places that are important to other cultures.

Tourists from other countries visit the United States, too. They visit national parks, amusement parks, aquariums, and other tourist sites. Tourist information is printed in many different languages to help visitors get around. Tourism connects Americans with cultures around the world.

The Inca city of Machu Picchu lies high in the Andes Mountains of Peru. It is very remote, but hundreds of thousands of tourists visit each year.

Trade

Advances in transportation have changed world trade. Goods from other countries used to be expensive. Now, faster and bigger ships carry more products in less time. This made these goods less expensive. Clothes made in Asia are sold in stores across the United States.

In the 1800s, mail order companies used railroads to connect with customers. They sent catalogs to people living far away. The catalogs showed hundreds of products such as plows, sewing machines, and furniture. Trains delivered these things to the people who bought them. Today, online companies are a lot like these early catalog companies. A buyer in Illinois can order items from China. The seller sends the items by cargo ship or airplane.

Transportation also lets people trade ideas. Experts in different fields can meet and learn from each other. Young people in different countries connect more easily, too. Some organizations arrange youth exchanges to help young people experience life in another country.

Many organizations bring together people from different cultures.

> ### ✓ Stop and Check
>
> **Talk** Identify the kinds of transportation you have read about. Discuss how each kind of transportation made communities and cultures more connected.
>
> **Find Details** As you read, add new information to the graphic organizer on page 125 in your Inquiry Journal.

RESEARCH COMPANION, pp. 128–129

Tourism/Trade

1 Inspect Have students read pp. 128–129 and identify ways that advances in transportation have affected trade.

2 Find Evidence Use the questions below to check comprehension.

Identify Cause and Effect In what ways did cars change family life? (Families did not need to stay in their community to work. They lived in suburbs outside cities and drove to other parts of the country for vacation.) **DOK 2**

Draw Conclusions How has the transportation revolution impacted the clothes you wear? (Answers will vary, but students should understand that with faster and cheaper transportation, most clothing comes from far away rather than being made locally.) **DOK 3**

3 Make Connections

Cite Evidence From what you have learned, explain how the transportation revolution connected communities around the world. (Students should understand that the transportation revolution made travel simpler and more affordable. People from the around the world visit the United States and people from the United States travel around the world, which connects people and communities.) **DOK 3**

✓ Stop and Check

Talk Remind students to include text evidence in their responses. (Types include boats, wagons, railroads, automobiles, airplanes; each kind of transportation made it faster to move people and things from place to place; people and cultures connected more easily and more often.)

Spotlight on Language

Words with Similar Meanings
The words *automobile* and *car* are often used as synonyms. However, automobile is more precise. A car may also be a compartment in a vehicle that carries people such as a trolley (streetcar), a train, a cable lift, and even an elevator.

 Digital Tools

Blended Learning
Students investigate curated resources and find evidence to answer the lesson question.

Interactive IMPACT

Students **Research** and find evidence using digital format texts.

Revolutions in Media

Communication

The world had a revolution in communication. In the past, if you wanted to learn about a different country, you might find a penpal. You would send your penpal a letter. It could take days or weeks to arrive. Trains, trucks, and airplanes moved the letter quickly, but it still took time to move it thousands of miles. Then you would wait for your penpal's reply.

Now technology allows people to communicate with each other instantly. The telegraph was the first kind of instant communication. News from one part of the country could be instantly spread to the rest of the country. Later, the telephone was invented. Over the next century, communities, states, and countries were connected to one another by miles of telephone and telegraph wire. People called neighbors close by and friends and families far away.

Instant communication is even more common thanks to the Internet. Now you do not need to wait on a letter from a penpal. You can communicate with someone from a different culture just by dialing a phone number or typing something into a computer.

A telegraph operator taps out a message. The message will be received at a telegraph office miles away.

Computers and cell phones let us communicate instantly with people far away.

International Events

Instant communication means that viewers in one country can watch something happening far away. People can watch hurricanes, tsunamis, and other events as they happen. People can watch news stories and sporting events live on televisions, computers, and cell phones. Communication happens immediately, and it is everywhere.

People from all over the world can watch live events, such as the Olympic opening ceremonies.

Did You Know?

Fifteen countries worked together to build the International Space Station! Astronauts from many different nations and cultures work there together.

✓ Stop and Check

Think What kinds of communication technology do you use every day? How do these help you connect with people?

RESEARCH COMPANION, pp. 130–131

Revolutions in Media

1 Inspect Have students read pp. 130–131 and identify three forms of communication in their daily lives.

2 Find Evidence Use the questions below to check comprehension.

Analyze How has writing and sending a letter changed in the past 100 years? (Letters used to always be written on paper and sent through the mail. Today, letters can be written on computers and sent electronically.) **DOK 2**

Infer How has the Internet brought together communities around the world? (The Internet provides instant communication, so things that happen in one part of the world are seen instantly in other places. People become closer to what is happening in other communities.) **DOK 3**

3 Make Connections

Draw Conclusions Which revolution in communication most impacts your life? Why? (Answers will vary, but students should provide a reasonable explanation of the technology's impact on their lives.) **DOK 3**

✓ Stop and Check

Think Have students discuss the question with a partner. (Students may identify cell phones, television, or the Internet; calling or texting friends, getting news, watching shows, and playing games.)

Social Emotional Learning

Social Awareness

Value Diversity Instant communication allows students today to be part of events around the world. Encourage students to actively participate by searching for the unique and interesting in other communities and cultures.

Academic Language

To help students understand the concept of perspectives on page 133, explain that this word has to do with how we look at things in the world. Tell students that a farmer might complain about a lack of rain. When we understand that no rain can hurt the farmer's crops, we develop a different perspective on the importance of rainy weather. Then discuss how understanding another culture might impact our perspective on that culture.

Entertainment

1 Inspect Have students read pp. 132–133 and identify the five types of entertainment discussed. (radio, movies, television, video games, books)

2 Find Evidence Use the questions below to check comprehension.

Make Observations Are movies always a good way to understand another culture? (Answers will vary but students should show that they understand that some movies, such as horror films or action movies, might not accurately reflect the culture of another country.) **DOK 2**

Infer How does today's gaming both connect and disconnect a person from their world? (A gamer is in his or her own house focused on the computer screen rather than outside connecting face-to-face with other people. However, the gamer is connecting virtually with people around the world.) **DOK 3**

3 Make Connections

Assess Which type of entertainment you read about, radio, movies, television, video games, and books, do you think is most helpful in connecting communities and why? (Answers will vary but should identify a helpful way in which radio, movies, television, gaming, or books connect communities.) **DOK 3**

✓ Stop and Check

Talk Remind students to use the text when discussing their answers. (Entertainment has moved from group gatherings to individuals' homes and even individuals' devices.)

What Is the IMPACT Today?

Draw Conclusions Discuss with students the ways in which revolutions in technology have connected cultures. (Students should identify an improvement in transportation or communication and present a valid reason why it is important in connecting cultures. For example, a student may identify the airplane because it takes people from one country to another and allows them to experience other cultures firsthand.)

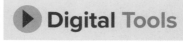

▶ Digital Tools

Blended Learning

Students investigate curated resources and find evidence to answer the Lesson Question.

Interactive IMPACT

Students choose from print or digital **Inquiry Tools** to take notes.

Entertainment

The world has also seen big changes in entertainment. People used to have to attend concerts, plays, or activities in person for entertainment. Radio, movies, and television changed this. People went to local theaters to see movies. Radio and television brought entertainment into people's homes.

Early filmmakers settled in Southern California. The film industry grew and became an important part of the Los Angeles area. Many people now think of movies and television when they hear the words "Hollywood" and "California."

American movies and television spread American culture to other countries. Americans watch foreign movies, too, and they affect how we view other cultures. Many people think of anime or Godzilla movies when they think of Japanese culture.

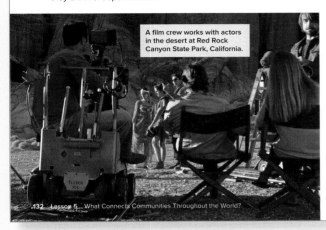

A film crew works with actors in the desert at Red Rock Canyon State Park, California.

Perspectives

Too Much Connection?

Is there such a thing as too much cultural connection? The more connected cultures become, the more alike they may become. Connecting with another culture is good if it helps you understand and appreciate other people. But each community and each culture has something special to offer the world. What if one culture dominates all other cultures?

The women in this picture combine traditions of their culture with modern technology.

Today, video games have become another way to connect with people. Gamers can form online friendships with people who do not even speak the same language. A gamer in Odessa, Texas, may be playing with someone in the house next door or someone in Odessa, Ukraine.

Books used to only be printed, bound, and sold in bookstores. Now you can buy a digital book and download it onto your device. You can even download an audiobook. Audiobooks allow you to listen to books on your device. Books are translated into many foreign languages, and this helps connect cultures, too.

✓ Stop and Check

Talk What are ways that technology has changed entertainment?

What Is the IMPACT Today? What do you think has been most helpful in connecting communities and cultures of today?

RESEARCH COMPANION, pp. 132–133

 ## English Learners SCAFFOLD

Use the following scaffolds to support student understanding of lesson concepts.

Entering and Emerging

Remind students that to make inferences, we use what we find in a text and what we already know about a topic. Provide support as needed to complete the Inferences column on their graphic organizers. Use sentence frames such as:

- Cars and planes help people travel _____.
- Computers let us communicate _____ with people around the world.
- Movies and television can help us learn about _____.

Developing and Expanding

To help students complete their graphic organizers, discuss with students how to use information in the text and prior knowledge to make inferences. Ask questions to help them complete the last column in their graphic organizer: *How has modern transportation helped people around the world learn about other cultures? How can modern technology and entertainment connect cultures?*

Bridging and Reaching

Review the process of making inferences with students. Then have them work in pairs or groups to fill out the first column of the graphic organizer. When they have finished, focus on the first entry. Ask: *How does faster transportation help communities connect to each other?* Have each pair or group do the same with their second and third entries and share their results with the class.

✓ Check for Success

Connect Can students identify the forms of transportation and media that connect communities throughout the world?

Differentiate

If Not, Review with students the left column of their graphic organizers on p. 125 of their Inquiry Journals. To help them make inferences, ask: *How can [item from column 1] help communities connect?*

LESSON 5 REPORT

What Connects Communities Throughout the World?

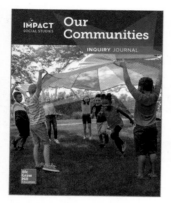

INQUIRY JOURNAL, pp. 126–127

Think About It

Remind students to review their research and think about how the transportation and media revolutions have changed the world. Encourage them to review the information in their graphic organizer as they answer the question. Direct students back to pp. 126–133 of their Research Companion if they need more information.

Write About It

Write and Cite Evidence Remind students to include the following elements in their responses:

- Identify at least one form of technology from transportation or media.
- Include observations about how the form of technology connects two cultures.
- Make inferences about how this connection will change each culture.

Discipline(s)	4	3	2	1
History **Geography**	Student provides evidence and details in a scene or in dialogue showing a strong understanding of how revolutions in transportation or media connect two communities.	Student includes details for some evidence in a scene or in dialogue showing a basic understanding of how revolutions in transportation or media connect two communities.	Student includes evidence but few supporting details in a scene or in dialogue showing a vague understanding of how revolutions in transportation or media connect two communities.	Student does not support evidence with details in a scene or in dialogue showing an understanding of how revolutions in transportation or media connect two communities.

Talk About It

Explain Pair classmates who have different levels of understanding and encourage them to ask one another questions to clarify thoughts and ideas.

Assessment Students can check their understanding with feedback from the **Lesson Test** available online.

Connect to the Essential Question

Consider Before students respond, remind them to think about the revolutions in technology that they learned about in the lesson, and how these new technologies connect cultures.

Inquiry Project Update Remind students to turn to Inquiry Journal pp. 84–85 for project information. If necessary, review the Project Checklist with students. At this point in the chapter, students should focus on the last item on the Checklist.

Think About It

Gather Evidence

Review your research. What are some forms of transportation or technologies that connect cultures? How do these connect people within different cultures?

Write About It

Write and Cite Evidence

Write a scene or dialogue about two cultures being connected by technology. How are the cultures connecting? Make inferences about how this connection affects each culture.

Answers will vary. An acceptable answer will discuss some of the transportation forms and communication technologies covered in the lesson.

Talk About It

Explain

Share your scene or dialogue with a partner.

Economics **Connect to the** EQ

Consider

How is your community connected with other communities? What are some products from your local community that are sold to other communities and countries? What products are brought into your community from other communities and countries? How does your community stay unique?

If students need help, have them think about the produce section in the grocery market. Also help them think about the products made or grown in the local community and how those make your community unique.

Inquiry Project Notes

INQUIRY JOURNAL, pp. 126–127

EL English Learners SCAFFOLD

Use the following scaffolds to support student understanding of writing a scene or dialogue.

Entering and Emerging

Review with students the meaning of _scene_ and _dialogue_. Discuss what a scene or dialogue would be like if it describes how two cultures connect. Practice a dialogue about the topic and then have them work in groups to plan a brief scene. Review their plans and provide writing support as needed.

Developing and Expanding

Review the meaning of scene and dialogue with students. Then organize the class into groups and assign half the groups one culture and half another culture that is distant from the first. Have groups representing each culture work together to create a two- or three-sentence dialogue about how technology can connect them.

Bridging and Reaching

Review with students the meaning of _scene_ and _dialogue_. Ask each student to write a two- or three-sentence dialogue on one form of technology and how it can connect two cultures. Have pairs of students dialogue with one another by reading their sentences.

✔ Check for Success

Infer Can students create a scene or dialogue by inferring ways in which technology connects two cultures?

Differentiate

If Not, Have students present their inferences about how cultures are connected by technology in a format other than a scene or dialogue, such as a drawing or list.

What Makes a Community Unique?

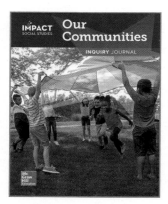

**INQUIRY JOURNAL,
pp. 128–129**

Inquiry Project Wrap-Up

Remind students that they are to have created a plan for a holiday or festival that celebrates at least three cultures.

Assessment Use the rubric on p. T169 to assess students' Inquiry Projects.

Complete Your Project

Have students work individually to review the Complete Your Project checklist. Remind them that if they have missed any of the items, now is their opportunity to make corrections or additions.

Share Your Project

If time allows, you may want to have students present their projects to the class. Provide the following presentation tips to students.

- Prepare and rehearse.
- Use notes to help you stay on topic when you present.
- Speak slowly and clearly. Make sure everyone can hear you.
- Make eye contact and speak directly to the audience.

Reflect on Your Project

Student reflection begins with thinking about the process for how they selected the three cultures and conducted their research. Students should focus not only on the results of the inquiry but also on the challenges and successes in the inquiry process. Students can apply those findings to future projects.

Chapter Connections can focus on anything that resonated with students about the chapter and their study of the people and cultures in communities. These connections may spark students to do further research on their own.

▶ Digital Tools

Blended Learning
Students use online checklists to prepare, complete, and reflect on their Inquiry Projects.

Chapter Assessments
Students can demonstrate content mastery with the feedback from the online **Chapter Test**.

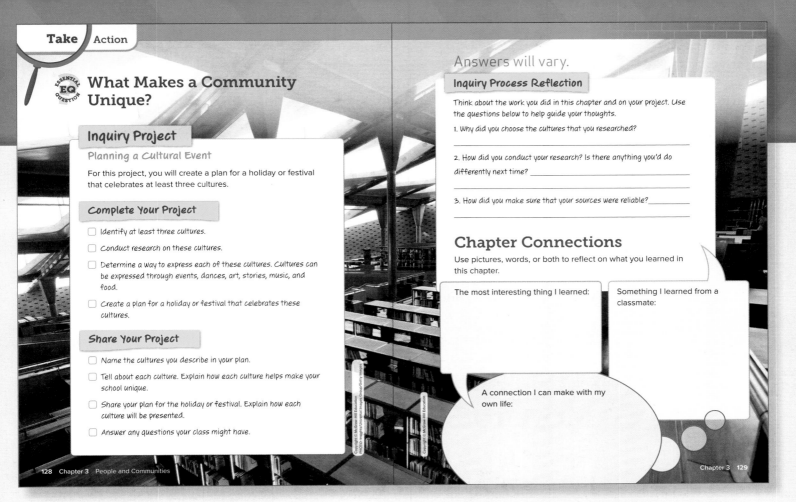

INQUIRY JOURNAL, pp. 128–129

 English Learners SCAFFOLD

Use the following scaffolds to support student presentation of their projects.

Entering and Emerging

Read aloud the project checklist and check students' understanding. Discuss any unfamiliar language. Help students practice presenting their holiday or festival plans. Encourage students to create notes based on important words in their presentations. Then, have partners take turns rehearsing their presentations.

Developing and Expanding

Have partners review the project checklist. As a class, talk about question words and sentence frames that could be used for discussing the holiday and festival presentations. Have students rehearse their presentations with a partner. Tell each partner to ask two questions about the presentation he or she hears.

Bridging and Reaching

Have partners review the project checklist and brainstorm ways to present their plans effectively. Have students practice presenting their plans with a partner.

✔ **Check for Success**

Describe Use your online rubric or the rubric found on p. T169 to check student progress. Did students present a plan for a holiday or festival that celebrates three cultures?

Differentiate

If Not, Have students create a poster for the holiday or festival that identifies the three cultures and what will be done to celebrate them.

TAKE ACTION
with RESEARCH COMPANION

**RESEARCH COMPANION,
pp. 134–135**

Connections in Action!

Think Lead a discussion about the different cultures students learned about in this chapter, or discuss the various cultures in your own community. Talk about the diverse traditions of these cultures and what each brings to the community.

Talk To help focus students' conversations, you may want to discuss the EQ with the entire class before partners discuss their ideas. Remind students to think about evidence they can provide that will support their ideas.

Share Invite students to share their small-group discussions with the class. Then talk about how we can learn about other cultures through stories, food, music, art, and dance. Explore what we can learn when we understand different cultures.

More to Explore

How Can You Make an IMPACT?

Mix and match the More to Explore activities to meet the needs of your classroom. Stretch students' thinking by offering alternative ways to demonstrate what they learned during the chapter.

These activities are flexible enough that you can assign one, two, or three activities to specific students or have students work in small groups. Remind students to use proper collaborative procedures when they work with partners.

Vocabulary Flash Cards

Before you begin, choose one vocabulary word and ask volunteers to provide a definition, use it in a sentence, and think of two synonyms.

Teacher Tip! **This activity can be used to monitor students' understanding of chapter vocabulary.**

Write a Letter

Remind students how to format a letter. Then, tell students that their letters should be persuasive. Students should use evidence and logical reasons to support their opinions. Before they write their letters, have students discuss their ideas with a partner and think of ways to persuade another person to attend their chosen events.

Teacher Tip! **This activity can be used to help students practice writing an opinion and supporting it with reasons.**

Give a News Report

Remind students that a news report gives facts about an event. It should tell *who, what, where, when,* and *why.* Students may wish to report on a recent event that occurred in the community. They also may consider an annual event, such as a festival.

Teacher Tip! **Use this activity to allow students to practice expository writing.**

▶ Digital Tools

Blended Learning

Students apply chapter concepts to extension activities and connect them to the Essential Question.

Interactive IMPACT

Review chapter vocabulary with **Word Play.**

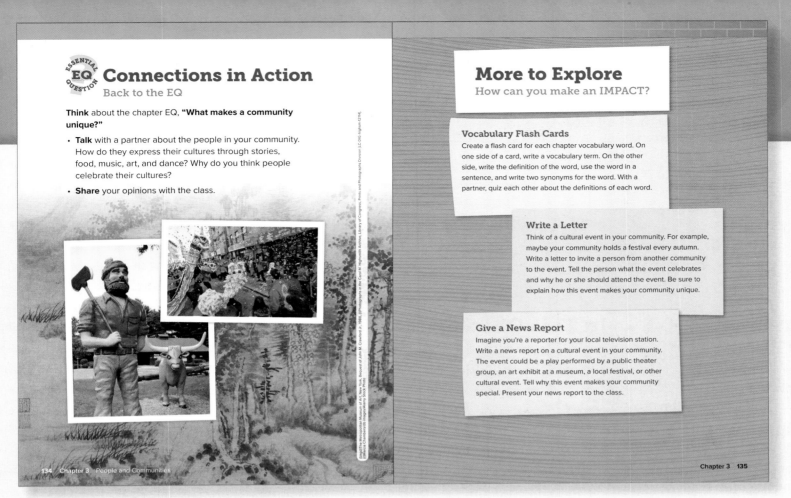

Connections in Action
Back to the EQ

Think about the chapter EQ, **"What makes a community unique?"**

- **Talk** with a partner about the people in your community. How do they express their cultures through stories, food, music, art, and dance? Why do you think people celebrate their cultures?

- **Share** your opinions with the class.

More to Explore
How can you make an IMPACT?

Vocabulary Flash Cards
Create a flash card for each chapter vocabulary word. On one side of a card, write a vocabulary term. On the other side, write the definition of the word, use the word in a sentence, and write two synonyms for the word. With a partner, quiz each other about the definitions of each word.

Write a Letter
Think of a cultural event in your community. For example, maybe your community holds a festival every autumn. Write a letter to invite a person from another community to the event. Tell the person what the event celebrates and why he or she should attend the event. Be sure to explain how this event makes your community unique.

Give a News Report
Imagine you're a reporter for your local television station. Write a news report on a cultural event in your community. The event could be a play performed by a public theater group, an art exhibit at a museum, a local festival, or other cultural event. Tell why this event makes your community special. Present your news report to the class.

RESEARCH COMPANION, pp. 134–135

 # English Learners SCAFFOLD

Use the following scaffolds to support student understanding of chapter content.

Entering and Emerging

To help students explore the chapter EQ, review chapter vocabulary, including *culture, ethnic groups, folktale,* and *heritage.* Then talk with students about cultural aspects that make your community unique. Provide sentence frames such as the following as needed:

- An important kind of food in our community is _____.
- In our community, we celebrate _____.
- When we have a celebration, we like to _____.

Developing and Expanding

Have students talk with partners or in a small group about different cultures and traditions that are a part of their community. Pose questions such as *What cultural traditions can you find in your community? What holidays are important? How do people celebrate cultural events?*

Bridging and Reaching

Have students share information about a cultural tradition that they celebrate or that they are familiar with in the community. Have them describe the tradition, and the events that are part of a celebration of the tradition. Discussions should include information about music, art, food, and stories associated with the tradition.

 ## Social Emotional Learning

Relationship Skills

Value Ideas of Others
As students discuss their ideas and supporting evidence, remind them of the importance of valuing other people's ideas. Explain that when they show that they value another person's contributions, they help build and maintain a good relationship with their classmates.

Chapter 4 OVERVIEW

ESSENTIAL EQ QUESTION

How Does the Past Impact the Present?

In This Chapter Students will investigate how and why communities grow. They will read about ways that communities can change. They also will explore the kinds of features that make communities unique.

Chapter Objectives

- **Explain** how Native Americans, European explorers, and American settlers shaped communities in the United States.

- **Explain** why people move to new places and how communities grow and change.

- **Compare** communities in the past with communities today.

- **Explain** how people and events have changed communities.

- **Compare and contrast** different communities to show change over time.

- **Use information** from a variety of sources to create a time line showing the development of a community.

Make Connections!

CONNECT TO SCIENCE
Millions of people today use cell phones to communicate with one another. Have students explore the technology related to cell phones, such as wireless technology, radio frequencies, liquid crystal displays, and fiber optics.

CONNECT TO MATH
Have students look at the line graph on page 145 of the Inquiry Journal. Ask them to calculate how many more people lived in Michigan in 1950 than in 1900.
(6,407,000 − 2,423,00 = 3,984,000)

Bibliography

Additional resources to aid student inquiry:

▶ **Hiawatha and the Peacemaker**
by Robbie Robertson; Abrams Books for Young Readers, 2015

▶ **The Transcontinental Railroad**
by John Perritano; Children's Press, 2010

▶ **Capitals**
by Taraneh Ghajar Jerven; Blueprint Editions, 2018

Go online at **my.mheducation.com** for a complete list of resources.

Chapter-At-A-Glance

EQ ESSENTIAL QUESTION How Does the Past Impact the Present?

1 ENGAGE

INQUIRY JOURNAL

pp. 130–133

- **Introduce the Chapter**
- **Chapter Inquiry Project**
- **Explore Words**

2 INVESTIGATE

RESEARCH COMPANION

pp. 136–195

- **Activate Knowledge**
- **How Has Life in Communities Changed?**
- **Connect Through Literature**
  Susanna's Promise
- **People You Should Know**
- **Lessons 1–6**

3 TAKE ACTION

INQUIRY JOURNAL
RESEARCH COMPANION

pp. 182–189 **pp. 196–197**

- **Inquiry Project Wrap-Up and Chapter connections**
- **Connections in Action!**
- **More to Explore**
- **The IMPACT Today**

Short on Time?

Engage with the content the way YOU want to teach—and *your* students want to learn!

Check out the three suggested **Flexible Instructional Pathways** on pages FM34–FM35.

The **IMPACT Explorer Magazine** supports students' exploration of the Essential Question and provides additional resources for the EQ Inquiry Project.

Digital Tools at my.mheducation.com

ePresentation

Teach the Engage, Investigate, and Take Action content to the whole class from ePresentations that launch directly from the chapter dashboard.

eBook

You can flip your instruction with the **IMPACT eBooks** found on your chapter dashboard.

Interactive IMPACT

Blend in digital content **when you want it** and **where you want it**. Blended Learning notes in the Teacher's Edition highlight ways to connect in-class work with online experiences to enhance learning.

Investigate current events with **IMPACT News**.

Introduce the EQ with the **IMPACT Chapter Video**.

Explore domain-based vocabulary with **Explore Words** and **Word Play** vocabulary activities.

MONITOR PROGRESS:
Know What Your Students Know

Choose the assessment options that work best for you and your students.

Chapter Pre-Test (Optional)

Begin the Chapter

Measure students' content knowledge before you begin the chapter with the following questions.

Quick Check

✔ What are some reasons that people in the last few centuries have moved to the United States?

✔ What kinds of technology have developed in the last few centuries that have helped communities grow?

✔ What are some examples of ways that people have helped make their communities better places in which to live?

1. When all students have responded, ask them to rate how confident they are in their answer on a scale from 1 (not very confident) to 5 (very confident).

2. Ask students to compare their responses. Determine what are some commonly held beliefs about the chapter content. Ask students to keep these in mind as they progress through the chapter.

3. **Don't Forget!** Throughout the chapter, revisit students' quick-check responses with them. If students change their responses, ask them to support the change with text evidence. You may wish to have students respond to a different prompt to measure students' content knowledge, such as *How has the automobile changed how communities grow in the United States?*

Ongoing Lesson Assessment

Use the lesson tools to monitor the **IMPACT** of your instruction.

☑ Stop and Check

Use the questions provided in the Stop and Check prompts to monitor students' comprehension of the core lesson content. The Stop and Check questions, found in the Research Companion, prompt students to engage in discussions to deepen their understanding of the content.

✔ Check for Success

Use this formative assessment tool to assess how well your students understand the material they are learning in class. The Check for Success questions, located at point of use in the Teacher's Edition, are not a test but a way to assess students' comprehension of a particular topic. A Differentiate strategy offers one activity that you can use to quickly adapt your instruction.

○ Report Your Findings

Use Report Your Findings in each lesson to measure student understanding of the lesson content and their ability to effectively express their understanding. See pp. T288, T304, T320, T336, T352, and T368 for task-specific evaluation rubrics. Report Your Findings is found in the Inquiry Journal.

▶ Digital Tools

Lesson Assessment

Use the **Lesson Test** to monitor students' understanding of the lesson content. Online Lesson Tests are customizable and available for every lesson. You will also find the tools you need to create your own assessments and to track your students' progress. A printable Lesson Test is available for use in class.

Chapter Assessment

Evaluate

Monitor student understanding of core chapter content with one or more of the following assessment options.

Connections in Action

Use the **Connections in Action** to evaluate student understanding of core chapter content through discussion in the Research Companion, pp. 196–197.

Inquiry Project

In this chapter's Inquiry Project, each student will research the history of a community he or she chooses, including key events that helped that community grow and where those events take place. Then each student will create an illustrated time line that shows important events in the community's growth. See pp. T264–T265 for more information.

Use the EQ Inquiry Project to measure student understanding of the chapter content and their ability to effectively express their understanding. A task-specific evaluation rubric is available in the Online Teacher Resources.

	4	3	2	1
Developing and Planning Inquiry	Project is focused on important events and places and explores specific aspects of them.	Project is focused on important events and places and explores some aspects of them.	Project is focused on important events and places but explorations lack focus.	Project is focused on important events and places but does not explore aspects of them.
Historical Understanding	Strong understanding of the events and places that influenced the community's growth	Adequate understanding of the events and places that influenced the community's growth	Uneven understanding of the events and places that influenced the community's growth	No understanding of the events and places that influenced the community's growth
Sources and Evidence	Project includes required and additional information and is supported with necessary evidence.	Project includes required information with some supporting evidence.	Project includes some required facts and evidence.	Required facts and supporting evidence are not included.
Communicating Conclusions	Project information is clearly supported with details and is easily understood.	Project information includes details and is understood with some explanation.	Project information is unclear due to lack of details.	Project does not include details necessary to communicate information.

ENGAGE
with INQUIRY JOURNAL

How Does the Past Impact the Present?

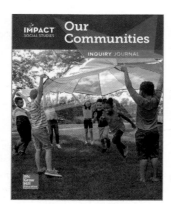

INQUIRY JOURNAL, pp. 130–131

Background Information

The U.S. population grew rather steadily from 1950 to 2018. The largest spike came in 1956, when the population rose by 1.8 percent. A second spike occurred in 1998, when the population rose by 1.27 percent. As of 2018, the U.S. population (over 328,000,000) is more than double what it was in 1950 (just over 154,000,000). This rise in population in the United States overall is not solely based on migration but is likely due to new births and more precise data-gathering techniques.

Talk About It

Read Have students read the opening page together. Prompt students to write three questions they would like to know the answers to after completing the reading. Allow students a chance to share their questions with a partner. You may wish to record these questions and revisit them throughout the chapter.

Inquiry Project

Community Time Line

Discuss the Inquiry Project with students. Review each step of the project from the **Project Checklist**. Tell students that they will use information from the chapter and from independent research to complete the project.

My Research Plan

Discuss the Essential Question with students. Ask students to think about how people and events in the past might have affected the way their community is today. Then have students work in pairs to brainstorm research questions that are "just right," neither too general nor too specific.

Design Your Own Inquiry Path (Optional)

You may wish to work with students to choose their own Essential Question, Inquiry Project, and related research questions. In addition to your feedback, have students preview chapter materials and discuss ideas with classmates to help develop possible questions, such as *What are the most important events in my community's history?*, *How do people in my community remember the past?*, or their own questions.

Have students explain why their Essential Question is important to them and to others. Have students record their question, project idea, and initial supporting research questions using the **Student EQ Inquiry Project** pages found at **my.mheducation.com**.

▶ Digital Tools

Blended Learning
Students engage with the chapter's Essential Question and launch their investigations.

Interactive IMPACT
Spark student interest with the **EQ Chapter Video**.

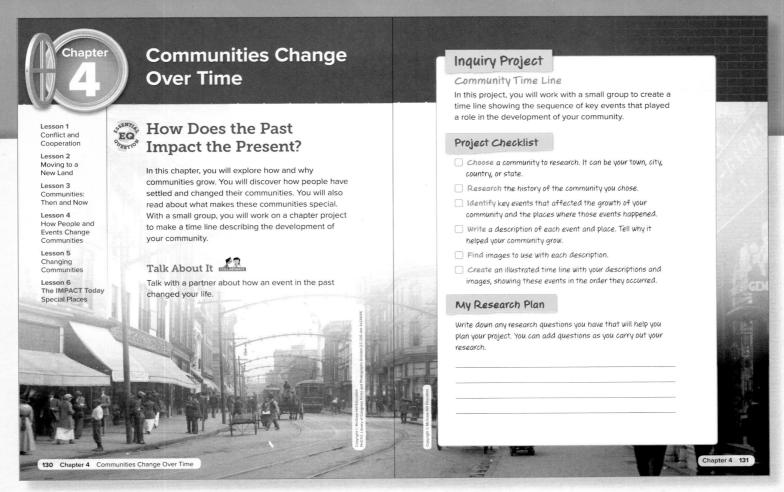

INQUIRY JOURNAL, pp. 130–131

Chapter **4**

Communities Change Over Time

Lesson 1
Conflict and Cooperation

Lesson 2
Moving to a New Land

Lesson 3
Communities: Then and Now

Lesson 4
How People and Events Change Communities

Lesson 5
Changing Communities

Lesson 6
The IMPACT Today Special Places

ESSENTIAL EQ QUESTION

How Does the Past Impact the Present?

In this chapter, you will explore how and why communities grow. You will discover how people have settled and changed their communities. You will also read about what makes these communities special. With a small group, you will work on a chapter project to make a time line describing the development of your community.

Talk About It

Talk with a partner about how an event in the past changed your life.

Inquiry Project

Community Time Line

In this project, you will work with a small group to create a time line showing the sequence of key events that played a role in the development of your community.

Project Checklist

☐ Choose a community to research. It can be your town, city, country, or state.

☐ Research the history of the community you chose.

☐ Identify key events that affected the growth of your community and the places where those events happened.

☐ Write a description of each event and place. Tell why it helped your community grow.

☐ Find images to use with each description.

☐ Create an illustrated time line with your descriptions and images, showing these events in the order they occurred.

My Research Plan

Write down any research questions you have that will help you plan your project. You can add questions as you carry out your research.

_____

_____

_____

_____

130 Chapter 4 Communities Change Over Time

Chapter 4 131

 English Learners SCAFFOLD

Use the following scaffolds to support student understanding of the Inquiry Project.

Entering and Emerging

Research and show students examples of illustrated time lines. Point to the different parts of the time line and relate them to the tasks that students will perform during this project. For example: *This time line shows the major events in the history of Philadelphia. Philadelphia is a city, and a community, in Pennsylvania. You will choose a community to research for your project.*

Developing and Expanding

Ask questions to check understanding of the Inquiry Project instructions and elicit answers. For example: *You will choose a community to research for this project. You will find out more about the important events that affected the community. What might be important in a community's history?*

Bridging and Reaching

Have students read through the Inquiry Project instructions with a partner. Then have partners talk about the types of information they will need to look for or the type of task they will need to complete for each item on the Project Checklist. Write examples of the information on the board for each item in the Project Checklist.

 Social Emotional Learning

Self-Regulation

Set Goals Explain that setting goals can help increase our motivation to succeed. Have students review the Inquiry Project checklist and set one learning goal that they would like to achieve in this chapter.

**INQUIRY JOURNAL,
pp. 132–133**

Explore Words

Academic/Domain-Specific Vocabulary Read the words aloud to students. Explain to students that these are words they will learn more about in the chapter.

Word Rater Have students place a checkmark in one of the three boxes below each word, indicating that they "Know It," "Heard It," or "Don't Know It." Explain to students that they will come back to this chart to add additional information about each word as they work through the chapter.

☐ **Know It!** Tell students that if they know the word, they should write its meaning on the lines provided.

☐ **Heard It!** Tell students that if they have heard, or are familiar with the word, they should write what they know about it on the lines provided. Remind them to take notes about the word as they encounter it.

☐ **Don't Know It!** If students do not know the word's meaning, tell them to write down its meaning when they encounter the word in the chapter.

Support Vocabulary

Return to the Word Rater as you come across vocabulary words in each lesson. Encourage students to use the "My Notes" section to include any of the following:

- definitions from the text
- deeper understandings
- synonyms
- other associations

Spanish Cognates

For Spanish speakers, point out the cognates:

decade = década

expedition = expedición

innovation = innovación

monument = monumeno

peninsula = península

Content Words	
boycott	a protest in which people refuse to buy, use, or participate in something
decade	ten years
drought	a shortage of water due to lack of rainfall
expedition	a journey, especially by a group of people, for a specific purpose
innovation	a new idea, piece of equipment, or method
monument	a building, statue, or other structure that honors a person, place, or event in history
peninsula	a piece of land surrounded by water on three sides
public services	something provided to the community, usually by the local government
strait	a narrow waterway connecting two larger bodies of water
taxes	money collected by a government

Complete this chapter's Word Rater. Write notes as you learn more about each word.

boycott
My Notes
☐ Know It! _____
☐ Heard It! _____
☐ Don't Know It! _____

decade
My Notes
☐ Know It! _____
☐ Heard It! _____
☐ Don't Know It! _____

drought
My Notes
☐ Know It! _____
☐ Heard It! _____
☐ Don't Know It! _____

expedition
My Notes
☐ Know It! _____
☐ Heard It! _____
☐ Don't Know It! _____

innovation
My Notes
☐ Know It! _____
☐ Heard It! _____
☐ Don't Know It! _____

monument
My Notes
☐ Know It! _____
☐ Heard It! _____
☐ Don't Know It! _____

peninsula
My Notes
☐ Know It! _____
☐ Heard It! _____
☐ Don't Know It! _____

public services
My Notes
☐ Know It! _____
☐ Heard It! _____
☐ Don't Know It! _____

strait
My Notes
☐ Know It! _____
☐ Heard It! _____
☐ Don't Know It! _____

taxes
My Notes
☐ Know It! _____
☐ Heard It! _____
☐ Don't Know It! _____

Copyright © McGraw-Hill Education

132 Chapter 4 Communities Change Over Time

Chapter 4 133

INQUIRY JOURNAL, pp. 132–133

English Learners SCAFFOLD

Use the following scaffolds to support student understanding of chapter vocabulary.

Entering and Emerging
Show students a picture that depicts each vocabulary word, and say the word aloud. Ask students to repeat the word after you. Then use simple sentences to describe the terms in context. For example: *The statue in the town square is a monument in our community.*

Developing and Expanding
Review vocabulary terms and definitions with students. Then organize students into two groups. One student from each group selects a vocabulary term and draws a picture of it on the board for the other group members to guess. Then the other team takes a turn. Repeat for all the vocabulary terms.

Bridging and Reaching
Have students read the vocabulary terms and find their definitions in the glossary. Then have partners take turns using each word in a complete sentence.

 Digital Tools

Blended Learning
Students investigate academic and domain-specific words they encounter in each lesson.

Interactive IMPACT
Throughout the chapter, encourage students to interact with the **Explore Words** cards and games.

How Does the Past Impact the Present?

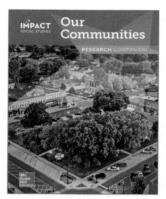

RESEARCH COMPANION, pp. 136–137

Activate Knowledge

Read and Discuss COLLABORATE Have students read the opening on p. 136 together. Ask: *What causes a community to change over time?* As students share their responses, you may wish to redirect misconceptions and inaccurate information.

How Has Life in Communities Changed?

- Have students read the text, focusing on both the photographs and the captions.
- What was life like for people who lived in the United States in the past? (Answers will vary, but students should use ideas from the text and consider how life differed for various groups of people.)
- How are hand-powered water pumps similar to the faucets we use today? How are they different? (Students should note specific similarities, such as the ability to bring water directly into the house, and specific differences, such as the ways that they are powered.)

Make Connections

- Based on what you have read, what conclusion can you draw about communities today compared to the past? (Answers will vary, but students should use details from the text to support their conclusions.)
- Imagine there is space on the page to describe another way that life in communities has changed. What would you add? Why? (Answers will vary.)

Perspectives Does new technology always make a community a better place to live? Why or why not? (Answers will vary, but students should include reasons to support their opinions.)

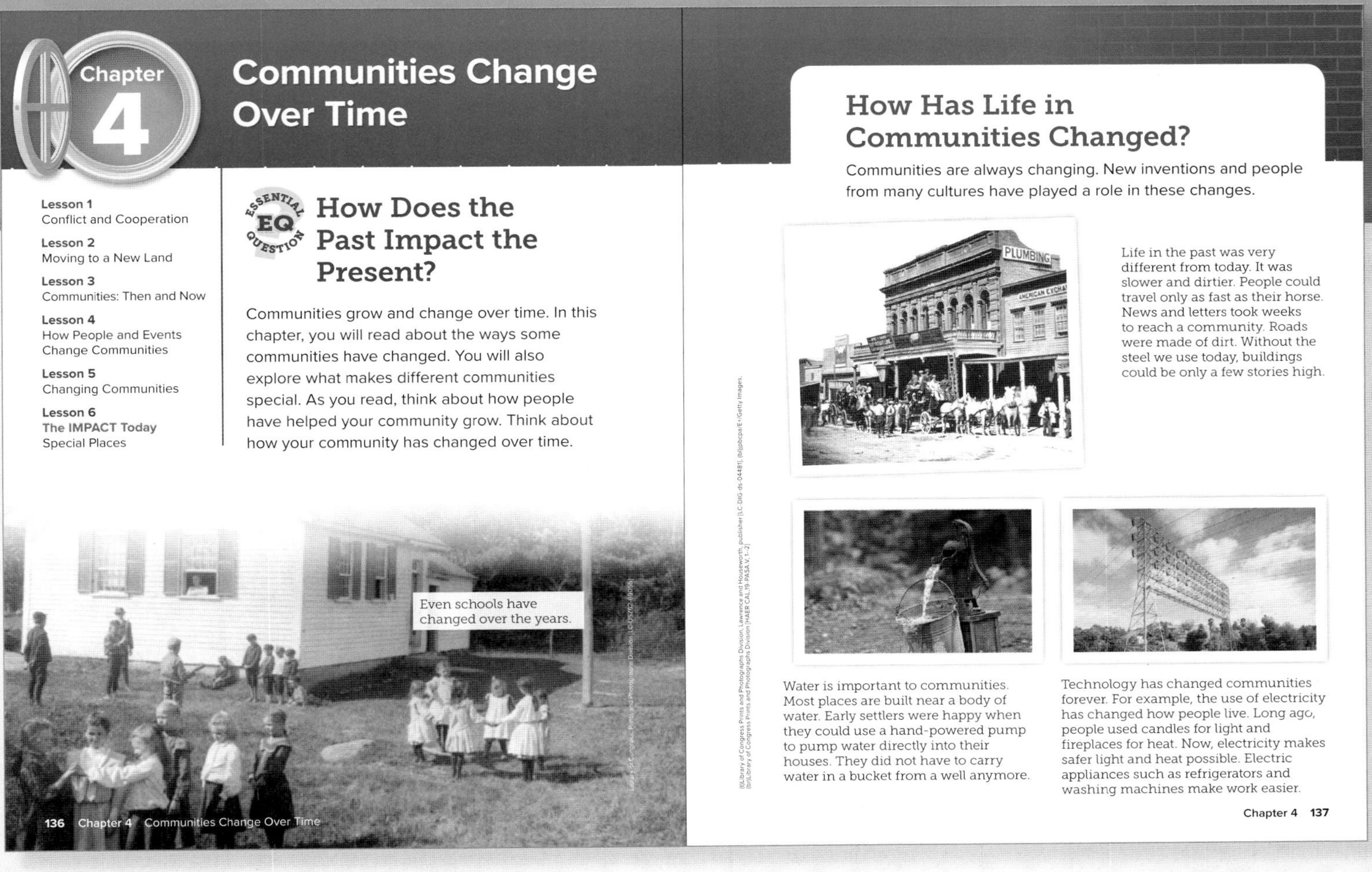

Chapter 4

Communities Change Over Time

ESSENTIAL QUESTION EQ

How Does the Past Impact the Present?

Communities grow and change over time. In this chapter, you will read about the ways some communities have changed. You will also explore what makes different communities special. As you read, think about how people have helped your community grow. Think about how your community has changed over time.

Even schools have changed over the years.

How Has Life in Communities Changed?

Communities are always changing. New inventions and people from many cultures have played a role in these changes.

Life in the past was very different from today. It was slower and dirtier. People could travel only as fast as their horse. News and letters took weeks to reach a community. Roads were made of dirt. Without the steel we use today, buildings could be only a few stories high.

Water is important to communities. Most places are built near a body of water. Early settlers were happy when they could use a hand-powered pump to pump water directly into their houses. They did not have to carry water in a bucket from a well anymore.

Technology has changed communities forever. For example, the use of electricity has changed how people live. Long ago, people used candles for light and fireplaces for heat. Now, electricity makes safer light and heat possible. Electric appliances such as refrigerators and washing machines make work easier.

RESEARCH COMPANION, pp. 136–137

English Learners SCAFFOLD

Use the following scaffolds to support students in activating their background knowledge.

Entering and Emerging

Point to each picture on p. 137 and ask: *What does this picture show?* Provide students with the following sentence frames:

- This picture shows how people ____________________. This technology *is used today/was used in the past.*

Ask students to find or draw a picture of how they get water or how they travel. Have each student share the picture with a partner and tell what it shows using the sentence frames above.

Developing and Expanding

Have students tell a partner what function each picture on p. 137 served/serves in a community. Ask students to think of the ways that people use technology in their community, and have them discuss their ideas with their partner.

Bridging and Reaching

Ask students to look at the pictures and read the captions. With a partner, have students discuss what the pictures have in common. Then ask partners to discuss how the people in their community use technology today.

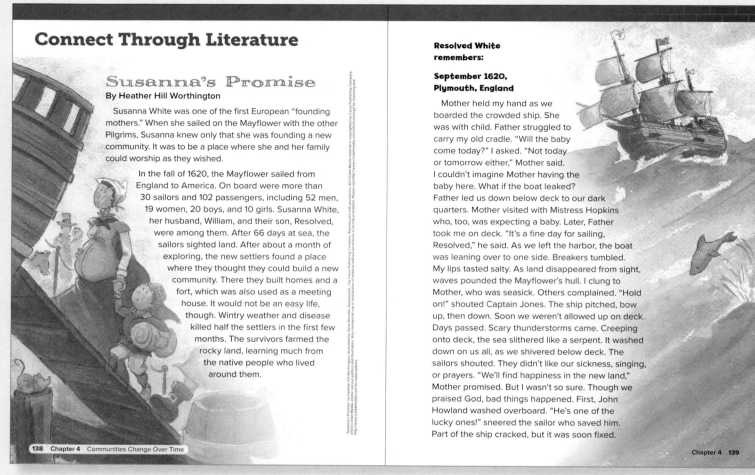

RESEARCH COMPANION, pp. 138–141

Connect Through Literature

Susanna's Promise
By Heather Hill Worthington

Susanna White was one of the first European "founding mothers." When she sailed on the Mayflower with the other Pilgrims, Susanna knew only that she was founding a new community. It was to be a place where she and her family could worship as they wished.

In the fall of 1620, the Mayflower sailed from England to America. On board were more than 30 sailors and 102 passengers, including 52 men, 19 women, 20 boys, and 10 girls. Susanna White, her husband, William, and their son, Resolved, were among them. After 66 days at sea, the sailors sighted land. After about a month of exploring, the new settlers found a place where they thought they could build a new community. There they built homes and a fort, which was also used as a meeting house. It would not be an easy life, though. Wintry weather and disease killed half the settlers in the first few months. The survivors farmed the rocky land, learning much from the native people who lived around them.

Resolved White remembers:

September 1620, Plymouth, England

Mother held my hand as we boarded the crowded ship. She was with child. Father struggled to carry my old cradle. "Will the baby come today?" I asked. "Not today or tomorrow either," Mother said. I couldn't imagine Mother having the baby here. What if the boat leaked? Father led us down below deck to our dark quarters. Mother visited with Mistress Hopkins who, too, was expecting a baby. Later, Father took me on deck. "It's a fine day for sailing, Resolved," he said. As we left the harbor, the boat was leaning over to one side. Breakers tumbled. My lips tasted salty. As land disappeared from sight, waves pounded the Mayflower's hull. I clung to Mother, who was seasick. Others complained. "Hold on!" shouted Captain Jones. The ship pitched, bow up, then down. Soon we weren't allowed up on deck. Days passed. Scary thunderstorms came. Creeping onto deck, the sea slithered like a serpent. It washed down on us all, as we shivered below deck. The sailors shouted. They didn't like our sickness, singing, or prayers. "We'll find happiness in the new land," Mother promised. But I wasn't so sure. Though we praised God, bad things happened. First, John Howland washed overboard. "He's one of the lucky ones!" sneered the sailor who saved him. Part of the ship cracked, but it was soon fixed.

138 Chapter 4 Communities Change Over Time

Chapter 4 139

Connect Through Literature

| **GENRE** | Historical Fiction "Susanna's Promise" is historical fiction that describes real people and events, but puts them in situations that are made up.

Have students read the selection on pp. 138–141. Then discuss the following question:

1. What did Susanna promise? (Susanna promised that her family would be happy in the new land.)

Have students reread the selection and ask:

2. What words would you use to describe how people felt on the journey? (Possible answers: excited, afraid, sad, hopeful, and so on.)

3. How does this story help us understand how life has changed for people in a community? (It describes how a community in the past started and some of the changes it went through.)

Perspectives How could the author know about what happened to the Pilgrims if she wasn't there? (Answers will vary.)

Background Information
Susanna White was an actual passenger on the *Mayflower*. She is known for two firsts in New England. In addition to giving birth to the first English baby in the colony, she also had the colony's first wedding when she married Edward Winslow after her husband died.

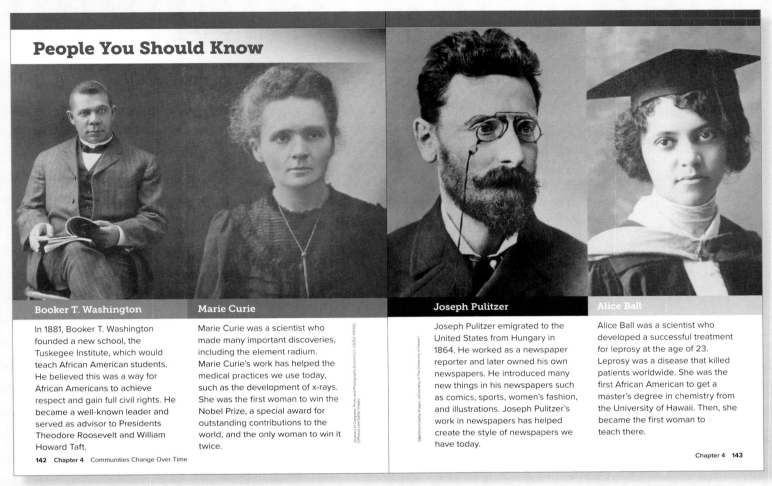

People You Should Know

Booker T. Washington

In 1881, Booker T. Washington founded a new school, the Tuskegee Institute, which would teach African American students. He believed this was a way for African Americans to achieve respect and gain full civil rights. He became a well-known leader and served as advisor to Presidents Theodore Roosevelt and William Howard Taft.

Marie Curie

Marie Curie was a scientist who made many important discoveries, including the element radium. Marie Curie's work has helped the medical practices we use today, such as the development of x-rays. She was the first woman to win the Nobel Prize, a special award for outstanding contributions to the world, and the only woman to win it twice.

Joseph Pulitzer

Joseph Pulitzer emigrated to the United States from Hungary in 1864. He worked as a newspaper reporter and later owned his own newspapers. He introduced many new things in his newspapers such as comics, sports, women's fashion, and illustrations. Joseph Pulitzer's work in newspapers has helped create the style of newspapers we have today.

Alice Ball

Alice Ball was a scientist who developed a successful treatment for leprosy at the age of 23. Leprosy was a disease that killed patients worldwide. She was the first African American to get a master's degree in chemistry from the University of Hawaii. Then, she became the first woman to teach there.

RESEARCH COMPANION, pp. 142–143

People You Should Know

How do personal stories IMPACT our understanding of how communities change over time?

Read Have students read the biographies. Tell them that they will read about the ways that communities can change because of people and technology.

Research Instruct students to choose one of these individuals and research his or her life and contributions. Tell students to gather facts about the individual's achievements, especially how that achievement may have affected or helped change communities.

Respond Have each student design a coin to commemorate a major achievement of the person he or she researched. On one side of the coin, each student should include a portrait of the person and, if possible, a quotation by or about that person. On the other side of the coin, the student should create an image that shows how that person's achievements influenced communities. Ask each student to write a paragraph that explains the achievement the coin commemorates and how that achievement affected communities.

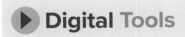 **Digital Tools**

Blended Learning

Students investigate and discuss curated news articles that extend the chapter content.

Interactive IMPACT

Connect to current events and people with **IMPACT News** and **More to Investigate**.

INVESTIGATE
with IMPACT EXPLORER MAGAZINE

IMPACT EXPLORER MAGAZINE, pp. 42–53

WordBlast

Remind students to look for the Word Blasts as they read the **IMPACT Explorer Magazine.**

Extend Knowledge Building

The **IMPACT Explorer Magazine** provides students another route to explore each chapter's Essential Question from a variety of perspectives as they dig deeper into the subject of how and why communities change over time. Additional questions and activities help students develop and deepen their understanding of the chapter's content.

Engage

Build background for students and share any information needed to provide a context for the chapter topic. Have students read the Essential Question and the Table of Contents.

Analyze the Visual Discuss the opening visual (photograph, photo essay, artwork) on the second page of the **IMPACT Explorer Magazine** chapter. Help students connect the visual to the chapter topic and the Essential Question.

Analyze the Sources

Students will read and analyze the leveled informational articles and literary texts, graphic texts, primary and secondary sources, photographs, maps, and other visual resources.

Read and Analyze Before reading, provide any additional information you think students will need about the topics. Then guide students through the three-step process to read and analyze the content.

1 Inspect

Have students skim the content on a page or multiple pages. Ask questions to help students recall and retell key ideas.

- What is this article mostly about?
- Who is _____?

2 Find Evidence

Have students reread the content and look for details they might have missed. Ask additional questions to help them read more closely.

- What details do you notice in the photographs?
- Why was _____ important?

3 Make Connections

Have students work in pairs or small groups to discuss prompts that help them connect the articles to other texts, their own lives, current ideas and issues, and other topics.

- How is _____ similar to what we do?
- How do you think _____ felt about what happened?
- What do you think about _____?

Chapter 4
Communities Change Over Time

ESSENTIAL EQ QUESTION

How does the past impact the present?

Table of Contents

42   Chapter 4   Communities Change Over Time

A Neighborhood
CHANGES

Just as we change and grow over time, so do our communities. New York City's Chinatown is one example of how a neighborhood evolves.

New York City's Chinatown began to form in the late 1800s, after Chinese immigrants moved to New York from the West. They settled close together in a few nearby streets. Later this area expanded and became known as Chinatown.

Today Chinatown is a busy neighborhood in New York City. Many Chinese Americans live here. Tourists also flock to Chinatown. It now has hundreds of restaurants, markets, and shops.

- What details do you see in these photos?
- How has New York City's Chinatown changed over time?

Chapter 4   43

IMPACT EXPLORER MAGAZINE, pp. 42–43

How to Use the IMPACT Explorer Magazine

Use the following scaffolds to support students' understanding and your classroom needs.

Whole Class

Use the **IMPACT Explorer Magazine** Teaching Guide to read and discuss one or more articles with the whole class.

Small Group

Have partners or small groups read articles connected to the day's core lesson and report back to the whole class about what they read.

Independent Work

Assign articles for students to extend and enrich their understanding of a topic, including during center time and independent reading time.

The online **IMPACT Explorer Magazine** Teaching Guide provides support for various implementation models as well as a three-step lesson plan for each article. The lesson plan includes background information, meaningful questions, vocabulary activities, scaffolded support for English learners, and collaborative conversation prompts.

Digital Tools

Blended Learning

Students extend the investigation of the Chapter Essential Question with highly visual, leveled articles and video.

eBook

Use the **IMPACT Explorer Magazine eBook** to extend knowledge building.

LESSON QUESTION

How Did Conflict and Cooperation Shape Early Communities?

Connect to the Essential Question

Tell students that this lesson provides key research into the Chapter Essential Question: **How Does the Past Impact the Present?** Explain that European explorers and settlers changed the shape of the Americas. While these settlers were able to build successful communities, they also had negative impacts on Native American communities.

Lesson Objectives

- **Identify** the different European explorers who traveled to the Americas.
- **Explain** how European settlers permanently changed the Americas.
- **Describe** early interactions between European settlers and Native Americans.
- **Write** an opinion about the positive and negative effects of cross-cultural interactions.

Make Connections!

CONNECT TO ELA

Reading Ask and answer questions to demonstrate understanding of a text and refer explicitly to the text as the basis for the answers.

Research Recall information from experiences or gather information from print and digital resources; take brief notes on sources and sort evidence into provided categories.

Writing Write opinion pieces on familiar topics or texts, supporting a point of view with reasons.

Speaking and Listening Engage effectively in a range of collaborative discussions with diverse partners on grade 3 topics and texts, building on others' ideas and expressing students' own ideas clearly.

Language Form and use comparative and superlative adjectives and adverbs, and choose between them depending on what is to be modified.

COMMUNITY CONNECTIONS

To further students' understanding of cross-cultural interactions within communities, have them research different cultural groups or festivals that are celebrated in the students' communities. Food festivals, street fairs, and parades are common in many communities for groups with a variety of cultural heritages. If possible, have students research events related to their own cultural backgrounds and share their findings with the class.

Lesson-At-A-Glance

1 ENGAGE — INQUIRY JOURNAL

pp. 134–139

- ▶ **Talk About It:** Illustration of explorers in the Americas
- ▶ **Analyze the Source:** A Clash of Cultures
- ▶ **Inquiry Tools:** Explore Chronology

2 INVESTIGATE — RESEARCH COMPANION

pp. 144–153

- ▶ **Explorers Arrive in the Americas**
- ▶ **European Explorers**
- ▶ **Explorers Settle in North America**
- ▶ **Impact of American Settlers**

3 REPORT — INQUIRY JOURNAL

pp. 140–141

- ▶ **Think About It**
- ▶ **Write About It:** Write an Opinion About Cultural Interactions; Cite Evidence from the Text
- ▶ **Talk About It**
- ▶ **Connect to the Essential Question**

ASSESSMENT

- ▶ **Online Lesson Test**
- ▶ **Printable Lesson Test**

For more details, see pages T262–T263.

▶ Digital Tools

at **my.mheducation.com**

ePresentation

Teach the **Engage**, **Investigate**, and **Report** content to the whole class from **ePresentations** that launch directly from the lesson dashboard.

eBook

You can flip your instruction with the **IMPACT eBooks** found on your lesson dashboard.

Interactive IMPACT

Blend in digital content **when you want it** and **where you want it**.

Blended Learning features in the Teacher's Edition highlight ways to connect in-class work with online experiences to enhance learning.

Investigate current events with **IMPACT News**.

Explore domain-based vocabulary with **Explore Words** and **Word Play** vocabulary activities.

pp. 42–53

Go Further with IMPACT Explorer Magazine!

The **IMPACT Explorer Magazine** supports students' exploration of the Essential Question and provides additional resources for the EQ Inquiry Project.

LESSON 1 LANGUAGE LEARNERS

How Did Conflict and Cooperation Shape Early Communities?

Introduce the Lesson

Set Purpose Explain to students that in this lesson, they will read informational texts to learn how European settlers lived with Native Americans.

Access Prior Knowledge Remind students that they already learned that Native Americans lived in North America long before the Europeans arrived. Ask: *Have you seen examples of Native American culture at a museum? What do you remember about Native American groups?*

Spark Curiosity Have students look at the photo of Chief Joseph on p. 152 of the Research Companion. Tell students that his Native American name was In-mut-too-yah-lat-lat, or Thunder-Traveling-Over-the-Mountains. Explain that the Nez Percé Indians were a powerful Native American group in the Pacific Northwest. They were initially friendly to the European settlers. Say: *Chief Joseph went to Washington, D.C., to speak to the president of United States. He asked that his people be allowed to live peacefully in their homeland, but they were never allowed to return.*

Build Meaning & Support Language

Inquiry Journal

Analyze the Source (pages 136–137) Tell students that in this lesson, they will read informational texts that give facts, dates, examples, and explanations about a topic. They include photographs and captions. As you read "A Clash of Cultures," explain any words that students don't know. Tell students that a bison is a very large wild animal that looks a little like a cow with a large, furry head and is sometimes called a buffalo. Support understanding of the photographs on pp. 136–137. Ask: *What are the differences between the two photos? How are the Native Americans dressed in the first photo? How are they dressed in the second photo?*

Inquiry Tools (pages 138–139) Remind students that **chronology** is telling the events that happened in the order in which they occurred. Tell students that they will identify the chronology of events as they read the selections in the Research Companion. Tell them that the graphic organizer will help them organize the information they read. Check that they understand the meaning of the column headings: *Time Period* and *Key Facts*. Explain that *Time Period* is a range of time, such as the 1800s. Ask: *What happened in the 1800s?* (Many states were added to the United States; Native Americans were pushed out of their homelands and onto reservations.) Say: *I will write these events under* Key Facts. Explain that the chart on page 139 will help students organize facts by time period as they read. If necessary, show students how to enter text in the right column that show facts for the time period in the left column.

Language Objectives

- Use newly acquired content and academic vocabulary to talk and write about European settlers and Native Americans.
- Form an opinion and write a paragraph describing positive and negative changes that happen when different cultures meet.
- Use comparative and superlative adverbs to describe actions.

Spanish Cognates

To support Spanish speakers, point out the cognates.

treaty = tratado

explore = explorar

route = ruta

mission = misión

conflict = conflicto

colony = colonia

Research Companion

Explorers Arrive in the Americas/European Explorers (pages 144–149) As you read, explain any words that students don't know. Read the last sentence on p. 146 beginning "These expeditions made Spain . . . ." Explain that the expeditions, or special trips for a purpose, were good for Spain, but they were harmful or bad for the native peoples. Point out that the word *but* shows a contrast or difference from what was said before it.

Explorers Settle in North America (pages 150–151) Direct students to study the map. Explain that the term *The Columbian Exchange* refers to the exchange of goods and ideas between Europe and the Americas that started with Christopher Columbus. Point out the connection between Columbian and Columbus. Ask: *What does the orange arrow show?* (goods coming from Europe to the Americas) *What does the blue arrow show?* (goods going from the Americas to Europe)

Impact of American Settlers (pages 152–153) Point out the map of Oklahoma. Make sure students understand that the map shows the tribal jurisdiction areas in Oklahoma. Explain that the journey from their homes in the Southeast to the land west of the Mississippi River became known as the Trail of Tears. Thousands of Native Americans did not survive the journey. Explain that the word *trail* means "path or small road." Ask: *How many different groups of Native Americans can you find on the map?*

Inquiry Journal

Report Your Findings (pages 140–141) Explain to students that to cite evidence means to base a response on information you have gathered about a topic. Students should include evidence and details from the texts in their responses. Encourage them to use the new vocabulary words they have learned. Check their answers for spelling and punctuation errors.

Language Forms & Conventions

Regular and Irregular Comparative and Superlative Adverbs Review with students that an adverb is a word that describes a verb, an adjective, or another adverb. In most cases, writers can compare two actions by using an adverb ending with *-er* or the word *more* and the adverb. Display the chart. Help students figure out the superlative word or phrase and add it to the chart.

Sentence	Adverb	Comparative Word or Phrase (Compares Two)	Superlative Word or Phrase (Compares More Than Two)
They could also move from place to place much faster. (p. 151)	fast	faster	fastest
They were able to hunt buffalo more effectively. (p. 151)	effectively	more effectively	most effectively

 Have students work in pairs to write sentences using the superlative words or phrases added to the chart.

LESSON 1 ENGAGE

 LESSON QUESTION

How Did Conflict and Cooperation Shape Early Communities?

INQUIRY JOURNAL, pp. 134–135

Bellringer

Ask: *What does it mean to cooperate?* (to work together with another person or group; to be helpful in order to make something happen) Explain that cooperation is needed to build things for a community, such as schools, public transportation, and libraries. Ask: *What might be an obstacle, or a challenge, to cooperation within a community?* (Answers will vary but might include that people might disagree on what a community needs or how those needs should be met.)

Lesson Outcomes

Discuss the lesson question and lesson outcomes with students.

- Make sure that students understand the words *conflict* and *cooperation*. Stress the social aspects of the two words and how they might apply to a community.
- Have students think about the population, government, economy, and culture of their own communities.

Talk About It

Have students look at the image and answer the questions in the Talk About It box. Encourage them to discuss their thoughts with a partner. Provide sentence frames as needed to help students complete the activity.

- The painting shows _____ and _____.
- The soldiers appear to be interested in _____.
- I think this because _____.

 Collaborative Conversations

Engage Have students discuss the following questions as a group. Ask students to build on each other's ideas, which requires them to both listen and think about what others are saying.

- How does our school reflect the community? In other words, how does our school look like the community or show the same values of the community?
- How is cooperation seen every day in our school?

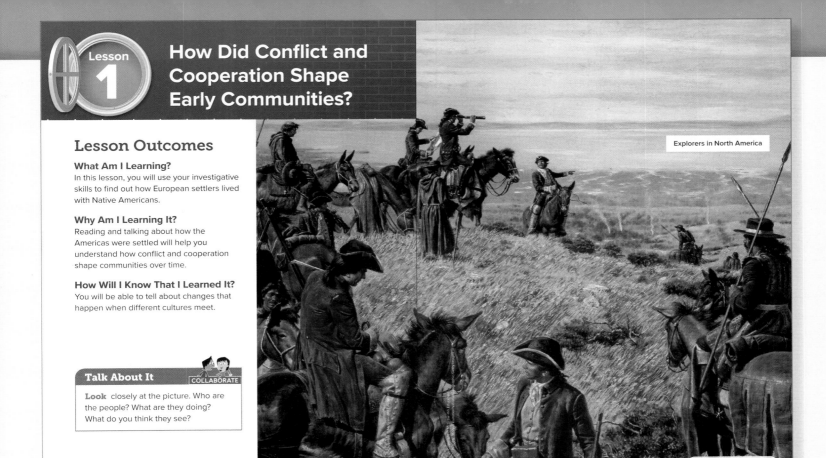

Lesson 1

How Did Conflict and Cooperation Shape Early Communities?

Lesson Outcomes

What Am I Learning?
In this lesson, you will use your investigative skills to find out how European settlers lived with Native Americans.

Why Am I Learning It?
Reading and talking about how the Americas were settled will help you understand how conflict and cooperation shape communities over time.

How Will I Know That I Learned It?
You will be able to tell about changes that happen when different cultures meet.

Talk About It COLLABORATE

Look closely at the picture. Who are the people? What are they doing? What do you think they see?

Explorers in North America

INQUIRY JOURNAL, pp. 134–135

English Learners SCAFFOLD

Use the following scaffolds to support student understanding of lesson outcomes.

Entering and Emerging
Have students think about what they would look for when settling a new area. Provide sentence frames as needed to help guide discussion.

- I would want to live where there is _____ and _____.
- I would make sure I could _____.
- If people were already living there, I would want to know _____.

Developing and Expanding
Have small groups discuss what would happen if they wanted to settle an area where people were already living. Ask: *How would you approach the people who were living there? What would you want to know? What could you do if they spoke a different language? What other challenges might you have?*

Bridging and Reaching
Have partners work together to make a list of what would be important to explorers and settlers—daily needs, as well as their long-term goals. Then have students write three ways those needs and goals are helped or hindered if people are already living in the area to be explored or settled.

 Social Emotional Learning

Self-Regulation

Set Goals To help students develop the habit of setting goals, remind them that setting small, achievable goals is important. These might include goals such as taking notes while they read. Ask: *Do you think explorers set goals? What kind of goals do you think they set?*

 Digital Tools

Blended Learning
Students engage with the lesson question and discussion prompts.

ePresentation

Discuss the **Lesson Question** and **Talk About It**.

A Clash of Cultures

1 Inspect

Read the first paragraph. What do you think this text will be about?

Read the article. Circle words you do not know.

Underline what the American settlers and government expected of the Native Americans.

Discuss with a partner how Native Americans changed because of American settlers.

My Notes

_____

_____

_____

_____

_____

_____

_____

Native Americans were the first people to live in what is now the United States. They had lived in the area for thousands of years. They had their own beliefs and ways of life. European settlers who came to North America brought their own cultures with them. Often, these cultures and ways of life were very different from how Native Americans lived.

Many settlers felt their cultures were the only way of life. They thought it would help the Native Americans to live as they did. They expected them to speak and dress like they did. They expected them to change their religions and give up their ways of life. Native Americans lost much of their culture during this time.

Potawatomi people gathered for a special occasion in 1906.

Native Americans had their own cultures and ways of life.

In the 1800s, many states were added to the United States—from Ohio to California. American settlers moved into those regions. They took the best land for themselves. They made the Native Americans move from their homelands. The United States government made the Native Americans live on small reservations.

One of these Native American groups was the Potawatomi. They lived in what is now Michigan, Indiana, and Illinois. When European settlers started arriving in the area, the Potawatomi moved west to Wisconsin. The government made treaties, or agreements, for the Native Americans to give up their land in return for payments. The Treaties of Fort Wayne in 1803 and 1809 particularly affected the Potawatomi. They were pushed to Kansas and then Oklahoma. As the Potawatomi moved west, they adapted to their new homeland. They learned from other Plains groups how to hunt bison.

2 Find Evidence

Reread How did the American settlers and government treat the Native Americans? What information from the text supports your ideas?

Look at the photographs. How do they help you understand how the lives of Native Americans changed?

3 Make Connections

Talk Why do you think settlers thought their cultures were the only way of life? Discuss your answer with a partner.

Connect to Now Do Native Americans live in your community today?

136 Lesson 1 How Did Conflict and Cooperation Shape Early Communities?

Chapter 4 Lesson 1 137

INQUIRY JOURNAL, pp. 136–137

Analyze the Source

1 Inspect

Read Have students read the first paragraph and predict what the rest of the text will be about. Remind them to circle words in the text with which they are unfamiliar.

- Underline details about what the European settlers and the U.S. government expected from Native Americans. (They usually expected Native Americans to live as they did, to speak and to dress like they did, and to change their religion and customs.)

Discuss As students discuss the subject, encourage them to revisit the text for specific examples of how life changed for Native Americans.

2 Find Evidence

Reread Have students refer to their underlined passages to help them understand the settlers' and the government's treatment of Native Americans.

Look Students should understand that the details in the photographs provide clues about culture, feelings, and ways of life.

3 Make Connections

Talk Encourage partners to discuss what happened to Native Americans. (Native Americans gave up much of their culture and customs. Many of them were also forced to move and to live on small reservations.)

Connect to Now If students are unfamiliar with local populations of Native Americans, work with them to discover this information via a local museum or expert.

Spotlight on Content

Scanning for Information

Have students work in pairs to trace the path of the Potawatomi by listing where they lived and where they moved. If possible, provide a map. Their path from Michigan, Indiana, and Illinois to Wisconsin, Kansas, and Oklahoma is representative of the struggles these groups faced.

Explore Chronology

Identifying the **chronology**, or the order in which events occur, will help you understand how events in history are connected.

1. **Read the text once all the way through.**
   This will help you understand what the text is about.

2. **Look at the section titles to see how the text is organized.**
   Titles may offer clues as to which important events are discussed.

3. **Watch for specific dates.**
   Are the events presented in chronological order? It may help to look for sentences that begin with a date. Note that dates could be specific, such as "In 1529." They could also express a range of time, such as "In the 1800s."

4. **Find key facts about the events.**
   While reading, ask yourself what key facts are most important to remember about the conflict and cooperation between the Europeans and Americans and the Native Americans.

 Based on the text you read, work with your class to complete the chart below.

Time Period	Key Facts
1800s	Many states were added to the United States. Native Americans were pushed out of their homelands and onto reservations.

138 Lesson 1 How Did Conflict and Cooperation Shape Early Communities?

 ## Investigate!

Read pages 144–153 in your Research Companion. Use your investigative skills to look for text evidence that tells you when and what happened. This chart will help you organize your notes.

Answers will vary, but students should record details from the Research Companion. Sample answers are shown below.

Time Period	Key Facts
1500s	Europeans explored the Americas. They claimed land, defeated native peoples in battle, and took resources.
1600s	Europeans explored Canada and the interior of the United States. Settlers began living in the United States.
1700s	Settlers and Native Americans fought as Europeans and Americans took over the land.
1800s	The Indian Removal Act (1839) forced Native Americans onto reservations.

Chapter 4 Lesson 1 139

INQUIRY JOURNAL, pp. 138–139

Inquiry Tools

Explore Chronology

Read Discuss with students the steps involved in identifying the chronology of events in history. Point out that understanding chronology requires them to pay attention to details within the text.

Guide Practice Have students review the text on pp. 136–137. Then work with them to complete the graphic organizer. Explain that they will use a similar graphic organizer to organize their independent research.

Check Understanding Confirm understanding of the inquiry skill, Explore Chronology. If students are having trouble grasping the concept, review the steps on p. 138.

Investigate!

Have students read pp. 144–153 in the Research Companion. Tell them the information will help them answer the lesson question *How Did Conflict and Cooperation Shape Early Communities?*

Sequence Tell students they should use the graphic organizer on p. 139 of the Inquiry Journal to take notes on when major events occurred that affected explorers, settlers, and Native Americans. If students have any empty spaces in their graphic organizers, suggest that they reread those the pages in their Research Companions.

 ### ▶ Digital Tools

Blended Learning

Students prepare for the lesson investigation with step-by-step instruction about how to identify chronology.

ePresentation

Use the **Inquiry Tools** to model and complete the lesson graphic organizer.

LESSON 1 INVESTIGATE

How Did Conflict and Cooperation Shape Early Communities?

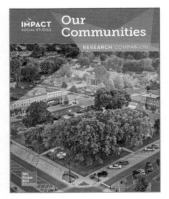

RESEARCH COMPANION, pp. 144–145

Background Information

European exploration and settlement was a complex affair that stretched over a hundred years. Students might have some of the following common misconceptions:

- The Caribbean islands Columbus first encountered had no people living on them.
- Native Americans living in the Americas were always happy to see the Spanish.
- European settlers and Native Americans always got along.
- Native Americans' lives were always better after their exposure to European technology.

Explorers Arrive in the Americas

1 Inspect Have students read pp. 144–145 and name the leader of the first Spanish exploration across the Atlantic.

2 Find Evidence Use the questions below to check comprehension. Remind students to support their answers with text evidence.

Explain What did Columbus discover instead of a route to Asia? (Instead of a route to Asia, Columbus discovered land that Europeans didn't know existed.) **DOK 2**

Speculate How do you think Native Americans felt after hearing the news that Spain had claimed ownership of their land? (Answers will vary, but students might guess that Native Americans were angry or scared; or maybe they were confused if they didn't understand what it meant.) **DOK 3**

3 Make Connections

Analyze How did the original purpose for exploring across the Atlantic Ocean change? (It changed from finding a route to Asia to exploring and gaining control of new land in the Americas.) **DOK 3**

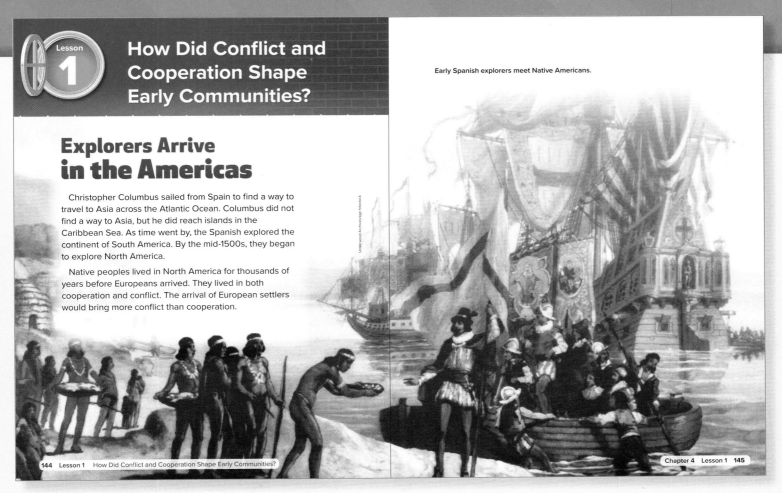

Lesson 1

How Did Conflict and Cooperation Shape Early Communities?

Early Spanish explorers meet Native Americans.

Explorers Arrive in the Americas

Christopher Columbus sailed from Spain to find a way to travel to Asia across the Atlantic Ocean. Columbus did not find a way to Asia, but he did reach islands in the Caribbean Sea. As time went by, the Spanish explored the continent of South America. By the mid-1500s, they began to explore North America.

Native peoples lived in North America for thousands of years before Europeans arrived. They lived in both cooperation and conflict. The arrival of European settlers would bring more conflict than cooperation.

144 Lesson 1 How Did Conflict and Cooperation Shape Early Communities?

Chapter 4 Lesson 1 145

RESEARCH COMPANION, pp. 144–145

English Learners SCAFFOLD

Use the following scaffolds to support student understanding of the lesson content.

Entering and Emerging
Help students describe details in the illustration. Read the caption and provide sentence frames:

- The people on the shore are _____.
- The people arriving in _____ are _____.
- The Native Americans have _____ and _____.
- The Spanish are holding _____.

Developing and Expanding
Have small groups discuss what is happening in the illustration. Ask questions to help them think about what it would be like to live in North America in the 1500s and to have European visitors for the first time. Ask: *How would you describe the Spanish arrival? What do you think the Native Americans thought? How are the Native Americans responding to their visitors?*

Bridging and Reaching
Have partners use details from the illustration to describe what Spanish explorers encountered in North America in the mid-1500s. Have them work together to write 3 or 4 sentences describing this scene from the Spanish point of view.

 Digital Tools

Blended Learning
Students investigate curated resources and find evidence to answer the lesson question.

Interactive IMPACT

Students choose from print or digital **Inquiry Tools** to take notes.

European Explorers

Many early explorers of the Americas came from Spain. Explorers like Christopher Columbus wanted to find trade routes to Asia. Instead, they found North and South America. They brought back to their homelands new products like sweet corn and coconuts. They called the native peoples Indians because they thought they had been sailing the Indian Ocean.

The Spanish continued to explore the Americas. In 1513, Juan Ponce de León explored the coasts of Florida. That same year, Vasco Núñez de Balboa discovered the Pacific Ocean. Later explorers found gold and silver in the Americas. The Spanish sent **expeditions** to take control of the land and the resources. An expedition is a journey for a specific purpose. In 1519, Hernán Cortés led an army to Mexico. They captured the gold and silver mines of the Aztec Empire. In 1529, Francisco Pizarro led an expedition to Peru. The Spanish took control of Inca silver mines. These expeditions made Spain very wealthy and powerful, but they were often harmful to native peoples.

Spanish explorer
Juan Ponce de León

During their exploration, the Spanish met several Native American groups. Sometimes the Native Americans traded goods with the Spanish. Sometimes they helped the Spanish repair their ships. At first, very little changed for the native people because of these explorers.

However, their lives began to change during the 1700s when the Spanish began to build settlements in what is now the United States. Often, the Native Americans and the Spanish fought. The Native Americans did not want the strangers taking over their land.

Did You Know?

The Spanish in New Mexico
About fifty years after discovering the Americas, the Spanish settled New Mexico. Artifacts they left behind show where the Spanish were and what they did. A Spanish cart from about 1845 was discovered in the sand dunes of a ranch in Las Cruces, New Mexico. The Spanish settlers used the cart to transport goods along El Camino Real, Spanish for "the royal road." El Camino Real was a major travel route.

This spur was used by an early Spanish settler.

✓ Stop and Check

Think Why did Spain send explorers to the New World?
Find Details As you read, add new information to the graphic organizer on page 139 in your Inquiry Journal.

RESEARCH COMPANION, pp. 146–147

European Explorers

1 Inspect Have students read pp. 146–147 and have them list one reason the Spanish explored the Americas.

2 Find Evidence Use the questions below to check comprehension.

Summarize How would you summarize Spain's efforts to explore the Americas? (In the beginning, Spanish explorers wanted to find trade routes to Asia, but found the Americas. They continued sailing to the Americas as they found new food products, gold, and silver. Eventually, the Spanish sent expeditions to take control of the land and resources belonging to the Native Americans.) **DOK 2**

Explain How did Spain become wealthy during this period? (Spain took control of the gold and silver mines belonging to the Aztecs and Incas.) **DOK 3**

3 Make Connections

Analyze Why do you think the author included so many facts about where the explorers went? (Answers will vary but should point out that location details support the main idea of exploration.) **DOK 3**

✓ Stop and Check

Think Encourage students to make inferences based on the text. (They were searching for a trade route to Asia. They discovered gold, silver, and other resources.)

Find Details Have students reread the text and scan the pages for specific dates and look for new key, related facts.

EL Spotlight on Vocabulary

Understanding Vocabulary

Guide students to identify the resources mentioned in the text: sweet corn, coconuts, gold, and silver. Ask students which resources made Spain wealthy.

▶ Digital Tools

Blended Learning
Students investigate curated resources and find evidence to answer the lesson question.

Interactive IMPACT
Students **Research** and find evidence using digital format texts.

Spain was not the only country to explore the New World. Great Britain, France, Portugal, and other countries sent expeditions across the Atlantic Ocean. At first, they searched for a route to Asia. Later, they focused on finding riches in the New World.

America is named after Italian explorer Amerigo Vespucci. He explored Brazil and other parts of South America for Spain. The Pacific Ocean was named by Portuguese explorer Ferdinand Magellan. In 1520, he was the first European to cross the Pacific Ocean.

English explorers looked for a northern route to Asia. In 1497, Italian explorer John Cabot explored the coast of Canada for England. In 1610, Henry Hudson sailed what is now the Hudson Bay. Later, England created the Hudson's Bay Company to sell fur.

Colonial ships arriving in North America

Biography

Robert Cavelier de La Salle
Robert Cavelier de La Salle was born in France in 1643. He moved to Canada in search of fortune. While trading furs, he heard about the land to the west. La Salle learned from the Native Americans how to survive on the land. He eventually canoed the Mississippi River to the Gulf of Mexico, claiming the area for France. He also tried to expand France's land by attacking the Spanish in part of Mexico but failed. On a later expedition, he was killed by his men.

☑ Stop and Check COLLABORATE

Talk How did European countries' reasons for exploring the Americas change? In your opinion, how did this change affect the native peoples?

RESEARCH COMPANION, pp. 148–149

European Explorers

1 Inspect Have students read pp. 148–149 and list other countries that explored the New World.

2 Find Evidence Use the questions below to check comprehension.

Compare How were other European explorers similar to the Spanish? (At first they searched for a new route to Asia, but later they focused on finding riches.) **DOK 2**

Predict How do you think the settlement of Europeans in the Americas affected the Native Americans already living there? (Answers will vary, but students might conclude that Native Americans suffered wherever the Europeans settle.) **DOK 3**

3 Make Connections

Compare How is Robert Cavelier de La Salle's background like that of many European explorers? (La Salle went to the New World in search of fortune, which eventually became the reason most European explorers went.) **DOK 3**

☑ Stop and Check COLLABORATE

Talk Have partners discuss different reasons for exploring the New World. (They changed from searching for trade routes to Asia to searching for ways to acquire more wealth.)

 Social Emotional Learning

Social Awareness

Value Diversity To encourage students to value diversity, remind them to consider different points of view. As students discuss issues as a class, tell them to listen to all viewpoints before forming opinions about them. Ask: *Do you think the European explorers considered the viewpoints of the native peoples they encountered?*

Explorers Settle in North America

By the 1600s, European settlers began living in North America. They built homes, farms, businesses, and forts. Some of the first permanent settlements were Spanish missions. There, priests like Father Junípero Serra in California worked to spread Christianity. The Spanish taught Native Americans about Christianity, European farming, cattle raising, and European ways of living. Sometimes they forced Native Americans to change religions, give up their land, and work at the mission.

European countries fought with one another over land claims. Settlers also fought with Native Americans over land, resources, and ways of life. Conflicts between the two groups often led to stolen cattle, burned crops, and battles. The Europeans had more effective weapons than the Native Americans. They also brought diseases like smallpox with them from Europe. These had a devastating impact on native peoples.

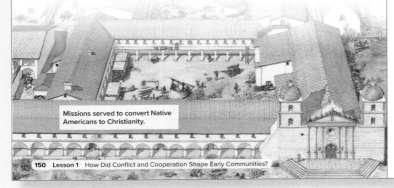

Missions served to convert Native Americans to Christianity.

Europeans found goods they had never seen, such as corn and potatoes. They also brought goods that were new to America. Settlers traded with Europe and with native peoples. Europeans brought horses to America. Native Americans could now hunt more effectively and move from place to place much faster. Settlers also brought goods like guns, metal cookware, tools, and cloth. Many Native Americans used European goods for everyday life.

InfoGraphic

THE COLUMBIAN EXCHANGE

Many goods were exchanged following Columbus's arrival in the Americas.

✓ Stop and Check

Talk Was European settlement in North America good or bad? Make a list of pros and cons.

RESEARCH COMPANION, pp. 150–151

Explorers Settle in North America

1 Inspect Have students read pp. 150–151 and name one positive outcome of European settlement in North America.

2 Find Evidence Use the questions below to check for comprehension.

Explain How did Spanish missions affect Native Americans? (Answers will vary but may include that the Spanish missionaries sometimes forced Native Americans to change religions, give up their land, and work at the mission.) **DOK 2**

Explain Why were Europeans able to conquer Native American forces so easily? (Europeans had better weapons; they brought diseases that killed Native Americans.) **DOK 2**

3 Make Connections

Analyze Visuals Study the map on p. 151. How did the Columbian Exchange provide benefits on both sides of the Atlantic? (Europeans found goods, such as new foods. Native Americans traded with Europeans and benefited from goods, such as horses.) **DOK 3**

✓ Stop and Check

Write As students make their lists, encourage them to consider multiple points of view, such as the impacts on communities when Native Americans had to give up their land. (Answers will vary, but pros might include exchange of goods and learning; cons might include conflicts, mistreatment of native peoples, and spread of diseases.)

 **Spotlight on Content**

Using Maps Use the map of the Columbian Exchange to emphasize that goods and ideas traveled both ways across the Atlantic.

 Digital Tools

Blended Learning Students explore lesson content through interactive activities.

Interactive IMPACT

Use the **More to Explore**.

Impact of American Settlers

American goods were very valuable to Europeans and American settlers. People wanted animal furs and tobacco. They also found that sugarcane grew much better in tropical areas of the Americas than in Europe. The trade of furs, sugar, and tobacco led to the growth of European settlements and communities. It also led to conflict that had negative affects on many communities.

Forests were cut down to make room for farms. Settlers in the Americas needed workers to build houses and farms. Indentured servants would work for several years in exchange for passage to the Americas. As communities expanded, however, European colonies began enslaving Native Americans and African people. They also claimed more and more land inhabited by Native Americans.

PRIMARY SOURCE

In Their Words...
Chief Joseph

"We gave up some of our country to the white men, thinking that then we could have peace. We were mistaken."

—Chief Joseph of the Nez Perce, speech in Washington, D.C., 1879

TEXT: Chief Young Joseph, "An Indian's Views of Indian Affairs," The North American Review 128, no. 269 (April 1879): 412-434.
PHOTO: Library of Congress Prints and Photographs Division; Edward S. Curtis Collection [LC-DIG-ppmsca-25872]

Oklahoma Tribal Jurisdiction Areas

Conflicts over land would continue. In 1830, President Andrew Jackson signed the Indian Removal Act. It forced Native Americans from their homes. It set up an Indian colonization zone which included what is now Iowa, Kansas, and Oklahoma. Native peoples were forced to march thousands of miles. Without enough food or supplies, many did not survive this journey. It became known as the Trail of Tears. The United States promised this territory would always belong to the Native Americans, but it didn't keep that promise. In 1907, Oklahoma became a state, taking more territory for the United States. Today, Native Americans still have territory and the right to govern themselves.

✓ Stop and Check
COLLABORATE

Talk Was the Indian Removal Act fair? Why or why not?

What Do You Think? How did conflict and cooperation with European explorers and settlers affect Native American communities?

RESEARCH COMPANION, pp. 152–153

Impact of American Settlers

1 Inspect Have students read pp. 152–153 and explain why Europeans cut down forests in the Americas.

2 Find Evidence Use the questions below to check for comprehension.

Summarize How did European colonists in the Americas expand their communities when they wanted more workers? (European colonists brought people to the Americas to work as indentured servants or enslaved people.) **DOK 2**

Analyze How would you describe the Indian Removal Act? (Answers will vary but students may point out the injustice in forcing Native Americans to leave their land and travel to other regions.) **DOK 2**

3 Make Connections

Analyze Visuals Study the map on p. 153. How did the United States use the Oklahoma territory to address their issues with Native Americans? (The government moved many Native American groups to Oklahoma. The government divided the territory among different groups.) **DOK 3**

✓ Stop and Check

COLLABORATE

Talk As partners discuss the Indian Removal Act, tell them to think about both the physical changes as well as emotional ones for Native Americans. (Answers will vary but could include that the Act was unfair as Native Americans were forced from their land.)

What Do You Think? (Answers will vary, but students should use text evidence to support their conclusions.)

✓ Check for Success

Explain Can students identify how conflict and cooperation help to shape their communities?

Differentiate

If Not, Have students review the completed graphic organizers on p. 139 of their Inquiry Journals and consider the effects of European settlement on Native Americans. Then have students discuss how conflict and cooperation can influence the success or failure of a community.

LESSON 1 REPORT

? LESSON QUESTION

How Did Conflict and Cooperation Shape Early Communities?

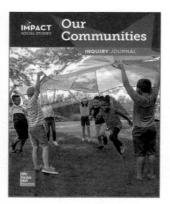

INQUIRY JOURNAL, pp. 140–141

Think About It

Remind students to review their research on the chronology of European exploration and settlement as they think about the forces that can shape a community. If students need more help, direct them to pp. 144–153 of the Research Companion.

Write About It

Write and Cite Evidence Remind students to include the following elements in their writing.

- Think about the ways Native American communities were affected when settlers arrived.
- Consider not just the short-term effects but also the long-term implications of the meeting of cultures.
- Use chapter vocabulary as appropriate.

Discipline(s)	4	3	2	1
Geography History	Written opinion clearly explains both positive and negative aspects of the meeting of the cultures	Written opinion adequately explains some positive aspects or negative aspects of the meeting of the cultures	Written opinion somewhat explains some positive or negative aspects of the meeting of the cultures	Poorly reasoned opinion fails to cover the positive and negative aspects of the meeting of the cultures

Talk About It

Defend Your Claim Remind students to use evidence as they present their opinions. Encourage students to listen closely to each other as they share and let each other finish before they respond.

Assessment Students can check their understanding with feedback from the **Lesson Test** available online.

Connect to the Essential Question

Pull It Together Before students respond, have them think about the long-term impacts of the arrival of European explorers and settlers. Prompt them to consider what the Americas were like before Europeans arrived and how things are different today.

Inquiry Project Update Remind students to turn to Inquiry Journal pp. 130–131 for project information. If necessary, review the Project Checklist with students. At this point in the chapter, students should focus on the first two items on the checklist.

Think About It

Gather Evidence

Review your research. Based on the information you have gathered, how did the lives of Native Americans change with the arrival of newcomers?

Write About It

Write and Cite Evidence

In your opinion, what are some positive things that happen when different cultures meet? What are some negative things?

Answers will vary, but students may suggest that positive things include trading for new items, helping new people, or learning new languages or ways of doing things. Negative things may include that one group's culture and way of life are lost or that groups may fight instead of working together.

Talk About It

Defend Your Claim

Take turns discussing your responses with a classmate. Do you think the meeting of cultures in the early years of the United States was more positive or negative?

History Connect to the **EQ**

Pull It Together

Think about the people and events you read and talked about in this lesson. How did they change things for the United States today?

Answers will vary but could include where and how Native Americans live today and how different cultures influenced the way of life and religion for many people in the United States.

EQ Inquiry Project Notes

140 Lesson 1 How Did Conflict and Cooperation Shape Early Communities?

Chapter 4 Lesson 1 141

INQUIRY JOURNAL, pp. 140–141

 # English Learners SCAFFOLD

Use the following scaffolds to support student writing.

Entering and Emerging

Have students think about what happens when different groups interact. Provide sentence frames, as needed, to help students form opinions:

- One culture might have a different _____ from another culture.
- It is good when different cultures meet because _____.
- It is sometimes bad when one culture _____.

Developing and Expanding

Ask questions to help students form opinions about what happens when different cultures meet. For example: *What might be different from one culture to another? What happens when different cultures meet? What is one good thing that could happen? What is one bad thing that could happen?*

Bridging and Reaching

Have partners discuss how communities are shaped by both conflict and cooperation. Ask: *How can different groups work together to make a community better? How can groups sometimes have conflict between themselves?* Guide students to write an opinion paragraph that includes positive and negative things about the meeting of cultures.

✔ Check for Success

Summarize Can students write an opinion paragraph expressing the positive and negative effects of the interactions between different cultures?

Differentiate

If Not, Have students present their opinion in an oral argument. Have them consider the case of settlers and Native Americans.

LESSON QUESTION

What Makes a Community Grow?

Connect to the Essential Question

Tell students that this lesson provides key research into the Chapter Essential Question: **How Does the Past Impact the Present?** Explain that they will learn why people choose to move to certain areas and understand the reasons why communities grow and change.

Lesson Objectives

- **Describe** reasons why people move to new communities.
- **Identify** features and events that cause communities to grow and change.
- **Explain** why a city's location is related to its growth.
- **Write** a paragraph about the main reason people move to new places.

Make Connections!

CONNECT TO ELA

Reading **Determine** the main idea of a text.
Recount the key details and explain how they support the main idea.

Research **Take** brief notes on sources and sort evidence into provided categories.

Writing **Develop** the topic with facts, definitions, and details.

Speaking and Listening **Determine** the main ideas and supporting details of a text read aloud or information presented in diverse media and formats, including visually, quantitatively, and orally.

COMMUNITY CONNECTIONS

To familiarize students with reasons why their own community has grown and changed over time, schedule a visit to a local history museum or invite a local historian to address the class.

Lesson-At-A-Glance

1 ENGAGE — INQUIRY JOURNAL

pp. 142–147

- ▶ **Talk About It:** Photograph of settlers arriving in Michigan
- ▶ **Analyze the Source:** Moving into Michigan; How to Read a Line Graph
- ▶ **Inquiry Tools:** Explore Main Ideas and Details

2 INVESTIGATE — RESEARCH COMPANION

pp. 154–161

- ▶ **Why People Move to New Places**
- ▶ **Communities Grow and Change**
- ▶ **Around the World: Dubai**

3 REPORT — INQUIRY JOURNAL

pp. 148–149

- ▶ **Think About It**
- ▶ **Write About It:** Write and Cite Evidence
- ▶ **Talk About It**
-  ▶ **Connect to the Essential Question**

ASSESSMENT

- ▶ **Online Lesson Test**
- ▶ **Printable Lesson Test**

For more details, see pages T262–T263.

▶ **Digital Tools**

at **my.mheducation.com**

ePresentation

Teach the Engage, Investigate, and Report content to the whole class from **ePresentations** that launch directly from the lesson dashboard.

eBook

You can flip your instruction with the **IMPACT eBooks** found on your lesson dashboard.

Interactive IMPACT

Blend in digital content **when you want it** and **where you want it**.

Blended Learning features in the Teacher's Edition highlight ways to connect in-class work with online experiences to enhance learning.

Investigate current events with **IMPACT News**.

Explore domain-based vocabulary with **Explore Words** and **Word Play** vocabulary activities.

pp. 42–53

Go Further with IMPACT Explorer Magazine!

The **IMPACT Explorer Magazine** supports students' exploration of the Essential Question and provides additional resources for the EQ Inquiry Project.

LESSON 2 LANGUAGE LEARNERS

What Makes a Community Grow?

Language Objectives

- Use newly acquired content and academic vocabulary to talk and write about how communities change over time.
- Identify and give examples of main ideas and details
- Use words that indicate a change in quantity.

Spanish Cognates

To support Spanish speakers, point out the cognates.

families = familias

disaster = desastre

industries = industrias

artists = artistas

miners = mineros

modern = moderno/a

Introduce the Lesson

Set Purpose Explain to students that in this lesson, they will read informational texts to find out why people migrate to new communities.

Access Prior Knowledge Have students work in groups to brainstorm and list what they have learned about how people change their environment. Review their ideas as a class. Discuss how the use of natural resources can change a community's landscape and impact its industry and population. Explain that in this lesson, they will read examples of how different communities have grown over time.

Spark Curiosity Have students examine the photograph on p. 155 of the Research Companion. Read the caption aloud. Ask: *What happens when more people move to a community?* (New buildings and roads are built, more resources are used, and the size of the community increases.)

Have pairs of students discuss what kinds of things are built when communities grow. Then have the pairs share their ideas. Be sure to discuss businesses, schools, community buildings, roads, and bridges.

Build Meaning & Support Language

Inquiry Journal

Analyze the Source (pages 144–145) Discuss the following excerpts from the text: *As the population grew, there were needs for other kinds of jobs, too. For example, a growing city needs teachers, firefighters, grocers, and carpenters.* Explain that *population* means "the number of people." Point out that one growing industry will affect many other parts of a community. Say: *Children need to learn, so teachers are needed. Emergency services are needed, so there must be police officers and firefighters. Food is essential, so grocers who manage food stores are needed. Buildings such as schools, city offices, and stores must be built by carpenters, plumbers, and bricklayers.*

Inquiry Tools (pages 146–147) Tell students they will explore the **Main Idea and Details** as they read the selections in the Research Companion. Explain that the diagram on p. 147 will help them record the main idea and details as they read. Say: *On p. 154 of the Research Companion we read that there are many reasons why people move. This is the main idea. Then there are examples of why people move, which provide details.* Show students how to enter the main idea in the center circle and the related details in surrounding circles. When students have completed their diagram, have them share their ideas with a group.

Research Companion

Why People Move to New Places (pages 154–157) Read aloud the first paragraph on p. 154. Explain that the terms *job, climate, family, situation*, and *disaster* found in this section gives key reasons why people move. Clarify meanings as needed. Read p. 156. Write and discuss the environments including *water, the Midwest*, and *mountains*. Ask: *Why did people move to each environment?* (water: travel and trade; Midwest: farming and ranching; mountains: mining) Read p. 157. Ask: *For what reason did most people move during the Great Depression?* (to find work)

Communities Grow and Change (pages 158–159) Read the first paragraph on p. 158. Ask: *How do communities grow larger?* (Businesses create jobs, and more people move there. New buildings and roads are built.) Explain that the Then and Now describes how Seattle has changed. Preview the word *lumber*. Read the section. Say: *Seattle, Washington, and Rapid City, South Dakota, have both changed since the late 1800s. Find the name of the event that caused both cities to grow.* (World War II) *What happened in each city?* (Seattle made airplanes. Rapid City had a new Air Force Base.)

Around the World: Dubai (pages 160–161) Point out on a map or globe the location of Dubai. Preview the words *skyscraper, bustling,* and *wealthiest*. Read the first paragraph on p. 160 and explain that today Dubai is crowded, busy, and wealthy, but fifty years ago it was small and quiet. Read the next paragraph. Ask: *Why did people move to Dubai in the 1800s?* (to trade and do business and not pay taxes) Read the next paragraph. Ask: *Why did Dubai change in the 1960s?* (Oil was discovered, many became wealthy, businesses grew, and buildings and roads were built.) Read p. 161. Ask: *What happened in the 1980s?* (Oil was hard to find, so Dubai developed tourism.)

Inquiry Journal

Report Your Findings (pages 148–149) Have students write sentences using the main ideas and details they have written. Then have them read their sentences to a partner as the partner determines if it is a main idea or detail. If partners disagree, have them discuss and come to an agreement.

For example: People move for many reasons. Sometimes they are looking for work.

      (main idea)   (detail)

Language Forms & Conventions

Words that Indicate Change Students should be able to identify and use words and phrases that indicate change in numbers. Key words like *double, increase,* and *grow* indicate that there is more of something. Words like *halve, decrease,* and *shrink* indicate there is less of something. Have students use an arrow pointing up as a reminder that a word means *more,* and an arrow pointing down as a reminder that a word means *less.*

Cross-Cultural Connection

Communities dominated by Native American cultures now have strong European influences. The settlements of Jamestown and Plymouth were the beginnings of the English-influenced culture we find in the United States today. French influence is strongest in the Canadian province of Quebec and the American state of Louisiana. Spanish influence is seen throughout the entire Southwest, from Texas to California, in states that were formerly part of Mexico, as well as in Florida.

Leveled Support

Entering & Emerging
Help students list ways in which different communities changed and how each change took place.

Developing & Expanding
Have students write sentences describing the changes that took place in a community and the reason for each one.

Bridging & Reaching
Encourage students to write a paragraph describing how and why a specific community changed.

Language Transfer

Intonation is important for distinguishing statements from questions in English. Questions end with rising intonation while statements have falling intonation. Speakers of tonal languages, such as Mandarin, Cantonese, Khmer, and Thai, do not use intonation. Model several statements and questions to demonstrate the differences in intonation. Have students repeat to practice using intonation in their speech.

LESSON 2 ENGAGE

LESSON QUESTION

What Makes a Community Grow?

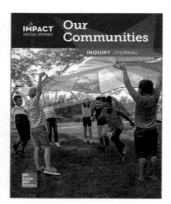

INQUIRY JOURNAL, pp. 142–143

Bellringer

Prompt students to retrieve information from the previous lesson. Say: *When people move to a new place, they sometimes change that place. You've read that Europeans explored and settled much of what is now the United States. How did Europeans change the places where they settled?* (They built houses, farms, and towns. They changed the lives of Native Americans who lived where they settled.)

Lesson Outcomes

Discuss the lesson question and lesson outcomes with students.

- Make sure students understand that people may choose to move to a new place for many different reasons. Ask: *What are some of the reasons you and your family live in this community? What are some other reasons people live in this community?*
- Tell students that by the end of the lesson, they will be able to write about the reasons why communities change and grow.

Talk About It

Explain that when we talk about photographs, we describe, analyze, and interpret them and present our ideas in our own words. Photographs can help readers predict what the text will be about. Captions tell us about what is happening in the photograph. Have students look at the photograph and read the caption. Ask:

- What details in the photograph tell you when it was taken? (the style of house, the setting, etc.)
- What other details in the photograph can you describe? (the line of horses, the newly built houses, etc.)

 Collaborative Conversations

Take Turns Talking As students engage in partner, small-group, and whole-class discussions, encourage them to

- Stay on topic.
- Connect their comments to the conversation using sentence starters, such as
  I agree with _____.
  That's a good idea. Let's think about changing it by _____.
- Listen carefully to others and expand on the information they share.

Lesson 2
What Makes a Community Grow?

Lesson Outcomes

What Am I Learning?
In this lesson, you will use your investigative skills to find out what makes a community grow.

Why Am I Learning It?
Reading and talking about the growth of communities will help you understand the reasons why communities grow and change.

How Will I Know That I Learned It?
You will be able to write a paragraph explaining the main reason people move to a new place.

Talk About It COLLABORATE

Look at the photograph on the next page. What words would you use to describe the buildings in the photo?

A lumbering camp in Michigan during the late 1800s

INQUIRY JOURNAL, pp. 142–143

English Learners SCAFFOLD

Use the following scaffolds to support student understanding of lesson outcomes.

Entering and Emerging

Have students respond to yes/no questions about the photograph by indicating thumbs up for *yes* and thumbs down for *no*. For example: *Is this photograph new? Is this a big town with lots of buildings?* Ask students what they think people are doing in the photo and accept one-word or short phrase answers.

Developing and Expanding

Ask students to look at the photograph and think about what is happening in it. Have pairs discuss their answers. Provide sentence frames to help facilitate their discussions:

The photograph shows _____.

I think these people are _____. I also think these people might be _____.

Bridging and Reaching

Ask students to look at the photograph and think about what is happening in it. Ask students to name one thing in the picture. Write the word where students can see it. Then ask students to give words that describe that thing. Make a web with the descriptions.

Social Emotional Learning

Social Awareness

Respect Showing respect for someone's opinion helps build good relationships with others. It also helps us build new understandings and perspectives. Remind students that, as they discuss the photograph, it is important to value the ideas of other students.

 Digital Tools

Blended Learning
Students engage with the lesson question and discussion prompts.

Interactive IMPACT

Discuss the **Lesson Question** and **Talk About It** with the whole class.

Moving into Michigan

1 Inspect

Look at the graph. What does it show?

Circle the year when Michigan's population was almost 3 million.

Place a box around the following:

- the point on the graph showing the population in 1920
- the point on the graph showing the population in 1950

My Notes

_____

_____

_____

_____

_____

_____

_____

_____

_____

_____

Why did Michigan's population more than double between 1900 and 1950? The most important reason is the car industry.

During the late 1800s, Michigan had a successful lumber industry. In order to move the large logs, workers needed strong wagons pulled by horses. There were many companies in Michigan that built wagons. In the early 1900s, demand began for a new type of vehicle: the car. Michigan's wagon companies were ready to build them.

By 1940, more than half of the world's cars were built in Detroit, Michigan. Almost every car company had a factory there. People came from all over the country to find work in the automobile industry. As the population grew, there were needs for other kinds of jobs, too. For example, a growing city needs teachers, firefighters, grocers, and carpenters.

Another reason Michigan's population increased was the Great Migration. During the first half of the 1900s, millions of African Americans left the South. They moved to get away from segregation, the practice of keeping people of different races separate. They also hoped to find better jobs. Many people came to Detroit for work. Between 1910 and 1920, Detroit's African American population grew six times greater.

Michigan's Population Change, 1900–1950

2,423,000
2,832,000
3,723,000
4,834,000
5,315,000
6,407,000

How to Read a Line Graph

To read a line graph, look at the graph's title and the labels. These tell you what the graph is about. The points, or dots, on the line show the information for each year. Trace the line connecting the points to see changes over time. On this graph, the line goes up. This means the population has grown. Some parts of the line are steeper than the others. When the line is steeper, it shows that the change in population was greater.

2 Find Evidence

Reread Look at the points for 1900 and 1950. What happened to Michigan's population during this time? Did more people live in Michigan in 1940 than in 1910? How do you know?

3 Make Connections

Talk Discuss with a partner how the graph supports the main idea of the article.

INQUIRY JOURNAL, pp. 144–145

Analyze the Source

Background Information

As in Michigan, the U.S. population grew steadily from 1900 to 1950, nearly doubling in that time. Immigration and a steady decline in death rates among children were major factors for the increasing population. Most years, the growth rate ranged from 0.5% to 2%, but 1918 was a stark exception. According to some sources, the U.S. population dropped that year. A half a million deaths caused by the influenza epidemic and another 100,000 deaths were due to World War I.

1 Inspect

Look Have students read the text about Michigan's growing population. Then have them read the text about the line graph and circle the year when Michigan's population was almost three million. (1910) Students should also place boxes around the points that show the populations in 1920 and 1950.

2 Find Evidence

Reread If necessary, point out that students can compare the heights or the values of the two points on the graph to answer the second question.

3 Make Connections

Talk Have students identify the main idea of the article. Then ask them to explain what the graph shows. Have students discuss how the graph supports the main idea of the article. (The main idea of the article is that Michigan's population grew between 1900 and 1950. The graph supports the main idea by showing how much the population grew between those years.)

 Spotlight on Language

Using Math Language

Help students identify words and phrases in the text that talk about changes in numbers. Point out *more than double*, *grew*, *increased*, and *grew six times greater*. Explain that *more than half* does not show a change in numbers.

▶ Digital Tools

Blended Learning

Students read informational texts and analyze primary sources.

Interactive IMPACT

Have students practice and apply the strategy of close reading as they analyze text.

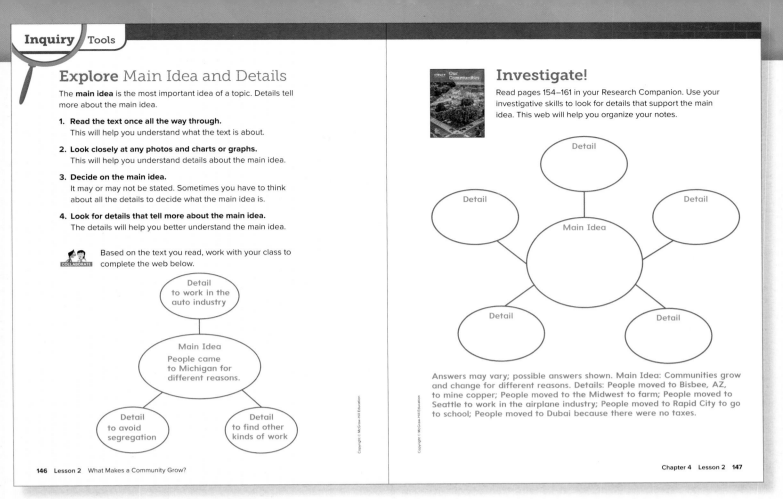

Inquiry Tools

Explore Main Idea and Details

Read Have students read aloud the step-by-step instructions about how to find the main idea and supporting details in a text. Point out to students that the population graph also has a main idea—Michigan's population grew from 1900 to 1950—and the statistics are the details that support the main idea. The graph as a whole also helps support the main idea of *Moving into Michigan*.

Guide Practice Read aloud the text on pp. 144–145. Guide students to decide on the main idea of the text by considering the details in the text. Ask: *What are the important details? What does that tell you about the main idea in the text?* Then work with students to complete the graphic organizer.

Check Understanding Confirm understanding of the inquiry skill, Explore Main Idea and Details. If students cannot identify the main idea and related details, review the steps on p. 146.

Investigate!

Have students read pp. 154–161 in the Research Companion. Tell them the information will help them answer the lesson question **What Makes a Community Grow?**

Take Notes Remind students to paraphrase, or use their own words, when they take notes. Remind students to look closely at the details in the text and ask themselves what main idea is being supported by these details.

 Spotlight on Content

Identifying Key Details

Encourage students to ask and answer *who, what, where, when, why,* and *how* questions about the text. Point out that the answers to these questions will help them identify key details.

LESSON 2 INVESTIGATE

LESSON QUESTION

What Makes a Community Grow?

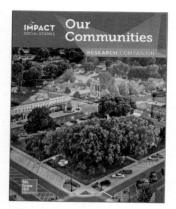

RESEARCH COMPANION, pp. 154–155

Background Information

Migration is fluid between countries, states, and cities. When the technology industry exploded in California in the 1990s, many people migrated to California for jobs. When the technology job market softened, many people who moved to California for jobs stayed for the weather or lifestyle. Natural disasters also cause people to migrate. For example, immediately after the devastation of Hurricane Katrina in 2005, New Orleans's population dropped by almost half. Today, the population has grown, but it is still almost 15 percent below its pre-Katrina numbers.

Why People Move to New Places

1 Inspect Have students read pp. 154–155 and identify reasons why someone might move to a new place.

2 Find Evidence Use the questions below to check comprehension. Remind students to support their answers with text evidence.

Summarize How would you summarize the text on p. 154? (Answers will vary, but students should mention that people move to new areas for many reasons, such as climate, jobs, loss of a home, and to be nearer to family and friends.) **DOK 2**

Explain Why is an earthquake an example of a natural disaster? (It is something that happens naturally and can cause damage and devastation.) **DOK 3**

3 Make Connections

Assess What are some reasons people might have moved to your community? (Answers will vary but might include jobs, schools, climate, recreational activities, etc.) **DOK 3**

Lesson 2 — What Makes a Community Grow?

Why People Move to New Places

Have you or a friend ever moved from one place to another? There are many reasons why people move. Some people move to find a better job. Others may choose to move to a place because of the weather. They want to live somewhere with a nice climate. Still others may move to be closer to their friends and families or to get away from a bad situation. Other people may need to find a new home after a natural disaster, such as an earthquake or a shortage of water called a **drought**.

Read on to learn more about why people have migrated to specific communities over the years.

Building a new house in a growing community

154 Lesson 2 What Makes a Community Grow?

Chapter 4 Lesson 2 155

RESEARCH COMPANION, pp. 154–155

English Learners SCAFFOLD

Use the following scaffolds to support student understanding of lesson content.

Entering and Emerging

Read aloud p. 154 and list reasons people move: *better jobs, better weather, family, safety*. Then display the following sentence frame to help students summarize the text:

- People need _____. People want _____. People move so they can have _____.

Have students use the sentence frame and the list to describe reasons why people move.

Developing and Expanding

In small groups, have students alternate reading aloud sentences from p. 154 while others listen for descriptive words. Have them complete a T-chart that shows opposites and compares *old* to *new*.

Bridging and Reaching

Have students generate a list of descriptive words that could be used to describe what they see happening in the photograph on p. 155. Then have them write a sentence describing the reason why they think the people in the photograph have moved to a new community.

Spotlight on Language

Understanding Language

over the years: in this context, *over* does not mean "above," but rather "across" or "through"

▶ Digital Tools

Blended Learning
Students explore lesson content through interactive activities.

Interactive IMPACT

Use the **More to Explore**.

In the past, people migrated to new places for many reasons. Some communities formed near water. Other communities were built in the Midwest where soil was good for growing crops and raising animals. Ranchers built communities farther west. The land was wide open, and few people lived there. Large herds of cattle and other livestock could roam for miles as they grazed. Some people traveled to the mountains looking for gold or other precious minerals. The discovery of oil deep underground brought people to new places as well.

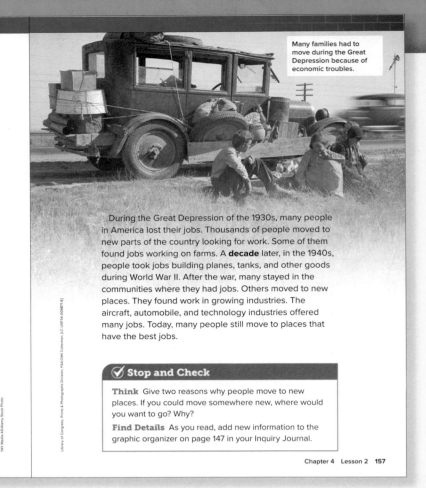

Many families had to move during the Great Depression because of economic troubles.

Did You Know?

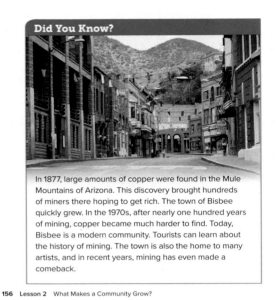

In 1877, large amounts of copper were found in the Mule Mountains of Arizona. This discovery brought hundreds of miners there hoping to get rich. The town of Bisbee quickly grew. In the 1970s, after nearly one hundred years of mining, copper became much harder to find. Today, Bisbee is a modern community. Tourists can learn about the history of mining. The town is also the home to many artists, and in recent years, mining has even made a comeback.

During the Great Depression of the 1930s, many people in America lost their jobs. Thousands of people moved to new parts of the country looking for work. Some of them found jobs working on farms. A **decade** later, in the 1940s, people took jobs building planes, tanks, and other goods during World War II. After the war, many stayed in the communities where they had jobs. Others moved to new places. They found work in growing industries. The aircraft, automobile, and technology industries offered many jobs. Today, many people still move to places that have the best jobs.

✓ Stop and Check

Think Give two reasons why people move to new places. If you could move somewhere new, where would you want to go? Why?

Find Details As you read, add new information to the graphic organizer on page 147 in your Inquiry Journal.

RESEARCH COMPANION, pp. 156–157

Why People Move to New Places

1 Inspect Have students read pp. 156–157 and explain why many people moved during the Great Depression.

2 Find Evidence Use the questions below to check comprehension.

Cause and Effect Why did ranchers choose to build communities farther west than the grassy plains where farmers had settled? (The land farther west was drier and not as good for farming, so it was wide open and few people lived there. It was good land for roaming herds of livestock.) **DOK 2**

Analyze How is the type of land in a place related to the reasons why people might want to move there? (Answers may vary but should focus on the resources available in different types of landscapes) **DOK 3**

3 Make Connections

Draw Conclusions How did the types of jobs available in Bisbee, Arizona, change after copper became harder to find? (There were fewer mining jobs but more jobs in tourism and art.) **DOK 3**

✓ Stop and Check

Think Have students consider the reasons people move and share their ideas of places where they would like to move and why. (Answers will vary but may include jobs, weather, or positive aspects of the landscape, such as scenery or recreational activities.)

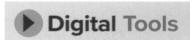 **Digital** Tools

Blended Learning
Students investigate curated resources and find evidence to answer the lesson question.

Interactive IMPACT

Students choose from print or digital **Inquiry Tools** to take notes.

Communities Grow and Change

Most communities begin as small settlements and grow slowly. As businesses open in a community, more people will move there to find jobs. As more people come to the community, new homes, stores, schools, and roads are built. The community becomes larger.

Then and Now

Seattle, Washington

Seattle is one community that has changed over time. It started as a small village with a lumber mill. During the late 1800s, Seattle grew quickly. Its location on the coast meant there were many jobs in fishing and shipping. Shipbuilding was also an important industry. During World War I, about one out of every five ships used in the war was built in Seattle. Workers from all over the world came to find jobs there. Later, during World War II, a company making airplanes moved to Seattle. Thousands of people found work in the airline industry. Today, many technology and Internet companies are located in Seattle.

Rapid City, South Dakota, is a town that has grown and changed over time. It is located near the Black Hills, a small mountain range rising from the surrounding plains. Originally, the Lakota lived on the land.

The first white settlers arrived in 1876 after gold was discovered in the Black Hills. Rapid City was founded soon after. It was a small supply town for miners heading into the mountains. It was nicknamed "the Gateway to the Black Hills."

In the 1880s, railroads were being built west across America. Rapid City's location made it a good stopping point along the way. This helped the city grow.

During the early 1900s, people began traveling by car. The Black Hills became a popular place for tourists. Then, in 1927, sculptor Gutzon Borglum chose Mount Rushmore in the Black Hills as the site of his giant carvings of presidents' faces. Gutzon's son, Lincoln Borglum, completed the work in 1941. Today, millions of people visit the monument each year.

The biggest impact on Rapid City's population was the Ellsworth Air Force Base. It was built during World War II, and the city's population almost doubled in just a decade.

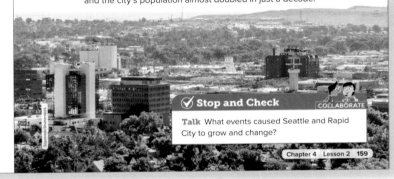

✓ **Stop and Check**

Talk What events caused Seattle and Rapid City to grow and change?

RESEARCH COMPANION, pp. 158–159

Communities Grow and Change

1 Inspect Have partners read pp. 158–159 and describe how Rapid City was founded.

2 Find Evidence Use the questions below to check comprehension.

Identify What event had the biggest impact on Rapid City's population? Explain. (The building of the Ellsworth Air Force Base. The base brought jobs and new residents which caused the population to double in one decade.) **DOK 2**

Cite Evidence Which details from the text support the idea that transportation helped Rapid City grow? (Rapid City's location made it a good stopping point for trains heading west. As more people owned cars, tourists began to drive to Rapid City.) **DOK 3**

3 Make Connections

Assess How do the photographs of Seattle support the text? (The text explains that Seattle changed over time. The photographs show how the city has changed.) **DOK 3**

✓ **Stop and Check**

Talk Once students have identified events, encourage them to find similarities between the events in both cities. (Answers will vary, but students may mention that Seattle and Rapid City both grew as businesses opened and people moved there to find jobs. Both Seattle and Rapid City first grew because of natural resources. They continued to grow because of their location. Finally, Seattle and Rapid City both grew during World War II.)

Social Emotional Learning

Relationship Skills

Build Relationships Students in a classroom setting function as a team with the shared goal of learning. Strong, supportive relationships among the "team members" will help facilitate positive learning outcomes. When pairing students for partner activities, be sure to vary the partnerships over time so students have a chance to work with and get to know a variety of their peers.

Around the World: Dubai

1 Inspect Read aloud pp. 160–161 and have students identify the natural resource that was discovered near Dubai in the 1960s.

2 Find Evidence Use the questions below to check comprehension.

Cause and Effect When the emir of Dubai declared that businesses would not have to pay taxes there, what was the effect? (Traders moved their businesses to Dubai, and the city's population doubled.) **DOK 2**

Draw Conclusions If oil had not been discovered near Dubai, how do you think the city might be different today? (Answers may vary but most likely will conclude that Dubai would still be a small city.) **DOK 3**

3 Make Connections

Compare and Contrast Choose one of the other cities you read about in this lesson. How are the reasons Dubai changed and grew similar to and different from those of your chosen city? (Answers will vary, but students should provide text evidence to support their responses.) **DOK 3**

✓ Stop and Check

Talk Students should find evidence in the text and in photographs to support their answers. (The desert is flat and mostly empty, so Dubai could spread easily across the land. Its coastal location allowed building materials and people to easily reach the city.)

What Do You Think?

Talk Have students share their ideas about how the reasons people move today are similar to the reasons people moved long ago. (Answers may vary, but students should cite text evidence.)

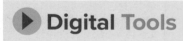

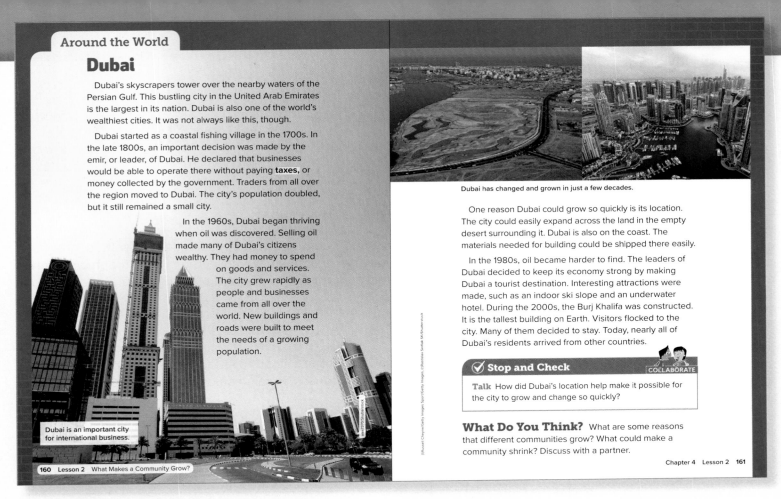

Around the World

Dubai

Dubai's skyscrapers tower over the nearby waters of the Persian Gulf. This bustling city in the United Arab Emirates is the largest in its nation. Dubai is also one of the world's wealthiest cities. It was not always like this, though.

Dubai started as a coastal fishing village in the 1700s. In the late 1800s, an important decision was made by the emir, or leader, of Dubai. He declared that businesses would be able to operate there without paying **taxes,** or money collected by the government. Traders from all over the region moved to Dubai. The city's population doubled, but it still remained a small city.

In the 1960s, Dubai began thriving when oil was discovered. Selling oil made many of Dubai's citizens wealthy. They had money to spend on goods and services. The city grew rapidly as people and businesses came from all over the world. New buildings and roads were built to meet the needs of a growing population.

Dubai is an important city for international business.

Dubai has changed and grown in just a few decades.

One reason Dubai could grow so quickly is its location. The city could easily expand across the land in the empty desert surrounding it. Dubai is also on the coast. The materials needed for building could be shipped there easily.

In the 1980s, oil became harder to find. The leaders of Dubai decided to keep its economy strong by making Dubai a tourist destination. Interesting attractions were made, such as an indoor ski slope and an underwater hotel. During the 2000s, the Burj Khalifa was constructed. It is the tallest building on Earth. Visitors flocked to the city. Many of them decided to stay. Today, nearly all of Dubai's residents arrived from other countries.

✓ Stop and Check COLLABORATE

Talk How did Dubai's location help make it possible for the city to grow and change so quickly?

What Do You Think? What are some reasons that different communities grow? What could make a community shrink? Discuss with a partner.

160 Lesson 2 What Makes a Community Grow?

Chapter 4 Lesson 2 161

RESEARCH COMPANION, pp. 160–161

English Learners SCAFFOLD

Use the following scaffolds to support student understanding of lesson content.

Entering and Emerging

Read aloud pp. 160–161 to students. Then draw a time line on the board with the following dates: 1700s, 1800s, 1960s, 1980s, 2000s. Have pairs of students scan the text for facts about how Dubai has changed, and then ask volunteers to provide information to label the timeline.

Developing and Expanding

Have partners scan the text for facts about how and why Dubai changed. Have them create a time line based on the text. Have pairs report to the class one of their events. Provide a sentence frame, as needed, to help students organize the information for their reports.

In _____, Dubai _____.

Bridging and Reaching

Have partners scan the text for facts about how and why Dubai changed. Have them list the information in a three-column chart with the headings *What Happened, When,* and *Why.* Have pairs describe to the class one of their events using a complete sentence that tells what, when, and why. Then have the whole group decide which event was most influential in the city's growth and justify their idea.

✓ Check for Success

Connect Can students identify reasons why people move to new communities?

Differentiate

If Not, Have students refer to the notes they took in their graphic organizers on Inquiry Journal pp. 146–147 and tell one reason people moved to a city featured in the texts.

LESSON 2 REPORT

LESSON QUESTION

What Makes a Community Grow?

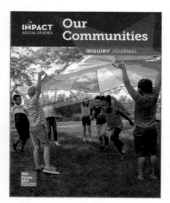

**INQUIRY JOURNAL,
pp. 148–149**

Think About It

Students will review their research and determine how communities are settled, grow, and change. Remind students to review the data they have collected in their graphic organizer as they answer the question. Direct students to pp. 154–161 of their Research Companion if they need more information.

Write About It

Write and Cite Evidence Read the prompt aloud to students. Encourage them to use vocabulary from the chapter in their responses. Remind students to include the following elements in their responses.

- Identify a reason why people might move to a new place.
- Cite specific evidence to support their answer.
- Include facts from their research, with page references for support.

Discipline(s)	4	3	2	1
History	Student provides evidence and details that show a strong understanding of why people move to a new region.	Student includes details for some evidence that show an adequate understanding of why people move to a new region.	Student includes evidence but few supporting details that show an uneven understanding of why people move to a new region.	Student does not provide support or details that show an understanding of why people move to a new region.

Talk About It

Explain Use students' comments in class to pair classmates who have different ideas about why people move to a community. Remind students to be respectful of one another's views.

Assessment Students can check their understanding with feedback from the **Lesson Test** available online.

Connect to the Essential Question

Pull It Together Before students respond, remind them to think about the reasons people moved to the cities they read about and how those communities changed over time.

Inquiry Project Update Remind students to turn to Inquiry Journal p. 131 for project information. If necessary, review the Project Checklist with students. At this point in the chapter, students should focus on the second and third items on the checklist.

Think About It

Gather Evidence
Based on your research, why do you think people migrate to a new place?

Write About It

Write and Cite Evidence
What do you think is the main reason people move to new places? Explain your choice.

Students' answers will vary, but students should provide reasonable explanations for their choices. Most will likely name an economic reason.

Talk About It

Explain
Compare your choice with the choice of a classmate. Take turns explaining your choices. Discuss why people often have several reasons for moving.

Connect to the EQ

Geography

Pull It Together
What are some ways that a community has changed over the years? What causes communities to change over time? How does that impact the present?

Students' answers will vary but should accurately reflect how and why communities can change over time.

Inquiry Project Notes

INQUIRY JOURNAL, pp. 148–149

English Learners SCAFFOLD

Use the following scaffolds to support student writing.

Entering and Emerging

Ask students to refer to their notes in the graphic organizers on Inquiry Journal p. 147. Ask students: *Why did people move to _____?* List the reasons on the board. Then survey students to determine which reason they think is most common. Model writing a simple paragraph supporting this reason with facts from the text. Have students use the paragraph as an example as they write their own paragraphs.

Developing and Expanding

Have students review the information they have learned about why people move. Survey students to determine which reasons they think are the main ones. Pair students who choose the same main reason. Have partners work together to write their explanation, supporting their opinion with facts and examples from the text.

Bridging and Reaching

After students have written their explanations, have them work with partners to review their writing. Have partners read each other's writing and offer constructive feedback. Students should first say one thing they like about their partner's writing. Then they should offer one suggestion for improvement about the content, grammar, spelling, or punctuation.

✔ Check for Success

Summarize Can students write an explanation supported by evidence of what they think the main reason is that people move to new communities?

Differentiate

If Not, Have students present their evidence in a different format, such as in a drawing or as an oral presentation.

LESSON QUESTION

How Do Communities of the Past Compare to Today?

Connect to the Essential Question

Tell students that this lesson provides key research into the Chapter Essential Question: **How Does the Past Impact the Present?** Explain that they will discover how people settled and changed their communities, what makes these communities special, and how their community's past affects it today.

Lesson Objectives

- **Describe** what life was like for a community in the past.
- **Identify** how innovations in transportation changed communities.
- **Explain** why communities change and grow.
- **Write** a paragraph about how a community today might be different than in the past.

Make Connections!

CONNECT TO ELA

Reading **Determine** the main idea of a text; recount the key details and explain how they support the main idea.

Compare and contrast the most important points and key details presented in two texts on the same topic.

Research **Conduct** short research projects that build knowledge about a topic.

Writing **Craft** informative/explanatory texts to examine a topic and convey ideas and information clearly.

Develop the topic with facts, definitions, and details.

Speaking and Listening **Engage** effectively in a range of collaborative discussions with diverse partners on grade 3 topics and texts, building on others' ideas and expressing students' own ideas clearly.

COMMUNITY CONNECTIONS

To enrich what students have learned about their community, plan a virtual field trip to an historic place, such as a building or a home of a prominent person of the community's past. The historic place should have artifacts and information about the community's past. Research to find a digital historic map that shows the layout of the community in the past.

Lesson-At-A-Glance

1 ENGAGE → INQUIRY JOURNAL

pp. 150–155

- ▶ **Talk About It:** Photographs of buildings in a community
- ▶ **Analyze the Source:** How the Past Can Be Seen Today
- ▶ **Inquiry Tools:** Explore Compare and Contrast

2 INVESTIGATE → RESEARCH COMPANION

pp. 162–171

- ▶ **Innovations in Transportation**
- ▶ **Communities Develop and Grow**
- ▶ **Communities in America: Then and Now**
- ▶ **Land and Water in Different Communities**

3 REPORT → INQUIRY JOURNAL

pp. 156–157

- ▶ **Think About It**
- ▶ **Write About It:** Write a Paragraph About How the Community Changed; Cite Evidence
- ▶ **Talk About It**
- ▶ **Connect to the Essential Question**

ASSESSMENT

- ▶ **Online Lesson Test**
- ▶ **Printable Lesson Test**

For more details, see pages T262–T263.

▶ Digital Tools

at **my.mheducation.com**

ePresentation

Teach the Engage, Investigate, and Report content to the whole class from **ePresentations** that launch directly from the lesson dashboard.

eBook

You can flip your instruction with the **IMPACT eBooks** found on your lesson dashboard.

Interactive IMPACT

Blend in digital content **when you want it** and **where you want it.**

Blended Learning features in the Teacher's Edition highlight ways to connect in-class work with online experiences to enhance learning.

Investigate current events with **IMPACT News.**

Explore domain-based vocabulary with **Explore Words** and **Word Play** vocabulary activities.

pp. 42–53

Go Further with IMPACT Explorer Magazine!

The **IMPACT Explorer Magazine** supports students' exploration of the Essential Question and provides additional resources for the EQ Inquiry Project.

LESSON 3 LANGUAGE LEARNERS

LESSON QUESTION

How Do Communities of the Past Compare to Today?

Language Objectives

- Use newly acquired content and academic vocabulary to compare communities of the past and present.
- In a written paragraph, compare and contrast two time periods using the support of a Venn diagram.
- Respond orally and in writing to questions using *can* and *could*.

 Spanish Cognates

To support Spanish speakers, point out the cognates.

innovation = innovación

common = común

west = oeste

train = tren

nation = nación

Introduce the Lesson

Set Purpose Explain to students that in this lesson, they will read informational texts that compare communities of the past to communities of today.

Access Prior Knowledge Before presenting the Lesson Outcomes, read the Lesson Question and find out what students already know about how communities of the past compare to communities today. Ask: *What is a community?* (city or town and the people who live there) Review with students how communities have changed since European and American settlers came. Ask: *What do you remember about Native American communities? How are they similar to and different from your community today?*

Spark Curiosity Have students study the photograph on pages 162–163 of the Research Companion. Read the caption aloud. Ask: *How do you think trains affected communities?* (made it easier for people to move; made it easier to build new communities at different places)

Have students work in pairs to explain some positive and some negative changes to communities over the years. Have them share their ideas with the group.

Build Meaning & Support Language

Inquiry Journal

Analyze the Source (page 152–153) Write the following sentence on the board and read it aloud: *The way a building looks can tell you who built it and when it was built.* Have students look closely at the sentence. Circle the words *who* and *when*. Say: Who *and* when *are question words.* Ask: *What does the word* when *ask about?* (time) *What does the word* who *ask about?* (a person) Underline the noun phrase *The way a building looks.* Point out to students that we can say it another way: *How a building looks* or *What a building looks like.* Ask: *What can we learn by looking at a building?* (We can learn who built it and when it was built.) Explain that the sentence means: *When we look at a building, we can learn something about the people who built it. We can also get information about when people built it.*

Inquiry Tools (pages 154–155) Tell students they will **Compare and Contrast** as they read about the past and present in the Research Companion. Point out the words on page 154 that signal comparisons and contrasts: *like, the same, both, unlike, different.* Explain that the graphic organizer on p. 155 will help them visualize similarities and differences. Show students how to add information to the diagram.

Research Companion

Innovations in Transportation (pages 162–165) Clarify the meaning of the word *transportation.* Read aloud the first paragraph on page 162. Ask: *What types of transportation are named?* (bike, bus, car) Explain that today people can easily travel by car, but many settlers going west traveled by wagon pulled by oxen. Ask: *How is a car different from a wagon?* (A car is faster and smoother; a wagon is slow and bumpy.) Point out that the word *innovation* often means "the introduction of something new," but it can also mean "a change made to something that already exists." The word *invention* has a similar meaning: "the discovery or product of someone's imagination."

As you read pages 163–164, clarify meanings for *steam locomotive, steamship, transcontinental, trolleys,* and *cable cars.* Then unlock the Primary Source on page 165. Point out the word *multitude,* and explain that it means "many people." Explain that Ford meant that many people would be able to buy the cars his company built.

Communities Develop and Grow/Communities in America: Then and Now (pages 166–169) Read the first two paragraphs. Explain that the word *goods* means "things" or "items." Ask: *What people and businesses did growing towns usually have?* (stores, miners, farmers, hotels, blacksmiths, doctors, newspapers, theaters, parks) Direct students to study the InfoGraphic on pages 168–169. Have students preview the headings and photos and predict what the text is comparing. Ask: *What do you think it was like to live in the 1800s?* Offer language support for *general store* (a store that sells all types of things) and *long-distance travel* (traveling far).

Land and Water in Different Communities (pages 170–171) Read the first paragraph and explain that land, water, and climate played important roles in community development. Point out the word *innovation* again and have students apply its meaning to rail transportation. Read the last paragraph on page 171, and explain that a canal is a man-made waterway that connects bodies of water.

Inquiry Journal

Report Your Findings (pages 156–157) Have students use the information in their graphic organizers to write sentences comparing and contrasting communities of the past and today. Explain that the information in the central section is true for both the past and the present. Remind them to use key words for comparing (*and, also, both*) and contrasting (*but, however*). For example: *In the past people traveled slowly with wagons, but today travel is faster with cars and airplanes.*

Language Forms & Conventions

Modals: *Could* and *Can* Innovations made developments possible. In order to speak about what was possible, and what became possible, students may need to practice using the words *could* and *can.* The word *can* means you are able to do something. The word *could* is sometimes used as a modal or conditional verb. So, *could* is used to show something is possible to do if conditions are met.

COLLABORATE

Provide examples of sentences that use *could* and *can.* Discuss the differences in meaning when using the two words. For example: *I can walk to the store. I could go to the store faster if I learned how to ride a bike.*

 Cross-Cultural Connection

Advancements in transportation changed the ways people travel, but transportation may be specific to a landscape or region. For example, the city of Venice in Italy is built on canals, so boats are essential for travel. In the Himalayas of Nepal, people use a bridge or zip-line basket to save time by crossing a deep gorge without descending a mountain. Ask: *How has the geography of your community affected the ways people travel?*

 Leveled Support

Entering & Emerging
Provide sentence frames: In the past, people traveled by _____. Today, people travel by _____. In the past, communities _____. Today, communities _____.

Developing & Expanding
Have small groups make a list of ways communities are different now than in the past. Have students write sentences describing the changes that took place in a community and the reason for each one.

Bridging & Reaching
Have partners describe their community and list three ways it might be different now than in the past.

 **Language Transfer**

Explain that the 's construction does not always mean possession. Sometimes it is used as a contraction for the word *is.* For example, the words *Pete's going* means "Pete is going." Explain that the word *its* is a possessive but the word *it's* is a contraction.

LESSON 3 ENGAGE

How Do Communities of the Past Compare to Today?

INQUIRY JOURNAL, pp. 150–151

Bellringer

Prompt students to retrieve information from the previous lessons. Say: *People move to new regions for different reasons. Native Americans had been living in the Americas for thousands of years before the Europeans arrived. How did the European settlers affect Native Americans?* (The new settlers claimed their land and made some Native Americans change how they lived. There was cooperation between the Europeans and Native Americans and also conflict.)

Lesson Outcomes

Discuss the lesson question and lesson outcomes with students.

- Help students understand that their community has changed over time. Give students a few examples of what their community was like in the past. Maybe the place where a major shopping center is located was once farmland. Perhaps the population of the community was much larger or smaller in the past.

- Explain that learning and talking about what life was like in the past will help them understand how and why a community changes.

Talk About It

Guide students to study the photographs, analyze them, and describe what they see. Provide sentence frames as needed to help students talk about the photographs.

- The two pictures show _____ .
- The two buildings are _____ and have _____ .
- The buildings were probably built _____ .
- These buildings are similar to / different from the buildings in my community because _____ .

 Collaborative Conversations

Listen Carefully As students engage in partner, small-group, and whole-class discussions, encourage them to follow discussion rules by listening carefully to speakers. Remind students to
- always look at the person who is speaking.
- respect others by not interrupting them.
- repeat peers' ideas to check understanding.

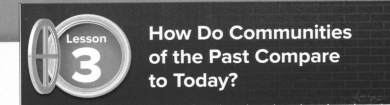

Lesson 3

How Do Communities of the Past Compare to Today?

Faneuil Hall in Boston, Massachusetts

Lesson Outcomes

What Am I Learning?
In this lesson, you will use your investigative skills to find out how a community changes over time.

Why Am I Learning It?
Reading and talking about what life was like in the past will help you learn how a community can change.

How Will I Know That I Learned It?
You will be able to write a paragraph about life in the past and explain how life is different today. You also will be able to give reasons why communities change.

The St. Louis Cathedral in New Orleans, Louisiana

Talk About It COLLABORATE

Look closely at the pictures. Describe the buildings. Do they look like the buildings you see in your community today? Do they seem old or modern?

150 Lesson 3 How Do Communities of the Past Compare to Today?

Chapter 4 Lesson 3 151

INQUIRY JOURNAL, pp. 150–151

 English Learners SCAFFOLD

Use the following scaffolds to support student understanding of lesson outcomes.

Entering and Emerging

Provide a list of words and phrases to help students describe the photos: *buildings, tall, large, old, modern, trees, statues, pointed towers, many windows.* Explain the word *modern* and then provide sentence frames:

- Both photos show _____.
- The building in the first photo is _____ and has _____.
- The building in the second photo is _____ and has _____.

Developing and Expanding

Guide small groups to work together to describe what they see in the photos. Ask questions similar to the following: *Do you think the buildings in the photos are modern or old? How is the first photo different from the second photo? How are the buildings similar? How are they different?*

Bridging and Reaching

Have partners study the two photos and write a list of words and phrases (nouns and adjectives) they would use to describe the buildings. Encourage students to include words that describe the age of the buildings, similarities and differences, and any specific features. Ask: *How do these buildings compare to buildings in your community?*

 Social Emotional Learning

Relationship Skills

Value Ideas of Others To grow intellectually, students must develop an interest in what others think about an issue. Encourage them to consider and respect other students' perspectives or views of the photos.

▶ **Digital Tools**

Blended Learning
Students engage with the lesson question and discussion prompts.

ePresentation

Discuss the **Lesson Question** and **Talk About It**.

How the Past Can Be Seen Today

1 Inspect

Read the title. What do you think this text will be about?

Highlight the names of two cities that show the places from which the early settlers came.

Underline the words that describe things in the different cultures that make up the United States.

Discuss with a partner what you think your community was like in the past.

My Notes

_____

_____

_____

_____

_____

_____

_____

_____

Read the names of these Florida cities: Boca Raton and Punta Gorda. The names are Spanish. This is because the Spanish formed these communities. The names help you understand the history of these cities. You can also learn about a community's history by looking at its buildings. The way a building looks can tell you who built it and when it was built. Buildings with red clay tile roofs and thick white walls are built in a Spanish style.

The population of the United States is diverse. Each community is made up of people from many different ethnic groups and backgrounds. Native Americans have lived in the United States for thousands of years. Other groups of people came more recently. The British settlers named many of the cities and states in New England after places in England. French settlers named New Orleans, Louisiana, after a city in France. German settlers named Fredericksburg, Texas, after a city in Germany. Today, people from all over the world make the United States home.

People from many ethnic groups have affected your community. The signs you see or even the house you live in can show your community's history. You may eat foods from different cultures. You may celebrate the holidays of other cultures. The people who lived in your community in the past helped make your community what it is like today.

Foods from many different cultures are available in the United States.

2 Find Evidence

Reread What features of a community today tell you about the cultures and people of its past?

Underline examples in the text of ethnic groups.

3 Make Connections

Talk Is there a part of your community named for something in the past? Why do you think it is important for a community to do things to show its history?

INQUIRY JOURNAL, pp. 152–153

Analyze the Source

1 Inspect

Read Have students read the title and predict what the text will be about. (how a place can tell us about its past) Then have them read pp. 152–153.

- How can city names show where the early settlers came from? (The names may be words from another language, or they may name cities in other countries.)

- Underline words that describe things from the different cultures in the United States. (Spanish-style buildings: red clay tile roofs, thick white walls; signs, names of cities and states, foods, holidays)

2 Find Evidence

Reread Guide students to identify features of a community that tell about its past. (houses or buildings in a community, the food people eat and their holidays)

- Underline examples of different groups that make up the United States. (Spanish, Native Americans, British, French, German)

- What different kinds of fruits and vegetables can you identify in the photograph? (Possible responses: peppers, radishes, celery, cabbage, onions, oranges, pineapples)

3 Make Connections

Talk Have partners discuss their community, who lived there in the past, how they know about its past, and how they think the past affected their community today. Have students compare their community to the one pictured in the photograph.

Spotlight on Vocabulary

Content Vocabulary

diverse: showing a great deal of variety

background: a person's family and life experience

culture: the beliefs, way of life, usual ways of doing things, and arts of a group of people

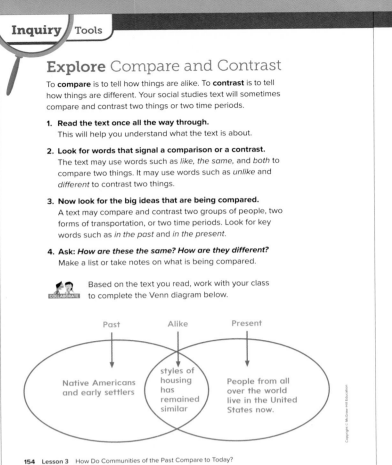

Explore Compare and Contrast

To **compare** is to tell how things are alike. To **contrast** is to tell how things are different. Your social studies text will sometimes compare and contrast two things or two time periods.

1. **Read the text once all the way through.**
   This will help you understand what the text is about.

2. **Look for words that signal a comparison or a contrast.**
   The text may use words such as *like, the same,* and *both* to compare two things. It may use words such as *unlike* and *different* to contrast two things.

3. **Now look for the big ideas that are being compared.**
   A text may compare and contrast two groups of people, two forms of transportation, or two time periods. Look for key words such as *in the past* and *in the present.*

4. **Ask: How are these the same? How are they different?**
   Make a list or take notes on what is being compared.

Based on the text you read, work with your class to complete the Venn diagram below.

Past — Alike — Present

Native Americans and early settlers / styles of housing has remained similar / People from all over the world live in the United States now.

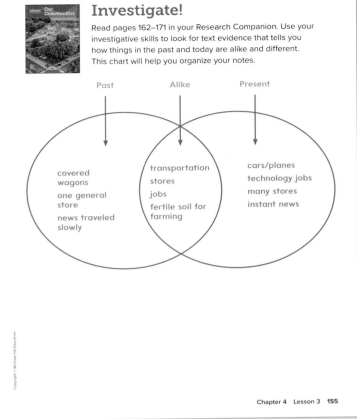

Investigate!

Read pages 162–171 in your Research Companion. Use your investigative skills to look for text evidence that tells you how things in the past and today are alike and different. This chart will help you organize your notes.

Past — Alike — Present

covered wagons / one general store / news traveled slowly

transportation / stores / jobs / fertile soil for farming

cars/planes / technology jobs / many stores / instant news

INQUIRY JOURNAL, pp. 154–155

Inquiry Tools

Explore Compare and Contrast

Read Have students read the step-by-step instructions about how to compare and contrast information or ideas. Explain that in social studies, sometimes the text compares or contrasts two things or two time periods. A text also can compare or contrast things of today with things in the past.

Guide Practice Have students review the text on pp. 152–153. Then work with students to complete the Venn diagram on p. 154. Explain that they will use a similar Venn diagram to organize their independent research.

Check Understanding Confirm understanding of the inquiry skill, Explore Compare and Contrast. If students have difficulty comparing and contrasting, review the steps on p. 154.

Investigate!

Have students read pp. 162–171 in the Research Companion. Tell them the information will help them answer the lesson question *How Do Communities of the Past Compare to Today?*

Take Notes Tell students they should take notes in the Venn diagram on p. 155 of the Inquiry Journal. Remind them that taking notes will help them understand and remember the information they learn. Remind students to look for clues that signal comparisons and contrasts when reading.

 Spotlight on Language

Prefixes

Compare starts with *com-,* a prefix that can indicate "together." Contrast is a special comparison that points out the differences. The prefix *contra-* means "against." It is related to words like controversy and contradict.

 Digital Tools

Blended Learning
Students prepare for the lesson with instruction about how to compare and contrast.

ePresentation
Use the **Inquiry Tools** to model and complete the lesson graphic organizer.

LESSON 3 INVESTIGATE

How Do Communities of the Past Compare to Today?

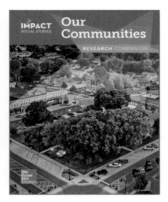

RESEARCH COMPANION, pp. 162–163

Background Information

- **Henry T. Williams** was editor and publisher of *The Pacific Tourist*, a travel guide for the Union and Central Pacific Railroads. The guide contained descriptions of railroad routes, resorts, towns, cities, U.S. forts, lakes, and mountains from the Atlantic to the Pacific. Also included was "all needful information for the pleasure traveler, miner, settler, or business man."

- The Model T was introduced in 1908. In less than 20 years, **Henry Ford's** Model T changed the lives of most people, connecting isolated farmers, stimulating the economy, and influencing the growth of cities and suburbs. This rapid change was made possible by Ford's assembly line technology and mass-production techniques, which allowed him to set prices low and meet the volume demands through efficiency.

Innovations in Transportation

1 Inspect Have students read pp. 162–163 and identify types of transportation.

2 Find Evidence Use the questions below to check comprehension. Remind students to support their answers with text evidence.

Explain Using the clues in the text, what do you think the word *innovation* means? (something new, a major improvement or change, a new invention) **DOK 2**

Cause and Effect What effects did the invention of the steam locomotive have? (People and goods reached their destinations faster and easier.) **DOK 2**

3 Make Connections

Compare How is transportation today similar to transportation in the 1800s? How is it different? (In the 1800s, people walked and traveled by wagon, train, and boat. People still travel by trains and ships now, but they are faster. Today, people also travel by car, bus, and airplane. Paved roads make traveling easier, too.) **DOK 3**

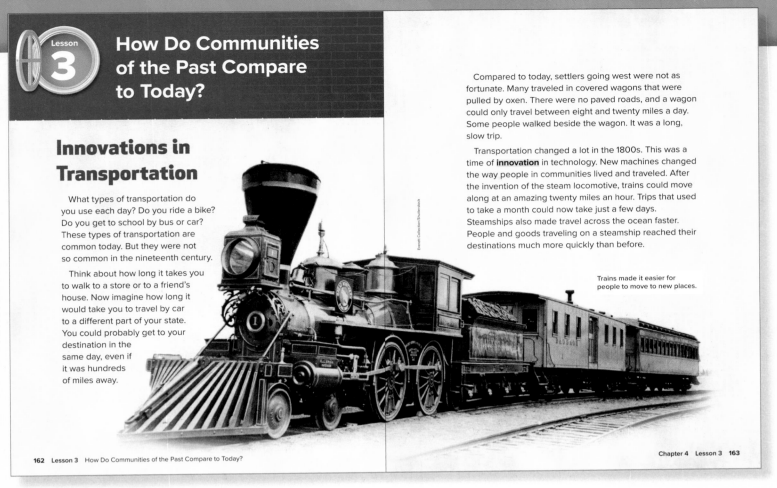

Innovations in Transportation

What types of transportation do you use each day? Do you ride a bike? Do you get to school by bus or car? These types of transportation are common today. But they were not so common in the nineteenth century.

Think about how long it takes you to walk to a store or to a friend's house. Now imagine how long it would take you to travel by car to a different part of your state. You could probably get to your destination in the same day, even if it was hundreds of miles away.

Compared to today, settlers going west were not as fortunate. Many traveled in covered wagons that were pulled by oxen. There were no paved roads, and a wagon could only travel between eight and twenty miles a day. Some people walked beside the wagon. It was a long, slow trip.

Transportation changed a lot in the 1800s. This was a time of **innovation** in technology. New machines changed the way people in communities lived and traveled. After the invention of the steam locomotive, trains could move along at an amazing twenty miles an hour. Trips that used to take a month could now take just a few days. Steamships also made travel across the ocean faster. People and goods traveling on a steamship reached their destinations much more quickly than before.

Trains made it easier for people to move to new places.

RESEARCH COMPANION, pp. 162–163

 English Learners SCAFFOLD

Use the following scaffolds to support student understanding of the lesson content.

Entering and Emerging

Work with students to understand the word *transportation* and the different kinds of transportation that people use. Provide sentence frames to help students describe transportation.

- In the 1800s, people traveled by _____.
- Today, people can travel using _____ or _____.

Developing and Expanding

Help students work in small groups to describe *transportation* and *innovation*. Ask: *What types of transportation did people use in the 1800s? What kinds of transportation do you use today? What is innovative about transportation today? What would make the transportation in your community even better? What innovations would make it faster or safer?* Encourage students to brainstorm innovative ideas.

Bridging and Reaching

Have partners discuss and make a list of the types of transportation available in their community. Ask: *What do you think transportation will be like in 50 years? What innovations will change how we travel?* Have students write short paragraphs comparing transportation today with transportation they think will be available in 50 years.

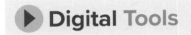 **Digital Tools**

Blended Learning

Students investigate curated resources and find evidence to answer the lesson question.

Interactive IMPACT

Students choose from print or digital **Inquiry Tools** to take notes.

In 1869, Americans celebrated when the final tracks in the nation's first transcontinental railroad were joined together. This new railroad connected the West Coast with the eastern part of the United States. It moved goods and people from one part of the nation to another. For the first time ever, farmers and ranchers could sell their fruits and vegetables across the nation. Goods made in factories in the East could be sold to people on the West Coast. This helped the nation's economy grow.

In communities across America, trolleys and cable cars had been pulled by horses. In the late 1800s, electricity provided the power. The electric trolley car made traveling around a community easier, cleaner, and faster.

Automobiles made another great change in the way people traveled. By 1900, inventors used the new technologies of steam, electricity, and gasoline engines to create "horseless carriages." In 1913, Henry Ford developed the assembly line. On an assembly line, a car moves down the line and each worker has a different job to do to build the car. This shortened the time it took to make a car. It cost less to make a car because it took less time. Cars became much cheaper to buy. More people could afford to buy a car.

TEXT: Williams, Henry T. The Pacific Tourist. Williams' Illustrated Trans-Continental Guide of Travel, from the Atlantic to the Pacific Ocean. New York: Henry T. Williams, Publisher, 1877. PHOTO: Library of Congress, Prints and Photographs Division. Photo by the Geo. R. Lawrence Co. [LC-USZ62-59207]

In Their Words... Henry T. Williams

"In no part of the world is travel made so easy and comfortable as on the Pacific Railroad. To travelers from the East it is a constant delight, and to ladies and families it is accompanied with absolutely no fatigue or discomfort."
—Henry T. Williams, *The Pacific Tourist*, 1876

In Their Words... Henry Ford

"I will build a motor car for the great multitude.... But it will be so low in price that no man making a good salary will be unable to own one."
—Henry Ford and Samuel Crowther, *My Life and Work*, 1922

As more people drove cars, new roads and highways were built. People could get to more places easily. Cars gave Americans new freedom. They could travel anywhere.

By the 1950s, the airplane became the fastest way to travel. A person could travel across the country on the same day. The makers of airplanes have made many innovations since then. Airplane travel is even faster today. Now, you can fly from Los Angeles to New York City in about five hours.

A modern Ford car

PHOTO: (t)MMarketing/Alamy Stock Photo; (b)Dmitriy Maksymenko Photography/Alamy Stock Photo

✓ Stop and Check

Talk What innovations in transportation were developed over the last hundred years? What were their benefits?

Find Details As you read, add new information to the graphic organizer on page 155 in your Inquiry Journal.

TEXT: Ford, Henry and Samuel Crowther. My Life and Work. New York: Doubleday, Page & Co. 1922.

RESEARCH COMPANION, pp. 164–165

Innovations in Transportation

1 Inspect Have students read pp. 164–165 and explain how electricity enabled travel in the late 1800s.

2 Find Evidence Use the questions below to check comprehension.

Explain What was important about the building of a transcontinental railroad? (It connected the East Coast and the West Coast of the nation, making it easier to move goods and people between coasts.) **DOK 2**

Cause and Effect How did Henry Ford's development of the assembly line lead to a change in how people traveled? (The invention of the assembly line enabled cars to be made faster, and more affordable. New highways and roads to hold all the new cars meant people could travel farther than before.) **DOK 3**

Interpret What did Henry Ford mean when he said that he would "build a car for the multitude"? (He meant he would build a car that the average person could afford to buy.) **DOK 2**

3 Make Connections

Draw Conclusions In the 1800s, how was the invention of new transportation related to the nation's economy? (The new transportation made it possible to ship and sell goods all over the country, so the economy grew.) **DOK 3**

✓ Stop and Check

Talk Have students discuss the question with a partner. (New highways were made which made travel easier and faster. Airplanes made it easier to travel long distances.)

 Spotlight on Vocabulary

Content Vocabulary

horseless carriages: the name for cars when they were first invented because they replaced carriages pulled by horses

trolley: an electric machine or vehicle that is used to carry people and goods that runs along the street on tracks

 Digital Tools

Blended Learning

Students investigate curated resources and find evidence to answer the Lesson Question.

Interactive IMPACT

Students **Research** and find evidence using digital format texts.

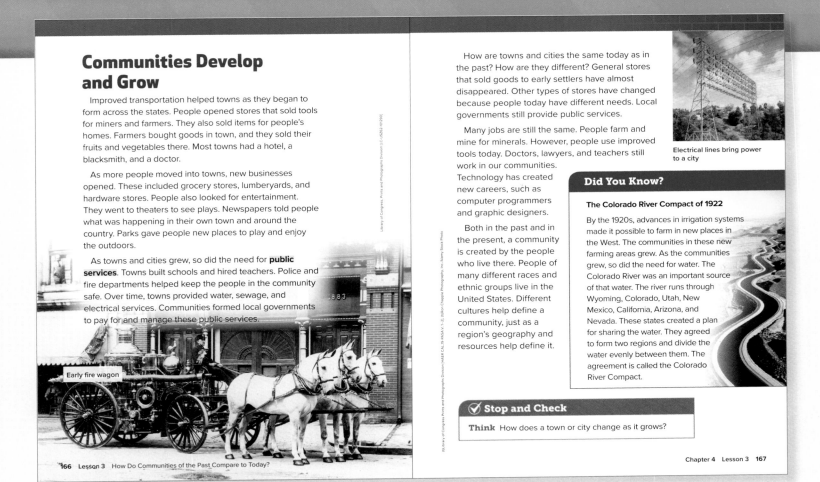

Communities Develop and Grow

Improved transportation helped towns as they began to form across the states. People opened stores that sold tools for miners and farmers. They also sold items for people's homes. Farmers bought goods in town, and they sold their fruits and vegetables there. Most towns had a hotel, a blacksmith, and a doctor.

As more people moved into towns, new businesses opened. These included grocery stores, lumberyards, and hardware stores. People also looked for entertainment. They went to theaters to see plays. Newspapers told people what was happening in their own town and around the country. Parks gave people new places to play and enjoy the outdoors.

As towns and cities grew, so did the need for **public services.** Towns built schools and hired teachers. Police and fire departments helped keep the people in the community safe. Over time, towns provided water, sewage, and electrical services. Communities formed local governments to pay for and manage these public services.

Early fire wagon

How are towns and cities the same today as in the past? How are they different? General stores that sold goods to early settlers have almost disappeared. Other types of stores have changed because people today have different needs. Local governments still provide public services.

Many jobs are still the same. People farm and mine for minerals. However, people use improved tools today. Doctors, lawyers, and teachers still work in our communities. Technology has created new careers, such as computer programmers and graphic designers.

Both in the past and in the present, a community is created by the people who live there. People of many different races and ethnic groups live in the United States. Different cultures help define a community, just as a region's geography and resources help define it.

Electrical lines bring power to a city

Did You Know?

The Colorado River Compact of 1922

By the 1920s, advances in irrigation systems made it possible to farm in new places in the West. The communities in these new farming areas grew. As the communities grew, so did the need for water. The Colorado River was an important source of that water. The river runs through Wyoming, Colorado, Utah, New Mexico, California, Arizona, and Nevada. These states created a plan for sharing the water. They agreed to form two regions and divide the water evenly between them. The agreement is called the Colorado River Compact.

✔ Stop and Check

Think How does a town or city change as it grows?

166 Lesson 3 How Do Communities of the Past Compare to Today?

Chapter 4 Lesson 3 167

RESEARCH COMPANION, pp. 166–167

Communities Develop and Grow

1 Inspect Have students read pp. 166–167 and describe public services.

2 Find Evidence Use the questions below to check comprehension.

Cause and Effect What were some of the effects of growing towns and cities? (People opened new businesses, local governments provided public services, and people looked for entertainment and new things to do.) **DOK 2**

Categorize Of the public services described in the text, which ones provide people with emergency services? (police and fire departments) Which ones provide essential things for everyday life? (water, sewage, and electricity services) How do public services help children? (build schools and hire teachers) **DOK 2**

3 Make Connections

Compare and Contrast How are towns and cities the same today as in the past? How are they different? (Answers will vary but should reference how stores are different, local government still provides public services, many jobs are the same, technology has improved tools and provided different jobs, and communities are still made up of many different people and cultures.) **DOK 3**

✔ Stop and Check

Talk Encourage students to think about what they know about schools, government, public services, jobs, stores, and different cultures. (Towns and cities grow to serve the needs of the people living there.)

Social Emotional Learning

Relationship Skills

Communicate Effectively
Remind students that when participating in a discussion, they need to politely communicate their ideas but also actively listen to others with respect. This involves listening closely to what others are saying and not interrupting the speaker. Part of communicating effectively is learning to listen intently to others.

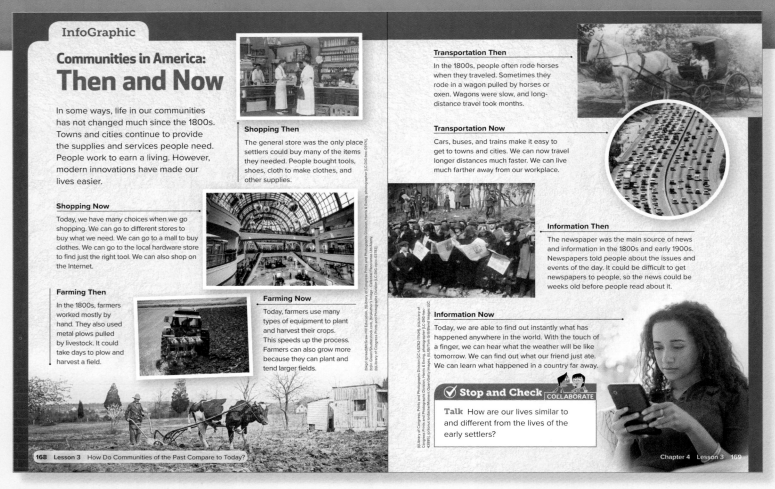

RESEARCH COMPANION, pp. 168–169

Communities in America: Then and Now

1 Inspect Have students read pp. 168–169 and explain how the pictures illustrate communities of the past and of today.

2 Find Evidence Use the questions below to check comprehension.

Interpret What has made our lives different from the 1800s? (stores for specific items, new machines and equipment, faster transportation, information technology) **DOK 2**

Infer Because farmers today use many types of equipment to farm, what can you infer about the size of farms today? (The farms are probably larger than in the past.) **DOK 3**

3 Make Connections

Draw Conclusions Based on the text about technology then and now, what can you conclude about today's technology for reporting news? (Today's news technology means people can get news from anywhere almost as soon as something happens, and it can be read throughout the world.) **DOK 3**

Stop and Check

Talk Guide students to think about a typical day in their lives and what would be the same or different if it were the 1800s. (People today have more shopping choices than early settlers. Technology today makes farming faster and easier. Cars, buses, and trains enable people to travel longer distances much faster than horses and wagons. People get the news as it is happening, but early settlers often had to wait weeks to hear news.)

Vocabulary

livestock: a compound word; farm animals, such as horses, cows, pigs

workplace: a compound word; the office or factory where people work

instantly: immediately, without delay

 Digital Tools

Blended Learning
Flip the research approach and find evidence in a digital format.

eBook

Students investigate using their **Research Companion** and **IMPACT Explorer Magazine eBooks** to find evidence.

Land and Water in Different Communities

Physical geography has played an important role in the development of the United States. People settled in places because of the land, water, and climate there. The geography continues to impact why people move and where they live.

Many settlers moved to new communities in search of fertile soil. By the mid-1800s, about half the population were farmers. Each region in the United States had good land for farming. As more farmers settled in an area, towns formed. Farmers sold their goods in town and purchased what they needed. This helped more businesses open. In this way, the towns continued to grow.

Innovations in rail transport meant farmers could ship their goods around the country. Later, new technology kept some train cars cool. This meant people in Idaho could eat blueberries grown in New Jersey or apples grown in New York. There are fewer farms in the United States today. Most of the towns formed around the early farms still remain.

Hammonton, New Jersey, is the blueberry capital of the world.

Water also played an important role in the development of communities in the United States. Many of the country's early communities were established along waterways, such as rivers or streams. Rivers and streams provided water for drinking and for crops. They also provided a way for people to transport goods to other communities.

Fort Wayne, Indiana, is one community that was impacted by water. The city was founded at the point where the St. Marys River and the St. Joseph River meet to form the Maumee River. These rivers helped Fort Wayne become a trade center in the early 1800s.

In the 1830s and 1840s, the Wabash & Erie Canal was built. The canal connected Lake Erie with the Ohio River. Fort Wayne was an important stop along the canal. Ships would sail into Orbison Basin, which was large enough for ships to turn around. This way the ships could return down the canal. Many immigrants came to help build the canal. Many others opened businesses in Fort Wayne along the canal. Fort Wayne grew as a result of its waterways. Today, Fort Wayne is the second-largest city in Indiana.

✓ Stop and Check

Talk How did land and water influence the growth and change of communities?

What Do You Think? How are communities today similar to and different from communities in the past?

RESEARCH COMPANION, pp. 170–171

Land and Water in Different Communities

1 Inspect Have students read pp. 170–171 and identify one way that water plays a role in the development of communities.

2 Find Evidence Use the questions below to check comprehension.

Cause and Effect What did it mean for farmers when new technology developed that cooled train cars? (It meant farmers could ship certain foods, like fruit that had to be kept cool, farther distances.) **DOK 2**

Draw Conclusions Why were waterways so important in the development of communities in the United States? (At a time when people traveled by wagon or by foot, waterways provided easier transportation for people and goods, as well as water for drinking and growing crops.) **DOK 2**

3 Make Connections

Identify Central Issues How did the building of the Wabash & Erie Canal impact Fort Wayne? (Many other businesses opened along the canal in Fort Wayne, and the city grew as a result of its waterways.) **DOK 3**

✓ Stop and Check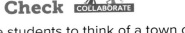

Talk Encourage students to think of a town or city in their region (or their own community) where land or water had a great impact on the growth of a community.

What Do You Think? Have students review the information on pp. 170–171 and consider how their own communities are different today than they were in the past.

✓ Check for Success

Compare and Contrast
Can students identify ways in which communities of the past are similar to and different from communities of today?

Differentiate

If Not, Guide students in reviewing their notes in the Venn diagram on p. 155 of their Inquiry Journals. Have students consider one big idea, such as transportation, and compare and contrast how it changed between the past and the present.

LESSON 3 REPORT

How Do Communities of the Past Compare to Today?

INQUIRY JOURNAL, pp. 156–157

Think About It

Remind students to review their research and think about how life in the 1800s was similar to or different from life today. Encourage students to review the information they included in their graphic organizer on p. 155. Direct students back to pp. 162–171 of their Research Companion if they need more information.

Write About It

Write and Cite Evidence Remind students to include the following elements in their response.

- Introduce the community and describe it.
- Identify two ways the community might be different today than it was in the past.
- Provide logical evidence supported by facts and details

Disciplines	4	3	2	1
History	Clear, complete description of their community; includes two ways the community might be different today than it was in the past; cites logical evidence, facts, and details	Brief but accurate description of their community; includes two ways the community might be different today than it was in the past; cites some logical evidence, some facts and details	Incomplete description of their community; mentions two ways the community might be different today than it was in the past; cites little evidence and few facts and details	Little or inaccurate description of their community; mentions one way their community might be different today than it was in the past; cites little or no facts and details

Talk About It

Share Your Ideas Have partners read their paragraphs to each other and talk about how their community today is different than it was in the past.

Assessment Students can check their understanding with feedback from the **Lesson Test** available online.

Connect to the Essential Question

Pull It Together Encourage students to think about innovations, technology, geography, natural resources, and population changes. Ask students which changes they think had the biggest impact on their community.

Inquiry Project Update Remind students to turn to Inquiry Journal pp. 130–131 for project information. If necessary, review the Project Checklist with students.

Think About It

Gather Evidence
What causes communities to change over time?

Write About It

Write and Cite Evidence
Write a paragraph telling two ways your community might be different now than in the past.

Answers will vary but should be supported with appropriate and well-reasoned evidence and reflect an understanding of how things have changed in your community.

Talk About It

Share Your Ideas
Read your paragraph to a partner. Then talk about how your community today is different from a century ago.

Connect to the EQ

Pull It Together
Think about the changes you have read and talked about in this lesson. Which change do you think had the biggest impact on your community?

Answers will vary but should reflect an understanding of the way innovations, technology, geographical features, natural resources, and population growth can change a community.

Inquiry Project Notes

156   Lesson 3   How Do Communities of the Past Compare to Today?

Chapter 4   Lesson 3   157

INQUIRY JOURNAL, pp. 156–157

English Learners   SCAFFOLD

Use the following scaffolds to support student writing.

Entering and Emerging

Guide students to think about transportation in the early 1800s and compare it with transportation in their community today. Have students draw pictures with short captions for their comparison. Provide students with sentence frames to help them write captions.

- In the 1800s many people traveled _____.
- Today, many people travel _____.

Developing and Expanding

Have small groups discuss their community today and how it might have changed from the 1800s. Ask questions to help them describe the differences. For example: *What is transportation like in your community today? What do you think it was like in the 1800s? How have the roads probably changed? How have cars changed?*

Bridging and Reaching

Have partners use a T-chart to list what their community is like now and how it might have been in the past. Encourage them to think about transportation, shopping, technology, jobs, buildings, and population. Then ask for volunteers to share one way their community is different. Guide students to write their paragraphs, describing two ways they think their community is different from the 1800s.

✔ Check for Success

Summarize Can students write a paragraph that explains two ways that a community today might be different now than in the past?

Differentiate

If Not, Have students use drawings and an oral presentation to compare the community's past and present.

LESSON QUESTION

How Can People and Events Change Communities?

 ## Connect to the Essential Question

Tell students that this lesson provides key research into the Chapter Essential Question: **How Does the Past Impact the Present?** Explain that they will learn about people who saw a problem and worked for a solution, invented a new technology, or overcame personal challenges, and how their efforts changed communities. Tell them they will read about important events that also caused changes and how all of these changes continue to impact people's lives today.

Lesson Objectives

- **Identify** problems faced by historical figures whose work for solutions changed their communities.
- **Describe** events that have changed communities and how technology provides solutions.
- **Identify** ways to find out about people and events in communities.
- **Write** a letter to a person in the lesson to explain his or her impact on the community.

Make Connections!

 ### CONNECT TO ELA

Reading
Ask and answer questions to demonstrate understanding of a text and refer explicitly to the text as the basis for the answers.

Research
Conduct short research projects that build knowledge about a topic.

Writing
Produce writing in which the development and organization are appropriate to task and purpose.

Speaking and Listening
Engage effectively in a range of collaborative discussions with diverse partners on grade 3 topics and texts, building on others' ideas and expressing students' own ideas clearly.

Language
Demonstrate command of the conventions of standard English grammar and usage when writing or speaking.

 ### COMMUNITY CONNECTIONS

To enrich what students have learned about people and events that change communities, identify a local event or person that changed the community. Have students visit a website connected with this person or event, or bring in a guest who can describe how this event or person impacted the community.

Lesson-At-A-Glance

1 ENGAGE
INQUIRY JOURNAL

pp. 158–163

- ▶ **Talk About It:** Photographs of cell phones over time
- ▶ **Analyze the Source:** Making Communication Mobile
- ▶ **Inquiry Tools:** Explore Problem and Solution

2 INVESTIGATE
RESEARCH COMPANION

pp. 172–179

- ▶ **People Can Change Communities**
- ▶ **Events Can Change Communities**
- ▶ **Finding Out About People and Events**

3 REPORT
INQUIRY JOURNAL

pp. 164–165

- ▶ **Think About It**
- ▶ **Write About It:** Write a Letter
- ▶ **Talk About It**
- ▶ **Connect to the Essential Question**

ASSESSMENT

- ▶ **Online Lesson Test**
- ▶ **Printable Lesson Test**

For more details, see pages T262–T263.

▶ Digital Tools

at **my.mheducation.com**

ePresentation

Teach the Engage, Investigate, and Report content to the whole class from **ePresentations** that launch directly from the lesson dashboard.

eBook

You can flip your instruction with the **IMPACT eBooks** found on your lesson dashboard.

Interactive IMPACT

Blend in digital content **when you want it** and **where you want it**.

Blended Learning features in the Teacher's Edition highlight ways to connect in-class work with online experiences to enhance learning.

Investigate current events with **IMPACT News**.

Explore domain-based vocabulary with **Explore Words** and **Word Play** vocabulary activities.

pp. 42–53

Go Further with IMPACT Explorer Magazine!

The **IMPACT Explorer Magazine** supports students' exploration of the Essential Question and provides additional resources for the EQ Inquiry Project.

LESSON 4 LANGUAGE LEARNERS

LESSON QUESTION

How Can People and Events Change Communities?

Language Objectives

- Use newly acquired content and academic vocabulary to talk and write about how people and events change communities.
- Write a letter using a standard letter format and formal language.
- Recognize and use synonyms and antonyms.

 Spanish Cognates

To support Spanish speakers, point out the cognates.

problem = problema

solution = solución

calculation = cálculo

publish = publicar

equal = igual

difficulty = dificultad

Introduce the Lesson

Set Purpose Explain to students that in this lesson, they will read informational texts to learn how people and events change communities.

Access Prior Knowledge Have students work in pairs to list ways that communities discussed in Lesson 3 are different than they were in the past. Review as a class the causes of those changes, including transportation, types of work, public services, and businesses. Ask students to describe changes they have seen in their communities and what they think led to those changes.

Spark Curiosity Have students look at the photograph on page 159 of the Inquiry Journal. Tell students that the earliest mobile phones were not portable; they were large and very heavy and were only installed in cars because they used so much power they had to be connected to a car battery. Marty Cooper demonstrated the first portable phone in 1973. It was nine inches long and weighed 2½ pounds. However, it took more than ten years before people could buy them in stores, and they cost thousands of dollars.

 Have groups of students discuss what additional features they think cell phones should have in the future.

Build Meaning & Support Language

Inquiry Journal

Analyze the Source (pages 160–161) Point to the Primary Source quote on page 160. Tell students that this is a statement by Martin Cooper, who created the first mobile phone that people could carry with them. Explain that the adjective *mobile* means "able to be moved." Define the word *gaped* as "looked at with an expression of surprise or shock." Read the sentence aloud. Explain that he is talking about walking down the street in New York while talking on a mobile phone at a time when no one had ever seen such a thing. Ask: *Why did other people gape at Cooper?* (Answers will vary, but students should understand that this was a new and unexpected sight that surprised and shocked people.)

Inquiry Tools (pages 162–163) Tell students they will explore **Problem and Solution** as they read the selections in the Research Companion about how people and events changed communities. Read aloud the steps listed on page 162 and the graphic organizer headings, and explain any words students don't understand. Then work with students to complete the graphic organizer on page 162 with information from "Making Communication Mobile." Tell students that the graphic organizer on page 163 will help them organize the information they read in the Research Companion. Say: *Several problems are described in the first box. As you read the Research Companion, look for what each person did to try to solve the problem. Write those steps in the second box. In the third box, write how the person solved the problem.*

Research Companion

People Can Change Communities (pages 172–175) After you read page 172, write the words *inequality*, *equal*, and *equally* on the board. Explain that *equal* is an adjective meaning "the same in some way." Here it describes the noun *African Americans*. Point out *equally* in the last paragraph. Tell students that it describes the verb *treated*. Then explain that *equal* can be made into a thing by adding *-ity* to form *equality*. Finally, tell students that the prefix *-in* means "not." Point out that the noun *inequality* means the opposite of *equality*.

Tell students that when someone *overcomes* something, he or she successfully deals with something difficult, such as a *disability*, a condition that limits a person's ability to do everyday things. After you read about Harriet Tubman, point out that *make a journey* means "take a trip." Explain to students that the Underground Railroad was a secret pattern of paths and hiding places that people used to helped enslaved people travel north and escape to freedom, but it was not an actual railroad and was usually not under the ground.

Events Can Change Communities (pages 176–177) Discuss the meaning of *natural disaster*. Explain that a *disaster* is a sudden event that causes much damage. A *natural disaster*, such as a flood, is caused by nature rather than humans. Another type of natural disaster is a *wildfire*, a large fire that burns in a wild, or natural, area. Explain that wildfires burn away trees and plants to leave bare soil, and later the rain makes the ground muddy. *Mudslides* happen when muddy soil on hillsides slides down onto roads or houses.

Finding Out About People and Events (pages 178–179) Explain that a *source* is a thing or person that supplies something wanted or needed. Ask: *What are news sources?* (places where people can get news; newspapers, websites, television) Tell students that the word *blog* is a shortened form of an earlier word *weblog*. Explain that a *blog* is a personal website that presents one person's thoughts. Check that students understand the difference between fact and opinion.

Inquiry Journal

Report Your Findings (pages 164–165) Explain to students that a formal letter is written to people one doesn't know. Review with students the standard parts of a formal letter. Explain that in the body of the letter, students should tell the person why they are writing, mention the problem and how the person solved it, and describe how it impacted the community. Choose a person from the lesson, and model for students how to restate the graphic organizer notes in the form of a letter to the person. Encourage students to use the new vocabulary words they have learned.

Language Forms & Conventions

Synonyms and Antonyms Explain to students that synonyms are different words that have the same or similar meanings. Using synonyms makes writing interesting because it avoids using the same word over and over. Antonyms are words with opposite or nearly opposite meanings. Using antonyms can show contrast or add emphasis to writing.

Example	Synonym	Antonym
illness	sickness	health

 Have students work in pairs to identify words in the text that have similar or opposite meanings. Have them add the words to the chart. Allow the use of a dictionary if necessary.

Cross-Cultural Connection

One of the largest natural disasters of the 20th century occurred in the Philippines when Mount Pinatubo erupted in 1991. It produced avalanches of gas, ash, and mudflows as well as a cloud of volcanic ash hundreds of miles wide. Scientists used technology to forecast the eruption, enabling many people living near the volcano to move to safer places. However, it dramatically changed the area as it buried numerous towns and villages.

Leveled Support

Entering & Emerging
Help students form complete sentences from their notes.

Developing & Expanding
Encourage students to use words such as *because*, *due to*, and *as a result* to signal how the person impacted the community.

Bridging & Reaching
Suggest that students include an introductory sentence to say why they are writing the letter or why they admire what the person has done.

Language Transfer

The abundance of synonyms in English proves particularly challenging for the non-native speaker. English has drawn vocabulary from several different language groups such as Anglo-Saxon, Latin, French, and Greek. This rich mixture has resulted in an unusually high number of synonyms and near-synonyms. However, other languages may have even more synonyms for particular words important in their culture. For example, Arabic has hundreds of words for *camel*.

LESSON 4 ENGAGE

LESSON QUESTION

How Can People and Events Change Communities?

INQUIRY JOURNAL, pp. 158–159

Bellringer

Prompt students to recall information discussed in the previous lesson. Say: *Communities today are different in many ways from communities of the past. What are some public services in your community today? What problem does each of those public services solve?* (Answers may include schools, police and fire departments, and utilities and the problem each solves.)

Lesson Outcomes

Discuss the lesson question and lesson outcomes with students.

- Explain to students that knowing about the people and events that have changed communities helps in understanding how the past influences communities today and the importance of recognizing problems and working for solutions.

- Ask students what they will be writing. (a letter to a person in the lesson about how he or she changed a community)

Talk About It

Guide students to look at the items in the photograph, read the caption, and answer the question. (Answers will vary, but students should understand that cell phones have become smaller, lighter, and can do more things.) Explain that the items are from different time periods, with the newest ones on the bottom half of p. 159. Provide sentence frames as needed.

- The items shown are _____.
- The items are similar because all the items _____.
- The items are different because some items _____.

 Collaborative Conversations

Take Turns Talking As students engage in partner, small-group, and whole-class discussions, encourage them to

- wait for a person to finish before they speak. They should not speak over others.
- quietly raise their hand to let others know they would like a turn to speak.
- ask others in the groups to share their opinions so that all students have a chance to share.

Lesson 4
How Can People and Events Change Communities?

Lesson Outcomes

What Am I Learning?
In this lesson, you will use your investigative skills to explore ways in which people and events change communities.

Why Am I Learning It?
Reading and talking about ways in which people and events have changed communities can help you understand your community better.

How Will I Know That I Learned It?
You will be able to write a letter to one of the people you have learned about in this lesson to explain how he or she has changed your community.

The cell phone has changed a lot since early cell phones.

Talk About It COLLABORATE

Look closely at the photos. What are some changes about the different devices that you notice?

INQUIRY JOURNAL, pp. 158–159

English Learners SCAFFOLD

Use the following scaffolds to support student understanding of lesson outcomes.

Entering and Emerging

Read the caption aloud. Work with individual students to help them describe each phone. Provide them with a list of simple nouns and adjectives to use when identifying details, such as *cell phone, flip phone, keypad, screen, large, small, heavy, light*. Guide students to use this sentence frame to describe each phone as they point to it: This _____ is _____.

Developing and Expanding

Have partners take turns pointing to two of the cell phones in the picture while the other partner compares the two. Provide them with a word list (*cell phone, flip phone, keypad, screen, large, small, heavy, light*) and sentence frames to identify details: This _____ is _____, but this _____ is _____.

Bridging and Reaching

Have partners view the picture and list nouns and adjectives that they can use to describe the cell phones. Direct each partner to choose one phone and write a sentence describing it. Have partners read their sentences aloud to one another. If time allows, have students write and read aloud sentences that compare two phones.

Social Emotional Learning

Social Awareness

Respect Collaborative discussions are an opportunity to teach skills such as respect. Remind students that they can show respect by listening attentively, waiting to take turns, and making positive comments about others' views.

 **Digital** Tools

Blended Learning
Students engage with the lesson question and discussion prompts.

Interactive IMPACT

Discuss the **Lesson Question** and **Talk About It** with the whole class.

Making Communication Mobile

PRIMARY SOURCE

In Their Words... Martin Cooper

"As I walked down the street while talking on the phone . . . New Yorkers gaped at the sight of someone actually moving around while making a phone call."

— Martin Cooper, 2011

Martin Cooper, inventor of the first truly mobile phone

To make a telephone call in the mid-twentieth century, you had to go where the phone was: in your home, in the school office, or in a phone booth. Phones were connected to the phone system by a telephone wire. If you moved to another city, you needed to get a new phone number.

1 Inspect

Read the title and the Primary Source. What do you think this text will be about?

Circle words you do not know.

Underline clues that will help you answer:
- Who is Martin Cooper?
- How did he change the way people live and do business?
- Why were New Yorkers surprised to see what Martin Cooper was doing?

My Notes

_____

_____

_____

_____

_____

Martin Cooper changed this forever. He and a team of engineers designed the first mobile phone a person could carry anywhere. Cooper made the first cell phone call in 1973. However, it took ten years before people could actually buy a cell phone.

The early mobile phones were big and heavy, but technology has improved them. Today's smartphone fits into a pocket. It can do many things. It is a camera, calendar, calculator, and notepad. You can text, e-mail, play games, or surf the web on your phone.

The graph below shows the number of people who owned cell phones over a period of thirty years.

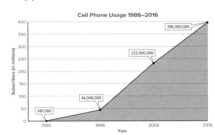

Cell Phone Usage 1986–2016

This graph shows how the number of cell phones has increased over a thirty-year period.

2 Find Evidence

Interpret the Graph Draw a straight line on the graph from the dot at 1986 to the dot at 2016. What do you notice about the line between 1986 and 2016?

Underline the dates and events in the text above.

Write the dates in the correct place on the graph.

Talk What are some possible reasons cell phone use changed so much between 1986 and 1996?

3 Make Connections

Talk How has the increased availability of cell phones solved problems? How has it created new problems?

INQUIRY JOURNAL, pp. 160–161

Analyze the Source

Spotlight on Content

Background Information

- Martin Cooper was an engineer and general manager of the communication systems division of a large telecommunications company.
- The first cell phone call was from Martin Cooper to his counterpart at a rival company, letting the competition know that Martin's company had succeeded.

1 Inspect

Read Have students read the quote, text, and captions. Remind them to circle unfamiliar words and underline clues that will help them answer the questions.

- What was the sequence of phone inventions that led to the pocket-sized cell phone? (phones connected to cords, car phones, large personal mobile phones, pocket-sized cell phones)

2 Find Evidence

Interpret the Graph Explain that the line on the graph shows a slower increase, or upward movement, between 1986 and 1996, but the increase is faster and steadier from 1996 to 2016.

3 Make Connections

Talk Have students share with a partner a situation they know of when a cell phone was used to ensure people's safety or to communicate urgent information.

Reading Numbers Aloud

Write a number 1 on the board and have students say it aloud. Write a zero to the right of it and have students say *ten*. Add another zero and say *one hundred*. Add a comma and a zero, say *one thousand*. Continue the process to *one million*.

▶ Digital Tools

Blended Learning

Students read informational texts and analyze primary sources.

Interactive IMPACT

Have students practice and apply the strategy of close reading as they analyze text.

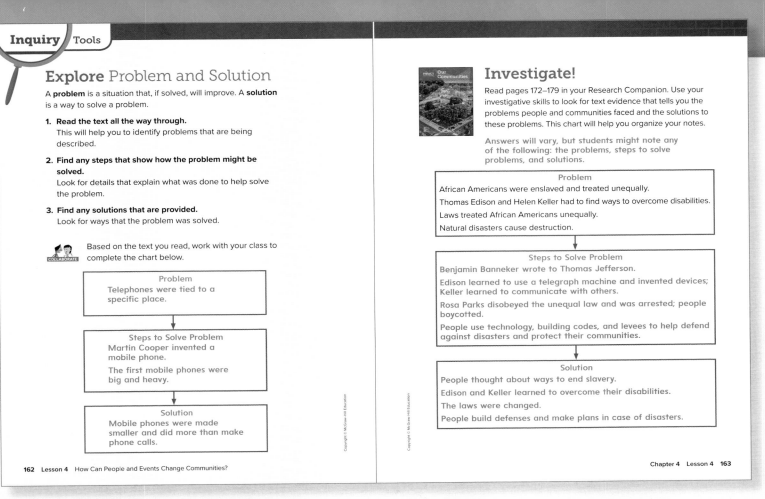

Explore Problem and Solution

A **problem** is a situation that, if solved, will improve. A **solution** is a way to solve a problem.

1. **Read the text all the way through.**
   This will help you to identify problems that are being described.

2. **Find any steps that show how the problem might be solved.**
   Look for details that explain what was done to help solve the problem.

3. **Find any solutions that are provided.**
   Look for ways that the problem was solved.

 Based on the text you read, work with your class to complete the chart below.

> **Problem**
> Telephones were tied to a specific place.

⬇

> **Steps to Solve Problem**
> Martin Cooper invented a mobile phone.
> The first mobile phones were big and heavy.

⬇

> **Solution**
> Mobile phones were made smaller and did more than make phone calls.

162   Lesson 4   How Can People and Events Change Communities?

Investigate!

Read pages 172–179 in your Research Companion. Use your investigative skills to look for text evidence that tells you the problems people and communities faced and the solutions to these problems. This chart will help you organize your notes.

Answers will vary, but students might note any of the following: the problems, steps to solve problems, and solutions.

> **Problem**
> African Americans were enslaved and treated unequally.
> Thomas Edison and Helen Keller had to find ways to overcome disabilities.
> Laws treated African Americans unequally.
> Natural disasters cause destruction.

⬇

> **Steps to Solve Problem**
> Benjamin Banneker wrote to Thomas Jefferson.
> Edison learned to use a telegraph machine and invented devices; Keller learned to communicate with others.
> Rosa Parks disobeyed the unequal law and was arrested; people boycotted.
> People use technology, building codes, and levees to help defend against disasters and protect their communities.

⬇

> **Solution**
> People thought about ways to end slavery.
> Edison and Keller learned to overcome their disabilities.
> The laws were changed.
> People build defenses and make plans in case of disasters.

Chapter 4   Lesson 4   163

INQUIRY JOURNAL, pp. 162–163

Inquiry Tools

Explore Problem and Solution

Read Discuss with students the steps for identifying and solving a problem. Encourage students to list details that signal important information.

Guide Practice Have students review the text on pp. 160–161. Then work with them to complete the graphic organizer on p. 162. Explain that they will use a similar graphic organizer to organize their independent research.

Check Understanding Confirm student understanding of the inquiry skill, Explore Problem and Solution. If students cannot identify the problems and solutions from the text, review the steps on p. 162.

Investigate!

Have students read pp. 172–179 in the Research Companion. Tell them the information will help them answer the lesson question *How Can People and Events Change Communities?*

Take Notes Tell students that they will take notes in the graphic organizer on p. 163 of the Inquiry Journal. Remind them that taking notes will help them understand and remember the information they learn. Explain to students the importance of thinking about problems as they take notes. This will help them identify the solution when they read about it.

LESSON 4 INVESTIGATE

LESSON QUESTION

How Can People and Events Change Communities?

RESEARCH COMPANION, pp. 172–173

Background Information

- **Benjamin Banneker's** grandmother was an indentured servant from England. She eventually became prosperous enough to buy and free two enslaved people, one of whom she married. Her daughter, Benjamin's mother, also married a freed enslaved person.
- After inventing the phonograph, **Thomas Edison** wanted to enhance it by linking it to photographic images that seemed to move. Although pairing sound with images proved too difficult, his Kinetoscope presented silent movies. A person could look through a peephole into a viewing box where a series of sequential photos flipped quickly to give the illusion of motion.
- **Drones** have many uses in natural disasters. Because they can fly over disaster areas and take high resolution pictures, drones are used to create maps for rescue and relief crews. In disaster areas where conditions prevent access, drones can quickly be deployed to deliver needed supplies and equipment.

People Can Change Communities

1 Inspect Have students read pp. 172–173 and describe Benjamin Banneker.

2 Find Evidence Use the questions below to check comprehension. Remind students to support their answers with text evidence.

Infer Based on the details you read about Banneker's inventions, what can you tell about him? (Answers will vary, but students should understand that he was curious, determined, and hardworking.) **DOK 2**

Cite Evidence What facts would you select to show that Banneker was upset about slavery and racial inequality? (He wrote a letter to Thomas Jefferson asking that Jefferson work toward ending slavery.) **DOK 3**

3 Make Connections

Draw Conclusions What conclusions can you draw about how Benjamin Banneker contributed to change in colonial America? (Banneker saw the problem of slavery and racial inequality around him. He educated himself and worked hard to be a productive citizen. He tried to persuade Thomas Jefferson to end slavery. Although he did not solve the slavery problem, he helped start the process.) **DOK 3**

Lesson 4 — How Can People and Events Change Communities?

People Can Change Communities

Benjamin Banneker changed our nation's capital and how early leaders of our nation viewed the African American community.

Banneker grew up seeing slavery and racial inequality all around him. Many people at the time did not think African Americans were equal with other people, but Banneker proved them wrong.

He was an inventor, an astronomer, an author, and a mathematician. At 15, he invented an irrigation system for his family farm. He later made the first clock in America. He went on to write an almanac with data about astronomy and comments about society.

In 1791, Banneker sent his almanac and a letter to Secretary of State Thomas Jefferson to show African Americans were equal to others. He told Jefferson that African Americans were not being treated equally and encouraged him to help end slavery. Jefferson later asked that Banneker be used to help plan the new capital, Washington, D.C. When the lead planner quit and took the city plans, Banneker saved the project by redoing all the lost plans from his memory!

172 Lesson 4   How Can People and Events Change Communities?

Benjamin Banneker was an American scientist. He also worked to end slavery and bring equality for all African Americans.

Chapter 4   Lesson 4   173

RESEARCH COMPANION, pp. 172–173

English Learners SCAFFOLD

Use the following scaffolds to support student understanding of the lesson content.

Entering and Emerging

Write this sentence on the board: *Many people at the time did not think African Americans were equal with other people, but Banneker proved them wrong.* Circle the word *but* and explain that it signals a contrast. Underline the words before and after *but* and read them aloud as separate sentences. Provide sentence frames to help students understand the contrast:

- Many people did _____ think African Americans were equal with other people. (not)

- Banneker proved them _____. (wrong)

Developing and Expanding

Have students follow along as you read aloud the second sentence of paragraph two. Point out that the word *but* signals a contrast between the words before and after *but*. Ask: *Did people believe African Americans were equal?* (no) *What did Banneker do?* (He proved them wrong.) *How did he do it?* (He became an inventor, an author, and helped develop Washington, D.C.)

Bridging and Reaching

Have students reread the second sentence of paragraph two. Point out that the word *but* signals a contrast. Ask students what Banneker did and how he did it.

Digital Tools

Blended Learning
Guide students as they investigate the lesson content.

Interactive IMPACT

Students choose from print or digital **Inquiry Tools** to take notes.

Thomas Edison was born in 1847. He was partially deaf, which made school difficult for him. Edison's mother taught him at home. While he was still in his teens, he learned to operate a telegraph machine. He began inventing devices to help him overcome his hearing difficulties. Eventually, he became a full-time inventor. He invented the phonograph that plays records, the light bulb, and more. His inventions transformed communities worldwide.

In 1882, when Helen Keller was almost two years old, she was very sick. This illness left her blind and deaf. Her teacher, Anne Sullivan, used finger signals developed for deaf people. She "spelled" words into the palm of Helen Keller's hand. Helen learned to connect the signals to the things around her. She learned to read Braille, a writing system for blind people that uses letters made of raised dots. Eventually, Keller even learned to speak aloud. She later went to college. Keller then became a writer, speaker, and leader for people with vision and hearing disabilities. Her life story and work showed that everyone should be treated as valuable members of our communities.

Harriet Tubman escaped slavery by running away to Philadelphia. She was free, but she did not forget the people she left behind. She made many dangerous journeys to help enslaved people escape to freedom. She led them along a route called the Underground Railroad. During the Civil War, she was a scout, nurse, and spy. After the war, she took care of orphans and elderly people. Tubman's work touched many lives and changed many communities.

Slavery ended almost fifty years before

Rosa Parks was born in 1913. However, African Americans were still treated unfairly. In Montgomery, Alabama, where Parks lived, there were laws forcing African Americans to ride in seats at the back of a bus. One day in 1955, a bus driver told Rosa Parks to give her seat to a white man. She refused. Her arrest and trial led to a very special kind of protest called a **boycott**. African Americans all over the Montgomery community stopped riding the bus. The boycott lasted until the Supreme Court of the United States told the community that its law was illegal. Rosa Parks changed her community and the nation.

✓ Stop and Check

Talk With a partner, discuss the problem each person you read about faced.

Find Details As you read, add new information to the graphic organizer on page 163 in your Inquiry Journal.

RESEARCH COMPANION, pp. 174–175

People Can Change Communities

1 Inspect Have students read pp. 174–175 and define the term boycott.

2 Find Evidence Use the questions below to check comprehension.

Compare What did Thomas Edison and Helen Keller have in common? How were they different? (Helen Keller and Thomas Edison both had disabilities. Edison was partially deaf, and Helen Keller was completely deaf and blind. Both overcame their disabilities and helped other people.) **DOK 3**

3 Make Connections

Draw Conclusions How did Benjamin Banneker and Helen Keller show that a person can succeed even when faced with challenges? (Many people thought African Americans were not equal, but Banneker became a scientist and wrote an almanac. Helen Keller's disabilities could have kept her from living a productive life or connecting with her world. However, she learned to communicate, read Braille, and became an example of how a person can overcome disabilities.) **DOK 3**

✓ Stop and Check

Talk (African Americans in Benjamin Banneker's time were enslaved and he experienced racial inequality. Thomas Edison was partially deaf, which made school difficult for him. Helen Keller was blind and deaf and struggled to communicate. Harriet Tubman had to escape slavery and faced dangers to help other enslaved people escape to freedom. Rosa Parks faced racial inequality and laws that were unfair to African Americans.)

Find Details Explain to students that they should note the facts and details that will help them answer the Essential Question.

Spotlight on Vocabulary

Content Vocabulary

disability: a condition in a person's body or mind that makes everyday activities difficult

inventor: someone who invents, or creates, something new

▶ Digital Tools

Blended Learning
Students investigate curated resources and find evidence to answer the lesson question.

Interactive IMPACT

Students **Research** and find evidence using digital format texts.

Events Can Change Communities

Events can change communities as well. A natural disaster is one event that can impact a community.

In 2017–2018, California experienced one of the largest wildfires in the state's history. The Thomas Fire burned 440 square miles. Thousands of people were evacuated from their homes. Entire neighborhoods were destroyed. The fires were followed by heavy rains and mudslides. Major roads were blocked, which made emergency response difficult. Homes and people were buried under rivers of mud.

Other parts of the country face hurricanes or tornadoes each year. There were more hurricanes and tornadoes than usual in 2017. That year, Hurricanes Harvey, Irma, and Maria ripped through the south Atlantic and Gulf states. Several Caribbean islands, Florida, Louisiana, and parts of Texas suffered damage.

Disasters change the appearance of communities. They destroy buildings and landscapes. Researchers are helping communities change in ways that make them safer during natural disasters. In areas with flooding, community money builds and repairs levees. Levees are high banks that hold back floodwaters. Levees protect communities from flooding, but they change the appearance of the landscape.

Flooding has impacted the people in this community.

Did You Know?

NASA's Earth Science Disasters Program uses satellites during disasters. Information from satellite images helps communities prepare, respond, and recover from disasters. Satellite images help track lava flows and hot spots in volcanoes. NASA also uses these images to measure rainfall and map flooding and mudslides.

Drones and robots are other technologies used during disasters. Both can go places where people cannot. Drones fly overhead and take pictures. They can locate people injured or lost in a disaster. They can help rescuers find paths and drop supplies if needed. They also help response teams see damages and make decisions for rebuilding. Robots are used for disaster search and rescue. They can go into areas that are unsafe for people. They carry cameras and sensors that send information to rescue teams.

The passage of a law is another event that can impact a community. In the past, for example, disabled Americans had been treated unfairly. The Americans with Disabilities Act of 1990 was passed to protect the civil rights of people with disabilities. Thanks to this law, people with mental or physical issues cannot be fired from their jobs simply because of their disabilities.

Stop and Check

Think How is technology providing rescue solutions in natural disasters?

RESEARCH COMPANION, pp. 176–177

Events Can Change Communities

1 Inspect Have students read pp. 176–177 and define natural disaster using their own words.

2 Find Evidence Use the questions below to check comprehension.

Summarize How do fires, floods, and other disasters change the appearance of a community? (Fires, tornadoes, hurricanes, and floods destroy buildings and landscapes; they can bury homes and roads under rubble or mud.) **DOK 2**

Assess Which form of technology described in the text do you think is most effective in saving lives? Why? (Answers will vary, but students should support their choices with text evidence.) **DOK 3**

3 Make Connections

Formulate What are two actions you think your community should take so it will be prepared for a natural disaster? (Answers will vary, but students should understand that food, water, shelter, and medical care are immediate needs in a disaster.) **DOK 3**

✓ Stop and Check

Think Encourage students to use specific details from the text to support their answers. (Satellites and drones can aid in showing the extent of damage; drones can take pictures, locate people, and drop supplies; robots can perform search and rescue.)

Social Emotional Learning

Relationship Skills

Teamwork Learning to work together as a team is essential to succeed in the classroom and in life. Remind students to allow each person to express ideas and propose possible solutions. Sharing ideas can prompt further creative thinking.

Spotlight on Language

Understanding Language

find out: to learn information

keep people informed: give people news and information about events

update: to add the most recent details about something; to change something to make it more modern

what is going on: what is happening

Finding Out About People and Events

1 Inspect Have students read pp. 178–179 and identify four types of news sources.

2 Find Evidence Use the questions below to check comprehension.

Categorize Have students write down the following headings: local newspaper, nearby big city newspaper, city government website. Ask them to write under the appropriate heading the best place to find the following news: city council meetings, street closures, trash pick-up schedule (city government website); national news, events in other states, international events (big city newspaper); events at the library, crime reports for the county, local gatherings (local newspaper) **DOK 2**

Differentiate What are the advantages of each newspaper format pictured in the illustrations? (Answers will vary, but students should understand that the electronic format is easily navigated and updated in real time, and that the paper format is easily portable and does not require a computer.) **DOK 3**

3 Make Connections

Compare How do you find out information about people and events at school? How is it similar to finding out about people and events in the community and world? (Take-home papers providing classroom and school news are similar to newspapers. Teacher and school websites also connect students and their parents to classroom and school events. Agendas and minutes from school board meetings are often available online) **DOK 2**

☑ Stop and Check

Talk (Answers may vary but should include that news sources from different places can be accessed to connect people with information.)

What Do You Think? (Answers will vary, but students should include supporting details from the lesson.)

▶ Digital Tools

Blended Learning

Students investigate curated resources and find evidence to answer the lesson question.

ePresentation

Students **Research** and find evidence using digital format texts.

Finding Out About People and Events

News sources are one way for you to learn about people and events in your community. News sources can tell about your community today or your community's past. Newspapers, websites, and television stations are just some of the ways people can get the news and connect with their communities.

Many large cities have newspapers and websites that are read across the country. Every day, newspapers publish articles about local, state, and national events. It helps keep people informed.

Smaller communities also have newspapers, websites, and blogs. The newspapers may be printed only once a week. However, a newspaper's website may be updated more often. Local news sources are important because people need to know what is going on in their communities. You can stay involved with events even while traveling.

Newspapers tell us what is going on in our community and in our nation.

The national, state, and local governments have websites that give information about the types of services they provide. They also tell community members about events in which they can give their ideas for improving the community.

Blogs are another way you can learn about people and events in your community. Sometimes, reporters for news organizations publish blogs on newspaper websites. Blogs may be updated daily or less often. A blog contains the reflections, opinions, and ideas of the writer. As a result, a blog may be biased. That means it may present information which favors a particular point of view.

Another way to find out about people and events in your community is through a historical society. A local historical society can tell how the community has changed and why. They can help connect people who are interested in the history of their communities.

Newspaper vending machines line this street.

✓ Stop and Check

Talk How do news sources help you find out about people and events in different communities?

What Do You Think? What are some ways people and events can change communities?

RESEARCH COMPANION, pp. 178–179

EL English Learners SCAFFOLD

Use the following scaffolds to support student understanding of language.

Entering and Emerging
As students consider the Stop and Check question, offer them a bank of words to for a word sort to describe newspapers and websites: *electronic, paper, current, local, national.*

Developing and Expanding
Have students come up with a list of words that describe a newspaper and another list that describe a website. Ask students to use one pair of words in a compound sentence that compares the two sources: A newspaper is _____ but a website is _____.

Bridging and Reaching
Have students find words or phrases that indicate what strengths newspapers or websites have. Have them form an opinion on which news source they would be most likely to use and justify that opinion.

✓ Check for Success

Explain Are students able to explain how people and events can change communities?

Differentiate

If Not, Have students identify one problem from the Problem box in the graphic organizer on p. 163 of the Inquiry Journal. Prompt students to state the problem, name a person who helped solve the problem, and identify what solutions they used.

LESSON 4 REPORT

How Can People and Events Change Communities?

Think About It

INQUIRY JOURNAL, pp. 164–165

Remind students to consider problems faced by the people they read about as well as the solutions to these problems. Encourage students to review the information in their graphic organizers. Direct students back to pp. 172–179 of their Research Companion if they need more information.

Write About It

Write and Cite Evidence Remind students to include the following elements in their responses.

- Identify the person from the lesson to whom they will write the letter.
- Review the problem faced by this person, the steps taken to solve the problem, and the solution to the problem.
- Describe specific ways in which this solution has impacted the student's community.
- Use chapter vocabulary as appropriate.

Discipline(s)	4	3	2	1
History	Student identifies a person from the lesson and provides evidence showing how the problem was solved and how it has impacted the student's community.	Student identifies a person and provides some evidence on how the problem was solved and how it has impacted the student's community.	Student identifies a person but fails to provide supporting details on how the problem was solved and/or how the student's community was impacted.	Student does not fully answer the question or provide evidence showing how the problem was solved and how the community was impacted.

Talk About It

Explain Remind students to actively listen to one another's reasons. Encourage them to ask for clarification of any points that are unclear.

Assessment Students can check their understanding with feedback from the **Lesson Test** available online.

Connect to the Essential Question

Pull It Together Before students respond, discuss ways in which their community has changed over time.

Inquiry Project Update Remind students to turn to Inquiry Journal p. 131 for project information. If necessary, review the Project Checklist with students. At this point in the chapter, students should focus on the fourth bullet.

Report Your Findings

Think About It

Gather Evidence

Review your research. Based on the information you have gathered, describe at least two problems people have faced. What were their solutions to these problems?

Write About It

Write and Cite Evidence

Write a letter to one of the people you have learned about in this lesson. Tell this person how he or she has impacted your community.

Students' answers will vary but should identify Benjamin Banneker, Thomas Edison, Helen Keller, Harriet Tubman, or Rosa Parks and explain his or her impact on the local community. They could also identify the people who make or use rescue technology.

Talk About It

COLLABORATE

Explain

Share your letter with a partner. Discuss why each of you wrote to the person you chose.

History

Connect to the ESSENTIAL QUESTION EQ

Pull It Together

What people and events have changed your community? List three ideas to share with others.

1. Answers should reflect the local
2. community. Encourage discussion of key
3. people and of natural disasters that have happened in your community or state.

ESSENTIAL QUESTION EQ

Inquiry Project Notes

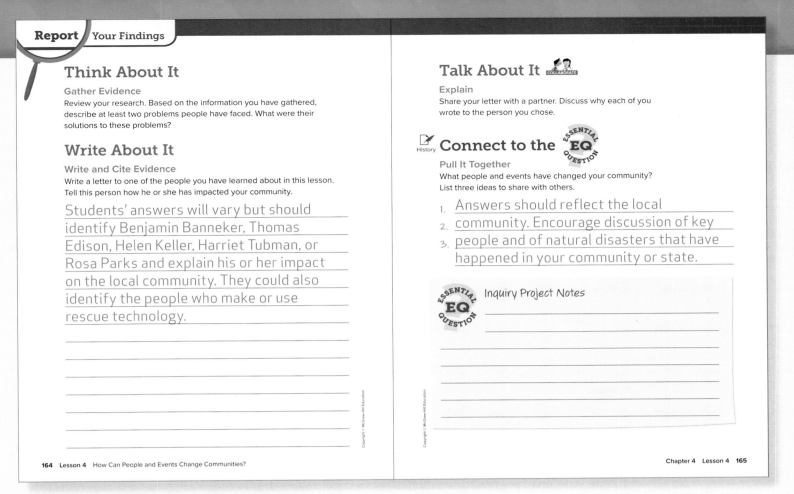

INQUIRY JOURNAL, pp. 164–165

EL English Learners SCAFFOLD

Use the following scaffolds to support student writing.

Entering and Emerging

Tell students that they will use formal language in their letters because they are writing to someone they do not know. Guide students in completing the following sentence frames for the body of the letter:

- I learned about you in ______________.
- I respect what you did about ______________.
- My community has changed because you ______________.

Developing and Expanding

Tell students that they will use formal language in their letters because they are writing to someone they do not know. Explain that they will write the main paragraph of the letter. Have students work with a partner to write a short sentence that answers each question. Ask: *Who are you writing to? What did the person do? Is your community different because of this person?*

Bridging and Reaching

Provide students with a "skeleton" letter that labels the standard parts of a formal letter: the date, writer's address, recipient's address, greeting, body text, closing, and signature. Have students work independently to write the body paragraph explaining who they chose and how he or she impacted the community. Have students exchange letters and give each other feedback.

✓ Check for Success

Summarize Can students write a letter to explain how a historical figure has impacted their community?

Differentiate

If Not, Have students discuss the assignment in groups and present their ideas as a public service announcement to the class.

What Can Comparing Different Communities Tell Us About How Communities Change Over Time?

Connect to the Essential Question

Tell students that this lesson will help them answer the Chapter Essential Question: **How Does the Past Impact the Present?** Explain that they will learn about how communities change over time. They will also generate a list of research topics about their community that takes into account features that would attract people to move there.

Lesson Objectives

- **Compare and contrast** Detroit and Kuala Lumpur.
- **Identify** ways communities change over time.
- **Explain** why groups work to save community landmarks.
- **Write** a research plan indicating what topics in their community interest students, and what might attract newcomers to the community.

Make Connections!

CONNECT TO ELA

Reading **Ask** and answer questions to demonstrate understanding of a text and refer explicitly to the text as the basis for the answers.

Research **Recall** information from experiences or gather information from print and digital sources; take brief notes on sources and sort evidence into provided categories.

Writing **Craft** opinion pieces on familiar topics or texts, supporting a point of view with reasons.

Speaking and Listening **Come to discussions prepared**, having read or studied required material; explicitly draw on that preparation and other information known about the topic to explore ideas under discussion.

Language **Use** sentence-level context as a clue to the meaning of a word or phrase.

COMMUNITY CONNECTIONS

To enrich what students have learned about saving landmarks in Detroit and Kuala Lumpur, research a landmark in the local community. Invite a speaker to talk about the role of the landmark and its preservation, or consider a field trip to explore the site further.

Lesson-At-A-Glance

1 ENGAGE — INQUIRY JOURNAL

pp. 166–171

▸ **Talk About It:** Photographs of Detroit Auto Museum and National Museum in Kuala Lumpur

▸ **Analyze the Source:** Charting History on Time Lines

▸ **Inquiry Tools:** Explore Summarizing

2 INVESTIGATE — RESEARCH COMPANION

pp. 180–187

▸ **Kuala Lumpur, Malaysia, and Detroit, Michigan**

▸ **Citizenship: Saving Community Landmarks**

3 REPORT — INQUIRY JOURNAL

pp. 172–173

▸ **Think About It**

▸ **Write About It:** Explain; Make a List

▸ **Talk About It**

 ▸ **Connect to the Essential Question**

ASSESSMENT

▸ **Online Lesson Test**

▸ **Printable Lesson Test**

For more details, see pages T262–T263.

▶ Digital Tools

at **my.mheducation.com**

ePresentation

Teach the Engage, Investigate, and Report content to the whole class from **ePresentations** that launch directly from the lesson dashboard.

eBook

You can flip your instruction with the **IMPACT eBooks** found on your lesson dashboard.

Interactive IMPACT

Blend in digital content **when you want it** and **where you want it**.

Blended Learning features in the Teacher's Edition highlight ways to connect in-class work with online experiences to enhance learning.

Investigate current events with **IMPACT News**.

Explore domain-based vocabulary with **Explore Words** and **Word Play** vocabulary activities.

pp. 42–53

Go Further with IMPACT Explorer Magazine!

The **IMPACT Explorer Magazine** supports students' exploration of the Essential Question and provides additional resources for the EQ Inquiry Project.

What Can Comparing Different Communities Tell Us About How Communities Change Over Time?

Language Objectives

- Use newly acquired content and academic vocabulary to compare how communities change over time.
- Identify and make a list of topics of interest.
- Employ spelling changes for plural nouns ending with -y.

 Spanish Cognates

To support Spanish speakers, point out the cognates.

technology = tecnología

history = historia

system = sistema

fertile = fértil

inhabitants = habitantes

control = controlar

Introduce the Lesson

Set Purpose Explain to students that in this lesson, they will read informational texts to compare how different communities change over time.

Access Prior Knowledge Help students to compile a list on the board of examples of people and events that changed communities in Lesson 4. Explain that in this lesson they will compare how two different communities change over time.

Spark Curiosity Point out the photographs on pages 180–181 of the Research Companion. Read the captions aloud. Ask: *How are these cities similar?* (tall buildings, many roads, crowded) Ask: *How are these cities different?* (Kuala Lumpur: capital city of Malaysia in Asia; Detroit: not the capital city, located in Michigan, U.S.A, North America)

 Have groups of students discuss how they think life may be similar and different for people living in Kuala Lumpur and Detroit. Have them share their ideas with the class.

Build Meaning & Support Language

Inquiry Journal

Analyze the Source (pages 168–169) Unpack the sentence: *A time line lists historical events in the order in which they occurred.* Review that historical events are things that happened in the past. Point out the time line on page 169. Explain that a short description of an event is written at each point and that the descriptions are ordered by when they happened.

Inquiry Tools (pages 170–171) Tell students they will explore **Summarizing** as they describe how communities changed over time. Explain that the chart on page 170 will help them list key events chronologically. Say: *Look at the chart on page 171. There are two columns of boxes—one to write main ideas about Kuala Lumpur and the other to write main ideas about Detroit. As you read the Research Companion, write the main idea of each paragraph you read. Using your information, write a summary in the last box.* Show them how to enter information in the diagram. When they have completed their diagram, have them discuss their ideas in a group.

Research Companion

Kuala Lumpur, Malaysia, and Detroit, Michigan (pages 180–181) Read aloud the first paragraph on page 180. Ask: *In what ways can communities change?* (can grow larger or smaller; people, businesses and technologies change) Ask: *Which communities will we learn about?* (Kuala Lumpur, Detroit)

Why People Moved to Detroit/Kuala Lumpur (pages 182–183) Read the first two sentences on page 182. Explain that *sits* means "is located." Read the rest of the page. Ask: *What does* Detroit *mean?* (strait) Say: *Describe a strait.* (narrow waterway connecting two bodies of water) Point out that *strait* and *straight* are homophones, words that are pronounced the same but have different meanings. Review the meaning of *straight*. Read the first paragraph on page 183. Display a map and point out the Malay Peninsula, Strait of Malacca, and Klang River so students have a visual to help them interpret the text.

Business in Detroit/Kuala Lumpur (pages 184–185) Read the first paragraph on page 184. Discuss the sentence: *Mills turned grain into flour to ship back East.* Explain that a *mill* is a building that has machines to grind grain, such as wheat, into flour. The phrase *back East* refers to the eastern United States. Detroit is located to the west of the states where the flour was shipped. Since settlers moved west from the eastern states as the nation expanded, traveling east is referred to as going *back East*.

Citizenship: Saving Community Landmarks (pages 186–187) Explain that landmarks are well-known places of historical importance. Point out and discuss the four landmarks pictured. Read the feature. Ask: *What are examples of landmarks in Kuala Lumpur and Detroit?* (Motown Museum, Joe Louis monument, Kuala Lumpur Railway Station, Medan Pasar)

Inquiry Journal

Report Your Findings (pages 172–173) Have students use the examples from their charts to write a summary of the main ideas of the reading. Then have them share with a partner and ask questions if anything is unclear.

Language Forms & Conventions

Plural Nouns: -y to -ies Remind students that most plural nouns end with *-s* or *-es*. Explain that some singular nouns end with *-y*. When there is a word that ends in *-y*, they should change the *y* to an *i* and add *-es*.

Singular	Plural
community	communities
technology	technologies
city	cities
library	libraries
family	families

Demonstrate changing *community* to *communities*. Then write the chart on the board and have students change the singular nouns to plurals. Review as a class. Ask students if they can find other words in the reading that form plurals in the same way.

Cross-Cultural Connection

The city of Hong Kong originally began as a village of farming, fishing, and salt production. By the nineteenth century it became an important port for trade. Britain was an influential trading partner. In 1898 the British and Chinese governments signed an agreement where the British would govern Hong Kong and surrounding islands. Hong Kong became an important manufacturing center. In 1997 it was returned to Chinese governance.

Leveled Support

Entering & Emerging
Have students create a two-column chart. In the first, they write details about Detroit; in the second, comparable details about Kuala Lumpur.

Developing & Expanding
Have students say comparisons about Detroit and Kuala Lumpur.

Bridging & Reaching
Have students say one sentence describing similarities in both cities and one sentence describing differences.

Language Transfer

Non-native speakers may overgeneralize the use of the plural *-s*. Examples are *mouse/mice, goose/geese, moose/moose* and *deer/deer*. These forms must be memorized. Provide examples and have students repeat.

LESSON 5 ENGAGE

What Can Comparing Different Communities Tell Us About How Communities Change Over Time?

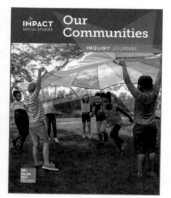

INQUIRY JOURNAL, pp. 166–167

Bellringer

Prompt students to retrieve information from the previous lesson. Say: *You have learned about how people and events change communities. How has the invention of the cell phone changed your community?* (Possible answers: People can now call for help or connect with friends more easily, but sometimes people use cell phones in public places in an inconsiderate way.)

Lesson Outcomes

Discuss the lesson questions and lesson outcomes with students.

- Make sure that students understand that a *time line* lists historical events in the order in which they occurred.
- Tell students that learning about what happened in their community in the past will help them understand the way the community is today. Explain that, over time, events help shape a community's development as well as the lives of its people.

Talk About It

Explain that when we talk about photographs, we describe, analyze, and interpret them and present our ideas in our own words. Provide sentence frames to help students form sentences as they talk about what they can learn from the photographs.

- The photographs show _____ and _____.
- The photograph of the museum in Detroit shows _____.
- The photograph of the museum in Kuala Lumpur shows _____.

 Collaborative Conversations

Add New Ideas As students engage in partner, small-group, and whole-class discussions, encourage them to

- stay on topic.
- connect their own ideas to things their peers have said.
- look for ways to connect their personal experiences or prior knowledge to the conversation.

Lesson 5

What Can Comparing Different Communities Tell Us About How Communities Change Over Time?

This Detroit museum shows the impact the automobile had on the development of the city.

Large murals span two outside walls of the National Museum in Malaysia's capital city, Kuala Lumpur. They show economic activities, cultural traditions, and events from the country's history.

Lesson Outcomes

What Am I Learning?
In this lesson, you will use your investigative skills to find out how communities change over time.

Why Am I Learning It?
Reading and talking about how communities change will help you understand how your community has become what it is today.

How Will I Know That I Learned It?
You will be able to create a list of topics you want to research about your own community.

Talk About It COLLABORATE

Look closely at the photos on the next page. What do you see? What can we learn about the past from these?

INQUIRY JOURNAL, pp. 166–167

English Learners SCAFFOLD

Use the following scaffolds to support student understanding of lesson outcomes.

Entering and Emerging

Read aloud the caption of the photo of the museum in Detroit. Then provide these sentence frames to help students describe the photo:

- This museum is located in _____.
- This museum shows _____.

Repeat the process for the caption and photo of the National Museum.

Developing and Expanding

Have a volunteer read the caption of each photograph. Then ask: *What can visitors to the museum in Detroit learn about the past? What can visitors to the National Museum learn about the past?* Have pairs of students work together to answer the questions.

Bridging and Reaching

Have students work in groups to discuss some facts about their own community. Ask each group to think about important people from the community and significant events that have happened there. Then have each group suggest a person or event from their community and explain why a museum should be built for that person/event.

Social Emotional Learning

Relationship Skills

Communicate Effectively
Tell students that when they engage in group discussions, they need to look at the person who is speaking, respect the speaker by not interrupting, and check their understanding by repeating peers' ideas.

 Digital Tools

Blended Learning

Students engage with the lesson question and discussion prompts.

Interactive IMPACT

Discuss the **Lesson Question** and **Talk About It** with the whole class.

Charting History on Time Lines

1 Inspect

Read the title and look at the chart. What do you think you will learn?

Underline clues that will help you answer:

- What is a time line?
- In what order does it list events?

Circle the events that happened first on each side of the time line.

Draw a box around the events that happened most recently on each side of the time line.

Read the dates and the events on the time line.

- What happened in 1998 in Kuala Lumpur?
- What year did Detroit become Michigan's capital?

My Notes

_____

_____

_____

_____

If you want to tell people what you did today, you would most likely list events in a certain order. You would tell what you did first, or earliest, in the day. Then you would describe later activities. You would end by explaining what you did most recently.

In history, we do the same thing with time lines. A time line lists historical events in the order in which they occurred. Events are listed from first, or those in the most distant past, to last, or those in the most recent past. The past refers to events that happened before now.

A time line most often lists information from left to right or from top to bottom. Study this example.

The steps at Batu caves in Kuala Lumpur

2 Find Evidence

Reread What does the time line tell you about the two communities?

Compare What is something the two communities have in common?

3 Make Connections

Talk Think about the photographs of Kuala Lumpur and Detroit shown on page 167. Where on the time line for these cities would you place the photographs? Why?

Time line:

Kuala Lumpur / Detroit

- 1701 — Antoine de la Mothe Cadillac founds Fort-Pontchartrain du Détroit.
- 1760 — Britain takes control of Detroit.
- 1805 — Detroit named capital of Michigan Territory
- 1837 — Detroit becomes first Michigan state capital. Lansing later made capital.
- 1857 — Chinese tin miners found settlement at Kuala Lumpur
- 1895 — Federal Malay States form under British rule; Kuala Lumpur becomes capital
- 1903 — Henry Ford starts the Ford Motor Company in Detroit, attracting many people to the city.
- 1957 — Federation of Malaysia wins independence; Kuala Lumpur remains the capital
- 1998 — Petronas Twin Towers completed

INQUIRY JOURNAL, pp. 168–169

Analyze the Source

1 Inspect

Read Have students read the title of the selection and predict what the article will be about. Make sure students understand what a time line is and that it lists events in the order in which they occurred. Have them circle the earliest events for each city on the time line. (Kuala Lumpur—1857: Chinese tin miners found settlement at Kuala Lumpur; Detroit—1701: Antoine de la Mothe Cadillac founds Fort Pontchartrain du Détroit)

- Which community was founded first? (Detroit)

2 Find Evidence

Reread Have students reread the text and answer the question.

Compare Students' responses may vary but might note that both communities were once ruled by the British.

3 Make Connections

Talk Encourage students to work with a partner to make inferences about where the photographs should be placed on the time line. (Students might suggest that these photographs appear to have been taken recently, so they would appear near the last events on the time line.)

Spotlight on Language

Time and Sequence Words

As you discuss the time line with students, point out the time and sequence words and phrases in the text, such as *first, then,* and *most recently.* Remind students that sequencing words put events in the order in which they happened. Write a few examples of time and sequence words on the board, such as *next* and *finally.* Then ask students to offer suggestions to add to the list on the board.

Inquiry Tools

Explore Summarizing

You can summarize a historical text, such as a time line. To do so, you tell the most important details in your own words.

1. **Read the text on the time line all the way through.** This will help you understand the events on the time line.
2. **Reread the time line. Look for how events connect.** See what happens from one date to the next.
3. **Retell the information in your own words.** Include the main ideas and the most important details.

COLLABORATE List key events for Detroit or Kuala Lumpur. Then summarize what you know about the city you chose.

Founded by Chinese tin miners in 1857.

↓

Ruled by the British from 1895 to 1957.

↓

Became capital of independent Federation of Malaysia in 1963.

↓

Summary
Kuala Lumpur began as a mining settlement in the mid-1800s. First founded by the Chinese, it was later ruled by Britain for more than 50 years. Kuala Lumpur became the capital of the independent Federation of Malaysia in 1963. It has continued to grow ever since.

Investigate!

Read pages 180–187 in your Research Companion. Use your investigative skills to look for text evidence that tells you more about how the communities of Kuala Lumpur and Detroit developed and changed over time. The charts will help you organize your information for each community.

French settlers build Fort-Pontchartrain du Détroit on the Detroit River.	Chinese start a tin mining settlement at what is now Kuala Lumpur.
Britain and then the United States take control of Fort Detroit.	British form independent Federation of Malaysia. Kuala Lumpur is its capital.
Detroit becomes capital of Michigan until the capital is moved to Lansing.	Federation of Malaysia wins independence. Kuala Lumpur remains capital.
Henry Ford launches the automobile industry in Detroit, attracting more people to the city.	Petronas Twin Towers are completed.
Summary Detroit began as a French fort on the Detroit River. The British and then United States took control of Detroit. Detroit became the first capital of Michigan until the capital moved to Lansing. Detroit grew when Henry Ford launched the automoblie industry and attracted more people to the city.	Summary Kuala Lumpur began as a mining settlement in the mid-1800s. First founded by the Chinese, it was later ruled by Britain. Kuala Lumpur became the capital of the independent Federation of Malaysia in 1963. It is now home to the Petronas Twin Towers.

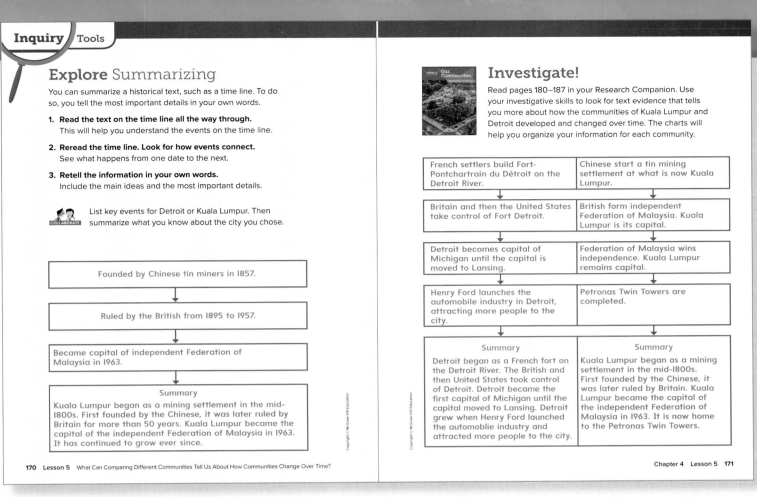

INQUIRY JOURNAL, pp. 170–171

Inquiry Tools

Explore Summarizing

Read Review with students what it means to *summarize*. Discuss the step-by-step instructions for summarizing the details in a text. Remind students that they can find important details in a text by examining headings, key words, captions, and names of people and places.

Guide Practice Have students review the text on pp. 168–169. Then work with them to complete the graphic organizer. Explain that they will use a similar graphic organizer to organize their independent research.

Check Understanding Confirm student understanding of the inquiry skill, Explore Summarizing. If students cannot summarize the text in their own words, review the steps on p. 170.

Investigate!

Have students read pp. 180–187 in the Research Companion. Tell them the information will help them answer the lesson question ***What Can Comparing Different Communities Tell Us About How Communities Change Over Time?***

Take Notes Tell students that they will take notes in the graphic organizer on p. 171 of the Inquiry Journal. Guide students to look for the main ideas and supporting details as they read the text in each section. Tell them that taking notes will help them understand and remember the information they learn. Remind students that they should use their own words when taking notes.

EL Spotlight on Content

Summarizing

Summarizing is a demanding task. As students summarize the text, guide them to notice words that indicate secondary details or opinions.

Digital Tools

Blended Learning

Students prepare for the lesson investigation with step-by-step instruction about how to summarize a text.

ePresentation

Use the **Inquiry Tools** to model and complete the lesson graphic organizer.

LESSON 5 INVESTIGATE

 LESSON QUESTION

What Can Comparing Different Communities Tell Us About How Communities Change Over Time?

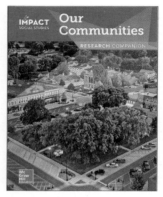

**RESEARCH COMPANION,
pp. 180–181**

Kuala Lumpur, Malaysia, and Detroit, Michigan

1 Inspect Have students read pp. 180–181 and identify some community features that change over time.

2 Find Evidence Use the questions below to check comprehension. Remind students to support their answers with text evidence.

Predict Based on the title, what will this selection be about? (The ways that the communities of Kuala Lumpur and Detroit have changed over time.) **DOK 2**

Compare Examine the photographs of Kuala Lumpur and Detroit. Based on the photos, in what ways are these two communities the same? (Answers may vary, but students should notice that both communities are large cities with many tall buildings.) **DOK 2**

Predict Based on the photographs of Kuala Lumpur and Detroit, what changes do you predict will happen in these cities in the future? (Answers may vary, but students should understand that both communities are large cities and may grow larger or smaller and may benefit from advances in technology.) **DOK 3**

3 Make Connections

Draw Conclusions The text states that understanding the history of Kuala Lumpur and Detroit will help you understand how communities grow and change. How do you think your own community has grown and changed? (Answers will vary, but students should support their ideas with facts.) **DOK 3**

Lesson 5

What Can Comparing Different Communities Tell Us About How Communities Change Over Time?

Kuala Lumpur is the capital city of Malaysia, a country in Southeast Asia.

Kuala Lumpur, Malaysia, and Detroit, Michigan

Communities around the world change over time. Often, they grow larger. Sometimes, they get smaller. People, businesses, and technologies change. Let's look at the history of two communities in different countries. Understanding their history can help us understand how our communities grow and change.

Detroit is a city in the state of Michigan in the United States.

RESEARCH COMPANION, pp. 180–181

English Learners SCAFFOLD

Use the following scaffolds to support student understanding of the lesson.

Entering and Emerging

Students may not be familiar with using countries' adjectives to describe people: the French, the British, the Wyandot, the Malay. Reinforce the idea that these words name groups of people who lived in Detroit or Kuala Lumpur. Ask for each city: *Who lived here first?* (the Wyandot, the Malay). *Who came later?* (the British, the French, or other European county)

Developing and Expanding

Students may not be familiar with the countries described by the adjectives in this lesson. Reinforce the idea that the people who came later came from other countries. Ask: *Who lived here first?* (the Wyandot, the Malay). Ask: *Who came later?* (the French, the British, the Chinese) *What country did they come from?* (France, Great Britain, China)

Bridging and Reaching

Have students work with partners to identify the people who came to inhabit Detroit and Kuala Lumpur and the countries where they originated. Have students use as many phrases as possible. Give an example: The British came from Great Britain and took control of Detroit.

▶ Digital Tools

Blended Learning
Students explore lesson content through interactive activities.

Interactive IMPACT

Use the **More to Explore**.

Lesson 5   **What Can Comparing Different Communities Tell Us About How Communities Change Over Time?   T347**

Why People Moved to Detroit

The city of Detroit lies near the Great Lakes in the United States. It sits on the Detroit River, a waterway between Lake Erie and the smaller Lake Saint Clair. The name Detroit comes from the French word for **strait**. A strait is a narrow waterway connecting two larger bodies of water.

People have lived in the area for thousands of years. Fertile land, forests, and fresh waterways provided important natural resources. The first inhabitants were Native Americans known as the Wyandot. They used the river and lakes to fish, travel, and trade.

Photograph of Detroit around 1920

In the early 1700s, French settlers built Fort Pontchartrain du Détroit along the river. They wanted to trade furs and other goods with the Wyandot. Later, the British took control of the site and called it Fort Detroit. The Detroit River and the Great Lakes became part of a large system of trade. Throughout the 1700s, more French and then British came. Many stayed to build homes and farms. The fort grew into a town.

Why People Moved to Kuala Lumpur

Kuala Lumpur is the capital city of Malaysia, a country in Southeast Asia. Kuala Lumpur lies on a **peninsula**, a piece of land surrounded by water on three sides.

Ancestors of the Malay ethnic group came to the region about three thousand years ago. They blended cultures in the area. In time, towns grew and formed governments. In the 1400s, the kingdom of Malacca formed.

Photograph of Kuala Lumpur around 1915

Starting in the 1500s, the Portuguese, Dutch, and British came to the region. They wanted to trade and start colonies. They built ports that grew rich from the spice trade. In 1857, the Chinese started a tin mining settlement at what is now Kuala Lumpur.

✓ Stop and Check

Talk What do Detroit and Kuala Lumpur have in common?

Find Details As you read, add new information to the graphic organizer on page 171 in your Inquiry Journal.

182 Lesson 5 What Can Comparing Different Communities Tell Us About How Communities Change Over Time?

Chapter 4 Lesson 5 **183**

RESEARCH COMPANION, pp. 182–183

Kuala Lumpur, Malaysia, and Detroit, Michigan

1 Inspect Have students read pp. 182–183 and differentiate between a strait and a peninsula.

2 Find Evidence Use the questions below to check comprehension.

Compare Why did the Portuguese, Dutch, and British come to the region of Kuala Lumpur in the 1500s? How do these reasons compare to the reasons the French settled near Detroit? (Europeans came to Kuala Lumpur in the 1500s to trade and start colonies; the French settlers near Detroit also wanted to trade.) **DOK 2**

Analyze Which details in the photographs indicate that the images are from long ago? (photos are in black-and-white; older styles of vehicles; older buildings) **DOK 3**

3 Make Connections

Draw Conclusions What geographical features made the areas around Detroit and Kuala Lumpur attractive places to build communities? (good land for farming, waterways for transportation and trade) **DOK 3**

✓ Stop and Check

Talk Have students find details in the text to support their answers. (People have lived in both areas for thousands of years. Both are located on rivers and other waterways. Europeans came to both regions to start colonies and trade.)

EL Spotlight on Vocabulary

Content Vocabulary

narrow: long and not wide

inhabitants: people who live in a particular place

colonies: areas controlled by a far-away country

▶ Digital Tools

Blended Learning
Students investigate curated resources and find evidence to answer the lesson question.

Interactive IMPACT
Students choose from print or digital **Inquiry Tools** to take notes.

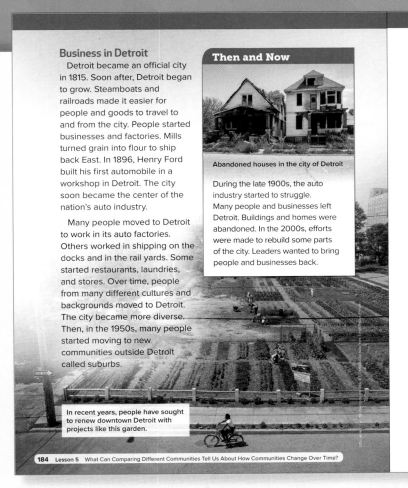

Business in Detroit

Detroit became an official city in 1815. Soon after, Detroit began to grow. Steamboats and railroads made it easier for people and goods to travel to and from the city. People started businesses and factories. Mills turned grain into flour to ship back East. In 1896, Henry Ford built his first automobile in a workshop in Detroit. The city soon became the center of the nation's auto industry.

Many people moved to Detroit to work in its auto factories. Others worked in shipping on the docks and in the rail yards. Some started restaurants, laundries, and stores. Over time, people from many different cultures and backgrounds moved to Detroit. The city became more diverse. Then, in the 1950s, many people started moving to new communities outside Detroit called suburbs.

Then and Now

Abandoned houses in the city of Detroit

During the late 1900s, the auto industry started to struggle. Many people and businesses left Detroit. Buildings and homes were abandoned. In the 2000s, efforts were made to rebuild some parts of the city. Leaders wanted to bring people and businesses back.

In recent years, people have sought to renew downtown Detroit with projects like this garden.

Business in Kuala Lumpur

In the 1800s, the British built the Klang–Kuala Lumpur Railway. Europeans started coffee, tea, and rubber plantations, or large farms. These supplied trade and business in the city. As in Detroit, many people moved to the city to work. In 1963, several British colonies formed the independent Federation of Malaysia.

In the late 1900s, Kuala Lumpur became a center of banking and trade. Malaysia's national oil company, Petronas, moved its headquarters to the city. The government built libraries, museums, and public transportation. A light-rail train made it easier to get around in the growing city. In 2016, the city had an estimated 1.76 million people.

Detroit and Kuala Lumpur are communities with exciting histories. You might like to learn about the history of your community and how it has changed over time. Here are some resources to help you:

- Check the local library. The librarian can help you find books and other resources about your town's history.
- Pay a visit to a local history museum.
- Stop at the local newspaper office. It might have news stories and photos from your town's past.
- Visit your town's website.

In 1998, the Petronas Twin Towers were completed. Each tower has 88 floors that house many offices and businesses.

> ☑ **Stop and Check**
>
> **Think** How did industry help Detroit and Kuala Lumpur grow?

RESEARCH COMPANION, pp. 184–185

Kuala Lumpur, Malaysia, and Detroit, Michigan

1 Inspect Have students read pp. 184–185 and identify two important businesses in both Detroit and Kuala Lumpur.

2 Find Evidence Use the questions below to check comprehension.

Define Use context clues to determine the meaning of the word *industry* in the text. (businesses that make a product or provide a service) **DOK 2**

Differentiate How would you compare the economies of Kuala Lumpur and Detroit in the late 1900s? (In the late 1900s, the auto industry in Detroit began to struggle and the city began to decline economically; by contrast, in the late 1900s, Kuala Lumpur became a center of banking and trade and the city's economy was thriving.) **DOK 3**

3 Make Connections

Assess Why does the text include suggestions for where you can learn about the history of your own community? (Answers will vary, but students might note that the lesson is about how communities develop over time. The suggestions will help us learn how our own community has developed over time.) **DOK 3**

☑ Stop and Check

Think Have students think about and answer the question using evidence from the text. (Industry attracted workers to cities. People came to work in factories and mills. They worked in trade. As more people came, more goods and services were needed. This brought more businesses.)

Social Emotional Learning

Decision-Making Skills

Analyze Problems Point out to students that Detroit's leaders are trying to turn around the city's economy. Have students practice problem-solving by offering their ideas about how the city's leaders might entice people and businesses to return.

Multiple-Meaning Words

Tell students that although the word *landmark* is used in the text to mean a well-known place that people like to visit, it is sometimes used in other ways. A *landmark* can also be an important historical event. For example, the Civil War might be described as a *landmark* of American history. Graduating high school might be a *landmark* event in a person's life.

Citizenship: Saving Community Landmarks

1 Inspect Have students read pp. 186–187 and define the term *landmark*.

2 Find Evidence Use the questions below to check comprehension.

Compare What do the photographs on these two pages have in common? (They are all monuments or historical landmarks that have been preserved or restored.) **DOK 2**

Draw Conclusions Why is it important to save landmarks? (to be able to remember our history; to draw tourists) **DOK 3**

3 Make Connections

Synthesize Based on the photograph of the Kuala Lumpur Railway Station, the information provided in the caption, and what you have learned so far in this chapter, why do you think the Kuala Lumpur Railway Station is considered a landmark? (Answers will vary, but students should recall that railroads were an important part of Kuala Lumpur's economy in the 1800s, and that the railway station combines British and Islamic building styles, which demonstrates both the city's colonial history and ethnic diversity.) **DOK 4**

 Stop and Check

Think As students work, remind them to give at least three reasons to support their opinion. (Answers will vary but should reflect the history and locations in their communities.)

What Do You Think? Have students think about how changes in Kuala Lumpur and Detroit may be alike and different to changes they are aware of in their community. (Answers will vary, but students should note that people build communities where they can access natural resources or to trade. People stay and start businesses, and more people join the community. These factors together help bring change to a community)

 Digital Tools

Blended Learning

Students investigate curated resources and find evidence to answer the lesson question.

Interactive IMPACT

Students **Research** and find evidence using digital format texts.

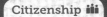 **Citizenship**

Saving Community
LANDMARKS

Historic landmarks in Detroit, Kuala Lumpur, and other communities remind people of the past. Landmarks are well-known places that people like to visit. They also highlight the roles of different cultures. Landmarks can be buildings or places that played a special role in historical events. They can also be museums and statues built to honor people in the past, or the time before now.

In 1959, Berry Gordy Jr. founded the Motown Record Corporation in Detroit. In 1985, Gordy's sister founded the Motown Museum when the company moved its headquarters to California.

Though no longer the main railway hub, the Kuala Lumpur Railway Station is a symbol of the city's mixed past.

Many groups work to save landmarks in Detroit and in Kuala Lumpur. The Detroit Historical Society helps identify and save landmarks. So, too, does Michigan's State Historic Preservation Office. Dozens of cultural and arts groups support local historic and other types of landmarks. In Malaysia, several agencies under the Ministry of Tourism and Cultures take care of the nation's cultural and historic sites. The National Museum in Kuala Lumpur saves much of the nation's history.

Joe Louis was a famous African American boxer. He grew up in Detroit and went on to win many championships. In 1986, the city built this statue to celebrate his life.

Medan Pasar, or Market Square, once served as the center of economic activity in Kuala Lumpur. Today, many modern cafés, shops, boutiques, and other businesses line the square.

✓ Stop and Check

Think Choose one old building in your community. Why do you think the building should be saved as an important historic landmark? Give at least three reasons for your opinion.

What Do You Think?

How does comparing Detroit and Kuala Lumpur help you understand how communities change?

186 Lesson 5 What Can Comparing Different Communities Tell Us About How Communities Change Over Time?

Chapter 4 Lesson 5 187

RESEARCH COMPANION, pp. 186–187

 English Learners SCAFFOLD

✓ Check for Success

Describe Can students describe ways that their communities have changed over the years?

Use the following scaffolds to support student understanding of the lesson.

Entering and Emerging

Read aloud the first paragraph of the selection. Then have students define the word *landmark* and name a landmark mentioned in the text using the following sentence frames:

- A landmark is _____.
- One example of a landmark is _____.

Differentiate

If Not, Review with students the graphic organizer on p. 171 of their Inquiry Journals. Discuss the key events that impacted Kuala Lumpur and Detroit. Help students identify similar changes that have taken place in their own community.

Developing and Expanding

Have students use their own words to craft a definition of the word *landmark*. Then ask them to write one sentence explaining why *landmarks* are important.

Bridging and Reaching

Organize students into groups and have them choose one of the landmarks pictured in the text. Ask them to conduct research to learn more about the landmark, its original use, why it was saved, and how it is used today. Have each group write a one-paragraph report of their findings.

LESSON 5 REPORT

LESSON QUESTION

What Can Comparing Different Communities Tell Us About How Communities Change Over Time?

INQUIRY JOURNAL, pp. 172–173

Think About It

Remind students to review their research and consider what they learned about Detroit and Kuala Lumpur. They will use that information to design a research plan to learn about their own community and identify features that might attract newcomers. Direct students back to pp. 180–187 of their Research Companion if they need more information.

Write About It

Explain Remind students to include the following as they craft their responses.

- List topics and features about their community that might attract newcomers.
- Include evidence from the lesson to support their selections.
- Use chapter vocabulary as appropriate.

Discipline(s)	4	3	2	1
History	Strong understanding of the community's features and why they might attract newcomers	Adequate understanding of the community's features and why they might attract newcomers	Uneven understanding of the community's features and why they might attract newcomers	Little or no understanding of the community's features and why they might attract newcomers

Talk About It

Explain Have student pairs compare and evaluate their lists. Encourage them to combine features from both lists to create a new list. Remind students to follow the rules of appropriate classroom conversation.

Assessment Students can check their understanding with feedback from the **Lesson Test** available online.

Connect to the Essential Question

Put It Together Before students respond, remind them Kuala Lumpur and Detroit have changed over the years and those changes impacted the people living there.

Inquiry Project Update Remind students to turn to Inquiry Journal p. 131 for project information. If necessary, review the Project Checklist with students. At this point in the chapter, students should focus on the third, fourth, and fifth items on the checklist.

Think About It

Gather Evidence
Based on your research about Kuala Lumpur and Detroit, what information do you want to find out about your community? What resources could you use to learn about your community and its history?

Answers will vary but should reflect students' interest in the community. Students might cite online historical societies, local museums and libraries, and reference materials like encyclopedias and guidebooks.

Write About It

Explain
Make a list of topics about your community that you want to research. How could you encourage someone to move to your community?

Answers will vary but should include specific features of the community. Features that might attract newcomers could include jobs and businesses, natural resources, parks and public services, and diverse cultural groups and events.

Talk About It

Explain
Compare lists with a partner. Pick features from both lists that you think would encourage people to move to your community.

Geography **Connect to the**

Pull It Together
Think about ways that your community has changed over the years. How have these changes affected the lives of people living in the community today?

Answers will vary but should include specific changes that have occurred within the community.

Inquiry Project Notes

172 Lesson 5 What Can Comparing Different Communities Tell Us About How Communities Change Over Time?

Chapter 4 Lesson 5 173

INQUIRY JOURNAL, pp. 172–173

 # English Learners SCAFFOLD

Use the following scaffolds to support student writing.

Entering and Emerging

Guide students as they scan the text for facts about how Detroit and Kuala Lumpur have changed and grown. Help them list the information they find in a three-column chart with the headings *Who, When,* and *Where.* Then have students use the list to think of similar facts they would like to learn about their own community.

Developing and Expanding

Have partners scan the text for facts about how Detroit and Kuala Lumpur have changed and grown. Have them list the information in a three-column chart with the headings *What, Where,* and *Why It's Interesting.* Then have students write *wh-* questions they have about their own community, based on what they have learned about Detroit and Kuala Lumpur.

Bridging and Reaching

Have groups scan the text for facts about how Detroit and Kuala Lumpur have changed and grown. Have them list the information in a three-column chart with the headings *What, Where,* and *Why It's Interesting.* Then have students write *wh-* questions they have about their own community and conduct research to find answers to those questions.

✓ Check for Success

Describe Can students list ideas for research topics about their community and make a list of features that might attract newcomers?

Differentiate

If Not, Have students bring in potential resources, including books, photographs, or videos, and present them to small groups.

LESSON 6 OVERVIEW

? LESSON QUESTION

What Makes My Community Special?

Connect to the Essential Question

Tell students that this lesson provides key research into the Chapter Essential Question: **How Does the Past Impact the Present?** Explain that they will use their investigative skills to discover how features of communities make them special. Tell students they will learn how these features have shaped their community, as well as communities around the world, over time.

Discuss The IMPACT Today

Discuss with students how history, geography, and culture impact communities. Encourage them to think about how these different elements impact communities in the lesson and their own community.

Lesson Objectives

- **Describe** the features that make different communities unique.
- **Identify** how geography, history, and cultures affect a community and its people.
- **Explain** how historic monuments and buildings show communities' changes over time.
- **Write** a blog post about the student's own community and why it is special.

Make Connections!

CONNECT TO ELA

Reading **Ask** and answer questions to demonstrate understanding of a text and refer explicitly to the text as the basis for answers.

Research **Recall** information from experiences or gather information from print and digital resources; take brief notes on sources and sort information into provided categories.

Writing **Craft** informative/explanatory texts to examine a topic and convey ideas and information clearly.

Speaking and Listening **Follow** agreed-upon rules for discussions (e.g., gaining the floor in respectful ways, listening to others with care, speaking one at a time about the topics and texts under discussion).

COMMUNITY CONNECTIONS

To further students' understanding of how history shapes communities, have students work in pairs to research a monument in their community. If possible, put them in contact with a local official who is knowledgeable about local history. Have students write a short journal entry about the purpose and history of the monument.

Lesson-At-A-Glance

1 ENGAGE — INQUIRY JOURNAL

▶ **Talk About It:** Photograph of a community celebration

▶ **Analyze the Source:** Linking to the Past

▶ **Inquiry Tools:** Explore Drawing Conclusions

pp. 174–179

2 INVESTIGATE — RESEARCH COMPANION

▶ **The Past Affects the Present**

▶ **Ways Communities Can Change**

▶ **Monuments Connect to the Past**

▶ **Field Trip: Pittsburgh, Pennsylvania**

pp. 188–195

3 REPORT — INQUIRY JOURNAL

▶ **Think About It**

▶ **Write About It:** Define What Makes a Community Special; Write a Blog Post

▶ **Talk About It**

 ▶ **Connect to the Essential Question**

pp. 180–181

ASSESSMENT

▶ **Online Lesson Test**

▶ **Printable Lesson Test**

For more details, see pages T262–T263

▶ Digital Tools

at **my.mheducation.com**

ePresentation

Teach the Engage, Investigate, and Report content to the whole class from **ePresentations** that launch directly from the lesson dashboard.

eBook

You can flip your instruction with the **IMPACT eBooks** found on your lesson dashboard.

Interactive IMPACT

Blend in digital content **when you want it** and **where you want it**.

Blended Learning features in the Teacher's Edition highlight ways to connect in-class work with online experiences to enhance learning.

Investigate current events with **IMPACT News**.

Explore domain-based vocabulary with **Explore Words** and **Word Play** vocabulary activities.

pp. 42–53

Go Further with IMPACT Explorer Magazine!

The **IMPACT Explorer Magazine** supports students' exploration of the Essential Question and provides additional resources for the EQ Inquiry Project.

 LESSON QUESTION

What Makes My Community Special?

Language Objectives

- Use newly acquired content and academic vocabulary to talk and write about what makes communities special.
- Write a blog based on conclusions about what makes a community a special place to live.
- Identify some regular and irregular plural nouns.

Spanish Cognates

To support Spanish speakers, point out the cognates.

special = especial

restaurant = restaurante

honor = honrar

statue = estatua

pioneer = pionero

city = ciudad

Introduce the Lesson

Set Purpose Explain to students that in this lesson, they will read informational texts to learn about communities, how they are special, and how this affects how communities change over time.

Access Prior Knowledge Before presenting the lesson outcomes, read the lesson question and find out what students already know about what makes their community special. First, check that they understand the word *special*. Say: *If something is special, it is important to us. Special people, places, and things make us happy.* Ask: *What do you think is one thing that makes our community special?* Accept suggestions of places, people, and events that are part of the fabric of your community.

Spark Curiosity Have students study the photo of the tower on page 188 of the Research Companion. Explain that a memorial can honor someone who did something that benefited his or her country or humankind. A memorial may also honor a significant event. Ask: *What do you know about Thomas Edison that would explain why people created this memorial?* (Answers will vary, but students may know that Edison was an inventor with his inventions including the phonograph, incandescent electric light bulb, and alkaline battery.)

 Have students work in pairs to discuss people they know or famous people who they think may someday be deserving of a memorial. Ask: *Why might these people deserve a memorial?*

Build Meaning & Support Language

Inquiry Journal

Analyze the Source (pages 176–177) Take a deeper look into the heading "Linking to the Past." Say: *The word* linking *means "connecting." What kinds of things connect people to their past?* (places, people, events) Read aloud the first sentence of each paragraph. Explain that the first sentence in the first paragraph tells about things New Orleans is known for. The first sentence of the second paragraph gives specific information about something New Orleans is known for that links it to its past. The first sentence of the third paragraph tells how this began to change in New Orleans. The first sentences of the fourth and fifth paragraphs tell how this continued to change. Ask: *Where do you think you will find details about why New Orleans became known for its streetcars?* (page 176)

Inquiry Tools (pages 178–179) Tell students they will be **Drawing Conclusions** as they read the selections in the Research Companion. Explain that the graphic organizer on page 179 will help them organize information to draw conclusions as they read. Check they understand the meaning of the column headings. Explain that *drawing a conclusion* means to make decisions based on the information they have. Discuss particularly the meaning of the verb *draw* in this context. Then provide support as students fill in the graphic organizer. After completing the graphic organizer, have each student share his or her ideas with a partner by stating his or her conclusion and text clues that support it.

Research Companion

The Past Affects the Present (pages 188–189) Read aloud the first paragraph on page 188. Explain that the multiple questions are to get readers to think about things that relate to a community. Then talk about the meaning of the phrase named for. Say: *Cities and streets have names. Sometimes, they are named for a person or a thing.* Point out examples in the text. Ask: *What is the difference between named and named for?*

Ways Communities Can Change (pages 190–191) Clarify that *sea level* refers to the average height of the sea or ocean. Land that is higher than the surface of the sea is above sea level. Land below this height is below sea level. Read the first sentence of the third paragraph on page 190. Point out that the word *breakwaters* is a compound word. Ask: *What are the two words that are linked together?* (*break* and *waters*) Have students find the meaning of the word in the text.

Monuments Connect to the Past (pages 192–193) Read the first sentence of the second paragraph on page 192. Explain that an oculus is a circular or oval eye-like opening. Then unlock the Primary Source. Check that students understand what the terrorist attacks refer to. Then read the last sentence of the quote. Point out that the word *steel* has two different meanings in this sentence. The first time it is used, it refers to a material used to make buildings; the second time it is used, it means "the quality of the human mind or spirit"—a firmness that suggests the strength of steel used in buildings.

Field Trip: Pittsburgh, Pennsylvania (pages 194–195) Read the last sentence of the first paragraph. Ask: *Will the reader actually take a trip to downtown Pittsburgh?* (no) *How will the trip happen?* (through the descriptive text and images) Have students scan the pages. Ask: *How many different things in Pittsburgh does the text describe?* (four)

Inquiry Journal

Report Your Findings (pages 180–181) Explain to students that one purpose of a blog post is to share information and opinions on a topic. Students should include reasons they think their community is special and evidence to support it. Evidence might include information about unique features and special places within their community.

Language Forms & Conventions

Regular and Irregular Plural Nouns Remind students that they make most nouns plural by adding -s or -es, or by changing y to -ies. These are all rules for regular plural nouns. Point out that some nouns are irregular. For some words, the spelling changes a lot when the word becomes plural.

Display the chart and point out the examples.

Regular Plural Nouns	Irregular Plural Nouns
language –> languages	life –> lives
church –> churches	hero –> heroes
community –> communities	man –> men
	person –> people

 Have students work in pairs to locate some regular plural or irregular plural nouns in the texts. Call on volunteers and add them to the chart.

 Cross-Cultural Connection

The United States has more than one hundred national monuments. President Theodore Roosevelt made Devil's Tower in Wyoming the first national monument in 1906. Some of the most popular monuments are the Statue of Liberty in New York Harbor, Fort Sumter in Charleston Harbor, the Washington Monument in Washington, D.C., and Muir Woods in California. Ask: *Have you visited a national monument? Is there a national monument in the region where you live?*

 Leveled Support

Entering & Emerging
Provide sentence frame: *I think my community is special because _____ and _____.*

Developing & Expanding
Help small groups make a list of special features in their community and name their favorite features. Have students listen as you repeat and paraphrase their answers.

Bridging & Reaching
Encourage partners to share with each other their opinions on the historic and geographical features that make their community special.

 **Language Transfer**

Point out that for plural nouns, many native languages may add an additional word rather than -s to the noun.

LESSON 6 ENGAGE

What Makes My Community Special?

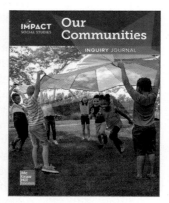

**INQUIRY JOURNAL,
pp. 174–175**

Bellringer

Prompt students to think about their community. Ask: *Does your community have any old buildings? How old do you think they are?* Be prepared to provide some examples with the approximate age of the buildings. (Answers will vary, but students should be aware that some buildings in the community are older than others.)

Lesson Outcomes

Discuss the lesson question and lesson outcomes with students.

- Make sure that students understand that the uniqueness of a community affects the people living there. Maybe the location or geographic environment of their community makes it special. Perhaps their community was the center of a historical event.

- Have students think about how history and culture have shaped their community. Discuss how their community is special.

Talk About It

Have students look at the photograph, read the caption, and describe what they see. Encourage them to look for specific details in the photo, including what people are doing and wearing. Provide sentence frames to help students talk about the photograph.

- The photograph shows _____ and _____.
- These details are interesting because _____.
- I think the photograph was included to show us _____.

 Collaborative Conversations

Activate Prior Knowledge Have students discuss the following questions as a group. Tell students to be respectful of each other and to let each person finish speaking before they speak.

- What cultural or historical festivals happen in your community?
- What do these festivals celebrate?

THE IMPACT TODAY

Lesson 6
What Makes My Community Special?

Lesson Outcomes

What Am I Learning?
In this lesson, you will use your investigative skills to find out how communities are special.

Why Am I Learning It?
Reading and talking about why a community is special will help you learn how geography, history, and cultures affect the people who live in a community.

How Will I Know That I Learned It?
You will be able to tell what makes a community special. You will be able to write about your own community and describe what makes it special.

Talk About It COLLABORATE

Look closely at the photo on the next page. What details in it do you find interesting? What do you think it shows about the community?

174 Lesson 6 What Makes My Community Special?

Native American dancers perform a traditional dance.

Chapter 4 Lesson 6 175

INQUIRY JOURNAL, pp. 174–175

English Learners SCAFFOLD

Use the following scaffolds to support student understanding of lesson outcomes.

Entering and Emerging

Read the photo caption and then provide sentence frames to help students describe the photograph:

- I see _____ and _____ in the photograph.
- Some of the people are _____.

Developing and Expanding

Have small groups work together to read the caption and identify details in the photograph. List these on the board. Have students describe the people and activity using familiar adjectives. Ask: *What do the people and activities tell you about their community?*

Bridging and Reaching

Have student pairs write a three-sentence story about what is happening in the photograph. Encourage students to think about what kind of community it is, who might live there, and what the dancers are celebrating.

Social Emotional Learning

Self-Awareness

Self-Confidence To help students develop self-confidence, encourage them to participate by answering in any format they feel comfortable with. Flexibility can make the classroom an active, fun environment where everyone can take part.

▶ Digital Tools

Blended Learning

Students engage with the lesson question and discussion prompts.

ePresentation

Discuss the **Lesson Question** and **Talk About It**.

Linking to the Past

New Orleans became known for streetcars, jazz clubs, and Mardi Gras during the 1900s. Tourists from around the world visited the city. Levees and canals were built to protect the city from flooding. Then Hurricane Katrina struck the city in 2005. The levees were no match for the storm. Much of New Orleans flooded. It took many years for New Orleans to rebuild again. New Orleans has kept links to its rich and interesting past. Let's look at one of those links.

New Orleans's streetcars are famous around the world. They are one of the oldest street railways still in operation. New Orleans was the first place west of the Allegheny Mountains to have a street railway service. Streetcars first began in 1835 to connect New Orleans and a suburb. They were powered by steam.

Streetcars are a symbol of New Orleans. Even today, they run on many New Orleans streets.

Much of New Orleans was rebuilt after Hurricane Katrina.

Steam trains were replaced by horse-drawn cars and then by electricity in 1893. New Orleans had more than 350 streetcars, that each held twenty-eight people, by the beginning of the 1900s. Some streetcars were painted olive green while others were painted red and gold.

During the 1930s, people preferred cars and buses. Fewer streetcars were needed. By the 1960s, most streetcars were retired. One streetcar line became a National Historic Landmark.

In 1988, New Orleans built a new streetcar line. Some people used the streetcars to get to work. Tourists found the streetcars charming and a great way to see some of New Orleans's historic sites. More and more people began using streetcars again. Today, streetcars are an important part of New Orleans transportation and history.

Analyze the Source

1 Inspect

Read Have students read the text and underline details that explain why streetcars are important to New Orleans. Remind them to circle words if they are unsure of the meaning.

- How does the text show that New Orleans today links with the past? (Streetcars were popular in the past and have become important to New Orleans again in recent times.)

2 Find Evidence

Reread Have students reread the text and identify why streetcars have once again become a popular from of transportation. (Tourists love the streetcars, so additional streetcars were added. Older lines became active, so more people began using them. It's a great way to see historic sites.)

Underline Tell students that the details in the article are important. Have them underline clues that support their answer to the Reread question.

3 Make Connections

Talk Have student discuss why the streetcars are an important part of New Orleans' history. (New Orleans was the first place west of the Allegheny Mountains to have a street railway service. They are one of the oldest street railways still in operation.) Then have students discuss what things from the past they still find in their communities. (Answers might include old buildings or other features of historic interest.)

EL Spotlight on Content

Scanning for Information

Have students take note of the dates present in this article. These dates are useful for organizing the content into a clear, understandable narrative. If students are unfamiliar with time lines, model a quick time line using dates from the article.

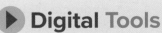 **Digital Tools**

Blended Learning

Students read informational texts and analyze primary sources.

Interactive IMPACT

Have students practice and apply the strategy of close reading as they analyze text.

Explore Drawing Conclusions

A **conclusion** is a decision you make about a topic. You use what you already know and information from what you are reading to draw a conclusion.

1. **Read the text.**
   Think about how the details and ideas in the text are connected.

2. **Think about what you already know about this topic.**
   Sometimes the author does not tell you everything. You have to use what you already know to understand the text.

3. **Draw a conclusion.**
   Draw a conclusion using what you read and what you know.

 Based on the text you read, work with your class to complete the chart below to answer the question: "How do the people of New Orleans feel about the streetcars?"

Text Clues and What I Already Know	Conclusion
Answers will vary, but students could mention that people liked it when new cable lines were added and that tourists and residents use them.	Answers will vary but may include that people are proud that they have the oldest street railways still in operation, and that New Orleans was the first place west of the Allegheny Mountains to have a street railway service.

Investigate!

 Read pages 188–195 in your Research Companion. Use your investigative skills to look for text evidence that tells you why communities are special. Then draw conclusions about what makes a community a special place. This chart will help you organize your notes.

Text Clues and What I Already Know About Communities	Conclusions
Answers will vary but could include these kinds of details: names of cities, roads, or street signs give clues about the past historic buildings and downtown areas keep history of community alive monuments and landmarks within communities often honor people, places, or events	Answers will vary but should be conclusions based on text clues and observation.

INQUIRY JOURNAL, pp. 178–179

Inquiry Tools

Explore Drawing Conclusions

Read Have students read the step-by-step instructions about how to draw conclusions. Point out that drawing conclusions often involves combining older information, or what we already know, with newer information that we have read or seen.

Guide Practice Have students review the text on pp. 176–177. Then work with students to complete the graphic organizer on p. 178. Explain that they will use a similar graphic organizer to organize their independent research.

Check Understanding Confirm understanding of the inquiry skill, Drawing Conclusions. If students are having trouble grasping the concept, review the steps on Inquiry Journal p. 178.

Investigate!

Have students read pp. 188–195 in the Research Companion. Tell them the information will help them answer the question **What Makes My Community Special?**

Take Notes Tell students they should use the graphic organizer on p. 179 of the Inquiry Journal to take notes on the key features of communities that they read about. Remind students that note taking involves recording the important details in a text. These details will help them draw conclusions about communities.

Spotlight on Language

Understanding Language

monument: a building, statue, or other structure that honors something important. The word is also the basis of the adjective *monumental*, which means "important."

LESSON 6 INVESTIGATE

What Makes My Community Special?

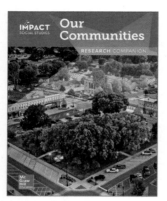

RESEARCH COMPANION, pp. 188–189

The Past Affects the Present

1 Inspect Have students read pp. 188–189 and list three street names that give clues about the community's history.

2 Find Evidence Use the questions below to check comprehension. Remind students to support their answers with text evidence.

Explain Why did the people of New Jersey change the name of Raritan Township? (They changed it to celebrate inventor Thomas Edison, who lived and worked there.) **DOK 2**

Relate What does Carteret Avenue tell us about Trenton, New Jersey's past? (Sir George Carteret is important to its past, because he was an early owner of New Jersey.) **DOK 2**

3 Make Connections

Infer What can you infer about the people and events that are honored with street names in a community? (People in the community believe these people and events were important parts of their history and should be remembered.) **DOK 3**

Apply Concepts Have students discuss the street names in their community. Ask: *Where do the names come from? Do they honor any person or event? What do the names tell about your community?* (Answers will vary, but students should be able to identify some connections between street names and their community's past.) **DOK 3**

THE IMPACT TODAY

Lesson 6 — What Makes My Community Special?

The Past Affects the Present

Look around your community. What do you see? Are there old buildings or old roads? What are the names on the street signs? What languages do you hear? What types of restaurants do you see? The answers help you understand what makes every community special.

For some communities, their names give us clues about people who lived and worked there. For example, Edison, New Jersey, was once called Raritan Township. However, in 1954, its name was changed to honor inventor Thomas Edison. The laboratory where he worked was in Menlo Park, part of the township.

Thomas Alva Edison Memorial Tower in Edison, New Jersey

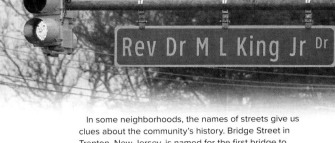

Rev. Dr. Martin Luther King Jr. Drive in Jersey City

In some neighborhoods, the names of streets give us clues about the community's history. Bridge Street in Trenton, New Jersey, is named for the first bridge to cross into Delaware from Trenton. Carteret Avenue is named for Sir George Carteret. He was an early owner of New Jersey.

Some streets are named for features that are found in the area. These include trees, plants, animals, or geographic features. Some of these places include Cedar Street, Briar Lane, and Quail Court in Bernards Township, New Jersey. Palisade Avenue in Englewood, New Jersey, is named for the steep cliffs that are found along part of the Hudson River.

Some streets are named for famous people who are important to our country's history. Martin Luther King Jr Drive in Jersey City, New Jersey, is named for a leader of the civil rights movement in the 1950s and 1960s. Rosa Parks Avenue in Montgomery, Alabama, is named for civil rights activist Rosa Parks.

These are just a few examples of how history affects a community.

RESEARCH COMPANION, pp. 188–189

English Learners SCAFFOLD

Use the following scaffolds to support student understanding of the lesson content.

Entering and Emerging

Have students look at the photos on pp. 188–189 and read the captions out loud to them. Have students complete the following sentence frames:

- The monument in Edison, New Jersey, was built to honor _____.
- The street sign was put up to celebrate the life of _____.

Developing and Expanding

Have small groups discuss how places and streets get their names. Ask: *Why might a community be named for a person? Why might a street be named for a bird or tree? Why do some communities name streets for famous people?* Have volunteers share their ideas using short sentences.

Bridging and Reaching

Have partners read the first paragraph on p. 188. Have them think about their community, discuss the questions, and then work together to make a list of their answers. Ask: *What do your answers tell you about your community?*

Digital Tools

Blended Learning

Students investigate curated resources and find evidence to answer the lesson question.

Interactive IMPACT

Students choose from print or digital **Inquiry Tools** to take notes.

Ways Communities Can Change

The geography of many communities throughout the United States has changed over time. People have changed the land in communities to meet their needs. Communities may make adjustments to their buildings to protect them from natural disasters. These changes can help make a community unique.

Many houses in New Orleans and other hurricane-prone communities use pilings to raise their houses.

Some cities are below sea level such as New Orleans, Louisiana. Levees were built to make it possible for people to live there. A levee is a wall meant to prevent water from flooding places during a storm. However, the levees did not protect New Orleans during Hurricane Katrina in 2005. A new levee system has been built since then. It has been designed to remain in place so less water is likely to escape onto the land.

Communities near the ocean have built walls called breakwaters to prevent flooding. Some breakwaters are called living breakwaters. They reduce flooding risks. They also help reef habitats and prevent erosion. A living breakwater is being developed on Staten Island, New York.

Some communities have changed the look of their houses to protect them from disasters. In New Orleans, some homes are placed on stilt-like structures called pilings. Pilings are meant to keep homes high enough off the ground to avoid flooding.

190   Lesson 6   What Makes My Community Special?

Communities Keep Histories Alive

Streets in communities can help us remember the past. Many streets in the United States were once paved with bricks. Some were widened and paved over with concrete. Many communities are fighting to keep the brick streets. They say brick streets keep the community's history alive.

Many communities look like they did long ago. Downtown Lanesboro, Minnesota, has many historic homes and old-fashioned shops. Buildings are built in a Spanish style in many Florida and California cities because the Spanish were early settlers in these communities.

✓ Stop and Check

Talk   Discuss with a partner how you can see the past in communities today.

Find Details   As you read, add new information to the graphic organizer on page 179 in your Inquiry Journal.

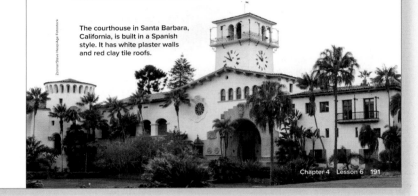

The courthouse in Santa Barbara, California, is built in a Spanish style. It has white plaster walls and red clay tile roofs.

Chapter 4   Lesson 6   191

RESEARCH COMPANION, pp. 190–191

Ways Communities Can Change

1 Inspect   Have students read pp. 190–191 and tell one way communities protect themselves from floods.

2 Find Evidence   Use the questions below to check comprehension.

Cite Evidence   What details in the text support the conclusion that people in some cities think it is important to remember the history of their community? (Some people fight to bring back brick streets. Some buildings are built in a style that reminds us who the early settlers were.) **DOK 3**

3 Make Connections

Analyze   Why do you think the author included so much information about the history of levees in New Orleans? (Answers will vary, but students might conclude that the author was trying to express how communities face challenges and must make changes to adapt to them.) **DOK 3**

✓ Stop and Check

Talk   Have students discuss how they can see the past in communities today. Tell them to think of specific locations in their community where they can see the past. (historical buildings, styles of architecture, street signs, landmarks, monuments)

Find Details   If students have trouble finding the appropriate facts to enter into the graphic organizer, suggest that they scan the pages for examples of changes that can happen within a community.

 Spotlight on Content

Scanning for Information

Have students work in small groups to find examples of changes that can occur in a community. Tell students to discuss which changes were a choice and which were a necessity. For example, changes made to adapt to floods are a necessity.

 Digital Tools

Blended Learning

Flip the research approach and find evidence in a digital format.

eBook

Students investigate using their **Research Companion** and **IMPACT Explorer eBooks** to find evidence.

Monuments Connect to the Past

Many **monuments** are found across the United States. A monument is a building, statue, or other structure that honors a person, place, or event in history. A monument is sometimes referred to as a memorial.

The Oculus in New York City is a monument that honors the victims of the terrorist attacks on September 11, 2001. On that day, the World Trade Center was destroyed. The Oculus is a transportation center. Part of the building is a 335-foot-long skylight. When the skylight is opened, it reminds people of what happened on that day. At 10:28 in the morning of September 11, 2001, the North Tower of the World Trade Center fell. Each year, the skylight will be opened at that time.

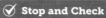

The Oculus in New York

> **PRIMARY SOURCE**
>
> **In Their Words...**
> George W. Bush
>
> "Terrorist attacks can shake the foundation of our biggest buildings, but they cannot touch the foundation of America. These acts shattered steel, but they cannot dent the steel of American resolve."
>
> —former president George W. Bush, 2001

Another important monument is the statue of a pioneer that stands on top of the Oregon State Capitol. This *Oregon Pioneer* is a symbol of Oregon's settlers. It stands for their determination and independence. This symbol has been part of the capitol building since 1938. The golden statue is twenty-three feet tall and weighs eight and a half tons. Visitors can reach it by climbing up a spiral staircase of 121 steps.

The pioneer statue stands on top of the Oregon State Capitol.

Did You Know?

Cloud Gate is a major work of art found in Chicago, Illinois. This sculpture is located in Millennium Park in the heart of the city. Indian-born British sculptor Anish Kapoor designed Cloud Gate. It was completed in 2006 and has become a highlight of the park. People from Chicago and visitors alike want to see its reflections and touch its surface.

Cloud Gate in Chicago

Cloud Gate's peculiar shape allows it to reflect the city's skyline. This reflection then bends the Chicago sky and skyline around its surface. The sculpture symbolizes a gate into the city. Most Chicagoans have nicknamed the sculpture "the Bean." The nickname is because of its unusual shape.

> ✓ **Stop and Check**
>
> **Talk** How do monuments reflect the past? Why are they important to people in a community?

RESEARCH COMPANION, pp. 192–193

Monuments Connect to the Past

1 Inspect Have students read pp. 192–193 and give an example of a monument cited in the text.

2 Find Evidence Use the questions below to check comprehension.

Compare How is the purpose of the Oculus in New York City different than the purpose of the *Oregon Pioneer* statue? (The purpose of the Oculus is to remember those who were affected by the terrorist attacks of 2001. The purpose of *Oregon Pioneer* is to celebrate Oregon's settlers.) **DOK 2**

Explain How does the location of the *Oregon Pioneer* statue add to its meaning? (The statue *Oregon Pioneer* is located on top of Oregon's capitol building. This adds to the statue's meaning as it is at the top of an important building in Oregon. The statue's location makes it easy to see.) **DOK 3**

3 Make Connections

Compare Think about a monument in your community. How is the statue *Oregon Pioneer* similar to or different than this monument? (Answers will vary, but students could compare how the monuments are made, where they stand, what they represent, and how they connect to the past.) **DOK 3**

✓ Stop and Check COLLABORATE

Talk Have partners discuss the purposes of monuments. (Answers will vary, but students should note that they honor people, places, or events. They are important to a community because of what these monuments represent or how they connect to the community's past.)

Social Emotional Learning

Self-Regulation

Maintain Focus To help students to develop their ability to maintain focus, help students create schedules before their independent work time. Allow students to list a time to begin and a time to end, and to create blocks of time to complete smaller tasks in between.

Field Trip: Pittsburgh, Pennsylvania

1 Inspect Have students read pp. 194–195 and tell the population and location of Pittsburgh.

2 Find Evidence Use the questions below to check for comprehension.

Draw Conclusions Why do you think the Cathedral of Learning was put on the National Historic Landmarks list? (Answers will vary, but students might mention that is was built in the early 1900s and is the tallest educational building in the Western Hemisphere.) **DOK 2**

Explain How does Market Square connect people to Pittsburgh's history? (Answers will vary, but students should mention that it has served as a meeting place for people since 1764.) **DOK 2**

Contrast How does the photograph of Phipps Conservatory contrast with the photographs of the other buildings on these two pages? (Answers will vary, but students might respond that it is not as tall, it is open and airy, more like a greenhouse and less like a building. They may explain that this is to help the plants inside.) **DOK 2**

3 Make Connections

Cite Evidence What two places would you recommend that visitors see if they want to learn what makes Pittsburgh a special community? Support your opinion with evidence from the text and photographs. (Answers will vary but should reflect what students have read in the text and seen in the photographs.) **DOK 3**

What Is the IMPACT Today?

Encourage students to explain any examples they give, and to think about examples they have seen in the text if they are stuck. (Answers will vary, but students might mention historic buildings, festivals, traditions, monuments or geographical features such as rivers or lakes.)

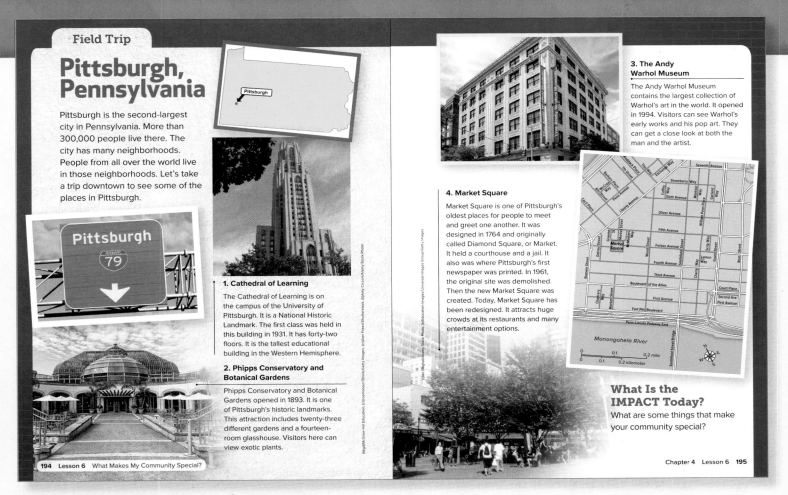

RESEARCH COMPANION, pp. 194–195

 English Learners SCAFFOLD

Use the following scaffolds to support student understanding of the lesson content.

Entering and Emerging

Have students describe places featured on pp. 194–195. Help students consider how the places are special. Provide sentence frames:

- The Cathedral of Learning is a _____ building.
- The Phipps Conservatory includes _____.
- The Andy Warhol Museum contains _____.
- People go to Market Square to _____.

Developing and Expanding

Have students look at the photos and maps associated with the Pittsburgh field trip. Ask questions to help students describe the different places. For example: *Why do people go to Market Square? What is special about the Cathedral of Learning? Which one of these places would you like to visit in Pittsburgh? Why?*

Bridging and Reaching

Have partners read the text about Pittsburgh, choose two places they would like to visit, and write a paragraph about those two places. The paragraph should include descriptive details and encourage others to visit. Ask: *What makes these places in Pittsburgh special? Why would you want to visit them?*

✓ **Check for Success**

Explain Can students explain what features make a community special?

Differentiate

If Not, Have students discuss one feature of communities that often sets them apart: history, culture, or location. If necessary, have students refer to their graphic organizers to review features of a community.

LESSON 6 REPORT

LESSON QUESTION

What Makes My Community Special?

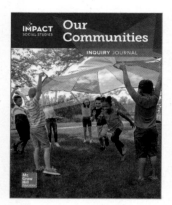

**INQUIRY JOURNAL,
pp. 180–181**

Think About It

Remind students to review their research and think about features that make a community special. As a refresher, have students look at their graphic organizers to review what they already knew about communities. Direct students back to pp. 188–195 of their Research Companion if they need more information.

Write About It

In Your Opinion Remind students to include the following as they craft their responses.

- Identify features and places of your community.
- List features of your community that are geographic, such as location, and features that developed over time, such as culture or architectural style.
- Explain why the people and places of your community are special.

Discipline(s)	4	3	2	1
Geography **History**	Blog post clearly explains how the community is special, including details about people and places.	Blog post somewhat explains how the community is special and includes a few details about people and places.	Blog post gives no explanation why the community is special but includes a few details about people or places.	Blog post fails to explain how the community is special, and details about people or places do not relate.

Talk About It

Compare and Contrast As students share ideas, tell them to take notes on any good ideas they have. Close, careful listening is key for this.

Assessment Students can check their understanding with feedback from the **Lesson Test** available online.

Connect to the Essential Question

Pull It Together Before students respond, encourage them to identify what they know about their local history. For example, they might know what language was spoken in the area and whether people farmed, fished, or worked in factories.

Inquiry Project Update Remind students to apply their knowledge from the chapter to their inquiry projects. At this point in the chapter, students should focus on the final items on the Project Checklist.

Think About It

Review
Recall what you have learned through your research.
Why do you think all communities are different?

Write About It

Define
What things can make a community special?

Answers will vary, but students should
show an understanding from their reading
about things such as people, location,
culture, and geography that can make a
community special.

In Your Opinion
Write a blog post about your community, its people,
and its places. List reasons why you think your community
is special.

Answers will vary but should provide
specific evidence to explain why the
student's community is special.

Talk About It

Compare and Contrast
Share your blog with a partner. Compare and contrast your ideas.
Then brainstorm additional reasons why your community is special.

Connect to the EQ
History
Pull It Together
Think about the role history has played in your community. How have events
and people of the past helped make your community special?

Answers will vary but should relate parts of
the community's history and accurately make
connections between past and present.

EQ Inquiry Project Notes

INQUIRY JOURNAL, pp. 180–181

English Learners SCAFFOLD

Use the following scaffolds to support student writing.

Entering and Emerging

Have students think about one thing in their community that they think is
special. Provide sentence frames to help students form ideas.

- Things that make a community special are _____.
- I think _____ is special about my community.
- One reason is _____.
- Another reason is _____.

Developing and Expanding

Explain that a blog post is information people publish on the Internet that
often contains the blogger's opinions. Ask questions to help students think
about features of their community that are special to them. Ask: *What feature
about your community do you like the most? Why is it special? How would you
describe it to someone who didn't know anything about it? What facts would
you include to show them it was special?*

Bridging and Reaching

Have partners discuss their favorite features, monuments, or places in their
community. Then ask for volunteers to share what is special about their community
and why they think so. Guide students to write a blog post that describes one or
two special features and provides facts to support their opinions.

✓ Check for Success

Summarize Can students
write a blog post about what
makes their community
special and support their
opinion with specific
evidence?

Differentiate

If Not, Have students list
facts about their community
and then identify which
facts make their community
special. Have students use the
identified facts to present a
visual report.

ESSENTIAL EQ QUESTION — How Does the Past Impact the Present?

**INQUIRY JOURNAL,
pp. 182–183**

Inquiry Project Wrap-Up

Remind students that they are to have created an illustrated time line featuring important events in a community's history.

Assessment Use the rubric on p. T263 to assess students' Inquiry Projects.

Complete Your Project

Have students work individually to review the Complete Your Project checklist. Remind them that if they have missed any of the criteria, now is their opportunity to make corrections or additions.

Share Your Project

If time allows, you may want to have students present their projects to the class. Provide the following presentation tips for students.

- Prepare and rehearse.
- Use notes to help you stay on topic when you present.
- Speak slowly and clearly. Make sure everyone can hear you.
- Make eye contact and speak directly to the audience.

Reflect on Your Project

Student reflections begin with thinking about the process for how they selected the key events that affected the community's growth and conducted their research. Students should focus on the results of the inquiry as well as the challenges and successes of the inquiry process. Students can apply those findings to future projects.

Chapter Connections can focus on anything that resonated with students about the study of their community's environment. These connections may spark students to do further research on their own.

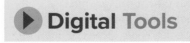

▶ Digital Tools

Blended Learning
Students use online checklists to prepare, complete and reflect on their Inquiry Projects.

Chapter Assessments
Students can demonstrate content mastery with the feedback from the online **Chapter Test**.

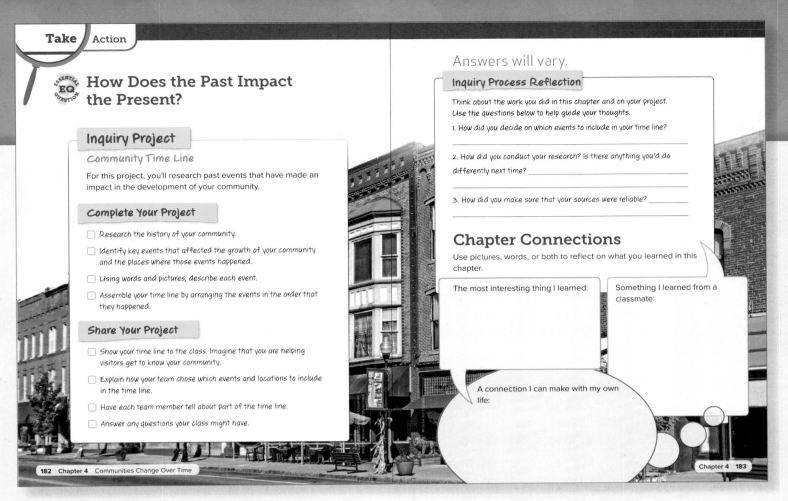

INQUIRY JOURNAL, pp. 182–183

 English Learners SCAFFOLD

Use the following scaffolds to support student presentation of their projects.

Entering and Emerging

Read aloud the project checklist and check students' understanding. Discuss any unfamiliar language. Then provide the following sentence frames to help students practice presenting their time lines:

- My time line shows how _____ changed.
- The community started when _____.
- People came to the community because _____.

Have students take turns presenting their time lines with a partner.

Developing and Expanding

Ask students to work with a partner to review the project checklist and determine whether they completed each item. As a class, make a list of question words or sentence frames that could be used for discussing the time lines. Have partners present their time lines to each other. Ask each student to ask two questions about his or her partner's time line.

Bridging and Reaching

Have students work in pairs to read the project checklist and brainstorm ways to present their time lines in a dynamic way. Give students time to practice presenting their time lines with their partners.

✔ Check for Success

Explain Use your online rubric or the rubric on p. T263 to record student progress. Can students use their time lines to explain how the community changed and grew?

Differentiate

If Not, Have students show how their community changed in a different way, such as a poster, play, or oral presentation.

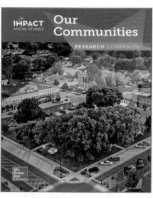

**RESEARCH COMPANION,
pp. 196–197**

Connections in Action!

Think Lead a discussion with students about how and why communities change. Select one of the ways that the students' community has changed and model how to determine what caused the change. Brainstorm how this change affected the people who live in the community.

Talk To help focus students' conversations, you may want to discuss the EQ with the entire class before students discuss their ideas with a partner. Remind students to think about evidence they can provide that will support their ideas.

Share Invite students to share their small group discussions with the class.

More to Explore

How Can You Make an IMPACT?

Mix and match the More to Explore activities to meet the needs of your classroom. Stretch students' thinking by offering alternative ways to demonstrate what they learned during the chapter.

These activities are flexible enough that you can assign one, two, or three activities to specific students or have students work in small groups. Remind students to use proper collaborative procedures when they work with partners.

Finish My Sentence
As a class, briefly review the definitions of the vocabulary words. If a team finishes early, challenge the partners to come up with more sentences using other vocabulary words.

Teacher Tip! **This activity can be used to monitor students' understanding of chapter vocabulary.**

My Community Then and Now
Bring in historical images of the community to share with the class after they have finished their drawings. Ask students to discuss how their drawings are similar to and different from the images.

Teacher Tip! **This activity can be used to monitor students' visual-spatial abilities.**

A Special Community
Brainstorm with students the places they find special in their community and reasons why these places are special. Have students use the information to write a letter to someone, encouraging him or her to visit these places. Explain that they can address their letters to real or imaginary people.

Teacher Tip! **Use this activity to help students practice writing about their opinions.**

▶ **Digital** Tools

Blended Learning
Students apply chapter concepts to extension activities and connect them to the Essential Question.

Interactive IMPACT

Review chapter vocabulary with **Word Play.**

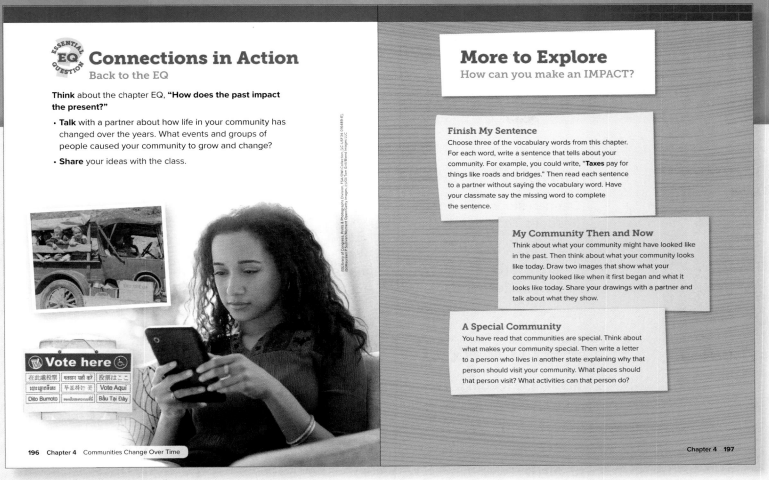

Connections in Action

Back to the EQ

Think about the chapter EQ, **"How does the past impact the present?"**

- **Talk** with a partner about how life in your community has changed over the years. What events and groups of people caused your community to grow and change?
- **Share** your ideas with the class.

More to Explore

How can you make an IMPACT?

Finish My Sentence

Choose three of the vocabulary words from this chapter. For each word, write a sentence that tells about your community. For example, you could write, **"Taxes** pay for things like roads and bridges." Then read each sentence to a partner without saying the vocabulary word. Have your classmate say the missing word to complete the sentence.

My Community Then and Now

Think about what your community might have looked like in the past. Then think about what your community looks like today. Draw two images that show what your community looked like when it first began and what it looks like today. Share your drawings with a partner and talk about what they show.

A Special Community

You have read that communities are special. Think about what makes your community special. Then write a letter to a person who lives in another state explaining why that person should visit your community. What places should that person visit? What activities can that person do?

RESEARCH COMPANION, pp. 196–197

English Learners SCAFFOLD

Use the following scaffolds to support student speaking and listening skills.

Entering and Emerging

Help students present an idea using supporting evidence from the text. Ask partners to work together to identify a big idea and then find evidence from the text to support it. Encourage students to use the following sentence frames to discuss their findings:

- In the past, our community had/was _____.
- Today, our community has/is _____.
- I read that some communities change when _____.
- Our community is *similar/different* because it changed when _____.

Developing and Expanding

Support students' attempt to use transition words by providing a list of words such as *then, next, because,* and *as a result of.* Encourage partners to practice using transition words as they discuss how and why their community has changed.

Bridging and Reaching

Support students' ability to connect ideas with supporting details and evidence. Have students create a list of transition words and allow them to refer to it as they present their ideas.

Social Emotional Learning

Relationship Skills

Teamwork Remind students of the importance of cooperating with others. Explain that people can achieve their goals more easily when they work together.

READER'S THEATER
with INQUIRY JOURNAL

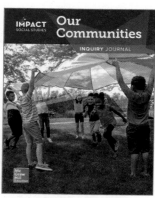

INQUIRY JOURNAL, pp. 184–189

Extend Learning

Deepen students' understanding of how and why communities change over time with the Reader's Theater selection "Step Back in Time."

> | **GENRE** | **Reader's Theater** is a form of drama in which actors do not memorize their lines. They use their voices rather than sets or costumes to help listeners understand the text.

Perform the Reader's Theater

Model the reading. Project the play with an interactive whiteboard or projector and read aloud as students follow along. As you read, use your voice to show how expression and rate can communicate meaning. Explain how exclamation points should affect expression.

Choose a few lines to examine. Discuss how a reader should read the lines:

- **Maria:** Airplane? Fly? What are you talking about?
  How should the character say this line? Why do you think so? (The character should say this line as if she's confused. She doesn't understand what Maya is talking about.)

- **Maya:** Wow! Life was very different in 1910!
  What does the exclamation point tell you to do? (The exclamation point tells me that the line should be read excitedly and slightly louder than the other lines.)

Practice the reading. Before students read aloud on their own, give them time to practice reading. Use techniques such as the following:

- **Choral Read**—Read together as a group to build fluency, practicing expression and pacing.

- **Echo Read**—Read a line and then have students repeat it.

Assign roles. Consider these strategies:
- Pair up students to read if some of your students are reluctant.
- Put students into performance groups so that every student has a chance to read a role.
- Have students mark up their scripts. They can highlight their dialogue, underline stage directions, and circle words they should emphasize when they speak.

Talk About It

As students discuss their ideas, have them think about how a school in a different country might differ from their school. Ask students to consider what it would be like if they didn't know anyone and didn't speak the language.

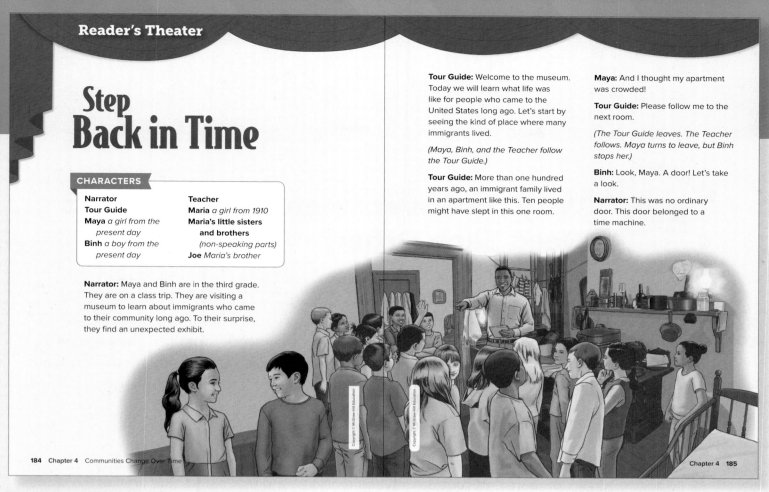

Step Back in Time

CHARACTERS

Narrator
Tour Guide
Maya *a girl from the present day*
Binh *a boy from the present day*

Teacher
Maria *a girl from 1910*
Maria's little sisters and brothers *(non-speaking parts)*
Joe *Maria's brother*

Narrator: Maya and Binh are in the third grade. They are on a class trip. They are visiting a museum to learn about immigrants who came to their community long ago. To their surprise, they find an unexpected exhibit.

Tour Guide: Welcome to the museum. Today we will learn what life was like for people who came to the United States long ago. Let's start by seeing the kind of place where many immigrants lived.

(Maya, Binh, and the Teacher follow the Tour Guide.)

Tour Guide: More than one hundred years ago, an immigrant family lived in an apartment like this. Ten people might have slept in this one room.

Maya: And I thought my apartment was crowded!

Tour Guide: Please follow me to the next room.

(The Tour Guide leaves. The Teacher follows. Maya turns to leave, but Binh stops her.)

Binh: Look, Maya. A door! Let's take a look.

Narrator: This was no ordinary door. This door belonged to a time machine.

184 Chapter 4 Communities Change Over Time

Chapter 4 185

INQUIRY JOURNAL, pp. 184–189

Reader's Theater Tips

- Allow students time to practice their lines before performing.
- Have students sit in a circle so they can hear each other as they read their lines.

Remind students of strategies for reading aloud:

- Speaking loudly so that other students can hear you.
- Speak at an appropriate rate.
- Use expression. Pay attention to punctuation.
- If you make a mistake, just keep going.

Connect to the Essential Question

Have students connect the Reader's Theater to the Essential Question. Ask: *How do Maya's and Binh's experience help you understand that communities change over time?* (Answers will vary, but students may suggest that when Maya and Binh traveled back in time, they learned that people in 1910 lived much differently than they do today. Students may cite Maria's reaction to airplanes and flying as evidence.)

 Digital Tools

Blended Learning
Students investigate how communities change over time with the online Reader's Theater.

Interactive IMPACT
Use the printable script for whole-class or small-group presentations.

Why Do Governments and Citizens Need Each Other?

In This Chapter Students will learn about the three branches of the United States government and how they work together. They also will explore the ways that communities in the United States govern themselves. Students will learn about citizenship and what it means to be a good citizen.

Chapter Objectives

- **Explain** what the Constitution is and why it was written.
- **Compare** and **contrast** governments in the United States and around the world.
- **Describe** the branches of government.
- **Explain** why communities need state and local governments.
- **Explain** the difference between rules and laws and why we have them.
- **Explain** what a hero is and give examples of people who are heroes.
- **Describe** what makes a good citizen, and explain how good citizens make a community strong.
- **Use information** from a variety of sources to create a constitution for your classroom.

Make Connections!

CONNECT TO SCIENCE

The National Archives Museum is the home of the original Declaration of Independence, U.S. Constitution, and Bill of Rights. Have students explore the technology related to preserving paper documents that are more than 200 years old, such as imaging techniques, oxygen removal, and moisture control.

CONNECT TO MATH

Tell students that each state has two senators. When the Constitution went into effect in 1789, the United States had 13 states. How many senators belonged to the U.S. Senate at that time? ($13 \times 2 = 26$) Today, the U.S. Senate has 100 members. How many more senators are there today than in 1789? ($100 - 26 = 74$)

Bibliography

Additional resources to aid student inquiry:

▶ **Hot Dog! Eleanor Roosevelt Throws a Picnic** by Leslie Kimmelman; Sleeping Bear Press, 2014

▶ **Heroes of History** by Anita Ganeri; little bee books, 2015

▶ **Miss Paul and the President: The Creative Campaign for Women's Right to Vote** by Dean Robbins; Knopf Books for Young Readers, 2016

Go online at **my.mheducation.com** for a complete list of resources.

Chapter-At-A-Glance

 EQ How Do Government and Citizens Work Together?

1 ENGAGE

INQUIRY JOURNAL

pp. 190–193

▶ **Introduce the Chapter**

▶ **Chapter Inquiry Project**

▶ **Explore Words**

 Short on Time?
Engage with the content the way YOU want to teach—and *your* students want to learn!

Check out the three suggested **Flexible Instructional Pathways** on pages FM34–FM35.

2 INVESTIGATE

RESEARCH COMPANION

pp. 198–257

▶ **Activate Knowledge**

▶ **What Does It Mean to Be a Good Citizen?**

▶ **Connect Through Literature** A Voice from Paris

▶ **People You Should Know**

▶ **Lessons 1–6**

 The **IMPACT Explorer Magazine** supports students' exploration of the Essential Question and provides additional resources for the EQ Inquiry Project.

3 TAKE ACTION

INQUIRY JOURNAL
RESEARCH COMPANION

pp. 242–243 pp. 258–259

▶ **Inquiry Project Wrap-Up and Chapter Connections**

▶ **Connections in Action**

▶ **More to Explore**

▶ Digital Tools at my.mheducation.com

ePresentation

Teach the Engage, Investigate, and Take Action content to the whole class from ePresentations that launch directly from the chapter dashboard.

eBook

You can flip your instruction with the **IMPACT eBooks** found on your chapter dashboard.

Interactive IMPACT

Blend in digital content **when you want it** and **where you want it**. Blended Learning notes in the Teacher's Edition highlight ways to connect in-class work with online experiences to enhance learning.

Investigate current events with **IMPACT News**.

Introduce the EQ with the **IMPACT Chapter Video**.

Explore domain-based vocabulary with **Explore Words** and **Word Play** vocabulary activities.

MONITOR PROGRESS:
Know What Your Students Know
Choose the assessment options that work best for you and your students.

Chapter Pre-Test (Optional)

Begin the Chapter
Measure students' content knowledge before you begin the chapter with the following questions.

Quick Check
✔ Why are there three branches of government? What are the three branches?

✔ How are local governments different from the federal government? How are they the same?

✔ What are examples of laws that are important for protecting citizens in your community?

1. Write each of the questions on separate sheets of poster paper. Have students volunteer answers and write all of their responses under the question.

2. Ask students to rate the answers on a scale from 1 (not very confident) to 5 (very confident).

3. Review the information on the posters for misconceptions, for factual errors, and to inform instruction. You may wish to hang the posters on the wall to review as students investigate Chapter 5.

4. **Don't Forget!** Throughout the chapter, revisit students' quick check responses with them. If students change their responses, ask them to support the change with text evidence. You may wish to have students respond to a different prompt to measure students' content knowledge, such as *What is expected of a citizen of the United States?*

Ongoing Lesson Assessment

Use the following lesson tools to monitor the **IMPACT** of your instruction.

☑ Stop and Check

Use the questions provided in the Stop and Check prompts to monitor students' comprehension of the core lesson content. The Stop and Check questions, found in the Research Companion, prompt students to engage in discussions to deepen their understanding of the content.

✔ Check for Success

Use this formative assessment tool to assess how well your students understand the material they are learning in class. The Check for Success questions, located at point of use in the Teacher's Edition, are not a test but a way to assess students' comprehension of a particular topic. A Differentiate strategy offers one activity that you can use to quickly adapt your instruction.

⌕ Report Your Findings

Use Report Your Findings in each lesson to measure student understanding of the lesson content and their ability to effectively express their understanding. See pp. T404, T420, T436, T450, T466, and T482 for task-specific evaluation rubrics. Report Your Findings is found in the Inquiry Journal.

▶ Digital Tools

Lesson Assessments
Use the **Lesson Test** to monitor students' understanding of the lesson content. Online Lesson Tests are customizable and available for every lesson. You will also find the tools you need to create your own assessments and to track your students' progress. A printable Lesson Test is available for use in class.

Chapter Assessment

Evaluate

Monitor student understanding of core chapter content with one or more of the following assessment options.

 ## Connections in Action

Use the **Connections in Action** to evaluate student understanding of core chapter content through discussion in the Research Companion, pp. 258–259.

 ## Inquiry Project

In this chapter's Inquiry Project, students will think about how they should behave in the classroom and create a constitution that sets rules that everyone in the class must follow. Students will also determine the consequences for breaking any of the rules before agreeing to follow the constitution. See pp. T380–T381 for more information.

Use the EQ Inquiry Project to measure student understanding of the chapter content and their ability to effectively express their understanding. A task-specific evaluation rubric is available in the Online Teacher Resources.

	4	3	2	1
Developing and Planning Inquiry	Classroom constitution has clear purpose, rules, and consequences.	Classroom constitution has mostly clear purpose, rules, and consequences.	Classroom constitution has some flaws in clarity, rules, or consequences.	Classroom constitution is unclear in terms of purpose, laws, or consequences.
Civics Understanding	Strong understanding of the purpose of a constitution	Adequate understanding of the purpose of a constitution	Uneven understanding of the purpose of a constitution	No understanding of the purpose of a constitution
Sources and Evidence	Rules and consequences based on thorough and convincing evidence	Rules and consequences based on adequate evidence	Rules and consequences based on uneven or only somewhat convincing evidence	Rules and consequences not based on supporting evidence
Communicating Conclusions	Provides clear reasons for decisions made in project	Provides reasons that mostly support decisions made in project	Loosely links reasons to work in the project	Does not link reasons to the project

ENGAGE
with INQUIRY JOURNAL

Why Do Governments and Citizens Need Each Other?

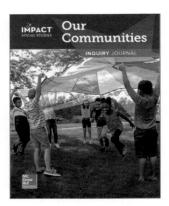

INQUIRY JOURNAL, pp. 190–191

Talk About It

Read Have students read the opening page together. Prompt students to write three questions to which they would like to know the answers after reading about how governments and citizens work together. Give students a chance to share their questions with a partner. You may wish to record these questions and refer back to them throughout the chapter.

Inquiry Project

Creating a Classroom Constitution

Discuss the Inquiry Project with students. Review each step of the project and the **Project Checklist** evaluation rubric. Tell students that they will use information from the chapter and from independent research to complete the project.

My Research Plan

Discuss the Essential Question with students and the reasons why people follow rules and laws. Then have students work in pairs to brainstorm research questions that are "just right," not too general nor too specific.

Design Your Own Inquiry Path (Optional)

You may wish to work with students to choose their own Essential Question, Inquiry Project, and related research questions. In addition to your feedback, have students preview chapter materials and discuss ideas with classmates to help develop possible questions, such as *What is the purpose of a constitution? What rules are students expected to follow?* or their own question.

Once chosen, have students explain why their Essential Question is important to them and to others. Have students record their question, project idea, and initial supporting research questions using the **Student EQ Inquiry Project** pages found at **my.mheducation.com**.

▶ Digital Tools

Blended Learning
Students engage with the chapter's Essential Question and launch their investigations.

Interactive IMPACT
Spark student interest with the **EQ Chapter Video**.

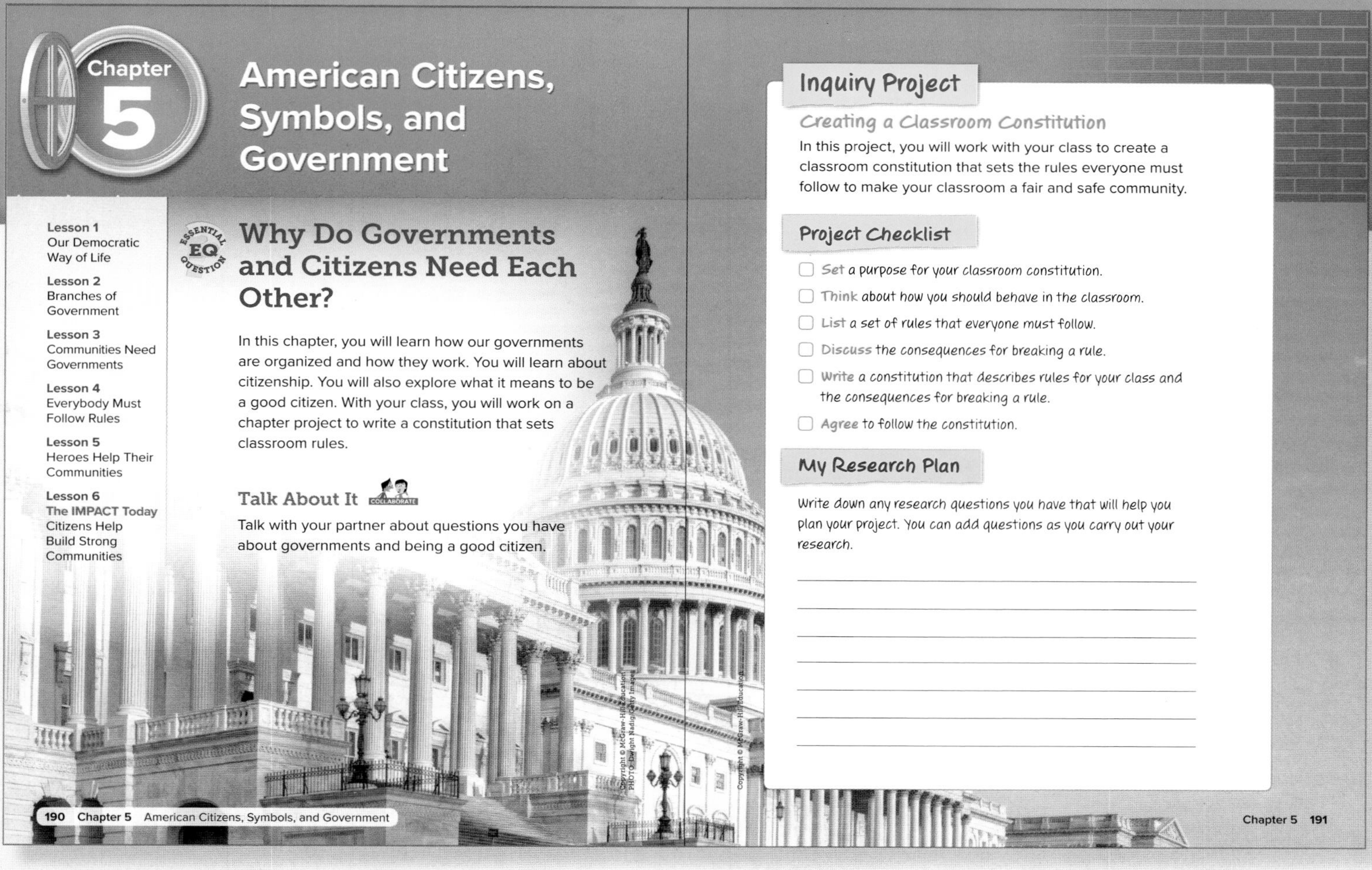
Chapter 5

American Citizens, Symbols, and Government

Lesson 1
Our Democratic Way of Life
Lesson 2
Branches of Government
Lesson 3
Communities Need Governments
Lesson 4
Everybody Must Follow Rules
Lesson 5
Heroes Help Their Communities
Lesson 6
The IMPACT Today
Citizens Help Build Strong Communities

ESSENTIAL EQ QUESTION

Why Do Governments and Citizens Need Each Other?

In this chapter, you will learn how our governments are organized and how they work. You will learn about citizenship. You will also explore what it means to be a good citizen. With your class, you will work on a chapter project to write a constitution that sets classroom rules.

Talk About It COLLABORATE

Talk with your partner about questions you have about governments and being a good citizen.

Inquiry Project

Creating a Classroom Constitution

In this project, you will work with your class to create a classroom constitution that sets the rules everyone must follow to make your classroom a fair and safe community.

Project Checklist

- ☐ Set a purpose for your classroom constitution.
- ☐ Think about how you should behave in the classroom.
- ☐ List a set of rules that everyone must follow.
- ☐ Discuss the consequences for breaking a rule.
- ☐ Write a constitution that describes rules for your class and the consequences for breaking a rule.
- ☐ Agree to follow the constitution.

My Research Plan

Write down any research questions you have that will help you plan your project. You can add questions as you carry out your research.

INQUIRY JOURNAL, pp. 190–191

English Learners SCAFFOLD

Use the following scaffolds to support student understanding of the Inquiry Project.

Entering and Emerging

Help students understand the Inquiry Project. Explain that the word *constitution* means "a document that tells about the laws or rules that people follow." Say: *The United States has a constitution. It tells the rules for the United States. Our state has a constitution, too. It tells the rules for our state.* Guide students in thinking about the purpose of a constitution. Ask students to use the following sentence frames:

The purpose of a constitution is to _________. People create a constitution because _________.

Developing and Expanding

Help students begin thinking about the Inquiry Project. Allow partners to read the project checklist together and restate each task in their own words.

Bridging and Reaching

Students should read the Inquiry Project instructions and checklist. Then have students explain the project to their partner in their own words. Students should listen for any differences in their explanation and discuss them.

Social Emotional Learning

Decision-Making Skills

Ethical Responsibility
As students consider rules to include in their classroom constitution, encourage them to think about how each rule might contribute to a better classroom experience. Explain that these rules also should show respect for the individual dignity and differences of their classmates.

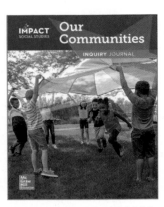

**INQUIRY JOURNAL,
pp. 192–193**

Explore Words

Academic/Domain-Specific Vocabulary Read the words aloud to students. Explain to students that these are words they will learn more about in the chapter.

Word Rater Have students place a checkmark in one of the three boxes below each word, indicating that they "Know It," "Heard It," or "Don't Know It." Explain to students that they will come back to this chart to add additional information about each word as they work through the chapter.

☐ **Know It!** Tell students that if they know the word, they should write its meaning on the lines provided.

☐ **Heard It!** Tell students that if they have heard, or are familiar with the word, they should write what they know about it on the lines provided. Remind them to take notes about the word as they encounter it.

☐ **Don't Know It!** If they do not know the word's meaning, tell them to write down its meaning when they encounter the word in the chapter.

Support Vocabulary

Return to the Word Rater as you come across vocabulary words in each lesson. Encourage students to use the "My Notes" section to include any of the following:

- definitions from the text
- deeper understandings
- synonyms
- other associations

 Spanish Cognates

federal = federal

hero = héroe

jury = jurado

justice = justicia

Content Words	
compromise	an agreement that people make when they have different ideas
executive branch	the part of government that makes sure that laws are carried out and followed
federal	national
hero	a person who has done great things or has behaved with great honor
judicial branch	the part of government that decides what the laws mean
jury	a group of citizens who are chosen to decide a legal case
justice	the fair and equal treatment under the law
legislative branch	the part of government that makes the laws
rights	things that are due to everyone
volunteer	to do a job or provide a service without pay

Complete this chapter's Word Rater. Write notes as you learn more about each word.

compromise
My Notes
☐ Know It!
☐ Heard It!
☐ Don't Know It!

executive branch
My Notes
☐ Know It!
☐ Heard It!
☐ Don't Know It!

federal
My Notes
☐ Know It!
☐ Heard It!
☐ Don't Know It!

hero
My Notes
☐ Know It!
☐ Heard It!
☐ Don't Know It!

judicial branch
My Notes
☐ Know It!
☐ Heard It!
☐ Don't Know It!

jury
My Notes
☐ Know It!
☐ Heard It!
☐ Don't Know It!

justice
My Notes
☐ Know It!
☐ Heard It!
☐ Don't Know It!

legislative branch
My Notes
☐ Know It!
☐ Heard It!
☐ Don't Know It!

rights
My Notes
☐ Know It!
☐ Heard It!
☐ Don't Know It!

volunteer
My Notes
☐ Know It!
☐ Heard It!
☐ Don't Know It!

Copyright © McGraw-Hill Education

INQUIRY JOURNAL, pp. 192–193

English Learners SCAFFOLD

Use the following scaffolds to support student understanding of chapter vocabulary.

Entering and Emerging

Show pictures for each vocabulary term, and name the vocabulary term that matches the picture. Have students say aloud the vocabulary term as you point to the picture. Then have students use the pictures and vocabulary terms to play a matching game. Make sure that students read aloud the term each time they make a match.

Developing and Expanding

Review the vocabulary terms and definitions with students. Then lead the class in a game of vocabulary charades. Organize the class into two groups. One student from each group selects a vocabulary term and then acts out the term for other group members to guess. Then the other team takes a turn. Repeat for all of the vocabulary terms.

Bridging and Reaching

Provide students with index cards to create vocabulary flashcards. On one side of the card, have students write the vocabulary term. On the other side, have students write their own definition or draw an image of the term.

▶ Digital Tools

Blended Learning

Explore Words engages students in the investigation of academic and domain-specific words they encounter in each lesson.

Interactive IMPACT

Throughout the chapter, encourage students to interact with the **Explore Words** cards and games.

ESSENTIAL EQ QUESTION

Why Do Governments and Citizens Need Each Other?

RESEARCH COMPANION, pp. 198–199

Activate Knowledge

Read and Discuss COLLABORATE Have students read the opening on p. 198 together. Ask: *Why do people form governments?* As students share their responses, you may wish to redirect misconceptions and inaccurate information.

What Does It Mean to Be a Good Citizen?

- Have students read the text, focusing on both the photographs and the captions.
- Describe some actions a good citizen might perform. (Answers will vary, but students might mention that good citizens are helpful to others, volunteer in the community, vote, and obey the law.)
- Why is it important to vote? (Voting is one way that citizens can participate in government. It gives citizens a voice on issues that are important to them and our country.)

Make Connections

- Identify some of the organizations that provide services to your community. What can you do to help them? (Answers will vary, but students should identify legitimate community services and reasonable ways to offer support.)
- **Perspectives** How does helping others make you a better citizen? (Answers will vary but should include reasons that support students' opinions.)

Chapter 5
American Citizens, Symbols, and Government

Lesson 1
Our Democratic Way of Life

Lesson 2
Branches of Government

Lesson 3
Communities Need Governments

Lesson 4
Everybody Must Follow Rules

Lesson 5
Heroes Help Their Communities

Lesson 6
The IMPACT Today
Citizens Help Build Strong Communities

 ESSENTIAL EQ QUESTION

Why Do Governments and Citizens Need Each Other?

We are responsible for making our community, state, and country fair and safe places to live. In this chapter, you will read about how our government was created and how it works today. You will learn why laws are important. You also will explore what it means to be a good citizen. As you read, think about what you can do to be a good citizen.

Citizens have the duty to vote in elections.

198 Chapter 5 American Citizens, Symbols, and Government

What Does It Mean to Be a Good Citizen?

A good citizen is part of the community, the state, and the country. What does it take to be a good citizen?

Good citizens are honest, polite, and kind. You can be a good citizen by doing simple tasks. A good citizen could hold the door open for someone or carry groceries for a neighbor. Behaving like a good citizen every day is easy.

Good citizens take part in government. They can help someone run for office or sign up people to vote. They can run for office themselves. They make sure they know about the people who are running for office before they vote. In a democracy, your vote is your voice in government.

Many citizens work for the common good. Some volunteer their time and energy to help others. A good citizen can make a community a better place by volunteering to lend a hand.

Chapter 5 199

RESEARCH COMPANION, pp. 198–199

 EL

English Learners SCAFFOLD

Use these scaffolds to support students in activating their background knowledge.

Entering and Emerging

Point to each picture on p. 199 and ask: *What does this picture show?* Allow students to answer without using complete sentences. Point out that all of the people in the pictures are good citizens. Remind students that a *citizen* belongs to a country and has the rights of that country. Ask students to draw a picture that shows how they are good citizens. Have each student share the picture with a partner and tell what it shows.

Developing and Expanding

Have students tell a partner what each picture on p. 199 shows. Then explain that each picture shows people who are good citizens. Ask students to think of ways that they can be good citizens, and have them discuss their ideas with their partner.

Bridging and Reaching

Ask students to look at the pictures and read the captions. With a partner, have students discuss what the pictures have in common. Then ask partners to discuss how they can be good citizens in their community.

Connect Through Literature

A VOICE *from Paris*

By Joy Dueland

Patsy Jefferson lifted up her long skirts and picked her way between the cartons of books spilling out of her father's study. What would the French servants think if she fell on her nose! A twelve-year-old daughter of an American diplomat had to mind her dignity. Since her mother's death two years ago she had tried to run her father's household, but it wasn't easy with servants who spoke only French. Patsy missed America.

Thomas Jefferson

Here in France to arrange trade treaties for the new United States, her father had made himself at home with his books as usual. He liked France far more than the old enemy, England. In Paris, he said to Patsy, a man could live his life without finding any rudeness.

But Thomas Jefferson missed America as much as his daughter did. He was in France because his country needed him here; the United States needed trade to grow strong. But Patsy knew how he longed right now to be in Philadelphia, where Americans would soon be framing their new Constitution.

Patsy stubbed her toe on a pile of books, and as they tumbled down the noise made her father look up. He smiled at her.

"Patsy, these are books for Mr. Madison. Have care, my child. He asked me to send him a few books to help him plan our new Constitution."

200 Chapter 5 American Citizens, Symbols, and Government

"A few books! Papa, these will fill several crates. How can he possibly read them before he goes to Philadelphia?"

"These books will give him direction," Patsy's father said. "He must convince the other delegates that protection of the people's rights is essential to the new Constitution."

Patsy's father had discussed with her his deep fears that the powerful and rich Americans back home would not care enough to protect the rights of the common people. It was obvious that here in France the ordinary people had few rights under the law. The king and his nobles could even throw a person in jail without a trial.

Jefferson believed the common people in America would make their wishes heard. He was speaking aloud as his goose quill scratched on a letter to be mailed to Madison.

"The only security of all is in a free press. The force of public opinion cannot be resisted."

Patsy listened as she bent down to put some volumes in their crates. Poor Mr. Madison. All this reading!

Weeks and months passed. The boats carrying mail between America and France were slow. Thomas Jefferson could guess at what was going on in Philadelphia, but any news he received was already many weeks old.

Chapter 5 201

RESEARCH COMPANION, pp. 200–203

Connect Through Literature

| **GENRE** | Historical Fiction "A Voice from Paris" is historical fiction. Historical fiction describes real people and events but puts them in situations that are made up.

Have students read the selection on pp. 200–203. Then discuss this question:

1. Why were Thomas Jefferson and James Madison writing to each other? (They were discussing the new Constitution of the United States.)

Have students reread the selection and ask:

2. How did Jefferson's time in France help him realize the importance of a Bill of Rights? (In France, Jefferson saw how common people had few rights under the law.)

3. In your opinion, is it important to have laws that protect the rights of the individual? Why or why not? (Answers will vary, but students should support their opinions with logical reasoning.)

Perspectives Why was it important to ratify the Constitution even though there was no Bill of Rights? (Without a constitution to provide laws and structure, the newly formed U.S. government could collapse.)

Background Information

Congress sent Thomas Jefferson to Paris in 1784, where he joined the United States' previous ambassadors Benjamin Franklin and John Adams. When Franklin returned to the United States in 1785, Jefferson took his place as the top U.S. diplomat.

People You Should Know

Alexander Hamilton

Alexander Hamilton was one of the founders of the United States. In 1787, he attended the Constitutional Convention. The people there helped create the U.S. Constitution. Hamilton believed the country should have a strong national government. He wrote essays that encouraged the states to approve the Constitution. His ideas helped shape the new government.

Cesar Chavez

Cesar Chavez was a Mexican American farmworker. The pay was low, and workers lived in crowded camps. Chavez wanted farmworkers to be treated better. He formed the National Farm Workers Association in 1962. This group helped farmworkers work for better treatment. Chavez has become a symbol for the rights of workers.

Thurgood Marshall

Thurgood Marshall was a lawyer who fought for the rights of African Americans. In the 1954 court case *Brown* v. *Board of Education*, Marshall argued that segregated schools were unfair. The Supreme Court agreed. The government made segregation against the law. In 1967, Marshall became the first African American judge to serve on the Supreme Court.

Sally Ride

Sally Ride was born in Los Angeles and studied physics at Stanford University. In 1978, she successfully applied for a job at NASA. A few years later she became the first American woman to travel into space. After her time at NASA, Ride worked as a professor of physics. Then, in 2001, she founded Sally Ride Science to inspire young people to study science and math.

RESEARCH COMPANION, pp. 204–205

People You Should Know

How do personal stories IMPACT our understanding of our government and citizenship?

Read Have students read aloud the biographies. Tell them that they will learn about these people and others throughout the chapter.

Research Prompt students to choose one of the individuals discussed in this section and do further research about his or her life, achievements, and opinions.

Respond Have students pick a particular incident from that person's life and write a blog from the person's point of view. The blog should have at least three short entries describing different aspects of the incident. It could be how the particular situation unfolded, how the person felt about the event, what happened afterward, and so on. Students can write the blog as a text document, a slide presentation, or a web page. They should use images and quotations to provide greater interest and context.

 **Digital Tools**

Blended Learning

Students investigate and discuss curated news articles that extend the chapter content.

Interactive IMPACT

Connect to current events and people with **IMPACT News** and **More to Investigate**.

IMPACT EXPLORER MAGAZINE, pp. 54–65

WordBlast

Remind students to look for the Word Blasts as they read the *IMPACT Explorer Magazine*.

Extend Knowledge Building

The **IMPACT Explorer Magazine** provides students another route to explore each chapter's Essential Question from a variety of perspectives as they dig deeper into the subject of the ways that government and citizens work together. Additional questions and activities help students develop and deepen their understanding of the chapter's content.

Engage

Build background for students and share any information needed to provide a context for the chapter topic. Read aloud the Essential Question and the Table of Contents.

Analyze the Visual Discuss the opening visual (photograph, photo essay, artwork) on the second page of the **IMPACT Explorer Magazine** chapter. Help students connect the visual to the chapter topic and the Essential Question.

Analyze the Sources

Students will read and analyze the leveled informational articles and literary texts, graphic texts, primary and secondary sources, photographs, maps, and other visual resources.

Read and Analyze Before reading, provide any additional information you think students will need about the topics. Then guide students through the three-step process to read and analyze the content.

1 Inspect

Have students skim the content on a page or multiple pages. Ask questions to help students recall and retell key ideas.

- What is this article mostly about?
- Who is _____?

2 Find Evidence

Have students reread the content and look for details they might have missed. Ask additional questions to help them read more closely.

- What details do you notice in the photographs?
- Why was _____ important?

3 Make Connections

Have students work in pairs or small groups to discuss prompts that help them connect the articles to other texts, their own lives, current ideas and issues, and other topics.

- How is _____ similar to what we do?
- How do you think _____ felt about what happened?
- What do you think about _____?

Chapter 5

American Citizens, Symbols, and Government

EQ Why do governments and citizens need each other?

Table of Contents

54 Chapter 5 American Citizens, Symbols, and Government

Chapter 5 55

CELEBRATE OUR SYMBOLS

Our national symbols stand for things we are proud of. What symbols of the United States do you see in the photos? What does each symbol represent?

IMPACT EXPLORER MAGAZINE, pp. 54–65

How to Use the IMPACT Explorer Magazine

Use the following scaffolds to support students' understanding and your classroom needs.

Whole Class

Use the **IMPACT Explorer Magazine** Teaching Guide to read and discuss one or more articles with the whole class.

Small Group

Have partners or small groups read articles connected to the day's core lesson and report back to the whole class about what they read.

Independent Work

Assign articles for students to extend and enrich their understanding of a topic, including during center time and independent reading time.

The online **IMPACT Explorer Magazine** Teaching Guide provides support for various implementation models as well as a three-step lesson plan for each article. The lesson plan includes background information, meaningful questions, vocabulary activities, scaffolded support for English learners, and collaborative conversation prompts.

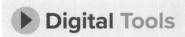 **Digital Tools**

Blended Learning

Students extend the investigation of the Chapter Essential Question with highly visual, leveled articles and video.

eBook

Use the **IMPACT Explorer Magazine eBook** to extend knowledge building.

LESSON QUESTION

What Makes Democracy Work?

Connect to the Essential Question

Tell students that this lesson provides key research into the Chapter Essential Question: **Why Do Governments and Citizens Need Each Other?** Explain that they will learn about the history of the U.S. Constitution and why it is an important and influential document. Tell them they will also look at the role democracy plays in our government and what some other governments around the world are like.

Lesson Objectives

- **Explain** why the U.S. Constitution was written.
- **Detail** important events related to the writing of the U.S. Constitution.
- **Describe** what it means for the United States to be a *representative democracy.*
- **Write** a list of items that might appear in a classroom constitution.

Make Connections!

CONNECT TO ELA

Reading **Determine** the main idea of a text; recount the key details and explain how they support the main idea.

Research **Conduct** short research projects that build knowledge about a topic.

Writing **Produce** writing in which the development and organization are appropriate to the task and purpose.

Speaking and Listening **Explain** students' own ideas and understanding in light of the discussion.

Language **Use** coordinating and subordinating conjunctions.

COMMUNITY CONNECTIONS

To enrich what students have learned about the United States Constitution, plan a field trip to a local government official's office to talk about how your local government is affected by the U.S. Constitution. Alternately, invite the local official to come to the class and address the students.

Lesson-At-A-Glance

1 ENGAGE INQUIRY JOURNAL

pp. 194–199

▶ **Talk About It:** Photograph of the Assembly Room in Independence Hall, Philadelphia

▶ **Analyze the Source:** Preamble of the United States Constitution

▶ **Inquiry Tools:** Explore Main Idea and Details

2 INVESTIGATE RESEARCH COMPANION

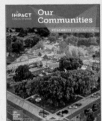

pp. 206–215

▶ **The History of the Constitution**

▶ **The Articles of Confederation**

▶ **The Constitutional Convention**

▶ **The Constitution Is Written**

▶ **Democracy and Our Country**

▶ **Around the World: Governments Around the World**

3 REPORT INQUIRY JOURNAL

pp. 200–201

▶ **Think About It**

▶ **Write About It:** Write a List of Ideas

▶ **Talk About It**

▶ **Connect to the Essential Question**

ASSESSMENT

▶ **Online Lesson Test**

▶ **Printable Lesson Test**

For more details, see pages T378–T379.

Digital Tools

at **my.mheducation.com**

ePresentation

Teach the **Engage**, **Investigate**, and **Report** content to the whole class from **ePresentations** that launch directly from the lesson dashboard.

eBook

You can flip your instruction with the **IMPACT eBooks** found on your lesson dashboard.

Interactive IMPACT

Blend in digital content **when you want it** and **where you want it**.

Blended Learning features in the Teacher's Edition highlight ways to connect in-class work with online experiences to enhance learning.

Investigate current events with **IMPACT News**.

Explore domain-based vocabulary with **Explore Words** and **Word Play** vocabulary activities.

pp. 54–65

Go Further with IMPACT Explorer Magazine!

The **IMPACT Explorer Magazine** supports students' exploration of the Essential Question and provides additional resources for the EQ Inquiry Project.

What Makes Democracy Work?

Language Objectives

- Use newly acquired content and academic vocabulary to talk and write about the United States Constitution.
- Write a list of ideas about a classroom constitution.
- Use sentences with *if* to talk about real situations and their results.

Spanish Cognates

To support Spanish speakers, point out the cognates.

democracy = democracia

constitution = constitucíon

government = gobierno

liberty = libertad

confederation = confederación

history = historia

Introduce the Lesson

Set Purpose Explain to students that in this lesson they will read informational texts to learn about the United States Constitution and why it was written.

Access Prior Knowledge Read the lesson question and find out what students already know about democracy and the United States Constitution. Ask: *Have you ever heard the words "We the People"?* Ask: *Where have you seen the words? What else did you see with the words? Where have you heard the words? What else did you hear with the words?*

Spark Curiosity Have students look at the image of Benjamin Franklin on p. 209 of the Research Companion. Explain that Benjamin Franklin was an author, a scientist, a leader, and one of America's founders. He helped write the Declaration of Independence and the U.S. Constitution. He discovered many things about electricity and invented bifocals. As a humorist, he is famous for many quotations, including the one on this page: ". . . nothing can be said to be certain, except death and taxes."

Have students work in small groups. Assign one of the following quotations by Benjamin Franklin and others to each small group and help them understand its meaning. Help each group find the pairs of opposite words in the quotations. Then have each small group explain the quote to the larger group. "Lost time is never found again"; "Tell me and I forget, teach me and I may remember, involve me and I learn"; "The Constitution only guarantees the American people the right to pursue happiness. You have to catch it yourself."

Build Meaning & Support Language

Inquiry Journal

Analyze the Source (pages 196–197) Tell students that in this lesson, they will read informational texts that give facts, examples, and explanations about a topic. As you read "Preamble of the United States Constitution," explain any words that students don't know. Use these easier-to-understand words and phrases to help students understand the reasons for the Constitution: insure = make sure; domestic tranquility = peace at home; provide = make available; defence (British spelling of defense) = protection; promote = help; general welfare = well-being of all; secure = get; liberty = freedom; posterity = our children and their children; ordain = order.

Inquiry Tools (pages 198–199) Tell students that they will **Explore Main Idea and Details** as they read the selections in the Research Companion. Tell them that the graphic organizer will help them organize the information they read. Review with students that the main idea is the most important idea the author presents about a topic and that details are pieces of information that support it. Model how to locate the main idea on p. 196 and show how it is recorded in the graphic organizer on p. 198. Say: *The main idea of the paragraph on page 196 is that the Preamble introduces the Constitution. This is written under Main Idea. Under Details I could write: "It lists reasons why the Constitution was written."*

Research Companion

The History of the Constitution (pages 206–207) Explain that this time line provides a history of the making of the Constitution of the United States. Have students find the year 1776. Ask: *What happened on July 4, 1776? Then what happened in 1777? What events happened in 1788 and 1791?*

The Articles of Confederation/The Constitutional Convention (pages 208–209) After you read the biography of Benjamin Franklin on p. 209, explain the meaning of the second paragraph. Tell students that he meant that the Constitution might appear to be permanent, or to last forever, but even the Constitution is not forever. He says the only things that are really certain in life are death and taxes (money that all citizens must pay to the government).

The Constitution Is Written (pages 210–211) After you read **Did You Know?** on p. 210, reread the last two sentences "Although the United States has had the same Constitution since it was founded, some states have had several. For example, Louisiana has rewritten its constitution eleven times." Point out the word *Although* in the first sentence. Display a simpler version of this sentence: *The United States has had the same Constitution since it was founded, but some states have had several constitutions.*

Democracy and Our Country (pages 212–213) Explain that the National Archives Museum is a museum that was built specifically to hold the founding documents of the United States. The word *rotunda* means a round room with a dome at the top. Ask: *Why do you think these documents are called the Charters of Freedom?*

Around the World: Governments Around the World (pages 214–215) After you read the first paragraph on p. 214, reread this sentence: "However, in a constitutional monarchy, the king or queen is more of a symbol for the country." Explain that the word *however* signals a difference from what was said before it. Tell students that the previous sentence said that the country was ruled by a king or queen, but the following sentence says that the king or queen is just a symbol for the country and does not have any power. Ask: *What do you remember about the word* symbol?

Inquiry Journal

Report Your Findings (pages 200–201) Explain to students that a classroom constitution should include the rules for the classroom and how everyone will make decisions. Encourage students to use the new vocabulary words and phrases that they have learned. Check their work for spelling and punctuation errors.

Language Forms & Conventions

Sentences with *if* Review with students that sentences that start with *if* talk about possible situations and what will happen as a result. The first part of the sentence, the *if* clause, shows a possible situation. The main, or result, clause shows the result of that situation. Write the chart on the board. Ask: *What happens if someone is accused of a crime? What happens if government leaders do a good job?*

If Part	Main Part
If someone is accused of a crime,	he or she has the right to a fair trial.
If government leaders do a good job,	the voters will reelect them.

 Have students work in pairs to locate another sentence with *if* on p. 213. Call on a volunteer to say the sentence aloud and add it to the chart.

 Cross-Cultural Connection

Since the United States Constitution was established, many countries have copied parts of it. But other countries have chosen to follow the British parliamentary system, where the prime minister has more power to run the government. More recently some countries have even added more rights than the U.S. Bill of Rights, such as the right to a healthy environment.

 Leveled Support

Entering & Emerging
Provide sentence frames:
Our classroom needs a constitution because _____.

We need a constitution in order to _____.

Developing & Expanding
Have small groups create a bank of words used to write a classroom constitution.

Bridging & Reaching
Remind students to use words that signal *if, then* situations:

If we have a classroom constitution, then we will have order in our classroom.

 **Language Transfer**

Point out that when the *if*-clause shows a real situation in the present tense, the result clause in English can be in the present tense or in the future tense. Also explain that the result clause can precede the *if* clause, in which case there is no comma.

LESSON 1 ENGAGE

LESSON QUESTION

What Makes Democracy Work?

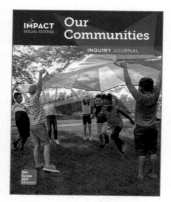

**INQUIRY JOURNAL,
pp. 194–195**

Bellringer

Ask students to think about what they learned in previous lessons. Ask: What are some examples of things the government does to help people? (Answers will vary but may include: helping people after a natural or human-caused disaster; taking care of land, such as forests or parks; helping newly arrived immigrants; or making our communities safe.)

Lesson Outcomes

Discuss the lesson question and lesson outcomes with students.

- Check that students understand the word *government*.

- To assess students' understanding, ask if they have heard the word before. Call on volunteers to define the term. Say: *A government has authority over a city, state, or country. It governs, or rules, the people in that city, state, or country. For example, we follow the laws made by the government in our state.*

Talk About It

Explain that you can study a photograph to learn more about what it shows. Have students ask themselves these questions:

- What do you think the room was used for? (meetings)

- What items in the photograph support your answer? (many tables with chairs all facing the front of the room, quill pens and paper on the tables to take notes, a raised platform with table and chair at the front facing out for the meeting leader)

 Collaborative Conversations

Ask and Answer Questions Encourage students to ask and answer questions as they discuss the concept. Remind them to

- ask questions to clarify ideas or comments they do not understand.

- wait a few seconds after asking a question to give others a chance to think before responding.

- answer questions thoughtfully with complete ideas, not one-word answers.

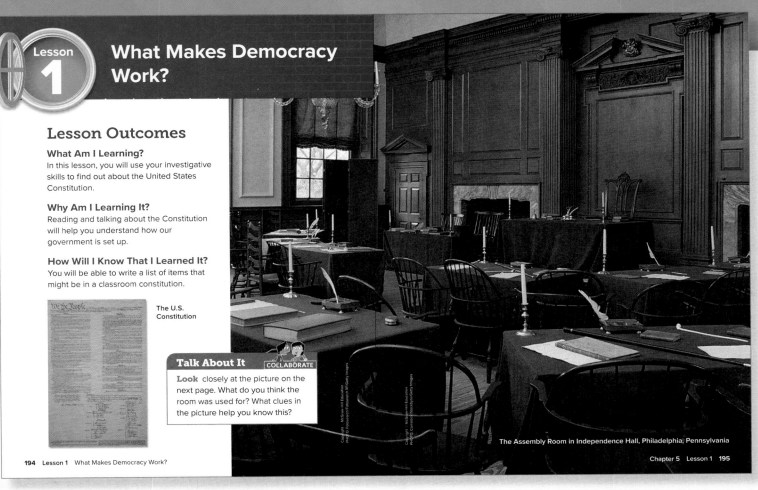

Lesson 1 — What Makes Democracy Work?

Lesson Outcomes

What Am I Learning?
In this lesson, you will use your investigative skills to find out about the United States Constitution.

Why Am I Learning It?
Reading and talking about the Constitution will help you understand how our government is set up.

How Will I Know That I Learned It?
You will be able to write a list of items that might be in a classroom constitution.

The U.S. Constitution

Talk About It COLLABORATE

Look closely at the picture on the next page. What do you think the room was used for? What clues in the picture help you know this?

The Assembly Room in Independence Hall, Philadelphia, Pennsylvania

194 Lesson 1 What Makes Democracy Work?

Chapter 5 Lesson 1 195

INQUIRY JOURNAL, pp. 194–195

English Learners SCAFFOLD

Use the following scaffolds to support student understanding of the lesson outcomes.

Entering and Emerging

Work with individual students to identify details in the photograph. Point to specific objects and ask questions to help students express ideas, such as: *Is this old or new? Do we still use a _____ like this one?* Also, ask more general questions about the room to prompt their ideas about its use: *Does this look like a place to play or work? Show me where the person in charge sits.*

Developing and Expanding

Guide partners to work together to describe details in the photograph. Have them study the photograph and write a list of words they can use in their discussion. Then have students write two to three sentences about the photograph using the list of words.

Bridging and Reaching

Encourage students to use their own words to write several sentences about the photograph. Suggest that they tell what they think the room was used for and during what time period. Ask if the room could have been used for other purposes. Provide students with a list of linking words and phrases to use in their writing: *and, also, because, for example, such as,* and *therefore.*

Social Emotional Learning

Self-Regulation

Maintain Focus To encourage listening as an active rather than passive role, have students restate what others have said before they respond with their own ideas.

Blended Learning

Students engage with the lesson question and discussion prompts.

Interactive IMPACT

Discuss the **Lesson Question** and **Talk About It** with the class.

Preamble of the United States Constitution

1 Inspect

Read the first paragraph. What is the preamble?

• **Circle** any words in the preamble that you do not know.

• **Underline** the words that tell *who* the Constitution is written for.

• **Discuss** with a partner the reasons *why* the Constitution was written. Then restate one of the reasons in your own words.

My Notes

_____
_____
_____
_____
_____
_____
_____
_____

Have you ever heard or seen the words "We the People"? You can find them at the beginning of our nation's Constitution. This part is called the preamble. The preamble introduces the Constitution. The opening words show that the United States government is run by its people and for its people. The preamble also lists the reasons why the Constitution was written. Let's read the preamble to find out more!

> ### PRIMARY SOURCE
>
> "We the People of the United States, in Order to form a more perfect Union, establish Justice, insure domestic Tranquility, provide for the common defence, promote the general Welfare, and secure the Blessings of Liberty to ourselves and our Posterity, do ordain and establish this Constitution for the United States of America."
> —Preamble to the United States Constitution

The United States Constitution begins with the words "We the People."

The preamble also tells about American beliefs. For example, the people of the United States are very important. The government gets its power from the people. Also, it is important for the states to join together. They are stronger as one country.

2 Find Evidence

Reread the preamble. How many reasons are listed for why the Constitution was written? Why do you think the founders listed so many reasons?

Think about the phrase "promote the general Welfare." What does the word *welfare* mean? Name a word that has a similar meaning.

3 Make Connections

Talk Discuss with a partner the reasons why the Constitution was written. Which do you think is most important? Why?

INQUIRY JOURNAL, pp. 196–197

Analyze the Source

1 Inspect

Read Ask students to skim the text, including the Primary Source, to focus on understanding the overall meaning. Remind them to circle words they do not know and underline words that tell them who the Constitution was written for.

• What three words begin the U.S. Constitution? (We the People) Why are these words important? (Answers will vary but should indicate that the Constitution was written for and by the people of the United States.)

2 Find Evidence

Reread Have students reread the text and the Primary Source.

Think Ask partners to take turns explaining their ideas to each other about the meaning of *general welfare*. (the health and happiness of the people of the nation)

3 Make Connections

Talk Point out to students that in the Preamble, the founders listed many reasons for why the Constitution was written. Have students discuss those reasons with a partner, including which reason they think is most important and why. (The nation needed a strong national government, and writing the Constitution made it clear and permanent. Students' ideas about which reason was most important will vary.)

Spotlight on Language

Understanding Language

run: Students will be more familiar with **run** as a verb meaning "move fast." In this case, **run** means "managed" or "controlled."

Explore Main Idea and Details

The topic is what a text is about. The **main idea** is the most important idea of a topic. **Details** tell more about the main idea.

1. **Read the text once all the way through.**
   This will help you understand what the text is about.

2. **Use section titles to identify topics.**
   A section title often tells you the topic of that section.

3. **Ask yourself: *What is the most important idea about this topic?***
   The most important idea is the main idea of the text.

4. **Look for information that tells more about the main idea.**
   These are details. They help you understand the main idea.

Based on the text you read, work with your class to complete the chart below.

Main Idea	Details
The preamble introduces the United States Constitution.	Possible answers: It tells who the Constitution was written for. It lists reasons why the Constitution was written.

Investigate!

Read pages 206–215 in your Research Companion. Use your investigative skills to look for details that tell more about the main ideas listed in the chart. This chart will help you organize your notes.

Main Ideas	Details
The Articles of Confederation was the first plan for the government of the United States.	Possible answers: It set up a weak national government. It was approved in 1777, during the Revolutionary War.
At the Constitutional Convention, a new constitution was written for the United States.	Possible answers: It created a system of government for the United States. People who helped write it include George Washington, Benjamin Franklin, James Madison, and Alexander Hamilton. It took effect in 1788.
Democracy is an important part of American government.	Possible answers: Democracy gives Americans the freedom to choose their leaders. Elections are held each year to either reelect representatives or elect new ones.
Other countries have governments that are similar to or different from ours.	Possible answers: The United Kingdom has a prime minister who is like a president but with more power. China has one leader with a lot of power. South Africa and the United Kingdom have parliaments with elected leaders, like the U.S. Congress.

INQUIRY JOURNAL, pp. 198–199

Inquiry Tools

Explore Main Idea and Details

Read Have students read aloud the step-by-step instructions about main ideas and supporting details. Tell them that supporting details give more information about the main idea. Explain that supporting details sometimes have signal words, such as *for example,* or *first, second,* or *third.*

Guide Practice Guide students to review the text on pp. 196–197. Then work with them to complete the graphic organizer. Explain that they will use a similar graphic organizer to organize their independent research.

Check Understanding Confirm understanding of the inquiry skill, Explore Main Idea and Details. If students cannot identify the main idea and supporting details from the text, review the steps on p. 198.

Investigate!

Have students read pp. 206–215 in the Research Companion. Tell them the information will help them answer the lesson question ***What Makes Democracy Work?***

Take Notes Tell students that they should use the graphic organizer on p. 199 of the Inquiry Journal to take notes on the history of the U.S. Constitution and democracy in America. Tell them that taking notes will help them understand and remember the information they learn.

Remind students that they are writing main ideas and supporting details. Review the importance of paraphrasing, or using their own words, when they take notes.

 Spotlight on Content

Main Idea and Details

Have students work in pairs or small groups. Provide a simple main idea, such as, *Cats are good pets.* Then have pairs or groups work together to brainstorm details that support the main idea.

 Digital Tools

Blended Learning

Students prepare for the lesson investigation.

ePresentation

Use the **Inquiry Tools** to model and complete the lesson graphic organizer.

LESSON 1 INVESTIGATE

LESSON QUESTION

What Makes Democracy Work?

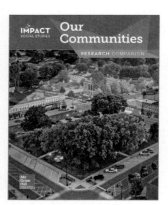

**RESEARCH
COMPANION,
pp. 206–207**

Background Information

- **The Loyalists** Although many American colonists were unhappy with Great Britain over taxes and a lack of freedom and independence, not all of the colonists were willing to declare independence or go to war. About one-third of the American colonists remained loyal to Great Britain. They were called Loyalists, or Tories.
- **Signers of the Constitution** Of the 55 delegates attending the Constitutional Convention, only 39 actually signed the Constitution. Some left the convention early for business reasons, because a family member was in failing health, or for other reasons. Several delegates refused to sign because the Constitution lacked a Bill of Rights, because they felt the federal government was too strong, or because they believed it violated states' rights.

The History of the Constitution

| TIME LINE | Invite students to look at the time line at the top of p. 207.

Analyze Which event happened before the Articles of Confederation were approved? (Colonies declared their independence from Great Britain.) **DOK 1**

1 Inspect Have students read pp. 206–207 and identify the name of our country's plan for running the government.

2 Find Evidence Use the questions below to check comprehension. Remind students to support their answers with text evidence.

Summarize What were the reasons American colonists were unhappy with Great Britain? (The British made them pay high taxes; the colonists wanted to rule themselves.) **DOK 2**

Draw Conclusions Our country has a written constitution. What might happen if a constitution is not written? (Students' answers should reflect that a written document is more consistent; an unwritten constitution might change from person to person, or parts of an unwritten constitution might be forgotten.) **DOK 3**

3 Make Connections

Cite Evidence Not everyone living in the colonies wanted to fight a war. What evidence can you find in the text to support this idea? (The text does not say that all people were unhappy, only that "many people" were unhappy with Great Britain.) **DOK 3**

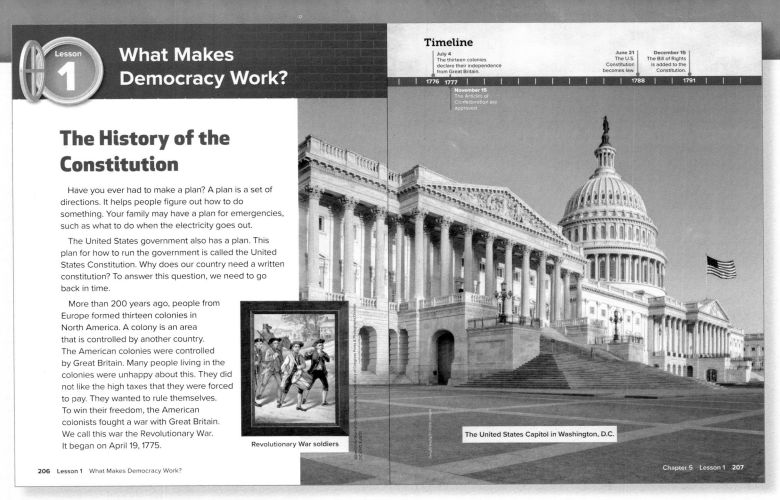

The History of the Constitution

Have you ever had to make a plan? A plan is a set of directions. It helps people figure out how to do something. Your family may have a plan for emergencies, such as what to do when the electricity goes out.

The United States government also has a plan. This plan for how to run the government is called the United States Constitution. Why does our country need a written constitution? To answer this question, we need to go back in time.

More than 200 years ago, people from Europe formed thirteen colonies in North America. A colony is an area that is controlled by another country. The American colonies were controlled by Great Britain. Many people living in the colonies were unhappy about this. They did not like the high taxes that they were forced to pay. They wanted to rule themselves. To win their freedom, the American colonists fought a war with Great Britain. We call this war the Revolutionary War. It began on April 19, 1775.

Revolutionary War soldiers

Timeline

July 4 The thirteen colonies declare their independence from Great Britain.

November 15 The Articles of Confederation are approved.

June 21 The U.S. Constitution becomes law.

December 15 The Bill of Rights is added to the Constitution.

1776 1777 1788 1791

The United States Capitol in Washington, D.C.

RESEARCH COMPANION, pp. 206–207

 Lesson 1 **What Makes Democracy Work?**

English Learners SCAFFOLD

Use the following scaffolds to support student understanding of lesson content.

Entering and Emerging

Guide students as a group to analyze the time line. Ask: *What happened in [year]?* Say the year a second time, and have students chorally repeat. Then read aloud the corresponding description for that year. Repeat a key phrase from the description, such as *declared independence* or *the Bill of Rights.* Have students chorally repeat the key phrase. Use this process for each date.

Developing and Expanding

Have partners echo read the time line text on Research Companion p. 207. If possible, pair students with differing levels of English language proficiency. Have the more fluent reader go first, reading aloud the first caption while the other student listens and follows along. Then have the second student echo read the same caption. Have them read the other captions. Allow partners to discuss the answers when you ask questions about the time line.

Bridging and Reaching

Display a list of time order words and phrases, such as *first, second, third, then, next, after, before.* Ask: *What happened in the United States between the years 1776 and 1791?* Have students write a brief summary of the information in the time line, using time order words to organize the information. Invite volunteers to read aloud their writing.

 **Digital Tools**

Blended Learning
Guide students as they investigate the lesson content.

Interactive IMPACT

Use the **More to Explore.**

The Articles of Confederation

While they were fighting the British, the American colonies needed to band together and form a government. In 1776, leaders from each colony met in Philadelphia, Pennsylvania. They talked about the best way to set up their new government.

Many Americans wanted a weak national government. They believed that the king of Great Britain had too much power. They did not want to give one person or group too much power in their new country. In 1777, American leaders approved a set of laws called the Articles of Confederation. This became the first plan of government for the new nation. The articles created a weak national government.

Eventually, many Americans came to believe that the United States government was too weak. When the Revolutionary War ended in 1783, they realized that the United States needed a stronger national government.

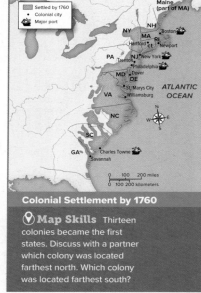

Colonial Settlement by 1760

Map Skills Thirteen colonies became the first states. Discuss with a partner which colony was located farthest north. Which colony was located farthest south?

The Constitutional Convention

In 1787, the leaders met again in Philadelphia. They called this meeting the Constitutional Convention. At this meeting, they discussed how to set up the government. How much power should each state have? How powerful should the national government be? Finally, they came to an agreement. They signed the United States Constitution into law on June 21, 1788. This written document states the duties of the government.

Biography

Benjamin Franklin
Benjamin Franklin worked on the writing of both the Declaration of Independence and the Constitution. He was eighty-one years old during the Constitutional Convention. He gave the other leaders advice on how to write the Constitution. A year later, he wrote to a French friend:

"Our new Constitution is now established, and has an appearance that promises permanency; but in this world nothing can be said to be certain, except death and taxes."

✓ Stop and Check

Talk Discuss with a partner why the United States Constitution was written.

Find Details As you read, add new information to the graphic organizer on page 199 in your Inquiry Journal.

The Articles of Confederation/ The Constitutional Convention

1 Inspect Have students read pp. 208–209 and tell what the Articles of Confederation were.

2 Find Evidence Use the questions below to check comprehension.

Cite Evidence What evidence shows that Americans thought the Articles of Confederation needed to be replaced? (The government under the Articles was designed to be weak; after the war, the country needed a stronger national government.) **DOK 3**

3 Make Connections

Compare How were the Articles of Confederation and the Constitution similar? How were they different? (Similar: Both were plans for the government written by a group of leaders; Different: The Articles created a weak national government, but the Constitution created a stronger national government.) **DOK 3**

Map Skills Project a large version of the map on p. 208. Help students identify each of the thirteen colonies. Guide students to identify the colony that was farthest north (Massachusetts) and the colony that was farthest south. (Georgia)

✓ Stop and Check

Talk (Many Americans believed the country needed a stronger national government.)

Spotlight on Language

Understanding Language

band together: get together; come together

called: named

states: used as both a noun meaning "political territories" and a verb meaning "expresses in writing." Help students clarify the difference.

The Constitution Is Written

The fifty-five men who wrote the United States Constitution are called the founders. These founders each have an important place in our country's history. George Washington led the meetings at the Constitutional Convention. He was our nation's first president. James Madison took careful notes during the meetings. He became our fourth president. Benjamin Franklin gave valuable advice. Alexander Hamilton suggested many new ideas. These representatives worked together to create a system of government that would work best for our country.

When the meetings ended, thirty-nine of the representatives signed the Constitution. It was then approved by each state. Today, the United States Constitution is the oldest national constitution that is still in use. Many other countries around the world have modeled their own written constitutions on it. Today, you can see our ideas for government in the constitutions of other countries.

Did You Know?

Each state has its own constitution. Like the United States Constitution, a state's constitution describes how the state's government works. It also includes the most important laws, ideas, and beliefs determined by the state's leaders. Although the United States has had the same Constitution since it was founded, some states have had several. For example, Louisiana has rewritten its constitution eleven times.

The Louisiana State Constitution

The founders argued for a long time about how the states would be represented in the new system of government. Some believed that states with more people should have more representatives than states with fewer people. Others believed that each state should have the same number of representatives, regardless of how many people lived in the state.

The founders eventually decided that Congress would have two parts. The Senate would have the same number of representatives from each state. It did not matter how many people lived in each state. The number of representatives a state could send to the House of Representatives would be based on state population. This is the system we still use today.

The Constitution was debated and signed in Independence Hall.

Stop and Check

Talk Discuss with a partner why the founders decided that Congress would have two parts.

RESEARCH COMPANION, pp. 210–211

The Constitution Is Written

1 Inspect Read aloud pp. 210–211 and ask students to name two of the founders.

2 Find Evidence Use the questions below to check comprehension.

Compare How are the Senate and the House of Representatives similar? (They both have representatives from each state.) **DOK 2**

Draw Conclusions What can you conclude about the U.S. Constitution, knowing that some countries around the world have used it as a model for their own constitutions? (Answers will vary, but students will most likely conclude that the U.S. Constitution is a fair and successful plan for a system of government.) **DOK 3**

3 Make Connections

State an Opinion Think back to the disagreement over how the states would be represented in the new government. Do you think the final decision was the best way to resolve it? (Answers will vary.) **DOK 3**

 Stop and Check

Talk Encourage students to use text evidence as they respond to the prompt. (The founders decided that Congress would have two parts because the founders disagreed on how states should be represented in the new system of government.)

Social Emotional Learning

Social Awareness

Flexible Behavior Learning to accept circumstances when they cannot be changed is an important skill that some students may still be developing. Some students may exhibit difficulty when their ideas do not fit within time constraints, the needs of other students, or other reasons. Support them by asking to hear their ideas fully and modeling empathy before asking them for ideas on how to make the situation work.

Democracy and Our Country

Today, the original Constitution of the United States is on display in the rotunda of the National Archives Museum in Washington, D.C. The Declaration of Independence and the Bill of Rights are also there. Together, these three documents are called the Charters of Freedom. They describe the most important ideas that America stands for.

The Constitution on display in the National Archives Museum

One of those ideas is that all people have the right to "life, liberty, and the pursuit of happiness." In other words, everyone has the right to live how they want and be happy. All Americans also have the right to **justice**. Each person is treated fairly and equally under the law. If someone is accused of a crime, he or she has the right to a fair trial.

The founders listed several specific freedoms in the Bill of Rights. They thought these freedoms needed to be protected. These freedoms include the freedoms of speech, religion, press, and assembly.

United States citizens also have the freedom to choose their leaders. America is a democracy. In a democracy, the people are in charge. They vote to make decisions about how the country is run. However, it would be impossible for people to vote on every decision that needs to be made. That is why the United States is a representative democracy. Citizens vote to elect people who will represent them in the government. Then the representatives vote to make decisions about running the nation.

Each November, elections are held all across the country. Voters choose the representatives who will work for them. The people who are elected serve for only a set amount of time. After they have served that time, they may choose to run again. If they have done a good job, the voters will reelect them. But if they have not done a good job, voters have the right to elect a new representative.

Elections are an important part of our democracy.

✓ Stop and Check

Think What is a democracy? What does it mean to say the United States is a representative democracy?

RESEARCH COMPANION, pp. 212–213

Democracy and Our Country

1 Inspect Have partners read pp. 212–213 and ask students to name the Charters of Freedom.

2 Find Evidence Use the questions below to check comprehension.

Generate Based on the text, how would you define the word *justice?* (Answers may include being treated fairly and equally and having the right to a fair trial.) **DOK 3**

Infer Why are elections an important part of living in a free and fair country? (Answers may vary but should indicate that elections allow citizens to choose the representatives who will work for them and support their values in Congress.) **DOK 2**

3 Make Connections

Draw Conclusions Why was the Bill of Rights added to the U.S. Constitution? (The founders thought certain freedoms needed to be protected.) **DOK 2**

✓ Stop and Check COLLABORATE

Think For support, simplify the question: how are a democracy and a representative democracy different? (In a democracy, people vote to make decisions. The United States is a representative democracy because Americans vote for people to represent them in government.)

 Spotlight on Language

Academic Language

Have students use knowledge of prefixes and context to explain the meaning of the word *reelect:*

. . . the voters will reelect them.

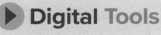 **Digital Tools**

Blended Learning

Students investigate curated resources and find evidence to answer the Lesson Question.

Interactive IMPACT

Students choose from print or digital **Inquiry Tools** to take notes.

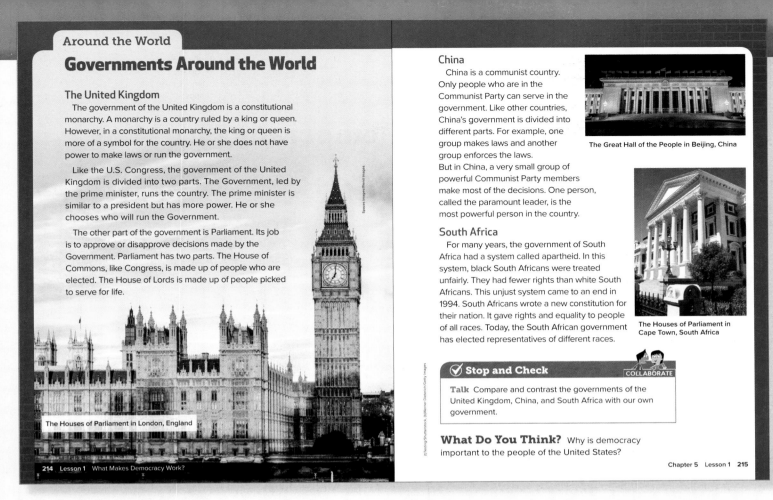

Around the World

Governments Around the World

The United Kingdom

The government of the United Kingdom is a constitutional monarchy. A monarchy is a country ruled by a king or queen. However, in a constitutional monarchy, the king or queen is more of a symbol for the country. He or she does not have power to make laws or run the government.

Like the U.S. Congress, the government of the United Kingdom is divided into two parts. The Government, led by the prime minister, runs the country. The prime minister is similar to a president but has more power. He or she chooses who will run the Government.

The other part of the government is Parliament. Its job is to approve or disapprove decisions made by the Government. Parliament has two parts. The House of Commons, like Congress, is made up of people who are elected. The House of Lords is made up of people picked to serve for life.

The Houses of Parliament in London, England

China

China is a communist country. Only people who are in the Communist Party can serve in the government. Like other countries, China's government is divided into different parts. For example, one group makes laws and another group enforces the laws. But in China, a very small group of powerful Communist Party members make most of the decisions. One person, called the paramount leader, is the most powerful person in the country.

The Great Hall of the People in Beijing, China

South Africa

For many years, the government of South Africa had a system called apartheid. In this system, black South Africans were treated unfairly. They had fewer rights than white South Africans. This unjust system came to an end in 1994. South Africans wrote a new constitution for their nation. It gave rights and equality to people of all races. Today, the South African government has elected representatives of different races.

The Houses of Parliament in Cape Town, South Africa

> ✓ **Stop and Check** COLLABORATE
>
> **Talk** Compare and contrast the governments of the United Kingdom, China, and South Africa with our own government.

What Do You Think? Why is democracy important to the people of the United States?

RESEARCH COMPANION, pp. 214–215

Around the World: Governments Around the World

1 Inspect Have students read pp. 214–215 and explain what apartheid is.

2 Find Evidence Use the questions below to check comprehension.

Compare How are the three governments similar? How are they different? (Answers will vary, but students should support their opinions with text evidence.) **DOK 3**

3 Make Connections

Draw Conclusions Why do you think the author chose to write about these three countries' governments? (Answers will vary but most likely will describe how the countries are good examples of different kinds of governments.) **DOK 2**

✓ Stop and Check COLLABORATE

Talk Have students discuss the prompt with a partner. (Answers will vary, but students may point out that all governments have the same function (running a country) and consist of multiple parts. Differences may include the amount of power individuals or groups have, the titles for leaders, etc.)

What Do You Think? (Answers may vary, but students should mention that it puts power in the hands of the citizens.)

✔ Check for Success

Details Can students identify the key reasons why democracy is an effective form of government?

Differentiate

If Not, Have students review their notes on the main ideas and supporting details about democracy in their graphic organizers in their Inquiry Journals.

LESSON QUESTION

What Makes Democracy Work?

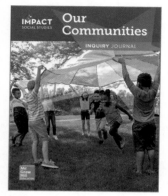

**INQUIRY JOURNAL,
pp. 200–201**

Think About It

Take a Stand Remind students to review their research and consider the value of a classroom constitution and what it would contain. Encourage students to review the main ideas and supporting details they have listed in their graphic organizers. Direct students back to pp. 206–215 of their Research Companion if they need more information.

Write About It

Write a List of Ideas Remind students to include the following elements in their responses.

- Introduce a topic.
- Provide logical rules supported by facts and details.
- Use transition words to link rules and evidence.

Discipline(s)	4	3	2	1
Civics	Strong understanding of items that should be in a classroom constitution	Adequate understanding of items that should be in a classroom constitution	Uneven understanding of items that should be in a classroom constitution	No understanding of items that should be in a classroom constitution

Talk About It

Compare and Contrast Encourage students to compare and contrast their ideas and explain why they believe certain rules are or are not important. Students can take turns discussing whether they agree or disagree with their classmates' ideas and explain why.

Assessment Students can check their understanding with feedback from the **Lesson Test** available online.

Connect to the Essential Question

Put It Together Before students respond, remind them to think about the purpose of a constitution and why we need laws and rules.

Inquiry Project Update Remind students to turn to Inquiry Journal p. 191 for project information. If necessary, review the Project Checklist with students. At this point in the chapter, students should focus on the first three items on the checklist.

Think About It

Take a Stand
Why might a constitution for your classroom be helpful?
Think about what might be contained in the constitution.

Write About It

Write a List of Ideas
Work with a partner to write a list of items that might be in a classroom constitution.

Responses will vary. Encourage students
to consider who will make the rules in the
classroom and how decisions will be made.

Talk About It

Compare and Contrast
Share your list with your classmates. Compare and contrast your ideas.
Then discuss which ideas are most important to include in a class constitution.

Connect to the EQ

Civics

Pull It Together
How does the Constitution help our government and its citizens to work together?

Responses will vary but should show
an understanding that the Constitution
sets up a system for making laws and
sharing power.

Inquiry Project Notes

INQUIRY JOURNAL, pp. 200–201

English Learners SCAFFOLD

Use the following scaffolds to support student writing.

Entering and Emerging

Elicit ideas from students for the list of items that could be in their classroom constitution. Provide simple sentence frames for students as needed: Students should _____.

List their ideas on the board. Next to each rule, add a supporting phrase frame:

- . . . because _____.

Developing and Expanding

Help partners generate reasons to support each item in their list. Display the following sentence frame:

- _____ is an important rule because _____.

Ask for an example from one of the lists.

Bridging and Reaching

Help partners list their ideas for the classroom constitution. Ask each pair to share one item from their list, including a supporting reason. Then have other students describe one thing they like about the rule and whether they think the supporting reason is valid. Remind students to be respectful as they express their opinions. After each pair has shared one rule and received feedback, have partners finish writing their lists.

✔ Check for Success

Opinion Can students write a list of items that they think should appear in a classroom constitution?

Differentiate

If Not, Have students share their lists in an oral presentation.

What Are the Different Parts of Government?

Connect to the Essential Question

Tell students that this lesson will help them answer the Essential Question: **Why Do Governments and Citizens Need Each Other?** Explain that by learning about what each branch of government does, they will understand more about how government and citizens work together.

Lesson Objectives

- **Tell** why volunteer service helps our country or community.
- **Explain** how the Constitution guides the U.S. government.
- **Describe** the three branches of government and how they work together.
- **Identify** reasons people choose public service jobs.
- **Write** an opinion paragraph telling which branch of government is the most important.

Make Connections!

CONNECT TO ELA

Reading **Ask and answer** questions to demonstrate understanding of a text and refer explicitly to the text as the basis for the answers.

Determine the main idea of a text; recount the key details and explain how they support the main idea.

Research **Recall** information from experiences or gather information from print and digital sources; take brief notes on sources and sort evidence into provided categories.

Writing **Craft** opinion pieces on familiar topics or texts, supporting a point of view with reasons.

Speaking and Listening **Engage** effectively in a range of collaborative discussions with diverse partners on grade 3 topics and texts, building on others' ideas and expressing students' own ideas clearly.

Language **Use** coordinating and subordinating conjunctions.

COMMUNITY CONNECTIONS

To enrich what students have learned about ways citizens give back, invite people with local public sector jobs to speak with the students or to submit a video showing where they work and what they do in the community.

Lesson-At-A-Glance

1 ENGAGE — INQUIRY JOURNAL

pp. 202–207

- **Talk About It:** Speech by President Theodore Roosevelt, 1902; Photograph of government workers
- **Analyze the Source:** State of the Union Address by President George H. W. Bush, 1991
- **Inquiry Tools:** Explore Main Idea and Details

2 INVESTIGATE — RESEARCH COMPANION

pp. 216–223

- **The Constitution Guides Our Government**
- **The Branches of Government**
- **Citizenship: Citizens Give Back Through Public Service**

3 REPORT — INQUIRY JOURNAL

pp. 208–209

- **Think About It**
- **Write About It:** Write an Opinion Paragraph; Cite Evidence from Text
- **Talk About It**
- **Connect to the Essential Question**

ASSESSMENT

- **Online Lesson Test**
- **Printable Lesson Test**

For more details, see pages T378–T379.

▶ Digital Tools

at **my.mheducation.com**

ePresentation

Teach the Engage, Investigate, and Report content to the whole class from **ePresentations** that launch directly from the lesson dashboard.

eBook

You can flip your instruction with the **IMPACT eBooks** found on your lesson dashboard.

Interactive IMPACT

Blend in digital content **when you want it** and **where you want it**.

Blended Learning features in the Teacher's Edition highlight ways to connect in-class work with online experiences to enhance learning.

Investigate current events with **IMPACT News**.

Explore domain-based vocabulary with **Explore Words** and **Word Play** vocabulary activities.

pp. 54–65

Go Further with IMPACT Explorer Magazine!

The **IMPACT Explorer Magazine** supports students' exploration of the Essential Question and provides additional resources for the EQ Inquiry Project.

LESSON 2 LANGUAGE LEARNERS

 LESSON QUESTION

What Are the Different Parts of Government?

Language Objectives

- Use newly acquired content and academic vocabulary to talk and write about the different branches of government.
- Write an opinion and give at least two reasons to support it.
- Write complete, compound sentences using linking words such as *because* and *even if.*

 Spanish Cognates

To support Spanish speakers, point out the cognates.

union = unión

judicial = judicial

responsibility = responsabilidad

elected = elegido

representative = representativo

to vote = votar

Introduce the Lesson

Set Purpose Explain to students that in this lesson, they will read informational texts to learn about the different parts of government and how they work together.

Access Prior Knowledge Read the Lesson Question and find out what students already know about their government. Say: *In the last lesson, you learned about how democracy works. The United States government is based on the Constitution. You also learned that the government is the people, as is stated in the Preamble to the Constitution. In this lesson, you will learn about the three branches of the government and how they work together.*

Spark Curiosity Draw students' attention to the photo of President Theodore Roosevelt on p. 202 of the Inquiry Journal. Tell students that Theodore Roosevelt, at the age of 42, was the youngest man to become president of the United States. He is known for his work in conservation, or protecting our natural resources. He wrote that we, as a people, needed to think about when our natural resources would come to an end. In 1901, he created the United States Forest Service (USFS). While president, Theodore Roosevelt protected about 230 million acres of public lands.

Build Meaning & Support Language

Inquiry Journal

Analyze the Source (pages 204–205) Tell students that in this lesson they will read informational texts that give facts, examples, and explanations about a topic. As you read "Working for the Future," unlock the Primary Source feature. Point out the prefix *re-* in the word *renewed*. Explain that *re-* means "again," so *renewed* means "made new again." Say: *President Bush talks about ways that citizens can help renew America, or help to solve its problems.* Ask: *What can an individual do to help?* (help someone learn to read, help build things for others and for the community, help those in need)

Inquiry Tools (pages 206–207) Tell students that they will **Explore Main Idea and Details** as they read the Research Companion. Review with students that the main idea is the most important idea that the author makes about a topic, whereas the details are pieces of information that support the main idea. Model how to locate the main idea on p. 204 and add it to the graphic organizer on p. 206. Work with students to complete the graphic organizer.

Research Companion

The Constitution Guides Our Government (pages 216–217) As you read, explain any words that students don't know. Point out the phrase *separates the power* in the first sentence. Explain that some power, or authority, is in each branch, or part, of the government. Break down the sentence "Each branch has its own duties, but the three branches must work together." Explain that *duties* are responsibilities, or jobs that each branch must do. Point out the word *but*, which signals a contrast to what was said before it. Say: *Each branch has its own work to do, but they all must work together.* Ask: *Why do you think the power is separated?*

The Branches of Government (pages 218–221) Read aloud the first sentence on p. 218. Explain that *responsibilities* are duties, or jobs, that each branch must do. After you read the second paragraph, explain that *carries out* means "enforces," or "does what it has been ordered to do." In the third paragraph, read aloud "While the president appoints cabinet members, the Senate must vote to approve them." Explain that the word *while* is used in this sentence to contrast two ideas: the first is that the president appoints, or names, cabinet members, and the second is that the Senate must vote to approve them. This vote is called a *confirmation*, or approval. Ask: *How does the Senate confirmation of cabinet members show a separation of power?*

Citizens Give Back Through Public Service (pages 222–223) Make sure students understand what a U.S. representative is. Then discuss what Representative Cathy McMorris Rodgers says about working in government: "We must remember that although we come from different backgrounds and ideologies, we're all part of this great experiment in self-governance." Point out that the word *ideologies* means "sets of ideas that describe a particular group of people." Explain that the word *although* shows a contrast and that what follows in the main part of the sentence may be surprising. Say: *We all have different backgrounds and ideas, but we still work together to govern ourselves.* Ask: *Do we need to always agree on how to reach our goals?*

Inquiry Journal

Report Your Findings (pages 208–209) Review what an opinion is, and emphasize that an opinion is easier to accept if it has good reasons to support it. Students should include details from the texts as support in their paragraphs. Encourage them to use new vocabulary words that they have learned. Check their work for spelling and punctuation errors.

Language Forms & Conventions

On p. 216 of the Research Companion, point out the last sentence of the first paragraph. The sentence has two parts, linked together by the word *but*. Some sentences are long because they are made of two complete ideas linked by words like *but*, *because*, *if*, or *even if*.

First Idea	Second Idea
California elects the most representatives to the House of Representatives	**because** it has the largest population of any state.
We're all united by common values of liberty, justice, and equality of opportunity,	**even if** we don't always agree on how to achieve them.

 Have students work in pairs to write two other sentences that have linking words.

Cross-Cultural Connection

In 1978, the government of Spain adopted a new constitution that favored diversity, or a variety of cultures. It granted autonomy, or some freedom, to many different regions in Spain, including Catalonia. In Catalonia, students learn in Catalan, with Spanish being taught as a foreign language. Ask: H*ow might it be different if schools in your region taught in a different language than schools in other regions?*

Leveled Support

Entering & Emerging
Provide sentence frames: I think the _____ branch is most important because _____.

Developing & Expanding
Encourage students to develop a bank of words used to describe reasons why they think a certain branch is the most important.

Bridging & Reaching
Remind students to use words that signal reasons for believing something (*because, therefore, as a result, so*) to explain why they think a certain branch of government is the most important.

Language Transfer

As in English, Spanish sentences can show a reason for doing something (with *porque*) or a contrast from the main part of the sentence.

LESSON 2 ENGAGE

What Are the Different Parts of Government?

**INQUIRY JOURNAL,
pp. 202–203**

Bellringer

Prompt students to retrieve information from the previous lesson. Say: *The U.S. Constitution is considered one of the Charters of Freedom. What makes it so important?* (The U.S. Constitution states the rules for the government and the form of government. It is over 200 years old and the oldest national written constitution still in use.)

Lesson Outcomes

Discuss the lesson question and lesson outcomes with students.

- Make sure that students understand the idea of *branches* as part of an organization or government.
- Tell students that learning about how the government is set up with different branches will help them understand how the government works.

Talk About It

Read the primary source with students and review the photographs. Ask: *Who spoke these words? When did he make this speech?* (President Theodore Roosevelt; 1902) *If the buildings in the photograph on p. 203 were destroyed, would the government still exist? Support your answer from the primary source.* (Yes, because the government is not the buildings: "Now, the Government is us—we are the Government, you and I.")

 Collaborative Conversations

Add New Ideas As students engage in partner, small-group, and whole-class discussions, encourage them to

- stay on topic.
- connect their own ideas to things their peers have said.
- look for ways to connect their personal experiences or prior knowledge to the conversation.

Lesson 2

What Are the Different Parts of Government?

Lesson Outcomes

What Am I Learning?
In this lesson, you will use your investigative skills to understand the branches of government.

Why Am I Learning It?
Reading and talking about how the government is set up will help you understand how the government works.

How Will I Know That I Learned It?
You will be able to support an opinion about which branch of government you think is most important.

PRIMARY SOURCE

In Their Words... Theodore Roosevelt

"We get in the habit of speaking of the Government as if it were something apart from us. Now, the Government is us—we are the Government, you and I. And the Government is going to do well or ill accordingly as we make up our minds that the affairs of the Government shall be managed."

—Speech by President Theodore Roosevelt given in Asheville, North Carolina, 1902, as recorded by Robert C. V. Meyers

People going to work in Washington, D.C.

Talk About It COLLABORATE

Read the primary source quotation. What does President Roosevelt mean when he says, "we are the Government"?

202 Lesson 2 What Are the Different Parts of Government?

Chapter 5 Lesson 2 203

INQUIRY JOURNAL, pp. 202–203

(EL) English Learners SCAFFOLD

Use the following scaffolds to support student understanding of lesson outcomes.

Entering and Emerging

Work with students to identify the details in the picture on p. 203. Explain that the building is called the Capitol. Read the caption. Provide sentence frames to help students describe what they see in the picture.

- I see _____ in the photograph.
- The people in the photograph are _____.

Developing and Expanding

Have small groups discuss the caption and identify details in the picture on p. 203. Ask questions to help them describe the photograph. For example: *Do you know the building in the photograph? What happens at this building? What are some jobs people might do in this building?*

Bridging and Reaching

Have partners reread the Primary Source on p. 202. Then have them write sentences to describe the picture on p. 203 and how it connects to what is said in the Primary Source—that the government is "us."

Social Emotional Learning

Relationship Skills

Engage with Others Ask students to imagine they are in the group of people headed to work at the Capitol. Then have students explain why it would be important to know how to communicate well and to actively listen to others.

▶ Digital Tools

Blended Learning

Students engage with the lesson question and discussion prompts.

ePresentation

Discuss the **Lesson Question** and **Talk About It**.

Analyze the Source

Analyze the Source

1 Inspect

Read President Bush's speech. What is he speaking about?

Underline the words you think are most important in the speech.

Discuss with a partner what President Bush thinks American citizens should do.

My Notes

_____

_____

_____

_____

_____

_____

_____

_____

_____

_____

Working for the Future

Read what President George H. W. Bush said in his 1991 State of the Union address.

> **PRIMARY SOURCE**

In Their Words... President George H. W. Bush

"We have within our reach the promise of a renewed America. We can find meaning and reward by serving some purpose higher than ourselves, a shining purpose, the illumination of a Thousand Points of Light. . .

. . . The problems before us may be different, but the key to solving them remains the same: it is the individual—the individual who steps forward. And the state of our Union is the union of each of us, one to the other—the sum of our friendships, marriages, families, and communities.

We all have something to give. So if you know how to read, find someone who can't. If you've got a hammer, find a nail. If you're not hungry, not lonely, not in trouble, seek out someone who is. Join the community of conscience. Do the hard work of freedom. That will define the state of our Union."

Copyright © McGraw-Hill Education. TEXT: George Herbert Walker Bush. "State of the Union Address." Washington, D.C. 29 January 1991.

George H. W. Bush was president of the United States from 1989–1992.

Copyright © McGraw-Hill Education. PHOTO: Larry Downing/Sygma/Getty Images

2 Find Evidence

Examine Reread the sentences, "Join the community of conscience. Do the hard work of freedom. That will define the state of our Union." Who does President Bush mean when he says, "the community of conscience?" Restate the sentences in your own words.

3 Make Connections

Talk Discuss with a partner why volunteering to help each other is important.

Connect to Now What can you do to help make your community stronger?

INQUIRY JOURNAL, pp. 204–205

Analyze the Source

Background Information

Article II, Section 3 of the U.S. Constitution lists the duties of the president. One of these duties is that the president "shall from time to time give to the Congress Information of the State of the Union, and recommend to their Consideration such Measures as he shall judge necessary and expedient." This information, delivered yearly, has officially been called the State of the Union Address since 1947.

1 Inspect

Read Have students read the Primary Source text and study the photograph on pp. 204–205. Remind them to underline the most important words in the speech.

- Have partners compare the words they underlined and then discuss what President Bush thinks American citizens should do. (volunteer, serve, help someone)

2 Find Evidence

Examine Students should understand that the phrase "community of conscience" refers to citizens working together, doing what is right for the common good.

3 Make Connections

Talk Have students work with a partner to discuss reasons why it is important to help others. (Everyone is important; it helps make the community stronger.) Have partners discuss ways they can help their community.

EL Spotlight on Language

Vocabulary

individual: single or separate; one person rather than a group, community, or family

▶ Digital Tools

Blended Learning

Students read informational texts and analyze primary sources.

Interactive IMPACT

Have students practice and apply the strategy of close reading as they analyze text.

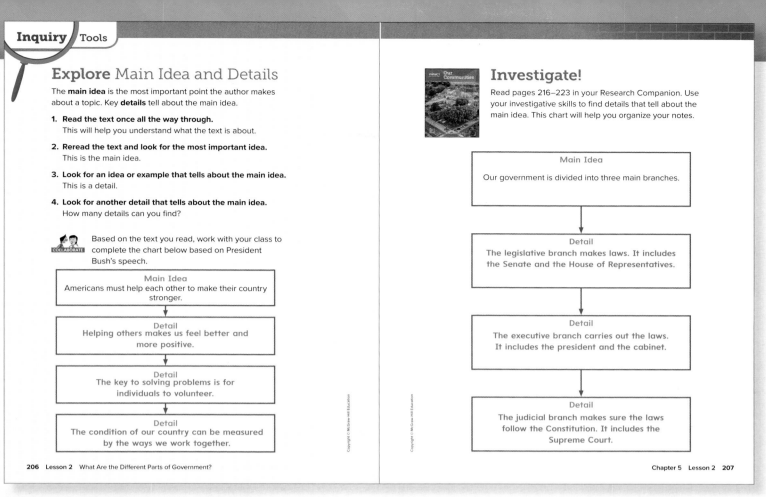

Explore Main Idea and Details

The **main idea** is the most important point the author makes about a topic. Key **details** tell about the main idea.

1. **Read the text once all the way through.**
   This will help you understand what the text is about.

2. **Reread the text and look for the most important idea.**
   This is the main idea.

3. **Look for an idea or example that tells about the main idea.**
   This is a detail.

4. **Look for another detail that tells about the main idea.**
   How many details can you find?

 Based on the text you read, work with your class to complete the chart below based on President Bush's speech.

> **Main Idea**
> Americans must help each other to make their country stronger.

> **Detail**
> Helping others makes us feel better and more positive.

> **Detail**
> The key to solving problems is for individuals to volunteer.

> **Detail**
> The condition of our country can be measured by the ways we work together.

Investigate!

Read pages 216–223 in your Research Companion. Use your investigative skills to find details that tell about the main idea. This chart will help you organize your notes.

> **Main Idea**
> Our government is divided into three main branches.

> **Detail**
> The legislative branch makes laws. It includes the Senate and the House of Representatives.

> **Detail**
> The executive branch carries out the laws. It includes the president and the cabinet.

> **Detail**
> The judicial branch makes sure the laws follow the Constitution. It includes the Supreme Court.

INQUIRY JOURNAL, pp. 206–207

Inquiry Tools

Explore Main Idea and Details

Read Discuss with students the steps for identifying a main idea and its supporting details. Explain that the main idea is usually the topic heading in a text or the first sentence in a paragraph.

Guide Practice Have students review the text and photograph on pp. 204–205. Then work with them to complete the graphic organizer. Explain that they will use a similar graphic organizer to organize their independent research.

Check Understanding Confirm student understanding of the inquiry skill, Explore Main Idea and Details. If students cannot identify a main idea and the key details, review the steps on p. 206.

Investigate!

Have students read pp. 216–223 in the Research Companion to gather more information that will help them answer the lesson question **What Are the Different Parts of Government?**

Take Notes Tell students that they should take notes about the main idea and supporting details in the graphic organizer on p. 207 of the Inquiry Journal. Remind students that taking notes in their own words will help them understand and remember the information they learn.

Spotlight on Content

Main Idea and Details
The main idea is usually stated first, with details following. Often a detail is an example that supports the main idea.

LESSON QUESTION

What Are the Different Parts of Government?

RESEARCH COMPANION, pp. 216–217

Background Information

- **Presidential Oath** The president's oath of office comes from Article II, Section 1, Clause 8 of the U.S. Constitution: "I do solemnly swear (or affirm) that I will faithfully execute the Office of President of the United States, and will to the best of my ability, preserve, protect and defend the Constitution of the United States."
- **Congressional Oath** The U.S. Constitution does not have an oath for members of the government other than the president, but it states that they "shall be bound by Oath or Affirmation to support this Constitution . . ." (Article VI, Clause 3). The congressional oath used today dates from the Civil War.
- **Judicial Oaths** Supreme Court justices take two oaths when they are appointed. The first is required by Article VI, Clause 3 of the Constitution. The second is a judicial oath in which they swear to "administer justice without respect to persons, and do equal right to the poor and to the rich" and to "faithfully and impartially discharge and perform all the duties" required by their position.

The Constitution Guides Our Government

1 Inspect Have students read pp. 216–217 and identify the three branches of the U.S. government.

2 Find Evidence Use the questions below to check comprehension. Remind students to support their answers with text evidence.

Interpret What do the three branches of government have in common? (Each has specific duties outlined in the U.S. Constitution, and all three branches must work together.) **DOK 2**

Explain How does the Constitution impact the duties of people who work in our government? (The Constitution contains the rules for the U.S. government. Members of the government must obey the Constitution. New laws cannot go against what is written in the Constitution.) **DOK 3**

3 Make Connections

Point of View Based on the text, how does this photograph mirror the way that our government works? (Answers will vary, but students could include ideas about people from all branches of government, as well as the people they represent, gathered to inaugurate the next president. The image represents the peaceful transfer of power.) **DOK 3**

What Are the Different Parts of Government?

The Constitution Guides Our Government

The Constitution separates the power of the government across three parts, or branches. The **legislative branch** is made up of the Senate and the House of Representatives. It makes our laws. The **executive branch**, led by the president, carries out the laws. The **judicial branch** is the nation's court system. This branch interprets the laws and decides whether the laws follow the Constitution. Each branch has its own duties, but the three branches must work together.

Who works in our government? In the United States, the people elect the government. Members of the government come from all over the country. They work in Washington, D.C., our nation's capital.

The people who work in our government promise to obey the Constitution. That means they cannot pass a law or act in any way that goes against the laws in the Constitution. They have to follow the laws that are written in the Constitution.

Crowds at the inauguration of President Barack Obama in 2009

216   Lesson 2   What Are the Different Parts of Government?

Chapter 5   Lesson 2   217

RESEARCH COMPANION, pp. 216–217

 English Learners SCAFFOLD

Use the following scaffolds to support student understanding of the lesson content.

Entering and Emerging

Have students look at the image on p. 217. Read the caption and provide sentence frames to help students describe what is happening in the photograph. Provide a word bank if needed.

- In this photograph, _____ is speaking to the audience.
- _____ came to see the new president.

Developing and Expanding

Help small groups work together to describe what is happening in the photograph on p. 217. Ask: *What is happening in the photograph? Who is speaking? Why did so many people come? What is on the tall tower in the middle of the crowd?*

Bridging and Reaching

Have partners discuss why people travel to see when a new person becomes president. Ask: *Where would they sit? What would they see? What would happen at the inauguration?*

 Digital Tools

Blended Learning

Students investigate curated resources and find evidence to answer the lesson question.

Interactive IMPACT

Students choose from print or digital **Inquiry Tools** to take notes.

The Branches of Government

Each of the three branches of government has its own responsibilities. All three branches work together to make sure our country runs smoothly.

Executive Branch

The executive branch is the part of government that carries out laws. The president of the United States is the head of the executive branch. The president leads our country. The president's main job is to make sure that the laws passed by Congress are being followed. The vice president supports the president. The vice president also leads the Senate.

People in the executive branch get their jobs in different ways. The president and the vice president are elected to serve for four years. The president appoints people to lead different departments of the executive branch. They are part of the president's cabinet. Cabinet members give advice to the president. While the president appoints cabinet members, the Senate must vote to approve them. That vote is called *confirmation*.

The president lives and works in the White House.

Legislative Branch

The legislative branch makes laws for everyone to follow. In the **federal** government, Congress makes laws for the entire country. Congress is made up of two parts—the Senate and the House of Representatives. Citizens elect members of Congress. Senators are elected every six years. Representatives are elected every two years.

Each state has two senators, so there are a hundred senators in the Senate. The House of Representatives is much bigger than the Senate. It has 435 members. The number of representatives from each state is based on the size of its population. California elects the most representatives to the House of Representatives because it has the largest population of any state.

Members of Congress work in the Capitol Building.

> **✓ Stop and Check**
>
> **Think** What is the main difference between the executive and legislative branches of our government?
>
> **Find Details** As you read, add new information to the graphic organizer on page 207 in your Inquiry Journal.

RESEARCH COMPANION, pp. 218–219

The Branches of Government

1 Inspect Have students read pp. 218–219 and explain what the president's cabinet is.

2 Find Evidence Use the questions below to check comprehension.

Summarize What does the president do? (heads the executive branch, leads the country, makes sure that laws passed by Congress are followed, appoints people to lead different departments of the executive branch) **DOK 2**

Compare and Contrast How is the House of Representatives different from the Senate? How is it similar? (The House has 435 members, but the Senate has 100 members. Representatives are elected every two years, but Senators are elected every six years. Both are part of the legislative branch, and both make laws.) **DOK 2**

3 Make Connections

Draw Conclusions How does the job of the vice president involve both the executive and legislative branches? (The vice president is part of the executive branch, but one of his jobs is to lead the Senate.) **DOK 3**

✓ Stop and Check   COLLABORATE

Think Encourage students to reference the text when formulating their responses. (The legislative branch makes the laws; the executive branch carries out the laws.)

 Spotlight on Vocabulary

Homophones

capital: a city in a state or country where the main government is located

capitol: the building in which the people who make the laws of a state or country meet

▶ **Digital Tools**

Blended Learning
Students explore lesson content through interactive activities.

Interactive IMPACT

Use the **More to Explore**.

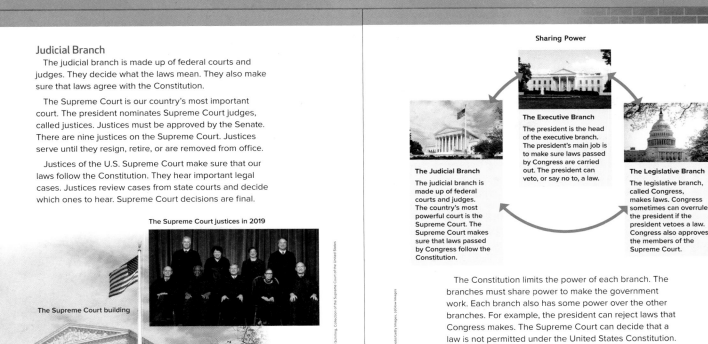

Judicial Branch

The judicial branch is made up of federal courts and judges. They decide what the laws mean. They also make sure that laws agree with the Constitution.

The Supreme Court is our country's most important court. The president nominates Supreme Court judges, called justices. Justices must be approved by the Senate. There are nine justices on the Supreme Court. Justices serve until they resign, retire, or are removed from office.

Justices of the U.S. Supreme Court make sure that our laws follow the Constitution. They hear important legal cases. Justices review cases from state courts and decide which ones to hear. Supreme Court decisions are final.

The Supreme Court justices in 2019

The Supreme Court building

Sharing Power

The Executive Branch
The president is the head of the executive branch. The president's main job is to make sure laws passed by Congress are carried out. The president can veto, or say no to, a law.

The Judicial Branch
The judicial branch is made up of federal courts and judges. The country's most powerful court is the Supreme Court. The Supreme Court makes sure that laws passed by Congress follow the Constitution.

The Legislative Branch
The legislative branch, called Congress, makes laws. Congress sometimes can overrule the president if the president vetoes a law. Congress also approves the members of the Supreme Court.

The Constitution limits the power of each branch. The branches must share power to make the government work. Each branch also has some power over the other branches. For example, the president can reject laws that Congress makes. The Supreme Court can decide that a law is not permitted under the United States Constitution. This keeps Congress from having too much power. Congress can refuse to pass a law that the president wants. This limits the power of the president.

✓ Stop and Check

Think Why does the Constitution limit the power of each branch of government?

220 Lesson 2 What Are the Different Parts of Government?

Chapter 5 Lesson 2 221

RESEARCH COMPANION, pp. 220–221

The Branches of Government

1 Inspect Have students read pp. 220–221 and describe the role of the judicial branch.

2 Find Evidence Use the questions below to check comprehension.

Infer How is the appointment process for a Supreme Court justice an example of the branches sharing power? (Justices are nominated by the president but must be approved by the Senate. All three branches share power in each appointment.) **DOK 3**

Explain How does the Constitution limit the power of each branch? (The president can veto laws made by Congress, Congress can refuse to pass a law that the president wants, and the Supreme Court can decide that a law does not follow the Constitution.) **DOK 2**

3 Make Connections

Draw Conclusions In what important way are Supreme Court decisions different from decisions in state courts? (Cases from state courts can go to the Supreme Court for another decision, but Supreme Court decisions are final—no other court can change decisions of the Supreme Court.) **DOK 3**

✓ Stop and Check COLLABORATE

Think Have students discuss the question with a partner. (Answers will vary, but students should conclude that the branches share power to make the government work, to maintain a balance of power, and to prevent one branch from having too much power.)

 Social Emotional Learning

Relationship Skills

Solve Problems Discuss how the government works to solve problems by thinking creatively to make laws that will benefit citizens. Each branch of government uses the Constitution to guide their plans and decisions. Ask: *How would our government work if each branch ignored our Constitution? What would our classroom be like if we ignored the class rules? Would it be difficult or easy to solve problems?*

Content Vocabulary

self-governance: a government that is under the control of the people it governs

equality of opportunity: the idea that all people should have the same opportunities or the same positive changes for their futures

Citizenship: Citizens Give Back Through Public Service

1 Inspect Have students read pp. 222–223 and identify two public service jobs.

2 Find Evidence Use the questions below to check comprehension.

Summarize According to President Obama, what does public service show about people? (It shows that people want to serve a cause beyond their own and give back to our nation.) **DOK 2**

Infer What would happen to your community if no one wanted to work in the government or public service? (Answers will vary but should indicate that the work of the city would not get done. The schools would not have teachers, there would be no police officers or firefighters, and city services would not be done.) **DOK 3**

3 Make Connections

Compare and Contrast How is being involved in your school government similar to what Cathy McMorris Rodgers is doing? (Cathy McMorris Rodgers is serving the people of Washington state, working to ensure a better future for the next generation. Working in a school government is a way to serve the school and to make it a better place for students.) **DOK 3**

✓ Stop and Check

Connect to Now Have students discuss the question with a classmate. (Answers will vary, but students might suggest helping to keep the country safe, working for better schools, or working for a cleaner environment.)

What Do You Think? Encourage students to review their notes as they answer this question.

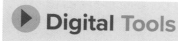

Blended Learning

Students investigate curated resources and find evidence to answer the lesson question.

Interactive IMPACT

Students **Research** and find evidence using digital format texts.

Citizenship

Citizens Give Back Through
Public Service

Why do people choose to work in the government? Many people want to help make a difference in other people's lives. Cathy McMorris Rodgers is a U.S. representative from Washington. Here is what she says about working in government: "We must remember that although we come from different backgrounds and ideologies, we're all part of this great experiment in self-governance. We're all united by common values of liberty, justice, and equality of opportunity, even if we don't always agree on how to achieve them."

Cathy McMorris Rodgers is a United States representative.

You do not have to work in government to make a difference. There are many different public service jobs. Firefighters, emergency medical technicians, and police officers help to protect our communities. Public school teachers help kids learn.

President Barack Obama once said of public service, "Public service is a calling which has meant so much to so many. It . . . reflects our drive to serve a cause beyond our own— to give back to our Nation, leave our mark, and nudge history forward. There is no greater opportunity to help more people or to make a bigger difference."

President Barack Obama

222 Lesson 2 What Are the Different Parts of Government?

How can you help make your school a better place? One way is by being involved in your school government. You can help bring about changes right where you learn!

You can continue to be involved in government when you grow up. People in local government work every day for better schools and medical care. They work for better transportation and for a cleaner environment. They work so all the people in their community can have better lives.

Remember to vote in your school elections!

✓ Stop and Check

Connect to Now What is a reason to choose a career in public service? Discuss your reason with a classmate.

What Do You Think? Describe the three branches of our government. How do the branches work together?

Chapter 5 Lesson 2 223

RESEARCH COMPANION, pp. 222–223

English Learners SCAFFOLD

Use the following scaffolds to support student understanding of lesson content.

Developing and Expanding

List the words *firefighters, police officers, teachers,* and *emergency medical technicians.* Explain each word and tell students that these are people who work in public service. Provide sentence frames to help students talk about what public servants do.

- _____ are people who work in public service.
- They help the community by _____.

Developing and Expanding

Have small groups make a list of public service jobs in their community. Ask questions to help them describe what each person does. For example: *What do firefighters do? How do police officers help the community? Why are public school teachers important? What do emergency medical technicians do? How do government leaders improve the community?*

Developing and Expanding

Have partners discuss the public service jobs that are mentioned in the text. Ask: *How are the jobs similar? How are they different?*

✓ Check for Success

Connect Can students identify and describe the different parts of government?

Differentiate

If Not, Have students review the details about each branch of government recorded in the graphic organizers on p. 207 of their Inquiry Journals.

LESSON QUESTION

What Are the Different Parts of Government?

INQUIRY JOURNAL, pp. 208–209

Think About It

Interpret Remind students to review their research and consider how the three branches of the U.S. government work together. Encourage students to review the key details they listed in their graphic organizer. Direct students to pp. 216–223 of their Research Companion if they need more information.

Write About It

Write and Cite Evidence Remind students to include the following elements in their responses.

- Introduce and describe the branch of government.
- Provide two reasons to support your opinion about the importance of the branch.
- Use transition words to link opinions and evidence.

Discipline(s)	4	3	2	1
Civics	Strong understanding of how the branches of government work together; clearly states ideas; examples given are thorough and convincing	Adequate understanding of how the branches of government work together; ideas and examples given are adequate and somewhat convincing	Uneven understanding of how the branches of government work; ideas somewhat unclear; examples given are uneven and only somewhat convincing	Little understanding of how the branches of government work together; ideas expressed do not always relate; examples are missing or do not support ideas

Talk About It

Defend Your Claim Have students pair up with a classmate who chose a different branch of the government from theirs. Have them take turns giving the reasons that helped them form their opinion and then discuss whether they agree or disagree with their partner's opinion and why.

Assessment Students can check their understanding with feedback from the **Lesson Test** available online.

Connect to the Essential Question

Pull It Together Remind students that different opinions of people in the three branches of government often affect how well the government works together.

Inquiry Project Update Remind students to turn to Inquiry Journal p. 191 for project information. If necessary, review the Project Checklist with students.

Think About It

Interpret
Review your research. Based on the information you have gathered, how do you think the three branches of government work together?

Write About It

Write and Cite Evidence
Write a paragraph telling which branch of government you think is most important. Give at least two reasons to support your opinion.

<u>Answers will vary, but students should give</u>
<u>two text-based reasons to support their</u>
<u>opinions.</u>

Talk About It

Defend Your Claim
Share your writing with a partner who wrote about a different branch of government. Take turns talking about your opinions. Do you agree or disagree with your partner's opinion? Why?

Connect to the EQ

Pull It Together
In what ways do you think the government can do a better job of working together? How can you help?

<u>Answers will vary but should show an</u>
<u>understanding of how the branches of</u>
<u>government work.</u>

Inquiry Project Notes

INQUIRY JOURNAL, pp. 208–209

English Learners   SCAFFOLD

Use the following scaffolds to support student writing.

Developing and Expanding

Explain to students that the word *opinion* means what someone thinks about something. Remind students that they will choose a branch of government, state their opinion about why it is the most important, and give two reasons for their choice. Provide sentence frames to help students as needed:

- I think _____ is the most important branch of government.
- _____ is important because _____.

Developing and Expanding

Explain to students that when giving an opinion about the branch of government they think is most important, they must state what they think and then give reasons for their opinion. Ask questions to help students begin to write: *Which branch of government is most important? How did you form this opinion? What other reasons do you have for having this opinion?*

Developing and Expanding

Have partners discuss the three branches of government, noting the reasons each branch is important. Then have students form an opinion about which branch is the most important and begin writing their paragraphs. Remind students to provide support for their opinion by citing at least two text-based reasons.

Check for Success

Summarize Can students write an opinion paragraph explaining which branch of government they think is most important and cite two text-based reasons for their opinion?

Differentiate

If Not, Have students present their opinion as a diagram of all three branches with graphics or annotations that show which branch of government they think is most important.

LESSON QUESTION

Why Do Communities Need Local Government?

Connect to the Essential Question

Tell students that this lesson provides key research into the Chapter Essential Question: **Why Do Governments and Citizens Need Each Other?** Explain that they will use their research skills to explore different kinds of local governments. Remind students that evidence of local government is all around them—from fire trucks to schoolteachers to librarians.

Lesson Objectives

- **Describe** the structures of local, state, and tribal governments.
- **Explain** why communities need governments in order to function.
- **Identify** services provided by state and local governments.
- **Write** a blog post describing a local government and explaining how it works.

Make Connections!

CONNECT TO ELA

Reading **Ask and answer** questions to demonstrate understanding of a text and refer explicitly to the text as the basis for the answers.

Research **Recall** information from experiences or gather information from print and digital resources; take brief notes on sources and sort evidence into provided categories.

Writing **Craft** informative/explanatory texts to examine a topic and convey ideas and information clearly.

Speaking and Listening **Follow** agreed-upon rules for discussions (e.g., gaining the floor in respectful ways, listening to others with care, speaking one at a time about the topics and texts under discussion).

Language **Form and use** possessives.

COMMUNITY CONNECTIONS

To further students' familiarity with local government, have student pairs contact a local official to conduct a short interview. The interview questions can cover basic topics, such as what kind of work they do, their normal day, and their educational background. Officials might include anyone from the mayor's office, city council, fire department, police department, library system, or parks department.

Lesson-At-A-Glance

1 ENGAGE — INQUIRY JOURNAL

▶ **Talk About It:** Photograph of lawmakers
▶ **Analyze the Source:** A Supreme Court Ruling
▶ **Inquiry Tools:** Explore Summarizing

pp. 210–215

2 INVESTIGATE — RESEARCH COMPANION

▶ **State Government**
▶ **Field Trip: Kansas State Capitol**
▶ **Local Governments**
▶ **Tribal Governments**

pp. 224–233

3 REPORT — INQUIRY JOURNAL

▶ **Think About It**
▶ **Write About It:** Write a Blog Post About Local Government and Explain How It Works
▶ **Talk About It**
 ▶ **Connect to the Essential Question**

pp. 216–217

ASSESSMENT

▶ **Online Lesson Test**
▶ **Printable Lesson Test**

For more details, see pages T378–T379.

▶ Digital Tools

at **my.mheducation.com**

ePresentation

Teach the Engage, Investigate, and Report content to the whole class from ePresentations that launch directly from the lesson dashboard.

eBook

You can flip your instruction with the **IMPACT eBooks** found on your lesson dashboard.

Interactive IMPACT

Blend in digital content **when you want it** and **where you want it**.

Blended Learning features in the Teacher's Edition highlight ways to connect in-class work with online experiences to enhance learning.

Investigate current events with **IMPACT News**.

Explore domain-based vocabulary with **Explore Words** and **Word Play** vocabulary activities.

Go Further with IMPACT Explorer Magazine!

The **IMPACT Explorer Magazine** supports students' exploration of the Essential Question and provides additional resources for the EQ Inquiry Project.

pp. 54–65

 LESSON QUESTION

Why Do Communities Need Local Government?

- Use newly acquired content and academic vocabulary to talk and write about state, local, and tribal governments in the United States.
- Write a blog post describing local government and how it works.
- Identify and use singular and plural possessives.

Introduce the Lesson

Set Purpose Explain to students that in this lesson, they will read informational texts to learn about local governments in the United States.

Access Prior Knowledge Remind students that a government exists to help its people live safely. It makes laws and provides services. Ask: *Why do we have local governments?* Compare a school community to a local community. Say: *Suppose our school was having a problem with too much noise in the halls. How could our school community solve that problem?*

Spark Curiosity Have students look at the illustration of services on p. 231 of the Research Companion. Explain that this illustration shows many of the services local governments provide for their citizens. Point out the different categories of services represented in the illustration. Ask: *Which services help you and your family?*

 Have students draw their own illustration showing the service category they believe they get the most benefit from. Ask them to share their ideas with a partner. Ask: *How would your life be more difficult without these services?*

Build Meaning & Support Language

Inquiry Journal

Analyze the Source (pages 212–213) Explain that Chief Justice John Marshall wrote a very important decision. By reading his own words in the Primary Source, we can understand how he came to his decision. John Marshall explained that the word *nation* means that the people are distinct or separate from others.

Inquiry Tools (pages 214–215) Tell students they will **Summarize** as they read the selections in the Research Companion. Remind students that when they summarize, they retell the most important parts of the text: the main idea and key details. Point out that the graphic organizer will help them organize the information they read. Ask students to preview the Research Companion text by reading the section headings and the topic sentences of paragraphs. Discuss what they think each section is about.

 Spanish Cognates

To support Spanish speakers, point out the cognates.

government = gobierno

local = local

constitution = constitución

governor = gobernador

court = corte

judge = juez

Research Companion

State Government (pages 224–227) Explain that the first paragraph on p. 224 compares state government to the federal government. Then point out that the second paragraph explains the role of each branch. Explain that pp. 226–227 tell some differences between state governments. Point out that in the second paragraph on p. 226, the words *Not all* and *For example* signal that the paragraph will explain some differences.

Field Trip, Kansas State Capitol (pages 228–229) Point out the sentence: *When you visit the state capitol, you can watch the House of Representatives and the Senate debate issues and vote on bills.* Explain that the sentence gives information about visiting the state capitol. Say: *The sentence explains how you can watch the Kansas House of Representatives and the Kansas State Senate in action. The first group of words says:* When you visit the state capitol. *The word* when *tells us that at the time you are in this place, something will happen.* Then break the sentence into shorter sentences to aid understanding: You visit the state capitol. You can watch the House of Representatives and the Senate. They will debate issues and vote on bills. Ask: *What does it mean to debate issues?* (It means to discuss them.)

Local Governments (pages 230–231) Point out the words *city council*, *city manager*, *mayor*, and *judge*. Say: Manager *and* leader *have similar meanings. When we talk about a person who works in government, we usually say* leader, *not* manager. Explain that in many cities, the mayor is an elected position whereas a city manager is appointed. Say: *A judge is a person in a court who makes decisions about laws.*

Tribal Governments (pages 232–233) Explain that tribal governments are different from other governments because they only relate to Native American groups. Point out that the word *treated* in the first paragraph means "acted toward." Review the structure of government. Point out that the federal government makes laws for the entire country, including Native Americans. However, just as each state government can make specific laws for its people, so too can tribal governments make laws for their members.

Inquiry Journal

Report Your Findings (pages 216–217) Explain to students that one purpose of a blog is to provide information about a topic. Students should tell about their local government and how it is organized. Encourage them to use new vocabulary from the chapter.

Language Forms & Conventions

Possessives Remind students that a possessive shows ownership and that an apostrophe is used to show possession for both singular and plural nouns. Display and discuss the chart.

Singular Possessives	Example	Plural Possessives	Example
state's	The state's budget was balanced.	states'	Several states' laws helped workers.
government's	The local government's monthly meeting was long.	governments'	Many governments' plans called for new services.
governor's	The governor's ideas were not approved.	governors'	Several governors' campaigns were successful.

Have student pairs locate possessives in the texts. If the possessive is singular, have them add it to the chart and write the plural possessive form, if appropriate. If the possessive is plural, have them add it to the chart and then write the singular possessive form.

Cross-Cultural Connection

The Navajo Nation covers 27,000 square miles in the states of Utah, Arizona, and New Mexico. Since 1989, the Navajo Nation has used a three-branch system of government (executive, legislative, and judicial). The council delegates represent communities. Council members often speak Navajo while the Council is in session. Ask: *How is the Navajo Nation government the same as a state government? How is it different?*

Leveled Support

Entering & Emerging
Provide sentence frames: One service my local government provides is _____. This service helps me by _____.

Developing & Expanding
Have small groups create a two-column chart. In the first column, have them write the names of services of their local government. In the second column, have them tell how the services help them.

Bridging & Reaching
Have partners write sentences describing their local government and the services it provides.

Language Transfer

Some students may form possessives incorrectly by avoiding the use of the 's. Point out that in some languages, possession is described using a prepositional phrase, such as "the book of my sister."

LESSON 3 ENGAGE

Why Do Communities Need Local Government?

INQUIRY JOURNAL, pp. 210–211

Bellringer

Prompt students to retrieve information from the previous lessons. Say: *The founders wrote the Constitution in a way that requires the three branches of government to work together. What are some ways the branches work together?* (The three branches work together to make and enforce laws. Congress passes laws, the executive branch enforces them, and the judicial branch reviews them.)

Lesson Outcomes

Discuss the lesson question and lesson outcomes with students.

• Make sure that students understand the connection between communities and local governments. Ask them to come up with synonyms for the word *community,* such as *small group, city,* or *town.* Say: *Local government refers to our town, county, or sometimes even our state.*

• Have students think about jobs that are done at the local level, such as firefighting and road maintenance. Tell students that they will discover the people and agencies that do these things.

Talk About It

Remind students that they can study a photograph to see what they can learn from it. Encourage students to ask themselves these questions about the photo on p. 211:

• What is happening in the photograph? (Lawmakers are having a discussion.)

• What parts of the photograph support the caption? (speaker, listeners at desks)

• What would you say in your own caption? (Answers will vary but should relate to the legislature.)

 Collaborative Conversations

Listen Carefully As students engage in partner, small-group, and whole-class discussions, encourage them to follow discussion rules by listening carefully to speakers. Remind students to

• always look at the person who is speaking.

• respect others by not interrupting them.

• repeat peers' ideas to check understanding.

Lesson 3
Why Do Communities Need Local Government?

Lesson Outcomes

What Am I Learning?
In this lesson, you will use your investigative skills to learn about local governments in the United States.

Why Am I Learning It?
Reading and talking about local governments in the United States will help you understand why communities need governments.

How Will I Know That I Learned It?
You will be able to write a blog post about your local government and how it serves your community.

Talk About It

Look at the picture and read the caption on the next page. How can the word "lawmaker" help you know if this is the executive, judicial, or legislative branch of government?

210   Lesson 3   Why Do Communities Need Local Government?

A discussion by lawmakers

INQUIRY JOURNAL, pp. 210–211

 English Learners **SCAFFOLD**

Use the following scaffolds to support student understanding of the lesson outcomes.

Entering and Emerging

Explain the difference between the noun *legislator* and the adjective *legislative*. Provide the following sentences to help students understand the two words:

- A _____ writes laws. (legislator)
- The workers in the photograph are part of the _____ branch of our government. (legislative)

Developing and Expanding

Review the difference between the noun *legislator* and the adjective *legislative*. Guide students to identify the endings that help differentiate the two words. (*-or, -ive*) Ask partners to work together to look at the photograph on p. 211 and then write a sentence using *legislator* and a sentence using *legislative*.

Bridging and Reaching

Elicit from students that *legislator* is a noun and *legislative* is an adjective that describes a noun. Have students write a paragraph about the photograph on p. 211. Direct them to use the words *legislator* and *legislative* in their writing.

 Social Emotional Learning

Relationship Skills

Solve Problems To help students learn problem-solving skills, tell them that working in a group can be very helpful. Once they have identified their problem, brainstorming is a good method to generate possible solutions.

▶ **Digital Tools**

Blended Learning

Students engage with the lesson question and discussion prompts.

Interactive IMPACT

Discuss the **Lesson Question** and **Talk About It**.

1 Inspect

Read the Primary Source quote. Who wrote this?

- **Circle** the subject of the page.
- **Underline** the important point John Marshall made about Native American nations.

My Notes

_____

_____

_____

_____

_____

_____

_____

A Supreme Court Ruling

The Cherokee Native Americans lived in the southeastern United States. In the early 1800s, leaders in the state of Georgia tried to make the Cherokee people move from their homelands. Samuel Worcester, a friend of the Cherokee, lived on their land. Leaders in Georgia did not want Worcester to help the Cherokee. They passed a law saying that only Cherokee people could live on Cherokee land. Worcester was arrested for breaking this law and sent to prison.

Worcester asked the Supreme Court to hear his case. In 1832, the Supreme Court ruled the Georgia law was wrong. John Marshall was the Chief Justice of the Supreme Court.

PRIMARY SOURCE

In Their Words... Chief Justice John Marshall

"Indian Nations have always been considered as distinct, independent political communities, retaining their original natural rights, as the undisputed possessors of the soil.... The very term 'nation' so generally applied to them, means 'a people distinct from others.'"

—United States Supreme Court, 1832

He wrote that Native American nations are separate and independent from the United States. Justice Marshall said that states could not tell a Native American nation what to do. It was an important decision.

Troy Fletcher, executive director of the Yurok people, meets with state officials to talk about how to manage the Klamath River land.

2 Find Evidence

Reread the statement "Indian Nations have always been considered as distinct, independent political communities." What does the word *independent* mean? Name a word that has the same meaning as *independent*.

3 Make Connections

Talk Summarize John Marshall's comments in your own words.

INQUIRY JOURNAL, pp. 212–213

Analyze the Source

Background Information

Chief Justice John Marshall served on the U.S. Supreme Court for 34 years during the Court's formative years. He served from 1801 until his death in 1835. He played a key role in establishing the power of the court, particularly the concept of judicial review. This is the idea that the courts have the power to determine whether the actions of the other branches of the government are constitutional.

1 Inspect

Read Have students read the entire text, including the Primary Source, to focus on understanding the overall meaning. Remind them to circle the topic of the page.

- Underline Chief Justice John Marshall's main idea concerning Native American nations. (distinct, independent political communities, retaining their original natural rights)

2 Find Evidence

Reread Have students reread the text and the Primary Source.

3 Make Connections

Talk Have students summarize John Marshall's comments and share their summaries with a partner. (Answers will vary but might point out that Marshall said that Native American nations are independent. They have the right to make their own laws and own their own land.)

Scanning for Information

Point out phrases in the Primary Source that are examples of formal, or official, language that a Supreme Court justice might use when making a decision about a law. Explain that people often use formal language when they are in a court.

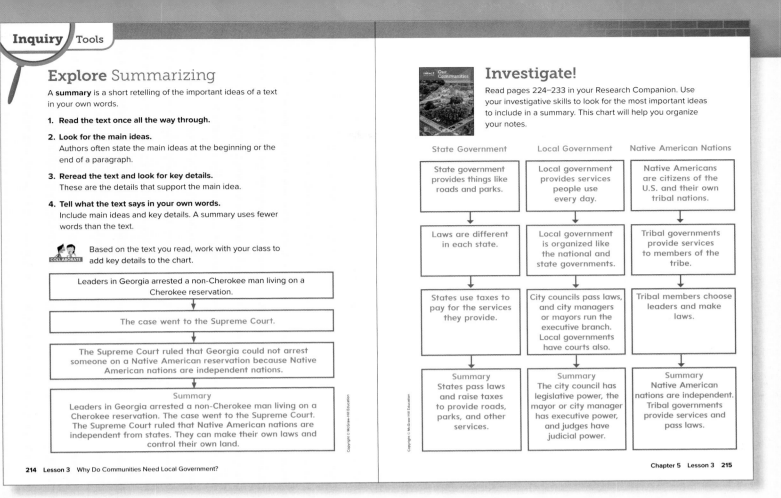

The image above shows the Inquiry Journal pages 214-215 containing:

Explore Summarizing

A **summary** is a short retelling of the important ideas of a text in your own words.

1. **Read the text once all the way through.**

2. **Look for the main ideas.**
   Authors often state the main ideas at the beginning or the end of a paragraph.

3. **Reread the text and look for key details.**
   These are the details that support the main idea.

4. **Tell what the text says in your own words.**
   Include main ideas and key details. A summary uses fewer words than the text.

Based on the text you read, work with your class to add key details to the chart.

Leaders in Georgia arrested a non-Cherokee man living on a Cherokee reservation.

↓

The case went to the Supreme Court.

↓

The Supreme Court ruled that Georgia could not arrest someone on a Native American reservation because Native American nations are independent nations.

↓

Summary
Leaders in Georgia arrested a non-Cherokee man living on a Cherokee reservation. The case went to the Supreme Court. The Supreme Court ruled that Native American nations are independent from states. They can make their own laws and control their own land.

214 Lesson 3 Why Do Communities Need Local Government?

Investigate!

Read pages 224–233 in your Research Companion. Use your investigative skills to look for the most important ideas to include in a summary. This chart will help you organize your notes.

State Government	Local Government	Native American Nations
State government provides things like roads and parks.	Local government provides services people use every day.	Native Americans are citizens of the U.S. and their own tribal nations.
Laws are different in each state.	Local government is organized like the national and state governments.	Tribal governments provide services to members of the tribe.
States use taxes to pay for the services they provide.	City councils pass laws, and city managers or mayors run the executive branch. Local governments have courts also.	Tribal members choose leaders and make laws.
Summary States pass laws and raise taxes to provide roads, parks, and other services.	**Summary** The city council has legislative power, the mayor or city manager has executive power, and judges have judicial power.	**Summary** Native American nations are independent. Tribal governments provide services and pass laws.

Chapter 5 Lesson 3 215

Inquiry Tools

Explore Summarizing

Read Discuss with students the steps for summarizing information provided in a text. Remind them that a summary covers only the information in the text, not their opinion of the information.

Guide Practice Have students review the text on pp. 212–213. Then work with students to complete the graphic organizer on p. 214. Explain that they will use a similar graphic organizer to organize their independent research.

Check Understanding Confirm understanding of the inquiry skill, Explore Summarizing. If students cannot retell the important ideas of a text, review the steps on p. 214.

Investigate!

Have students read pp. 224–233 in the Research Companion. Tell them the information will help them answer the lesson question *Why Do Communities Need Local Government?*

Take Notes Tell students they should use the graphic organizer on p. 215 of the Inquiry Journal to take notes on state, local, and tribal governments. Remind students that taking notes will help them understand and remember the information they learn. Explain to students the importance of summarizing when they take notes.

 Spotlight on Language

Understanding Language

decision: a ruling by a court. Students may recognize the everyday use of *decision* that means "a conclusion reached after some thought." Help students recognize the slight difference between the two meanings.

 Digital Tools

Blended Learning

Students prepare for the lesson investigation with step-by-step instruction about how to summarize.

ePresentation

Use the **Inquiry Tools** to model and complete the lesson graphic organizer.

LESSON 3 INVESTIGATE

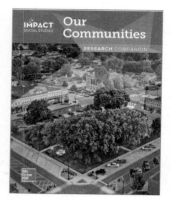

RESEARCH COMPANION, pp. 224–225

Why Do Communities Need Local Government?

Background Information

Sovereignty refers to the authority of a state to govern itself. Native American groups in Oklahoma and other states retain their sovereignty. Tribal members can choose their leaders and make their laws. States also have a degree of sovereignty because they can set laws and collect taxes.

State Government

1 Inspect Have students read pp. 224–225 and identify the main purpose of the legislative branch of government.

2 Find Evidence Use the questions below to check comprehension. Remind students to support their answers with text evidence.

Compare In what ways are all state governments alike? (They each have their own government and constitution.) **DOK 2**

Identify What is the title of the head of a state's executive branch? What do you think this person might do as part of the job? (Governor; Answers will vary but might point out that the governor would be in charge of state workers and carrying out state laws.) **DOK 2**

Cite Evidence How does the state judicial branch work with the legislative branch? Use evidence from the text to support your answer. (The legislative branch makes state laws, and the judicial branch reviews those laws to see if they are fair.) **DOK 3**

3 Make Connections

Compare How are most state governments like the federal government? (Both have three branches, and all three branches help the government run smoothly. The three branches are legislative, executive, and judicial. In both governments, the legislative branch is usually made up of two parts.) **DOK 3**

Lesson 3

Why Do Communities Need Local Government?

State Government

Every state, including your state, has its own government and its own constitution. Your state's government is similar to the federal government. The state government has three branches, just like the federal government. All three branches work together to help your state run smoothly.

The legislative branch makes the laws in your state. In every state but Nebraska, the legislative branch is made up of two parts. Nebraska has just one part. The legislative branch meets in your state's capital. The head of your state's executive branch is called the governor. The judicial branch reviews state laws to see if they are fair. The judicial branch includes all of the state courts.

Former South Carolina Governor Nikki Haley signs a bill into law.

RESEARCH COMPANION, pp. 224–225

English Learners SCAFFOLD

Use the following scaffolds to support student understanding of the lesson content.

Entering and Emerging

Use a graphic organizer of a tree to help make the word branch clear. Label the tree *government*. Ask students to name the branches. Make smaller sticks off the branches for people and roles.

Developing and Expanding

Provide a word bank: *state legislature, state courts, state laws, branch, executive, legislative, judicial,* and *governor*. Ask questions to help students in small groups sort them into categories.

Bridging and Reaching

Provide a word bank: *state legislature, state courts, state laws, branch, executive, legislative, judicial,* and *governor*. Have partners take turns asking and answering questions about state governments. Direct students to answer in complete sentences.

Digital Tools

Blended Learning

Students investigate curated resources and find evidence to answer the Lesson Question.

Interactive IMPACT

Students choose from print or digital **Inquiry Tools** to take notes.

State and local governments hire police officers, pave the streets, and set speed limits.

Speed Limit **55**

The state government meets different needs than the federal government. The state government takes care of state roads and parks. It also helps to decide what you learn in school. State laws say how old you must be to drive a car and get married. Lawyers and other professionals have to pass state tests before they can do their jobs in the state. The state also sets up elections for its citizens. These are issues that directly affect people every day.

Not all states have the same laws. For example, in Missouri, you can get an instruction permit to drive when you are 15 years old and an intermediate license when you are 16. In Iowa, you can get a learner's permit when you are 14.

Where does the state get the money to pay for things like roads, parks, and schools? It comes from taxes. A tax is money that people must pay to support the government. People pay a sales tax when they buy certain items. They pay an income tax on the money they earn from a job. Taxes are used to pay for things that benefit everyone in the state.

Biography

Governor Eric Holcomb

Eric Holcomb became Indiana's fifty-first governor in January 2017. Before that, he served as lieutenant governor. Governor Holcomb wants all Indiana schools to provide computer science for its students. He wants to make sure that students have the skills to succeed in future jobs. Governor Holcomb has also focused on increasing Indiana's role in the global economy. He has encouraged foreign corporations to do business in the state.

The United States Constitution divides power between the federal and state governments. Only the federal government can do certain things, such as declare war and print money. State governments control things the United States Constitution does not specify as a power of the federal government. Both federal and state governments can pass laws, raise taxes, and borrow money. Sometimes the federal government directs all states to follow the same rule, such as to reduce air pollution. State governments work together with local governments to provide services. Local governments are created by the state. They must follow the state constitution and all state laws.

✓ Stop and Check   COLLABORATE

Talk What are some services provided by the state government? Discuss your ideas with a partner.

Find Details As you read, add new information in the graphic organizer on page 215 in your Inquiry Journal.

RESEARCH COMPANION, pp. 226–227

State Government

1 Inspect Have students read pp. 226–227 and identify three responsibilities of a state government.

2 Find Evidence Use the questions below to check comprehension.

Identify What is a tax and why is it necessary? (A tax is money people must give the government. This money is spent to pay for government services.) **DOK 2**

Summarize What are some needs that the state government meets? (State governments take care of state roads and parks, help educate students in school, make laws for citizens to follow, and set up elections.) **DOK 2**

Compare What can the federal government do that the state government cannot? What are some things both governments can do? (Only the federal government can declare war and print money; both can pass laws, raise taxes, and borrow money.) **DOK 3**

3 Make Connections

Compare Have students read the biography feature on p. 227. Ask: *How do you think Governor Holcomb's work might be similar to or different from the work your governor does?* (Answers will vary, but students might say that their governor is also working to improve education and employment. Differences might arise if the students' state has priorities that are different than Indiana's, such as those for a coastal state.) **DOK 3**

✓ Stop and Check   COLLABORATE

Talk Students should use evidence from the text to support their answer. (Answers will vary but may include roads, parks, schools, and the state highway patrol.)

EL Spotlight on Content

Scanning for Information
Have students work in small groups to scan the text for one thing the state and federal government both do.

▶ Digital Tools

Blended Learning
Flip the research approach and find evidence in a digital format.

eBooks

Students investigate using their **Research Companion** and **IMPACT Explorer Magazine** eBooks to find evidence.

Kansas State Capitol

The Kansas State Capitol is in Topeka. This building is home to Kansas's state government. The Kansas House of Representatives and the Kansas State Senate meet in this building to make laws. The governor also has an office here.

When you visit the state capitol, you can watch the House of Representatives and the Senate debate issues and vote on bills. Visitors must be quiet and not interrupt the legislators. Watching the legislators at work can help you understand how ideas turn into laws.

Kansas lawmakers at work

A view of the dome from inside the Kansas State Capitol

Visitors can take tours of the state capitol, its grounds, and its dome. Tour guides share information about the building's history and its artwork. The dome tour involves a 296-step climb to the inner and outer domes. From the highest point, visitors get a wide view of the city of Topeka.

Fun Facts

- The Kansas State Capitol took 37 years to complete. It was started in 1866. A major renovation was completed in 2014. The work restored the original look of the building.
- The state capitol has a large round room called a rotunda. It is covered by a domed roof. People visiting the top of the dome can walk along its outside balcony.
- A sculpture called *Ad Astra* is on top of the dome. It is a figure of a Native American warrior. His arrow is pointed toward the North Star. The name comes from the state motto, *Ad Astra per Aspera*. It means "to the stars through difficulties."
- The Kansas State Capitol was featured in a 1989 movie. The building portrayed the Indiana statehouse.

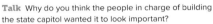

Many people also enjoy visiting Capitol Square. It contains memorials. One memorial is in honor of the state's pioneer women. Another honors law enforcement officials. It features a ring of tablets with the names of those who have died in the line of duty. The Veterans Memorial and Walk honors the state's soldiers. Another Walk of Honor recognizes people who have made major contributions to Kansas. People can also see a statue of Abraham Lincoln and a small Statue of Liberty.

Capitol Square in Topeka

✓ Stop and Check

Talk Why do you think the people in charge of building the state capitol wanted it to look important?

RESEARCH COMPANION, pp. 228–229

Field Trip: Kansas State Capitol

1 Inspect Have students read pp. 228–229 and describe one of the memorials in Capitol Square.

2 Find Evidence Use the questions below to check comprehension.

Identify Where is Kansas's state capitol building? How would you describe its design? (Topeka; it looks like many other state capitols, as well as the U.S. Capitol.) **DOK 2**

Cite Evidence What type of behavior is expected of visitors watching the House of Representatives and the Senate at work? (Visitors must be quiet and not interrupt the legislators.) **DOK 2**

3 Make Connections

Infer How can a visit to a state capitol building help you learn more about state government? (You can see where laws are made, learn from tour guides about how state government works, and watch a legislature debate and vote on bills.) **DOK 3**

✓ Stop and Check

Talk Prompt students to use the word *symbol* in their response. (Answers will vary but may mention that the building symbolizes—or stands for—the importance of the state and its government.)

Social Emotional Learning

Social Awareness

Respect To encourage students to develop respect for others, remind them that visitors watching a debate in the House of Representatives or Senate must be quiet and not interrupt the legislators. Ask: *How does this behavior show respect to legislators? How does this kind of behavior show respect during class discussions?*

Local Governments

Who hires firefighters and police officers? Who decides if a street corner needs a traffic light? Your local government does! Local governments affect our everyday lives.

Local city governments have executive and legislative branches, just like our federal and state governments. The legislative branch of a local government is usually called a city council. The city council makes laws for the city. The mayor is the head of the city council. Citizens vote for the mayor and city council members.

In some cities throughout the country, the executive branch is headed by a city manager. The city manager carries out the city council's plans. In some larger cities, such as Chicago and New York, the mayor is the head of the executive branch.

Most cities don't have their own court system. They use the county courts. Many minor crimes, such as traffic tickets, are judged in local courts. A judge listens to the issues brought before him or her and follows the law to make fair decisions.

A city council meeting

Local governments provide many services.

libraries · parks · road repair · local museums · fire departments · police

Most local city councils meet every week at the city hall. Citizens can attend city council meetings. At each meeting, the council listens to the concern of citizens. Then the council decides what actions to take. In some locations, citizens can watch city council meetings on television.

Like state government, local governments provide important services to people. One major difference between state and local government is in the sharing of power. Local governments have only the power that the state gives to them.

 Stop and Check

Think Why do you think some cities put their city council meetings on television?

Local Governments

1 Inspect Have students read pp. 230–231 and explain what a city council does.

2 Find Evidence Use the questions below to check for comprehension.

Cite Evidence What types of cases are heard by the local government's judicial branch? (minor crimes, such as traffic tickets) **DOK 2**

Compare How are federal, state, and local governments alike? How are they different? (All have a legislative, executive, and judicial branch; local government deals with local needs such as fire, police, streets, and schools; state government handles state needs; federal government handles national needs.) **DOK 3**

3 Make Connections

Infer How can citizens make sure their elected officials are working for them? (They can attend city council meetings and speak about their concerns. In some places, they can watch these meetings on television.) **DOK 2**

 Stop and Check
COLLABORATE

Think Encourage students to think about the priorities of local officials and their reason for being in office. (Answers will vary but should point out that putting the meetings on television allows people to learn what local government is doing. It also encourages participation.)

EL Spotlight on Content

Using Visuals

Have students look at the graphic on p. 231. Discuss how this graphic helps explain the text. Ask for a volunteer to explain what the graphic represents.

 Digital Tools

Blended Learning

Students investigate curated resources and find evidence to answer the lesson question.

Interactive IMPACT

Students **Research** and find evidence using digital format texts.

Tribal Governments

When European settlers came to America hundreds of years ago, they treated Native American groups as independent nations. They often signed treaties with the nations. A treaty is a formal agreement between nations. The United States made many promises in the treaties it signed with Native Americans. In one treaty, the United States promised Native Americans that they could continue to govern themselves. The United States Constitution recognizes that tribal nations have the right to govern themselves.

Native Americans are citizens of the United States. They are also citizens of their own tribal nations. As American citizens, they are citizens of the state where they live. They vote in national, state, and local elections. Native Americans also follow local, state, and national laws.

Native Americans also have their own governments. Tribal members choose leaders and make laws. States cannot tell tribal governments what to do. However, the federal government can pass laws that affect tribal affairs.

A tribal chairman speaking at a meeting

Tribal governments work like other local and state governments. They provide community services to Native Americans who live on the reservations.

Tribal governments also encourage businesses to come to the community. And they work to preserve their own cultures and to support education.

Perspectives

A large area of land in Oklahoma is claimed by both the Muscogee (Creek) Nation and the state of Oklahoma. Who owns it? Questions like this are sometimes decided by the United States Supreme Court. The case involves a claim about the original Creek Nation's reservation. The state claims that the land has not belonged to the Creek Nation since Oklahoma became a state. The Creek Nation claims that its reservation was never officially taken away. This is an example of a time when the federal government makes decisions that impact tribal affairs.

The U.S. Supreme Court sometimes hears cases involving tribal lands.

Stop and Check

Talk What are some ways tribal governments are the same as state governments?

What Do You Think? Why do we need state and local governments?

RESEARCH COMPANION, pp. 232–233

Tribal Governments

1 Inspect Have students read pp. 232–233 and explain which laws Native Americans follow.

2 Find Evidence Use the questions below to check for comprehension.

Cite Evidence Why do Native Americans have their own governments? (The U.S. Constitution granted them the right to have their own governments. This right allows them to govern themselves in many ways.) **DOK 2**

3 Make Connections

Compare How are tribal governments and local governments alike? How are they different? (Tribal governments and local governments both provide services such as water, roads, police, and community courts, and they encourage businesses to locate in their communities. They are different in that tribal governments can govern their communities as independent nations.) **DOK 3**

 Stop and Check

Talk (Answers will vary, but students may mention that tribal governments also have elected leaders and make laws, provide services for their communities, and encourage businesses to come to their community.)

What Do You Think? Have students discuss with a partner what state, local, and tribal governments do. (Answers will vary, but students should describe functions these governments perform for citizens.)

✓ **Check for Success**

Explain Can students identify the need for state and local governments?

Differentiate

If Not, Have students review their notes on local government in their graphic organizers in their Inquiry Journals.

LESSON QUESTION

Why Do Communities Need Local Government?

INQUIRY JOURNAL, pp. 216–217

Think About It

Remind students to review their research on local government and think about how this level of government is different from state and national government. Encourage them to look at their graphic organizers to review different services provided by local governments. If students need more help, have them review pp. 224–233 of the Research Companion.

Write About It

Describe and Explain Remind students to include the following elements in their responses.

- Provide a description of local government.
- Cite logical evidence supported by facts and details.
- Use transition words to link opinions and evidence.
- Use chapter vocabulary as appropriate.

Discipline(s)	4	3	2	1
Civics	Clearly describes local government, provides key details from the text, and accurately and completely explains how local government works	Somewhat clearly describes local government, provides details from the text, and adequately explains how local government works	Incomplete description of local government, provides few details from text, and explanation of how government works is unclear	Unclear description of local government, includes no details from the text, and explanation of how government works is inaccurate

Talk About It

Explain Encourage students to be specific and to discuss the services provided by local governments.

Assessment Students can check their understanding with feedback from the **Lesson Test** available online.

Connect to the Essential Question

Pull It Together Before they respond, remind students to think about how local government is different from state and national governments.

Inquiry Project Update Remind students to turn to Inquiry Journal p. 191 for project information. If necessary, review the Project Checklist with students. At this point in the chapter, students should focus on the second and third items on the checklist.

Think About It

Contrast

Review your research on local government. How is it different from state and national governments? What kinds of services do local governments provide?

Write About It

Describe and Explain

Write a blog post describing your local government and explaining how it works.

Answers will vary, but should be written in the style of a blog post and include details about the student's local government.

Talk About It

Explain

Share your blog post with a partner. Discuss the services local government provides in your community.

Connect to the EQ

Pull It Together

How do local governments help communities?

Answers will vary, but students should understand that local governments are equipped to deal with local issues and problems.

Inquiry Project Notes

INQUIRY JOURNAL, pp. 216–217

English Learners SCAFFOLD

Use the following scaffolds to support student writing.

Entering and Emerging

Help students think about local government and how it is different from other levels of government. Provide sentence frames:

- Our local government is different from the state and national government because _____.

- Our local government provides services such as _____ and _____.

- Our local government makes decisions about _____.

Developing and Expanding

Ask questions to help students explain how their local government works. Questions might include: *What does the local government do for your community? What services does it provide? How is your local government organized? Who makes decisions about laws? Who is in charge of the executive branch?*

Bridging and Reaching

Have students work in pairs to discuss their local government, what it does, and how it works. Then guide students to write a blog that clearly explains what local government is, includes examples of important services, and provides details about how it is organized.

✔ Check for Success

Summarize Can students write a blog post describing their local government and what it does?

Differentiate

If Not, Have students create a poster or digital photo album that uses images and captions to describe the services their local government provides to its citizens.

LESSON QUESTION

Why Do We Follow Rules?

Connect to the Essential Question

Tell students that this lesson will help them answer the Chapter Essential Question: **Why Do Governments and Citizens Need Each Other?** Explain that they will learn about the rules and laws everyone follows and why they are important. Tell them they will also learn about cause and effect by discussing the consequences that occur when rules are broken.

Lesson Objectives

- **Explain** the difference between laws and rules.
- **Describe** some familiar rules and **explain** why they are important.
- **Identify** the consequences that occur when rules are broken.
- **Discuss** what it means to be a good citizen.
- **Write** about the importance of rules and the consequences for breaking them.

Make Connections!

CONNECT TO ELA

Reading **Use** information gained from illustrations and the words in a text to demonstrate understanding of the text (e.g., where, when, why, and how key events occur).

Research **Recall** information from experiences or gather information from print and digital sources; take brief notes on sources and sort evidence into provided categories.

Writing **Write** informative/explanatory texts to examine a topic and convey ideas and information clearly.

Speaking and Listening **Engage** effectively in a range of collaborative discussions (one-on-one, in groups, and teacher-led) with diverse partners on grade 3 topics and texts, building on others' ideas and expressing their own clearly.

Language **Determine** or clarify the meaning of unknown and multiple-meaning words and phrases based on grade 3 reading and content, choosing flexibly from a range of strategies.

COMMUNITY CONNECTIONS

To enrich what students have learned about rules and laws in your community, invite a law enforcement officer to speak to the class. You can also guide students to explore their local law enforcement website and discuss its mission statement and services to the community.

Lesson-At-A-Glance

1 ENGAGE — INQUIRY JOURNAL

▶ **Talk About It:** Photograph of a crossing guard helping students

▶ **Analyze the Source:** Safety Rules and Laws

▶ **Inquiry Tools:** Explore Cause and Effect

pp. 218–223

2 INVESTIGATE — RESEARCH COMPANION

▶ **Obeying Rules and Laws**

pp. 234–239

3 REPORT — INQUIRY JOURNAL

▶ **Think About It**

▶ **Write About It:** Describe Rules and Their Consequences; Explain the Importance of Rules

▶ **Talk About It**

 ▶ **Connect to the Essential Question**

pp. 224–225

ASSESSMENT

▶ **Online Lesson Test**

▶ **Printable Lesson Test**

For more details, see pages T378–T379.

▶ Digital Tools

at **my.mheducation.com**

ePresentation

Teach the Engage, Investigate, and Report content to the whole class from ePresentations that launch directly from the lesson dashboard.

eBook

You can flip your instruction with the **IMPACT eBooks** found on your lesson dashboard.

Interactive IMPACT

Blend in digital content **when you want it** and **where you want it**.

Blended Learning features in the Teacher's Edition highlight ways to connect in-class work with online experiences to enhance learning.

Investigate current events with **IMPACT News**.

Explore domain-based vocabulary with **Explore Words** and **Word Play** vocabulary activities.

Go Further with IMPACT Explorer Magazine!

The **IMPACT Explorer Magazine** supports students' exploration of the Essential Question and provides additional resources for the EQ Inquiry Project.

pp. 54–65

 LESSON QUESTION

Why Do We Follow Rules?

Language Objectives

- Use newly acquired content and academic vocabulary to talk and write about rules and laws.
- In writing, describe rules and consequences at home, using phrases such as *breaking the rules* or *following a rule*.
- Identify the time frame in sentences with *when* and *while*.

 Spanish Cognates

To support Spanish speakers, point out the cognates.

obey = obedecer

respect = respetar

protect = proteger

consequence = consecuencia

Introduce the Lesson

Set Purpose Explain to students that in this lesson, they will read informational texts to learn more about rules and laws we must follow every day and why we must follow them.

Access Prior Knowledge Read the Lesson Question and find out what students already know about rules and laws they must follow. Ask: *What are some games or sports that have rules? Why do you think they have these rules?* Point out the need for fairness and the possibilities of being injured or causing injury. Compare this to laws about driving. Ask: *Why are there stop signs, speed limit signs, and traffic signals?*

Spark Curiosity Direct students to p. 237 of the Research Companion. Point out the photo and ask students what they notice about the rider. (The rider is wearing a helmet.) Explain that many states require bicycle riders to wear a helmet if they are younger than a certain age. Point out that even if their state does not require a helmet, the city that they live in may require one, so it is important to know the local laws about wearing a helmet. Ask: *Why do you think many states require wearing a helmet when riding a bicycle? Does our state require it? Do you think a helmet should be required for riding a scooter?*

Build Meaning & Support Language

Inquiry Journal

Analyze the Source (pages 220–221) Tell students that in this lesson they will read informational texts that give facts, examples, and explanations about a topic. The texts include headings and photographs with captions. As you read "Safety Rules and Laws," explain words that students don't know. After you read the paragraph on p. 221, reread the sentence: *Wearing a seat belt can mean the difference between life and death in an accident.* Rephrase it in simpler language: "If you wear a seat belt, you are more likely to survive an accident. If you don't wear a seat belt, you are more likely to die in an accident." Explain that the term "buckle up" means "fasten your seat belt." Explain that *Click It or Ticket* means "If you don't make the 'click' sound by fastening your seat belt, you may get a ticket." Point out that the word *ticket* in this context means a notice that a person has broken a law and may have to pay money as punishment.

Inquiry Tools (pages 222–223) Tell students that they will **Explore Cause and Effect** as they read the selections in the Research Companion. Explain that an effect answers the question "What happened?" and a cause answers the question "Why did it happen?" Point out the signal words listed on p. 222 (*because* and *as a result*) that students can use to identify cause-and-effect relationships in the texts. Provide an example sentence: *The laws of your community are created to protect people's safety.* What happened? (The community created laws.) Why did it happen? (to protect people's safety) Ask volunteers to find other cause-and-effect relationships.

Research Companion

Obeying Rules and Laws (pages 234–237) As you read, explain any words students don't know. After you read the first paragraph on p. 234, reread this sentence: *Before you can speak in class, you must raise your hand.* Ask: *What must you do first?* (raise your hand) *Then what can you do?* (speak in class) Explain that *before* plus a phrase tells that something else is first; the other part of the sentence tells what comes first or what happened first.

After you read the first paragraph on p. 237, reread this sentence: *Your family may have a rule that you must do your homework before you watch your favorite show.* Rephrase this sentence in a simpler way: "You must do your homework first. Then you can watch TV." Be sure students understand that a *consequence* is a result. Ask: *What is the consequence of not doing your homework?* (You can't watch your favorite TV show.) Then take a poll: *What else must you do before watching shows at your home?*

Being a Good Citizen (pages 238–239) Be sure students understand that *common good* in paragraph two on p. 238 means the well-being of all the people in the community or country. Point out that the examples in the paragraph are what citizens can do for the common good. Read aloud the last sentence: *They do what they can to make their communities better places to live.*

After you read the second paragraph on p. 239, reread this sentence: *A jury is a group of citizens who are chosen to decide a court case.* Rephrase it in simpler terms: "A court case is when a person accused of a crime goes to a judge. A jury is a group of citizens. They are selected to be on the jury. The jury listens to what the judge says and what both sides say. Then the jury votes to decide if the person is guilty or innocent of the crime."

Inquiry Journal

Report Your Findings (pages 224–225) Review what a cause-and-effect relationship is. Remind students that they should describe two rules and what the effects or results are if they don't follow them. Encourage them to use signal words such as *because* and *as a result*, or an *if-then* sentence, such as *If I don't do my homework, then I can't watch TV.* Check their work for spelling and punctuation errors.

Language Forms & Conventions

Sentences with *While* and *When* Tell students that *while* and *when* can be connecting words that tell when something happens. Write the chart on the board. Ask: *What does the "when" or "while" part of the sentence tell about the other part?* (the time when it happens)

What?	When?
Seat belts keep us safe	**when** we ride in a car.
Car seats help keep babies safe	**while** they are in the car.

COLLABORATE

Have students work in pairs to find two sentences on p. 234 in their Research Companion that use the connecting word *when*. Point out that the word *when* can be at the beginning of the sentence. Have students explain what is happening and when it happens.

Cross-Cultural Connection

Some countries have laws that are different from ours, but their laws exist for the common good. For example, chewing gum is not allowed in Singapore. This law is enforced to keep the public spaces clean. The only exception is gum for medical reasons.

Leveled Support

Entering & Emerging
Have students give examples of a classroom rule and a rule at home by completing these sentence frames:

At school we have to _____.
At home I cannot _____.

Developing & Expanding
Have small groups use the word *because* to write one sentence about consequences of breaking a rule and the phrase *as a result* to write one sentence about the consequences of following rules.

Bridging & Reaching
Have students write three sentences describing rules for a sport or a game and the consequences for breaking each rule.

Language Transfer

As in English, Spanish sentences can be complex, with a main clause and a subordinate clause. In both languages, the subordinate clause can be the first part or the second part of a sentence. If it is the first part, it is followed by a comma.

LESSON 4 ENGAGE

Why Do We Follow Rules?

**INQUIRY JOURNAL,
pp. 218–219**

Bellringer

Help students recall information they have previously learned by reminding them that we have government at different levels. Ask: *What are the basic levels of government?* (federal, state, local, tribal) *What are the three branches of the federal government?* (legislative, executive, judicial)

Lesson Outcomes

Discuss the lesson question and lesson outcomes with students.

- Make sure students understand the difference between the terms *rules* (guides we agree to follow) and *laws* (rules created by a government that everyone must follow).

- Remind students that they have already learned about different levels of government. Explain that part of the job of these governments is to make and enforce rules and laws. Tell students that in this lesson they will explore how rules and laws allow us to live together in communities.

Talk About It

Explain that analyzing photographs can help us better understand a situation. Give students a few moments to examine the photograph of the crossing guard helping students. Provide sentence frames to help students form sentences as they analyze the photo.

- The purpose of the crossing guard is _____. (to help the students safely cross the street)

- The students have a responsibility to _____. (obey the crossing guard and stay within the crosswalk)

- The driver of the car has a responsibility to _____. (obey the crossing guard)

Have partners or groups briefly discuss what they think would happen if there was no crossing guard and report back to class.

 ## Collaborative Conversations

Be Open to All Ideas As students engage in partner, small-group, and whole-class discussions, remind them

- that all ideas, questions, or comments are important and should be heard.
- not to be afraid to ask a question if something is unclear.
- to respect the opinions of others.
- not to be afraid to offer opinions, even if they are different from others' viewpoints.

Lesson 4

Why Do We Follow Rules?

Lesson Outcomes

What Am I Learning?
In this lesson, you will use your investigative skills to learn about the rules and laws we must follow each day.

Why Am I Learning It?
Reading and talking about rules and laws will help you understand how they keep people in your community safe.

How Will I Know That I Learned It?
You will be able to write about some rules you follow and tell why they are important.

Talk About It

Look closely at the picture on the next page. What rules are being followed? Why are these rules needed in the community?

A crossing guard stops traffic for children walking to school.

INQUIRY JOURNAL, pp. 218–219

 English Learners SCAFFOLD

Use the following scaffolds to support student understanding.

Entering and Emerging

Explain that the word *rule* can be a verb, meaning "to govern or lead," or a noun, meaning "a way to behave." Point out that the word *follow* is a verb that can mean "to obey" or "to go after something." Reread the text aloud. Have students state the meaning of *rule* and *follow* each time they hear the terms, using sentence frames such as:

- *In this sentence, the word rule means _____. In this sentence, the word follow means _____.*

Developing and Expanding

Explain that the word *rule* can be a verb, meaning "to govern or lead," or a noun, meaning "a way to behave." Point out two common meanings of *follow:* "to obey" or "to go after something." Have partners work together to use the words *rule* and *follow* to write a sentence for each of the meanings of the terms.

Bridging and Reaching

Help students understand the multiple meanings of the words *rule* and *follow*. Have students use the words *rule* and *follow* to write a sentence for each of the meanings of the terms. Then have partners exchange their sentences and underline the context clues that helped them identify the meaning of *rule* or *follow* in each sentence.

 Social Emotional Learning

Relationship Skills

Communicate Effectively
To strengthen their oral communication skills, students need to take a moment to think about how best to convey information. Model an example of a long, rambling sentence and a shorter, focused sentence.

▶ **Digital** Tools

Blended Learning
Students engage with the lesson question and discussion prompts.

Interactive IMPACT

Discuss the **Lesson Question** and **Talk About It** with the class.

Safety Rules and Laws

1 Inspect

Read the title and look at the photographs. What do you think this text will be about?

- **Circle** the word *fine*. What clues help you figure out what it means?
- **Underline** clues that tell you why sports have rules about wearing safety equipment.
- **Highlight** what could happen to people who do not wear their seat belts.

My Notes

_____

_____

_____

_____

_____

_____

Have you ever played football or soccer? These sports have rules that players must follow. In football, you must wear a helmet and pads to play. In soccer, you usually wear shin guards. Why do you think sports have these rules? The rules are to help keep the players safe.

The laws of your community also help keep you safe. Here's an example. People who wear seat belts are less likely to get hurt in a car accident. All states have laws about wearing a seat belt when riding in a car. If people do not wear one, they could get a ticket and pay a fine.

Car seats help keep babies safe while they are in a car.

Thousands of people are hurt in car accidents every year. Wearing a seat belt can mean the difference between life and death in an accident. Laws help make sure drivers and passengers stay safe by wearing a seat belt. Advertisements remind drivers and passengers to "Buckle Up." Police follow a "Click It or Ticket" program to protect people in cars. In many states, police officers can stop a driver if they see someone in the car not wearing a seat belt. A parent can be fined hundreds of dollars if a child is not buckled up! The police take car safety very seriously. You should too! Communities make rules and laws to keep people safe.

Seat belts keep us safe when we ride in a car.

2 Find Evidence

Reread Why is it important to obey laws?

Examine What are the consequences of breaking seat belt laws?

3 Make Connections

Talk Why do police follow a "Click It or Ticket" program? Do you think this program will make people wear seat belts?

INQUIRY JOURNAL, pp. 220–221

Analyze the Source

Many safety laws can be used to demonstrate the concept of cause and effect. In the United States, vehicle crashes are a leading cause of death among teens. In 2016, more than half of those who died in crashes were not wearing seat belts. For adults and children who are big enough to wear seat belts, being properly restrained by a seat belt is the most effective way to save lives and reduce injuries. However, millions of people still do not wear them every time they take a car trip.

1 Inspect

Read Have students read the title of the selection and look at the photographs. Then have them predict what the article will be about.

2 Find Evidence

Reread Have students reread the text and tell why people should obey laws.

Examine Make sure students understand the meaning of the word *consequences*. (results, effects) They should recognize that breaking seat belt laws results in being more likely to be injured as well as possibly having to pay a fine.

3 Make Connections

Talk Encourage students to work with a partner to draw conclusions about the purpose of the "Click It or Ticket" program and its possible effects. (Answers will vary, but students may say the program could be effective because the slogan is easy to remember and helps people understand the consequences of not wearing a seat belt.)

 Spotlight on Language

Talking about Possibility

Have students locate the following words and phrases in the passage that indicate a possibility rather than a proven fact: *less likely, could get, can mean, can stop,* and *can be.*

 Digital Tools

Blended Learning

Students read informational texts and analyze primary sources.

Interactive IMPACT

Have students practice and apply the strategy of close reading as they analyze text.

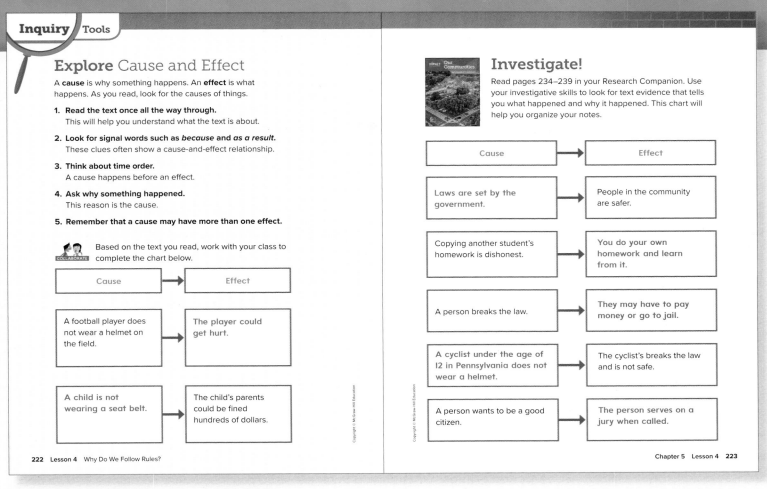

Inquiry Tools

Explore Cause and Effect

Read Tell students that text is sometimes structured around cause and effect. The text explains reasons for or the effects of an action or event. Remind students that events can have multiple effects and that effects can also be called consequences or results. Have students read the step-by-step instructions for finding cause and effect in a text.

Guide Practice Have students review the text on pp. 220–221. Then work with them to complete the graphic organizer. Explain that they will use a similar graphic organizer to organize their independent research.

Check Understanding Confirm student understanding of the inquiry skill, Explore Cause and Effect. If students cannot identify the cause-and-effect relationships from the text, review the steps on p. 222.

Investigate!

Have students read pp. 234–239 in the Research Companion. Tell them the information will help them answer the lesson question *Why Do We Follow Rules?*

Take Notes Tell students they should use the graphic organizer on p. 223 of the Inquiry Journal to take notes on causes and effects in the text. Remind them that taking notes will help them understand and remember the information they learn. Remind students to always use their own words when taking notes.

Spotlight on Language

Signal Words

Tell students that words and phrases such as *because*, *the reason for*, *on account of*, *led to*, *due to*, and *since* are often clues that show the causes in a cause-and-effect relationship. Words and phrases such as *as a result*, *outcome*, *finally*, *therefore*, *for this reason*, *then*, and *so* frequently signal the effects in such a relationship.

LESSON QUESTION

Why Do We Follow Rules?

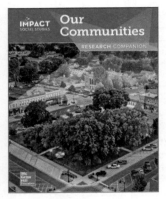

**RESEARCH
COMPANION,
pp. 234–235**

Background Information

John Locke Political philosopher John Locke believed that all people were free and equal. However, he also stated that people could transfer some of their rights to the government in order to enjoy stable lives that allowed them to live with a reasonable amount of liberty. Locke referred to this agreement between the governed and the government as a social contract. These governments exist to promote the public good and to protect people's rights.

Obeying Rules and Laws

1 Inspect Have students read pages 234–235 and identify who usually makes rules and who sets laws.

2 Find Evidence Use the questions below to check comprehension. Remind students to support their answers with text evidence.

Use Context Clues What do you think the word *respect* means? (consideration, caring about the other person) **DOK 2**

Predict What do you think would happen if there were no laws? Why? (Answers will vary, but students should understand that without laws many people would do whatever they wanted and there would be chaos, people would not be treated equally, and those who were stronger or had more money might take over.) **DOK 2**

Compare How is a law different from a rule? (A rule helps people get along well and work together, whereas a law is set by the government to keep people safe and make sure that people are treated equally.) **DOK 3**

3 Make Connections

Cite Evidence How are the students who are raising their hands in the picture on p. 235 showing respect for their classmates? (Answers will vary, but students should include that the students are showing their willingness to take turns and allow others to share their ideas and opinions.) **DOK 3**

Lesson 4

Why Do We Follow Rules?

Obeying Rules and Laws

When you ride your bike, you must stop at a light. Before you can speak in class, you must raise your hand. Do you know which of these examples is a rule and which is a law?

Rules are set by people like your parents or your teacher. Rules help people get along well and work together. They help teach you right from wrong. Rules can also help you learn to respect one another.

Laws are set by the government. They are the rules that you and all the members of your community must follow. Laws help keep people safe. They also make sure people are treated equally.

People set rules when they want to solve a problem or improve a situation. Parents and teachers can just tell others the new rule or write it down. Government officials cannot do that. They have to talk about the law to make sure it is good and fair. Then they vote on it. Sometimes their idea becomes a law, and sometimes it does not.

Rules help make sure that everyone in the class is heard.

234   Lesson 4   Why Do We Follow Rules?

Chapter 5   Lesson 4   235

RESEARCH COMPANION, pp. 234–235

 # English Learners   SCAFFOLD

Use the following scaffolds to support student understanding of lesson content.

Entering and Emerging

Use the photograph on p. 235 to help students understand the difference between a rule and a law. Guide students to complete sentence frames, such as:

- The people in the photo are _____. (students and their teacher) They are in a _____. (classroom)

- The students want to speak, so they are _____. (raising their hands)

- Students must raise their hands to speak because that is a _____. (rule)

- Classroom rules are set by the _____ (teacher) A law is set by the _____. (government)

Developing and Expanding

Have partners use the photograph on p. 235 to help them understand the difference between a rule and a law. Guide them to explain to each other who the people are, where they are, and what they are doing. Ask partners to tell each other how they know the students are following a rule instead of a law.

Bridging and Reaching

Have small groups play a guessing game to help them explain the difference between rules and laws. Students take turns naming a rule or a law. Other students guess if it is a rule or a law and explain their answer.

 **Digital** Tools

Blended Learning
Guide students as they investigate the lesson content.

ePresentation

Investigate with the whole class or small groups.

Rules help people get along and treat each other fairly.

Rules are important because they teach people how to behave and how to treat others. Your classroom rules help you learn about fairness and honesty. You do not cut in line because it is unfair. You do not copy another student's homework because it is dishonest. There are also rules against bullying. People who follow the rules try to do what is best at all times.

The laws of your community are created to protect people's safety. It is against the law to drive faster than the speed limit. This law protects walkers and other drivers. Restaurant workers must wash their hands. This protects the health of their customers. Laws also protect our property. For example, it is against the law to go into a house and take something without permission.

A driver who speeds is breaking a law. He or she may have to pay a fine.

What keeps people from breaking a rule or law? All rules and laws have consequences. A consequence is something that happens as a result of something else. If you know what the consequence will be, you might not break a rule. Your family may have a rule that you must do your homework before you watch your favorite show. You know the consequence for not doing your homework is that you cannot watch your favorite show. This means that you will probably do your homework. People who break laws are punished. They may have to pay money or go to jail.

Did You Know?

In Pennsylvania, there are many laws about bicycles. Your bike must have a brake. You cannot carry a passenger unless your bike is designed to hold a passenger. Also, you must wear a helmet whenever you ride a bike if you are under the age of 12. If you are caught without a helmet, your parent or guardian might have to pay a fine of $25.

Obeying bike laws

✓ Stop and Check

Talk With a partner, discuss how a law is different from a rule. What are the consequences of breaking a law?

Find Details As you read, add new information to the graphic organizer on page 223 in your Inquiry Journal.

RESEARCH COMPANION, pp. 236–237

Obeying Rules and Laws

1 Inspect Have students read pp. 236–237 and name three reasons why classrooms need to have rules.

2 Find Evidence Use the questions below to check comprehension.

Use Context Clues What do you think the word *property* means? (anything a person owns, such as clothing, computer, cell phone, car, house) **DOK 2**

Draw Conclusions Think of a rule that you must follow at school. What are the advantages of obeying the rule? What are any disadvantages? (Answers will vary.) **DOK 3**

3 Make Connections

Develop a Logical Argument If your school had no rules against bullying, what might you say to adults to encourage them to create these rules? Give specific reasons. (Answers will vary, but students should understand the reasons to make a rule: to make certain no one is treated unfairly or has their feelings hurt, and to create a more pleasant school where students get along.) **DOK 3**

✓ Stop and Check

Talk (A law is made by the government and must be followed by everyone. You could pay a fine or go to jail if you disobey a law.)

Find Details Explain to students that after they read and take notes, they should review and think about how the facts and details will help them answer the Essential Question.

 Spotlight on Content

Scanning for Information
Have students work in pairs to find different examples of laws or rules and their possible consequences. Have students list their findings and then enter them into the graphic organizer.

 **Digital Tools**

Blended Learning
Students explore lesson content through interactive activities.

Interactive IMPACT

Use the **More to Explore**.

Being a Good Citizen

Good citizens follow the rules and laws of their communities. They know that rules and laws protect everyone. They respect the **rights** and opinions of others. They are also honest and trustworthy.

Good citizens believe in the common good. This means that they do what is best for their communities. They might serve as government leaders. They might **volunteer** to help clean up their local parks. They do what they can to make their communities better places to live.

Most importantly, citizens support the rules and laws of the United States. Good citizens know that every American has the right to worship as they wish. Every American has the right to an opinion. Every American has the right to be treated fairly. Good citizens follow the laws to protect everyone's rights and differences.

Being good citizens

Citizens serving on a jury

American citizens have certain responsibilities. A responsibility is a duty or job. All American citizens have the responsibility to vote. When citizens vote, they choose the people who will make and enforce the laws. Good citizens follow the news to stay informed about the issues that affect their communities. This helps them make good choices about what their communities need.

American citizens are required to serve on a **jury** if they are asked. A jury is a group of citizens who are chosen to decide a court case. A jury helps make sure that a person who is accused of a crime has a fair trial.

A good citizen pays taxes. Taxes help pay for the services in your community. Taxes pay for services such as schools, libraries, and police and fire departments.

> **✓ Stop and Check** COLLABORATE
>
> **Talk** What does it mean to be a good citizen? Discuss your answer with a partner.
>
> **Find Details** As you read, add new information to the graphic organizer on page 223 in your Inquiry Journal.

What Do You Think? What are some rules that we must follow? Why is it important to follow these rules?

RESEARCH COMPANION, pp. 238–239

Obeying Rules and Laws

1 Inspect Have students read pp. 238–239 and name three things a good citizen does.

2 Find Evidence Use the questions below to check comprehension.

Use Context Clues What do you think the word *rights* means? (something that is due to everyone, such as the right to be treated fairly or to express an opinion) **DOK 2**

Infer Why is paying taxes an important responsibility of a good citizen? What would happen if citizens refused to pay their taxes? (Taxes help pay for services the community needs; if people did not pay taxes, many services might have to be reduced or eliminated.) **DOK 3**

3 Make Connections

Develop a Logical Argument What do you think is the most important responsibility of a good citizen? (Answers will vary, but students should provide logical reasons supported by text evidence.) **DOK 3**

✓ Stop and Check   COLLABORATE

Talk (Answers will vary, but students should include that good citizens follow rules and laws, do what is best for their communities, and fulfill their responsibilities such as voting, serving on a jury, and paying taxes.)

What Do You Think? Review rules in school and the community to help students identify reasons for following rules. (Answers will vary, but students should support the rules they mention with logical reasons for their importance.)

✓ Check for Success

Explain Can students explain why we follow rules and laws?

Differentiate

If Not, Ask students to review their notes on causes and effects of following rules and laws in their Inquiry Journals.

LESSON 4 REPORT

LESSON QUESTION

Why Do We Follow Rules?

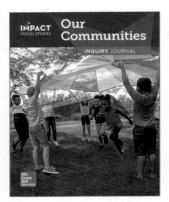

**INQUIRY JOURNAL,
pp. 224–225**

Think About It

Students will review their research and consider why they think it is important to have rules and laws. Remind students to review the causes and effects they have listed in their graphic organizer. Direct students back to pp. 234–239 of their Research Companion if they need more information.

Write About It

Describe and Explain Remind students to include the following elements in their responses:

- Describe two rules they follow and the consequences for breaking them.
- Explain why it is important to have rules.
- Use chapter vocabulary as appropriate.

Discipline(s)	4	3	2	1
Civics	Strong understanding of the rules we must follow and the consequences if we do not	Adequate understanding of the rules we must follow and the consequences if we do not	Uneven understanding of the rules we must follow and the consequences if we do not	No understanding of the rules we must follow and the consequences if we do not

Talk About It

Discuss Have students pair up with a classmate to talk about the reasons that rules are important. Remind students to take turns discussing their reasons and to state whether they agree or disagree with their partner's reasons and explain why.

Assessment Students can check their understanding with feedback from the **Lesson Test** available online.

Connect to the Essential Question

Pull It Together Before students respond, ask them to think about how government and citizens work together to create rules and laws.

Inquiry Project Update Remind students to turn to Inquiry Journal p. 191 for project information. If necessary, review the Project Checklist with students. At this point in the chapter, students should focus on the third and fourth items on the checklist.

Think About It

Ask Yourself
Why do you think it is important to have rules and laws?

Write About It

Describe
What are some rules you follow at home? Describe two rules and what might happen if you do not follow them.

Answers will vary, but students should list valid rules that parents would set for their children and describe the consequences of breaking them.

Explain
Based on what you have read in this lesson, why do you think it is important to have rules?

Students may suggest that the rules are created with their safety and well-being in mind.

Talk About It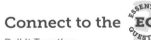

Discuss
Share your rules and the possible consequences if you do not follow them. How are your rules similar to or different from your partner's rules?

🏛 Connect to the EQ
Civics

Pull It Together
Think about what you read in this lesson. How do rules and laws help us all live together?

Answers will vary, but students should show an understanding that rules and laws keep communities safe and secure.

EQ Inquiry Project Notes

INQUIRY JOURNAL, pp. 224–225

 # English Learners SCAFFOLD

Use the following scaffolds to support student writing.

Entering and Emerging

Help students understand how to combine clauses to make connections between ideas. Support them as they answer the questions about rules and laws on pp. 224–225 by helping them create compound sentences using the words *and*, *but*, and *so*. Use sentence frames such as:

- A rule I follow at home is _____, but if I break it, _____.

Developing and Expanding

Review with small groups how to combine clauses to make connections between ideas. Guide them to create compound sentences using the words *and*, *but*, and *so* as they write their responses to the questions on pp. 224–225.

Bridging and Reaching

Review how to combine and condense clauses to make connections between ideas using the words *and*, *but*, and *so*. Guide students to create compound, precise, and detailed sentences as they express their responses to the questions on pp. 224–225.

✔ **Check for Success**

Explain Can students describe rules they must follow and the importance of having rules?

Differentiate

If Not, Have students present their information in a series of drawings or in an oral presentation.

LESSON QUESTION

How Have Heroes Helped Communities?

Connect to the Essential Question

Tell students that this lesson provides key research into the Chapter Essential Question: **Why Do Governments and Citizens Need Each Other?** Explain that they will use their investigative skills to learn about real people who helped make their communities and the nation better.

Lesson Objectives

- **Identify** heroes who took action and how they made a difference.
- **Describe** ways in which people work together to solve problems in a community.
- **Write** about people who worked to solve issues and about the effects of their actions.

Make Connections!

CONNECT TO ELA

Reading **Use** language that pertains to time, sequence, and cause/effect to describe the relationship between a series of historical events, scientific ideas or concepts, or steps in technical procedures in a text.

Research **Recall** information from experiences or gather information from print and digital sources; take brief notes on sources and sort evidence into provided categories.

Writing **Craft** informative/explanatory texts to examine a topic and convey ideas and information clearly.

Speaking and Listening **Engage** effectively in a range of collaborative discussions with diverse partners on grade 3 topics and texts, building on others' ideas and expressing students' own ideas clearly.

Language **Demonstrate** command of the conventions of standard English capitalization, punctuation, and spelling when writing.

COMMUNITY CONNECTIONS

To enrich what students have learned about heroes in communities, invite a hero from your community (police officer, firefighter, nurse, or representative from a community service organization) to speak to the class.

Lesson-At-A-Glance

1 ENGAGE — INQUIRY JOURNAL

pp. 226–231

- ▶ **Talk About It:** Picture of Anne Hutchinson on trial
- ▶ **Analyze the Source:** Anne Hutchinson: A Hero for Freedom
- ▶ **Inquiry Tools:** Explore Cause and Effect

2 INVESTIGATE — RESEARCH COMPANION

pp. 240–249

- ▶ **What Is a Hero?**
- ▶ **Around the World:** Humanitarian Heroes Around the World
- ▶ **Biography: Eleanor Roosevelt**

3 REPORT — INQUIRY JOURNAL

pp. 232–233

- ▶ **Think About It**
- ▶ **Write About It:** Write a Cause and Effect Paragraph
- ▶ **Talk About It**
- ▶ **Connect to the Essential Question**

ASSESSMENT

- ▶ **Online Lesson Test**
- ▶ **Printable Lesson Test**

For more details, see pages T378–T379.

▶ Digital Tools

at **my.mheducation.com**

ePresentation

Teach the Engage, Investigate, and Report content to the whole class from **ePresentations** that launch directly from the lesson dashboard.

eBook

You can flip your instruction with the **IMPACT eBooks** found on your lesson dashboard.

Interactive IMPACT

Blend in digital content **when you want it** and **where you want it**.

Blended Learning features in the Teacher's Edition highlight ways to connect in-class work with online experiences to enhance learning.

Investigate current events with **IMPACT News**.

Explore domain-based vocabulary with **Explore Words** and **Word Play** vocabulary activities.

Go Further with IMPACT Explorer Magazine!

pp. 54–65

The **IMPACT Explorer Magazine** supports students' exploration of the Essential Question and provides additional resources for the EQ Inquiry Project.

LESSON 5 LANGUAGE LEARNERS

How Have Heroes Helped Communities?

Language Objectives

- Use newly acquired content and academic vocabulary to talk and write about heroes.
- Write about an issue in the past and how people worked to solve it, using cause-and-effect language.
- Use correct subject-verb agreement.

Spanish Cognates

To support Spanish speakers, point out the cognates.

equality = igualdad

escape = escapar

organize = organizar

segregation = segregación

humanitarian = humanitario

universal = universal

Introduce the Lesson

Set Purpose Explain to students that in this lesson, they will read informational texts to learn about people who have helped make their communities and the world better.

Access Prior Knowledge Read the Lesson Question and find out what students already know about community heroes. Ask: *What is a hero?* Point out that when people do heroic acts, there is often a story about them in the newspaper or on television. Ask: *Why do you think people like to read or hear stories about heroes?* Ask students to give some examples of heroic acts.

Spark Curiosity Point to the photo of Linda Brown on p. 248 of the Research Companion. Explain that when she was in third grade, her family lived in a diverse neighborhood. The white children she played with went to a school nearby, but it was an all-white school. Linda Brown could not attend it because she was not white. Her father thought it was wrong that she had to go all the way across town to attend a school. It took many years for the case to move through the courts and finally reach the Supreme Court. Linda Brown didn't get to attend that neighborhood school, but her sisters were able to go to integrated schools. Her case shows that even a young person can have an effect that can change the whole nation.

Build Meaning & Support Language

Inquiry Journal

Analyze the Source (pages 228–229) Tell students that in this lesson they will read informational texts that give facts, examples, and explanations about a topic. As you read "Anne Hutchinson: A Hero for Freedom," explain any words that students don't know. Make sure students understand that a *trial* is where people bring evidence to show if a person is guilty or innocent of a crime. Point out that *stood by* means "defended." Look closely at the sentence *She left, but she never gave up her ideas or her right to think for herself.* Rephrase it in simpler language: "She left, but she didn't stop believing in her ideas." Ask: *What was Anne's crime?* (Her ideas were different from those of the people in her community.) *Did she give up her ideas?* (No)

Inquiry Tools (pages 230–231) Tell students they will **Explore Cause and Effect** as they read the selections in the Research Companion. Remind them that the graphic organizer will help them organize the information they read. Point out the column headings. Say: *A cause is why something happens; an effect is what happens.* Model locating a cause and an effect on p. 228. Add them to the graphic organizer on p. 230. Say: *The second paragraph on p. 228 tells the cause:* Anne Hutchison's ideas were different from the ministers' ideas. *On p. 230, that sentence is written under "Cause" in the graphic organizer. The third paragraph tells what happened:* Anne was arrested and put on trial. *I will write that sentence under "Effect."* Remind students that there are some words we can use to talk about cause and effect. List on the board *because, therefore, as a result,* and *so.* Guide students to form a cause-and-effect sentence using each word.

Research Companion

What Is a Hero? (pages 240–241) After you read p. 240, explain any unfamiliar words. Tell students that *everyday people* means any person. Read aloud the first paragraph on p. 241, emphasizing the repeated word *fought*. Explain that *fought* is the past tense of *fight*. Ask for another way to say *fought*.

American Heroes (pages 242–244) After you read the third paragraph on p. 242, explain that *emancipation* means "freedom from slavery" and *proclamation* is "an official announcement by a leader." Support understanding of the Primary Source on p. 243. Explain that *I do order and declare* is a formal way of saying "I announce"; that *henceforward* is a formal way to say "from now on"; and that *shall* is a formal way to say "will."

Around the World (pages 245) After you read the first paragraph on p. 245, explain that a *nickname* is an informal name that a person's friends or family give to that person. Tell students that a *battlefield* is a place where soldiers fight each other. Ask: *Why do you think Clara Barton earned the nickname "angel of the battlefield"?* (She helped soldiers who were wounded.)

Biography: Eleanor Roosevelt (pages 246–247) After reading the second paragraph on p. 246, explain to students that polio is a disease that causes muscle weakness and that a person with polio usually cannot walk.

After reading the third paragraph on p. 246, tell students that the United Nations is an international organization where countries work together to keep peace and encourage cooperation around the world. Support understanding of the Primary Source. Explain that *purport* means "claim to be" even if the claim may not be true. Tell students that *It . . . does not purport to be a statement of law . . .* means "it does not claim to be a law."

Inquiry Journal

Report Your Findings (pages 232–233) Review with students what a cause-and-effect relationship is. Tell students that when they write about an issue, their writing should include a clear statement of the issue, how it caused people to take action, and the effects of their actions. Encourage students to use new vocabulary words they have learned. Have them check their writing for spelling and punctuation errors.

Language Forms & Conventions

Subject-Verb Agreement Remind students that subjects and verbs must agree, or match, in number. If the subject is singular, or is one person or thing, the verb must agree in number and be a singular verb. If the subject is plural, or is more than one person or thing, the verb must agree in number and be a plural verb. Display the chart. Model using correct subject-verb agreement: *Some heroes <u>work</u> to make the world a better place. Clara Barton <u>was</u> one of these heroes.*

One (singular)	More Than One (plural)
Anne **was** born in England.	Her ideas **were** different.
Harriet Tubman **was** an enslaved person.	Both Harriet Tubman and Frederick Douglass **were** born into slavery.
She **works** for a better world.	Some heroes **work** to make the world a better place.

 Have students work in pairs to locate some examples of subject-verb agreement in the texts. Call on volunteers to say them aloud.

Cross-Cultural Connection

Have students discuss heroes from other countries that they may know about. They may mention people such as Malala Yousafzai (Pakistan), Nelson Mandela (South Africa), and Mahatma Gandhi (India).

Leveled Support

Entering & Emerging
Help students form complete sentences from their notes.

Developing & Expanding
Encourage students to use cause-and-effect words and phrases such as *because* and *as a result* to show the effects of the actions that people took to solve an issue.

Bridging & Reaching
Have students swap responses with a partner. Ask partners to make suggestions about where to add more detail about the issue and the effects of people's actions to solve it.

Language Transfer

In some languages, such as Chinese, Haitian Creole, Hmong, Korean, and Vietnamese, the verb does not change for person and number. A student may say: *She work for a better world.*

LESSON 5 ENGAGE

LESSON QUESTION

How Have Heroes Helped Communities?

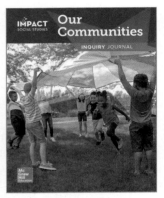

INQUIRY JOURNAL, pp. 226–227

Bellringer

Prompt students to recall what they have learned in the previous lesson. Say: *You have learned about rules and laws. Good citizens follow rules and laws because they keep us safe. What are some other things good citizens do?* (respect others and their beliefs, stay informed about issues, vote, serve on juries, pay taxes, volunteer)

Lesson Outcomes

Discuss the lesson question and lesson outcomes with students.

- To help students understand the meaning of the word *hero*, identify specific heroes such as historical figures, firefighters, and police officers and ask students what these people do or have done to be called heroes.

- Explain to students that knowing about heroes of both the past and the present helps in understanding the importance of standing up for what you believe in and helping our communities and our country be better places to live.

Talk About It

Remind students that studying artwork can help us understand events that happened long ago. Explain that this image shows Anne Hutchinson in court. Emphasize that she is standing up for her beliefs. Ask: *Do you think standing up for her beliefs was easy for Anne Hutchinson? Based on this scene, how did you reach this conclusion?* (Answers will vary, but students should note that the men in the picture look very stern and disapproving of Hutchinson.)

 Collaborative Conversations

Add New Ideas As students engage in partner, small-group, and whole-class discussions, encourage them to add new ideas to their conversations. Remind students to

- stay on the topic of American heroes.
- connect their own ideas to things their peers have said.
- look for ways to connect their own experiences of heroes who have personally affected them to the conversation.

Lesson 5 — How Have Heroes Helped Communities?

Anne Hutchinson defends her actions during her trial in the colony of Massachusetts.

Lesson Outcomes

What Am I Learning?
In this lesson, you will use your investigative skills to learn about real people who helped make their communities and the world better.

Why Am I Learning It?
Reading and talking about heroes will help you understand how people have solved problems.

How Will I Know That I Learned It?
You will be able to write about how people helped solve a problem in the world, nation, or their communities.

Talk About It COLLABORATE

Look closely at the picture on the next page. Who is the most important person? Why do you think that?

INQUIRY JOURNAL, pp. 226–227

EL English Learners SCAFFOLD

Use the following scaffolds to support student understanding of lesson outcomes.

Entering and Emerging

Read aloud the caption. Explain that as used here, *defends* means "speaks to support." Have students study the picture on p. 227 and choose the best word to complete the following sentences. Discuss their responses.

- The men in the picture are (listening/talking) _____.
- Anne Hutchinson is (listening/talking) _____.
- Anne Hutchinson is (afraid/fearless) _____.

Developing and Expanding

Have students study the picture on p. 227. Read aloud the caption and guide students to discuss what is happening. Have partners work together to write a sentence describing what is happening.

Bridging and Reaching

Have students study the picture on p. 227 and read the caption. Then have them write a few sentences to answer the following questions:

- Who is the hero in the picture?
- How do you know?

Social Emotional Learning

Decision-Making Skills

Ethical Responsibility
Explain that ethical responsibility is making the decision to do what you know is right. As they read the lesson, have students identify how each hero demonstrated ethical responsibility.

 Digital Tools

Blended Learning
Students engage with the lesson question and discussion prompts.

ePresentation

Discuss the **Lesson Question** and **Talk About It** with the class.

1 Inspect

Read the text all the way through.

Circle words you do not know.

Underline clues that tell you who Anne Hutchinson was.

Highlight clues that tell you where she lived.

Discuss with a partner why Anne Hutchinson was on trial.

My Notes

_____
_____
_____
_____
_____
_____
_____
_____
_____

Anne Hutchinson: A Hero for Freedom

Anne Hutchinson was born in England. Her father taught her to think for herself and to speak her mind. Anne sailed to Massachusetts with her family in 1634. They settled in Boston.

Anne was very religious. She began to have meetings in her home. At these meetings, she talked about religion. She believed God taught everyone, not just ministers and men. Her ideas were different from what the people in her community taught and believed.

The ministers who disagreed with Anne had her arrested. She was put on trial. During her trial, Anne Hutchinson stood by what she believed. She said only God could be her judge.

The court ordered Anne to leave the community. She left, but she never gave up her ideas or her right to think for herself.

PRIMARY SOURCE

In Their Words...
Anne Hutchinson

"Now, if you do condemn me for speaking what in my conscience I know to be truth I must commit myself unto the Lord."

—The Examination of Mrs. Anne Hutchinson at the Court at Newton, 1637

The court orders Anne Hutchinson to leave Boston.

2 Find Evidence

Reread the quote from Anne Hutchinson. How does this show her beliefs?

Underline words and sentences from the text that show how Anne stood up for her beliefs.

3 Make Connections

Talk Discuss with a partner why it is important to stand up for something you believe in.

Connect to Now Who is someone today who stands up for what he or she believes?

INQUIRY JOURNAL, pp. 228–229

Analyze the Source

Background Information
Anne Hutchinson lived from around 1591 to 1643, a time when women were expected to be silent and when their opinions were considered to be inferior to those of men. Religious leaders in Boston became alarmed that many women supported Hutchinson. When she was banished from the Massachusetts colony, she and her husband moved to what is now Rhode Island, which was more tolerant of various religious viewpoints.

1 Inspect

Read Have students read the text, the Primary Source, and the caption. Remind them to circle words in the text they do not know.

2 Find Evidence

Reread Read aloud the quote from Anne Hutchinson.

- How does the Primary Source reveal Hutchinson's beliefs? (Answers will vary, but should include that Hutchinson says that she is speaking her conscience and what she knows to be the truth.) Based on its context in this quote, what does the word *condemn* mean? (pronounce guilty, convict, sentence, criticize)

3 Make Connections

Talk Have students discuss whether they think Anne Hutchinson was right to stand up for her beliefs, considering the price she paid. Ask: *Why is it important to stand up for something you believe in?* (Answers will vary.)

Connect to Now Who is someone today who stands up for what he or she believes in? (Answers will vary.)

EL Spotlight on Language

Understanding Language

think for herself: to have opinions or make decisions without others' help

speak her mind: to say her true thoughts or beliefs

stood by: kept believing that her beliefs were still correct

stand up for: to defend a person or belief that is being attacked

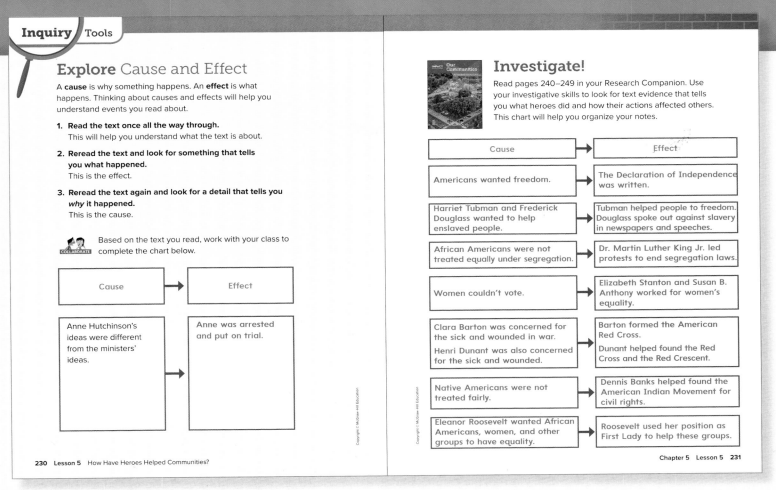

Explore Cause and Effect

A **cause** is why something happens. An **effect** is what happens. Thinking about causes and effects will help you understand events you read about.

1. **Read the text once all the way through.**
   This will help you understand what the text is about.

2. **Reread the text and look for something that tells you what happened.**
   This is the effect.

3. **Reread the text again and look for a detail that tells you _why_ it happened.**
   This is the cause.

Based on the text you read, work with your class to complete the chart below.

Cause	Effect
Anne Hutchinson's ideas were different from the ministers' ideas.	Anne was arrested and put on trial.

230 Lesson 5 How Have Heroes Helped Communities?

Investigate!

Read pages 240–249 in your Research Companion. Use your investigative skills to look for text evidence that tells you what heroes did and how their actions affected others. This chart will help you organize your notes.

Cause	Effect
Americans wanted freedom.	The Declaration of Independence was written.
Harriet Tubman and Frederick Douglass wanted to help enslaved people.	Tubman helped people to freedom. Douglass spoke out against slavery in newspapers and speeches.
African Americans were not treated equally under segregation.	Dr. Martin Luther King Jr. led protests to end segregation laws.
Women couldn't vote.	Elizabeth Stanton and Susan B. Anthony worked for women's equality.
Clara Barton was concerned for the sick and wounded in war. Henri Dunant was also concerned for the sick and wounded.	Barton formed the American Red Cross. Dunant helped found the Red Cross and the Red Crescent.
Native Americans were not treated fairly.	Dennis Banks helped found the American Indian Movement for civil rights.
Eleanor Roosevelt wanted African Americans, women, and other groups to have equality.	Roosevelt used her position as First Lady to help these groups.

Chapter 5 Lesson 5 231

INQUIRY JOURNAL, pp. 230–231

Inquiry Tools

Explore Cause and Effect

Read Have students read the step-by-step instructions for how to identify cause and effect. Tell students that when they determine cause and effect, they are explaining how events are related to one another.

Guide Practice Have students review the text on pp. 228–229. Then work with them to complete the graphic organizer. Explain that they will use a similar graphic organizer to organize their independent research.

Check Understanding Confirm student understanding of the inquiry skill, Explore Cause and Effect. If students cannot identify the cause and/or effect, review the steps on p. 230.

Investigate!

Have students read pp. 240–249 in the Research Companion to gather more information that will help them answer the lesson question **_How Have Heroes Helped Communities?_**

Take Notes Tell students that they will use the graphic organizer on p. 231 of the Inquiry Journal to take notes on causes and effects as they read each section. Remind them that taking notes will help them understand and remember the information they learn. Taking notes will also make it easier to identify causes and effects.

EL Spotlight on Content

Cause and Effect

Have students write down the names of people as they read through the text. Then have them look for _what_ the person did and _why_ the person took this action. This will help them find the cause and effect. Have students practice with the text on pp. 228–229.

▶ **Digital Tools**

Blended Learning

Students prepare for the lesson investigation with step-by-step instruction about how to determine cause and effect.

ePresentation

Use the **Inquiry Tools** to model and complete the lesson graphic organizer.

LESSON 5 INVESTIGATE

How Have Heroes Helped Communities?

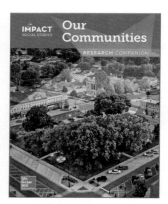

RESEARCH COMPANION, pp. 240–241

Background Information

- Many of the heroes discussed here, such as Dr. Martin Luther King, Jr., sacrificed a great deal for their beliefs. In 1963, Dr. King was arrested for protesting segregation in Birmingham, Alabama. He was in jail for about a week, and during that time he wrote his well-known "Letter from Birmingham Jail." In the letter, King stated that individuals had a moral responsibility to directly protest unjust laws, such as laws that enforced segregation. King said that nonviolent protests were vital because he believed that injustice, no matter where it occurred, threatened justice everywhere.

- There are heroic organizations that are attempting to make the world a better place. One of these is Doctors Without Borders (Médecins Sans Frontières), which works to respond quickly to humanitarian crises anywhere they occur. Since its beginning, Doctors Without Borders has treated more than 100 million people and today has offices in multiple countries.

- *Brown* v. *Board of Education* consisted of five different cases concerning whether the Constitution allowed public schools to be segregated. Under the leadership of Chief Justice Earl Warren, the Court came to a unanimous decision in favor of desegregating public schools, determining that segregated schools were inherently unequal.

What Is a Hero?

1 Inspect Have students read pp. 240–241 and define the word *hero*.

2 Find Evidence Use the questions below to check comprehension. Remind students to support their answers with text evidence.

Infer Why are people who have fought for equality considered heroes? (Answers will vary, but students should understand that the equality of all people is an important part of what the United States stands for, so people who work for equal rights are considered heroes.) **DOK 2**

Cite Evidence Why is being able to solve problems an important part of being a hero? Ask students to cite evidence from the text in their answer. (Answers will vary, but students should understand that being able to solve problems helps people improve their communities.) **DOK 3**

Cause and Effect What are some of the ways you can be a hero in your family? Give specific examples. (Answers will vary, but students should provide specific reasons for their answers.) **DOK 3**

3 Make Connections

Relate Using what you have learned here, who would you say is one of your heroes? Why? (Answers will vary, but students should provide specific reasons for their answers.) **DOK 3**

How Have Heroes Helped Communities?

What Is a **Hero?**

Heroes are people who make the world better for other people. They may be people who have done great things or behaved with great honor. They may be young or old, boys or girls. They may be famous people or everyday people. Teachers, firefighters, police officers, nurses, and others in your community are heroes. A hero could simply be someone who helps you feel better if you are having a bad day. Think about some of your everyday heroes.

A firefighter can be a hero.

History is filled with heroes. Women and men fought for the freedoms we enjoy every day. They fought for freedom of speech, the right to vote, and the right to attend school. They fought so that all Americans would have equality, or equal rights.

In this lesson, you will read about some of our nation's heroes. Many of them risked their lives to change their communities. They also changed our nation and the world. The stories of their lives will help you understand how people can solve problems and create positive changes.

Dr. Martin Luther King, Jr.

Thomas Jefferson

240 Lesson 5 How Have Heroes Helped Communities?

Chapter 5 Lesson 5 **241**

RESEARCH COMPANION, pp. 240–241

 English Learners **SCAFFOLD**

Use the following scaffolds to support student understanding of lesson content.

Entering and Emerging

Have students copy these simple definitions for these domain-specific nouns: *honor* (ideas about the right way to act), *freedom* (being able to do what you want), and *equality* (being equal to others). Then guide students to complete these sentence frames:

- Heroes often make choices based on their _____. (honor)
- Many heroes work for _____ and _____. (freedom; equality)

Developing and Expanding

Provide students with simple definitions for these domain-specific nouns: *honor* (ideas about the right way to act), *freedom* (being able to do what you want), and *equality* (being equal to others). Have partners discuss the meanings of the terms and work together to create illustrated dictionary entries for them.

Bridging and Reaching

Discuss with students the definitions for these domain-specific nouns: *honor* (ideas about the right way to act), *freedom* (being able to do what you want), and *equality* (being equal to others). Have individual students write a paragraph using these terms to tell about a hero in the future.

 Digital Tools

Blended Learning
Students explore lesson content.

Interactive IMPACT
Use the **Lesson Video**.

American Heroes

Thomas Jefferson and Benjamin Franklin are heroes who helped create our country. They worked together with others to write the Declaration of Independence. This document is dated July 4, 1776. It lists the reasons why Americans wanted to be free from Great Britain. Jefferson was a skilled writer who wrote most of the document.

Benjamin Franklin was also important because of the work he did to form our government. Franklin was a member of the Constitutional Convention. He and other leaders organized the government of the new nation. Franklin asked Congress to end slavery in our new nation, but Congress refused. It took more than seventy years for another American hero named Abraham Lincoln to bring an end to slavery in the United States.

On January 1, 1863, President Abraham Lincoln issued the Emancipation Proclamation. This was an executive order that freed our country's enslaved people. Lincoln spoke out against slavery and worked to end it.

Franklin and Jefferson working on the Declaration of Independence

PRIMARY SOURCE

In Their Words... Abraham Lincoln

"I do order and declare that all persons held as slaves within said designated States, and parts of States, are, and henceforward shall be free; and that the executive government of the United States, including the military and naval authorities thereof, will recognize and maintain the freedom of said persons."

—from the Emancipation Proclamation

Abraham Lincoln

Harriet Tubman and Frederick Douglass also worked to end slavery. Both were born into slavery. They were able to escape and then worked to free others. Tubman risked her life leading enslaved people to freedom. The routes she followed and the houses where people could hide were known as the Underground Railroad. Tubman helped many people to freedom.

Frederick Douglass taught himself to read and write. He started a newspaper to speak out against slavery. He gave speeches to tell how he suffered in slavery. Even after slavery became illegal, African Americans were not given the same rights as other people. Douglass continued to work for equality for all people.

✓ Stop and Check

Talk How were Tubman and Douglass similar?

Find Details As you read, add new information to the graphic organizer on page 231 in your Inquiry Journal.

RESEARCH COMPANION, pp. 242–243

What Is a Hero?

1 Inspect Have students read pp. 242–243 and tell what the text was about.

2 Find Evidence Use the questions below to check comprehension.

Compare How were Jefferson and Franklin similar? (Both helped create our country, and both helped write the Declaration of Independence.) **DOK 3**

Infer Based on what you read, what do you think the term *executive order* means? (a written command given by a president) **DOK 2**

Differentiate Describe the different plans Tubman and Douglass used to end slavery. (Answers will vary, but students should recognize that Tubman took direct action to free enslaved people while Douglass wrote and spoke to encourage change.) **DOK 3**

3 Make Connections

Compare and Contrast How were Abraham Lincoln and Frederick Douglass similar? How were they different? (Both helped gain the freedom of enslaved African Americans. Douglass was an African American who was a former enslaved person, while Lincoln was white and a U.S. president.) **DOK 3**

✓ Stop and Check

Talk Have students think about how Tubman and Douglass took similar actions in their cause. (Both were former enslaved people who worked to free others.)

EL Spotlight on Vocabulary

Content Vocabulary

emancipation: setting someone free

proclamation: official announcement

henceforward: from now on

 Digital Tools

Blended Learning
Students investigate curated resources and find evidence to answer the lesson question.

Interactive IMPACT
Students choose from print or digital **Inquiry Tools** to take notes.

As you have read, African Americans were not treated equally even after slavery ended. It took another one hundred years and the work of heroes, such as Dr. Martin Luther King, Jr., to bring equality to African Americans. Dr. King was an African American minister. He spoke out against segregation. This is the separation of people by the color of their skin. Dr. King asked government leaders to end this separation. He led peaceful protest marches. He refused to use violence to meet his goals. Dr. King was killed in 1968 while working for civil rights. The country celebrates his birthday each January.

Many other American heroes risked their lives to bring equality to people. Before 1920, women in the United States were not allowed to vote. Elizabeth Cady Stanton and Susan B. Anthony worked to change that. They worked to bring equal rights to all women.

Dennis Banks is another American hero. He helped found the American Indian Movement. The goal of this organization was to bring civil rights to Native Americans. Banks fought for fair and equal treatment for Native Americans.

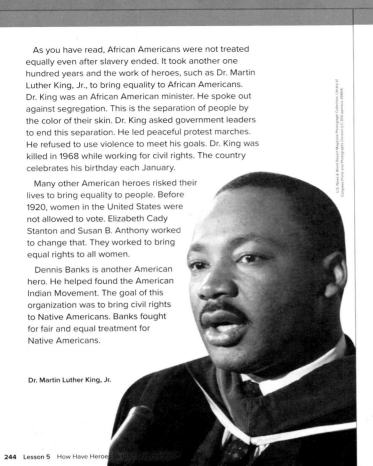
Dr. Martin Luther King, Jr.

Around the World

Humanitarian Heroes Around the World

Some heroes work to make the world a better and safer place to live. These people are called humanitarian heroes. Clara Barton was one of these heroes. She helped get medicine and supplies to soldiers who were sick and hurt during the Civil War. She earned the nickname "angel of the battlefield." When a war started in Europe, Barton helped provide supplies for people there. Barton also convinced people in the government to sign the Geneva Conventions. This is an agreement on how to treat sick and wounded soldiers. In 1881, she started the organization that is now known as the American Red Cross.

The American Red Cross and other national groups are now part of an international group. It is called the International Red Cross and Red Crescent Movement. This group was the idea of Henri Dunant. He was a humanitarian hero from Switzerland. The International Red Cross and Red Crescent Movement helps people around the world during war and natural disasters. The organization brings food and medical supplies, sets up places for people to stay, and helps them find loved ones who are missing.

Clara Barton, a pioneer in nursing

A national Red Cross organization in action

✓ Stop and Check

Think Compare the heroes you have read about. How did the actions of these heroes make a difference?

RESEARCH COMPANION, pp. 244–245

What Is a Hero?/Around the World

1 Inspect Have students read pp. 244–245 and describe the way Dr. Martin Luther King, Jr., fought segregation.

2 Find Evidence Use the questions below to check comprehension.

Classify Which group did each of the following help achieve equality: Dennis Banks, Elizabeth Cady Stanton, Dr. Martin Luther King, Jr., Susan B. Anthony? (Banks: Native Americans; Stanton: women; King: African Americans; Anthony: women) **DOK 2**

3 Make Connections

Make an Argument Why does the caption say that Clara Barton was a pioneer in nursing? Do you agree? (Answers will vary, but students should note her role in the Geneva Conventions and the Red Cross.) **DOK 3**

Draw Conclusions Tell students that the Geneva Conventions are written treaties. Why was it important to humanitarians such as Clara Barton that the U.S. government sign the Geneva Conventions? (Humanitarians cared about sick, wounded, and injured people no matter which side they fought on. In the treaties, countries agreed on how to treat sick and wounded people, including enemy soldiers, during wars.) **DOK 3**

✓ Stop and Check

Think Compare humanitarian heroes to heroes for justice. How did the actions of these heroes make a difference? (Heroes for justice work to bring fairness and equality to all people. Humanitarian heroes make the world a better, safer place to live. King, Stanton, Anthony, and Banks all helped bring fair and equal treatment to people. Barton and Dunant brought medical assistance and aid to people around the world during war and natural disasters.)

Social Emotional Learning

Social Awareness

Build Empathy Explain that empathy is the ability to share or understand someone else's feelings. Humanitarian heroes have empathy for people who are sick, injured, or in need. Heroes for justice have empathy for people who are treated unfairly. Have students discuss how learning about heroes helps build empathy.

Eleanor Roosevelt

Eleanor Roosevelt was born in New York in 1884. In 1905, she married Franklin D. Roosevelt. Her husband began working in politics. She helped him with his work. Franklin Roosevelt became governor of New York in 1929. He was elected president in 1932.

Eleanor Roosevelt changed the role of First Lady. She often traveled around the country for President Roosevelt. This was because Franklin had a disease called polio. This made it hard for him to walk and to travel. When she returned from her trips, she told the president what she had seen. She also wrote a newspaper column and spoke at meetings. As First Lady, Mrs. Roosevelt worked for the rights of women, African Americans, and other groups.

Eleanor Roosevelt continued to work for Americans even after she was no longer the First Lady. She worked at the United Nations. There, she helped write the Universal Declaration of Human Rights.

Eleanor Roosevelt receiving a pin from the Red Cross

This document lists basic rights that all people should have. It says that all people have the right to life, liberty, and security. Many of the rights listed in this document are also found in the United States Bill of Rights. Eleanor Roosevelt spent her life helping others. The work she did helped to bring equality to many people.

PRIMARY SOURCE

In Their Words... Eleanor Roosevelt

"It is not a treaty; it is not an international agreement. It is not and does not purport to be a statement of law or of legal obligation. It is a Declaration of basic principles of human rights and freedoms, to be stamped with the approval of the General Assembly by formal vote of its members, and to serve as a common standard of achievement for all peoples of all nations."

—a speech on the adoption of the Universal Declaration of Human Rights (1948)

Mrs. Roosevelt holding a large copy of the Universal Declaration of Human Rights in 1947

 Stop and Check COLLABORATE

Talk Why is the Universal Declaration of Human Rights important?

246 Lesson 5 How Have Heroes Helped Communities?

Chapter 5 Lesson 5 247

RESEARCH COMPANION, pp. 246–247

Biograpy: Eleanor Roosevelt

1 Inspect Have students read pp. 246–247 and tell why Eleanor Roosevelt traveled around the country.

2 Find Evidence Use the questions below to check comprehension.

Infer Based on Eleanor Roosevelt's activities as First Lady, how do you think the role of previous First Ladies was different? (Answers will vary, but students should understand that previous First Ladies would not have been as politically active and would have played a less public role.) **DOK 2**

Cite Evidence What does Eleanor Roosevelt say is the purpose of the Universal Declaration of Human Rights? (It lists standards of human rights and freedoms that all countries should achieve.) **DOK 2**

3 Make Connections

Draw Conclusions Would you describe Eleanor Roosevelt as a good citizen? Why or why not? (Answers will vary, but students may likely say yes, citing her work as First Lady and as a citizen fighting for people's equality and rights.) **DOK 3**

 Stop and Check COLLABORATE

Talk Have students discuss what basic human rights they think are important as they think about the Universal Declaration of Human Rights. (Answers will vary, but students should understand that it describes rights that all people throughout the world should have.)

 Spotlight on Language

Understanding Language

Read aloud the sentence beginning *This was because*. Explain that *this* is a pronoun that refers to something already stated, such as *She often traveled*. Point out *This* in the next sentence. Guide students to see that it refers to *Franklin had a disease*.

▶ Digital Tools

Blended Learning

Students investigate curated resources and find evidence to answer the lesson question.

Interactive IMPACT

Students **Research** and find evidence using digital format texts.

Heroes Make Changes in Their Communities

Heroes are found everywhere. Some heroes fought for equality in education. Before the 1950s, African American students and white students in many states were not allowed to go to school together. They were segregated, or legally separated.

Linda Brown lived in Topeka, Kansas. She had to attend school a mile from her home, even though there was one much closer. The school near her home was for white children only. She was not allowed to go there. She had to attend a school for African American students. In 1954, the United States Supreme Court heard her case. The case was called *Brown* v. *Board of Education*.

Linda Brown answering questions from the press in 1984

Did You Know?

Before *Brown* v. *Board of Education*, Sylvia Mendez's family fought against school segregation in California. In 1943, students of Mexican descent were not allowed to go to school with white students. Her case, *Mendez* v. *Westminster* ended segregation in California schools. The case was argued by Thurgood Marshall, the same lawyer who argued Linda Brown's case in *Brown* v. *Board of Education*.

Sylvia Mendez became a civil rights activist as an adult.

In *Brown* v. *Board of Education*, the Supreme Court ruled that in education, separate can never be equal. It ended the legal segregation of schools. Linda Brown's court case changed segregation laws. As an adult, Linda Brown continued to speak out against segregation.

Not all heroes become famous. Heroes are people who take action when they see a problem in their communities. They may clean trash from the side of a road or the local park. Some heroes visit the elderly and help them with chores. Other heroes plant new seeds on hillsides after a large fire. All of these people do what they can to make their communities better places to live. Sometimes only a few people know what they have done, but they are still heroes.

Helping someone who needs assistance

✓ Stop and Check

Think What can you do to be a local hero?

What Do You Think? What are ways heroes have helped communities? Who do you think is a hero in your community?

RESEARCH COMPANION, pp. 248–249

Everyday Heroes

1 Inspect Have students read pp. 248–249 and tell what Linda Brown was fighting for.

2 Find Evidence Use the questions below to check comprehension.

Make Observations What do you think students gain by going to school with others of different races and backgrounds? (Answers will vary, but students should include learning about what people have in common.) **DOK 2**

Develop a Logical Argument Imagine you were a lawyer fighting to end segregated schools in 1954. What would you say in favor of ending segregation? (Answers will vary, but students should understand that the Constitution says everyone should be treated equally under the law.) **DOK 3**

3 Make Connections

Hypothesize The Supreme Court ruled that in education, separate can never be equal. What do you think was not equal in the segregated schools? Give specific reasons for your answer. (Answers will vary, but students should give reasons to support their answers.) **DOK 3**

✓ Stop and Check

Think Have students discuss the question with a partner. (Answers will vary, but students should mention things that would improve the community or the lives of the people who live in their community.)

What Do You Think? Who do you think is a hero in your community? (Answers will vary, but students should give reasons to support their choices.)

✓ Check for Success

Explain Can students identify real heroes and explain the problems they solved and the effects their actions had on local communities?

Differentiate

If Not, Guide students to identify the problems, solutions, and heroes they noted in their Inquiry Journals to help them summarize lesson goals.

LESSON 5 REPORT

LESSON QUESTION

How Have Heroes Helped Communities?

INQUIRY JOURNAL, pp. 232–233

Think About It

Remind students to review their research and think about how heroes of the past and of today have made our communities, our country, and the world better places to live. Encourage students to review the causes and effects they have listed in their graphic organizers. Direct students back to pp. 240–249 of their Research Companion if they need more information.

Write About It

Cause and Effect Remind students to include the following elements in their responses.

- Describe the issue in detail.
- Discuss the people who worked to solve the issue and the actions they took.
- State the effects of their actions and cite evidence that supports these effects.
- Use chapter vocabulary as appropriate.

Discipline(s)	4	3	2	1
Civics	Strong understanding of how some heroes helped their communities and the effect of their actions	Adequate understanding of how some heroes helped their communities and the effect of their actions	Uneven understanding of how some heroes helped their communities and the effects of their actions	No understanding of how some heroes helped their communities and the effects of their actions

Talk About It

Defend Your Claim Explain that students should talk with a partner about their issue and its effects. Encourage partners to compare the issues they wrote about. Have them take turns talking about their issues and the resulting effects.

Assessment Students can check their understanding with feedback from the **Lesson Test** available online.

Connect to the Essential Question

Pull It Together Before students respond, ask them to think about the heroes they learned about, the ways those heroes helped their communities, and the ways in which everyone can be a hero.

Inquiry Project Update Remind students to turn to Inquiry Journal p. 191 for project information. If necessary, review the Project Checklist with students. At this point in the chapter, students should have completed the first four steps in the checklist and be writing a constitution.

Think About It

Examine

Review your research. What are some problems in the past that people have tried to solve?

Write About It

Cause and Effect

Choose one of the issues in the past that caused people to take action. What was the issue? How did people work to solve the issue? What were the effects of their actions?

Answers will vary, but students should show a clear understanding of the issue they chose and have a grasp of causes and effects.

Talk About It COLLABORATE

Defend Your Claim

Share your paragraph with a partner. Discuss how the person or people you wrote about helped make the world a better place.

🏛 Connect to the EQ

Civics

Pull It Together

In what ways can people work together to solve problems in a community?

Students' answers will vary but may include working together to respond to a disaster or writing to make people see the problem and to bring change to laws.

EQ Inquiry Project Notes

INQUIRY JOURNAL, pp. 232–233

EL English Learners SCAFFOLD

Use the following scaffolds to support student writing.

Entering and Emerging

Explain that an issue is something important that people talk about and that sometimes an issue, such as segregation, is a problem. Work with students to organize their ideas for their paragraph by completing these sentence frames:

- _____ was an issue.
- _____ worked to solve this issue.
- The things he/she/they did were _____.
- The effect of this work was _____.

Developing and Expanding

Guide partners to write an outline to organize their paragraph. Direct them to start with a sentence that names the problem or issue. Then have them name the person or group who took action and describe the steps taken to solve the problem. Tell them that the last sentence should describe the effects of the action.

Bridging and Reaching

Have students write a brief response to each question in Write About It to create an outline for their writing. Remind them to include the name of the person or group who worked to solve the issue. Tell students to exchange outlines with a partner and give each other feedback for revision.

✔ Check for Success

Cause and Effect Are students able to write a paragraph identifying a past issue that caused people to take action, how people solved the issue, and the effects of their actions?

Differentiate

If Not, Have partners present their information as a news segment, in a mock interview, or in another type of oral presentation.

LESSON 6 OVERVIEW

LESSON QUESTION

How Can You Help Build Strong Communities?

Connect to the Essential Question

Tell students that this lesson provides information about government in the Essential Question: **Why Do Governments and Citizens Need Each Other?** Explain that they will use investigative skills to explore what makes a strong community and how people can make a difference in their communities.

Discuss The IMPACT Today

Tell students that this lesson shows how they can directly make an impact in their communities. Encourage students to think about issues in their community. Provide ideas, such as cleaning up a local park.

Lesson Objectives

- **Explain** what features strengthen communities.
- **Discuss** characteristics of good citizens and leaders.
- **Draw conclusions** about ways to build strong communities.
- **Write** a paragraph identifying a problem in the community and proposing a solution.

Make Connections!

CONNECT TO ELA

Reading **Ask and answer** questions to demonstrate understanding of a text, referring explicitly to the text as the basis for the answers.

Use language that pertains to time, sequence, and cause/effect to describe the relationship between a series of historical events, scientific ideas or concepts, or steps in technical procedures in a text.

Research **Conduct** short research projects that build knowledge about a topic.

Recall information from experiences or gather information from print and digital sources; take brief notes on sources and sort evidence into provided categories.

Writing **Write** informative/explanatory texts to examine a topic and convey ideas and information clearly.

Speaking and Listening **Ask** questions to check understanding of information presented; stay on topic: have students link their comments to the remarks of others.

COMMUNITY CONNECTIONS

To enrich what students have learned about improving the community, guide them to explore community or nonprofit websites for programs such as community gardens, cleanup projects, arts festivals, or animal shelters. Have students report on their findings to the class.

Lesson-At-A-Glance

1 ENGAGE — INQUIRY JOURNAL

pp. 234–239

- **Talk About It:** Photographs of students picking up litter; primary source quote by Dorothy Height
- **Analyze the Source:** Building Community
- **Inquiry Tools:** Explore Drawing Conclusions

2 INVESTIGATE — RESEARCH COMPANION

pp. 250–257

- **What Makes a Community Strong?**
- **Learning to Become a Good Citizen**
- **What Makes a Good Leader?**
- **Ways to Make a Difference**
- **Biography: Gaylord Nelson**

3 REPORT — INQUIRY JOURNAL

pp. 240–241

- **Think About It**
- **Write About It:** Write an Informational Paragraph
- **Talk About It**
- **Connect to the Essential Question**

▶ Digital Tools

at my.mheducation.com

ePresentation

Teach the **Engage**, **Investigate**, and **Report** content to the whole class from **ePresentations** that launch directly from the lesson dashboard.

eBook

You can flip your instruction with the **IMPACT eBooks** found on your lesson dashboard.

Interactive IMPACT

Blend in digital content **when you want it** and **where you want it**.

Blended Learning features in the Teacher's Edition highlight ways to connect in-class work with online experiences to enhance learning.

Investigate current events with **IMPACT News**.

Explore domain-based vocabulary with **Explore Words** and **Word Play** vocabulary activities.

ASSESSMENT

- **Online Lesson Test**
- **Printable Lesson Test**

For more details, see pages T378–T379.

pp. 54–65

Go Further with IMPACT Explorer Magazine!

The **IMPACT Explorer Magazine** supports students' exploration of the Essential Question and provides additional resources for the EQ Inquiry Project.

LESSON 6 LANGUAGE LEARNERS

How Can You Help Build Strong Communities?

Language Objectives

- Use newly acquired content and academic vocabulary to talk and write about building strong communities.
- Write a paragraph to describe a problem in your community and how to solve it.
- In formal writing, use compound sentences with the coordinating conjunctions *and* and *but*.

 Spanish Cognates

To support Spanish speakers, point out the cognates.

recycle = reciclar

honest = honesto

preserve = preservar

conserve = conservar

difference = diferencia

Introduce the Lesson

Set Purpose Explain to students that in this lesson, they will read informational texts to learn about how they can be good citizens and help make communities better.

Access Prior Knowledge Read the Lesson Question and find out what students already know about how citizens can build strong communities. Ask: *What makes a community strong?* Point out one of the most important aspects of a strong community is citizen participation. Ask: *How can citizens take part in their community to make it stronger?*

Spark Curiosity Point to the image of Gaylord Nelson on p. 255 of the Research Companion. Tell students that for that first Earth Day in 1970, Senator Nelson insisted that the activities be organized by individual citizens and local groups in their own communities, not by the federal government. The response was far beyond Senator Nelson's wildest expectations. Twenty million Americans from 10,000 elementary and high schools, 2,000 colleges, and more than 1,000 communities across the nation participated in the festivities. Today, more than a billion people worldwide celebrate Earth Day.

Build Meaning & Support Language

Inquiry Journal

Analyze the Source (pages 236–237) Tell students that in this lesson they will read informational texts that give facts, examples, and explanations about a topic. The texts include headings and photographs with captions. Point to the heading on p. 236 and the photo and caption on p. 237. As you read "Building Community," explain any words students don't know. After you read the second paragraph on p. 236, reread the sentence *A community is made up of different kinds of people.* Explain that *made up* means "different things combined." Rephrase the sentence as: *Different kinds of people combine to form a community.* Support students' understanding of the photograph on p. 237. Ask: *What does the photo show?*

Inquiry Tools (pages 238–239) Tell students that they will **Explore Drawing Conclusions** as they read the selections in the Research Companion. Remind them that a conclusion is a decision you make about a topic using what you already know and the information you learn from what you read. Explain that they can draw conclusions from information not only in texts, but also in charts, maps, and images and their captions. Tell them that the graphic organizer will help them organize the information they read. Check that they understand the meanings of the column headings: *Text Clues and What I Already Know* and *Conclusions*. Then model how to find text clues and add them to the graphic organizer. Say: *The fourth paragraph on page 236 names many ways to build a strong community. I will list these clues in the first box in the graphic organizer.* Work with students to complete the list. (following rules and laws, working together, solving problems, volunteering, getting along with neighbors)

Research Companion

What Makes a Community Strong? (pages 250–251) After you read p. 250, explain any unfamiliar words. Be sure students understand that a *leader* is a person who guides a group of people, such as a community. Explain that the *citizens* are members of the community who work with their leaders to help make their community better. Ask: *How do leaders and citizens in a community work together?*

Learning to Become a Good Citizen (pages 252–253) Point out the word *compromise* on p. 252. Explain that a compromise is an agreement between people or groups, in which each person or group gets part of what they wanted. Each person gives up a little to the other person until they reach an agreement. Ask: *If your group has three project ideas, but you can only do one, how do you reach a compromise?*

What Makes a Good Leader? (pages 254–255) After you read p. 254, take a closer look at this sentence in the fifth paragraph: *They ask people in the community to help because they know a strong team is important.* Remind students that the word *because* comes before a cause, or reason, for doing something. Ask: *Why do they ask people in the community to help?*

Ways to Make a Difference (pages 256–257) After you read p. 256, explain any words that students don't know. Walk through this sentence in the third paragraph: *If you like to talk, you can ask to speak at a town meeting.* Explain that the first part of the sentence beginning with *if* tells a condition, *if you like to talk.* If the first part is true, the second part of the sentence tells what you can do, such as *ask to talk at a town meeting.*

Inquiry Journal

Report Your Findings (pages 240–241) Explain that problems often make people decide to take action in order to find a solution. Review solutions to problems such as reducing waste by recycling, cleaning up trash in the community, or teaching others how to protect the environment. Encourage students to use the new vocabulary words they have learned. Check their work for spelling and punctuation errors.

Language Forms & Conventions

Coordinating Conjunctions Explain to students that a compound sentence contains two separate sentences, or independent clauses, that are joined by a coordinating conjunction. The seven coordinating conjunctions are *and, but, for, nor, or, so,* and *yet.* Display the chart. Point out the comma before *and* or *but.* Ask: *How are the sentences similar or different?* (*and* joins similar ideas; *but* joins two different ideas)

First Clause of a Compound Sentence	Second Clause of a Compound Sentence
Your classroom is your community,	**and** you are one of its citizens.
Your group has three ideas for a project,	**but** the group can create only one project.

 Have students work in pairs to find two other sentences that have the coordinating conjunction *and* or *but* in them. (one on p. 253 in the second paragraph and one on p. 254 in the first paragraph) Call on volunteers to say them aloud and add them to the chart. As a challenge, have students tell whether the conjunction shows similar or different ideas.

 Cross-Cultural Connection

Have students discuss how communities in other countries may have problems similar to or different from those of communities in the United States.

 Leveled Support

Entering & Emerging
Provide sentence frames:
_____ is a problem because _____.
We can solve the problem by _____.

Developing & Expanding
Encourage students to use words and phrases such as *because, due to,* and *as a result* to signal the reasons why the problem must be solved.

Bridging & Reaching
Have students exchange papers with a partner. Ask partners to make suggestions about where to add more details to their reasons for solving the problem.

 **Language Transfer**

In Hmong, verbs can be used consecutively without conjunctions or punctuation. For example, a student may say: *I took a book went studied at the library.*

LESSON 6 ENGAGE

 LESSON QUESTION

How Can You Help Build Strong Communities?

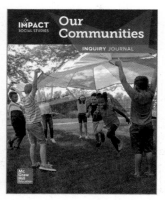

INQUIRY JOURNAL, pp. 234–235

Bellringer

Write *hero* on the board. Prompt students to retrieve information from the previous lesson. Ask: *What does it mean to be a hero?* (Answers will vary, but students should understand that a hero is someone who has done great things, behaved with great honor, or solved difficult problems.) Explain to students that they will be learning how they can be heroes by helping to make their communities stronger.

Lesson Outcomes

Discuss the lesson question and lesson outcomes with students.

- Make sure students understand what makes a community. Guide them to understand that a community can be a place or a group of people. Say: _____ *is the name of our community. In this classroom, we are a community of learners.*

- Tell students that people build a strong community by working together to meet the needs of everyone living there and by trying to treat everyone fairly. Say: *Think of our classroom as a small community. How do we work together to make it a good place to learn? What do we do to make things fair and to meet everyone's needs?*

Talk About It

Analyze the Primary Source Explain that when we read a quote, we try to understand the meaning of what the person is saying. Read aloud the quote by Dorothy Height. Point out that a *beneficiary* is a person who is helped by something. Ask: *What does the word* serve *mean?* (provide service or help) Then have students study the photograph. Provide sentence frames to help students form sentences as they talk about the quote and the photograph.

- Based on the quote, "community service" is _____. (serving or helping the community)

- The people in the photo help their community by _____. (keeping public places clean)

 ## Collaborative Conversations

Add New Ideas As students engage in partner, small group, and whole-class discussions, encourage them to

- stay on the topic of how strong communities can be built.
- connect their own ideas to things their classmates have said.
- look for ways to connect their own experiences or prior knowledge to the conversation.

THE IMPACT TODAY

How Can You Help Build Strong Communities?

Lesson Outcomes

What Am I Learning?
In this lesson, you will use your investigative skills to explore how people strengthen their communities.

Why Am I Learning It?
Reading and talking about how people work together to take care of and improve their communities will help you understand how you can make a difference in your community.

How Will I Know That I Learned It?
You will be able to describe the characteristics of good leaders. You will also be able to write a paragraph proposing ways that you can help strengthen your community.

Talk About It
COLLABORATE

Read the quote from Dorothy Height. What is she suggesting that young people should do today? Why do you think that is?

Look closely at the photos. What are the young people doing? How do you think this activity helps the community?

Litter and other trash not only make a place look bad but also contribute to pollution and harm local plant and animal life. Pollution dirties the air, water, and land around us.

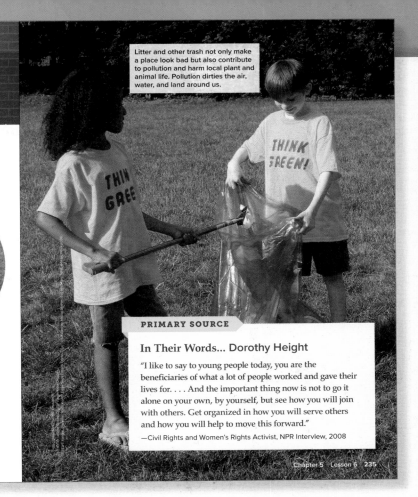

PRIMARY SOURCE

In Their Words... Dorothy Height

"I like to say to young people today, you are the beneficiaries of what a lot of people worked and gave their lives for. . . . And the important thing now is not to go it alone on your own, by yourself, but see how you will join with others. Get organized in how you will serve others and how you will help to move this forward."

—Civil Rights and Women's Rights Activist, NPR Interview, 2008

INQUIRY JOURNAL, pp. 234–235

EL English Learners SCAFFOLD

Use the following scaffolds to support student understanding of lesson outcomes.

Entering and Emerging
List these words on the board: *students, plastic bag, park, trash, clean.* Make sure students understand their meanings by reading it aloud and having them point to the item in the photograph. Then have students complete the following sentence frames: The two _____ are working together in a _____. (students; park) They pick up _____ and put it into a _____. (trash; plastic bag) They help keep their community _____. (clean)

Developing and Expanding
Have small groups brainstorm and write a list of words that describe the photo on p. 235. Direct group members to work together and use their word list to write two sentences about how the people in the photo are building a strong community. Then have students discuss whether this is a good way to make a difference and give reasons for their opinions.

Bridging and Reaching
Have student partners take turns sharing their opinions about how the people in the photo on p. 235 are building a strong community. Remind them to support their opinions with reasons. Then have each student write a sentence stating his or her opinion and the reasons.

Social Emotional Learning

Relationship Skills

Value Ideas of Others Sharing ideas can enhance learning and stimulate new ones. Have each student write down one idea for a volunteer activity. Then, have partners take turns sharing their ideas and discussing why each would make the community a better place.

Digital Tools

Blended Learning
Students engage with the lesson question and discussion prompts.

Interactive IMPACT

Discuss the **Lesson Question** and **Talk About It** with the class.

Building Community

1 Inspect

Read the text and look at the photo.

- **Circle** words you do not know.
- **Underline** words and phrases that help you understand rights and responsibilities.
- **Summarize** in a sentence what the text is about.

My Notes

_____

_____

_____

_____

_____

_____

_____

_____

_____

_____

_____

We are all part of a community. When someone asks where we live, we might say the name of our town or state. We might also say we live in the United States. All three answers are correct.

A community can also be a neighborhood, a school, or even a classroom. A community is made up of different kinds of people. But the people in a community all share certain beliefs, rights, and responsibilities. Rights are things people can claim. Responsibilities are things people are expected to do.

Think about the different communities to which you belong. What kinds of beliefs, rights, and responsibilities do you share with other people in those communities? American citizens have many rights, like such as the freedom to share ideas. In exchange, they also have important responsibilities, such as obeying laws.

In a strong community, people try to do what is best for everybody. They follow rules and laws to help keep people safe. They work together to solve problems to improve life for everyone. Many people also volunteer to help make their community a better place for all who live there. To **volunteer** means to do a job or provide a service without pay.

What are some ways you can help make your community better?

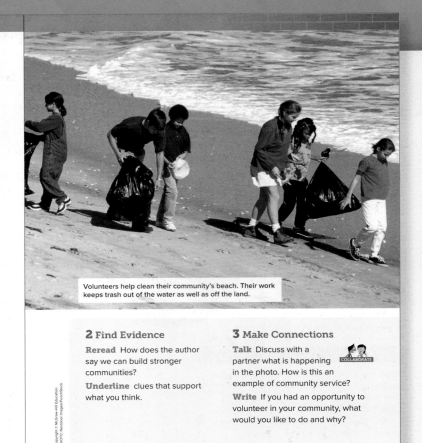

Volunteers help clean their community's beach. Their work keeps trash out of the water as well as off the land.

2 Find Evidence

Reread How does the author say we can build stronger communities?

Underline clues that support what you think.

3 Make Connections

Talk Discuss with a partner what is happening in the photo. How is this an example of community service?

Write If you had an opportunity to volunteer in your community, what would you like to do and why?

INQUIRY JOURNAL, pp. 236–237

Analyze the Source

1 Inspect

Read Have students read the text and examine the photo. Remind them to circle words in the text with which they are unfamiliar.

- What are some words and phrases that help you understand what a community is? ("where we live," "name of our town or state," "made up of different kinds of people," and "all share certain beliefs, rights, and responsibilities")

2 Find Evidence

Reread Have students reread the text.

Underline Discuss that the selection's main idea is ways to build stronger communities. Ask partners to take turns describing how people can build stronger communities, citing evidence from the text.

3 Make Connections

Talk Have partners discuss what is happening in the photo and why it is an example of community service. (Cleaning the beach makes it a safe place for people to use.) Then have students work in pairs to list other ways that people can volunteer to serve their communities. Call on pairs to share their ideas with the class.

Write Instruct individual students to choose one of the ideas they listed as their topic.

Spotlight on Vocabulary

neighborhood a small section of a city or town

service work that a person or company does for others that is not making a product

▶ Digital Tools

Blended Learning

Students read informational texts and analyze primary sources.

Interactive IMPACT

Have students practice and apply the strategy of close reading as they analyze text.

Explore Drawing Conclusions

A **conclusion** is a decision you make about a topic. You use what you already know and information from what you read or observe to draw your conclusion. We draw conclusions when we read. We also draw conclusions from information we see in maps, charts, graphs, and photos.

1. **Read the title of the selection and captions for images.**
   This will help you know what the topic is.

2. **Read the text all the way through and look closely at images.**
   This will help you understand important ideas about the topic.

3. **Think about what you read or saw.**
   Ask: What information do the text and images give about the topic? What do I already know about the topic?

4. **Draw a conclusion.**
   Use information from the text as well as what you already know to draw a conclusion about the topic.

 Based on the text, work with your class to draw a conclusion about what makes a strong community. Then work with your class to complete the chart below.

What Makes a Strong Community

Text Clues and What I Already Know	Conclusions
following rules and laws, solving problems, volunteering, getting along with neighbors, working together	A strong community has people who follow laws and are willing to work together to solve problems and help others.

238 Lesson 6 How Can You Help Build Strong Communities?

Investigate!

 Read pages 250–257 in your Research Companion. Use your investigative skills to look for text evidence that tells you how citizens can build strong communities. This chart will help you organize your notes.

Answers will vary. Sample answers are shown.

Text Clues and What I Already Know	Conclusions
Becoming a good citizen: My classroom is a community, and I'm expected to follow the rules. At school, I learn to be honest, trustworthy, and loyal.	How to build a strong community: To build a strong community, I can learn about being a good citizen at school. I can know how good leaders should act and encourage leaders to be good. I can also find out or point out problems in my community and suggest ways to solve that problem. I can choose a problem to help with and decide how to work on the problem with others in my community.
Characteristics of good leaders: Characteristics include being a hard worker, being honest and trustworthy, solving problems, having good ideas, communicating effectively, asking for help, and being willing to work with everyone.	
Problems in my community: Students should list problems related to leaders, schools, jobs, neighborhood safety, respect for people, business, air and water quality, trash, hunger and poverty, and other community concerns.	
Ways to make a difference in my community: I can write a letter or an e-mail, call leaders, make a flyer, speak at a town meeting, organize people for a cause, join a group helping my community, pick up trash, follow rules and laws, and be kind to others.	

Chapter 5 Lesson 6 239

INQUIRY JOURNAL, pp. 238–239

Inquiry Tools

Explore Drawing Conclusions

Read Review with students the meaning of the word *conclusion*. Discuss the step-by-step instructions for drawing conclusions found on p. 238 of the Inquiry Journal. Emphasize that students can use both written and visual information in a text combined with what they already know in order to draw a conclusion.

Guide Practice Have students review the text on pp. 236–237. Then work with them to complete the graphic organizer. Explain that they will use a similar graphic organizer to organize their independent research.

Check Understanding Confirm understanding of the inquiry skill, Explore Drawing Conclusions. If students cannot draw an appropriate conclusion from the information, review the steps on p. 238 of the Inquiry Journal.

Investigate!

Have students read pp. 250–257 in the Research Companion. Tell them the information will help them answer the lesson question *How Can You Help Build Strong Communities?*

Take Notes Tell students that they will use the graphic organizer on p. 239 of the Inquiry Journal to take notes as they read. Explain that taking notes will help them understand and remember the information they learn. Remind students that they should use their own words when they take notes.

 Spotlight on Language

Draw a Conclusion

Point out that *draw a conclusion* is an idiom in which the meaning of *draw* is different from its usual meaning, "make a picture." *Draw a conclusion* means "make a decision using available information." *To conclude* means "to decide something based on information you have." A *conclusion* is the decision that is made.

LESSON 6 INVESTIGATE

How Can You Help Build Strong Communities?

RESEARCH COMPANION, pp. 250–251

Background Information

A number of organizations work throughout the United States and around the world to strengthen communities.

- The National Science Foundation (NSF) encourages Native Americans to connect to their heritage and work to preserve their lands, forming stronger community bonds. The NSF Tribal Colleges and Universities Program promotes STEM (science, technology, engineering and math) education.

- The National Urban League began during the 1900s as many African Americans moved North to escape economic and political domination in the South. However, northern cities were also hard places to live. The National Urban League tried to make this transition easier. Today, the organization works toward the goal of making certain that every individual receives a good education, is paid a living wage, and has access to affordable health care.

- Habitat for Humanity began as a local community effort near Americus, Georgia. During its early years, this organization aimed to bring together people who needed adequate shelter with volunteers to work together building affordable homes. Decades later, Habitat works across the United States as well as in 70 other countries, and has helped provide homes for millions of people.

What Makes a Community Strong?

1 Inspect Have students read pp. 250–251 and define *community*.

2 Find Evidence Use the questions below to check comprehension.

Use Context Clues What do you think the word *opinions* means? (views, beliefs) **DOK 2**

Infer Why is it important that citizens share their opinions with community leaders? (Leaders need to know what citizens are thinking and what their needs are in order to make decisions that will help them.) **DOK 3**

Draw Conclusions How do you think good jobs can make a community strong? (People will want to live in the community because they know they will be able to support their families and have a good life.) **DOK 3**

3 Make Connections

Assess Study the photograph on p. 251. How are the students strengthening their community? (They are working to protect the environment and making their community a cleaner place by not being wasteful. They also are working together toward a common goal.) **DOK 3**

Point of View Based on what you have read, what do you think would happen if everyone in a community was not treated equally? (Answers will vary, but students should describe specific effects they think would result from unfair treatment of people in a community.) **DOK 3**

Lesson 6

How Can You Help Build Strong Communities?

What Makes a Community Strong?

A community is a group of people who live in the same area. Families shop at the same stores and go to the same parks. The children in a community often go to the same schools. To make a community strong, people need to work together. Leaders serve the community. They listen to citizens, or members of the community, and work to improve life for everyone. The people in the community trust them to make good decisions.

Citizens help their leaders by giving their opinions and volunteering their time. People in communities work with leaders to provide good schools for their children. They work together to build businesses and provide jobs for people. They also work with their leaders and with one another to take care of the environment. Community members respect one another and make sure everyone is treated fairly. Everyone in the community benefits from having a safe, kind, and fun place to live.

To *recycle* means to make trash ready to use again.

Recycling is good for a community's environment because it reduces waste.

RESEARCH COMPANION, pp. 250–251

English Learners   SCAFFOLD

Use the following scaffolds to support student understanding of the lesson content.

Entering and Emerging

Help students understand how leaders and citizens work together in a community. Guide them to complete these sentence frames. If time permits, encourage them to illustrate each sentence.

- I am a community leader. I _____ (listen to citizens; work with people) to help our community.
- I am a citizen. I _____ (give my opinions; volunteer) to help our community.

Developing and Expanding

Have partners role play a conversation between a leader and a citizen of a community. Ask them to take turns saying what they each will do to help the community. Direct them to refer to the text to get ideas. To extend the activity, have each pair work together to write one sentence that each student said.

Bridging and Reaching

Have partners use a t-chart with the headings *Leaders* and *Citizens* to list ways in which each group helps a community. Encourage students to refer to the text for information. Have each partner use the information from a different side of the t-chart and write a short paragraph explaining how leaders or citizens help the community.

▶ Digital Tools

Blended Learning

Guide students as they investigate the lesson content.

eBook

Students investigate using their **Research Companion** and **IMPACT Explorer Magazine eBooks** to find evidence.

Learning to Become a Good Citizen

Students working on a group project

Learning how to become a good citizen starts at school. Your classroom is your community, and you are one of its citizens. As its citizen, you are expected to follow the rules. Before you speak, you must raise your hand. You form a line before going to recess. You are expected to listen when your teacher speaks. Your teacher may ask you to work with other classmates in a group. You get to share ideas and listen to your classmates' ideas when you work in a group. You learn to cooperate by working together.

You also learn how to **compromise** when your group has different opinions. A compromise is an agreement that people make when they have different ideas. Each person or group gives up something they wanted to make an agreement. For example, imagine your group has three ideas for a project. Finding a compromise could include combining some of the ideas into one project.

Pledging allegiance

Your classroom also teaches you to care about our country. You show that you care when you say the Pledge of Allegiance. When you say the Pledge of Allegiance, you promise to support and defend the values of the United States.

You may be too young to vote for issues in your community, but you can vote for class leaders. Before you vote, you should think about the qualities you want in a leader. Do you want a leader who listens to other people's ideas, or do you want a leader who makes all of the decisions? You can use that information to make an informed choice.

 Stop and Check

Think What do you think is the most important characteristic of a good citizen in your classroom?

Find Details As you read, add new information to the graphic organizer on page 239 in your Inquiry Journal.

252 Lesson 6 How Can You Help Build Strong Communities?

Chapter 5 Lesson 6 253

RESEARCH COMPANION, pp. 252–253

Learning to Become a Good Citizen

1 Inspect Have students read pp. 252–253 and summarize what the text is about. Remind them to study the images and read the captions.

2 Find Evidence Use the questions below to check comprehension.

Draw Conclusions How do you think being a good citizen at school can help all students? (Following rules, respecting others, and working together helps make school a safe, kind, and pleasant place to learn.) **DOK 3**

Infer Why might people working together on a project want to compromise? What might happen if they don't compromise? (A compromise would enable them to cooperate and finish the project. Otherwise, they might stop working and not reach their goal.) **DOK 2**

3 Make Connections

Assess How does being a good citizen in the classroom prepare you for being an adult member of the community? (Classroom activities such as following rules, working together, and voting give students practice using the skills that they will need as adult citizens of their community.) **DOK 3**

 Stop and Check

Think Encourage students to consider how the characteristic they chose helps make the classroom a good place for learning. (Answers will vary, but students should provide reasons for their choice.)

EL Spotlight on Content

Scanning for Information

Have pairs scan each paragraph for key words and phrases that tell the main idea (follow rules, work in a group, compromise, care about country, vote). Have pairs discuss what they recall about each topic.

▶ Digital Tools

Blended Learning

Students investigate curated resources and find evidence to answer the lesson question.

Interactive IMPACT

Students choose from print or digital **Inquiry Tools** to take notes.

What Makes a Good Leader?

Good leaders who want their communities to grow work hard with everyone else. Good leaders are honest. They say what they mean, and they keep their promises. They encourage others to do the same.

Good leaders understand the needs of diverse, or different, people. They can help the community make sure it meets everyone's needs.

Good leaders think about what the community needs to be a good place to live. They work with citizens and other leaders to find solutions to problems.

Good leaders know how to communicate their ideas. They encourage people to work together to develop ideas that are good for the community. They promote fairness and kindness among people in the community.

Good leaders know they cannot do everything by themselves. They ask people in the community to help because they know a strong team is important.

How can you be a good leader in your community?

Leaders can be people who work in the government and protect the community, like firefighters and police officers.

254 Lesson 6 How Can You Help Build Strong Communities?

Biography

Gaylord Nelson

On April 22, 1970, the United States celebrated its first Earth Day. Gaylord Nelson, a United States senator from Wisconsin, founded Earth Day. He wanted to focus attention on the environment. Nelson hoped more people would work to preserve and conserve the nation's natural resources. To *preserve* means to set aside and protect. To *conserve* means to limit use and save for the future. Nelson served in the U.S. Senate for eighteen years. During that time, he supported many laws to protect the environment and plant and animal life.

Gaylord Nelson

Did You Know?

Earth Day takes place every year on April 22. On Earth Day, millions of people participate in activities to celebrate Earth. These include festivals, planting trees, and volunteering to clean up trash. How will you celebrate Earth Day this year?

✓ Stop and Check

Think How did Gaylord Nelson show that he was a good leader?

Write How do events like Earth Day encourage community service?

Chapter 5 Lesson 6 255

RESEARCH COMPANION, pp. 254–255

What Makes a Good Leader?

1 Inspect Have students read pp. 254–255 and name some examples of leaders.

2 Find Evidence Use the questions below to check comprehension.

Summarize What qualities do good leaders have? (Good leaders are honest, keep their promises, and understand what the people in their community need. They can talk about their ideas and encourage others to cooperate. They also know that they need to rely on others in order to make the community strong.) **DOK 2**

Predict What do you think might happen if a leader was not honest with a community's citizens? (Answers will vary, but students should understand that citizens would no longer believe the leader and would not support him or her, which could weaken the entire community.) **DOK 3**

3 Make Connections

Develop a Logical Argument Based on what you have read, which of the qualities of a good leader do you think is most important? Defend your choice. (Answers will vary, but students should provide specific reasons for their choices.) **DOK 3**

✓ Stop and Check

Think (He saw a problem and convinced people to work together to preserve and conserve natural resources.)

Write (They draw attention to important issues and inspire people to work together to solve problems.)

Social Emotional Learning

Relationship Skills

Teamwork Good leaders are team builders. They know how to bring people together to accomplish a task or goal. Ask students to discuss in groups how they would bring people together to celebrate Earth Day or accomplish a similar goal.

Phrasal Verbs Explain that some verbs have more than one word. They include a main verb and either a preposition or an adverb, and the meaning is different than what the main verb alone means.

find out learn something by trying to get the answer

pick up lift something from the ground or floor

Ways to Make a Difference

1 Inspect Have students read pp. 256–257 and describe the purpose of the text.

2 Find Evidence Use the questions below to check comprehension.

Infer Why does improving the community start with doing research? (Doing research allows you find out what things in the community need to be improved.) **DOK 2**

Summarize What should you include in a letter to the editor or a letter to a community or state leader? (You should include what the problem is, ideas for solving the problem, and any research you have done on the problem.) **DOK 2**

Compare and Contrast How is writing a letter to a community leader similar to attending a town meeting? How are the two experiences different? (Both writing a letter and attending a town meeting allow you to tell community leaders about problems in your community. However, you can speak with a leader directly at a town meeting. You also may ask questions to get answers to your concerns.) **DOK 3**

3 Make Connections

Evaluate Which way to make a difference mentioned in the text do you think would help your community the most? Why? (Answers will vary, but students should choose one of the ways to make a difference discussed in the text and explain why they believe that it would help the community the most.) **DOK 3**

✓ **Stop and Check** COLLABORATE

Talk Have students discuss the question with a partner. (Answers should include specific ways to make a difference in a community.)

What Is the IMPACT Today?

(Answers should include ways students can use their skills in the community.)

Ways to Make a Difference

How can you make a difference in your community? First, you should do research to find out about good things in your community and things that need to be better. Then you can think about ways to help make things better. There are many ways you can make a difference.

You can write a letter to the editor of your local newspaper to let more people know about a problem. You can also write a letter to a community or state leader. Your letter should clearly explain the problem. It should also give ideas for possible solutions. Include any research you have done when you send your letter.

If you like to talk, you can ask to speak at a town meeting. A town meeting is a time when members of a community come together to talk about issues that face the community. A town meeting is a good place to talk directly to the leaders of your community. It is also a good place to ask questions.

Citizens attend town meetings to ask questions, find out information, and share their ideas with local leaders.

Another way to make a difference is by organizing people. You can organize a rally to tell your community about a problem. A rally is a public gathering. You can talk with business owners about ways to improve the community. You can organize a group to pick up trash one day a week in the public areas of your neighborhood.

You can also find out about groups in your community that are already making a difference. Some groups build houses for people, run food pantries, and collect used clothing to give to people in need. Other groups collect toys for children in the hospital. Look for a group that is working to fix a problem you see. Ask them how you can help.

Young people can help organizations build homes for people in the community.

Stop and Check

Talk What are some ways to make a difference in a community?

What Is the IMPACT Today? What skills do you have? How can you use your skills to help your community make a change for the better?

RESEARCH COMPANION, pp. 256–257

English Learners SCAFFOLD

Use the following scaffolds to support student understanding of the lesson content.

Entering and Emerging

Write a list of lesson-specific vocabulary words and phrases on the board: *town meeting, community, leaders,* and *make a difference.* Help students choose the correct words to complete the following sentence frames: People in a _____ can find ways to _____ . (community; make a difference) They went to a _____ and talked to the _____ about a problem. (town meeting; leaders)

Developing and Expanding

Write a list of lesson-specific vocabulary words and phrases on the board: *town meeting, community, leaders,* and *make a difference.* Ask: *What are a group of people living in the same area called?* (a community) *Who are the elected people in the community?* (leaders) *Where can citizens talk about issues?* (at a town meeting) *Why do people work to solve problems in their community?* (to make a difference)

Bridging and Reaching

Write a list of lesson-specific vocabulary words and phrases on the board: *town meeting, community, leaders,* and *make a difference.* Tell students that they have volunteered to write an announcement for the community website about a public meeting. Direct students to use these words and others from the text to write a short paragraph to persuade people to attend the meeting.

✔ Check for Success

Synthesize Can students identify what makes a strong community and explain ways to build a strong community?

Differentiate

If Not, guide students in filling out the Text Clues and What I Already Know, and Conclusions columns in the graphic organizer on p. 239 of their Inquiry Journals for one aspect of strong communities.

LESSON 6 REPORT

 LESSON QUESTION

How Can You Help Build Strong Communities?

**INQUIRY JOURNAL,
pp. 240–241**

Think About It

Remind students to review the items they have listed in their graphic organizer. Students may want to ask adults, such as their parents and neighbors, for ideas about problems affecting their communities. Direct students to pp. 250–257 of their Research Companion if they need more information.

Write About It

Explain Remind students to include the following as they craft their responses.

- Begin by stating the problem clearly.
- Describe how you would work to solve the problem.
- Explain how you would get others to help you to achieve your solution.
- Use appropriate vocabulary from the chapter.

Discipline(s)	4	3	2	1
Civics	Strong understanding of a problem in the community and a proposal for a solution	Adequate understanding of a problem in the community and a proposal for a solution	Uneven understanding of a problem in the community and a weak proposal for a solution	No understanding of a problem in the community and no proposal for a solution

Talk About It

Discuss and Compare Remind students to share their proposed solutions and then to offer any different solutions to their partner. Encourage them to chart benefits and drawbacks for their solutions as they evaluate their choices.

Assessment Students can check their understanding with feedback from the **Lesson Test** available online.

Connect to the Essential Question

Pull It Together Before they respond, remind students to think about the different ways that people can help their communities. Tell them to consider how community service helps create a strong and safe place to live.

Inquiry Project Update Remind students to turn to Inquiry Journal p. 191 for project information. If necessary, review the Project Checklist with students. At this point in the chapter, students should focus on the last two items on the checklist.

Think About It

Identify

Review your research and the problems discussed in the lesson. Think about a problem that affects your community right now.

Write About It

Explain

Write a paragraph describing a problem that exists in your community today. How would you solve the problem?

Answers will vary, but students should
identify a problem and propose a solution.

Talk About It

Discuss and Compare

Share your paragraph with a partner. Compare your problems and solutions. Ask for a different solution to the problem you wrote about. Offer a different solution for your partner's problem. If time permits, discuss the benefits and drawbacks for each solution. Which solution might best address each problem, and why?

Connect to the EQ

Civics

Pull It Together

Remember that citizens have rights and responsibilities. Think about how these ideas relate to volunteering and community service. Why is community service an important part of being a citizen?

Answers will vary, but should show an
understanding that all citizens benefit
from community service.

Inquiry Project Notes

INQUIRY JOURNAL, pp. 240–241

English Learners SCAFFOLD

Use the following scaffolds to support student writing.

Entering and Emerging

Model making a plan for writing a paragraph. Remind students that a paragraph usually begins with a topic sentence that tells what the paragraph is about, followed by details about the topic. Provide the following sentence frames for students to help them write a topic sentence and details about the solution.

- A problem in our community is _____.
- One way to solve the problem is _____.

Developing and Expanding

Direct students to the photograph on p. 237 of the Inquiry Journal. Ask: *What is the problem? What are people doing to solve the problem?* Have partners brainstorm to think of a problem in their community and how they might solve it. Remind students to begin their paragraphs with a topic sentence and include details about their solution.

Bridging and Reaching

Have individual students choose a community problem and decide on one way to solve it. Remind students to begin their paragraphs with a topic sentence and include details about their solution. Then have them exchange paragraphs with another student to offer constructive feedback.

✔ Check for Success

Explain Can students write a paragraph describing a community problem and suggesting how they would solve it?

Differentiate

If Not, Guide students to recall a problem mentioned in the text and brainstorm possible ways to solve it.

TAKE ACTION
with INQUIRY JOURNAL

Why Do Governments and Citizens Need Each Other?

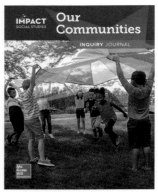

INQUIRY JOURNAL, pp. 242–243

Inquiry Project Wrap-Up

Remind students that they are to have created a classroom constitution that lists rules that everyone in the class should follow and provides consequences for breaking the rules.

Assessment Use the rubric on p. T379 to assess students' Inquiry Projects.

Complete Your Project

Have students work individually to review the Complete Your Project checklist. Remind them to mark each item on the list as they complete it. If they have missed any of the criteria, now is their opportunity to make corrections or additions.

Share Your Project

If time allows, you may want to have students present their projects to the class. Provide the following presentation tips for students.

- Prepare and rehearse.
- Use notes to help you stay on topic.
- Speak slowly and clearly. Make sure everyone can hear you.
- Make eye contact and speak directly to the audience.

Reflect on Your Project

Student reflections begin with thinking about the process for how they selected the rules for the classroom and appropriate consequences for breaking them. Students should focus on the results of the inquiry as well as the challenges and successes of the inquiry process. Students can apply those findings to future projects.

Chapter Connections can focus on anything that resonated with students about the study of how citizens work with the government. These connections may spark students to do further research on their own.

▶ Digital Tools

Blended Learning
Students use online checklists to prepare, complete, and reflect on their Inquiry Projects.

Chapter Assessments
Students can demonstrate content mastery with the feedback from the online **Chapter Test**.

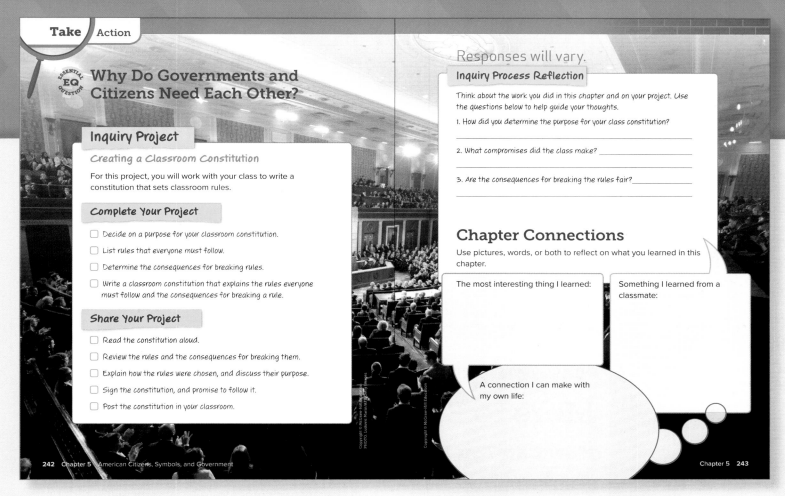

INQUIRY JOURNAL, pp. 242–243

The inquiry journal pages shown contain:

Take Action

Why Do Governments and Citizens Need Each Other?

Inquiry Project

Creating a Classroom Constitution

For this project, you will work with your class to write a constitution that sets classroom rules.

Complete Your Project

- ☐ Decide on a purpose for your classroom constitution.
- ☐ List rules that everyone must follow.
- ☐ Determine the consequences for breaking rules.
- ☐ Write a classroom constitution that explains the rules everyone must follow and the consequences for breaking a rule.

Share Your Project

- ☐ Read the constitution aloud.
- ☐ Review the rules and the consequences for breaking them.
- ☐ Explain how the rules were chosen, and discuss their purpose.
- ☐ Sign the constitution, and promise to follow it.
- ☐ Post the constitution in your classroom.

242 Chapter 5 American Citizens, Symbols, and Government

Responses will vary.

Inquiry Process Reflection

Think about the work you did in this chapter and on your project. Use the questions below to help guide your thoughts.

1. How did you determine the purpose for your class constitution?

2. What compromises did the class make?

3. Are the consequences for breaking the rules fair?

Chapter Connections

Use pictures, words, or both to reflect on what you learned in this chapter.

The most interesting thing I learned:

Something I learned from a classmate:

A connection I can make with my own life:

Chapter 5 243

 English Learners SCAFFOLD

Use the following scaffolds to support student presentation of their projects.

Entering and Emerging

Pair English learners with fluent English speakers. Partners should take turns sharing their rules. Students may want to use sentence frames to support their presentation:

- The first rule of our constitution is _____.
- I chose this rule because _____.
- If a student breaks this rule, then _____.

Developing and Expanding

Have partners read the project checklist to guide their presentation to each other. Encourage partners to alternate presenting each rule.

Bridging and Reaching

Have partners use the checklist to organize their presentation. Encourage partners to alternate presenting each rule. After they present, have partners ask each other at least one question about the presentation.

✓ **Check for Success**

Use Rubric Use your online rubric or the rubric on p. T379 to record student progress. Can students describe the purpose of their constitution and explain how they chose the rules and their consequences?

Differentiate

If Not, Have students design a poster that illustrates the rules and their consequences as described in the constitution. Ask students to use the pictures to explain why the constitution is necessary.

**RESEARCH COMPANION,
pp. 258–259**

Connections in Action

Think Lead a discussion with students about how the government and citizens work together in a community. Select one of the ways that citizens in your community work with the government, and model how to determine why citizens cooperate with the government in this way. Brainstorm the benefits of government and citizens working together.

Talk To help focus students' conversations, you may want to discuss the EQ with the entire class before students discuss their ideas with a partner. Remind students to think about evidence they can provide that will support their ideas.

Share Invite students to share their discussions with the class.

More to Explore

How Can You Make an IMPACT?

Mix and match the More to Explore activities to meet the needs of your classroom. Stretch students' thinking by offering alternative ways to demonstrate what they learned during the chapter.

These activities are flexible enough that you can assign one, two, or three activities to specific students or have students work in small groups. Remind students to use proper collaborative procedures when they work with partners.

Write a Letter to the Mayor

Ask the class to come up with ideas about how to make the community a better place to live. Write students' ideas on the board. Students may use one of these suggestions for their letters or come up with one of their own.

Teacher Tip! **Use this activity to help students practice supporting their ideas with logical reasoning.**

Citizenship in Action

Have students perform skits about they can be good citizens in assigned groups or groups of their choosing. Allow time for students to rehearse their skits before performing them. If possible, give groups the option to record their performances.

Teacher Tip! **This activity can be used to monitor students' relationship skills.**

Guess the Word

List the vocabulary words on the board. Then model the activity for students by saying the definition for one of the words and asking volunteers to guess the word you are defining.

Teacher Tip! **This activity can be used to monitor students' understanding of chapter vocabulary.**

▶ **Digital Tools**

Blended Learning
Students apply chapter concepts to extension activities and connect them to the EQ.

Interactive IMPACT

Review chapter vocabulary with **Word Play**.

Connections in Action
Back to the EQ

Think about the chapter EQ, **"Why do governments and citizens need each other?"**

• **Talk** with a partner about the ways American citizens and the government work together. List ways that students your age could work with your community's government. What could government leaders learn from working with students? What could students learn from working with government leaders?

• **Share** your list with the class.

More to Explore
How can you make an IMPACT?

Write a Letter to the Mayor
Think about how your community could be a better place to live. Write a letter to the mayor describing your ideas. Begin your letter with a short summary of your ideas. Then tell why you think your ideas will improve your community. Use at least one vocabulary word in your letter.

Citizenship in Action
Think of ways that you and your classmates can be good citizens. Then work with a partner or small group to create a skit that shows how to be a good citizen. Write a script, and make sure that each of you has a role. Perform the skit for the class.

Guess the Word
Choose three of the vocabulary words from this chapter. For each word, write a simple definition. Then join one or two classmates and take turns reading your definitions. See if the others can correctly guess the word based on the definition.

258 Chapter 5 American Citizens, Symbols, and Government

Chapter 5 259

RESEARCH COMPANION, pp. 258–259

English Learners SCAFFOLD

Use the following scaffolds to support student speaking and listening skills.

Entering and Emerging

Assign groups that encourage interaction between an English learner and a fluent English speaker. Give groups images from the unit, including people, buildings, and settings. Ask them to name each image and sort them into groups based on the branch of government. Then ask partners to sort them into groups based on the government level.

Developing and Expanding

Assign groups that encourage interaction between an English learner and a fluent English speaker. Give groups images and vocabulary words from the unit, including people, buildings, and settings. Ask them to sort them into groups based on the branch of government. Then ask partners to sort them into groups based on the government level.

Bridging and Reaching

Assign groups that encourage interaction between an English learner and a fluent English speaker. Give groups vocabulary words from the unit, including people, buildings, and settings. Ask them to sort them into groups based on the branch of government. Then ask partners to sort them into groups based on the government level.

Social Emotional Learning

Relationship Skills

Build Relationships Remind students of the importance of capitalizing on the partnerships they have already established with their classmates. By tapping into available partnerships, students will more easily be able to ask for and give help when needed.

How Do People in a Community Meet Their Wants and Needs?

In This Chapter Students learn about economics and the resources businesses use to make profits for themselves and help strengthen their community's economy. Students will also learn what a budget is and how to live within their means.

Chapter Objectives

- **Define** economics.
- **Name** the types of resources businesses use, and **describe** how they are used.
- **Explain** what goods and services are.
- **Describe** how people use trade to get the goods they want and need.
- **Describe** how goods and services have changed over time.
- **Explain** how people earn and use money.
- **Write a blog** about a business in the community using information from a variety of sources.

Make Connections!

CONNECT TO SCIENCE

Economics is based on processes, like much of science. Have students team up to research a manufacturing process that interests them. Ask each team to create a presentation that shows the resources needed to create the product.

CONNECT TO MATH

Have students find out the cost of an item that they really want to buy. It should be under $200. Tell them that they can use an allowance of $20 a week to purchase the item. Have students calculate how many weeks it would take for them to afford the item.

Bibliography

Additional resources to aid student inquiry:

► **Let's Chat About Economics!**
by Michelle A. Balconi and Dr. Arthur Laffer, 2014

► **Do I Need It? or Do I Want It?**
by Jennifer S. Larson; Lerner Classroom, 2010

► **Round and Round the Money Goes**
by Melvin Berger and Gilda Berger; Ideals Publications, 2001

Go online at **my.mheducation.com** for a complete list of resources.

Chapter-At-A-Glance

 EQ How Do People in a Community Meet Their Wants and Needs?

1 ENGAGE

INQUIRY JOURNAL

pp. 244–247

▶ **Introduce the Chapter**
▶ **Chapter Inquiry Project**
▶ **Explore Words**

Short on Time?
Engage with the content the way **YOU** want to teach—and *your* students want to learn!

Check out the three suggested **Flexible Instructional Pathways** on pages FM34–FM35.

2 INVESTIGATE

RESEARCH COMPANION

pp. 260–301

▶ **Activate Knowledge**
▶ **How Do People Meet Their Needs?**
▶ **Connect Through Literature**
  Clothes with an IQ
▶ **People You Should Know**
▶ **Lessons 1–5**

The **IMPACT Explorer Magazine** supports students' exploration of the Essential Question and provides additional resources for the EQ Inquiry Project.

3 TAKE ACTION

INQUIRY JOURNAL
RESEARCH COMPANION

pp. 288–295   pp. 302–303

▶ **Inquiry Project Wrap-Up and Chapter Connections**
▶ **Reader's Theater**
▶ **Connections in Action**
▶ **More to Explore**

▶ Digital Tools at my.mheducation.com

ePresentation

Teach the Engage, Investigate, and Take Action content to the whole class from ePresentations that launch directly from the chapter dashboard.

eBook

You can flip your instruction with the **IMPACT eBooks** found on your chapter dashboard.

Interactive IMPACT

Blend in digital content **when you want it** and **where you want it**. Blended Learning notes in the Teacher's Edition highlight ways to connect in-class work with online experiences to enhance learning.

Investigate current events with **IMPACT News**.

Introduce the EQ with the **IMPACT Chapter Video**.

Explore domain-based vocabulary with **Explore Words** and **Word Play** vocabulary activities.

MONITOR PROGRESS:
Know What Your Students Know

Choose the assessment options that work best for you and your students.

Chapter Pre-Test (Optional)

Begin the Chapter

Measure students' content knowledge before you begin the chapter with the following questions.

Quick Check

✔ Why are people one of the most important resources for a successful business?

✔ How do businesses help the community's economy grow?

✔ What is a budget?

1. When all students have responded, ask them to rate how confident they are in their answers on a scale from 1 (not very confident) to 5 (very confident).

2. Ask students to compare their responses. Determine what are commonly held beliefs about business and the economy. Ask students to keep these in mind as they progress through the chapter.

3. **Don't Forget!** Throughout the chapter, revisit students' Quick Check responses with them. If students change their responses, ask them to support the change with text evidence. You may wish to have students respond to a different prompt to measure their content knowledge, such as *What are imports and exports?*

Ongoing Lesson Assessment

Use the lesson tools to monitor the **IMPACT** of your instruction.

☑ Stop and Check

Use the questions provided in the Stop and Check prompts to monitor students' comprehension of the core lesson content. The Stop and Check questions, found in the Research Companion, prompt students to engage in discussions to deepen their understanding of the content.

✔ Check for Success

Use this formative assessment tool to assess how well your students understand the material they are learning in class. The Check for Success questions, located at point of use in the Teacher's Edition, are not a test but a way to assess students' comprehension of a particular topic. A Differentiate strategy offers one activity that you can use to quickly adapt your instruction.

⌕ Report Your Findings

Use Report Your Findings in each lesson to measure student understanding of the lesson content and their ability to effectively express their understanding. See pp. T516, T532, T546, T560, and T576 for task-specific evaluation rubrics. Report Your Findings is found in the Inquiry Journal.

▶ Digital Tools

Lesson Assessments
Use the **Lesson Test** to monitor students' understanding of the lesson content. Online Lesson Tests are customizable and available for every lesson. You will also find the tools you need to create your own assessments and to track your students' progress. A printable Lesson Test is available for use in class.

Chapter Assessment

Evaluate

Monitor student understanding of core chapter content with one or more of the following assessment options.

Connections in Action

Use the **Connections in Action** to evaluate student understanding of core chapter content through discussion in the Research Companion, pp. 302–303.

Inquiry Project

In this chapter's Inquiry Project, students will select a local business and conduct an interview with the business owner. Then students will use their findings to create a blog about the business, adding pictures, charts, or graphs to support their ideas. See pp. T492–T493 for more information.

Use the EQ Inquiry Project to measure student understanding of the chapter content and their ability to effectively express their understanding. A task-specific evaluation rubric is available in the Online Teacher Resources.

	4	3	2	1
Developing and Planning Inquiry	Project is focused on a local business, and interview questions explore many aspects of that business.	Project is focused on a local business, and interview questions explore some aspects of that business.	Project is focused on a local business, and interview questions explore only a few aspects of that business.	Project is focused on a local business, and interview questions do not explore aspects of that business.
Economic Understanding	Project shows strong understanding of how businesses are run.	Project shows adequate understanding of how businesses are run.	Project shows uneven understanding of how businesses are run.	Project shows no understanding of how businesses are run.
Sources and Evidence	Descriptions are based on thorough and convincing evidence.	Descriptions are based on adequate evidence.	Descriptions are based on uneven or only somewhat convincing evidence.	Descriptions are not based on supporting evidence.
Communicating Conclusions	Project information is clearly supported with details and is easily understood.	Project information includes details and is understood with some explanation.	Project information is unclear due to lack of details.	Project does not include details necessary to communicate information.

ESSENTIAL EQ QUESTION

How Do People in a Community Meet Their Wants and Needs?

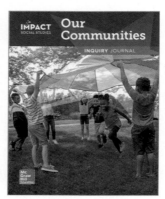

INQUIRY JOURNAL, pp. 244–245

Talk About It COLLABORATE

Read Have students read the opening page together. Prompt them to write three questions they would like to know the answers to after reading about the economics of communities. Give students a chance to share their questions with a partner. You may wish to record these questions and refer back to them throughout the chapter.

Inquiry Project

Blogging About a Local Business

Discuss the Inquiry Project with students. Review each step of the project and the **Project Checklist** evaluation rubric. Tell students that they will use information from the chapter and from independent research to complete the project.

My Research Plan

Discuss the Essential Question with students and ways in which people in their community meet their wants and needs. Then have students work in pairs to brainstorm research questions that are "just right," neither too general nor too specific.

Design Your Own Inquiry Path (Optional)

You may wish to work with students to choose their own Essential Question, Inquiry Project, and related research questions. Have students preview chapter materials and discuss ideas with classmates to help develop possible questions, such as *What resources are necessary to run a particular business in my community?, What are the characteristics of successful business owners?,* or their own questions.

Have students explain why their Essential Question is important to them and to others. Have students record their question, project idea, and initial supporting research questions using the **Student EQ Inquiry Project** pages found at **my.mheducation.com.**

▶ Digital Tools

Blended Learning
Students engage with the chapter's Essential Question and launch their investigations.

Interactive IMPACT

Spark student interest with the **EQ Chapter Video.**

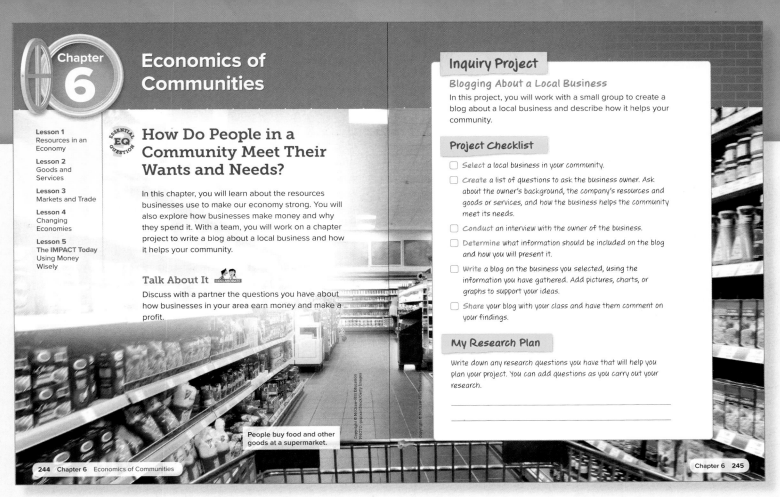

INQUIRY JOURNAL, pp. 244–245

The image above shows the Inquiry Journal pages:

Chapter 6 — Economics of Communities

Lesson 1 Resources in an Economy
Lesson 2 Goods and Services
Lesson 3 Markets and Trade
Lesson 4 Changing Economies
Lesson 5 The IMPACT Today Using Money Wisely

ESSENTIAL EQ QUESTION

How Do People in a Community Meet Their Wants and Needs?

In this chapter, you will learn about the resources businesses use to make our economy strong. You will also explore how businesses make money and why they spend it. With a team, you will work on a chapter project to write a blog about a local business and how it helps your community.

Talk About It

Discuss with a partner the questions you have about how businesses in your area earn money and make a profit.

People buy food and other goods at a supermarket.

244 Chapter 6 Economics of Communities

Inquiry Project

Blogging About a Local Business

In this project, you will work with a small group to create a blog about a local business and describe how it helps your community.

Project Checklist

☐ Select a local business in your community.

☐ Create a list of questions to ask the business owner. Ask about the owner's background, the company's resources and goods or services, and how the business helps the community meet its needs.

☐ Conduct an interview with the owner of the business.

☐ Determine what information should be included on the blog and how you will present it.

☐ Write a blog on the business you selected, using the information you have gathered. Add pictures, charts, or graphs to support your ideas.

☐ Share your blog with your class and have them comment on your findings.

My Research Plan

Write down any research questions you have that will help you plan your project. You can add questions as you carry out your research.

_____

_____

Chapter 6 245

 # English Learners **SCAFFOLD**

Use the following scaffolds to support student understanding of the Inquiry Project.

Entering and Emerging

Help students understand what's expected in the Inquiry Project. Explain that the term *blog* is a shortened form of the word *weblog*, which is a log that is published on the Internet. Say: *A blog is like a journal. It's a website where a person writes about what he or she thinks, feels, or does.* Then walk through the steps of the Inquiry Project to make sure students understand what's expected. Talk about local businesses that students might like to learn more about.

Developing and Expanding

Review the definition of the term *blog* with students. Then ask questions to check understanding of the Inquiry Project instructions, and elicit answers. Say: *You're going to select a business in the community and write questions that you will use to interview the owner. What would you like to know about a local business? What questions could you ask the owner? Then you'll use the information from the interview to create a blog about the local business.*

Bridging and Reaching

Read through the Inquiry Project instructions with students. Ask students if they are familiar with any blogs. Then have partners talk about the types of questions they could ask a local business owner in an interview. Share examples of different question stems students can use to develop their interview questions.

 Social Emotional Learning

Relationship Skills

Engage with Others To develop students' relationship skills, make sure they understand how to engage in positive interactions with others. Before students begin to write interview questions, explain that good interviewers know how to listen attentively to the person they are interviewing. Ask: *How can you show that you are listening attentively when another person is speaking?*

ENGAGE
with INQUIRY JOURNAL

**INQUIRY JOURNAL,
pp. 246–247**

Explore Words

Academic/Domain-Specific Vocabulary Read the words aloud to students. Explain to students that these are words they will learn more about in the chapter.

Word Rater Have students place a checkmark in one of the three boxes below each word, indicating that they "Know It," "Heard It," or "Don't Know It." Explain to students that they will come back to this chart to add additional information about each word as they work through the chapter.

☐ **Know It!** Tell students that if they know the word, they should write its meaning on the lines provided.

☐ **Heard It!** Tell students that if they have heard, or are familiar with the word, they should write what they know about it on the lines provided. Remind them to take notes about the word as they encounter it.

☐ **Don't Know It!** If they do not know the word's meaning, tell them to write down its meaning when they encounter the word in the chapter.

Support Vocabulary

Return to the Word Rater as you come across vocabulary words in each lesson. Encourage students to use the "My Notes" section to include any of the following:

- definitions from the text
- deeper understandings
- synonyms
- other associations

 Spanish Cognates

For Spanish speakers, point out the cognates.

benefits = beneficios

capital resources = recursos de capital

economy = economía

export = exportar

human capital = capital humano

human resources = recursos humanos

import = importar

Content Words	
benefits	things that help a person
capital resource	a good such as a tool or a machine that a business uses to provide a good or service
economy	the production, buying, and selling of goods and services
entrepreneur	a person who starts and runs his or her own business
export	to send goods to another country for sale; an item transported to another country for sale there
human capital	the skills and knowledge a person has to do a job
human resources	people in a business who provide valuable skills
import	to bring goods into a country from another country to sell; an item brought into a country for sale there
scarcity	a limited amount of a good or service that many people want
specialize	to focus on a specific subject or task

Explore Words

Complete this chapter's Word Rater. Write notes as you learn more about each word.

benefits   My Notes
- ☐ Know It!
- ☐ Heard It!
- ☐ Don't Know It!

capital resource   My Notes
- ☐ Know It!
- ☐ Heard It!
- ☐ Don't Know It!

economy   My Notes
- ☐ Know It!
- ☐ Heard It!
- ☐ Don't Know It!

entrepreneur   My Notes
- ☐ Know It!
- ☐ Heard It!
- ☐ Don't Know It!

export   My Notes
- ☐ Know It!
- ☐ Heard It!
- ☐ Don't Know It!

human capital   My Notes
- ☐ Know It!
- ☐ Heard It!
- ☐ Don't Know It!

human resource   My Notes
- ☐ Know It!
- ☐ Heard It!
- ☐ Don't Know It!

import   My Notes
- ☐ Know It!
- ☐ Heard It!
- ☐ Don't Know It!

scarcity   My Notes
- ☐ Know It!
- ☐ Heard It!
- ☐ Don't Know It!

specialize   My Notes
- ☐ Know It!
- ☐ Heard It!
- ☐ Don't Know It!

INQUIRY JOURNAL, pp. 246–247

English Learners SCAFFOLD

Use the following scaffolds to support student understanding of chapter vocabulary.

Entering and Emerging

Display and read aloud a definition for each word in the list. Discuss each word and its meaning, and then work with students to write definitions in their own words. Guide students to use each word in a context sentence.

Developing and Expanding

Read aloud sentences that describe each term without saying the term itself. Have students work individually or in pairs to identify the terms. For example: *Companies hire workers. The workers use their skills to make products the company sells. These workers are an example of this.* (human resources)

Bridging and Reaching

Provide students with paper to create vocabulary flashcards. On one side, students can write the term. On the other side, students can write their own definition, provide a synonym, or draw a picture. Have them work in pairs and use the flashcards to quiz each other on the terms.

▶ **Digital Tools**

Blended Learning

Students investigate academic and domain-specific words they encounter in each lesson.

Interactive IMPACT

Throughout the chapter, encourage students to interact with the **Explore Words** cards and games.

INVESTIGATE
with RESEARCH COMPANION

How Do People in a Community Meet Their Wants and Needs?

RESEARCH COMPANION, pp. 260–261

Activate Knowledge

Read and Discuss **COLLABORATE** Have students read the opening on p. 260 together. Ask: *What is the difference between a want and a need?* To verify understanding of the meaning of each term, have students provide examples of wants and needs and discuss why each is a want or a need.

How Do People Meet Their Needs?

- Have students read the text, focusing on the photographs and the captions.

- How does spending money at local stores help the community? (The money that's spent provides an income for storeowners and employees, which they can then spend at other businesses in the community. It also provides tax money for the community.)

- Why do we import some goods? (If we can't make or grow a product, we have to import it from elsewhere. Sometimes it is cheaper to import products from other places.)

Make Connections

- What are some products that you use that are imported to the United States? What products does the United States export? (Answers will vary, but students should understand that probably most clothing they wear is imported. The United States exports many farm products.)

- Your friend has an old phone that works well, but it's not as fast or cool as the new model. He decided he *has* to get the new model even though he doesn't have enough savings. How would you advise your friend? (Answers will vary, but students should differentiate between a need and a want and explain why some purchases may need to be put off.)

Perspectives What are some ways that people can keep track of how they spend money? (Answers will vary, but students might mention keeping a budget and thinking about what they want and what they need.)

Chapter 6 Economics of Communities

Lesson 1
Resources in an Economy

Lesson 2
Goods and Services

Lesson 3
Markets and Trade

Lesson 4
Changing Economies

Lesson 5
The IMPACT Today
Using Money Wisely

How Do People in a Community Meet Their Wants and Needs?

ESSENTIAL EQ QUESTION

People work to earn money. This allows them to buy the things they want and need. In this chapter, you will read about the goods and services provided by businesses. You will learn how people and businesses make and spend money. You will also explore how tradeoffs affect our spending choices. As you read, think about how you can make good choices when you spend your money.

Even you can earn money selling goods and services.

260 Chapter 6 Economics of Communities

How Do People Meet Their Needs?

Today, people buy many of the things they need. But first they must have money to do so.

Spending money at local stores helps people in your community. The money you spend provides an income for the business owners and their employees. The money they earn can be spent on items that they need or want. In this way, everybody in your community can meet their needs.

Earning money takes time and effort. You may wish to spend your money as soon as you get it. But you should think before you buy. You may need money later to buy something that you really need. Sometimes, saving money rather than spending it is how people can best meet their needs.

Importing goods helps people get items from other countries that their country can't make or grow. This helps both the business that exports the goods and the people buying them. The business makes money and the buyers get the goods they need.

Chapter 6 261

RESEARCH COMPANION, pp. 260–261

English Learners SCAFFOLD

Use these scaffolds to support students in activating their background knowledge.

Entering and Emerging

To help students understand the concept of economics, make sure they understand the words *want, need, income,* and *earn*. Help student look up each word in a dictionary. Discuss the meaning of each word. Then have partners take turns using each word in the following sentence frames:

- *The word _____ means_____.*
- *An example of _____ is _____.*

Developing and Expanding

Display the words *want, need, income,* and *earn*. Have students work with partners to find each word in a dictionary and discuss its definition. Have partners take turns using each word in a sentence they create. If necessary, ask questions such as the following to facilitate discussion: *If you already own a bike that is in great shape, is a new bike a want or a need? What are some ways that you can earn an income?*

Bridging and Reaching

Point out the content-specific vocabulary words *income, earn, want,* and *need* in the text. Have students ask each other open-ended questions to build their understanding of each word. Provide question examples, such as *What are some things you need to live? How would you like to earn an income?*

INVESTIGATE
with RESEARCH COMPANION

Connect Through Literature

Clothes with an IQ
by Meg Moss
Art by Dave Clark

Smarty Pants

Some new fabrics can track your body's motions and functions. These e-textiles don't look much different from ordinary clothing, even though they have electronic components and electrical circuits woven right in. Some monitor heart rate and blood pressure. This is great for people with heart problems. Runners may someday wear pants that measure their speed, distance, and gait. Or how about a backpack that knows what you've forgotten? These work with computer chips that can be programmed to identify all the stuff you want to carry and alert you when something is missing.

Super Suits

In space, one tiny hole in your suit can be deadly. Astronauts working outside their spacecraft depend on their suits. Space suits help keep their bodies properly pressurized. Some researchers have developed a suit layered with high-tech fabrics and gel. If a smidge of space debris punctures the suit, the gel oozes into the hole to seal it up. If a larger hole opens up, tiny computers in the fabric alert the astronaut to head for the nearest space capsule.

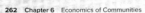

262　Chapter 6　Economics of Communities

Plug It In

Ever want a piece of toast on the beach or a hair dryer on the ski slope? We aren't there yet, but some companies are developing jackets that can charge your electronic toys. Just strap on a solar panel and plug in your phone or tablet. Another jacket charges batteries and powers devices by turning the vibrations of your body into electrical energy.

Better Than Skin

For superheroes and ski racers, it's all about speed. The developers of this new fabric studied the skin of sharks and the dimples on golf balls. They wanted to find out what kind of surface helps an object move the fastest. The result is a stretchy, skintight material that is carefully woven in a special pattern to lower wind resistance. For clumsy superheroes and ski racers, the fabric can be made with remarkable padding that hardens on impact and then softens up again.

Think About It

1. What are some ways "clothes with an IQ" can help keep us safe?

2. Why do you think it's dangerous for an astronaut's suit to have a hole in it?

3. Which of the "clothes with an IQ" do you think is most useful? Use details from the text to explain your choice.

Chapter 6　263

RESEARCH COMPANION, pp. 262–263

Connect Through Literature

| **GENRE** | Informational Article "Clothes with an IQ" is an informational article, which is usually a short piece of nonfiction written for a newspaper, magazine, or website.

Have students read the selection on pp. 262–263. Then discuss these questions.

1. What are some ways "clothes with an IQ" can help keep us safe? (They can monitor heart rate, blood pressure, patch holes in space suits, and give padding to ski racers.)

Have students reread the selection and ask:

2. Why do you think it's dangerous for an astronaut's suit to have a hole in it? (Possible answer: The astronaut would not have oxygen needed to breathe.)

3. Which of the "clothes with an IQ" do you think is most useful? (Student responses should show an understanding of the function of the clothing they chose.)

Perspectives Why is this article called "Clothes with an IQ"? (IQ measures intelligence, so the clothes described in the article make "intelligent" decisions that help the wearer.)

▶ Digital Tools

Blended Learning

Students explore the chapter content by making connections to literature.

eBook

Have students use the **eBook** to interact with engaging literary selections.

People You Should Know

Steve Jobs

Steve Jobs was a designer and inventor. He cofounded a personal computer company in 1976. Before the company moved to its first office, work was done from Steve Jobs's family garage! Now it has offices and stores all over the world. Steve Jobs also helped build a company that produces many movies.

Cher Wang

Cher Wang was born in Taiwan and studied economics at the University of California, Berkeley. In 1997, she cofounded a company which makes computers and smartphones. In 2011, she founded Guizhou Forerunner College. This is a college in China which provides free or low-cost education, and also supports projects to help communities recover from disasters.

Oprah Winfrey

Oprah Winfrey started her work in television as a news presenter and reporter. In 1984, she hosted her own talk show on television. It was very popular, and soon she formed her own television company and film company. Oprah Winfrey continues to do a lot of work to help people. She was awarded the Presidential Medal of Freedom in 2013.

Jerry Yang

Jerry Yang moved to California from Taiwan in 1978 when he was 10 years old. He studied at Stanford University and went on to cofound a technology company. It started as a listing of favorite web pages, but grew to provide many different Internet services such as news, a way to search the Internet, and e-mail.

RESEARCH COMPANION, pp. 264–265

People You Should Know

How do personal stories IMPACT our understanding of the economics of communities?

Read Explain to students that they will learn about people and their role in the economy. Then have students read through all the biographies and select one individual that interests them.

Research Ask students to research that person's life, achievements, and opinions. Tell students to gather facts and some memorable stories about the individual.

Respond Using details from their research, each student will write a magazine profile about the person he or she researched. The profile should give details about major events in the person's life and describe how the person became successful. Students may also wish to incorporate quotations and photographs into their magazine profiles.

 **Digital Tools**

Blended Learning

Students investigate and discuss curated news articles that extend the chapter content.

Interactive IMPACT

Connect to current events and people with **IMPACT News** and **More to Investigate**.

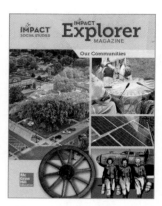

IMPACT EXPLORER MAGAZINE, pp. 66–79

WordBlast

Remind students to look for the Word Blasts as they read the **IMPACT Explorer Magazine**.

▶ Digital Tools

Blended Learning
Students investigate Magazine content in video format.

ePresentation
Use the **IMPACT Explorations Video**.

Extend Knowledge Building

The **IMPACT Explorer Magazine** provides students another route to explore each chapter's Essential Question from a variety of perspectives as they dig deeper into the subject of the economics of communities. Additional questions and activities help students develop and deepen their understanding of the chapter's content.

Engage

Build background for students and share any information needed to provide a context for the chapter topic. Read aloud the Essential Question and the Table of Contents.

Analyze the Visual Discuss the opening visual (photograph, photo essay, artwork) on the second page of the **IMPACT Explorer Magazine** chapter. Help students connect the visual to the chapter topic and the Essential Question.

Analyze the Sources

Students will read and analyze the leveled informational articles and literary texts, graphic texts, primary and secondary sources, photographs, maps, and other visual resources.

Read and Analyze Before reading, provide any additional information you think students will need about the topics. Then guide students through the three-step process to read and analyze the content.

1 Inspect

Have students skim the content on a page or multiple pages. Ask questions to help students recall and retell key ideas.

- What is this article mostly about?
- Who is _____?

2 Find Evidence

Have students reread the content and look for details they might have missed. Ask additional questions to help them read more closely.

- What details do you notice in the photographs?
- Why was _____ important?

3 Make Connections

Have students work in pairs or small groups to discuss prompts that help them connect the articles to other texts, their own lives, current ideas and issues, and other topics.

- How is _____ similar to what we do today?
- How do you think _____ felt about what happened?
- What do you think about _____?

IMPACT EXPLORER MAGAZINE, pp. 66–67

How to Use the IMPACT Explorer Magazine

Use the following scaffolds to support students' understanding and your classroom needs.

Whole Class

Use the **IMPACT Explorer Magazine** Teaching Guide to read and discuss one or more articles with the whole class.

Small Group

Have partners or small groups read articles connected to the day's core lesson and report back to the whole class about what they read.

Independent Work

Assign articles for students to extend and enrich their understanding of a topic, including during center time and independent reading time.

The online **IMPACT Explorer Magazine** Teaching Guide provides support for various implementation models as well as a three-step lesson plan for each article. The lesson plan includes background information, meaningful questions, vocabulary activities, scaffolded support for English learners, and collaborative conversation prompts.

Digital Tools

Blended Learning

Students extend the investigation of the Chapter Essential Question with highly visual, leveled articles and video.

eBook

Use the **IMPACT Explorer Magazine eBook** to extend knowledge building.

LESSON QUESTION

How Can Communities Use Their Resources?

Connect to the Essential Question

Tell students that this lesson will help them answer the Chapter Essential Question: **How Do People in a Community Meet Their Wants and Needs?** Explain that they will use their investigative skills to find out what kinds of resources businesses use. They will understand how businesses in the United States provide goods and services and describe how a local business uses resources to help meet people's needs.

Lesson Objectives:

- **Explain** how businesses use resources to provide goods and services.
- **Identify** some local businesses, and **describe** the ways they use resources.
- **Recognize** the ways local businesses help people meet their needs.
- **Write** a paragraph about a local business that depends on community resources.

Make Connections!

CONNECT TO ELA

Reading **Ask and answer** questions to demonstrate understanding of a text, by citing references from the text.
Determine the main idea of a text; recount the key details and explain how they support the main idea.

Research **Recall** information from experiences or gather information from print and digital sources; take brief notes on sources and sort evidence into provided categories.

Writing **Craft** informative/explanatory texts to examine a topic and convey ideas and information clearly.

Speaking and Listening **Follow** agreed-upon rules for discussions (e.g., gaining the floor in respectful ways, listening to others with care, speaking one at a time about the topics and texts under discussion).

Language **Acquire and use accurately** grade-appropriate conversational, general academic, and domain-specific words and phrases, including those that signal spatial and temporal relationships.

COMMUNITY CONNECTIONS

To enrich what students have learned about the resources businesses use, invite a business owner from your community to speak to the class. Students may also visit a local business, such as a bakery or coffee shop, to witness firsthand how the business uses resources to meet customer needs.

Lesson-At-A-Glance

1 ENGAGE — INQUIRY JOURNAL

pp. 248–253

- **Talk About It:** Photographs of fishing, mining, logging, and farming
- **Analyze the Source:** Agriculture Depends on Resources
- **Inquiry Tools:** Explore Main Idea and Details

2 INVESTIGATE — RESEARCH COMPANION

pp. 266–273

- **What Is Economics?**
- **How Businesses Use Resources**
- **A Day in the Life: A Restaurant Owner**

3 REPORT — INQUIRY JOURNAL

pp. 254–255

- **Think About It**
- **Write About It:** Describe a Community Business
- **Talk About It**
- **Connect to the Essential Question**

ASSESSMENT

- **Online Lesson Test**
- **Printable Lesson Test**

For more details, see pages T490–T491.

▶ Digital Tools

at **my.mheducation.com**

ePresentation

Teach the Engage, Investigate, and Report content to the whole class from **ePresentations** that launch directly from the lesson dashboard.

eBook

You can flip your instruction with the **IMPACT eBooks** found on your lesson dashboard.

Interactive IMPACT

Blend in digital content **when you want it** and **where you want it**.

Blended Learning features in the Teacher's Edition highlight ways to connect in-class work with online experiences to enhance learning.

Investigate current events with **IMPACT News**.

Explore domain-specific vocabulary with **Explore Words** and **Word Play** vocabulary activities.

pp. 66–79

Go Further with IMPACT Explorer Magazine!

The **IMPACT Explorer Magazine** supports students' exploration of the Essential Question and provides additional resources for the EQ Inquiry Project.

How Can Communities Use Their Resources?

Language Objectives

• Use newly acquired content and academic vocabulary to talk and write about resources that help businesses in the United States provide goods and services.

• Describe a business and how the environment affects it.

• Use articles correctly.

Introduce the Lesson

Set Purpose Explain to students that in this lesson, they will read informational texts to learn about different kinds of resources businesses use and how they provide goods and services.

Access Prior Knowledge Read the lesson question and remind students that resources are things that are useful. Natural resources are things that occur in nature, such as sunlight, soil, minerals, and water. Ask: *What things can be produced using sunlight, water, and soil?* (plants, including trees, fruit, vegetables) Guide students to brainstorm what they already know about natural resources. Explain that in addition to natural resources they will learn about other kinds of resources businesses use.

Spark Curiosity Have students look at the photos of different regions on pp. 248–249 of the Inquiry Journal. Explain that these photos provide a glimpse at different ways people use the resources found in the different regions of the United States. Walk through each picture with students, making sure they understand that these show industries that use important natural resources. The man in the boat is in the fishing industry. The men in the field are most likely in agriculture. The picture next to this shows the importance of lumber as a resource. The large picture of rocks and canyons suggests the importance of minerals that come from the earth.

 Have pairs of students discuss the resources they see in each image and why these resources are important to people. Have them consider which of these resources they can find near where they live.

Build Meaning & Support Language

Inquiry Journal

Analyze the Source (pages 250–251) Unpack the heading "Agriculture Depends on Resources." Say: *In this heading, the word* agriculture *means "farming," or "growing crops" and* depends on *means "needs."* Read aloud the first sentence of the section. Explain that a major industry is one that makes important contributions to the country. Explain that agriculture contributes to the nation's economy because thousands of people work in the industry and produce goods that people throughout the country and the world need. Have students look at the photograph. Ask: *What resources does agriculture depend on?* (soil, water, and sun)

Inquiry Tools (pages 252–253) Tell students they will explore **Main Idea and Details** as they read sections in the Research Companion. Explain that the graphic organizer will help them organize the information as they read. Check to see that they understand that the main idea goes in the first column and details that support the main idea go in the second column. Say: *We know that the main idea from p. 250 is that* agriculture *is a major industry in the United States. It is the first sentence, and it tells what everything else on the page describes.* Then read the rest of the text as students follow along and help them identify details to support the main idea. Work with students to complete the graphic organizer on p 252.

Research Companion

What Is Economics? (pages 266–267) Unpack the first sentence in the second paragraph. *The study of how people use money, goods, resources, and services to meet their needs is called economics.* Explain that in this sentence *study* means to analyze something. Make sure that students understand the terms *goods, resources,* and *services.* Then explain that people who study economics look at how people acquire and use money, goods, resources, and services. Point out that buying and selling things is an example of economics. Then help students to rewrite the sentence with *economics* as the subject: *Economics is the study of how people use money, goods, resources, and services to meet their wants and needs.*

How Businesses Use Resources (pages 268–271) Before reading the selection, discuss the terms *natural resources, human resources, human capital,* and *capital resources* with students and make sure students understand each one. Work with them to write definitions in their own words. Then discuss how businesses rely on each of these to be successful.

A Day in the Life: A Restaurant Owner (pages 272–273) Display the section and read it aloud as students follow along. On the board, draw three boxes labeled *natural resources, human resources,* and *capital resources.* Then read through the selection again and have students identify examples of each type of resource to put in each box.

Inquiry Journal

Report Your Findings (pages 254–255) Explain to students that in a description they should provide information that tells about the business in their community, including the products or services it provides. Then they should describe the resources this business needs to create its products or services. Encourage students to use new vocabulary in their writing. Provide support for grammar and spelling as students write.

Language Forms & Conventions

Articles Tell students that *a, an* and *the* are called articles, and they come before a noun. Point out that the word *the* is a definite article because it limits the meaning of a noun to a specific thing, such as *the house.* Explain that the articles *a* and *an* are indefinite articles because they refer to a general idea. Have them recall that *a* is used before a word that begins with a consonant and *an* is used before a word that begins with a vowel. Model using articles to talk about economics: *Economics is the study of how people use money, goods, resources, and services. A person who sells you music lessons provides a service.*

The	A, An
the economy	a good
the country	a service
the community	an architect
the machine	an orange grove

Have students work in pairs to locate some articles in the texts. Call on volunteers to say them aloud and add them to the chart. As a challenge, ask pairs to write a word that begins with each vowel and add the article *an* in front of it.

Cross-Cultural Connection

While the United States has many resources that businesses use for the production of goods and services, it is still not self-sufficient. This means it imports some goods to meet its needs. Some imported goods are not based on need but preference or cost. These goods include computers, telecommunications equipment, and vehicles. Some services are also imported.

Leveled Support

Entering & Emerging
Provide sentence frames: *The business makes _____. The resources it depends on are _____ and _____.*

Developing & Expanding
Provide sentence frames: *A business in my community is _____. It depends on _____. It depends on these resources because _____.*

Bridging & Reaching
Provide sentence frames: *An important business in my community is _____. A natural resource it depends on is _____. A human resource it depends on is _____. A capital resource it depends on is _____. It needs these resources to _____.*

Language Transfer

In some languages there is no article or no difference between *a* and *the,* so students may omit articles. Also, in some languages *a* and *an* are the same words, so students may use them differently or mistake one for the other.

LESSON 1 ENGAGE

LESSON QUESTION

How Can Communities Use Their Resources?

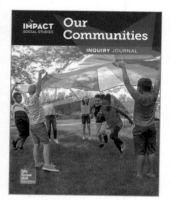

**INQUIRY JOURNAL,
pp. 248–249**

Bellringer

Prompt students to retrieve information from the previous lesson. Say: *Governments provide education, build roads, and provide other services. They pay for these services with money they receive from taxes. Governments use taxes as a resource for meeting people's needs. How do people meet their own personal needs? What is one important resource they use?* (People have jobs to earn money to buy the things they need. Money is an important resource that they use.)

Lesson Outcomes

Discuss the lesson question and lesson outcomes with students.

- Make sure students understand the words *business* and *industry*. Explain that a *business* is a store, company, or factory that makes, buys, or sells goods or services in exchange for money. An *industry* is a group of businesses that provide a particular product or service.

- Provide the following context for the words *business* and *industry*. *Your grocery store is a business that sells vegetables and fruit. The vegetables and fruit are supplied by the agricultural industry.* Then have students name other businesses or industries in their community.

Talk About It

Explain that when we talk about photographs, we describe, analyze, and interpret them and present our ideas in our own words. Give students a few moments to examine the photographs of the various industries. Provide sentence frames to help students form sentences as they analyze each photo.

- This photograph shows _____ and _____.
- _____ is an industry that needs _____.
- This photograph shows a region that has _____ that is used as a resource.

 Collaborative Conversations

Be Prepared As students engage in partner, small-group, and whole-class discussions, encourage them to:

- make sure they have read the material.
- use what they know to explore the topic being discussed.
- explain their understanding of the topic's main ideas and details.

Lesson 1

How Can Communities Use Their Resources?

Lesson Outcomes

What Am I Learning?
In this lesson, you will use your investigative skills to find out what kinds of resources businesses use.

Why Am I Learning It?
Reading and talking about resources will help you understand how businesses in the United States provide goods and services.

How Will I Know That I Learned It?
You will be able to describe a business in your community that is affected by the environment.

Talk About It COLLABORATE

Look closely at the photographs. In what type of community do you think each industry takes place? How do you know?

Different communities have important industries.

INQUIRY JOURNAL, pp. 248–249

EL English Learners SCAFFOLD

Use the following scaffolds to support student understanding of lesson content.

Entering and Emerging

Ask students to look at the photographs. Discuss the term *natural resources* and explain that the photos show different natural resources. Help students list the resources they see in the photos. Provide sentence frames to help them as needed:

- In this photograph, I see _____. It is used for _____.

Provide specific words as needed.

Developing and Expanding

Guide partners to choose two of the resources they see in the photographs. Ask them to form sentences describing what communities might use those resources. For example: *Fish come from the water, but crops come from the land. These communities might be in the Northwest and the Midwest.*

Bridging and Reaching

Have students write captions for each of the photographs. Encourage them to include details about the geography, landscape, and resources that they see in the photos.

Social Emotional Learning

Decision-Making Skills

Analyze Situations To help students sharpen their decision-making skills, ask them to think about problems people working in the pictured industries might face (e.g., fishers might not catch many fish). Then ask what decisions the workers might make to solve the problem.

▶ Digital Tools

Blended Learning

Students engage with the lesson question and discussion prompts.

Interactive IMPACT

Discuss the **Lesson Question** and **Talk About It**.

Analyze the Source

1 Inspect

Read Have students read the text and the photo caption. Remind them to circle the names of major crops grown in the United States.

- Underline details that explain how agriculture affects the U.S. economy and specific regions within the country. (Agriculture is a major industry in the United States. Students should identify other details within the text.)

2 Find Evidence

Reread Have students reread the text.

Examine Ask students to note the regions that are mentioned in the passage and list the crops produced in each region. Then have students identify which crops are grown in more than one region. (Potatoes are grown in the Midwest, Northeast, Southwest, and West. Tomatoes are grown in the Midwest, Northeast, Southeast, and West. Rice is grown in the Southeast and the Southwest.)

3 Make Connections

Talk Encourage partners to discuss the different ways agriculture can help the economy of a region and the country. (Answers will vary, but students should understand that agriculture can help a region's economy by providing jobs and tax revenue.)

 Spotlight on Language

Content Vocabulary

major: very important

fertile: able to support plant growth

produce: to make or create something

export: to sell a product to another country

Explore Main Idea and Details

The **main idea** is what the text is about. **Details** tell you more about the main idea.

1. **Read the text all the way through.**
   This will help you understand what the text is about.

2. **Reread the text and look for the most important point.**
   The most important point is the main idea. Look for a sentence that states the main idea.

3. **Look for ideas that tell you more about the most important point.**
   These ideas are the details.

Based on the text you read, work with your class to complete the chart.

Main Idea	Details
Agriculture is a major industry in the United States.	Sample answer: About half of the corn used throughout the world is produced in the United States. Agriculture benefits every region of the United States. Different crops are grown in each region. The United States exports agricultural products to other countries.

Investigate!

Read pages 266–273 in your Research Companion. Use your investigative skills to look for text evidence that tells you how businesses use resources. This chart will help you organize your notes.

Main idea and details statements will vary. Examples:

Main Idea	Details
Businesses in the United States use many natural resources.	Farmers sell goods to people all across the world.
Businesses in communities use human resources.	Workers help businesses make goods or provide services.
Businesses in communities use capital resources.	Tools and machines help businesses provide products, such as milk and airplanes, or services, such as transporting goods and serving food.
Businesses in communities use many resources.	A restaurant buys natural resources to make food, uses tools to prepare food, has workers to serve food, and uses money to pay workers and buy supplies.

INQUIRY JOURNAL, pp. 252–253

Inquiry Tools

Explore Main Idea and Details

Read Discuss with students the steps for finding the main idea and details of a text. Remind students that the main idea of a text is what the text is about. Explain that they can find details by asking *wh-* questions about the text, e.g, *who? what? when? where? why?*

Guide Practice Have students review the text on pp. 250–251. Then work with them to complete the graphic organizer. Explain that they will use a similar graphic organizer to organize their independent research.

Check Understanding Confirm understanding of the inquiry skill, Explore Main Idea and Details. If students cannot identify the main idea and related details, review the steps on p. 252.

Investigate!

Have students read pp. 266–273 in the Research Companion. Tell them the information will help them answer the lesson question *How Can Communities Use Their Resources?*

Take Notes Tell students that they will take notes in the graphic organizer on p. 253 of the Inquiry Journal. Remind them that taking notes will help them remember the information they learn. When taking notes, they should write the information from the text in their own words.

 Spotlight on Content

Asking Questions

Encourage students to make note of words they do not understand as they read the text, and look for answers to questions such as *who? what? when? where? why?* and *how?*

 Digital Tools

Blended Learning

Students prepare for the lesson investigation with step-by-step instruction about how to explore main idea and details.

ePresentation

Use the **Inquiry Tools** to model how to complete the lesson graphic organizer.

LESSON 1 INVESTIGATE

How Can Communities Use Their Resources?

RESEARCH COMPANION, pp. 266–267

Background Information

There are almost 30 million businesses in the United States. They can be large or small. One of the largest businesses in the country employs over 19 million people worldwide. However, most American businesses are much smaller. Well over 99 percent of all businesses in the United States have fewer than 500 employees. But all businesses, whether large or small, make money by selling a good or service.

What Is Economics?

1 Inspect Have students read pp. 266–267 and explain the difference between wants and needs.

2 Find Evidence Use the questions below to check comprehension. Remind students to support their answers with text evidence.

Relate What are some goods and services that you use regularly? (Answers will vary, but should show that students can distinguish between a good and a service. For goods, students may point out items that they buy in stores or online. For services, students might mention such things as lessons they take, or a doctor or dentist.) **DOK 2**

Infer What can you infer about the boy and his money shown in the photograph? (Answers will vary, but students might infer that the boy has earned money, has saved money, or has money to spend.) **DOK 3**

3 Make Connections

Develop a Logical Argument Look at the amount of money that Alex has in the photograph. In what way does it illustrate the benefits of saving money in order to buy something you want? (Answers will vary, but students might note that by saving money people build a supply of money that allows them to buy more expensive goods or services that they may want.) **DOK 3**

Lesson 1

How Can Communities Use Their Resources?

What Is Economics?

Alex walks his neighbor's dog to earn money. What will he do with the money? His parents pay for the things he needs. Needs are things you cannot live without, like food and clothing. So Alex can spend the money on things he wants. Wants are things that you do not really need but are nice to have. Maybe he will buy goods or services. Goods are things you can use, like comic books. Services are things a person does for you. For example, a person might give you a guitar lesson.

The study of how people use money, goods, resources, and services to meet their wants and needs is called economics. Sellers provide goods and services. Buyers pay for these goods and services. Buyers and sellers work together so people can get what they want and need.

Alex has saved his money. Now he can spend it on goods and services.

266 Lesson 1 How Can Communities Use Their Resources?

Chapter 6 Lesson 1 267

RESEARCH COMPANION, pp. 266–267

English Learners SCAFFOLD

Use the following scaffolds to support student understanding of lesson content.

Entering and Emerging

Draw a two-column chart on the board with the headings **Needs** and **Wants.** Explain that *needs* are things people need to survive and *wants* are things that people like to have. Write examples of each in the chart. Then ask volunteers to come to the board and write a need or a want in the chart. Have them explain if the item is a need or a want, using this sentence frame:

- _____ is a need/want.

Developing and Expanding

Ask partners to write a pair of sentences that describe needs and wants. Guide students in their writing using these sentence frames:

- _____ is something people need.
- _____ is something people want.

Have students work with a partner to compare sentences.

Bridging and Reaching

Have partners collaborate to write a short paragraph naming two needs and describing why each item is a need. Repeat for two wants. Ask volunteers to share their paragraphs.

Digital Tools

Blended Learning
Students explore lesson content through interactive activities.

Interactive IMPACT

Use the **More to Explore**.

How Businesses Use Resources

The United States has a very large **economy**. In fact, some states have larger economies and produce more goods than other countries in the world. Economy is the way a country uses its money, goods, resources, and services. Why is the United States' economy so large? The country has many resources that it uses to make goods and provide services.

Natural Resources

The United States has many natural resources. The United States has fertile soil and a mild climate. As a result, every U.S. region has the ability to produce goods from the land. Fruits, vegetables, and livestock are grown and raised on farms. Farmers sell these goods to people all across the world. The United States also has rivers that people use to ship these goods.

Fruits and vegetables are grown in many regions of the United States.

PRIMARY SOURCE

In Their Words... Aldo Leopold

"When we see land as a community to which we belong, we may begin to use it with love and respect."

—from *A Sand County Almanac*, 1949

The United States also has other natural resources. Lumber comes from the forests of many states. These include Oregon, Washington, and California. The Southeast and Northeast regions also provide timber. Seafood is caught off the Atlantic and Pacific Oceans. It is also found off the Gulf of Mexico. Minerals are mined in many states. Nevada, Arizona, Texas, California, and Minnesota are the top five mineral-producing states. Energy resources are also important to the country's economy. The United States has nonrenewable energy sources, such as oil, coal, and natural gas. It also uses renewable energy sources, such as solar, wind, and water.

Every community has different natural resources that help its economy. Using these resources benefits both businesses and the people who live and work in the community. For example, in Dubuque, Iowa, community leaders realized that the Mississippi River was a valuable resource. They developed attractions such as riverboat rides along the river and the National Mississippi River Museum & Aquarium. These attractions bring people to their community and create new jobs. As a result of using this natural resource, the community benefits.

✓ Stop and Check

Talk Discuss with a partner the kinds of natural resources found in your community and the United States. How do people use these resources?

Find Details As you read, add new information to the graphic organizer on page 253 in your Inquiry Journal.

RESEARCH COMPANION, pp. 268–269

How Businesses Use Resources

1 Inspect Have students read pp. 268–269 and identify three natural resources found in the United States.

2 Find Evidence Use the questions below to check comprehension.

Categorize What natural resources provide the United States with energy? (oil, coal, natural gas, sunlight, wind, water) **DOK 2**

Analyze the Primary Source Rephrase Leopold's statement in your own words. In what ways do we use the land "with love and respect"? (Answers will vary. Students might rephrase the statement as follows: *People try to protect the environment to make sure that the land and its natural resources will be available for people in the future.*) **DOK 3**

3 Make Connections

Cite Evidence What evidence from the text supports the idea that natural resources in all regions of the United States are important to the country's economy? (Answers will vary, but students might point out that lumber from the West, Southeast, and Northeast; seafood from the Gulf, Atlantic, and Pacific coasts; minerals from the West and Midwest; and agricultural products from around the nation are all produced as goods.) **DOK 3**

✓ Stop and Check

Talk Have partners discuss the kinds of natural resources found in the United States. (Answers will vary, but students may mention that people in the United States grow many kinds of crops, which farmers sell to people to eat.)

Spotlight on Content

Using Maps

Provide students a map of the United States. Help students categorize the areas into states, bodies of water, and regions.

▶ Digital Tools

Blended Learning

Students investigate curated resources and find evidence to answer the Lesson Question.

Interactive IMPACT

Students choose from print or digital **Inquiry Tools** to take notes.

Human Resources

Communities throughout the United States have many **human resources**. Human resources are the people who work for a business or person. People with ideas and skills provide services. Teachers instruct students. Doctors work to keep people healthy. Architects design buildings. Factory workers turn cotton into clothing. These workers are all important resources.

Manufacturing is a major part of our country's economy. Manufacturing is making products with machinery. The money that consumers spend on products helps our economy. The jobs that manufacturing provides also help the economy. In parts of Pennsylvania, Michigan, Indiana, and Ohio, workers manufacture cars, trucks, metals, and machines. Workers in Texas produce computers, bricks, foods, and petroleum products. Some Massachusetts, Connecticut, and New Hampshire workers make electronics, appliances, chemicals, and medical equipment. Human resources used to make products in the United States help keep our economy strong.

Human Capital

Businesses look for people with the skills, knowledge, and experience to do a job well. These characteristics are known as **human capital**. A person's human capital can add value to a business. If a person lacks skills or experience, it can take away value. As we learn, we gain skills, knowledge, and experience. This helps us develop our human capital.

Students develop their human capital.

Capital Resources

The dairy industry is important to the United States. For example, many people who work in the dairy industry work with cows. But how does the milk get from the cow into the carton you have in your refrigerator? Many farmers milk the cows with a milking machine. Then the milk is stored in a refrigerated tank. Farmers and other workers use trucks to haul the milk to factories. People who work in the factory operate machines that make the milk safe to drink. Then the milk is delivered to stores.

A milking machine is an example of a **capital resource**. Capital resources are the tools and machines that people use to make products. Businesses need capital resources to make goods. Often, business will borrow the money to purchase these capital resources from banks. When businesses borrow something, they receive something of value now and agree to pay it back over time.

✓ Stop and Check

Talk Discuss with a partner the difference between human resources and capital resources. Why are both needed to create products?

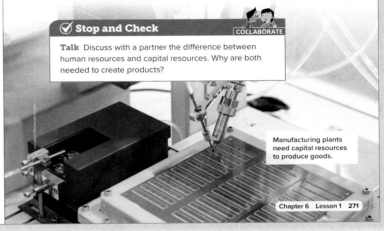
Manufacturing plants need capital resources to produce goods.

RESEARCH COMPANION, pp. 270–271

Background Information

Capital Resources Capital resources are not just machines or tools. Any item that a company uses to make or sell its goods or services is considered a capital resource. These include buildings, equipment such as computers and delivery trucks, and basic supplies such as shipping boxes.

Social Emotional Learning

Relationship Skills

Teamwork To succeed in the workplace, teamwork skills are vital. Read aloud the first paragraph on p. 271 and point out how different workers operate as a team to get milk from the farm to the grocery. Ask students to think of similar examples with other products, such as baked goods, clothing, or automobiles.

How Businesses Use Resources

1 Inspect Have students read pp. 270–271 and define capital resources.

2 Find Evidence Use the questions below to check comprehension.

Assess Do human resources provide goods or services? (They provide both. Some workers make goods to be sold and other workers provide services to customers.) **DOK 3**

Summarize What are the different types of resources used by businesses and how would you describe them? (natural resources: items grown or available in nature; human resources: people who make goods and services; capital resources: tools and machines that people use to create goods and services) **DOK 2**

3 Make Connections

Draw Conclusions What do you think is the best way for a person to improve their human capital? (getting an education) **DOK 3**

✓ Stop and Check

Talk (Answers will vary, but students should recognize that human resources are needed to run machines and use tools. The machines and tools are needed to create products.)

Understanding Language

The word *wait* may be familiar to students as a verb that means "to stay in a place until something happens" Point out the phrase *waiting on tables* in the text and explain that the phrase means "to serve food or drinks to a customer in a restaurant."

A Day in the Life: A Restaurant Owner

1 Inspect Have students read pp. 272–273 and tell what this selection is about.

2 Find Evidence Use the questions below to check comprehension.

Categorize What capital resources does Camilla use? (lights, oven, mixer) **DOK 2**

Draw Conclusions Why do you think people love to go to Camilla's restaurant? (Answers will vary, but students might say that Camilla makes good food, gives good service, and provides what her customers want.) **DOK 3**

Summarize How does Camilla use the money she earns from her business? (She pays her workers, she pays for her capital resources, she buys more natural resources, she pays taxes, and she keeps some for herself.) **DOK 2**

3 Make Connections

Draw Conclusions What do you think is the main goal of Camilla's business? (Answers will vary, but students should recognize that Camilla's main goal is to earn money to buy the things she needs and wants.) **DOK 3**

 Stop and Check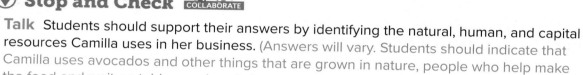

Talk Students should support their answers by identifying the natural, human, and capital resources Camilla uses in her business. (Answers will vary. Students should indicate that Camilla uses avocados and other things that are grown in nature, people who help make the food and wait on tables, and capital resources such as the machine she uses to make the guacamole.)

What Do You Think? Businesses use natural, human, and capital resources. Which are most expensive? Which are most important? (Answers will vary, but students should know that there is a cost associated with each resource. In addition, all the resources are important and are dependent on each other for success.)

 Digital Tools

Blended Learning
Students investigate curated resources and find evidence to answer the lesson question.

Interactive IMPACT
Students **Research** and find evidence using digital format texts.

A Day in the Life

A RESTAURANT OWNER

Camilla owns a restaurant. She needs resources to run it. She uses natural resources to make the food. Camilla buys avocados at a farmers' market. When she goes to the market, she is the buyer. She uses the avocados to make guacamole. In the kitchen, Camilla turns on the lights and washes her hands at a faucet. Her mixer makes it easy to make large batches of guacamole. She uses these capital resources to make meals for her customers.

Camilla helps her community when she buys goods from local farmers.

Camilla uses many resources to provide her customers with meals.

People love to go to Camilla's restaurant. When she is working, Camilla is the seller. She serves her customers food and they pay her for it. But Camilla needs help. The workers she hires are the human resources she needs. The workers provide services, such as greeting customers, waiting on tables, and washing dishes. Camilla is also an employer.

At the end of the day, the restaurant has earned money. Camilla uses some of the money to pay workers. She saves some money to buy more avocados and to pay taxes for services provided by the government. She keeps some for herself. She can spend this money on things she wants and needs. Camilla has had a busy day!

✓ Stop and Check — COLLABORATE

Talk What resources does Camilla use in her business? Identify the natural resources she uses. Then identify the human resources and capital resources she uses.

What Do You Think? Businesses use natural, human, and capital resources. Which are most expensive? Which are most important?

272 Lesson 1 How Can Communities Use Their Resources?

Chapter 6 Lesson 1 273

RESEARCH COMPANION, pp. 272–273

 ## English Learners SCAFFOLD

Use the following scaffolds to support student understanding of lesson content.

Entering and Emerging
Help students find the words natural resources, human resources, and capital resources in the text. Have students act out one way that Camilla uses each type of resource.

Developing and Expanding
Have students first find where each type of resource is mentioned in the text. Then, together with a partner, have them act out each type of resource, narrating their actions.

Bridging and Reaching
Partners should identify how Camilla uses the resources. Have students act out an interview, with one person as Camilla, and the other asking Camilla questions about those resources.

✓ Check for Success

Identify Can students identify the natural, human, and capital resources used by communities?

Differentiate

If Not, Guide students to the graphic organizer on p. 253 of their Inquiry Journals. Review with students the main ideas and details about the ways businesses in a community use local resources.

LESSON 1 REPORT

 LESSON QUESTION

How Can Communities Use Their Resources?

INQUIRY JOURNAL, pp. 254–255

Think About It

Students will review their research and list the types of businesses found in their community. They will also reflect on how those businesses use resources to help people meet their needs. Remind students to review the main ideas and details they have listed in their graphic organizers as they answer the question. Direct students back to pp. 266–273 of their Research Companion if they need more information.

Write About It

Describe Remind students to include the following elements in their response:

- Open with a topic sentence that introduces the subject of their paragraph.
- Describe a local business and the resources it depends on.
- Use chapter vocabulary as appropriate.
- Provide a concluding statement.

Discipline(s)	4	3	2	1
Economics	Student provides evidence and supporting details showing how communities and businesses use resources to meet people's needs.	Student includes some evidence and details showing how communities and businesses use resources to meet people's needs.	Student includes evidence but few supporting details showing how communities and businesses use resources to meet people's needs.	Student does not support evidence with details showing how communities and businesses use resources to meet people's needs.

Talk About It

Give Reasons Remind students to take turns discussing their opinions and state whether they agree or disagree with their partner's reasons, explaining why.

Assessment Students can check their understanding with feedback from the **Lesson Test** available online.

Connect to the Essential Question

Pull It Together Before students respond, ask students to think about the basic needs people have and how local businesses use resources to help people meet those needs.

Inquiry Project Update Remind students to turn to Inquiry Journal p. 245 for project information. If necessary, review the Project Checklist with students. At this point in the chapter, students should focus on the first two items on the checklist.

Think About It

Examine
Based on your research, what types of businesses are found in your community?

Write About It

Describe
Write a paragraph describing a business in your community that depends on the resources found there. Give reasons to support your answer.

Answers will vary, but students should describe the business and the resources it depends on.

Talk About It

Give Reasons
Talk to a classmate who chose a different business. Take turns discussing your business and reasons why you chose that business. Do you agree or disagree with your partner's reasons?

Economics Connect to the EQ

Pull It Together
How do businesses in your community use resources to help people meet their needs?

Answers will vary, but students should mention that businesses provide goods and services to help people meet their needs.

Inquiry Project Notes

INQUIRY JOURNAL, pp. 254–255

English Learners SCAFFOLD

Use the following scaffolds to support student writing.

Entering and Emerging
Use the following sentence frames to help students describe local businesses and the resources they use:

- One type of local business is _____.
- This business uses resources such as _____.

Developing and Expanding
Have students write about how local businesses use resources to meet people's needs. Ask each student to choose three local businesses and write a sentence about each, using the following sentence frames for each business:

- _____ is a local business that uses resources such as _____.
- The resources help the business to _____.

Bridging and Reaching
Have partners discuss one local business and how it uses resources to meet people's needs. Then have them collaborate to write a paragraph explaining what the business does and how it helps its customers. Remind students to include supporting details in their paragraphs to tell more about the main idea.

✔ Check for Success

Describe Can students write a paragraph describing how businesses in their community use resources to help people meet their needs?

Differentiate

If Not, Have students present their information in a format other than a paragraph, such as in a comic strip or an oral presentation.

How Do Businesses and Communities Provide Goods and Services?

Connect to the Essential Question

Tell students that this lesson provides key research into the Chapter Essential Question: **How Do People in a Community Meet Their Wants and Needs?** Explain that they will use their investigative skills to find out how businesses and people around the world make money by providing goods and services.

Lesson Objectives

- **Describe** goods and services that businesses and communities provide.
- **Explain** how and why businesses and communities provide goods and services.
- **Describe** what entrepreneurs do.
- **List** examples of businesses around the world.
- **Write** a paragraph describing a new business they would start in their community.

Make Connections!

CONNECT TO ELA

Reading **Ask and answer** questions to demonstrate understanding of a text and refer explicitly to the text as the basis for the answers.

Research **Conduct** short research projects that build knowledge about a topic.

Writing **Write** informative/explanatory texts to examine a topic and convey ideas and information clearly.

Speaking and Listening **Ask and answer** questions about information from a speaker, offering appropriate elaboration and detail.

Language **Demonstrate** command of the conventions of standard English grammar and usage when writing or speaking.

COMMUNITY CONNECTIONS

To enrich what students have learned about how businesses make money by providing services or goods, invite a chief financial officer or owner of a community business to speak to the class.

Lesson-At-A-Glance

1 ENGAGE
INQUIRY JOURNAL

▶ **Talk About It:** Picture of someone selling flowers

▶ **Analyze the Source:** The American Dream

▶ **Inquiry Tools:** Explore Making Inferences

pp. 256–261

2 INVESTIGATE
RESEARCH COMPANION

▶ **How Goods Are Made**

▶ **Providing Services**

▶ **What's In It for Businesses and Communities?**

▶ **Businesses Around the World**

pp. 274–281

3 REPORT
INQUIRY JOURNAL

▶ **Think About It**

▶ **Write About It:** Identify Goods and Services; Write about a Business You Would Start

▶ **Talk About It**

 ▶ **Connect to the Essential Question**

pp. 262–263

ASSESSMENT

▶ **Online Lesson Test**

▶ **Printable Lesson Test**

For more details, see pages T490–T491.

▶ Digital Tools

at **my.mheducation.com**

ePresentation

Teach the **Engage**, **Investigate**, and **Report** content to the whole class from **ePresentations** that launch directly from the lesson dashboard.

eBook

You can flip your instruction with the **IMPACT eBooks** found on your lesson dashboard.

Interactive IMPACT

Blend in digital content **when you want it** and **where you want it**.

Blended Learning features in the Teacher's Edition highlight ways to connect in-class work with online experiences to enhance learning.

Investigate current events with **IMPACT News**.

Explore domain-based vocabulary with **Explore Words** and **Word Play** vocabulary activities.

Go Further with IMPACT Explorer Magazine!

The **IMPACT Explorer Magazine** supports students' exploration of the Essential Question and provides additional resources for the EQ Inquiry Project.

pp. 66–79

How Do Businesses and Communities Provide Goods and Services?

Language Objectives

- Use newly acquired content and academic vocabulary to talk and write about how businesses and communities provide goods and services.
- Write a description of a business the student might start that provides goods or services.
- Understand and use compound words.

 Spanish Cognates

To support Spanish speakers, point out the cognates.

services = servicios

lesson = lección

computer = computador, computadora

consumer = consumidor

restaurant = restaurante

necessary = necesario

Introduce the Lesson

Set Purpose Explain to students that in this lesson, they will read informational texts to learn how businesses and communities provide goods and services.

Access Prior Knowledge Before presenting the lesson outcomes, read the lesson question and have students work in groups to list the types of resources they learned about in Lesson 1, such as natural, human, and capital resources. Then have them provide one example of each type of resource. Explain that in this lesson they will learn how those resources help businesses and communities provide goods and services.

Spark Curiosity Have students study the photograph on pp. 274–275 of the Research Companion. Read the caption aloud. Ask: *Are the jeans shown a type of good or service?* (good) Ask: *What three types of resources are mentioned?* (natural, human, capital)

 Have students work with a partner to brainstorm possible examples of natural, human, and capital resources that are used to make jeans. For example, a capital resource might be a sewing machine. Have two partner groups share their ideas with each other and then report their ideas to the rest of the class.

Build Meaning & Support Language

Inquiry Journal

Analyze the Source (pages 258–259) Unlock the Primary Source. Most students may know the word *dream* as it refers to images during sleep. Point out that in this context it means "a hope for the future." Note that the comparatives *richer* and *fuller* have literal and figurative meanings. A person can be rich with money but also rich with life experiences. A full life could be a busy life or a content, satisfied life. The phrase *according to ability or achievement* means that what a person gets from life compares to the amount of talent, work, and effort the person puts into it.

Inquiry Tools (pages 260–261) Tell students they will explore **Making Inferences** as they learn how businesses and communities provide goods and services. Explain that in the graphic organizer on p. 261 they will write information from the text and their own knowledge in the left column. Using this information, they will write what they think the text means. Work through an example together. When students have completed their graphic organizer, have them discuss their ideas in a group.

Research Companion

How Goods Are Made (pages 274–275) Explain that the word *goods* refers to physical things. The adjectives *good* and *bad* are not related to this word. Ask: *What kind of goods do we see in the picture?* (blue jeans) Read aloud the second sentence on p. 274. Explain that *make money* is a figurative phrase that means "earn money." People are not physically making bills and coins. Read the last paragraph. Ask: *What are examples of capital resources for making jeans?* (machines, tools, factory building)

Providing Services (pages 276–277) Read the first three sentences on p. 276. Explain that the word *consumers* comes from the word *consume*. *Consume* means "to eat or use up" something. Consumers are using goods and services. Ask: *What are examples of goods and services that consumers use?* (teaching skills, restaurant services, transportation, health care, haircuts, police and fire protection, utilities) Read the main paragraph on p. 277. Discuss the meaning of the word *profit*. Ask: *What is profit?* (money made by a business after costs are paid)

What's In It for Businesses and Communities? (pages 278–279) Read the section title. Explain that the phrase *what's in it* means "how does someone benefit." In this section we learn how businesses and communities benefit. Explain that a tax is money charged by the government to pay for services. Ask: *What are examples of how taxes are used?* (police and fire departments)

Businesses Around the World (pages 280–281) Read the first paragraph on p. 280. Explain that the word *exist* means "are." Point out that *to run a business* means "to lead a business." The physical activity of running is not involved. Read the last paragraph on p. 280. Explain that *meet the demand* means "complete, satisfy, or fulfill." Read the paragraph on p. 281. Explain that *anywhere* means "in every possible place." Ask: *What two words make the word* anywhere? (any, where)

Inquiry Journal

Report Your Findings (pages 262–263) Ask students to think about what they read and what they know about their own community. Based on this information, what goods do they think their community would use? Have them complete pp. 262–263.

Language Forms & Conventions

Compound Words Remind students that compound words are two words put together to form one word. Display the chart. Say: *The word* railroad *is made from two words*, rail *and* road. Provide an example of a sentence that uses the word *railroad*.

Compound Word	Part 1	Part 2
railroad	rail	road
airplane		
website		
online		
something		
sometimes		

 Have students complete the chart. Have pairs of students work together to write a sentence using each word.

Cross-Cultural Connection

Chocolate was a good produced and used by people on the west coast of Mexico as early as 1900 B.C. Chocolate is made from cocoa beans. Today, two-thirds of the world's cocoa production occurs in West Africa. Due to trade, what was once a food unique to Central America is now produced and enjoyed throughout the world.

Leveled Support

Entering & Emerging
Provide sentence frames:
A type of goods is _____.
A type of service in my community is _____.

Developing & Expanding
As small groups read, have them list the goods and services mentioned in the text.

Bridging & Reaching
Have partners write a short description of the goods and services provided by their community and another of the goods and services provided by businesses.

Language Transfer

Sometimes a compound word does not reflect the meanings of the separate words from which they are made. For example, a butterfly is not a fly made of butter. Explain that the meanings of these types of compound words must be memorized.

LESSON 2 ENGAGE

How Do Businesses and Communities Provide Goods and Services?

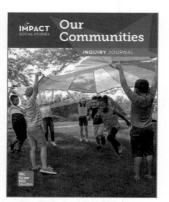

**INQUIRY JOURNAL,
pp. 256–257**

Bellringer

Prompt students to retrieve information from the previous lesson. Say: *You learned that businesses use resources to make goods and provide services. Identify the three main categories of resources and an example of each.* (natural resources: food, lumber, energy sources; human resources: people, various types of workers; capital resources: tools and machines used to make products)

Lesson Outcomes

Discuss the lesson questions and lesson outcomes with students.

- Confirm that students understand the terms *goods* and *services*. Have volunteers provide definitions and examples for each term.
- Explain that in the past, most businesses made money by selling goods to local communities, but that today many businesses sell their goods all over the world.

Talk About It

Have students study the photograph, read the caption, and answer the questions. Explain that the image illustrates the most common way people meet their needs—the buying and selling of goods and services. Provide sentence frames to help students connect this photograph to what they know about resources.

- The _____ are capital resources. (Computer, cash register, store counters)
- The _____ is a human resource. (Flower salesperson)
- The _____ are natural resources. (Flowers, soil)

 Collaborative Conversations

Ask and Answer Questions Encourage students to ask and answer questions as they discuss the concept. Remind them to:

- ask questions to clarify ideas or comments they do not understand.
- wait a few seconds after asking a question to give others a chance to think before responding.
- answer questions thoughtfully with complete ideas, not one-word answers.

Lesson Outcomes

What Am I Learning?
In this lesson, you will use your investigative skills to find out how businesses and communities provide goods and services.

Why Am I Learning It?
Reading and talking about how businesses and communities provide goods and services will help you better understand where the goods and services in your own life come from.

How Will I Know That I Learned It?
You will be able to write a paragraph explaining what goods and services you would imagine providing to your community in a successful business.

Talk About It COLLABORATE

Look closely at the photo. What are these people doing? What kind of business is this? How can you tell?

Workers in a business sell goods and services.

256 Lesson 2 How Do Businesses and Communities Provide Goods and Services?

Chapter 6 Lesson 2 257

INQUIRY JOURNAL, pp. 256–257

 English Learners SCAFFOLD

Use the following scaffolds to support student understanding of lesson outcomes.

Entering and Emerging

Read the photo caption and review the meaning of *goods* and *services*. Provide sentence frames to help students describe what is happening in the photograph.

- I see _____ in the photograph.
- People are buying _____.
- The business in the photograph is providing _____ for the community.

Developing and Expanding

Have small groups work together to read the caption and answer the Talk About It questions. Ask: *Is this business providing goods or a service? Could this business be providing both goods and services?*

Bridging and Reaching

Have partners talk about what is happening in the photograph. Then have them write a short story about the people in the photo, what they might be thinking or saying, and what the occasion might be.

 Social Emotional Learning

Self-Regulation

Self-Motivation The ability to motivate oneself is an important job skill. Explain that one must be motivated to show up to work on time, dressed appropriately, and ready to do the job. Students can learn how to be self-motivated. Encourage them to practice completing tasks without reminders.

▶ **Digital Tools**

Blended Learning

Students engage with the lesson question and discussion prompts.

Interactive IMPACT

Discuss the **Lesson Question** and **Talk About It.**

The American Dream

1 Inspect

Read the article "The American Dream" and the Primary Source quote.

Underline examples of success in the article.

Circle words in the quote you do not know.

My Notes

_____
_____
_____
_____
_____
_____
_____
_____
_____
_____

Many people want the "American Dream." They want to have the chance to succeed—to get a good job, own a home, or run their own business. The economy of the United States is based on the success of its citizens. People must have jobs and earn money in a successful economy. Businesses create jobs. They hire people to make and sell their goods and services.

> **PRIMARY SOURCE**

In Their Words... James Truslow Adams

"The American Dream is that dream of a land in which life should be better and richer and fuller for everyone, with opportunity for each according to ability or achievement."

—James Truslow Adams, *The Epic of America*

All the workers in a business help the business succeed.

Workers are important to any business. A business cannot operate without people doing their jobs. A good business will have many different kinds of workers. They may have different skills. Some workers will make the goods. Others will provide a service. When people work together, it makes the business a better place to work. The work they do allows the business to earn money. This way, both the workers and the business are successful. Success gives people the opportunity to improve their lives.

2 Find Evidence

Reread the quote. Who does the historian James Truslow Adams think should benefit from the American Dream?

Underline the three words describing what life should be.

Circle the words describing what opportunity should be based on.

3 Make Connections

Talk Discuss with a partner different ways in which a worker's ability and achievement help the worker and the business succeed.

258 Lesson 2 How Do Businesses and Communities Provide Goods and Services?

Chapter 6 Lesson 2 259

INQUIRY JOURNAL, pp. 258–259

Analyze the Source

Background Information
James Truslow Adams, 1878–1949, was a businessman who became an author. He created the term "The American Dream" in his book *The Epic of America*, published in 1931.

1 Inspect

Read Have students read the entire text, including the Primary Source, and describe what they think it is about. Remind them to circle words that are unfamiliar.

- Underline examples of success in the article. (opportunities for people and businesses to earn money and for people to improve their lives)

2 Find Evidence

Reread Have students reread the Primary Source.

Have students underline three words describing what life should be. (better, richer, fuller) Then ask students to circle words describing what opportunity should be based on. (ability or achievement)

3 Make Connections

Talk Have students discuss with a partner why a business depends on workers in order to be successful. (Answers will vary, but students should realize that the workers make the goods and/or provide the services. Workers' abilities and achievements can make the business more successful.)

 Spotlight on Vocabulary

Content Vocabulary
ability: talent, skill, or training in a task

achievement: a successfully completed task

Point out that Adams links these words by *or*, not *and*. Discuss the difference.

▶ Digital Tools

Blended Learning
Students read informational texts and analyze primary sources.

Interactive IMPACT

Have students practice and apply the strategy of close reading as they analyze text.

Explore Making Inferences

When you read, you often make inferences about the text. An **inference** is a decision you make about the meaning of the text. To make an inference, you can do the following.

1. **Read the text once all the way through.**
   This will help you understand what the text is about.

2. **Think about what you read.**
   An author may not always tell you everything. What questions do you have?

3. **Think about what you already know about this topic.**

4. **Make a decision about the text.**
   Base your decision on what you know and what you read.

Based on the text you read, work with your class to complete the chart below.

Text Clues and What I Already Know	Inferences
James Truslow Adams says that the American Dream is of a better life for everyone according to ability or achievement. I know: Answers will vary, but students should connect what Adams says to the idea that people need to work to achieve their dreams.	Adams means that: Answers will vary, but students should understand that Adams means that the American Dream is when everyone has the opportunity to work for a fuller, richer life.

Investigate!

Read pages 274–281 in your Research Companion. Use your investigative skills to make inferences about how businesses and communities provide goods and services. This chart will help you organize your notes.

Text Clues and What I Already Know	Inferences
Manufacturing goods uses capital resources and human resources. I know: Answers will vary, but students may know that capital resources and human resources cost the manufacturer money.	This means that: The money I pay for blue jeans includes the cost of the capital resources and human resources just to make the blue jeans before they even get to the store.
Services have value to the people who use them. I know: Answers will vary, but students may know that service workers have some level of training or education to help them do their job.	This means that: Service workers are as valuable to the community as manufacturing workers.
Communities need strong, healthy businesses to survive. I know: Answers will vary, but students may know of local businesses and their support for community activities such as sports teams.	This means that: Shopping in my community helps my community.

INQUIRY JOURNAL, pp. 260–261

Inquiry Tools

Explore Making Inferencs

Read Review with students the meaning of the word *inference*. Explain that an inference is a decision about the text which is based on evidence and personal knowledge. Then have students read the step-by-step instructions for how to make inferences.

Guided Practice Have students review the text on pp. 258–259. Then work with them to complete the graphic organizer. Explain that they will use a similar graphic organizer to organize their independent research.

Check Understanding Confirm student understanding of the inquiry skill, Explore Making Inferences. If students cannot make reasonable inferences about the text, review the steps on p. 260.

Investigate!

Have students read pp. 274–281 in the Research Companion. Tell them the information will help them answer the lesson question *How Do Businesses and Communities Provide Goods and Services?*

Take Notes Tell students that they will take notes in the graphic organizer on p. 261 of the Inquiry Journal. Remind them that taking notes will help them understand and remember the information they learn.

Explain to students the importance of paraphrasing, or using their own words, when they take notes. This will help them identify what they already know, so they can make inferences.

Spotlight on Language

Understanding Language

Help students define the words *American* and *dream*. Point out that when the words are used together, their meaning changes to a specific idea of being able to improve one's life through skill or hard work.

LESSON QUESTION

How Do Businesses and Communities Provide Goods and Services?

How Goods Are Made

RESEARCH COMPANION, pp. 274–275

Background Information

Manufacturing According to the U.S. Census Bureau, California's manufacturing industry is the largest in the nation, with over one million employees statewide. These employees made products worth a little over $493 billion in 2016. Texas has the second largest manufacturing industry (725,255 employees, $523 billion in value in 2016), followed by Ohio, Michigan, Illinois, and Pennsylvania.

Service Industry The U.S. Census Bureau also tracks data on eleven sectors of the service industry in the United States. The sectors, by highest to lowest revenue for 2015, are finance and insurance; health care and social assistance; professional, scientific, and technical services; information; transportation and warehousing; real estate, rental and leasing; admin and support, waste management and remediation services; other services; utilities; art, entertainment, and recreation; and educational services.

1 Inspect Have students read pp. 274–275 and describe what a manufacturing business does.

2 Find Evidence Use the questions below to check comprehension. Remind students to support their answers with text evidence.

Make Observations Look at the photograph of the blue jeans factory. What are some examples of the factory's use of natural resources, capital resources, and human resources? (natural resources: cotton cloth; capital resources: factory building, equipment; human resources: worker) **DOK 2**

3 Make Connections

Hypothesize Apart from the goods listed in the text, what goods do you think are manufactured in a factory? (Answers will vary but may include goods such as automobiles, sports equipment, books, canned foods, and tools.) **DOK 3**

Infer Based on what you know from the picture, what kinds of skills would this worker need? (Answers will vary, but students may identify computer skills, reading, matching, and looking for details.) **DOK 3**

Lesson 2
How Do Businesses and Communities Provide Goods and Services?

How Goods Are Made

You have learned that businesses and communities provide many goods and services. In this lesson, you will look more closely at how businesses make money.

Some businesses manufacture goods. To *manufacture* means to make goods using machinery. Factories manufacture computers, clothes, airplane parts, electronics, and many other things.

Let's look at how a company manufactures blue jeans. The company uses cotton to make cloth. Cotton is a natural resource. First, the company uses machines and other tools to turn the cloth into blue jeans. Machines and tools are capital resources. The factory building is also a capital resource. People design the blue jeans and run the machines that make them. These human resources are also necessary to make blue jeans.

It takes natural resources, capital resources, and human resources to make a pair of blue jeans.

274 Lesson 2 How Do Businesses and Communities Provide Goods and Services?

Chapter 6 Lesson 2 275

RESEARCH COMPANION, pp. 274–275

English Learners SCAFFOLD

Use the following scaffolds to support student understanding of lesson content.

Entering and Emerging

Guide students to understand how blue jeans are manufactured. Provide sentence frames to help students as needed:

- The blue jean business needs natural resources, such as _____.
- It also needs capital resources, such as _____.
- People needed to help run the business are called _____ resources.

Developing and Expanding

Help small groups describe what it means to manufacture goods. Ask: *What kinds of goods do manufacturers make? What are some examples of natural resources manufacturers need? What capital resources are needed to make goods? Why does the manufacturing process need human resources? What can you infer about how the manufacturer will pay for the needed resources?*

Bridging and Reaching

Have partners discuss what it means to manufacture something. Then have them choose a type of good (cell phone, shoes, hat, water bottle, etc.) and write three or four sentences describing what the process might be for manufacturing it. Ask: *What natural resources are needed? What capital resources are needed? What human resources are needed? What can you infer about how the cost of these resources will affect the price of the item?*

 Digital Tools

Blended Learning

Flip the research approach and find evidence in a digital format.

eBook

Students investigate using their **Research Companion** and **IMPACT Explorer Magazine eBooks** to find evidence.

Providing Services

You have read that businesses sell goods. Businesses also provide many kinds of services. The people who buy these goods and services are called consumers. Some businesses have people who teach different skills, such as how to dance or ride a horse. Workers at a restaurant provide a service, too. When you go out to dinner, servers take your order, bring your food, and clear the table. Transportation is another service. A bus driver takes you from one place to another. Doctors and nurses take care of your health. A barber or hair stylist provides a service when he or she gives you a haircut. When people pay for these services, the businesses earn money.

Communities also provide services. Some services are paid for through tax money. Police and fire protection are community services. Utilities such as water, sewers, and trash collection are often provided by the community. The city or county government sets a price for these services.

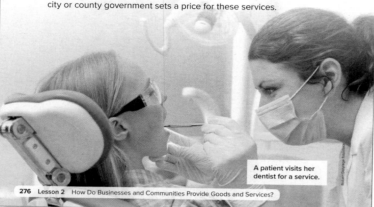

A patient visits her dentist for a service.

Perspectives

Some businesses like to sell their services online. It does not cost much to get started. It is easy to set up a website. Consumers can visit the website anytime, day or night. And the business can sell its services to people all over the country and around the world.

Some businesses find it hard to sell their services online. There may be other businesses selling the same service. Also, some consumers do not like to buy services online. This can make it harder for a business to earn a profit.

Businesses and individuals produce goods and services to make money. They set a price that covers how much they spend to provide the product. Then they charge a little more to make a profit. Profit is the amount of money left after costs are paid. This profit allows people to grow their businesses.

A chef at his restaurant

✓ Stop and Check

Talk What is a service? With a partner, list examples of service businesses in your community.

RESEARCH COMPANION, pp. 276–277

Providing Services

1 Inspect Have students read pp. 276–277 and explain how people selling services make a profit.

2 Find Evidence Use the questions below to check comprehension.

Infer What is a service? (work provided to a customer; work that does not involve an actual product but meets the needs of a buyer) **DOK 2**

Draw Conclusions Why do different services, such as restaurants, dentists, and hair stylists, cost different amounts of money? (The amount businesses charge includes the cost of the resources they need to supply the service—capital and human resources. A person in a profession that requires more training can demand a higher wage, and so the service can cost more.) **DOK 3**

3 Make Connections

Compare How is a service different from a good? (A service does not provide an actual product. A good is a product.) **DOK 2**

✓ Stop and Check

Talk Have partners discuss what a service is and list examples of service businesses in their community. (A service is work that somebody does for you. Students' examples will vary but may include dentists, lawyers, repair shops, tourism, cleaning services, car washes, babysitting, plumbers, electricians, and so forth.)

Spotlight on Vocabulary

Content Vocabulary

Compare the words *consume* and *consumer*. *Consume* means "to eat or use up," and a *consumer* is the person who eats or uses up something. Apply these words to *goods* and *services*. Explain that with *services*, a person pays for *using up* a portion of the seller's time or using the person's skill.

▶ Digital Tools

Blended Learning

Students investigate curated resources and find evidence to answer the lesson question.

Interactive IMPACT

Students choose from print or digital **Inquiry Tools** to take notes.

What's In It for Businesses and Communities?

Why do businesses and communities provide goods and services? Communities provide some services because it does not work well to have several providers. For example, if your house is on fire, you don't want to have to decide which fire department to use! Police and fire departments are run by tax money. They do not make a profit.

Most businesses provide goods and services for profit. Business costs include wages to employees and rent for the building. Other costs are utilities, advertising, and taxes. Anything left after these are paid is profit.

How do businesses know how much to charge for goods and services? This is based in part on the law of supply and demand. Supply is the amount of something available. Demand is how much people want it. Think about supply and demand in terms of dentists. If there are lots of dentists in town, cleaning your teeth will cost roughly the same at each office. If there are not enough dentists in town, they can charge more for their services. A dentist will also want to charge enough to cover the costs of running the business.

Stores hold sales to draw in customers.

How do businesses affect a community? Businesses provide work to people who live there. The businesses and the workers pay money for rent, utilities, and taxes. Businesses provide goods and services to consumers in the community. People who live and work in the community usually spend their money there. They buy food at the local grocery and clothes at local stores. This puts money back into the community.

Thriving local businesses make a community strong and healthy.

What happens when a new clothing store opens in a nearby community? Perhaps they sell clothing much more cheaply than the store in your community. If enough people go to the new store, the store in your town will not make any money. Without money, the store may close. The workers need to find new jobs and have less money to spend at stores in the community. These stores have less money and may begin to close. Then, people go to other communities to shop because there are fewer local stores. With less tax money in the community, the local government has less money to spend for community services. People may leave the community.

When local businesses close, the whole community suffers.

✓ Stop and Check

Think Why are businesses important to local communities?

278 Lesson 2 How Do Businesses and Communities Provide Goods and Services?

Chapter 6 Lesson 2 279

RESEARCH COMPANION, pp. 278–279

What's In It for Businesses and Communities?

1 Inspect Have students read pp. 278–279 and describe the kinds of businesses found in communities.

2 Find Evidence Use the questions below to check comprehension.

Make Inferences Why can a dentist charge more for their services in a town with not enough dentists compared to a town with a lot of dentists? (Answers may include that dentists have to compete with lower prices in towns with a lot of dentists.) **DOK 3**

Compare What are the positives of the new clothing store in a nearby community? Can they outweigh possible negatives for your community? (Answers will vary, but students may weigh possible better prices and more clothing options with the impact on local jobs.) **DOK 3**

3 Make Connections

Hypothesize How might the closure of one of your town's large grocery stores impact your community? (It might help the smaller grocery stores get more business, but employees of the closed store would have to find new work, and there would be less tax money. If the former employees transfer their shopping to another community, the local community could suffer.) **DOK 3**

✓ Stop and Check

Think (Local businesses provide goods and services, jobs, taxes, and other income.)

Social Emotional Learning

Relationship Skills

Teamwork Remind students that relationship skills are important beyond the classroom and playground. Teamwork is important to a successful business. The business and the community are a team and when they support one another, both succeed. Ask: *How do you think people practice teamwork in businesses? How do you think teamwork helps businesses?*

The word *organic* has many meanings. One meaning relates to "being made from living compounds." Chemicals are not made from living compounds. Therefore, organically grown food does not use chemical fertilizers or pesticides.

Businesses Around the World

1 Inspect   Have students read pp. 280–281 and explain what a "mom and pop" shop is.

2 Find Evidence   Use the questions below to check comprehension.

Interpret   What examples of "mom and pop" shops can you think of? (Answers will vary but could include the examples in the text and students' own ideas.) **DOK 2**

Cause and Effect   How does growing organic food help the environment? (There are no chemicals used in organic farming, so the environment is unharmed by the farms.) **DOK 2**

Hypothesize   How has the Internet changed how people run a business? (With Internet businesses, people are no longer tied to a particular location. They can work from home in whatever country they live in and sell products around the world. They can also work the hours that best fit their needs.) **DOK 3**

3 Make Connections

Compare   Besides size, how are small stores and large companies alike and different? How do they help a community in different ways? (Answers will vary, but students may say both small stories and large companies provide goods and services and work to make a profit. Students may say small stores can fit individual community needs while large companies can provide more complex goods and services such as transportation or technology.) **DOK 3**

 **Stop and Check**

Write   Have students write about what an entrepreneur is and describe what they think an entrepreneur needs to do to be successful. (Student paragraphs should define *entrepreneur* and include an opinion on what is required to succeed.)

What Do You Think?   Ask students to think of different businesses in their community, the goods and services these businesses provide, and how they think these businesses make money. (Students should demonstrate an understanding of how businesses make money or a profit, charging enough money for their goods and services to more than cover their costs.)

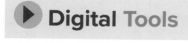 **Digital Tools**

Blended Learning
Students explore lesson content through interactive activities.

Interactive IMPACT

Use the **More to Explore**.

Businesses Around the World

Businesses exist all over the world. Everywhere you go, you will find stores, offices, restaurants, and factories. An **entrepreneur** is a person who starts and runs a business. Entrepreneurs run businesses all over the world.

Many businesses are small stores such as grocery stores and hair salons. They are sometimes called "mom and pop" shops. This is because a family started the business. There may be a local deli or grocery store on a corner near your house. In India, "mom and pop" grocery stores are common. These businesses sell fruit and vegetables to people who can walk to the store. This means that people do not have to drive to larger stores to buy food.

A "mom and pop" store in India

Some Cambodian farmers are learning to grow rice organically.

As you have already learned, rice is an important product in Cambodia. Consumers around the world are asking for organically grown rice. Organic food is grown without chemicals. Farmers in Cambodia are changing their farming methods to meet this demand. They learn how to use natural methods to protect their crop from pests and disease. Their organic rice is exported to world markets.

Where in the World?

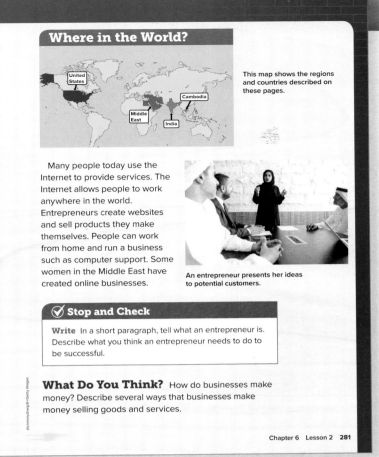
This map shows the regions and countries described on these pages.

Many people today use the Internet to provide services. The Internet allows people to work anywhere in the world. Entrepreneurs create websites and sell products they make themselves. People can work from home and run a business such as computer support. Some women in the Middle East have created online businesses.

An entrepreneur presents her ideas to potential customers.

✓ Stop and Check

Write In a short paragraph, tell what an entrepreneur is. Describe what you think an entrepreneur needs to do to be successful.

What Do You Think? How do businesses make money? Describe several ways that businesses make money selling goods and services.

RESEARCH COMPANION, pp. 280–281

English Learners SCAFFOLD

Use the following scaffolds to support student understanding of lesson content.

Entering and Emerging

Help students understand and describe "mom and pop" shops. Use sentence frames to help students as needed:

- A "mom and pop" shop is owned by _____.
- The size of a "mom and pop" shop is _____.
- Because a "mom and pop" shop is close by, a person can _____.

Developing and Expanding

Work with small groups to compare "mom and pop" shops to larger stores. Identify a "mom and pop" shop and a larger chain store that sells the same general goods. Have each group answer the following questions for one type of store: *Why do people shop at this store? How does this store help the local community? Where do the owners and employees of this store live?* Then compare the answers.

Bridging and Reaching

Have partners identify a "mom and pop" shop and a larger chain store selling the same general products. Ask them to write a paragraph answering the following questions: *What goods does each store sell? Why do people shop at each store? If the "mom and pop" shop closed, where would people shop? Who would be most affected if it closed? How would its closing affect the community?*

✓ Check for Success

Examine Can students explain how businesses and their community provide goods and services?

Differentiate

If Not, Have students review the text clues and inferences about services, goods, and businesses that they recorded in their Inquiry Journals.

LESSON QUESTION

How Do Businesses and Communities Provide Goods and Services?

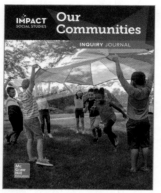

INQUIRY JOURNAL, pp. 262–263

Think About It

Remind students to review their research and describe how businesses and communities provide goods and services. Have students review the data they have collected in their graphic organizers as they answer the question. Direct students back to pp. 274–281 of their Research Companion if they need more information.

Write About It

Identify Guide students to identify goods and services and reasons why people use them.

Write and Cite Evidence Remind students to include the following elements in their responses.

- Include the type of business and specific goods and services their business would provide.
- Provide valid reasons why the business would be successful in the community.
- Use chapter vocabulary as appropriate.

Discipline(s)	4	3	2	1
Economics	Student provides evidence and details including a clear description of the start-up business; logical reasons for the success of the business.	Student includes details for some evidence including a somewhat clear description of the start-up business; some reasons for the success of the business.	Student includes evidence but few supporting details and an unclear description of the start-up business; few reasons for the success of the business.	Student does not support evidence with details and has an incomplete description of the start-up business; no logical reasons for the success of the business.

Talk About It

Explain Remind students that they should listen to and build upon their partners' ideas.

Assessment Students can check their understanding with feedback from the **Lesson Test** available online.

Connect to the Essential Question

Look at Our Community Before they respond, remind students that successful businesses help the local community. Review examples as needed.

Inquiry Project Update Remind students to turn to Inquiry Journal pp. 244–245 for project information. If necessary, review the Project Checklist with students. At this point in the chapter, students should focus on the second and third items on the checklist.

Think About It

Examine
Based on your research, how do you think businesses are able to earn money to make a profit?

Write About It

Identify
What kinds of goods or services do you think people in your community would use?

Answers will vary, but students should identify practical goods and services and reasons why people in the community would use them.

Write and Cite Evidence
Imagine that you want to start a business in your community. Describe what kind of business you would start and what kinds of goods or services you would provide. Tell why you think your imaginary business would be successful.

Answers will vary, but students should identify goods and services and practical ways to provide these to the community for profit.

Talk About It

Explain
Share your business idea with a partner. Discuss how the goods and services you and your partner identified would benefit your community.

Economics Connect to the EQ

Look at Our Community
How can successful businesses help people in a community meet their needs and wants?

Answers will vary, but students should show an understanding that successful businesses employ people within a community. This allows those people to earn money to buy the items they need and want. It also gives them opportunities to succeed in business and have a fulfilling life.

Inquiry Project Notes

262 Lesson 2 How Do Businesses and Communities Provide Goods and Services?

Chapter 6 Lesson 2 263

INQUIRY JOURNAL, pp. 262–263

English Learners SCAFFOLD

Use the following scaffolds to support student writing.

Entering and Emerging

Show students a picture of a business district, preferably in their community. Have students identify the businesses and the goods and services they provide. Provide sentence frames to help student writing.

- In my community, there are _____ and _____ businesses.
- In my community, there are no _____ businesses.
- I think my community needs a business that _____, because _____.

Developing and Expanding

Have students work in groups to identify the businesses where they, their family, and their friends usually shop. Ask: *What product or service do you wish you could find more easily in your community? What could you do to make your business successful?*

Bridging and Reaching

Have partners research a list of businesses in a nearby community (online maps/search). Guide them to ask the following questions before they begin to write: *Which businesses provide goods or services not available in my community? Would people in my community like to buy these goods and services closer to home? If I sold these goods or services in my community, how could I make my business a place where people would like to shop?*

✓ Check for Success

Describe Are students able to write about what type of business they would start in their community and why they think it would be successful?

Differentiate

If Not, Have two students work together as business partners and brainstorm businesses that they would like to start. Have them choose one and then create a poster to advertise their new business.

LESSON QUESTION

How Do People Get What They Want and Need?

Connect to the Essential Question

Tell students that this lesson provides key research into the Chapter Essential Question: *How Do People in a Community Meet Their Wants and Needs?* Explain that they will learn about markets and the buying and selling of goods. They will also analyze how goods are made in one part of the world and then sold in another part.

Lesson Objectives

- **Explain** the multiple meanings of *market*.
- **Describe** how trade helps people get what they need.
- **Tell** how importing and exporting helps companies and communities.
- **Detail** the sequence of events that leads to profit.
- **Write** a story describing how an imported item in the classroom came to be there.

Make Connections!

CONNECT TO ELA

Reading **Use** language that pertains to time, sequence, and cause/effect to describe the relationship between a series of historical events, scientific ideas or concepts, or steps in a technical procedure in a text.

Research **Recall** information from experiences or gather information from print and digital sources; take brief notes on sources and sort evidence into provided categories.

Writing **Craft** narratives to develop real or imagined experiences or events using effective technique, descriptive details, and clear event sequences.

Speaking and Listening **Engage** effectively in a range of collaborative discussions with diverse partners on grade 3 topics and texts, building on others' ideas and expressing students' own ideas clearly.

COMMUNITY CONNECTIONS

To enrich what students have learned about scarcity, trade, and how goods move around the globe, invite a community retail business owner to speak to the class about how the business obtains the goods it sells.

Lesson-At-A-Glance

1 ENGAGE
INQUIRY JOURNAL

pp. 264–269

- **Talk About It:** Photograph of an outdoor market
- **Analyze the Source:** What Do We Mean When We Say *Market?*
- **Inquiry Tools:** Explore Sequence

2 INVESTIGATE
RESEARCH COMPANION

pp. 282–287

- **What Happens When Nothing Is Available?**
- **Where Goods Come From**
- **Making Money From Imports**
- **Where Does Your T-Shirt Come From?**

3 REPORT
INQUIRY JOURNAL

pp. 270–271

- **Think About It**
- **Write About It:** Describe; Write a Story
- **Talk About It**
- **Connect to the Essential Question**

ASSESSMENT

- **Online Lesson Test**
- **Printable Lesson Test**

For more details, see pages T490–T491.

Digital Tools

at **my.mheducation.com**

ePresentation

Teach the Engage, Investigate, and Report content to the whole class from **ePresentations** that launch directly from the lesson dashboard.

eBook

You can flip your instruction with the **IMPACT eBooks** found on your lesson dashboard.

Interactive IMPACT

Blend in digital content **when you want it** and **where you want it**.

Blended Learning features in the Teacher's Edition highlight ways to connect in-class work with online experiences to enhance learning.

Investigate current events with **IMPACT News**.

Explore domain-based vocabulary with **Explore Words** and **Word Play** vocabulary activities.

pp. 66–79

Go Further with IMPACT Explorer Magazine!

The **IMPACT Explorer Magazine** supports students' exploration of the Essential Question and provides additional resources for the EQ Inquiry Project.

 LESSON QUESTION

How Do People Get What They Want and Need?

Language Objectives

- Use newly acquired content and academic vocabulary to discuss how people get what they want and need.
- Write a story about how an item from another country made it into the classroom.
- Understand and use key sequencing words.

 Spanish Cognates

To support Spanish speakers, point out the cognates.

fruit = fruta

price = precio

reason = razón

car = carro (in some countries)

producer = productor

port = puerto

Introduce the Lesson

Set Purpose Explain to students that in this lesson, they will read informational texts to learn how people get what they want and need.

Access Prior Knowledge Have students work in groups to list types of transportation they are familiar with or have learned about in earlier lessons. Then have groups share their lists as you create a combined class list. Explain that in this lesson, students will learn how transportation helps people get what they want and need.

Spark Curiosity Have students study the photograph on pp. 282–283 of the Research Companion. Read the caption aloud. Ask: *Why do you think the shelves are empty?* (Answers will vary but may include high demand, lack of transportation, or a natural disaster.)

Have students work with a partner to brainstorm possible reasons that goods may be difficult to get. Have two pairs share their ideas with each other, then report their group's ideas to the class.

Build Meaning & Support Language

Inquiry Journal

Analyze the Source (pages 266–267) Unpack the sentences: *A market is not always a physical place. It can also be an imaginary area where trade happens.* Explain that a market may be a place like a grocery store or a mall. Say: *People buy and sell things at a market. However, a market does not always have a building. For example, people can buy and sell goods online.* Explain that all markets involve buying and selling things, but they don't always happen in a physical location.

Inquiry Tools (pages 268–269) Tell students they will explore **Sequence** as they learn how people get what they want and need. Explain that the graphic organizer on p. 268 will help them practice recording information in order or sequence as they read. Check that students understand the words *First, Next,* and *Last.*

Research Companion

What Happens When Nothing Is Available? (pages 282–283) Explain that the word *scarce* means "few" or "not many." Sometimes a type of good is easy to get in one region but scarce in another. Explain that the word *trade* means "exchange." Trade helps people get goods that may not exist in their region. Compare this to a familiar situation such as trading cards. In a market, trade happens when one person sells and another buys. Read the last paragraph. Ask: *What is an example of local trade?* (artist sells painting in the same town) *Global trade?* (person buys an electronic device made in another country)

Where Goods Come From (pages 284–285) Help students with the meanings of the words *export* and *import* by looking at prefixes. Say: *The prefix im- sounds like* in. On the board, write: *When you import, you bring goods into the country*. Say: *The prefix ex- has the same beginning as the word* exit, *which is the way out of a building*. On the board, write: *When you export, you move goods out of the country*. Ask: *What are examples of U.S. imports?* (oil, electronic parts, cars, clothing) *Exports?* (soybeans) Read the second paragraph on p. 285. Discuss ways that imports and exports move. Have students compare the examples with the lists they generated in the Access Prior Knowledge activity.

Making Money From Imports / Where Does Your T-Shirt Come From? (pages 286–287) In Lesson 2, students looked at the phrases *make money* and *profit*. Review their meaning if needed. Have students study the infographic. Point out that in this graphic, the pictures are numbered, and there are arrows to show the order in which things happened. Ask: *What happens first?* (Step 1) *What happens next?* (Steps 2–5) *What happens last?* (Step 6)

Inquiry Journal

Report Your Findings (pages 270–271) Review with students the meaning of *manufactured* ("made"). Ask students to look for items in the classroom that were manufactured in another country and exported to the United States. Remind them to think about the sequence of events that brought these items to the classroom.

Language Forms & Conventions

Sequencing Vocabulary Explain that when you write more than one sentence about events, words that mark the order of those events are helpful to make your writing clear. The beginning, middle, and end of your writing will use different words to mark the order in which events occur. The chart has examples of words you may want to use.

Beginning	Middle	End
first	next, then	last

 Have students work in pairs to write short sentences to describe the process pictured on p. 287 of the Research Companion. For example: *First, cotton is grown. Next, it is sent to Indonesia to make yarn. Then . . . . Last . . . .*

Cross-Cultural Connection

Honduras is the second poorest country in Central America. For much of its history, the country's economy has depended on the exports of bananas and coffee. Lately, though, Honduras also exports apparel, or clothing, and is the largest supplier of wire harnesses to the U.S. automobile industry. Ask: *How does more industry and exports help people who are poor?*

Leveled Support

Entering & Emerging
Provide sentence frames: *First, _____ is made. Then, it travels by _____. Last, it arrives at _____.*

Developing & Expanding
Have small groups make a list of the steps in the process of moving goods from one country to another.

Bridging & Reaching
Have partners choose an item that might come from another country to the United States and write a short description of the process.

Language Transfer

English learners will master simple sentence structure before they are able to combine ideas into compound or complex sentences. Words that mark sequence will help them describe chronological events, and conjunctions will help them link ideas. Provide students with words that help them expand their sequencing vocabulary, such as *in/at the beginning, later,* and *finally*. Then demonstrate the use of conjunctions that help combine ideas, such as *and, but, however, also,* and *while*.

LESSON QUESTION

How Do People Get What They Want and Need?

INQUIRY JOURNAL, pp. 264–265

Bellringer

Say: *In the previous lesson, you learned about the goods and services your community provides. The main goal of businesses is to sell their goods and services to make money. Think about the clothes you are wearing. How many businesses earned money from these purchases? Think about how your clothes were made. Now how many businesses do you think earned money? Did your answer change? Why?* (Answers will vary, but students may initially suggest that one or two stores made money. When they think again, they may realize that several more businesses made money if they think about materials used, the manufacturing process, and the transportation and retail businesses involved.)

Lesson Outcomes

Discuss the lesson question and lesson outcomes with students.

- Make sure students understand the terms *local* and *global*. Have volunteers provide definitions.

- To relate *local* and *global* to the lesson context, explain that in the past, most businesses made money by selling goods to local communities. However, today many businesses sell their goods all over the world.

Talk About It

Have students study the photograph. Explain that the image shows a common way people meet their needs—the buying and selling of goods. Provide sentence frames to help students talk about the photograph.

- The photograph shows _____ .
- People are buying _____ .
- People are selling _____ .

 ## Collaborative Conversations

Share Ideas As students engage in partner, small-group, and whole-class discussions, encourage them to:
- take turns describing their ideas with supporting details.
- tell a story or share an experience that supports their reasoning.
- listen to and provide feedback on the ideas of others.

How Do People Get What They Want and Need?

Lesson Outcomes

What Am I Learning?
In this lesson, you will use your investigative skills to learn how markets and trade provide people with what they want and need.

Why Am I Learning It?
Reading and talking about markets and trade will help you understand how the items in your life got to you from other places.

How Will I Know That I Learned It?
You will be able to write a story telling how an item in your classroom came to be there.

Talk About It COLLABORATE

Look closely at the picture. Where are these people? What do you think they are doing?

264 Lesson 3 How Do People Get What They Want and Need?

Buyers and sellers at a marketplace

INQUIRY JOURNAL, pp. 264–265

EL English Learners SCAFFOLD

Use the following scaffolds to support student understanding of lesson outcomes.

Entering and Emerging

Clarify the meanings of *buyer* and *seller*. Write both words on the board. Have students describe items in the photograph that people are buying or selling. Provide sentence frames:

- When people need something, they give money to a _____.
- When people need to earn money, they receive money from a _____.

Developing and Expanding

Provide a list of words: *buying, selling, goods, trade, money, market.* Have small groups discuss the photograph. Ask questions to introduce the words in context: *What are people buying in the market? What are people selling? What will the buyers and sellers trade?* (goods and money)

Bridging and Reaching

Have student pairs take on the role of one of the sellers pictured in the photograph. Encourage students to describe what he or she is selling, where the goods came from, how the goods made it to the marketplace, and what the seller is thinking or hoping.

Social Emotional Learning

Self-Regulation

Set Goals Encourage students to create their own benchmarks for success so they become personally invested in their own learning experience. Ask students to make a list of what they hope to learn by the end of the lesson and revisit their lists later to see whether their expectations were met.

 Digital Tools

Blended Learning

Students engage with the lesson question and discussion prompts.

ePresentation

Discuss the **Lesson Question** and **Talk About It.**

What Do We Mean When We Say Market?

Read the title. What do you think this text will be about?

Circle words you do not know.

Underline clues that tell you:
• **What** is a market?
• **What** kinds of markets are there?
• **Why** are markets helpful?

My Notes

_____
_____
_____
_____
_____
_____
_____
_____
_____
_____
_____

A market is a place where things are bought and sold. You may have visited an outdoor farmers' market before. Local growers bring fresh fruits and vegetables to the market to sell. People from the community come to the market to buy these goods.

A market can also be a store inside a building. The store may have some local things for sale, but many of the items came from other places. Canned and jarred foods may have come from other parts of the United States. Toys and electronics most likely came from other countries.

A market is not always a physical place. It can also be an imaginary area where trade happens. For example, the American housing market is not an actual place. It refers to the buying and selling of all houses in America.

A market can be a physical place where people buy fruits and vegetables.

The stock market is another example of a market that's not an actual place. When people buy stocks, they buy a small ownership in a company. Companies sell stocks to raise money.

All markets help people get the things they want or need. First, sellers bring goods or services to a market, which may be a real place or an imaginary one. Then, they sell their goods or services. Next, the sellers receive money from the buyers. Finally, the sellers become buyers. They use the money they received to buy different goods.

Stock prices often go up and down throughout the day.

2 Find Evidence

Reread How can someone be both a buyer and a seller?

Draw a box around the sentences that provide the answer.

3 Make Connections

Talk Look at the photograph on page 265. What type of market does it show? How do you know?

INQUIRY JOURNAL, pp. 266–267

Analyze the Source

1 Inspect

Read Have students read the title first. Ask them to share their ideas of what the text will be about. Then have them read the text, circling any words they do not know.

• Underline clues that tell you what a market is, what kinds of markets there are, and why markets are helpful. (a place where things are bought and sold; markets include stores, a place or area where trade happens; people get what they want or need)

2 Find Evidence

Reread Have students reread the text, thinking about how someone can be both a buyer and a seller.

Draw Tell students to draw a box around the sentences that provide the answer. (Finally, the sellers become buyers. They use the money they received to buy different goods.)

3 Make Connections

Talk Have students talk with a partner about the photograph on Inquiry Journal pp. 264–265. Remind them to think about the kinds of markets they read about in the text. (Answers will vary but should relate to an outdoor produce market.)

Spotlight on Language

Understanding Language

imaginary: exists in the mind only

actual: existing in the world

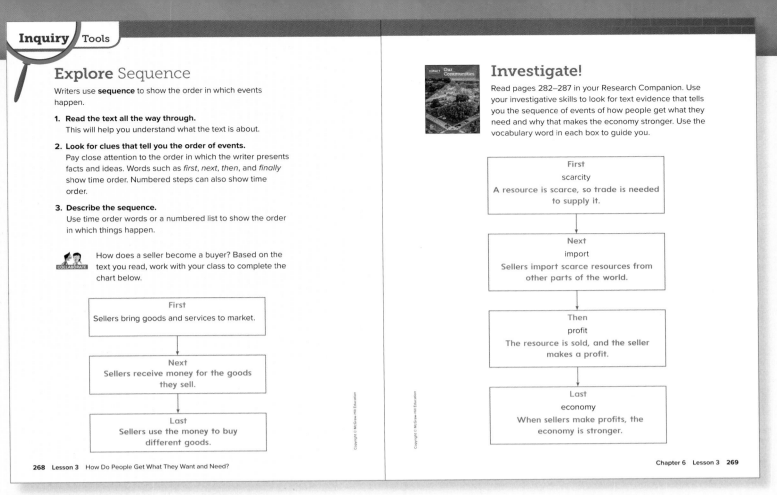

Inquiry Tools

Explore Sequence

Read Have students read the step-by-step instructions about how to analyze sequence in a text. Tell students that as they read, they should pay attention to words and phrases that show time order, or the order in which events happen.

Guide Practice Have students review the text on pp. 266–267. Then work with them to complete the graphic organizer. Explain that they will use a similar graphic organizer to organize their independent research.

Check Understanding Confirm student understanding of the inquiry skill, Explore Sequence. If students cannot identify the sequence of events, review the steps on p. 268.

Investigate!

Have students read pp. 282–287 in the Research Companion. Tell them the information will help them answer the lesson question *How Do People Get What They Want and Need?*

Take Notes Tell students that they should use the chart on p. 269 of the Inquiry Journal to keep track of the sequence of events that lead to a stronger economy. These notes will help students understand the information they have read and will be helpful when they write about how and why items made in other parts of the world can be found in their classroom.

 Spotlight on Content

Sequence Chart

Have students work in pairs or small groups to fill in a chart like the one on Inquiry Journal p. 269 to describe a simple sequence of events, such as how they got to school.

 **Digital Tools**

Blended Learning

Students prepare for the lesson investigation with step-by-step instructions about how to identify sequence.

ePresentation

Use the **Inquiry Tools** to model how to complete the lesson graphic organizer.

LESSON 3 INVESTIGATE

LESSON QUESTION

How Do People Get What They Want and Need?

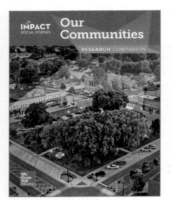

RESEARCH COMPANION, pp. 282–283

Background Information

Global Manufacturing The T-shirt example on p. 287 in the Research Companion is not unusual. In today's global economy, many products we use every day are manufactured in stages. Employees across the globe play roles in the creation of cars, computers, cell phones, clothing, and many other everyday items. For example, an aircraft may be assembled in Washington, but the wings may have been manufactured in a factory in Asia, the engine built in another part of the United States, and the seats shipped in from another location. Eventually, all the parts are brought together in one factory where the final product is constructed.

What Happens When Nothing Is Available?

1 Inspect Have students read pp. 282–283 and explain the meaning of *scarcity*.

2 Find Evidence Use the questions below to check comprehension. Remind students to support their answers with text evidence.

Contrast In a marketplace, how are the buyer's goals and the seller's goals different? (The buyer needs to find someone who has what they want or need; the seller needs to find someone who wants or needs what they already have.) **DOK 2**

Predict If a seller has what a buyer wants, but the buyer thinks the seller's price is too high, what might happen next? (Answers may vary but might include the seller lowering the price to make a sale or the buyer looking for another seller with a lower price.) **DOK 3**

Interpret Think of a time when you traded something with someone else. How was that like the kind of trade described in the text? (The two people trading had to agree on a fair value for each item being traded.) **DOK 2**

3 Make Connections

Draw Conclusions How are the photograph and its caption on p. 283 related to the main text? (Answers may vary, but students will most likely conclude that the photograph shows a real-world example of scarcity, and the caption prompts the reader to think about trade's role in getting items back on the shelves.) **DOK 3**

How Do People Get What They Want and Need?

What Happens When Nothing Is Available?

Scarcity occurs because we do not have enough resources to satisfy everyone's needs and wants. For example, in many places, fruits and vegetables do not grow during winter. Although these goods are not available locally, many people still want them. One way a community can get scarce goods is through trade.

Trade is the buying and selling of goods and services. It works two ways. Sellers must find people who want or need what they are trying to sell. Buyers must find people who have what they want or need. When a seller and a buyer agree on a fair price, then trade happens.

Trade happens both locally and globally. An artist might sell a painting to someone who lives in the same town. Another person might buy an electronic device that was made in another country. Trade is the reason many things are available.

Where do the items come from that will fill these shelves?

RESEARCH COMPANION, pp. 282–283

English Learners SCAFFOLD

Use the following scaffolds to support student understanding of lesson content.

Entering and Emerging

Work with students to understand *scarcity* and *trade*. Provide sentence frames:

- Scarcity means there are enough/are not enough goods or services that people want.
- Sometimes scarcity is caused because _____.
- A community can get scarce goods by _____.

Developing and Expanding

Guide small groups of students to discuss *scarcity* and *trade*. Ask: *What is opposite of scarce? When might there be a scarcity of fresh fruit? How can a community get fresh fruit if it is scarce? What does the community need to find if they want to buy fresh fruit?*

Bridging and Reaching

Have partners discuss and define *scarcity* and *trade* in their own words. Ask: *How does scarcity affect trade? How does trade affect scarcity?*

Social Emotional Learning

Decision-Making Skills

Solving Problems To help students build problem-solving skills, say: *Look at the photo on p. 283. There is a scarcity of eggs. What are ways a community can get eggs when they are scarce?*

 Digital Tools

Blended Learning

Flip the research approach and find evidence in a digital format.

eBook

Students investigate using their **Research Companion** and **IMPACT Explorer Magazine eBooks** to find evidence.

Where Goods Come From

In the past, people made or grew most of the things they needed in their communities. Today, people buy some goods that are produced locally, while other goods are made in different places around the world. Countries **import** goods that they cannot grow or make. To *import* means to bring in goods from another country.

The United States imports goods such as oil, electronic parts, cars, and clothing. These goods come from countries such as China, Vietnam, Mexico, and Canada. Most of the clothing you wear was probably imported.

Many goods are imported and exported on huge cargo ships.

The United States **exports** many goods as well. *To export* means to send goods to another country to sell. For example, the United States is one of the world's top producers of soybeans. Farmers grow more soybeans than our country needs. American farmers export the extra soybeans to other countries to be sold.

The United States imports clothing from other countries.

Goods are moved around the world in many ways. Airplanes move some goods. But most goods are moved to and from the United States on cargo ships. The United States has several ports that are used by cargo ships. There are large ports in the cities of Los Angeles, Houston, Miami, New Orleans, and Detroit. Once the goods arrive at the port, they are transported to a factory or store.

Countries all over the world depend on trade to get many of the products they need. Trade is the exchange of goods. International trade is trade that happens between countries. Countries sell goods they make and buy goods they cannot make. Exporting goods is one way that businesses make money.

✓ Stop and Check

Talk How does exporting goods help companies? How does importing goods help communities?

Find Details As you read, add new information to the chart on page 269 in your Inquiry Journal.

RESEARCH COMPANION, pp. 284–285

Where Goods Come From

1 Inspect Have students read pp. 284–285 and explain why the United States imports goods.

2 Find Evidence Use the questions below to check comprehension.

Compare and Contrast How are imports and exports similar? How are they different? (They both involve the transportation of goods. Imports are things brought into a country for sale. Exports are goods transported outside a country for sale.) **DOK 2**

Hypothesize What do you think are the benefits of importing goods? What might be the costs? (benefits: items that cannot be made in a country are available to consumers, access to more goods, more choices, lower prices; costs: money goes to businesses outside of the country, more competition among businesses) **DOK 3**

3 Make Connections

Draw Conclusions What do you think would happen if U.S. soybean growers did not export their extra soybeans? (Answers will vary but may include that they would grow fewer soybeans or the extras would be wasted; they would grow something else; or countries that could not grow soybeans would have to do without.) **DOK 3**

✓ Stop and Check

Talk Have students discuss the question with a partner. (Answers will vary, but students should understand that companies make money from selling goods to other countries and that communities benefit by receiving goods they cannot make or grow themselves.)

 Spotlight on Vocabulary

Academic Vocabulary

cargo: goods moved by ships, trucks, or airplanes

ports: places where large ships dock and unload cargo

 Digital Tools

Blended Learning

Students investigate curated resources and find evidence to answer the lesson question.

Interactive IMPACT

Students choose from print or digital **Inquiry Tools** to take notes.

Making Money From Imports

Businesses in the United States import goods so they can earn a profit. Let's look at a T-shirt as an example. A business might buy the shirt from a factory in Bangladesh and sell it in the United States at a higher price. After paying for the shirt and transportation costs, the money that remains is called a profit.

Businesses then decide how they want to use these profits. They can build more factories or plant more crops. They can pay their workers higher wages or they can hire new workers. Businesses use profits to continue to grow.

Making and selling goods makes the economy stronger. A strong economy means people have jobs and money to spend. Trade helps the economy of the United States grow.

The United States exports airplane parts.

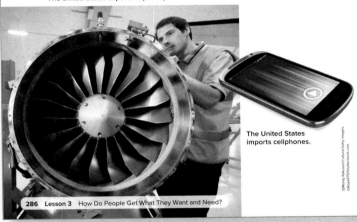

The United States imports cellphones.

286 Lesson 3 How Do People Get What They Want and Need?

InfoGraphic
Where Does Your T-Shirt Come From?

The trip a T-shirt makes from cotton to a store near you is a long one.

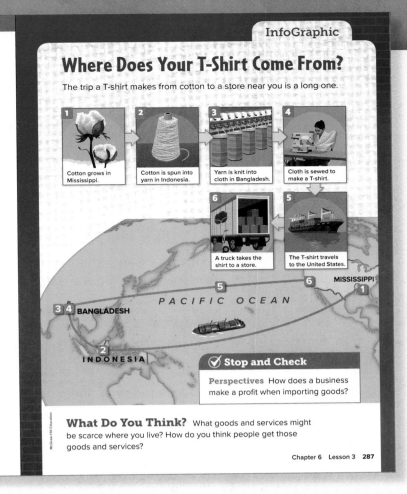

1. Cotton grows in Mississippi.
2. Cotton is spun into yarn in Indonesia.
3. Yarn is knit into cloth in Bangladesh.
4. Cloth is sewed to make a T-shirt.
5. The T-shirt travels to the United States.
6. A truck takes the shirt to a store.

✓ Stop and Check

Perspectives How does a business make a profit when importing goods?

What Do You Think? What goods and services might be scarce where you live? How do you think people get those goods and services?

Chapter 6   Lesson 3   287

RESEARCH COMPANION, pp. 286–287

Making Money From Imports/Where Does Your T-Shirt Come From?

1 Inspect Have students read pp. 286–287 and define the word *profit*.

2 Find Evidence Use the questions below to check comprehension.

Draw Conclusions Why do you think a U.S. company is able to buy an item from another country and then sell it at a higher price? (Answers will vary, but students may suggest that the price of the imported item may be less than the price of a similar item made locally.) **DOK 3**

Make Observations According to the infographic, what is Mississippi's role in the T-shirt trade? (Farmers in Mississippi grow the cotton that will make cloth for the T-shirts.) **DOK 2**

3 Make Connections

Assess T-shirts often have a "Made in _____" label, which tells where the T-shirt was sewn. Why is this only part of the story for a T-shirt in the infographic? (The label tells only the country the shirt was sewn. Many other countries are involved in the process.) **DOK 3**

✓ Stop and Check

Perspectives (Students should understand that businesses make a profit by charging more for the item than it cost them to buy, transport, and sell.)

What Do You Think? (Answers will vary but should identify goods and services that are scarce in the community and suggest that people get these items through trade.)

✓ Check for Success

Summarize Can students explain why trade helps people get the things they need and want?

Differentiate

If Not, Have students review the sequence chart on Inquiry Journal p. 269. Help students define the vocabulary appearing at the top of each box. Then, out of order, write four sentences describing the sequence. Have students renumber the sentences 1–4 to show the correct sequence.

LESSON 3 REPORT

LESSON QUESTION

How Do People Get What They Want and Need?

INQUIRY JOURNAL, pp. 270–271

Think About It

Examine Guide students in examining classroom objects for labels identifying the point of manufacture. Create a chart that lists each item and where it was originally made.

Write About It

Describe Remind students to include the following elements in their responses.

- Choose an item in the classroom that was made in another country.
- Develop a story about how the item came to be in the classroom.
- Include time-order words and phrases to clearly show the sequence of events.

Discipline(s)	4	3	2	1
Economics	Student shows strong understanding of how goods move globally to reach a local market; includes well-thought-out description with good use of sequencing words.	Student shows adequate understanding of how goods move globally to reach a local market; includes good description using sequencing words.	Student shows uneven understanding of how goods move globally to reach a local market; includes incomplete description with some use of sequencing words.	Student shows little or no understanding of how goods move globally to reach a local market; includes unclear description with little use of sequencing words.

Talk About It

Explain Have students share their stories with partners and discuss how and why an object made in another part of the world has come to be in their classroom.

Assessment Students can check their understanding with feedback from the **Lesson Test** available online.

Connect to the Essential Question

Look at Our Community Before students respond, remind them to think about why goods are imported and what need is being met by the item they chose to write about.

Inquiry Project Update Remind students to to turn to Inquiry Journal pp. 244–245 for project information. If necessary, review the Project Checklist with students. At this point in the chapter, students should focus on the second and third items on the checklist.

Think About It

Examine
Where were the things in your classroom made? Look for labels showing the countries where they were manufactured.

Write About It

Describe
Choose something from your classroom that was made in another country. Write a story telling about how it traveled from that country to your classroom.

Stories will vary, but most students will describe how the object traveled on a ship, landed at a port city, and then made its way, most likely by truck, to their classroom.

Talk About It 👥

Explain
Share your story with a partner. Discuss how and why objects made in one part of the world end up in another place.

Economics
Connect to the EQ

Look at Our Community
How does trade help the people in your community meet their wants and needs? How is your story an example of this?

Answers will vary, but students should show an understanding that trade, both locally and globally, helps relieve scarcity of resources. They should point out that their story is an example of a classroom need being met through a specific aspect of trade: the importing of goods.

Inquiry Project Notes

INQUIRY JOURNAL, pp. 270–271

English Learners SCAFFOLD

Use the following scaffolds to support student writing.

Entering and Emerging

Model a sequence of steps for a simple task, such as brushing teeth, using *first, then, next,* and *last.* Then help students use the sentence frames to write a sequence of events that tells the story of the classroom item they chose. Encourage students to replace the word *item* with the name of the item they chose.

- First, materials for the item _____. Then, the item was _____.
- Next, the item traveled by _____. Last, the item _____.

Developing and Expanding

Have small groups discuss ideas for their stories using the words *first, then, next,* and *last.* Ask questions to help students think about the sequence of events: *What item is your story about? Where did the item come from? Where do you think the materials for the item came from? Where do you think the item might have been made or put together? How did it get to our classroom?*

Bridging and Reaching

Have partners discuss the "trip" that a classroom item might have taken, referring to the infographic on p. 287 if needed. Then guide students to write their stories, using the words *first, then, next,* and *last.* Encourage students to include adjectives in their stories to make their writing more detailed and interesting to read.

✓ Check for Success

Describe Can students write a story describing the sequence of events that begins with an item being made in another country and ends with the item arriving in the classroom?

Differentiate

If Not, Have students act out the sequence. Assign roles as the manufacturer, the shipper, the importer, the truck driver, and so on. Work with students to create a short play demonstrating the sequence of events.

LESSON QUESTION

What Makes a Community's Economy Change?

Connect to the Essential Question

Tell students that this lesson provides key research into the Chapter Essential Question: **How Do People in a Community Meet Their Wants and Needs?** Explain that they will learn how goods and services in the United States have changed over time. Tell them they will understand how our nation's communities use goods and services and how people have adjusted to changes in the economy.

Lesson Objectives

- **Explain** how buying and selling goods and services have changed over time.
- **Compare and contrast** how people shopped in the past with the ways people shop today.
- **Discuss** examples of economic changes in the community and their effects.
- **Describe** goods and services provided by different types of businesses.
- **Write** a journal entry describing the economy of a community in the past.

Make Connections!

CONNECT TO ELA

Reading **Determine** the main idea of a text; recount the key details and explain how they support the main idea.
Describe the logical connection between particular sentences and paragraphs in a text.

Research **Recall** information from experiences or gather information from print and digital sources; take brief notes on sources and sort evidence into provided categories.

Writing **Create** narratives to develop real or imagined experiences or events using effective technique, descriptive details, and clear event sequences.

Speaking and Listening **Engage** effectively in a range of collaborative discussions with diverse partners on grade 3 topics and texts, building on others' ideas and expressing students' own ideas clearly.

Language **Form and use** the simple (e.g., *I walked; I walk; I will walk*) verb tenses.

COMMUNITY CONNECTIONS

To enrich what students have learned about a community's economy today, challenge them to interview family, friends, and neighbors about how they obtain goods they need or want. Encourage students to ask about specific goods, such as food, clothing, or appliances. Questions might include *Where do you buy food? Do you use the computer, the Internet, or your phone to obtain goods and services?*

Lesson-At-A-Glance

1 ENGAGE — INQUIRY JOURNAL

pp. 272–277

▶ **Talk About It:** Photograph of People Buying Tickets at an Amusement Park

▶ **Analyze the Source:** Shopping Long Ago and Today

▶ **Inquiry Tools:** Explore Comparing and Contrasting

2 INVESTIGATE — RESEARCH COMPANION

pp. 288–293

▶ **Goods and Services Change Over Time**

▶ **Then and Now: The Music Industry Over Time**

3 REPORT — INQUIRY JOURNAL

pp. 278–279

▶ **Think About It**

▶ **Write About It:** Write a Journal Entry

▶ **Talk About It**

▶ **Connect to the Essential Question**

ASSESSMENT

▶ **Online Lesson Test**

▶ **Printable Lesson Test**

For more details, see pages T490–T491.

▶ Digital Tools

at **my.mheducation.com**

ePresentation

Teach the **Engage**, **Investigate**, and **Report** content to the whole class from **ePresentations** that launch directly from the lesson dashboard.

eBook

You can flip your instruction with the **IMPACT eBooks** found on your lesson dashboard.

Interactive IMPACT

Blend in digital content **when you want it** and **where you want it**.

Blended Learning features in the Teacher's Edition highlight ways to connect in-class work with online experiences to enhance learning.

Investigate current events with **IMPACT News**.

Explore domain-based vocabulary with **Explore Words** and **Word Play** vocabulary activities.

Go Further with IMPACT Explorer Magazine!

pp. 66–79

The **IMPACT Explorer Magazine** supports students' exploration of the Essential Question and provides additional resources for the EQ Inquiry Project.

 LESSON QUESTION

What Makes a Community's Economy Change?

Language Objectives

• Use newly acquired content and academic vocabulary to discuss how buying and selling goods and services have changed over time.

• Compare and contrast economies of different times.

• Understand and use simple past tense.

Spanish Cognates

To support Spanish speakers, point out the cognates.

economy = economía

nation = nación

gas = gas

petroleum = petróleo

specialize = especializar

lemon = limón

Introduce the Lesson

Set Purpose Explain to students that in this lesson, they will read informational texts to learn how buying and selling goods and services have changed over time.

Access Prior Knowledge Read the lesson question and find out what students already know about how buying and selling goods and services have changed over time. Make sure students understand the meaning of *goods* and *services*. Ask: *What products do we buy now that we didn't buy many years ago? Where do we buy products today that is different from long ago? Are there services that used to exist but don't anymore? In the past, how did people pay for things? What are some new ways people pay for things today?*

Spark Curiosity Direct students to the photograph on p. 290 of the Research Companion. Read the caption aloud. Explain that the first programmable computer was completed in 1946 to make numerical calculations during World War II. It had forty panels. Each panel was eight feet tall and two feet wide. It lined three walls of a room measuring fifty feet by thirty feet, probably larger than an average classroom, and required specially trained technicians to operate it. Personal computers did not exist until 1970.

 Have students work with a partner to compare and contrast the computer pictured on p. 290 with a tablet computer. Ask: *How are they similar and different?* (Both process information faster than humans can, but tablets are smaller, process more data, and have many different applications.)

Build Meaning & Support Language

Inquiry Journal

Analyze the Source (page 274–275) Tell students that in this lesson, they will read informational texts that give facts, examples, and explanations about a topic. The texts include headings and photographs with captions. As you read "Shopping Long Ago and Today," explain any words that students don't know. Point out the phrase *Long ago* that begins the first paragraph. Explain that it means "in the past." Then call students' attention to the word *Today* on p. 275 and say: *The text following* Long ago *tells about shopping in the past, and the information that follows* Today *is about how people shop now. The text is comparing and contrasting shopping at different times.* Support understanding of the text by asking questions such as: *Where did people shop long ago? Where do people shop today?*

Inquiry Tools (pages 276–277) Tell students they will explore **Comparing and Contrasting** as they learn how a community's economy changes. Explain that the graphic organizer on p. 276 will help them record information as they read. Say: *In one circle write examples from long ago, and in the other circle write examples from today. If the example makes sense for both times, write it in the middle section where the circles overlap.* Explain that they will use the diagram on p. 277 to record examples as they read the Research Companion.

Research Companion

Goods and Services Change Over Time (pages 288–291) Explain that the economy is the total activity of buying and selling goods and services in a place. Read the first paragraph on p. 288. Ask: *What activities were part of the economy in 1776?* (farming, working small businesses, raising crops, cutting trees for lumber, mining coal) Explain that the words *oil* and *petroleum* refer to the same thing.

Read the first paragraph on p. 290. Ask: *What activities made up the economies of different regions?* (New England: fishing, shipbuilding; the South: raising cotton, rice, sugar; the Great Plains: raising grains, herding cattle) Explain that today's economy includes many industries that did not exist long ago. Read p. 291. Ask: *What industries are examples from today's economy?* (travel, entertainment, computers, electronics, banking, advertising, news)

The Music Industry Over Time (pages 292–293) Help students with the meaning of the word *over* in the section title. Explain that it does not mean "above" but means "during" or "throughout." Read the first sentence and explain that *vast* means "very large." Read the page, and discuss the meanings of the phrases *live music* and *sound recordings*. Say: *As we complete the reading, notice the different ways that people listened to sound recordings.* Read the rest of the feature. Ask: *What different ways have people listened to sound recordings over time?* (phonograph/record player, tapes/tape recorders, CDs, MP3s, computers, phones)

Inquiry Journal

Report Your Findings (pages 278–279) Explain to students that a journal entry, like a diary, is a place for someone to write about their experiences and thoughts. Remind students to write sentences using the information they recorded about goods and services of the economies of different times. Tell students that when they write about long ago they must use past-tense verbs. Encourage students to use new vocabulary words they have learned. Provide support as needed with spelling and punctuation.

Language Forms & Conventions

Simple Past Tense Tell students that when they describe something that happened in the past, they must use a verb in the past tense. Say: *The usual way to make a verb past tense is to add the ending -ed or -d.* Explain that *-d* is added to verbs that end in *e*. Provide this example: *Long ago Americans farm<u>ed</u> and work<u>ed</u> small businesses.* Write on the board the chart of verbs from the text.

Verb	Past Tense	Verb	Past Tense
change	changed	provide	
raise		develop	
mine		discover	
drill		fish	

Have students work in pairs to write the past tense for each verb. Point out that they can find each correct form in the text. Then have them search for and record other past tense verbs ending in *-ed* or *-d* that are used in the text. Have them write short sentences using the present and past tense form of each verb.

Cross-Cultural Connection

Tourism is a much larger part of many countries' economies today than it was a century ago. It grew during the twentieth century with the development of air travel and cruise ships. With the growth of the middle class and increased disposable income, travel for pleasure became more widespread.

Leveled Support

Entering & Emerging
Help students form complete sentences from the notes they took in their graphic organizers.

Developing & Expanding
Have students write sentences that describe the activities that were part of the economy of long ago.

Bridging & Reaching
Have students work with partners to brainstorm words they can use in their writing to describe the goods and services available 100 years ago.

Language Transfer

English learners may find it challenging to correctly pronounce past tense verbs ending in *-ed*, as there are three variations. When a verb ends with *d* or *t* and *-ed* is added, the ending is pronounced as the new syllable *-ed*, as in the word *provided*. At times it is pronounced simply as the sound /d/, as in *farmed* and *raised*. And at other times it is pronounced as the sound /t/, as in *talked* and *walked*.

LESSON 4 ENGAGE

LESSON QUESTION

What Makes a Community's Economy Change?

INQUIRY JOURNAL, pp. 272–273

Bellringer

Say: *In the previous lesson, you learned that businesses import and export goods.* Invite students to identify examples of goods the United States imports and exports. Then, ask: *What effects do you think innovations in technology have had on the goods that are available in communities?* (Technological innovations have made it easier for communities to get goods from all over the world. Many of these goods may not have been available in the community in the past.)

Lesson Outcomes

Discuss the lesson questions and lesson outcomes with students.

- Have students define *change* in their own words.

- Explain that to recognize how something has changed over time students need to know what something was like in the past. Say: *Letters that took weeks to arrive used to be the only way people could communicate, but that changed with the invention of the telephone. Now people can reach each other instantly.*

Talk About It

Have students look at the image of the ticket window. Explain that the image represents an important industry to the economy of many communities in the United States—tourism. Ask: *What is tourism?* (Tourism means traveling for pleasure, and the tourism industry is made up of businesses that provide goods and services to travelers.) Say: *This industry provides both goods and services.* Have students think about what happens at an amusement park. Provide sentence frames to help student partners give examples of goods and services at an amusement park.

- _____ *is an example of a service because* _____.
- *The person who is* _____ *is selling/buying a good.*

 Collaborative Conversations

Be Prepared As students engage in partner, small-group, and whole-class discussions, encourage them to:

- build on a conversation by linking their comments with those of others.
- offer opinions and negotiate with others in conversations by using basic phrases, such as "I think . . ." and "I agree with _____, but . . ."
- continue a conversation through multiple exchanges.

Lesson 4

What Makes a Community's Economy Change?

Lesson Outcomes

What Am I Learning?
In this lesson, you will use your investigative skills to explore how buying and selling goods and services have changed over time.

Why Am I Learning It?
Reading and talking about these changes will help you understand how sales and shopping work in communities today.

How Will I Know That I Learned It?
You will be able to write and talk about the goods and services you would have used in your community one hundred years ago.

Talk About It COLLABORATE

Look closely at the photo on the next page. Are these people buying goods or services? Who provides them?

When you buy a ticket to a show, you're paying for entertainment. Other people perform in concerts, plays, and movies for your enjoyment!

At an amusement park, people buy tickets to see shows and ride on rides.

INQUIRY JOURNAL, pp. 272–273

English Learners SCAFFOLD

Use the following scaffolds to support student understanding of lesson outcomes.

Entering and Beginning
Ask students to think back to previous lessons in this chapter. Then have partners take turns completing the following sentence frames:

- A good is something that people _____. (make) A service is something that people _____. (do)
- Examples of goods include _____, _____, and _____.
- Examples of services include _____, _____, and _____.

Developing and Expanding
Ask students to list goods and services that are related to the tourism industry in a T-chart. Ask: *What might you buy in a gift shop at a theme park?* (hat, sweatshirt) *What might you do if you are unfamiliar with a city you are visiting?* (go on a tour) *How might you get meals if you are visiting a place far from home?* (buy food at a store or restaurant)

Bridging and Reaching
Have students work with partners to list goods and services they use everyday, such as things they use at school or play, the local library, or a playground. Have them write sentences describing but not naming each good or service. Then have partners read their descriptions to another pair to see if they can name the good or service.

Social Emotional Learning

Decision-Making Skills

Reflect An important part of making decisions is reflecting on those choices. Thinking about what went well or what did not will help students make better decisions. After a group discussion or activity, ask each student to reflect on the experience.

 Digital Tools

Blended Learning
Students engage with the lesson question and discussion prompts.

Interactive IMPACT

Discuss the **Lesson Question** and **Talk About It** with the whole class.

Shopping Long Ago and Today

1 Inspect

Read the title and look at the photos. What do you think you will learn?

- **Circle** words you do not know.
- **Underline** words and phrases that tell you what shopping was like long ago and what shopping is like today.
- **Summarize** how shopping has changed over time.

My Notes

_____

_____

_____

_____

_____

_____

_____

_____

_____

Long ago, most towns had only a few small stores. Each store carried only a few different items. Most of the items were made nearby. Items that came from far away were expensive and not easy to get. Customers who walked to a store could buy only a few items at a time. Customers are people who buy goods and services. Customers who rode in wagons could bring home more food, clothing, tools, and other items. Most people paid for goods in cash. Some traded their own goods for others.

In the past, most people shopped in small stores in their communities. They might buy food at one store, tools at another, and clothing at another.

Today, people can buy goods from their computer and telephone. The goods arrive on the doorstep or in the mailbox!

Today, customers have more choices among goods. The same items are available all year. Many customers drive to the store. This makes it easier to reach stores farther away. People can also bring many things home at one time.

Customers use the Internet to buy goods from stores that have websites. Online shopping allows people to buy goods from stores in other states and countries. Goods ordered online are shipped to people's homes and businesses.

People have many ways to pay for goods and services. They can use cash, checks, and credit cards. Credit cards let customers charge goods that they must pay for later.

2 Find Evidence

Reread the text. How do changes in how people shop affect the local economy?

Draw a box around clues that support what you think.

3 Make Connections

Talk Discuss with a partner why people might shop online. What goods and services do they get online?

INQUIRY JOURNAL, pp. 274–275

Analyze the Source

 Spotlight on Language

Background Information
Most rural communities between the 1800s and early 1900s had one main store, known as the general store, where people could buy the items that they couldn't make for themselves. By the late 1880s, mail-order businesses printed catalogs to sell people items they couldn't get locally. Today, retail websites present digital catalogs on the Internet for online shopping.

1 Inspect

Read Have students read the text, study the photos, and read the captions. Remind students to circle words in the text with which they are unfamiliar.

- Underline words and phrases that tell what shopping was like long ago (a few small stores; only a few different items) and today. (more choices among goods; items available all year; use the Internet to buy goods)

2 Find Evidence

Reread Have students reread the text and answer the question.

Draw Students should draw boxes around relevant details that support their answer.

3 Make Connections

Talk Have partners take turns sharing ideas about why people might shop at large stores, at malls, and online. Have them list goods and services that they might buy with each method.

Descriptive Modifiers

Explain that some adjectives describe quantities, or amounts. Guide students to identify words in the text that describe *how much* or *how many* of something. Invite students to practice making sentences using one or more of the modifiers.

▶ Digital Tools

Blended Learning

Students read informational texts and analyze primary sources.

Interactive IMPACT

Have students practice and apply the strategy of close reading as they analyze text.

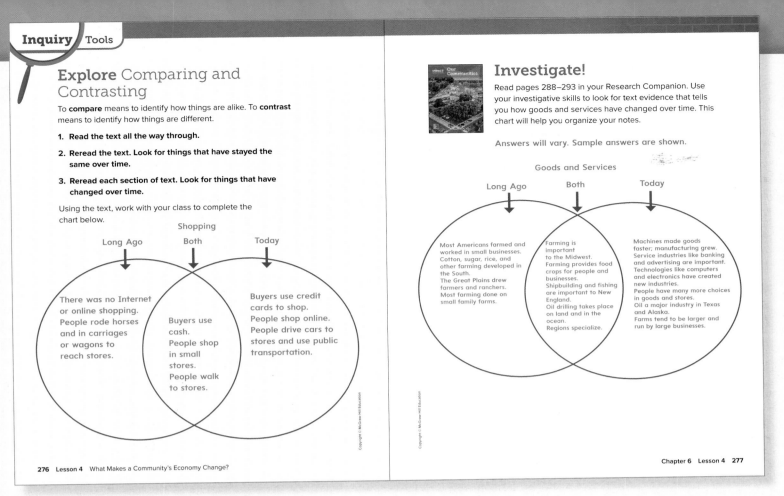

Inquiry Tools

Explore Comparing and Contrasting

Read Have students read the step-by-step instructions about how to compare and contrast. Have them look for words that signal differences between the past and present, such as *then, now, after, before, long ago,* and *today* as they reread the text.

Guide Practice Have students review the text on pp. 274–275. Then work with them to complete the graphic organizer. Explain that they will use a similar graphic organizer to organize their independent research.

Check Understanding Confirm student understanding of the inquiry skill, Explore Comparing and Contrasting. If students cannot identify similarities and differences between the past and present, review the steps on p. 276.

Investigate!

Have students read pp. 288–293 in the Research Companion. Tell them the information will help them answer the lesson question *What Makes a Community's Economy Change?*

Take Notes Tell students that they will take notes in the Venn diagram on p. 277 of the Inquiry Journal as they read. Remind students that taking notes will help them understand and remember the information they learn.

Explain that they will contrast by looking for things that are different and compare by looking for things that have stayed the same.

Spotlight on Language

Academic Language

A *similarity* is a way in which two or more things are almost alike.

A *difference* is a feature that makes two or more things not like each other.

Often, two or more things will have both similarities and differences.

LESSON 4 INVESTIGATE

LESSON QUESTION

What Makes a Community's Economy Change?

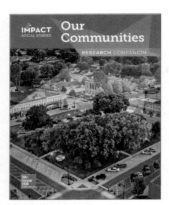

RESEARCH COMPANION, pp. 288–289

Background Information

- **The Service Economy** Goods, services, and agriculture are the main U.S. economic sectors for which the U.S. Bureau of Labor Statistics tracks employment. Today, American service industries employ the most people. More than eighty percent of workers are employed in service businesses, which include retail trade, transportation, education, health care, professional services, and government.

- **Decline in Goods Producing** Employment in the goods-producing sector—manufacturing, construction, and mining—has declined by about three percent in the past decade, to twelve percent today. Oil and gas extraction workers make up about one-fourth of mining employment. The agriculture sector employs only 1.5 percent of total U.S. workers, but the use of advanced technologies such as GPS and robotic systems facilitate robust production. The remaining workers are self-employed.

- **Digitization of Music** Until the 1990s, the only way to sell recorded music was on a record, CD, or tape cassette. Technology changed that. Now people can download albums or listen to them on streaming services for a much smaller cost than paying for an album or cassette. This means music companies and musicians make less money from these purchases. Technology allows musicians and music companies to find other ways to make money off of music. For example, they can sell their songs for people to use as ringtones for their phones.

Goods and Services Change Over Time

1 Inspect Have students read pp. 288–289 and have them identify goods and services in the U.S. economy.

2 Find Evidence Use the questions below to check comprehension. Remind students to support their answers with text evidence.

Compare and Contrast Look at the photograph of the oil fields in 1906. Describe the similarities and differences of mining oil between then and now. (Answers should note similarities, such as pumping oil out of the ground, changing the land, and dirty work, and differences, such as the material used for equipment, the type of equipment, drilling at sea, how oil is kept and transported, concern for the land, and technological advances.) **DOK 2**

Draw Conclusions What do you think contributed to the discovery and development of new oil fields? (The nation's growing population and subsequent industrial growth led to a need for more energy, which made it worthwhile for energy companies to search for new sources and to build more production facilities.) **DOK 3**

3 Make Connections

Analyze Which of the industries discussed in the text are important to your community's economy today? (Answers will vary, but students should accurately describe the natural resources that are still important to their local economy.) **DOK 3**

Lesson 4
What Makes a Community's Economy Change?

Goods and Services Change Over Time

The economy of the United States has changed greatly over time. When the United States became a nation in 1776, most Americans farmed and worked in small businesses. Many raised food crops. Others cut down trees for lumber. Still others mined coal. Later, some Americans drilled for oil and natural gas. People sold these natural resources to provide energy and to make other goods. Shopkeepers and merchants ran businesses to sell these goods. Community members like doctors, teachers, bankers, and lawyers provided other important services.

Modern Americans still work in farming, mining, and drilling. The American oil industry first developed in Pennsylvania and California. Later, petroleum—or oil—was discovered in other states. Texas and Alaska became large oil producers. Today, drilling takes place at sea as well as on land. People and businesses rely on oil for fuel as well as for plastics and other goods.

Oil fields, 1906

RESEARCH COMPANION, pp. 288–289

English Learners SCAFFOLD

Use the following scaffolds to support student understanding of the lesson content.

Entering and Emerging

Explain that the text on p. 288 uses time-related words to signal changes that happened over a long time. Read the text aloud one sentence at a time, pointing out the time-related words and phrases: *in 1776, Later, Modern Americans, first, Later,* and *Today*. For each word or phrase, ask individual students to read aloud what change happened.

Developing and Expanding

Explain that the text on p. 288 uses time-related words to signal changes that happened over a long time. Read the text aloud slowly, and have students raise their hands when they hear a time-related word or phrase: *in 1776, Later, Modern Americans, first, Later,* and *Today*. For each word or phrase, ask students what change happened. Provide a three-column chart with the headings *Long Ago, Later,* and *Today*. Have students work in groups to list changes in the appropriate column.

Bridging and Reaching

Explain that the text on p. 288 uses time-related words to signal changes that happened over a long time. Ask students to name the time-related words and phrases: *in 1776, Later, Modern Americans, first, Later,* and *Today*. Have students work with a partner to write three sentences to explain how the American oil industry has changed over time.

Social Emotional Learning

Self-Regulation

Set Goals To deal effectively with daily tasks and challenges, students must practice setting and achieving goals. Ask them to set one or two goals before they begin taking notes. When students have finished, ask: *Did you accomplish your goals?*

Digital Tools

Blended Learning
Find evidence in a digital format.

Interactive IMPACT
Use the **Lesson Video**.

Differences in natural resources and climate led regions to **specialize**, or focus on different activities. New Englanders on natural harbors built ships and fished. In the South, rich soil and warm weather led people to raise cotton, rice, and sugar. On the Great Plains, farmers raised grains like wheat and corn. Ranchers herded cattle for meat.

Farms now cover what was once open prairie in the Midwest. Most farms used to be small family businesses. Today, big businesses run much larger farms. They provide food for stores, restaurants, and homes. Small farmers still raise their own food and sell goods in their communities.

Manufacturing, or the making of goods, grew. Machines enabled people to make goods faster and cheaper. Now, many people work in retail, or businesses that sell goods. People have many choices of goods and places to shop.

The earliest computers were big. They took up entire rooms.

Technology has also led to new economic activities. Travel, especially on airplanes, is a big business today. Technology also impacted entertainment. Television became a part of many homes in the mid-1900s. Today, people view television shows from many providers.

Computers and other electronics are major industries that did not exist in the past. Many people and companies design computers and computer programs. Tech support people help customers figure out problems with their computers and other electronics. They provide a service. Many people work in other service industries fixing the goods that people buy.

As more people started saving money and taking out loans, banking spread. Today, many banks exist that offer their services to everyone. Advertising, which draws attention to goods and services, developed as companies wanted to reach more customers. Newspapers and magazines provide a good—the printed material—and a service—information. Today, many publications no longer rely on printing. They have websites.

Today's computers fit on a desk and in your lap. Some even fit in your hand as a tablet or a smartphone!

✓ Stop and Check

Talk Why do some regions specialize in certain goods?

Find Details As you read, add new information to the graphic organizer on page 277 in your Inquiry Journal.

290 Lesson 4 What Makes a Community's Economy Change?

Chapter 6 Lesson 4 291

RESEARCH COMPANION, pp. 290–291

---

1 Inspect Have students take turns reading the text on pp. 290–291 and tell about one new industry or product.

2 Find Evidence Use the questions below to check comprehension.

Hypothesize Why do you think some stores sell goods made in the United States as well as imported goods? (They can offer their customers a wider selection or cheaper prices by selling goods from different places.) **DOK 3**

Infer Why have the products of farming remained much the same while the methods have changed? (Americans eat most of the same foods as they have in the past, but machines and technology have improved industry processes.) **DOK 2**

Analyze What main idea in the text do the two images on pp. 290–291 illustrate? (The two images show how technology has changed over time by making computers smaller, more portable, and easier to use.) **DOK 3**

3 Make Connections

Hypothesize Why do you think many newspapers and magazines now have websites instead of offering only a paper publication? (They can reach more people more quickly at less cost on their websites because they don't have to spend time and money on printing and distributing their publications.) **DOK 3**

✓ Stop and Check

Talk Ask students to think about the natural resources and the climate in their region and how those features contribute to economic activities. (Answers will vary but should note that natural resources and climate affect what minerals and energy resources can be extracted and what types of crops can be grown.)

 Spotlight on Vocabulary

Content Vocabulary

prairie: a large, flat land area in North America that is covered in grasses and has few trees

harbor: an area of the ocean or a lake beside the land that is protected by the land and is deep enough for ships to stay

 Digital Tools

Blended Learning

Students investigate curated resources and find evidence to answer the lesson question.

Interactive IMPACT

Students **Research** and find evidence using digital format texts.

Then and Now

The Music Industry Over Time

Music is one part of a vast entertainment industry. How do you listen to music today? Perhaps you listen to the radio and CDs in a car. You might listen to music on a phone or a computer.

Long ago, the only way to listen to music was to make it—or to listen to someone else making it. People sang and played musical instruments. This is called live music. Musicians performed in homes, churches and other religious gatherings, and in restaurants and clubs. They formed bands that held concerts.

The first sound recordings didn't happen until the late 1850s. In 1877, Thomas Edison invented the first phonograph, or record player. In the 1930s, new technologies produced tapes and tape recorders. Then came compact discs (CDs) in the 1980s. Finally, digital recordings and audio devices like MP3 players were developed in the 1990s. *Digital* means electronic or computerized. People could listen to music on their phones or computers.

Most people used to go to clubs to hear jazz music live.

Albums were the main type of sound recording until the late 1900s. People have started buying albums and record players again.

Each new technology lets people share more music. Musicians did not have to play live for people to hear their music. New kinds of music could reach more listeners. Bands and singers gained fans who had never seen them perform.

Today, many people use digital devices to listen to music from all over the world. They can buy individual songs instead of entire albums. They listen on smartphones and computers. They listen in their homes, cars, and businesses. They listen while they walk, bike, and run. However, fans still go to concert halls, festivals, stadiums, and other places to hear music. Ticket sales to music events are a big part of the entertainment industry today.

Headphones and digital devices let people listen to music just about anywhere, anytime.

✓ Stop and Check

Talk Why do you think live music and recorded music are such big industries?

What Do You Think? What are some ways the economy of a community can change?

292 Lesson 4 What Makes a Community's Economy Change?

Chapter 6 Lesson 4 293

Then and Now: The Music Industry Over Time

1 Inspect Have students read pp. 292–293 and define *digital* in their own words.

2 Find Evidence Use the questions below to check comprehension.

Explain How did recording devices change the music industry? (The ability to record music created the opportunity for new businesses and allowed people to purchase music rather than attend performances or make their own music.) **DOK 2**

Relate What image would you add to the pages to show how you enjoy music? (Answers will vary.) **DOK 3**

3 Make Connections

Hypothesize Why do you think music fans still go to live performances at concert halls and other venues? (Possible answer: Fans enjoy the experience of going out together, enjoying the music as it is performed, and watching the musicians at their work.) **DOK 3**

✓ Stop and Check

Talk Encourage students to use background knowledge to consider why people listen to music. (Many people enjoy music, so they are willing to pay for recorded music that they can listen to any time as well as to pay for the experience of enjoying live music.)

What Do You Think? (Answers will vary, but students should formulate an appropriate response based on evidence from the text and their community's development and current economic conditions.)

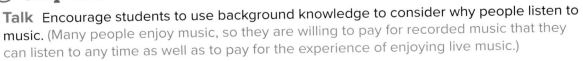

✓ Check for Success

Connect Can students identify similarities and differences about economic activities in the past and present?

Differentiate

If Not, Guide students in filling out one comparison and one contrast in the Goods and Services Venn diagram on p. 277 of the Inquiry Journal.

LESSON 4 REPORT

What Makes a Community's Economy Change?

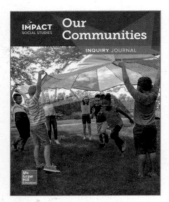

INQUIRY JOURNAL, pp. 278–279

Think About It

Remind students to review their research about the types of goods and services provided by businesses in the United States. Encourage them to begin reflecting on what goods and services the businesses in their community provide and how these goods and services have changed over time. Direct students back to pp. 288–293 of their Research Companion if they need more information.

Write About It

Imagine Remind students to include the following elements in their responses.

- Describe the types of goods and services used based on the community's economic development.
- Explain how easy or hard it is to get the needed goods and services.
- Use chapter vocabulary as appropriate.

Discipline(s)	4	3	2	1
Economics **History**	Student shows a strong understanding of the community's economy and the goods and services used at that time.	Student shows an adequate understanding of the community's economy and the goods and services used at that time.	Student shows an uneven understanding of the community's economy and the goods and services used at that time.	Student shows no understanding of the community's economy and the goods and services used at that time.

Talk About It

Discuss Have students discuss how changes in goods and services have impacted the community. Remind them to support their opinions with prior knowledge or text evidence.

Assessment Students can check their understanding with feedback from the **Lesson Test** available online.

Connect to the Essential Question

Evaluate Before students respond, remind them to compare and contrast present and past ways of making, selling, and buying goods and services in the community.

Inquiry Project Update Remind students to turn to Inquiry Journal pp. 244–245 for project information. If necessary, review the Project Checklist with students. At this point in the chapter, students should focus on the fourth and fifth items on the checklist.

Think About It

Examine
Based on your research, what goods and services have businesses in the United States provided?

Answers will vary but should reflect the content of the text, including food crops, manufactured goods, and services such as banking, medical care, education, tech support, and retail.

Write About It

Imagine
What if you lived one hundred years ago? Write a journal entry describing the goods and services you would have used in your community at that time.

Answers will vary but should reflect the specific economic development of their community. Most responses should show a greater emphasis on farming, manufacturing, and mining rather than on services in the past.

Talk About It

Discuss
Share your paragraph with a partner. Discuss how the goods and services in your community have changed over time. How do you think those changes have shaped your community?

Economics Connect to the

Evaluate
What are the benefits and drawbacks to the ways people make, sell, and buy goods and services in your community today?

Answers will vary but should discuss how people have many more choices in goods as well as in providers of goods and services.

 Inquiry Project Notes

_____
_____
_____
_____
_____

INQUIRY JOURNAL, pp. 278–279

 # English Learners SCAFFOLD

Use the following scaffolds to support student writing.

Entering and Beginning

Ask students to think of themselves as workers living in the community one hundred years ago. Have them complete the following sentence frames:

- If I lived one hundred years ago, I would have worked as a _____.
- I would have used _____ to do my work.

Developing and Expanding

Ask students to think of themselves as a worker living in the community one hundred years ago. Have student pairs take turns asking and answering these questions: *What kind of work did you do? What did you use to do your work? How did you get what you needed?*

Bridging and Reaching

Ask partners to discuss how life and work in the community were different one hundred years ago. Have them write sentences that compare something that was easier with something that was harder. For example, *It took longer to take the wagon to town, but it was easier to decide what soap to buy.*

✔ Check for Success

Imagine Can students write a journal entry describing goods and services used in the community one hundred years ago?

Differentiate

If Not, Have students work in pairs or small groups to present their ideas in a different format such as a dialogue, a skit, or a Q&A session.

LESSON 5 OVERVIEW

LESSON QUESTION

How Can You Use Money Wisely?

Connect to the Essential Question

Tell students they will use their investigative skills to explore how people choose to spend money. It will help them answer the Essential Question: **How Do People in a Community Meet Their Wants and Needs?** Also, by reading and talking about how others choose to spend their money, students will understand how to make good choices about how to spend their own money.

Discuss The IMPACT Today

Tell students that this lesson will help them see how economics impacts the choices people and communities make today. Encourage them to consider the choices they will need to make in order to use money wisely.

Lesson Objectives

- **Identify** ways people earn money.
- **Explain** ways people choose to use their money.
- **Describe** ways to build personal human capital.
- **Write** a list of questions to ask before spending money.

Make Connections!

CONNECT TO ELA

Reading Ask and answer questions to demonstrate understanding of a text and refer explicitly to the text as the basis for the answers.

Determine the main idea of a text; recount the key details and explain how they support the main idea.

Research Recall information from experiences or gather information from print or digital sources; take brief notes on sources and sort evidence into provided categories.

Writing Craft informative/explanatory texts to examine a topic and convey ideas and information clearly.

Develop the topic with facts, definitions, and details.

Speaking and Listening Engage effectively in a range of collaborative discussions with diverse partners on grade 3 topics and texts, building on others' ideas and expressing students' own ideas clearly.

Language Form and use regular and irregular verbs.

COMMUNITY CONNECTIONS

To enrich what students learn about spending their money wisely, invite a financial advisor or banker from the community to speak with the class about the importance of budgeting and saving money.

Lesson-At-A-Glance

1 ENGAGE
INQUIRY JOURNAL

pp. 280–285

- ▶ **Talk About It:** Photograph of young people considering a purchase
- ▶ **Analyze the Source:** Good Money Choices
- ▶ **Inquiry Tools:** Explore Main Idea and Details

2 INVESTIGATE
RESEARCH COMPANION

pp. 294–301

- ▶ **Using Money**
- ▶ **Earning Money to Help Others**
- ▶ **Making Economic Choices**
- ▶ **Building Your Own Capital**

3 REPORT
INQUIRY JOURNAL

pp. 286–287

- ▶ **Think About It**
- ▶ **Write About It:** Write a List of Questions; Cite Evidence from Text
- ▶ **Talk About It**
- ▶ **Connect to the Essential Question**

ASSESSMENT

- ▶ **Online Lesson Test**
- ▶ **Printable Lesson Test**

For more details, see pages T490–T491.

▶ Digital Tools

at **my.mheducation.com**

ePresentation

Teach the Engage, Investigate, and Report content to the whole class from **ePresentations** that launch directly from the lesson dashboard.

eBook

You can flip your instruction with the **IMPACT eBooks** found on your lesson dashboard.

Interactive IMPACT

Blend in digital content **when you want it** and **where you want it**.

Blended Learning features in the Teacher's Edition highlight ways to connect in-class work with online experiences to enhance learning.

Investigate current events with **IMPACT News**.

Explore domain-based vocabulary with **Explore Words** and **Word Play** vocabulary activities.

pp. 66–79

Go Further with IMPACT Explorer Magazine!

The **IMPACT Explorer Magazine** supports students' exploration of the Essential Question and provides additional resources for the EQ Inquiry Project.

How Can You Use Money Wisely?

Language Objectives

- Use newly acquired content and academic vocabulary to discuss and write about how to use money wisely.
- Write questions to consider before making a purchase.
- Understand and use irregular past tense verbs.

Spanish Cognates

To support Spanish speakers, point out the cognates.

value = valor

video = video

equal = igual

construction = construcción

receive = recibir

future = futuro

Introduce the Lesson

Set Purpose Explain to students that in this lesson they will read informational texts to learn how to use money wisely.

Access Prior Knowledge Find out what students already know about how people choose to spend money. Review the terms *needs* and *wants*. Ask: *What are some things that people often spend money on? What do they* need *to spend money on? What do they* want *to spend money on? What should people think about before they decide to spend money?*

Spark Curiosity Have students study the photographs on p. 295 of the Research Companion and read the caption. Ask: *What kinds of things are people buying? What type of store do you think this is?* (food, fruits and vegetables; a grocery store)

Have students work with a partner to brainstorm types of things that people buy and the types of stores they buy them from. Have two pairs share their ideas with each other, and then report their group's ideas to the class.

Build Meaning & Support Language

Inquiry Journal

Analyze the Source (pages 282–283) As you read "Good Money Choices," explain any words that students don't know. Make sure they understand the term *benefits*. Then work with students to unlock the Primary Source. Tell students that this is a quote from a book called *Poor Richard's Almanack*. The *Almanack* came out every year and provided a variety of information, such as calendars, weather information, and advice for living. Explain that the quote is called an *analogy*. An analogy is a comparison between two unlike things. Tell students that in this analogy, a hole in a ship is compared to small expenses. Help students understand that Benjamin Franklin is saying many small expenses can lead to financial difficulty, just as a small hole can sink a very large ship

Inquiry Tools (pages 284–285) Tell students they will explore **Main Idea and Details** as they read selections about how to use money wisely. Read through the steps on p. 284 about finding the main idea and key details. Then work with students to complete the graphic organizer on p. 284. Explain that they will use the graphic organizer on p. 285 to record information as they read the Research Companion.

Research Companion

Using Money (pages 294–296) Explain that the word *earn* means "receive money for work done." Then discuss with students the concept of allowance. Read the first paragraph on p. 296. Ask: *What are some examples of how people earn money?* (work in construction, as bankers, teachers, truck drivers) Have students suggest other jobs that people do to earn money. Explain that the phrase *left over* does not refer to food. In this context it is extra money a person has after they have paid for needs.

Earning Money to Help Others (page 297) Clarify the meanings of the words *volunteer* and *citizen*. Explain that *raise money* is another way to describe earning money and is typically used when people want money for a special purpose. Read the first two paragraphs. Ask: *What are examples of ways the students raised money?* (sold bracelets, had bake sales, conducted a walk) You may want to discuss how events such as walks are often used as a way to raise money for a cause.

Making Economic Choices (pages 298–299) Explain that *tradeoff* means "exchange." Divide it into two words to show how it is a compound word. Read p. 298 and look at the photos. Discuss with students the order in which they should read the captions on the photo on p. 298. Then talk about the pros and cons of buying each item.

Building Your Own Capital (pages 300–301) Discuss the meanings of the terms *income* and *human capital* with students and help them see how the two terms are connected. Explain that income is money we earn for doing work. The skills, experience, and knowledge we have make up our human capital. Human capital is what helps us get a job and earn an income.

Inquiry Journal

Report Your Findings (pages 286–287) Before they write their list of questions, have students discuss with partners ways they can decide what to buy and when to buy it. Remind students that questions end with a question mark.

Language Forms & Conventions

Irregular Past-Tense Forms Check that students understand the meaning of *past* and *present*. Review past and present tense. Remind students that many past-tense verbs are formed by adding *-d* or *-ed*, but others, called irregular verbs, have a different form in the past tense. Display the chart below. Name the irregular action words and model forming the past tense of each.

Present	Past
sell	sold
hold	held
spend	spent

Have pairs scan the text for examples of past-tense verbs. Have them write sentences that show their meaning. Then have them use the irregular verbs from the chart and repeat the activity.

Cross-Cultural Connection

Money is different in many countries. In the United States we use the U.S. dollar. However, our neighbors have their own money. Canada uses the Canadian dollar, and Mexico uses the Mexican peso. In some tourist areas of these countries, they will accept the U.S. dollar to pay for things. However, there is an exchange rate that determines how much of a U.S. dollar is needed to pay for Canadian or Mexican goods. Some countries share money. In Europe countries in the European Union use the euro to pay for goods and services.

Leveled Support

Entering & Emerging
Provide the following sentence frame: *If I want to buy something, I should think about _____.*

Developing & Expanding
Have small groups create a list of ideas or questions to consider before purchasing an item.

Bridging & Reaching
Have partners identify an item they would like to buy and write three questions to ask themselves before purchasing it.

Language Transfer

It is common for students to use incorrect past-tense verb forms by overgeneralizing the use of the *-ed* ending. Introduce appropriate forms when hearing words such as *selled* (sold), *spended* (spent), or *holded* (held) by restating the student's idea using the correct verb form.

LESSON QUESTION

How Can You Use Money Wisely?

**INQUIRY JOURNAL,
pp. 280–281**

Bellringer

Prompt students to retrieve information from the previous lessons. Say: *Businesses make money by selling goods and services. People must earn money to buy those goods and services to meet their needs. But money is often limited. Most people have to decide how to spend their money. What do you think about when you choose to spend money on something?* (Answers will vary, but students may suggest that they just buy something when they want it without thinking about the consequences, or they may suggest that they take time before buying something to ensure it is something they really need or want.)

Lesson Outcomes

Discuss the lesson questions and lesson outcomes with students.

- Check to make sure that students understand the concept of analyzing costs and benefits. Have volunteers provide definitions for *cost* and *benefit*. Explain that everyone needs to think about the costs and benefits of buying things before they make a choice about how to spend their money. By doing so, they make sure that the choice they make is the best one.

- Explain to students they will be able to write a list of questions that they should ask themselves before spending their money.

Talk About It

Have students look at the photograph on pp. 280–281 of the Inquiry Journal. Explain that the image illustrates a typical economic choice: *Which of these items should I buy?* Have students think about and discuss the choices they need to make and what they need to do to make their decision. Ask: *When you go to spend money, what influences your choices the most?*

 Collaborative Conversations

Take Turns Talking As students engage in partner, small-group, and whole-class discussions, encourage them to:
- wait for a person to finish before they speak.
- quietly raise their hand to let others know they would like a turn to speak.
- ask others in the groups to share their opinions so that all students have a chance to share.

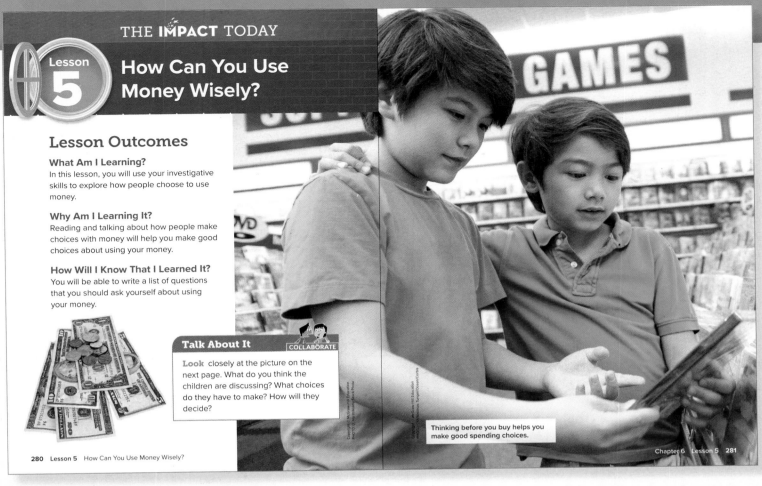

Lesson 5 — How Can You Use Money Wisely?

Lesson Outcomes

What Am I Learning?
In this lesson, you will use your investigative skills to explore how people choose to use money.

Why Am I Learning It?
Reading and talking about how people make choices with money will help you make good choices about using your money.

How Will I Know That I Learned It?
You will be able to write a list of questions that you should ask yourself about using your money.

Talk About It COLLABORATE

Look closely at the picture on the next page. What do you think the children are discussing? What choices do they have to make? How will they decide?

Thinking before you buy helps you make good spending choices.

280 Lesson 5 How Can You Use Money Wisely?

Chapter 6 Lesson 5 281

INQUIRY JOURNAL, pp. 280–281

EL English Learners SCAFFOLD

Use the following scaffolds to support student understanding of lesson outcomes.

Entering and Emerging

Work with students to describe details in the picture on p. 281 of the Inquiry Journal. Read the caption and explain that the boys have choices: whether to buy something and what they should buy. Provide sentence frames to help students describe what they see in the photograph.

- Two boys are thinking about _____.
- I think the boys are considering _____ before they buy something.

Developing and Expanding

Have small groups work together to read the caption and describe what is going on in the photograph. Ask: *What does the phrase* good spending choices *mean? What do you think the boys are thinking about buying? What should the boys consider before they spend their money?*

Bridging and Reaching

Have student pairs discuss the photograph. Ask: *If you were one of those boys, how would you decide which video game to buy or if you needed to buy a video game?* Then have students write sentences to describe two things they would consider before buying a game.

Social Emotional Learning

Relationship Skills

Engage with Others Point out to students that the ability to listen well and take one's turn to speak helps build strong relationships with others. Remind students that listening carefully to what others have to say can help them learn new things or see a situation from a different point of view.

 Digital Tools

Blended Learning
Students engage with the lesson question and discussion prompts.

Interactive IMPACT

Discuss the **Lesson Question** and **Talk About It.**

Analyze the Source | THE IMPACT TODAY

Good Money Choices

1 Inspect

Read the title. What do you think this text will be about?

- **Underline** questions you should ask before buying something.

My Notes

_____

_____

_____

_____

_____

_____

_____

_____

_____

_____

_____

How do you decide how to use your money? Do you save some or spend it all? When you spend money, do you buy something you need or something you want? Do you take time to think about your purchase before making it? It is important to ask yourself some questions before you buy something. You might ask: Is this something I really need? Is the most expensive item the best choice? Will a less expensive item be just as good? Do I have enough money? Should I save my money for something else I really need or want?

PRIMARY SOURCE

In Their Words... Benjamin Franklin

"Beware of little expenses, a small leak will sink a great ship."

—*Poor Richard's Almanack*

People spend money on things that they need and on things that they want.

Earning money takes time and effort. So, people need to make good choices about how to use their money. They might save, donate, or spend some of their money.

People buy things they need, such as food. They buy other things because they want them, like games and toys. People need to think about the costs and **benefits** of buying an item because every choice involves a tradeoff. It's easy to spend money on a want without thinking about it. But that could mean they may not have enough to buy something they really need later.

2 Find Evidence

Reread What is the difference between a want and a need?

Examine the text. What examples does it give of wants and needs?

3 Make Connections

Talk With a partner, discuss Benjamin Franklin's statement. What does it mean? Do you agree? Why or why not?

282 Lesson 5 How Can You Use Money Wisely?

Chapter 6 Lesson 5 283

INQUIRY JOURNAL, pp. 282–283

Analyze the Source

Background Information

Benjamin Franklin was born in Boston, Massachusetts, in 1706 into a poor family of seventeen children. He soon left Boston for Philadelphia where he prospered. Using the pen name Poor Richard, he wrote, edited, printed, and sold the popular *Poor Richard's Almanack* from 1732–1757. He became so successful, that he retired at age forty-two and devoted his time to public service and the study of science.

1 Inspect

Read Have students read the text, including the Primary Source.

- Underline questions to consider before buying something. (the costs and benefits of buying that item)

2 Find Evidence

Reread Have students reread the text, study the image, and answer the question.

Examine Have students circle some needs and wants mentioned in the text. (Needs: food; Wants: games and toys)

3 Make Connections

Talk Have students discuss Benjamin Franklin's statement, determine what they think it means, and explain whether or not they agree with it and why. (Students should understand that small amounts of money spent over many days could add up to a lot of money spent on things that are unnecessary.)

EL Spotlight on Language

Understanding Language

most expensive: means the item costs more than any other item like it

less expensive: means the item does not cost as much as another item like it

Explore Main Idea and Details

The **main idea** is the most important idea of a paragraph, a section, or an article. **Details** tell more about the main idea. When you read, it is helpful to focus on the main ideas.

1. **Read the text all the way through.**
   This will help you understand what the text is about.

2. **Think about what you read.**
   Ask yourself: *What is it about? What is the author trying to say?*

3. **In each section of the text, look for a main idea.**
   Section titles will give you clues. Sometimes the first or last paragraph in a section contains the main idea.

4. **Look for key details that tell more about the main ideas.**

Based on the text you read, work with your class to complete the chart.

	Main Idea	Details
Wise Money Choices	People need to make good choices when they spend money.	Answers will vary, but students should provide some details from the article, such as thinking about whether you really need the item, how much it costs, etc.

284 Lesson 5 How Can You Use Money Wisely?

 ## Investigate!

Read pages 294–301 in your Research Companion. Use your investigative skills to look for text evidence that tells you the main ideas and their supporting details. This chart will help you organize your notes.

Statements of main ideas will vary. Below are examples.

	Main Idea	Details
Using Money	People earn money and make decisions about how to spend it.	Answers should provide details about earning an income and spending money on needs and wants.
Earning Money to Help Others	People can make a difference by giving money to help others.	Answers should provide details about how the students in San Anselmo raised money to help communities in Ecuador.
Making Economic Choices	Before buying something, you need to think about the costs and benefits of your choices.	Answers may include the costs and benefits of a specific choice or how to use a budget to make economic choices.
Building Your Own Capital	Building our human capital will make us more valuable in our communities and our jobs.	Answers should provide details such as studying in school and being involved in activities in and out of school.

Chapter 6 Lesson 5 285

INQUIRY JOURNAL, pp. 284–285

Inquiry Tools

Explore Main Idea and Details

Read Have students read the step-by-step instructions about how to identify main ideas and details. Tell students that a text is usually structured around a main idea with supporting details. Sometimes each paragraph in a text is based on a specific topic. This topic is the main idea of the paragraph. In a selection, the main idea may be directly stated in the first paragraph but could also be stated elsewhere in the selection. The details that support this main idea are described in the rest of the selection's content.

Guide Practice Have students review the text on pp. 282–283. Then work with them to complete the graphic organizer. Explain that they will use a similar graphic organizer to organize their independent research.

Check Understanding Confirm student understanding of the inquiry skill, Explore Main Idea and Details. If students cannot identify the main idea and details, review the steps on p. 284.

Investigate!

Have students read pp. 294–301 in the Research Companion. Tell them the information will help them answer the lesson question *How Can You Use Money Wisely?*

Take Notes Tell students that they will take notes in the graphic organizer on p. 285 of the Inquiry Journal. Remind students that making notes in their own words of what they have read will help them keep track of the main ideas and details described in the lesson. These notes will help them when they write about how they can make good money choices.

 ## Spotlight on Content

When Details Are Clues to the Main Idea

Tell students that sometimes a main idea is not directly stated. In that case, they need to determine the main idea by deciding what the key details have in common or how they are connected.

▶ Digital Tools

Blended Learning

Students prepare for the lesson investigation with step-by-step instruction about how to determine the main idea and details.

ePresentation

Use the **Inquiry Tools** to model and complete the lesson graphic organizer.

LESSON 5 INVESTIGATE

How Can You Use Money Wisely?

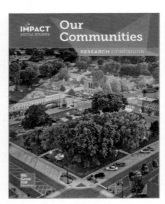

RESEARCH COMPANION, pp. 294–295

Background Information

- Before the invention of a **medium of exchange** such as money, most people bartered. They exchanged goods or services that had a value that both parties agreed on. Eventually, the use of a currency, such as beads and shells, developed and were used as money is used today. Money works today because buyers, sellers, and earners accept its symbolic value.
- A person's **income** mainly depends on their **education**. The more education people have, the more likely it is that they earn a large income. The Bureau of Labor Statistics reports that anesthesiologists and surgeons have the highest annual wages, while cooks and fast food workers have the lowest. But despite this wage gap, Americans donate money to help others. In 2015, Americans gave over $268 billion in charitable donations.
- Budgets are an important tool for **financial planning**. They keep track of income and expenses. People, businesses, and governments use budgets to plan for their futures. Today, an important part of people's financial planning is preparing for their future to ensure they have enough funds saved for retirement.
- Developing our **human capital** cannot be overstated. The highly technical world of today makes having a college or graduate degree and specialized skills a must for job candidates. The more education, skills, and experience people can list on their résumés, the more marketable they become and the more attractive they are to potential employers.

Using Money

1 Inspect Have students read pp. 294–295 and explain how people use money.

2 Find Evidence Use the questions below to check comprehension. Remind students to support their answers with text evidence.

Interpret Use the clues in the text to determine the definition of the word *value*. (the monetary worth of something) **DOK 2**

Make Observations Look at the photograph on p. 295. Would you describe the items being purchased as wants or needs? Explain your answer. (The people in the photograph are in line buying food at a grocery store. Food is something that everyone needs to survive, so the people are purchasing needs.) **DOK 2**

3 Make Connections

Hypothesize What do you think would happen if a business tried to sell an item at a higher price than buyers thought it was worth? (Answers will vary, but students may conclude that people would not purchase the item or that the business would not be able to sell the item and may reduce the price.) **DOK 3**

THE IMPACT TODAY

Lesson 5

How Can You Use Money Wisely?

Using Money

How do you earn money? Maybe you get a weekly allowance or get paid for chores. Why do you need money? Money has a value because it is scarce. Money is something we use to buy goods and services. Perhaps you have traded a book or a game with a friend. You traded because the items had the same value. Would you trade a video game for a baseball cap? Probably not. They have very different values. We use money because it is an easy way to exchange things of equal value. If a video game costs $50, you exchange that amount of money for the game. It is an equal exchange.

People use money to buy things they need, such as food and clothing. They also use money to buy things they want.

People buy many things every week.

RESEARCH COMPANION, pp. 294–295

English Learners SCAFFOLD

Use the following scaffolds to support student understanding of lesson content.

Entering and Emerging

Review with students the definition of *needs* and *wants*. Then have students study the photographs on pp. 294–295. Provide sentence frames to help them identify wants and needs pictured in the photos.

- I see a _____, which is a want.
- I see a _____, which is a need.

Developing and Expanding

Have small groups work together to review the text and look at the photographs on pp. 294–295. Ask: *How do people your age earn money? What items in the photos are needs? What items in the photos are wants? Are the photos showing someone buying goods or services?*

Bridging and Reaching

Have students work in pairs to discuss the photograph on p. 295. Then have them write a sentence for each person in the photo. Encourage them to include what each person is buying or selling and whether the buyers are purchasing needs or wants.

▶ Digital Tools

Blended Learning

Flip the research approach and find evidence in a digital format.

eBook

Students investigate using their **Research Companion** and **IMPACT Explorer Magazine eBooks** to find evidence.

Most people need to work to get money. You may earn money by doing chores. Adults earn money by working at jobs. There are many types of jobs, such as construction workers, bankers, teachers, or truck drivers. People have jobs to earn an income. An income is the money a person receives for work.

By earning an income, people get money to spend. Most money is spent on needs such as a place to live, food, or clothing. But sometimes there is money left over. This can be spent on something that is nice to have, or it can be saved. When people choose to save their money, they can buy things in the future.

Earning income in an office

A forklift operator

296   Lesson 5   How Can You Use Money Wisely?

Citizenship

Earning Money to Help Others

A good citizen tries to help people in need. Sometimes this means helping communities in other countries. Students in San Anselmo, California, created the Ross Valley Free the Children Club. Its members volunteer and raise money to help other people nearby and around the world.

The group learned that some communities in Ecuador could not get clean water. The club decided to raise money to buy equipment that would provide clean water to those communities. Students organized many events to raise funds. They made and sold bracelets, held bake sales, and conducted a Walk for Water. In the end, the club raised over $20,000 for the clean-water systems.

People can help make a difference by giving money for a good reason. Would you make the choice to give some of your money to help others?

A walk to raise money for charity

✓ Stop and Check

Think Why is it sometimes good to save money rather than spend it right away?

Find Details As you read, add new information to the graphic organizer on page 285 in your Inquiry Journal.

Chapter 6   Lesson 5   297

RESEARCH COMPANION, pp. 296–297

Earning Money to Help Others

1 Inspect Have students read pp. 296–297 and explain how people earn money.

2 Find Evidence Use the questions below to check comprehension.

Summarize What is the benefit of saving money? (People have money available so they can buy things they need or want in the future.) **DOK 2**

Interpret What can people do to make a difference and help others? (People can give money to organizations that help with the needs of others.) **DOK 2**

3 Make Connections

Hypothesize Imagine there's a group or an organization that you and your classmates would like to support. What are some things that you could do to raise money? (Answers will vary. Encourage students to think of realistic activities, such as a walk-a-thon, bike-a-thon, or a rummage sale.) **DOK 3**

✓ Stop and Check   COLLABORATE

Think Ask partners to discuss what might happen if they spent their money as soon as they earned it. (Students should understand that saving money allows them to have money to spend on future needs and wants.)

Find Details Explain to students that after they read and take notes, they should review and think about how the facts and details will help them answer the Essential Question.

 Spotlight on Language

Verbs Ending in -ed

learned; earned; raised: These are verbs that have *-d* or *-ed* added to the root verb. Remind students that the *-ed* tells us the action happened in the past. We say that they are verbs written in the past tense. To find the root verb drop the *-d* or *-ed*.

 Digital Tools

Blended Learning
Students investigate curated resources and find evidence to answer the lesson question.

Interactive IMPACT
Students choose from print or digital **Inquiry Tools** to take notes.

Making Economic Choices

Before you buy something, you need to think about the costs and **benefits** of your choices. Every buying choice involves a tradeoff. You may give up something you want when you buy something else.

Look at Jamie's choices. Which should Jamie buy? First, look at the cost of each item. Jamie has enough to buy either one. If Jamie buys the tablet, he would have to spend all of his savings. Now, what are the benefits of each item? Jamie could use the tablet to do research and play games. Jamie could use the bike to get to school and to soccer practice. Buying choices are not always simple. Jamie must decide what is more important to him.

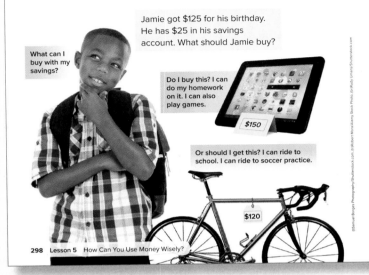

Jamie got $125 for his birthday. He has $25 in his savings account. What should Jamie buy?

What can I buy with my savings?

Do I buy this? I can do my homework on it. I can also play games.

$150

Or should I get this? I can ride to school. I can ride to soccer practice.

$120

Another way to help make buying decisions is to keep a budget. A budget is a plan for using money. It shows all the income expected in a week or month. It also shows all the expenses that must be paid each week or month. The money left over can be used for anything.

But should this leftover money be spent? What happens if a family has an expense it did not expect? A family needs to decide how to handle this leftover money. They may choose to save some so they are ready for an unexpected expense.

Knowing that there is only so much money to spend helps people make decisions on what to buy. Sometimes a buyer's decision may be not to spend any money at all.

Some families choose to spend money at restaurants.

✓ Stop and Check

Talk With a partner, discuss the decision Jamie has to make. If you were Jamie, what decision would you make? Why?

RESEARCH COMPANION, pp. 298–299

Making Economic Choices

1 Inspect Have students read pp. 298–299 and define the word *tradeoff*.

2 Find Evidence Use the questions below to check comprehension.

Infer What do you think makes Jamie's decision so difficult? (He has enough money to buy either item, but he has to decide whether he wants to use all his birthday money and savings to buy the more expensive item.) **DOK 2**

Draw Conclusions What are the benefits of making a budget? (A budget enables a person to know exactly how much income he or she has, how much he or she has in expenses, and how much money he or she is likely to have left over.) **DOK 2**

3 Make Connections

Hypothesize Think about an expensive item that you really want. Would you be willing to tradeoff all of the things you could buy with your money if you had to save up for three months to buy the expensive item? Would you be willing to tradeoff some lesser items if it took you longer to save for the expensive item? Give reasons. (Answers will vary.) **DOK 3**

✓ Stop and Check

Talk Encourage students to consider the costs and benefits of each decision before determining the choice they would make. (Answers will vary; there is no right decision. Students should determine what decision they would make and explain why. They also should show that they understand the benefits of each choice.)

Spotlight on Language

leftover money: money that is left after you have paid for your needs

unexpected expense: a cost, or expense, that you did not plan on

RESEARCH COMPANION, pp. 300–301

Social Emotional Learning

Self-Regulation

Set Goals The ability to set and work toward academic and personal goals is a very important attribute for students to have. Setting goals and developing their own human capital go hand-in-hand. Ask: *What do you want to learn or what skill do you want to improve? How will that goal build your human capital?*

 Digital Tools

Blended Learning
Students investigate curated resources and find evidence to answer the lesson question.

Interactive IMPACT

Students **Research** and find evidence using digital format texts.

Building Your Own Capital

1 Inspect Have students read pp. 300–301 and list what makes up human capital.

2 Find Evidence Use the questions below to check comprehension.

Infer What skills or experiences do you think the children in the pictures are gaining? (Answers will vary but may include learning how to use tools, how to build things, and how to work together to accomplish a goal.) **DOK 2**

Assess Think of three subjects you are currently studying in school. What skills are you learning from them and how are they developing your human capital? (Possible answers: math is teaching me how to solve equations; reading is teaching me how to read as well as analyze text; social studies is helping me know what has happened in the past and how it affects the present.) **DOK 3**

3 Make Connections

Draw Conclusions What do you think would be the best way to develop your human capital? (Answers will vary, but students may recognize that getting a good education is the best way to develop their human capital.) **DOK 3**

 **Stop and Check**

Talk Ask students to think of a skill, an experience, or knowledge that they would like to have. Then have students discuss how they would go about learning it. (Answers will vary, but students should point out that *human capital* refers to your skills, experiences, and knowledge that will help you when you have a job. Students may point out that they may build human capital by learning as much as possible at school. They may also build human capital by joining clubs and activities at school or in their community.)

What Is the IMPACT Today?

Encourage students to think about why it is important to spend money wisely. (Answers will vary, but students may mention that people could spend money wisely by keeping a budget and considering the costs and benefits of the items they want to buy.)

Building Your Own Capital

You have learned that people get paid an income for the work they do. They use their income to buy the things they need and want and to save for the future. However, we don't always get paid for the jobs we do.

Your job right now is to go to school. You don't get paid an income for the work you do in school, but you are earning in other ways. The subjects you study in school help you "earn" or gain knowledge. This kind of earning is known as developing your human capital. Human capital is made up of the skills, experiences, and knowledge that will help you when you have a job and earn your own income. As you learn, you develop the tools you'll need to do different kinds of jobs.

There are different ways to develop your own human capital. One way is by going to school to learn new things and find out what interests you. Another way to develop your human capital is by being involved in activities in school and in your community. This will give you many different experiences. You'll learn new things from your different experiences. All the things you learn help you build your human capital. As a result, you become more valuable in your community and in your job.

A school project also builds human capital.

Did You Know?

The word *capital* has many different meanings. In this lesson, *capital* means things that have value, such as human capital, money in the bank, and property that someone owns.

Capital also means the city in a state or country where the government is located. Atlanta is the *capital* of Georgia.

In writing, a *capital* is an uppercase letter. Always begin a sentence with a *capital* letter.

What other meanings can you find for the word *capital*?

Stop and Check

COLLABORATE

Talk Discuss with a partner what *human capital* means. What could you do to build your own human capital?

What Is the IMPACT Today? What are things people can do today to spend money wisely?

A workshop can help you build human capital.

RESEARCH COMPANION, pp. 300–301

English Learners SCAFFOLD

Use the following scaffolds to support student understanding of lesson content.

Entering and Emerging

Review the meaning of the term *human capital*. Say: *Human capital is the knowledge, skills, and experiences a person has.* Have students think about the ways they are developing their human capital each day at school. Provide sentence frames to help students as needed:

- At school, I am learning about _____.
- I am also learning to _____.
- Someday, this will help me _____.

Developing and Expanding

Review the meaning of the term *human capital*. Have small groups discuss the kinds of skills they are developing at school. Then have them make a list of ways they can use these skills in the future. Ask: *What skills are you developing in school? How will those skills help you when you are an adult? What activities can you do now to help you develop more human capital?*

Bridging and Reaching

Have partners discuss what human capital is and how a person develops more human capital. Then have them talk about what they would like to do when they grow up and the knowledge, skills, and experiences they are developing now that will help them. Have partners report back to the larger group.

✔ Check for Success

Explain Can students explain how people earn money and decide how to use their money?

Differentiate

If Not, Review with students the graphic organizer on p. 285 of their Inquiry Journals. Guide students to find the main ideas in the text about using and earning money and identify the details about how to make good choices with money.

LESSON 5 REPORT

How Can You Use Money Wisely?

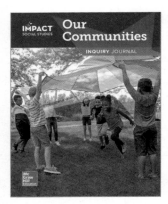

**INQUIRY JOURNAL,
pp. 286–287**

Think About It

Have students review and examine their research to create a list of questions that can help them decide what to buy and when to buy it. Remind students to review the text and images as well as their graphic organizers for evidence to support their answers. Direct students back to pp. 294–301 of their Research Companion if they need more information.

Write About It

Write and Cite Evidence Remind students to include the following elements in their responses.

- Determine an order for your questions.
- Include details that support your list of questions.
- Provide an explanation for why you chose each question.

Discipline(s)	4	3	2	1
Economic Understanding	Student shows strong understanding of wants and needs and the questions a person should ask before spending money.	Student shows adequate understanding of wants and needs and the questions a person should ask before spending money.	Student shows uneven understanding of wants and needs and the questions a person should ask before spending money.	Student shows no understanding of wants and needs and the questions a person should ask before spending money.

Talk About It

Discuss Remind students to take turns discussing their opinions. Explain that they do not necessarily need to agree on which questions are the most important, but they should explain their reasoning for their choices.

Assessment Students can check their understanding with feedback from the **Lesson Test** available online.

Connect to the Essential Question

Look at Our Community Before they respond, remind students to think about how someone makes good choices about money and how the choices of one person can affect a community.

Inquiry Project Update Remind students to turn to Inquiry Journal pp. 244–245 for project information. If necessary, review the Project Checklist with students. At this point in the chapter, students should focus on the final two items on the checklist.

Think About It

Examine
Based on your research, what will help you make wise choices about using money?

Write About It

Write and Cite Evidence
What questions should you consider before you buy something? Use details from the text to explain your response.

Answers will vary, but students may include:
1. Is this a need or a want?
2. How much does it cost?
3. Is the item worth the price?
4. Will a cheaper product do?
5. Do I have other purchases I need more?

Talk About It

Discuss
Compare your list with a partner. Discuss why these questions are important. Which questions do you and your partner think are most important?

Connect to the EQ

Economics

Look at Our Community
How does making good money choices help people in your community meet their needs?

Answers will vary, but students may suggest that using money responsibly means that people are able to meet their needs themselves and possibly help others in their community.

EQ Inquiry Project Notes

INQUIRY JOURNAL, pp. 286–287

EL English Learners SCAFFOLD

Use the following scaffolds to support student writing.

Entering and Emerging

Help students define *want* and *need*. Then provide sentence frames to help them write questions they should consider before they buy something.

- Before I buy something, I should make sure _____.
- It is smart to ask myself _____ before spending money.

Developing and Expanding

Work with students to brainstorm questions they should ask before buying something. Then have them choose and organize their questions in a logical order. Tell students they can use words that show the order in which the questions should be asked, such as *first, second, third,* and *fourth* or the words *then, next,* and *finally*. Remind students to use details from the text to explain their lists.

Bridging and Reaching

Have partners talk about how to make good money choices. Remind them to look at their graphic organizers and review the text to provide support for their questions. Ask: *What is something you should do before you buy something? What can you ask that will help you weigh the benefits and costs? How would having a budget help you make a good money decision?*

✔ Check for Success

Summarize Are students able to write a list of questions they should consider before using money and give supportive details from the text for those questions?

Differentiate

If Not, Have students present their questions as an oral presentation that includes a chart with graphics or illustrations about a specific buying decision.

TAKE ACTION
with INQUIRY JOURNAL

 EQ ESSENTIAL QUESTION

How Do People in a Community Meet Their Wants and Needs?

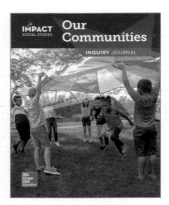

**INQUIRY JOURNAL,
pp. 288–289**

Inquiry Project Wrap-Up

Remind students that they are to have created a blog about a local business and explain how the business helps the community.

Assessment Use the rubric on p. T491 to assess students' Inquiry Projects.

Complete Your Project

Have students work individually to review the Complete Your Project checklist. Remind them that if they have missed any of the criteria, now is their opportunity to make corrections or additions.

Share Your Project

If time allows, you may want to have students present their projects to the class. Provide the following tips to students before they present to the class.

- Prepare and rehearse.
- Use notes to help you stay on topic.
- Speak slowly and clearly. Make sure everyone can hear you.
- Make eye contact and speak directly to the audience.

Reflect on Your Project

Student reflections begin with thinking about the process for how they selected the business to research and crafted interview questions for the owner. Students should focus on the results of the inquiry as well as the challenges and successes of the inquiry process. Students can apply those findings to future projects.

Chapter Connections can focus on anything that resonated with students about their study of the economics of a community and how people meet their wants and needs. These connections may spark students to do further research on their own.

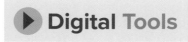 **Digital Tools**

Blended Learning

Students use online checklists to prepare, complete and reflect on their Inquiry Projects.

Chapter Assessments

Students can demonstrate content mastery with the feedback from the online **Chapter Test**.

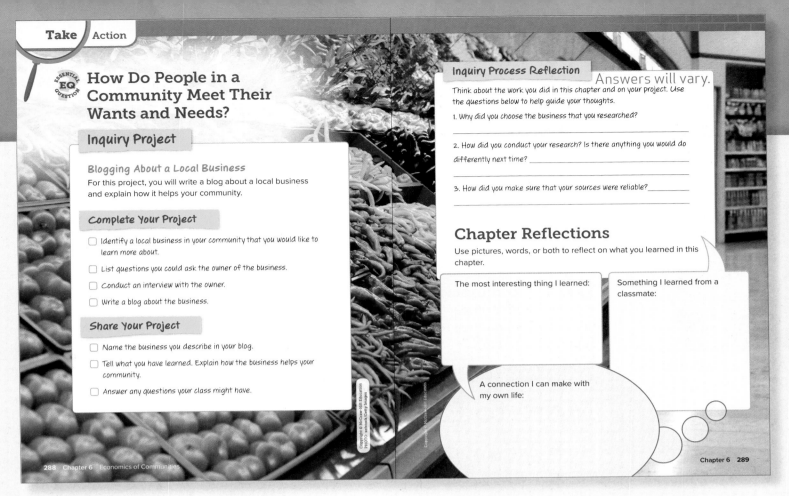

Take Action

How Do People in a Community Meet Their Wants and Needs?

Inquiry Project

Blogging About a Local Business

For this project, you will write a blog about a local business and explain how it helps your community.

Complete Your Project

☐ Identify a local business in your community that you would like to learn more about.

☐ List questions you could ask the owner of the business.

☐ Conduct an interview with the owner.

☐ Write a blog about the business.

Share Your Project

☐ Name the business you describe in your blog.

☐ Tell what you have learned. Explain how the business helps your community.

☐ Answer any questions your class might have.

Inquiry Process Reflection

Answers will vary.

Think about the work you did in this chapter and on your project. Use the questions below to help guide your thoughts.

1. Why did you choose the business that you researched? _____

2. How did you conduct your research? Is there anything you would do differently next time? _____

3. How did you make sure that your sources were reliable? _____

Chapter Reflections

Use pictures, words, or both to reflect on what you learned in this chapter.

The most interesting thing I learned:

Something I learned from a classmate:

A connection I can make with my own life:

INQUIRY JOURNAL, pp. 288–289

 ## English Learners SCAFFOLD

Use the following scaffolds to support students' project reflections

Entering and Emerging

Provide sentences frames such as the following to help students reflect on the work they did in this project:

- We chose to interview the owner of _____ business.
- We chose this business because _____.
- We shared the work by having each group member _____.
- The best part about this project was _____.

Developing and Expanding

Provide the following questions for students to answer as part of the project reflection: *Which local business did you choose? What part of the project did you enjoy the most? What was the most important thing you learned during this project?*

Bridging and Reaching

Have partners review the project checklist and explain how they shared the tasks among the group members. Have students identify and explain tasks they found interesting and tasks they found difficult to complete.

✔ Check for Success

Use your online rubric or the rubric found on p. T491 to record student progress. Can students name a local business and tell how it helps the community?

Differentiate

If Not, Have students create a diagram with the name of the local business in the center and branches that list the ways that business helps the community.

**RESEARCH COMPANION,
pp. 302–303**

Connections in Action

Think Lead a discussion about how people in a community meet their wants and needs. Use your community or another community with which students are familiar. Identify the types of jobs available to the people in that community and how they use their earnings to obtain goods and services.

Talk To help focus students' conversations, brainstorm a list of technological innovations that have had an impact on your community. Then have students choose one of these to discuss with a partner. Remind students to think about evidence they can provide that will support their ideas.

Share Invite students to share their small group discussions with the class.

More to Explore

How Can You Make an IMPACT?

Mix and match the More to Explore activities to meet the needs of your classroom. Stretch student's thinking by offering alternative ways to demonstrate what they learned during the chapter.

These activities are flexible enough that you can assign one, two, or three activities to specific students or have students work in small groups. Remind students to use proper collaborative procedures when they work with partners.

Give Advice

Bring in some ads for different cars so that students can compare prices of various models. Discuss other features that might affect the purchase of a car, such as gas mileage, insurance costs, safety records, warranties, or special packages.

Teacher Tip! **This activity can be used to monitor students' critical thinking and analysis skills.**

Create a Sketch

Review the terms *capital resources, human resources,* and *natural resources* with students. Then list local businesses, and discuss the types of resources each business uses. Have students work with partners to choose a business and sketch the resources.

Teacher Tip! **Use this activity to monitor students' understanding of chapter vocabulary.**

Write a "Want Ad"

Project some real want ads for students to see. Then list possible careers with students. Invite students to make suggestions about what should be in the want ad for each career. Have students work with partners to write the want ad for one of the careers.

Teacher Tip! **Use this activity to allow students to practice setting goals.**

▶ Digital Tools

Blended Learning

Students apply chapter concepts to extension activities and connect them to the EQ.

Interactive IMPACT

Review chapter vocabulary with **Word Play**.

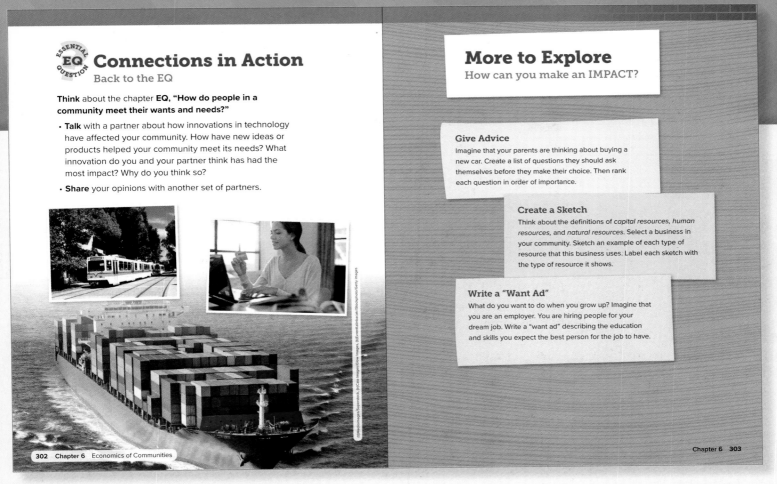

Connections in Action
Back to the EQ

Think about the chapter EQ, "How do people in a community meet their wants and needs?"

• **Talk** with a partner about how innovations in technology have affected your community. How have new ideas or products helped your community meet its needs? What innovation do you and your partner think has had the most impact? Why do you think so?

• **Share** your opinions with another set of partners.

More to Explore
How can you make an IMPACT?

Give Advice
Imagine that your parents are thinking about buying a new car. Create a list of questions they should ask themselves before they make their choice. Then rank each question in order of importance.

Create a Sketch
Think about the definitions of *capital resources, human resources,* and *natural resources.* Select a business in your community. Sketch an example of each type of resource that this business uses. Label each sketch with the type of resource it shows.

Write a "Want Ad"
What do you want to do when you grow up? Imagine that you are an employer. You are hiring people for your dream job. Write a "want ad" describing the education and skills you expect the best person for the job to have.

302 Chapter 6 Economics of Communities

Chapter 6 303

RESEARCH COMPANION, pp. 302–303

 # English Learners SCAFFOLD

Use the following scaffolds to support student understanding of chapter content.

Entering and Emerging

Explain to students that the term *innovation* means a new idea, a new device, or a new way of doing something. Work with students to identify some innovations in technology, such as bluetooth or cloud computing. Provide the following sentence frames to facilitate discussion:

• Some innovations in technology that I know about are _____.

• Our community has used new technology to improve _____.

• This has helped the community because _____.

Developing and Expanding

Work with students to write a definition of *innovation.* Then discuss innovations in technology with which they are familiar. Ask questions to facilitate discussion: *What new kinds of technology do you see being used in your community? Which one do you think has had the greatest impact on the community? Why?*

Bridging and Reaching

Have students work with partners to write a definition of *innovation* in their own words. Then have partners discuss different technological innovations they know about and which of these are in use in the community. Have them list ways that different kinds of technology can be used to have a positive impact on the community.

 ## Social Emotional Learning

Relationship Skills
Communicate Effectively
Remind students that to communicate effectively, they need to share ideas with others, listen actively, use clear and precise language, and address any questions their listeners might have. Explain that effective communication will help them cooperate with others and negotiate conflict when it arises.

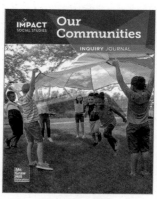

**INQUIRY JOURNAL,
pp. 290–295**

Extend Learning

Deepen students' understanding of economics with the Reader's Theater selection, "Studying the Stars." First, analyze the ideas in the text. Then prepare and read the text as a Reader's Theater.

> | **GENRE** | Reader's Theater Reader's Theater is a form of drama in which actors do not memorize their lines. They use their voices rather than sets or costumes to help listeners understand the text.

Perform the Reader's Theater

Model the reading. Project the play with an interactive whiteboard or projector and read aloud as students follow along. As you read, use your voice to show how expression and rate can communicate meaning. Explain how exclamation points should affect expression.

Choose a few lines to examine. Discuss how a reader should read the lines:

- **Dad:** A telescope? Really? Is that something you need or just something you want? *How should the character read this line? Why do you think so?* (The sentences end in question marks, so they should be asked like questions. But "Really?" indicates that the father is surprised by Ava's statement, so he might sound like he doesn't believe her.)

- **Beth:** Yuk! *How should the character read this line? Why do you think so?* (The exclamation point means that the character should read this line loudly. Since the line before is about cleaning up after a dog, it should also show disgust.)

Practice the reading. Before students read aloud on their own, give them time to practice reading. Use techniques such as the following:

- Echo Read—Read a line and then have students repeat it.
- Partner Read—Have students work in pairs and take turns reading the lines of the play out loud. They can correct each other but should do it in a helpful, collaborative way.

Assign roles. Consider these strategies:

- Pair up students to take turns reading a role if some of your students are reluctant to participate.
- Put students into performance groups, and let them try out different roles.
- Have students mark up their scripts. They can highlight their dialogue, underline stage directions, and circle words they should emphasize when they speak.

Talk About It

As students discuss their experiences, they should consider an item that they wanted to buy and the plan they put in place to get that item. Ask students to discuss what they had to give up to get the item. For example, did students have to forgo buying something else they wanted in order to have enough money to buy the item?

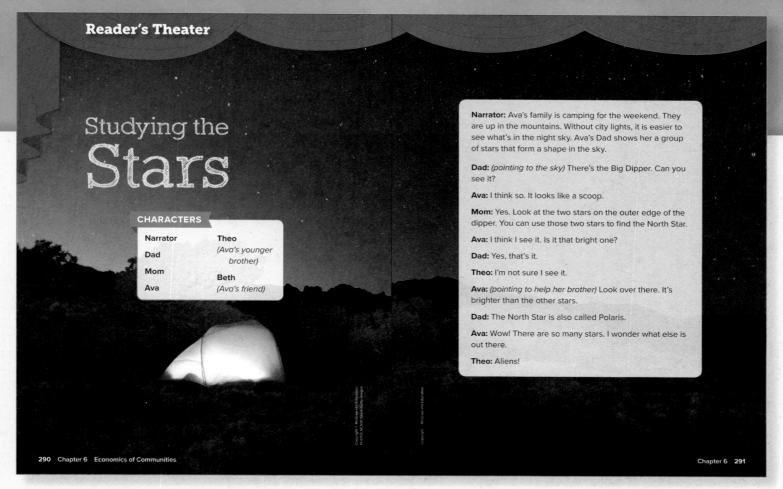

Studying the Stars

CHARACTERS

Narrator	Theo
Dad	*(Ava's younger brother)*
Mom	
Ava	Beth
	(Ava's friend)

Narrator: Ava's family is camping for the weekend. They are up in the mountains. Without city lights, it is easier to see what's in the night sky. Ava's Dad shows her a group of stars that form a shape in the sky.

Dad: *(pointing to the sky)* There's the Big Dipper. Can you see it?

Ava: I think so. It looks like a scoop.

Mom: Yes. Look at the two stars on the outer edge of the dipper. You can use those two stars to find the North Star.

Ava: I think I see it. Is it that bright one?

Dad: Yes, that's it.

Theo: I'm not sure I see it.

Ava: *(pointing to help her brother)* Look over there. It's brighter than the other stars.

Dad: The North Star is also called Polaris.

Ava: Wow! There are so many stars. I wonder what else is out there.

Theo: Aliens!

INQUIRY JOURNAL, pp. 290–295

Reader's Theater Tips

- Allow students time to practice their lines before performing.
- Have students sit in a circle so they can hear each other as they read their lines.

Remind students of these strategies for reading aloud:

- Speak loudly so that other students can hear you.
- Speak at an appropriate rate.
- Use expression. Pay attention to punctuation.
- If you make a mistake, just keep going.

 Digital Tools

Blended Learning

Students investigate how communities change over time with the online Reader's Theater.

Interactive IMPACT

Use the printable script for whole-class or small-group presentations.

Connect to the Essential Question

Have students connect the Reader's Theater to the Essential Question. Ask: *How does reading Ava's story help you understand why an income and budget are important?* (Answers will vary, but students may say that Ava thought about her purchase and then considered her budget and income. She was willing to work harder and save for what she wanted to buy.)

Teacher Notes

References Sources

Celebrate Holidays

Communities Celebrate Holidays

Throughout the year, people in communities around our country come together to celebrate holidays that are important to them. Holidays help us remember and celebrate different cultures, important people, and events.

In this special section you will read about many holidays. You will see how people all across our country celebrate holidays.

R2

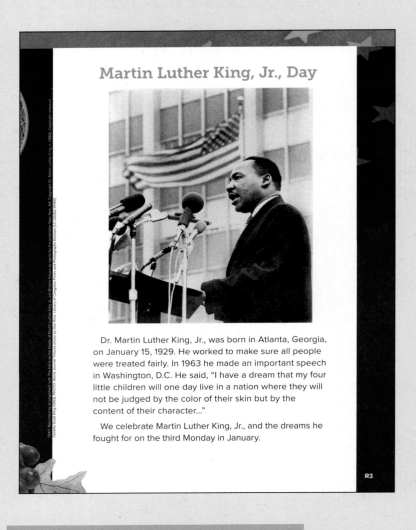

Martin Luther King, Jr., Day

Dr. Martin Luther King, Jr., was born in Atlanta, Georgia, on January 15, 1929. He worked to make sure all people were treated fairly. In 1963 he made an important speech in Washington, D.C. He said, "I have a dream that my four little children will one day live in a nation where they will not be judged by the color of their skin but by the content of their character..."

We celebrate Martin Luther King, Jr., and the dreams he fought for on the third Monday in January.

R3

Background Information

Communities Celebrate Holidays There are many kinds of holidays that people celebrate throughout the United States. Thanksgiving is a cultural holiday that many people like to celebrate with their families. Veterans Day is a patriotic holiday that honors people who have served in the United States military. Some holidays are also officially recognized by federal and state governments. Typically, the U.S. Congress or a state legislature must pass legislation in order to make something a federal or state holiday.

Background Information

Martin Luther King, Jr., Day
Dr. Martin Luther King, Jr., was perhaps the most influential leader of the civil rights movement that took place in the United States during the 1950s and 1960s. Dr. King led a bus boycott in Birmingham, Alabama, after an African American woman named Rosa Parks refused to give up her seat on a bus to a white person. He organized the March on Washington, D.C., in 1963. At the event, he gave his "I Have a Dream" speech. This march was a key event that led to the signing of the Civil Rights Act in 1964.

We celebrate George Washington (top) and Abraham Lincoln (bottom) on Presidents' Day.

Presidents' Day

Presidents' Day is celebrated on the third Monday in February. On this day we honor the work of all people who have served as President of the United States. Schools, banks, government offices and many businesses are closed to show respect for the people who have led our country.

R4

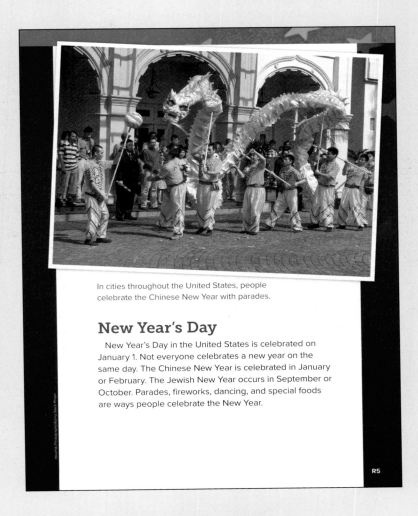

In cities throughout the United States, people celebrate the Chinese New Year with parades.

New Year's Day

New Year's Day in the United States is celebrated on January 1. Not everyone celebrates a new year on the same day. The Chinese New Year is celebrated in January or February. The Jewish New Year occurs in September or October. Parades, fireworks, dancing, and special foods are ways people celebrate the New Year.

R5

Background Information

Presidents' Day Presidents' Day is celebrated each year on the third Monday in February. Although the holiday has a confusing history, many people today recognize Presidents' Day as a celebration of all of America's presidents. The holiday was originally celebrated on Washington's birthday, February 22. But instead of being called Presidents' Day, it was called Washington's Birthday. President Chester Alan Arthur signed a bill establishing Washington's Birthday as a federal holiday in 1885. In 1968, Congress decided to move the holiday from February 22 to the third Monday in February. Over the years, many states have chosen to include Lincoln's birthday in the celebration because he was also born in February. Although Congress never officially changed the name of the holiday from Washington's Birthday to Presidents' Day, millions of Americans now recognize this holiday as a celebration of all presidents.

Background Information

New Year's Day New Year's Day every year is celebrated on January 1 in the United States. The celebration and choice of January 1 dates back to the days of Julius Caesar and the Julian calendar. January itself was named after the Roman god Janus. Janus was the Roman god with two faces, one looking forward and one looking back. The first marking of the new year on January 1 took place in 46 B.C. In the Middle Ages, celebrating New Year's Day fell out of practice. In 1582, the Roman Catholic Church adopted the Gregorian calendar and the practice of celebrating New Year's Day on January 1 returned.

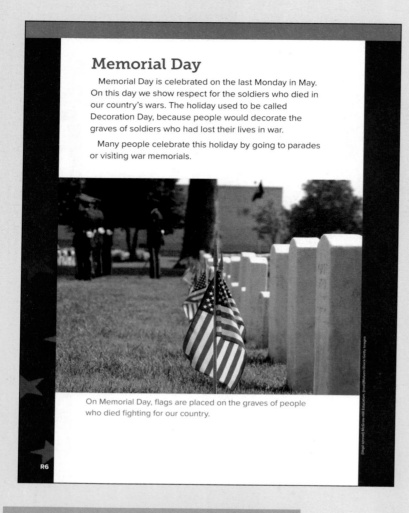

Memorial Day

Memorial Day is celebrated on the last Monday in May. On this day we show respect for the soldiers who died in our country's wars. The holiday used to be called Decoration Day, because people would decorate the graves of soldiers who had lost their lives in war.

Many people celebrate this holiday by going to parades or visiting war memorials.

On Memorial Day, flags are placed on the graves of people who died fighting for our country.

R6

Independence Day

Independence Day, or the Fourth of July, honors our country's birthday. We remember that on July 4, 1776, we declared our independence from Great Britain. We celebrate with parades and fireworks to show that we are proud to be Americans.

R7

Background Information

Memorial Day Memorial Day began as a holiday commemorating the soldiers who died during the Civil War. However, many southern states did not acknowledge Memorial Day until after World War I. Instead, some southern states honored their fallen soldiers on a different day. After World War I, Memorial Day was changed to recognize all soldiers who died serving the United States. Since the Revolutionary War, more than a million Americans have lost their lives serving their country.

Background Information

Independence Day The first battle in the Revolutionary War took place on April 19, 1775, which was before the colonists officially declared independence from Great Britain. The colonies later voted in favor of independence on July 2, 1776. Independence Day—celebrated on July 4 each year—commemorates the signing of the Declaration of Independence in 1776. The Revolutionary War ended in the spring of 1783. On September 3 of that year, Great Britain recognized the colonies as an independent nation by signing the Treaty of Paris.

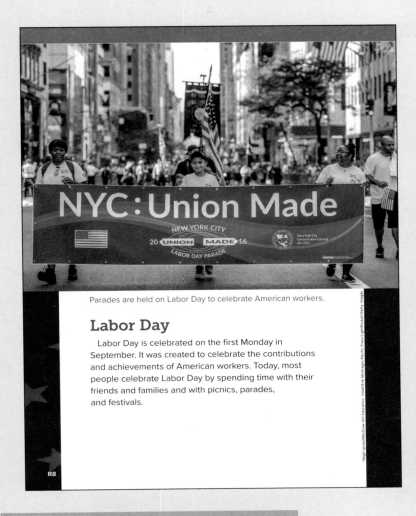

Parades are held on Labor Day to celebrate American workers.

Labor Day

Labor Day is celebrated on the first Monday in September. It was created to celebrate the contributions and achievements of American workers. Today, most people celebrate Labor Day by spending time with their friends and families and with picnics, parades, and festivals.

Thanksgiving

Thanksgiving is celebrated on the fourth Thursday in November. On this day we remember the feast shared by the Pilgrims and the Native Americans. We share a meal with family and friends and enjoy parades and celebrations. It is a time for us to be thankful for the many good things in our lives.

Background Information

Labor Day The very first Labor Day was celebrated in New York City with a parade on September 5, 1882. The idea was conceived by a man named Peter J. Maguire, who in 1881 had founded the United Brotherhood of Carpenters and Joiners. Maguire wanted to celebrate the contributions of American workers. The holiday soon gained support across the country from working people and labor groups, including the Knights of Labor. In 1887, Oregon became the first state to officially recognize Labor Day. Not long after this, Colorado, Massachusetts, New Jersey, and New York also recognized the holiday. On June 28, 1894, Congress officially made Labor Day a national holiday. Labor Day is now celebrated each year in both the United States and Canada. In many countries around the world, they celebrate a holiday similar to Labor Day called May Day.

Background Information

Thanksgiving In 1620, the Pilgrims sailed from Europe to North America and became the first English settlers in what is now the state of Massachusetts. Once there, the Pilgrims encountered the Wampanoag people. In October of 1621, the Pilgrims and Wampanoag people held a three-day feast, sharing food such as deer, duck, goose, and wild turkey. This celebration is commonly referred to as the first Thanksgiving. However, both the English and the Wampanoag people had celebrated rich harvests by giving thanks before.

All page numbers shown here are from the student Research Companion.

Geography Handbook

The Themes of Geography

Geography is the study of Earth and the way people, plants, and animals live on it. Geographers divide geography into five themes. These themes are location, place, region, movement, and human interaction. They help us to think about the world around us.

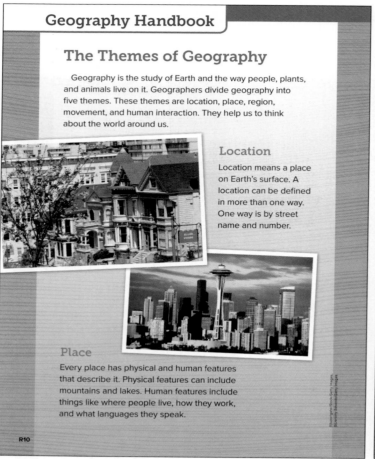

Location

Location means a place on Earth's surface. A location can be defined in more than one way. One way is by street name and number.

Place

Every place has physical and human features that describe it. Physical features can include mountains and lakes. Human features include things like where people live, how they work, and what languages they speak.

R10

Region

A region is bigger than a place or a location. Regions cover large areas of land that share physical or human characteristics.

Movement

Geographers study why people have moved from place to place. They look at how movement changes the culture and physical landscape of an area.

Human Interaction

Geographers study how people and places change each other. People change the environment to meet their needs. For example, people build bridges to make travel easier.

R11

Dictionary of Geographic Terms

1 **CANAL** A channel built to carry water for irrigation or transportation

2 **CANYON** A deep, narrow valley with steep sides

3 **COAST** The land along an ocean

4 **DAM** A wall built across a river, creating a lake that stores water

5 **DELTA** Land made of soil left behind as a river drains into a larger body of water

6 **DESERT** A dry environment with few plants and animals

7 **GLACIER** A huge sheet of ice that moves slowly across the land

8 **GULF** Part of an ocean that extends into the land; larger than a bay

9 **HARBOR** A sheltered place along a coast where boats dock safely

10 **HILL** A rounded, raised landform; not as high as a mountain

11 **ISLAND** A body of land completely surrounded by water

12 **LAKE** A body of water completely surrounded by land

13 **MOUNTAIN** A high landform with steep sides; higher than a hill

14 **MOUNTAIN PASS** A narrow gap through a mountain range

15 **MOUNTAIN RANGE** A row or chain of mountains

R12

16 **MOUTH** The place where a river empties into a larger body of water

17 **OASIS** A fertile area in a desert that is watered by a spring

18 **OCEAN** A large body of salt water; oceans cover much of Earth's surface

19 **PEAK** The top of a mountain

20 **PENINSULA** A body of land nearly surrounded by water

21 **PLAIN** A large area of nearly flat land

22 **PLATEAU** A high, flat area that rises steeply above the surrounding land

23 **PORT** A city where ships load and unload goods

24 **RESERVOIR** A natural or artificial lake used to store water

25 **RIVER** A stream of water that flows across the land and empties into another body of water

26 **RIVER BASIN** All the land that is drained by a river and its tributaries

27 **SOURCE** The starting point of a river

28 **TRIBUTARY** A smaller river that flows into a larger river

29 **VALLEY** An area of low land between hills or mountains

30 **VOLCANO** An opening in Earth's surface through which hot rock and ash are forced out

R13

All page numbers shown here are from the student Research Companion.

United States: Political

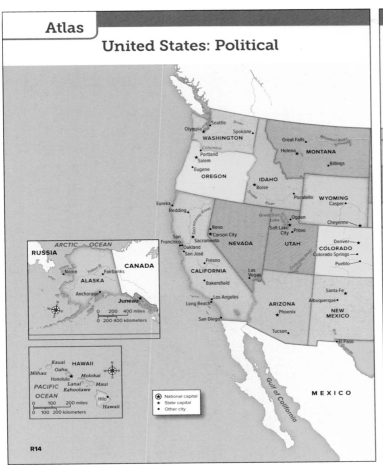

R14

R15

United States: Physical

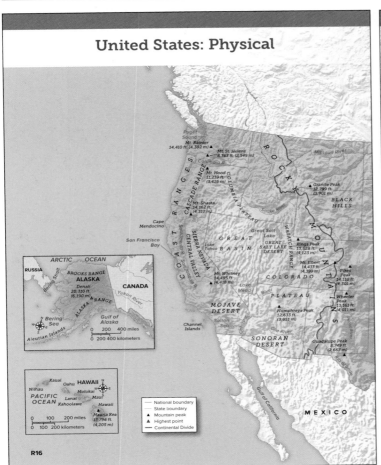

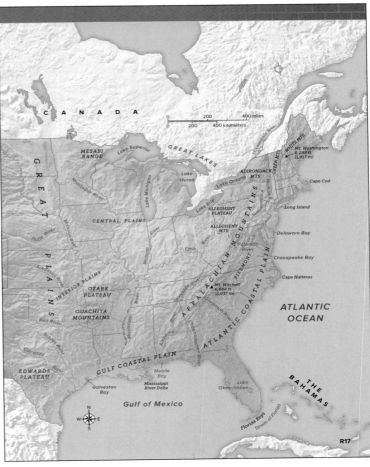

R16

R17

GEOGRAPHY HANDBOOK

All page numbers shown here are from the student Research Companion.

World: Political

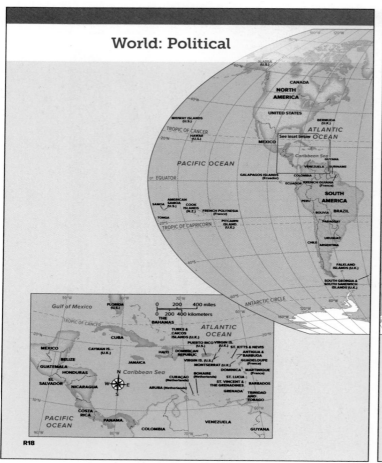

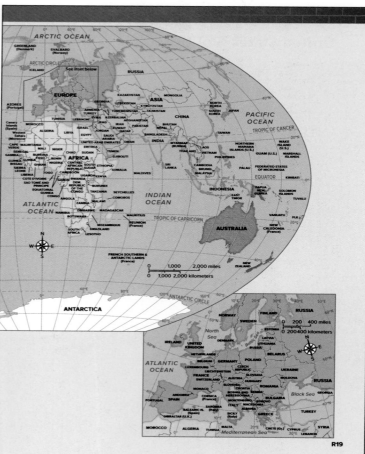

North America: Political

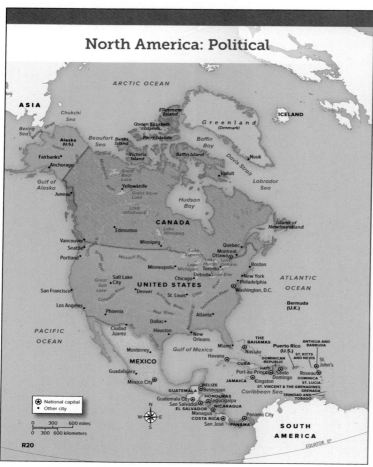

South America: Political

All page numbers shown here are from the student Research Companion.

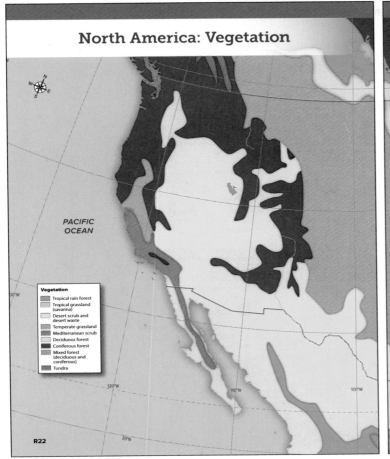

North America: Vegetation

Vegetation
- Tropical rain forest
- Tropical grassland (savanna)
- Desert scrub and desert waste
- Temperate grassland
- Mediterranean scrub
- Deciduous forest
- Coniferous forest
- Mixed forest (deciduous and coniferous)
- Tundra

PACIFIC OCEAN

120°W

110°W

100°W

20°N

R22

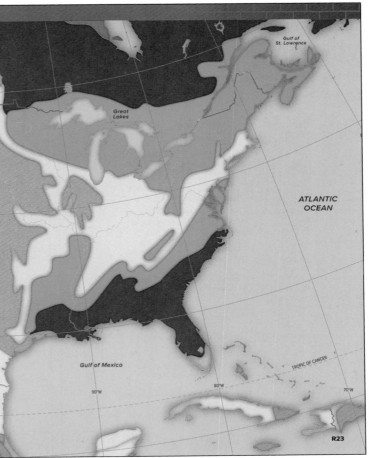

Great Lakes

Gulf of St. Lawrence

ATLANTIC OCEAN

Gulf of Mexico

90°W

80°W

TROPIC OF CANCER

70°W

R23

GLOSSARY

All page numbers shown here are from the student Research Companion.

Glossary

A

apartheid a system of racial inequality and segregation

artifact an object that was used by people in the past

atmosphere the layer of gases that surround a planet, such as Earth

B

benefits something that helps a person

boycott a special kind of protest where people decide to stop doing, using or buying something

C

capital resource the tools and machines that people use to make products or provide services

citizen a person who lives in a community or is a member of a country

climate the weather a place has over a long period of time

community the place where people live, work, and play

compromise an agreement that people make when they have different ideas

culture the values, beliefs, and other ways of life shared by a group of people

D

decade ten years

deforestation the loss of forests

drought a shortage of water due to lack of rainfall

E

economy the way a country uses its money, goods, resources, and services

ecosystem the plants and animals that live in a particular place

elevation how high an area of land is above sea level

endangered an animal that is at risk of becoming extinct

entrepreneur a person who starts and runs a business

erosion the wearing away of Earth's surface over a period of time

ethnic group a group of people who share the same culture

E

executive branch the part of government that makes sure that laws are carried out and followed

expedition a journey, especially by a group of people, for a specific purpose

export to send goods to another country to sell

extinct a type of animal that has no more living members

F

federal national

folktale a story handed down over the years

H

habitat the home of an animal or plant

heritage a person's background or tradition

hero a person who helps make the world better for other people

human capital the skills and knowledge a person has to do a job

human resource the people who work for a business or person

humidity a measure of how much moisture is in the air

hydroelectric dam a type of dam, or barrier, that turns the energy of moving water into electric power

I

import to bring in goods from another country to sell

innovation a new idea, piece of equipment, or method

J

judicial branch the part of government that decides what the laws mean

jury a group of citizens who are chosen to decide a legal case

justice treating people fairly and equally under law

L

landform a physical feature of the land, such as mountains, valleys, and coasts

legislative branch the part of government that makes the laws

M

monument a building, statue, or other structure that honors a person, place, or event in history

N

natural disaster an event that occurs in nature that damages the environment and may harm living things, such as a hurricane, earthquake, or tornado

natural resource something found in nature that people use

O

oral tradition stories and poems that are spoken rather than written

ozone layer a layer in the Earth's atmosphere that absorbs the sun's harmful rays and helps keep Earth's temperature controlled

P

peninsula a piece of land mostly surrounded by water

pioneer a person who settled in wilderness areas

population the number of people who live in one place

precipitation water that falls to the ground as rain, snow, sleet, or hail

public services a service supplied to all members of a community

R

region an area of land with certain features that make it different from other areas

rights things that are due to everyone

S

scarcity when there is a limited amount of a good or service that many people want

specialize to focus on providing a particular product or service

strait a narrow waterway connecting two larger bodies of water

T

taxes money collected by a government

technology the use of knowledge to invent new tools that make life easier and solve problems

tolerance accepting something different from your own beliefs and customs

V

volunteer to do a job or provide a service without pay

INDEX

This index lists many topics that appear in this book. It also tells you the page numbers where to find those topics. Page numbers after a *c* refer you to a chart; after an *m* refer you to a map; after a *ptg* refer you to illustrations, paintings, and artwork; and after a *p* refer you to photographs or similar pictures.

INDEX

INDEX

INDEX